1st EMNLP Workshop BlackboxNLP: Analyzing and Interpreting Neural Networks for NLP 2018

Brussels, Belgium
1 November 2018

ISBN: 978-1-5108-7421-3

EMNLP 2018

The 2018 EMNLP Workshop BlackboxNLP: Analyzing and Interpreting Neural Networks for NLP

Proceedings of the First Workshop

November 1, 2018
Brussels, Belgium

Sponsored by:

 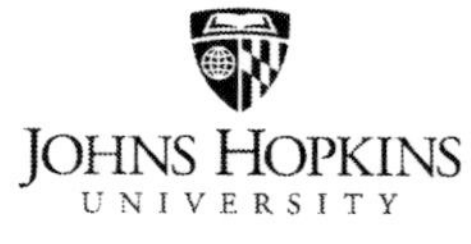

Order copies of this and other ACL proceedings from:

Association for Computational Linguistics (ACL)
209 N. Eighth Street
Stroudsburg, PA 18360
USA
Tel: +1-570-476-8006
Fax: +1-570-476-0860
acl@aclweb.org

Introduction

BlackboxNLP is the first workshop on analyzing and interpreting neural networks for NLP, hosted by the 2018 Conference on Empirical Methods in Natural Language Processing (EMNLP 2018) in Brussels, Belgium.

The goal of this workshop is to bring together people who are attempting to peek inside the neural network black box, taking inspiration from machine learning, psychology, linguistics and neuroscience. Neural networks have rapidly become a central component in language and speech understanding systems in the last few years. The improvements in accuracy and performance brought by the introduction of neural networks has typically come at the cost of our understanding of the system: what are the representations and computations that the network learns?

We received an impressive number of 76 submissions (including both archival papers and extended abstracts), suggesting that the issue of interpretability of neural networks is timely and important within the NLP community. The final program contains three keynote talks, eight oral presentations and 47 posters. We hope this workshop provides a venue for bringing together ideas and stimulate new ways of building methods and resources for facilitating better analysis and understanding of the inner-dynamics of neural networks for NLP.

BlackboxNLP would not have been possible without the dedication of its program committee. We would like to thank them for their invaluable effort in providing high-quality reviews in a very short period of time and for a higher number of submission originally expected. We are also grateful to our invited speakers, Leila Wehbe, Graham Neubig and Yoav Goldberg for contributing to our program. Finally, we are very thankful to our sponsors, Amazon and the Department of Cognitive Science, Johns Hopkins University for supporting the workshop.

Tal Linzen, Grzegorz Chrupała and Afra Alishahi

Organizers:

Tal Linzen, Johns Hopkins University
Grzegorz Chrupała, Tilburg University
Afra Alishahi, Tilburg University

Program Committee:

Željko Agić, IT University of Copenhagen
Niranjan Balasubramanian, Stony Brook University
Roberto Basili, University of Roma, Tor Vergata
Laurent Besacier, LIG
Yonatan Belinkov, MIT CSAIL
Or Biran, n-Join
Pravesh Biyani, IIIT Delhi
Arianna Bisazza, Leiden University
Samuel Bowman, New York University
Bill Byrne, University of Cambridge
Kyunghyun Cho, New York University
Ryan Cotterell, Johns Hopkins University
Barry Devereux, Queen's University, Belfast
Ewan Dunbar, Ecole Normale Supérieure et Ecole des Hautes Etudes en Sciences Sociales
Indranil Dutta, The English and Foreign Languages University
Allyson Ettinger, University of Maryland
Antske Fokkens, VU Amsterdam
Robert Frank, Yale University
Alona Fyshe, University of Alberta
Lieke Gelderloos, Tilburg University
Yoav Goldberg, Bar Ilan University
John Hale, Cornell University and Google DeepMind
David Harwath, Massachusetts Institute of Technology
Ákos Kádár, Tilburg University
Philipp Koehn, Johns Hopkins University
Adhiguna Kuncoro, University of Oxford and DeepMind
Ignacio Iacobacci, Sapienza University of Rome
Angeliki Lazaridou, DeepMind
Miryam de Lhoneux, Uppsala University
Nelson F. Liu, University of Washington
Adam Lopez, University of Edinburgh
David Mareček, Charles University in Prague
Rebecca Marvin, Johns Hopkins University
Paola Merlo, University of Geneva
Marie-Francine Moens, KU Leuven
Yves Peirsman, NLP Town
Mohammad Taher Pilehvar, University of Cambridge
Barbara Plank, IT University of Copenhagen
Delip Rao, Johns Hopkins University
Brian Roark, Google Inc.

Jan Šnajder, University of Zagreb
Whitney Tabor, University of Connecticut
Adina Williams, New York University
Fabio Massimo Zanzotto, University of Rome Tor Vergata
Willem Zuidema, University of Amsterdam

Invited Speakers:

Yoav Goldberg, Bar Ilan University
Graham Neubig, Carnegie Mellon University
Leila Wehbe, Carnegie Mellon University

Table of Contents

Keynote Talks

Archival Papers

Conference Program

09:00-09:10   **Opening Remarks**

09:10-10:00   **Invited Talk: Yoav Goldberg**

10:00-11:00   **Poster Session 1**

When does deep multi-task learning work for loosely related document classification tasks?
Emma Kerinec, Chloé Braud and Anders Søgaard

Analyzing Learned Representations of a Deep ASR Performance Prediction Model
Zied Elloumi, Laurent Besacier, Olivier Galibert and Benjamin Lecouteux

Learning Explanations from Language Data
David Harbecke, Robert Schwarzenberg and Christoph Alt

Nightmare at test time: How punctuation prevents parsers from generalizing
Anders Søgaard, Miryam de Lhoneux and Isabelle Augenstein

How much should you ask? On the question structure in QA systems.
Barbara Rychalska, Dominika Basaj, Anna Wróblewska and Przemyslaw Biecek

Does it care what you asked? Understanding Importance of Verbs in Deep Learning QA System
Barbara Rychalska, Dominika Basaj, Anna Wróblewska and Przemyslaw Biecek

Interpretable Textual Neuron Representations for NLP
Nina Poerner, Benjamin Roth and Hinrich Schütze

Evaluating Textual Representations through Image Generation
Graham Spinks and Marie-Francine Moens

On the Role of Text Preprocessing in Neural Network Architectures: An Evaluation Study on Text Categorization and Sentiment Analysis
Jose Camacho-Collados and Mohammad Taher Pilehvar

Language Models Learn POS First
Naomi Saphra and Adam Lopez

Jump to better conclusions: SCAN both left and right
Joost Bastings, Marco Baroni, Jason Weston, Kyunghyun Cho and Douwe Kiela

10:30-11:00   **Coffee Break**

11:00-12:30   **Oral Presentations**

Interpretable Structure Induction via Sparse Attention
Ben Peters, Vlad Niculae and André F. T. Martins

Understanding Convolutional Neural Networks for Text Classification
Alon Jacovi, Oren Sar Shalom and Yoav Goldberg

Extracting Syntactic Trees from Transformer Encoder Self-Attentions
David Mareček and Rudolf Rosa

Context-Free Transductions with Neural Stacks
Yiding Hao, William Merrill, Dana Angluin, Robert Frank, Noah Amsel, Andrew Benz and Simon Mendelsohn

Explaining non-linear Classifier Decisions within Kernel-based Deep Architectures
Danilo Croce, Daniele Rossini and Roberto Basili

Firearms and Tigers are Dangerous, Kitchen Knives and Zebras are Not: Testing whether Word Embeddings Can Tell
Pia Sommerauer and Antske Fokkens

12:30-14:00   **Lunch Break**

14:00-14:50   **Invited Talk: Graham Neubig**

14:50-16:00   **Poster Session 2**

State Gradients for RNN Memory Analysis
Lyan Verwimp, Hugo Van hamme, Vincent Renkens and Patrick Wambacq

LISA: Explaining Recurrent Neural Network Judgments via Layer-wIse Semantic Accumulation and Example to Pattern Transformation
Pankaj Gupta and Hinrich Schütze

Analysing the potential of seq-to-seq models for incremental interpretation in task-oriented dialogue
Dieuwke Hupkes, Sanne Bouwmeester and Raquel Fernández

An Operation Sequence Model for Explainable Neural Machine Translation
Felix Stahlberg, Danielle Saunders and Bill Byrne

Introspection for convolutional automatic speech recognition
Andreas Krug and Sebastian Stober

Keynote Talk

Trying to Understand Recurrent Neural Networks for Language Processing.

Yoav Goldberg

Bar Ilan University

Abstract

Recurrent neural networks (RNNs), and in particular LSTM networks, emerge as very capable learners for sequential data. Thus, my group started using them everywhere, achieving strong results on many language understanding and modeling tasks. However, little is known about how RNNs represent sequences, what they actually encode, and what they are capable representing. In this talk, I will describe some attempts at trying to shed light on the inner-working of RNNs. Particularly, I plan to describe at least two of the following: a method for comparing what is captured in vector representations of sentences based on different encoders (Adi et al, ICLR 2017, and more generally the notion of diagnostic classification), a framework for extracting a finite-state automata from trained RNNs (Weiss et al, ICML 2018), and a formal difference between the representation capacity of different RNN variants (Weiss et al, ACL 2018).

Biography of the Speaker

Yoav Goldberg is a Senior Lecturer at Bar Ilan University's Computer Science Department. Before that, he was a Research Scientist at Google Research New York. He works on problems related to Natural Language Processing and Machine Learning. In particular he is interested in syntactic parsing, structured-prediction models, learning for greedy decoding algorithms, multilingual language understanding, and cross domain learning. Lately, he is also interested in neural network based methods for NLP. He recently published a book on the subject.

Keynote Talk

Learning with Latent Linguistic Structure

Graham Neubig

Carnegie Mellon University

Abstract

Neural networks provide a powerful tool to model language, but also depart from standard methods of linguistic representation, which usually consist of discrete tag, tree, or graph structures. These structures are useful for a number of reasons: they are more interpretable, and also can be useful in downstream tasks. In this talk, I will discuss models that explicitly incorporate these structures as latent variables, allowing for unsupervised or semi-supervised discovery of interpretable linguistic structure, with applications to part-of-speech and morphological tagging, as well as syntactic and semantic parsing.

Biography of the Speaker

Graham Neubig is an assistant professor at the Language Technologies Intitute of Carnegie Mellon University. His work focuses on natural language processing, specifically multi-lingual models that work in many different languages, and natural language interfaces that allow humans to communicate with computers in their own language. Much of this work relies on machine learning to create these systems from data, and he is also active in developing methods and algorithms for machine learning over natural language data. He publishes regularly in the top venues in natural language processing, machine learning, and speech, and his work occasionally wins awards such as best papers at EMNLP, EACL, and WNMT. He is also active in developing open-source software, and is the main developer of the DyNet neural network toolkit.

Keynote Talk

Language representations in human brains and artificial neural networks

Leila Wehbe

Carnegie Mellon University

Abstract

When studying language in the brain, it has become more common to image the brain of humans while they process naturalistic language stimuli consisting of rich, natural text. To analyse the brain representation of such complex stimuli, vector representations derived from various NLP methods are extremely useful as a model of the information being processed in the brain. The recent deep learning revolution has ignited a lot of interest in using artificial neural networks as a source of high dimensional vector representation for modeling brain processes. However, these representations are hard to interpret and the problem becomes increasingly difficult: how do we study complex brain activity – a black box we want to understand – using hard-to-interpret artificial neural network representations – another black box we want to understand? In this talk, I will summarize the recent effort in modeling the brain processing of language, the use of artificial neural networks in this process, and how inferences about brain processes and about artificial neural network representations can still be made under this setup.

Biography of the Speaker

Leila Wehbe is an assistant professor of Machine Learning at Carnegie Mellon University. Previously, we was a postdoctoral researcher at the Gallant Lab in the Helen Wills Neuroscience Institute at UC Berkeley. She obtained her PhD from the Machine Learning Department and the Center for the Neural Basis of Cognition at Carnegie Mellon University, where she worked with Tom Mitchell. She works on studying language representations in the brain when subjects engage in naturalistic language tasks. Specifically, she combines functional neuroimaging with natural language processing and machine learning tools to build spatiotemporal maps of the information represented in the brain during language processing.

When does deep multi-task learning work for loosely related document classification tasks?

Emma Kerinec
École Normale Supérieure
de Lyon
Lyon, France
`emma.kerinec@ens-lyon.fr`

Anders Søgaard
Dpt. of Computer Science
University of Copenhagen
`soegaard@di.ku.dk`

Chloé Braud[*]
Université de Lorraine,
CNRS, LORIA
Nancy, France
`chloe.braud@loria.fr`

Abstract

This work aims to contribute to our understanding of *when* multi-task learning through parameter sharing in deep neural networks leads to improvements over single-task learning. We focus on the setting of learning from *loosely related* tasks, for which no theoretical guarantees exist. We therefore approach the question empirically, studying which properties of datasets and single-task learning characteristics correlate with improvements from multi-task learning. We are the first to study this in a text classification setting and across more than 500 different task pairs.

1 Introduction

Multi-task learning is a set of techniques for exploiting synergies between related tasks, and in natural language processing (NLP), where there is an overwhelming number of related problems, and different ways to represent these problems, multi-task learning seems well-motivated. Since multi-task learning, by exploiting related tasks, also reduces the need for labeled data, multi-task learning is also often seen as a way to obtain more robust NLP for more domains and languages.

Multi-task learning has seen a revival in recent years, amplified by the success of deep learning techniques. Multi-task learning algorithms have been proven to lead to better performance for similar tasks, e.g., Baxter and others (2000), such as models of individual patients in health care, but recently multi-task learning has been applied to more loosely related sets of tasks in artificial intelligence. Examples include machine translation and syntactic parsing (Kaiser et al., 2017) or fixation prediction and sentence compression (Klerke, Goldberg, and Søgaard, 2016). Reported results

have been promising, but in the case of loosely related tasks, often also with different label spaces, we have no guarantees that multi-task learning will work.

Recent studies have tried to study empirically *when* multi-task learning leads to improvements (Alonso and Plank, 2017; Bingel and Søgaard, 2017). These preliminary studies have argued – Bingel and Søgaard (2017) most clearly – that multi-task learning is particularly effective when the target task otherwise plateaus faster than the auxiliary task. This study compliments these studies, considering new tasks and architectures, and our findings are largely supportive of this conclusion. In text classification, however, performance also depends crucially on the divergence between the marginal distributions of words in the target and auxiliary task.

Document classification comes in many different flavors, including spam detection, sentiment analysis, customer support ticket routing, and diagnosis support based on patient records, but in this paper we focus on **topic-level multi-way classification**. We use the 20 Newsgroups dataset, a corpus of newsgroup posts that are labeled by the topics of the newsgroups. One key challenge in document classification is the high number of feature dimensions introduced by n-gram features, often outnumbering the number of document instances in the training corpus. Specifically, it is easy to overfit to the training corpus in high dimensions.

Multi-task learning (Caruana, 1993) has strong regularization effects and can therefore potentially make our models less prone to overfitting. Previous empirical meta-studies of multi-task learning have focused on sequence tagging problems and recurrent neural networks, but there is no guarantee that results extend to document classification. This work, which extends previous work on recur-

---

This work was done, when the third author was affiliated with Dpt. of Computer Science, University of Copenhagen.

1

Proceedings of the 2018 EMNLP Workshop BlackboxNLP: Analyzing and Interpreting Neural Networks for NLP, pages 1–8
Brussels, Belgium, November 1, 2018. ©2018 Association for Computational Linguistics

rent neural networks, is thus motivated by a) an interest in whether previous findings generalize to document classification algorithms – in our case, **multi-layered perceptrons**, b) a practical consideration that any recommendations coming out of a study of document classification would be helpful to a wider audience.

As already said, our focus on topic-level classification is motivated by the observation that this is an extremely common problem, and key to structuring content on websites, customer support ticket routing, intelligent email, etc. Also, the 20 Newsgroups corpus uses a set of 20 labels that are hierarchically organized (see Figure 1), which we can exploit to extract a large set of task pairs.

The problem that we consider is the following: *If we have two topic-level classification datasets that are loosely related – i.e, contrasts the same upper level classes in the hierarchy in Figure 1 – and we have run single-task experiments for each of these, when does multi-task learning help, keeping hyper-parameters fixed?* We approach this as a prediction problem, trying to predict gains or losses based on meta features such as dataset characteristics and features of the single-task learning curves. This approach was first introduced in (Bingel and Søgaard, 2017).

1.1 Contributions

Our contributions are as follows: a) We present the first study of when multi-task learning works in the context of document classification. b) This is, to the best of our knowledge, also the first meta-study that focuses on hard parameter sharing in multilayered perceptrons, although this approach to multi-task learning goes all the way back to (Caruana, 1993). c) We find that many of the results obtained with other types of deep neural networks scale to our case, but also that distributional divergence is strongly, negatively correlated with performance gains; something not observed with sequence tagging problems. Finally, we make all our code available at [anonymized].

2 Related Work

Document classification has a very long history and is one of the most fundamental applications of machine learning. It is extremely important to many industries, from customer support to medical diagnosis support.

The standard approach to document classifica-tion is to represent documents by what is known as *bags of words*, i.e., vector representations where each dimension encodes the presence or relative frequency of a particular n-gram (sequence of words). In this work, we use TF-IDF scores and only encode the presence of unigrams (words). Each document is thus a $|V|$-dimensional array of floats, where $|V|$ is the size of our vocabulary.

The dataset that we use, is 20 Newsgroups.[1] It has been used in several comparisons of classification algorithms (Dredze, Crammer, and Pereira, 2008; Crammer and Chechik, 2012), and some of the best results have been achieved with random forests and multi-layered perceptrons (deep learning models). The dataset, however, is also known to allow for over-fitting (Ribeiro, Singh, and Guestrin, 2016). Such overfitting can be remedied by multi-task learning. In this paper, we focus on multi-task learning with multi-layered perceptrons.

Multi-task learning comes in many different flavors, but most approaches can be cast as ways of doing matrix regularization. To see this, construct a $m \times n$ matrix for m models with n parameters. Multi-task learning corresponds to jointly fitting the m models penalized by a regularization term defined over this matrix. One common approach to multi-task learning, for example, is *mean-constrained ℓ_2-regularization*. The penalty in this case is the sum of the ℓ_2-distances of the m models to their mean.

In this paper, we focus on *hard parameter sharing*, in which we jointly learn m multi-layered perceptrons that share the parameters of their hidden layers. This is also the kind of architecture discussed in (Collobert et al., 2011), one of the seminal papers in multi-task learning for natural language processing. See Ruder (2017) for a more complete overview of multi-task learning algorithms used in natural language processing.

Hard parameter sharing comes with several guarantees when applied to closely related tasks (Baxter and others, 2000), including a reduction in Rademacher complexity (Maurer, 2006). These guarantees, however, do not apply to our case of more loosely related tasks. For example, (Baxter and others, 2000) requires the tasks to have shared optimal hypothesis classes; which does not have to be the case in 20 Newsgroups.

---

[1] http://qwone.com/~jason/20Newsgroups/

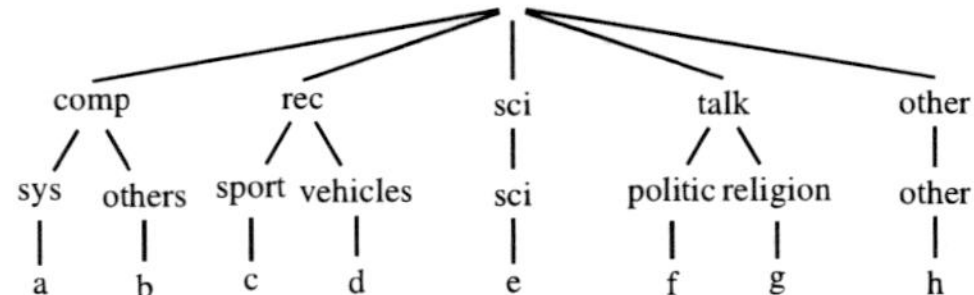

Figure 1: Hierarchical structure of 20 Newsgroups, with a= ibm.pc.hardware, mac.hardware; b= graphics, os.ms-windows.misc, windows.x; c= baseball, hockey; d= autos, motorcycles; e= crypt, electronics, med, space; f= misc, guns, mideast; g= misc, atheism, christian, h= forsale.

3 Methodology

We begin with a brief summary of our methodology: We sample pairs of tasks from 20 Newsgroups. The documents are represented as TF-IDF vectors, and we train single-task and multi-task multilayered perceptrons to predict topics from such vectors. We then run meta-experiments using logistic regression classifiers to predict the sign of the relative difference between multi-task and single-task performance, from features derived from the data and the single-task runs. We are primarily interested in the coefficients of the logistic regression meta-models, which tell us what characteristics of the data and the single-task experiments are predictive of multi-task learning gains.

3.1 20 Newsgroups

The 20 Newsgroups data set is a collection of approximately 20,000 newsgroup documents, partitioned across 20 different topics. It contains about 60,000 different words in total.

Some of the newsgroups are very closely related and can be seen as subtopics of the same topic, while others are highly unrelated. The topics can be represented as a 3-level hierarchy: The first level partitions the set of topics into 5 classes (e.g. `comp`, `rec`...), the second one into 8 subclasses (e.g. `sys`, `others`, `sport`...), and at the leaf nodes we have the 20 topics (e.g. `ibm.pc.hardware`, `baseball`...); see Figure 1.

3.2 Classification tasks

Based on the 20 Newsgroups' structure, we define pairs of tasks in ways similar to previous studies (Søgaard and Johannsen, 2012). We do this in two different ways, leading to Problem 1 and 2, defined below.

3.2.1 Problem 1 (RELATED TOPICS)

The main task is to distinguish between two topics A and B (third level) that have the same ancestor at the first level of the above hierarchy, i.e. they pertain to the same class, but to different subclasses. An auxiliary task is to distinguish between two topics C and D, with the following constraints: C has the same father as A, and D the same as B.

A task pair example would be: A=`baseball` and B=`autos` for the main task since; C=`hockey` and D=`motorcycles` for the auxiliary task (see 2). We obtained 52 unique such pairs of main-auxiliary tasks for problem 1.

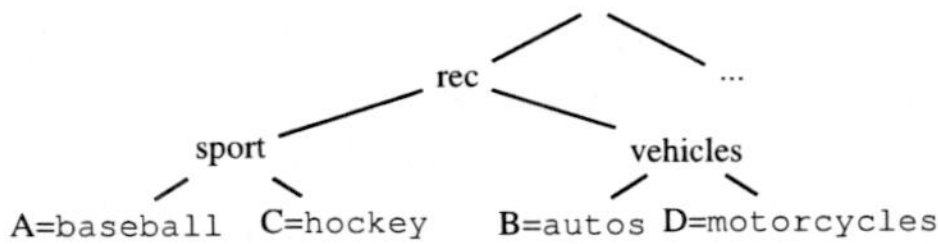

Figure 2: Problem 1 (Related topics): A and B are the main tasks, C and D the auxiliary ones.

3.2.2 Problem 2 (UNRELATED TOPICS)

For the second problem, we keep the constraints that C has the same father as A and D the same as B, and that A and B have different fathers. However, A and B are not forced to have the same ancestor at the first level anymore. In this setting, the main and auxiliary tasks could be about distinguishing texts corresponding to unrelated topics, but they still share topics pertaining to the same classes, making multi-task learning a relevant framework.

An example of pairs of tasks would be: A=`guns` and B=`autos` for the main task; C=`Mideast` and D=`motorcycles` for the auxiliary task (see Figure 3).

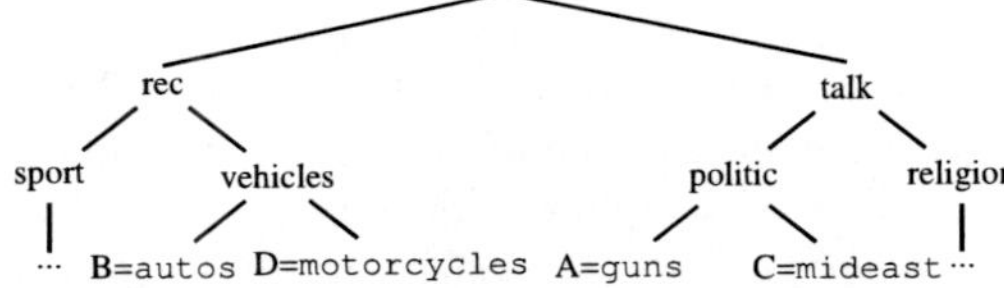

Figure 3: Problem 2 (Unrelated topics):A and B are the main tasks, C and D the auxiliary ones.

We obtained 516 different pairs of main-auxiliary tasks for UNRELATED TOPICS.

Note that the instances (i.e. pairs of main-auxiliary tasks) of RELATED TOPICS are included in the set of instances of UNRELATED TOPICS. We have many more instances for UNRELATED

3

TOPICS than for RELATED TOPICS, which means that we have many more training points when trying to predict the performance of multi-task learning.

3.3 Representation of the data

We use TF-IDF (term frequency-inverse document frequency) over the bag-of-words to represent the data. The TF-IDF value increases proportionally to the number of times a word appears in a document, but is offset by the frequency of the word in the corpus, which helps to adjust for the fact that some words appear more frequently in general. This representation is known to be efficient (Salton and Buckley, 1988; Aizawa, 2003); especially in the case of text classification (Zhang, Yoshida, and Tang, 2011). We keep the 10,000 most frequent features, the frequency being computed on the training data available for the entire 20 Newsgroups corpus.

3.4 Models

Both our single and multi-task learning architectures consist of a multi-layered perceptron with two hidden layers. In the case of multi-task learning, those layers are shared across all tasks. This setting is known as hard parameter sharing. Hard parameter sharing was first introduced by (Caruana, 1993) and used with success for different tasks, for example in (Collobert et al., 2011; Klerke, Goldberg, and Søgaard, 2016; Plank, Søgaard, and Goldberg, 2016). Hard parameter sharing greatly reduces the risk of overfitting. In fact, Baxter and others (2000) showed that the risk of overfitting the shared parameters is an order n where n is the number of tasks smaller than overfitting the task-specific parameters, i.e. the output layers.

The input is thus a 10,000-dimensional TF-IDF vector representation of the texts. A training step consists of sampling a random batch of 32 instances, i.e. texts (for both main and auxiliary task in the case of multi-task learning) and minimizing the binary cross-entropy loss using an Adam optimizer (Kingma and Ba, 2014).

We tune the following hyper parameters of the single-task architectures on a similar document classification problem, using data from Amazon reviews,[2] and, following (Bingel and Søgaard,

---

[2] https://www.cs.jhu.edu/~mdredze/datasets/sentiment/index2.html

2017), we apply *the same* hyper-parameter values to multi-task learning: number of hidden layers (2) and layer size (100). See §4.1 for number of epochs (100).

3.5 Meta-analysis

We want to investigate whether we can predict gains from multi-task learning given features of the data sets and single-task learning characteristics, as well as understand how gains correlate with data set and single-task learning characteristics. For each problem instance, we thus extract several features from the datasets and the learning curves of the single task models. These features are similar to those used in (Bingel and Søgaard, 2017):

- Jensen-Shannon Divergence between the (unigram) word distributions of the target and auxiliary task training sets, as well as internally (between target and test data) for each task,

- Gradients of the loss curve at 10, 25, 50 and 75 percent of a training of 150 epochs, for each single-task, as well as the relative differences in the learning curve gradients,

- Type-token ratios and out-of-vocabulary rates in the target and auxiliary task training sets, and their relative difference,

- Finally, we fit logarithmic functions to the (log-like) loss curves, where the function is of the form: $a \cdot ln(c \cdot i + d) + b$, and we include a and c as features. Both parameters relate to the steepness of the loss curve, reflecting when training plateaus or comes with diminishing returns.

In total, for each problem instance we have 30 features that we normalize to the $[0, 1]$ interval. We use logistic regression to predict benefits or detriments of multi-task learning setups based on the features computed above.

4 Experiments

We run single-task and multi-task learning experiments for all pairs of main and auxiliary tasks, as described in Section 3.2. We then extract data characteristics and features from the logs of the single-task learning experiments. We train a meta-learning model to predict gains from doing multi-task learning over single-task performance using

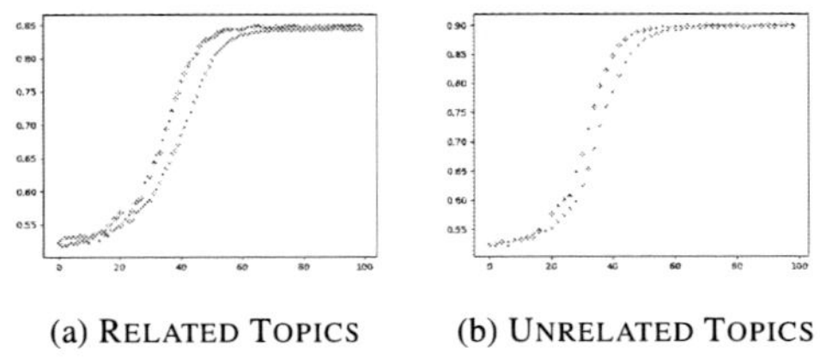

(a) RELATED TOPICS   (b) UNRELATED TOPICS

Figure 4: Mean F_1 over the number of epochs, for single-task (crosses/blue) and multi-task learning models (points/orange), for classification problems 1 and 2.

the above features. Then we build a final model to predict gains from multi-task learning using these pairs as instances. We use the 20 Newsgroups for both RELATED TOPICS and UNRELATED TOPICS, as explained above. We use 200 topics for each class for training, and the rest of each dataset for testing (5-700 data points, depending on the topics).

4.1 Hyper-parameters

Hyper-parameters were tuned using the Amazon data, as described in §3.4. Our models are trained with two layers of size 100. The input is a 10,000 dimensional TF-IDF vector, and the output is a probability distribution from a softmax layer, whose predictions are evaluated using cross-entropy loss.

Figures 4a and 4b plot the impact of the number of epochs on the F_1 scores. This parameter was not optimized on the Amazon data, but set such that multi-task learning gains were reasonably balanced.

In meta-learning, when predicting the gains from multi-task learning, we use the mean performance of 100 runs of randomized five-fold cross-validation with logistic regression.

4.2 Evaluation

We train single-task models for all tasks, as well as multi-task learning models for all combinations of target and auxiliary tasks. We report the F_1 gains obtained for multi-task learning over single-task learning below.

Our real aim, however, is to try to predict the gains one can get from doing multi-task learning. This is a meta-learning problem, and here, the above experiments are our instances, i.e., one instance for each of the main-auxiliary task pairs,

meaning that we have 52 instances for RELATED TOPICS and 516 for UNRELATED TOPICS. In order to compensate for the small number of training instances, we repeat our RELATED TOPICS experiments five times with random initializations, and report means over the results. We use the same procedure for UNRELATED TOPICS, also. F_1 scores, obtained by a logistic regression model over 100 runs using a 5-fold cross-validation procedure, are reported at the end of the next section.

5 Results

We first discuss the performance of our multi-task learning models on the 20 NEWSGROUPS data, and then present the results of our meta-learning experiments.

5.1 Multi-task versus single-task learning

As mentioned above, we report averages over five runs. The mean F_1 scores across all the problems, and five runs, are presented in Table 1. We observe that on average, multi-task learning leads to slight improvements over single-task learning. This holds for both our problems, also for RELATED TOPICS. The number of epochs needed to train the multi-task models is slightly greater than the one for the single-task ones (Figures 4a and 4b), and the global stabilization occurs after approximatively 75 epochs. We can also observed that UNRELATED TOPICS, where tasks to differentiate are in general theoretically more different, has better result than RELATED TOPICS (for both single-task and multi-task learning) see Table 1.

For RELATED TOPICS, we see improvements in more than 70% of the cases, and the mean gain is about 5%. Figure 5a presents the relative gains and losses over the different high-level classes of the RELATED TOPICS problem. Note there is a lot of variance. Some class pairs exhibit a lot of synergy, with gains doing multi-task learning, while others seem relatively immune to multi-task learning. For UNRELATED TOPICS, multi-task learning leads to improvements in about 57% of all cases.

5.2 Predicting gains from multi-task learning

In our meta-learning experiment, the objective is to predict multi-task learning gains given the dataset and single-task learning characteristics. This is not only because it is of practical importance to be able to predict whether multi-task learning is worthwhile, when dealing with massive

5

	Single-task	Multi-task	Improvements
RELATED	0.834	0.843	0.719
UNRELATED	0.893	0.897	0.572

Table 1: Mean F_1 score for single-task and multi-task models, with average fraction of datasets with improvements.

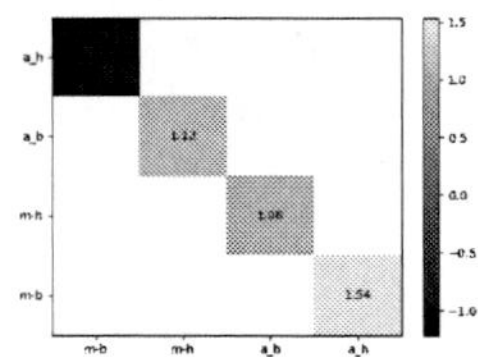

(a) "rec": VEHICLES (motorcycles and autos) vs. SPORTS (hockey and baseball).

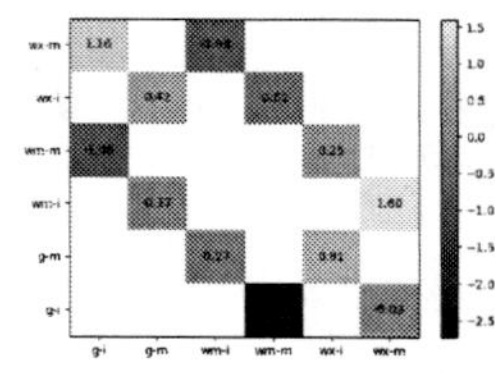
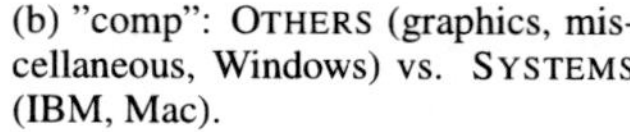

(b) "comp": OTHERS (graphics, miscellaneous, Windows) vs. SYSTEMS (IBM, Mac).

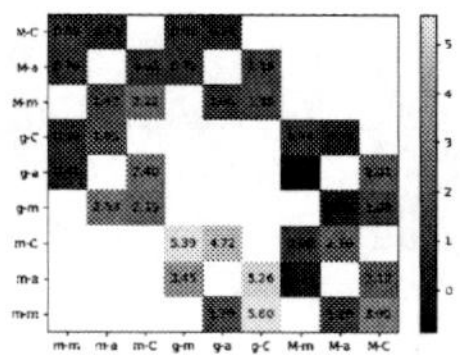

(c) "talk": POLITICS (miscellaneous, guns, Middle East) vs. RELIGION (miscellaneous, atheism, Christianity).

Figure 5: Relative F_1 gains from multi-task learning for *Related Topics*

datasets or thousands of tasks. More importantly, our meta-learning models implicitly learn correlations between such characteristics and gains, giving us insights as to *when* and *why* multi-task learning works. If a dataset characteristic, for example, is highly predictive of gains, this can either be a feature that puts single-task learning at a disadvantage, or something that multi-task learning can exploit.

The mean scores over 100 runs (5-fold CV) of our logistic regression model for different feature combinations are listed in Table 2. The results show that generally, features extracted from the loss curves are more predictive of gains than any other features. This confirms findings in Bingel and Søgaard (2017).

	RELATED TOPICS	UNRELATED TOPICS
Using all features	0.67	0.57
Not using curve features	0.66	0.53
Only using curve features	0.71	0.58
Only using ratio features	0.69	0.57

Table 2: Mean performance across 100 runs of 5-fold CV logistic regression.

6 Discussion

The mean score (inverse rank) of each predictor is given in Table 4a; and the coefficients of the predictors in Table 4b. The JSD features either capture divergences between target and auxiliary tasks, in general, or between the classes, or between target and auxiliary with respect to either positive or negative class. Other features include the number of words in the training and test set, their relative numbers, or the relative numbers between target and auxiliary tasks (equivalent to type-token ratios). Finally, the curve-related features come in two flavors. One set is simply the gradients of the loss curve at different time steps. The other set is the parameters a and c from a log-curve fitted to the entire loss curve.

6.1 Most predictive features

The most predictive features across both tasks are Jensen-Shannon divergences, and the fitted loss curve parameters a and c. OOV rate is also predictive of gains, i.e., correlated with gains from multi-task learning, which makes sense, since our embedding parameters are updated during training, leading to better representations for rare words that occur more frequently in the auxiliary data.

Jensen-Shannon Divergence (JSD) We compute JSD between training and test, in both tasks, and their relative ratio, as well as between classes. JSD between training and test is strongly negatively correlated with gains from multi-task learning. In other words, the more divergence between your target and your auxiliary task, the *less* likely multi-task learning is to work. The importance of JSD is very interesting – and per-

Feature	Data	Inverse rank
JSD pos. class	main	23
Curve param a	main	21
JSD pos. class	ratio	21
Curve gradient 10%	main	20
Curve gradient 10%	ratio	18
JSD between classes	aux	17
# words	ratio	17
OOV rate	all	17
Curve param c	aux	16
Curve gradient 50%	ratio	16
JSD neg. class	aux	16
# words	main	15
Curve gradient 75%	main	14
Curve gradient 25%	aux	14
JSD between classes	ratio	14
Curve gradient 75%	ratio	14
JSD neg. class	all	14
Curve gradient 25%	ratio	13
Curve gradient 50%	aux	12
Curve gradient 75%	aux	12
Curve param a	aux	11
Curve param a	ratio	11
# words	test	11
Curve gradient 50%	main	10
Curve param c	ratio	10
JSD pos. class	all	10
Curve param c	main	9
# words	aux	9
Curve gradient 10%	aux	9
Curve gradient 25%	main	8

(a) Inverse ranks for RELATED TOPICS

Feature	Data	Coefficient
JSD pos. class	all	-0.93
JSD neg. class	all	-0.88
OOV rate	all	0.81
JSD between classes	all	0.64
JSD between classes	aux	0.63
JSD between classes	main	0.58
# words	test	-0.49
# words	train	-0.47
Curve param a	ratio	0.34
Curve param a	aux	-0.31
Curve gradient 75%	ratio	0.26
Curve param c	ratio	0.24
# words	aux	-0.21
Curve param c	main	-0.17
Curve gradient 75%	main	0.17
# words	main	0.13
Curve gradient 50%	aux	-0.11
Curve gradient 75%	aux	0.10
JSD neg. class	aux	-0.08
Curve gradient 50%	main	-0.07
Curve param a	main	0.07
JSD pos. class	aux	0.07
Curve gradient 25%	aux	-0.05
Curve gradient 10%	ratio	0.04
Curve gradient 25%	ratio	0.04
Curve gradient 25%	main	0.03
Curve gradient 50%	ratio	-0.03
Curve gradient 10%	aux	-0.02
Curve param c	aux	-0.02
Curve gradient 10%	main	0.01

(b) Coefficients for UNRELATED TOPICS

Table 3: Average inverse ranks and average logistic regression coefficients of various predictors of gains from multi-task learning

haps a bit surprising in the light of recent results for sequence tagging (Alonso and Plank, 2017; Bingel and Søgaard, 2017). These recent results suggested that JSD is not predictive of multi-task learning performance *at all*. Of course, JSD over unigram occurrences is more closely related to the model bias arising when training document classification models on loosely related tasks, than to the model bias in sequence models. After all, transition probabilities are typically at least as important as emission probabilities in statistical sequence tagging models.

Loss curve gradients were shown in (Bingel and Søgaard, 2017) to be the best predictors of multi-task learning gains. The intuition offered there is that multi-task learning is more likely to work when the target task quickly plateaus, but the auxiliary task keeps pounding, eventually letting the target task out of a potentially suboptimal local optimum. Multi-task learning leads to a smoother loss landscape, where it is harder to get trapped, and when randomly sampling from the auxiliary task, also, there is ample chance to be led out of poor, local optima. Note that in our experiments the good predictors based on loss curve gradients are found in the last regions of the curve, just before early stopping.

Stability Some features are highly correlated, which can produce instability – and poor results and misleading coefficients – when training logistic regression models. Note, however, that we report averages over multiple models. This is similar to the idea of using *stability selection* (Meinshausen and Bühlmann, 2010), though averaging over multiple problems is arguably more robust than doing it over bootstrap samples with replacement.

7 Conclusion

We have investigated the performance of single-task and multi-task multi layer perceptrons for text classification using a TF-IDF representation of documents. We ran experiments on the 20 Newsgroups corpus and took advantage of the class hierarchy in this dataset, to extract hundreds of pairs of loosely related documents, for which no theoretical guarantees exist.

Based on this data, we conduct meta-learning experiments, trying to predict when multi-task learning works, and when it does not. We inspect the coefficients of such meta models to estimate the contribution of various dataset features or learning characteristics to such gains. Our experiments show the importance of loss curve gradients and out-of-vocabulary rates, supporting recent findings from sequence tagging (Bingel and Søgaard, 2017), but we also see that biases in the marginal distribution of the data, as measured by JSD, are predictive of multi-task learning gains in document classification.

References

Aizawa, A. 2003. An information-theoretic perspective of tfidf measures. *Information Processing and Management*.

Alonso, H. M., and Plank, B. 2017. When is multitask learning effective? semantic sequence prediction under varying data conditions. In *EACL*.

Baxter, J., et al. 2000. A model of inductive bias learning. *Journal of Artificial Intelligence Research (JAIR)* 12:3.

Bingel, J., and Søgaard, A. 2017. Identifying beneficial task relations for multi-task learning in deep neural networks. In *EACL*.

Caruana, R. 1993. Multitask learning: a knowledge-based source of inductive bias. In *ICML*.

Collobert, R.; Weston, J.; Bottou, L.; Karlen, M.; Kavukcuoglu, K.; and Kuksa, P. 2011. Natural language processing (almost) from scratch. *The Journal of Machine Learning Research* 12:2493–2537.

Crammer, K., and Chechik, G. 2012. Adaptive regularization of weight matrices. In *ICML*.

Dredze, M.; Crammer, K.; and Pereira, F. 2008. Confidence-weighted linear classification. In *ICML*.

Kaiser, L.; Gomez, A.; Shazeer, N.; Vaswani, A.; Parmar, N.; Jones, L.; and Uszkoreit, J. 2017. One model to learn them all. In *https://arxiv.org/abs/1706.05137*.

Kingma, D. P., and Ba, J. 2014. Adam: A method for stochastic optimization. *arXiv preprint arXiv:1412.6980*.

Klerke, S.; Goldberg, Y.; and Søgaard, A. 2016. Improving sentence compression by learning to predict gaze. In *NAACL*.

Maurer, A. 2006. Bounds for linear multi-task learning. *Journal of Machine Learning Research* 6:117–139.

Meinshausen, N., and Bühlmann, P. 2010. Stability selection. *Journal of the Royal Statistical Society: Series B (Statistical Methodology)* 72(4):417–473.

Plank, B.; Søgaard, A.; and Goldberg, Y. 2016. Multilingual part-of-speech tagging with bidirectional long short-term memory models and auxiliary loss. In *ACL*.

Ribeiro, M. T.; Singh, S.; and Guestrin, C. 2016. Why should I trust you - explaining the predictions of any classifier. In *NAACL*.

Ruder, S. 2017. An overview of multi-task learning in deep neural networks. *CoRR*.

Salton, G., and Buckley, C. 1988. Term-weighting approaches in automatic text retrieval. *Information Processing and Management*.

Søgaard, A., and Johannsen, A. 2012. Robust learning in random subspaces: equipping NLP for OOV effects. In *COLING*.

Zhang, W.; Yoshida, T.; and Tang, X. 2011. A comparative study of tf*idf, lsi and multi-words for text classification. *Expert Systems with Applications*.

Analyzing Learned Representations of a Deep ASR Performance Prediction Model

Zied Elloumi[1,2]   Laurent Besacier[2]   Olivier Galibert[1]   Benjamin Lecouteux[2]

[1]Laboratoire national de métrologie et d'essais (LNE) , France
[2]Univ. Grenoble Alpes, CNRS, Grenoble INP, LIG, F-38000 Grenoble, France
`firstname.name@lne.fr`
`firstname.name@univ-grenoble-alpes.fr`

Abstract

This paper addresses a relatively new task: prediction of ASR performance on unseen broadcast programs. In a previous paper, we presented an ASR performance prediction system using CNNs that encode both text (ASR transcript) and speech, in order to predict word error rate. This work is dedicated to the analysis of speech signal embeddings and text embeddings learnt by the CNN while training our prediction model. We try to better understand which information is captured by the deep model and its relation with different conditioning factors. It is shown that hidden layers convey a clear signal about speech style, accent and broadcast type. We then try to leverage these 3 types of information at training time through multi-task learning. Our experiments show that this allows to train slightly more efficient ASR performance prediction systems that - in addition - simultaneously tag the analyzed utterances according to their speech style, accent and broadcast program origin.

1 Introduction

Predicting automatic speech recognition (ASR) performance on unseen speech recordings is an important Grail of speech research. In a previous paper (Elloumi et al., 2018), we presented a framework for modeling and evaluating ASR performance prediction on unseen broadcast programs. CNNs were very efficient encoding both text (ASR transcript) and speech to predict ASR word error rate (WER). However, while achieving state-of-the-art performance prediction results, our CNN approach is more difficult to understand compared to conventional approaches based on engineered features such as *TransRater*[1] for instance. This lack of interpretability of the representations learned by deep neural networks is a

general problem in AI. Recent papers started to address this issue and analyzed hidden representations learned during training of different natural language processing models (Mohamed et al., 2012; Wu and King, 2016; Belinkov and Glass, 2017; Shi et al., 2016; Belinkov et al., 2017; Wang et al., 2017).

Contribution. This work is dedicated to the analysis of speech signal embeddings and text embeddings learnt by the CNN during training of our ASR performance prediction model. Our goal is to better understand which information is captured by the deep model and its relation with conditioning factors such as speech style, accent or broadcast program type. For this, we use a data set presented in (Elloumi et al., 2018) which contains a large amount of speech utterances taken from various collections of French broadcast programs. Following a methodology similar to (Belinkov and Glass, 2017), our deep performance prediction model is used to generate utterance level features that are given to a shallow classifier trained to solve secondary classification tasks. It is shown that hidden layers convey a clear signal about speech style, accent and show. We then try to leverage these 3 types of information at training time through multi-task learning. Our experiments show that this allows to train slightly more efficient ASR performance prediction systems that - in addition - simultaneously tag the analyzed utterances according to their speech style, accent and broadcast program origin.

Outline. The paper is organized as follows. In section 2, we present a brief overview of related works and present our ASR performance prediction system in section 3. Then, we detail our methodology to evaluate learned representations in section 4. Our multi-task learning experiments for ASR performance prediction are presented in section 5. Finally, section 6 concludes this work.

---

[1]`https://github.com/hlt-mt/TranscRater`

9

Proceedings of the 2018 EMNLP Workshop BlackboxNLP: Analyzing and Interpreting Neural Networks for NLP, pages 9–15
Brussels, Belgium, November 1, 2018. ©2018 Association for Computational Linguistics

2 Related works

Several works tried to understand learned representations for NLP tasks such as Automatic Speech Recognition (ASR) and Neural Machine Translation (NMT).

(Shi et al., 2016) and (Belinkov et al., 2017) tried to better understand the hidden representations of NMT models which were given to a shallow classifier in order to predict syntactic labels (Shi et al., 2016), part-of-speech labels or semantic ones (Belinkov et al., 2017). It was shown that lower layers are better at POS tagging, while higher layers are better at learning semantics. (Mohamed et al., 2012) and (Belinkov and Glass, 2017) analyzed the feature representations from a deep ASR model using t-SNE visualization (Maaten and Hinton, 2008) and tried to understand which layers better capture the phonemic information by training a shallow phone classifier. Also relevant is the work of (Wang et al., 2017) who proposed an in-depth investigation on three kinds of speaker embeddings learned for a speaker recognition task, i.e. i-vector, d-vector and RNN/LSTM based sequence-vector (s-vector). Classification tasks were designed to facilitate better understanding of the encoded speaker representations. Multi-task learning was also proposed to integrate different speaker embeddings and improve speaker verification performance.

3 ASR performance prediction system

In (Elloumi et al., 2018), we proposed a new approach using convolution neural networks (CNNs) to predict ASR performance from a collection of heterogeneous broadcast programs (both radio and TV). We particularly focused on the combination of text (ASR transcription) and signal (raw speech) inputs which both proved useful for CNN prediction. We also observed that our system remarkably predicts WER distribution on a collection of speech recordings.

To obtain speech transcripts (ASR outputs) for the prediction model, we built our own French ASR system based on the KALDI toolkit (Povey et al., 2011). A hybrid HMM-DNN system was trained using 100 hours of broadcast news from *Quaero*[2], *ETAPE* (Gravier et al., 2012), *ESTER 1 & ESTER 2* (Galliano et al., 2005) and *REPERE*

(Kahn et al., 2012) collections. ASR performance was evaluated on the held out corpora presented in table 2 (used to train and evaluate ASR prediction) and its averaged value was 22.29% on the TRAIN set, 22.35% on the DEV set and 31.20% on the TEST set (which contains more challenging broadcast programs).

Figure 1 shows our network architecture. The network input can be either a pure text input, a pure signal input (raw signal) or a dual (text+speech) input. To avoid memory issues, signals are downsampled to 8khz and models are trained on six-second speech turns (shorter speech turns are padded with zeros). For text input, the architecture is inspired from (Kim, 2014) (green in Figure 1): the input is a matrix of dimensions 296x100 (296 is the longest ASR hypothesis length in our corpus ; 100 is the dimension of pre-trained word embeddings on a large held out text corpus of 3.3G words). For speech input, we use the best architecture (*m18*) proposed in (Dai et al., 2017) (colored in red in Figure 1) of dimensions 48000 x 1 (48000 samples correspond to 6s of speech).

For WER prediction, our best approach (called $CNN_{Softmax}$) used *softmax* probabilities and an external fixed WER_{Vector} which corresponds to a discretization of the WER output space (see (Elloumi et al., 2018) for more details). The best performance obtained is 19.24% MAE[3] using text+speech input. Our ASR prediction system is built using both *Keras* (Chollet et al., 2015) and *Tensorflow*[4].

In the next section, we analyze the representations learnt in the higher layers (3 blocks colored in yellow and dotted in Figure 1) for pure text (TXT), pure speech (RAW-SIG) and both (TXT+RAW-SIG).

4 Evaluating learned representations

4.1 Methodology

In this section, we attempt to understand what our best ASR performance prediction system (Elloumi et al., 2018) learned. We analyze the text and speech representations obtained by our architecture. Alike (Belinkov and Glass, 2017), the joint text+speech model is used to generate utterance

---

[2] http://www.quaero.org

[3] Mean Absolute Error (MAE) is a common metric to evaluate WER prediction ; it computes the absolute deviation between the true and predicted WERs, averaged over the number of utterances in the test set.

[4] https://www.tensorflow.org

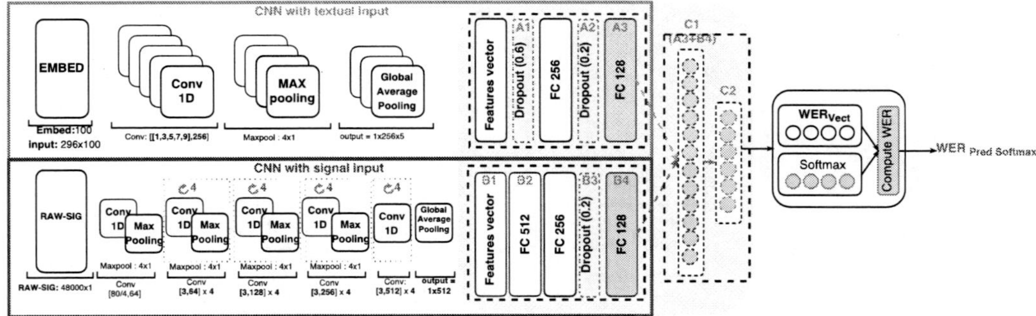

Figure 1: Architecture of our CNN with text (green) and signal (red) inputs for WER prediction

level features (hidden representations of speech turns colored in yellow in Figure 1) that are given to a shallow classifier trained to solve secondary classification tasks such as:

- **STYLE:** classify the utterances between (*spontaneous* and *non spontaneous*) styles (see table 1),

- **ACCENT:** classify the utterances between *native* and *non native* speech (see also table 1, we used the speaker annotations provided with our datasets in order to label our utterances in native/non native speech),

- **SHOW:** classify the utterances in different broadcast programs (as described in table 2, each utterance of our corpus is labeled with a *broadcast program name*).

As a more visual analysis, we also plot an example of hidden representations projected to a 2-D space using t-distributed Stochastic Neighbor Embedding (t-SNE) (Maaten and Hinton, 2008).[5]

4.2 Shallow classifiers

We built three shallow classifiers (SHOW, STYLE, ACCENT) with a similar architecture. The classifier is a feed-forward neural network with one hidden layer (size of the hidden layer is set to 128) followed by dropout (rate of 0.5) and a ReLU non-linearity. Finally, a $softmax$ layer is used for mapping onto the label set size. We chose this simple formulation as we are interested in evaluating the quality of the representations learned by our ASR prediction model, rather than optimizing the secondary classification tasks.

The network input size depends on which layer to analyze (see figure 1). Training is performed using *Adam* (Kingma and Ba, 2014) (using default parameters) over shuffled mini-batches in order to minimize the cross-entropy loss. The models are trained for 30 epochs with a batch size of 16 speech utterances. After training, we keep the model with the best performance on DEV set and report its performance on the TEST set. The classifier outputs are evaluated in terms of accuracy.

4.3 Data

A data set from (Elloumi et al., 2018) was employed in our experiments, divided into three subsets: training (TRAIN), development (DEV) and test (TEST). Speech utterances come from various French broadcast collections gathered during projects or shared tasks: *Quaero*, *ETAPE*, *ESTER 1 & ESTER 2* and *REPERE*.

The TEST set contains unseen broadcast programs that are different from those present in TRAIN and DEV (Elloumi et al., 2018).

Category	TRAIN	DEV	TEST
Non Spontaneous	54250	6101	**3109**
Spontaneous	**13277**	**1403**	3728
Native	44487	4945	5298
Non Native	**23040**	**2559**	**1539**

Table 1: Distribution of our utterances between non spontaneous and spontaneous styles, native and non native accents

Tables 1 and 2 show the whole data set in terms of speech turns available for each classification task. We clearly see that the data is unbalanced for the three categories (STYLE, ACCENT, SHOW). Since we are interested in evaluating the discriminative power of our learned representations for

Show	TRAIN	DEV
FINTER-DEBATE	7632	833
FRANCE3-DEBATE	928	77
LCP-PileEtFace	**4487**	525
RFI	25565	2831
RTM	24198	2745
TELSONNE	4717	**493**
Total	67527	7504

Table 2: Number of utterances for each broadcast program

these 3 tasks, we extracted a balanced version of our TRAIN/DEV/TEST sets by filtering among over-represented labels (final number of kept utterances corresponds to bold numbers in table 1 and 2). Table 3 shows the distribution of our final balanced TRAIN/DEV/TEST sets as well as the number of categories for each task.[6]

	#Catg	Turns of speech per category		
		TRAIN	DEV	TEST
SHOW	5	$4487_{\times5}$	$493_{\times5}$	-
STYLE	2	$13277_{\times2}$	$1403_{\times2}$	$3109_{\times2}$
ACCENT	2	$23040_{\times2}$	$2559_{\times2}$	$1539_{\times2}$

Table 3: Description of our balanced data set for each category

4.4 Results

For each classification task, we build a shallow classifier using the hidden representations of *TXT*, *RAW-SIG* and *TXT+RAW-SIG* blocks as input. The experimental results are presented in table 4 for both DEV and TEST sets separated by two vertical bars ($\|$).

Classification performance is all above a random baseline accuracy ($>50\%$ for STYLE and ACCENT and $>20\%$ for SHOW). This shows that training a deep WER prediction system gives representation layers that contain a meaningful amount of information about speech style, speech accent and broadcast program label. Predicting utterance style (spontaneous/non spontaneous) is slightly easier than predicting accent (native/non native) especially from text input. One explanation might be that speech utterances are short ($< 6s$) while accent identification needs probably longer sequences. We also observe that using both text and speech improves the learned representations for the STYLE task while it is

---

[6]For the *SHOW* classification task, the *FRANCE3-DEBATE* shows were finally removed since they represent a too small amount of speech turns.

less clear for the ACCENT task (for which improvement seen on DEV is not confirmed on TEST). Finally, text input is significantly better than speech input whereas we could have expected better performance from speech for the SHOW task (speech signals convey information about the audio characteristics of a broadcast program). It means that text input contains correlated information with broadcast-program type, speech style and speaker's accent. In case of SHOW task, our performance prediction system is able to capture information (vocabulary, topic, syntax, etc.) about a specific broadcast program type, based on textual features and to differ it from others (radio programs, TV debate programs, phone calls, broadcast news programs, etc.). Likewise, the textual information captured is very different between spontaneous/non-spontaneous speech styles and native/non-native speaker's accents.

Among the representations analyzed, the outputs of the CNNs (A1,B1) lead to the best classification results, in line with previous findings about convolutions as feature extractors. Performance then drops using the higher (fully connected) layers that do not generate better representations for detecting style, accent or show.

Layer	Dim.	SHOW	STYLE	ACCENT
		TXT		
A1	1280	**57.12**$\|$-	**80.72**$|$68.99	**70.75**$|$66.54
A2	256	54.89$\|$-	80.01$\|$**69.56**	69.30$|$69.43
A3	128	51.04$\|$-	79.23$|$68.27	68.25$\|$**70.89**
		RAW-SIG		
B1	512	**42.35**$\|$-	**72.92**$\|$**58.64**	64.60$\|$**55.85**
B2	512	41.22$\|$-	72.20$|$58.41	64.44$|$54.84
B3	256	41.22$\|$-	72.38$|$58.44	64.50$|$54.65
B4	128	40.77$\|$-	72.38$|$58.52	**64.74**$|$54.87
		TXT + RAW-SIG		
C1 (A3+B4)	256	**57.04**$\|$-	**81.29**$|$70.36	**71.41**$\|$**65.98**
C2	128	53.06$\|$-	79.62$\|$**70.55**	70.01$|$65.20
Random	-	**20.00**	**50.00**	**50.00**

Table 4: Show/Style/Accent classification accuracies using representations from different layers learned during the training of our ASR WER prediction system.

We visualize an example of utterance representations from C2(TXT+RAW-SIG) layer in figure 2 using the t-SNE. For a fixed utterance duration $4s\leq D<5s$ (716 speech turns) and $5s\leq D<6s$ (489 speech turns), non spontaneous utterances are plotted in blue while spontaneous ones are in pink. The C2 layer produces clusters which shows that spontaneous utterances are in the upper-left part

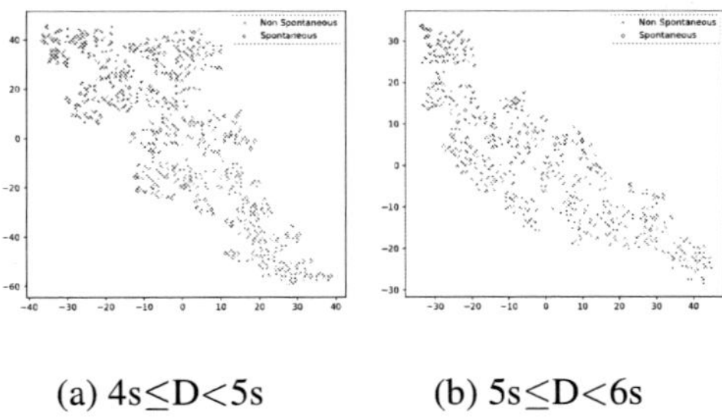

(a) 4s≤D<5s   (b) 5s≤D<6s

Figure 2: Visualization of utterance representations from C2 layer for different speech styles (S spontaneous - NS non spontaneous) - (a) utt. length is 4s≤D<5s and (b) 5s≤D<6s

of the 2D space. This suggests that C2 hidden representation captures a weak signal about speaking style.

Finally, figure 3 is the confusion matrix produced using C2(TXT+RAW-SIG) layer. The classifiers very well predicted *TELSONNE* category (Accuracy of 82%), which contains many phone calls from the radio listeners. This show is rather different from the 4 other shows in DEV (broadcast debates and news).

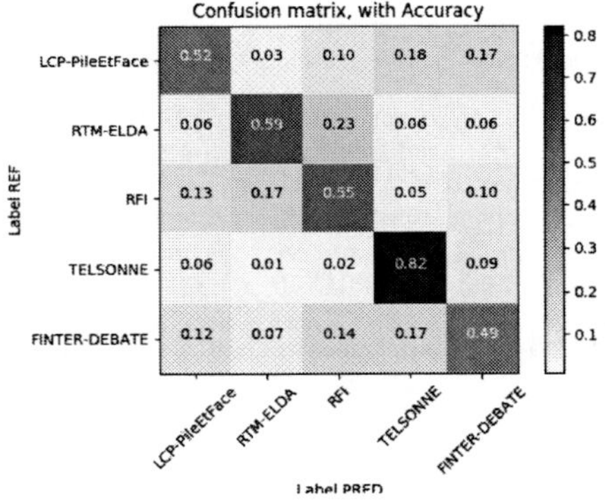

Figure 3: Confusion matrix for SHOW classification using C2(TXT+RAW-SIG) layer as input, evaluated on DEV

5 Multi-task learning

We have seen in the previous section that, while training an ASR performance prediction system, hidden layers convey a clear signal about speech style, accent and show. This suggests that these 3 types of information might be useful to structure the deep ASR performance prediction models. In this section, we investigate the effect of knowledge of these labels (style, accent, show) at training time on prediction systems qualities. For this, we perform multi-task learning providing the additional information about broadcast type, speech style and speaker's accent during training. The architecture of the multi-task model is similar to the single-task WER prediction model of Figure 1 but we add additional outputs: a $softmax$ function is added for each new classification task after the last fully connected layer (C2). The output dimension depends on the task: 6 for SHOW and 2 for STYLE and ACCENT tasks.

We use the full (unbalanced) data set described in tables 1 and 2. Training of the multitask model uses $Adadelta$ update rule and all parameters are initialized from scratch (8.70M). Models are performed for 50 epochs with batch size of 32. MAE is used as the loss function for WER prediction task while cross-entropy loss is used for the classification tasks.

In the composite (multitask) loss, we assign a weight of 1 for MAE loss (main task) and a smaller weight of 0.3 (tuned using a grid search on DEV dataset) for cross-entropy (secondary classification task) loss(es).

After training, we take the model that lead to the best *MAE* on *DEV* set and report its performance on TEST. We build several models that simultaneously address 1, 2, 3 and 4 tasks. The models are evaluated with a specific metric for each task: MAE & Kendall[7] for WER prediction task and Accuracy for classification tasks.

Table 5 summarizes the experimental results on DEV and TEST sets, separated by two vertical bars (||). We considered the mono-task model described in (Elloumi et al., 2018) (and summarized in section 3) as a baseline system.

We recall that we evaluated the SHOW classification task only on the DEV set (TEST broadcast programs are new and were unseen in the TRAIN).

First of all, we notice that performance of classification tasks in muti-task scenarios are very good: we are able to train efficient ASR performance prediction systems that simultaneously tag the analyzed utterances according to their speech style, accent and broadcast program origin. Such multitask systems might be useful diagnostic tools to analyze and predict ASR on large speech collections. Moreover, our best multi-task systems dis-

---

[7]Correlation between true ASR values and predicted ASR values

Models	Performance prediction task		Classification tasks		
	MAE	Kendall	SHOW	STYLE	ACCENT
Baseline: Mono-task					
WER (Elloumi et al., 2018)	15.24||19.24	45.00||46.83	-	-	-
2-task					
WER SHOW	**14.83**||19.15	**47.25**||47.05	**99.29**||-	-	-
WER STYLE	15.07||19.66	45.92||45.49	-	99.01||65.24	-
WER ACCENT	15.05||19.60	46.17||45.60	-	-	91.72|| 75.30
3-task					
WER STYLE ACCENT	15.12||20.23	45.75||44.09	-	98.63||69.07	88.99|| **77.46**
WER SHOW ACCENT	14.94||19.76	46.19||43.61	98.38||-	-	89.87||71.44
WER SHOW STYLE	14.90||**19.14**	45.87||**47.28**	99.12||-	**99.47**||**81.98**	-
4-task					
WER SHOW STYLE ACCENT	15.15||19.64	45.59||45.42	99.04||-	99.29||81.55	**91.92**||73.60
WER ALL COMBINED OUTPUTS	**14.50** ||**18.87**	**48.16**||**48.63**	-	-	-

Table 5: Evaluation of ASR performance prediction with multi-tasks models ($DEV\|\|TEST$) computed with MAE and Kendall - secondary classification tasks accuracy is also reported

play a better performance (MAE, Kendall) than the baseline system, which means that the implicit information given about style, accent and broadcast program type can be helpful to structure the system's predictions. For example, in 2-task case, the best model is obtained on WER+SHOW tasks with a difference of +0.41%, +2.25% for MAE and Kendall respectively (on DEV) compared to the baseline on WER prediction task. However, it is also important to mention that the impact of multi-task learning on the main task (ASR performance prediction) is limited: only slight improvements on the test set are observed for MAE and Kendall metrics. Anyway, the systems trained seem complementary since their combination (averaging, over all multi-task systems, predicted WERs at utterance level) leads to significant performance improvement (MAE and Kendall).

6 Conclusion

This paper presented an analysis of learned representations of our deep ASR performance prediction system. Experiments show that hidden layers convey a clear signal about speech style, accent, and broadcast type. We also proposed a multi-task learning approach to simultaneously predict WER and classify utterances according to style, accent and broadcast program origin.

References

Yonatan Belinkov and James Glass. 2017. Analyzing hidden representations in end-to-end automatic speech recognition systems. In *Advances in Neural Information Processing Systems*, pages 2438–2448.

Yonatan Belinkov, Lluís Màrquez, Hassan Sajjad, Nadir Durrani, Fahim Dalvi, and James Glass. 2017. Evaluating layers of representation in neural machine translation on part-of-speech and semantic tagging tasks. In *Proceedings of the Eighth International Joint Conference on Natural Language Processing (Volume 1: Long Papers)*, volume 1, pages 1–10.

François Chollet et al. 2015. Keras. `https://github.com/fchollet/keras`.

Wei Dai, Chia Dai, Shuhui Qu, Juncheng Li, and Samarjit Das. 2017. Very deep convolutional neural networks for raw waveforms. In *Acoustics, Speech and Signal Processing (ICASSP), 2017 IEEE International Conference on*, pages 421–425. IEEE.

Zied Elloumi, Laurent Besacier, Olivier Galibert, Juliette Kahn, and Benjamin Lecouteux. 2018. Asr performance prediction on unseen broadcast programs using convolutional neural networks. In *IEEE International Conference on Acoustics, Speech and Signal Processing (ICASSP)*.

Sylvain Galliano, Edouard Geoffrois, Djamel Mostefa, Khalid Choukri, Jean-François Bonastre, and Guillaume Gravier. 2005. The ester phase ii evaluation campaign for the rich transcription of french broadcast news. In *Interspeech*, pages 1149–1152.

Guillaume Gravier, Gilles Adda, Niklas Paulson, Matthieu Carré, Aude Giraudel, and Olivier Galibert. 2012. The etape corpus for the evaluation of speech-based tv content processing in the french language. In *LREC-Eighth international conference on Language Resources and Evaluation*, page na.

Juliette Kahn, Olivier Galibert, Ludovic Quintard, Matthieu Carré, Aude Giraudel, and Philippe Joly. 2012. A presentation of the repere challenge. In *Content-Based Multimedia Indexing (CBMI), 2012 10th International Workshop on*, pages 1–6. IEEE.

Yoon Kim. 2014. Convolutional neural networks for sentence classification. *arXiv preprint arXiv:1408.5882*.

Diederik P. Kingma and Jimmy Ba. 2014. Adam: A method for stochastic optimization. *CoRR*, abs/1412.6980.

Laurens van der Maaten and Geoffrey Hinton. 2008. Visualizing data using t-sne. *Journal of machine learning research*, 9(Nov):2579–2605.

Abdel-rahman Mohamed, Geoffrey Hinton, and Gerald Penn. 2012. Understanding how deep belief networks perform acoustic modelling. In *Acoustics, Speech and Signal Processing (ICASSP), 2012 IEEE International Conference on*, pages 4273–4276. IEEE.

Daniel Povey, Arnab Ghoshal, Gilles Boulianne, Lukas Burget, Ondrej Glembek, Nagendra Goel, Mirko Hannemann, Petr Motlicek, Yanmin Qian, Petr Schwarz, et al. 2011. The kaldi speech recognition toolkit. In *IEEE 2011 workshop on automatic speech recognition and understanding*, EPFL-CONF-192584. IEEE Signal Processing Society.

Xing Shi, Inkit Padhi, and Kevin Knight. 2016. Does string-based neural mt learn source syntax? In *Proceedings of the 2016 Conference on Empirical Methods in Natural Language Processing*, pages 1526–1534.

Shuai Wang, Yanmin Qian, and Kai Yu. 2017. What does the speaker embedding encode? In *Interspeech*, volume 2017, pages 1497–1501.

Zhizheng Wu and Simon King. 2016. Investigating gated recurrent neural networks for speech synthesis. *CoRR*, abs/1601.02539.

Explaining non-linear Classifier Decisions within Kernel-based Deep Architectures

Danilo Croce and **Daniele Rossini** and **Roberto Basili**
Department of Enterprise Engineering
University of Roma, Tor Vergata
{croce,basili}@info.uniroma2.it

Abstract

Nonlinear methods such as deep neural networks achieve state-of-the-art performances in several semantic NLP tasks. However epistemologically transparent decisions are not provided as for the limited interpretability of the underlying acquired neural models. In neural-based semantic inference tasks epistemological transparency corresponds to the ability of tracing back causal connections between the linguistic properties of a input instance and the produced classification output.

In this paper, we propose the use of a methodology, called *Layerwise Relevance Propagation*, over linguistically motivated neural architectures, namely *Kernel-based Deep Architectures* (KDA), to guide argumentations and explanation inferences. In such a way, each decision provided by a KDA can be linked to real examples, linguistically related to the input instance: these can be used to motivate the network output. Quantitative analysis shows that richer explanations about the semantic and syntagmatic structures of the examples characterize more convincing arguments in two tasks, i.e. question classification and semantic role labeling.

1 Introduction

Nonlinear methods such as deep neural networks achieve state-of-the-art performances in several challenging problems, such as image classification or natural language processing (NLP). However the traditional AI criticism still holds: they are not epistemologically transparent, as for the limited interpretability of the neural inferences.

In a question classification (QC) task, e.g. (Li and Roth, 2006), this is particularly evident. The category describing the target of a request is relevant in question answering to optimize the later stages of search and answer detection, and its interpretation depends on a variety of semantic and syntactic properties of the question. Epistemological transparency corresponds here to the ability of tracing back the connections between linguistic properties of the input question and the proposed question category. An example-driven machine learning model should be able to provide causal relations between the input semantic aspect and the properties of the question.

For example, given the prediction *"What is the capital of Zimbabwe?"* refers to a Location, we would like the system to motivate it with a sentence such as: *Since it seems similar to "What is the capital of California?" which also refers to a* Location.

Notice how in neural learning, as for example in Multilayer Perceptrons, Long Short-Term Memory Networks, (Hochreiter and Schmidhuber, 1997), or the more recent Attention-based Networks (Larochelle and Hinton, 2010), the network parameters have no clear conceptual counterpart.

Using the *Layerwise Relevance Propagation* (LRP) (Bach et al., 2015) approach, the classification decisions of a multilayer perceptron are decomposed backward across the network layers, and evidence about the contribution of individual input fragments (i.e. layer 0) to the final decision is gathered. Evaluation against images (i.e. the MNIST and ILSVRC data sets) suggests that LRP activates meaningful associations between input and output fragments, and this corresponds to tracing back meaningful causal connections.

In this paper, we propose the use of a similar mechanism over the linguistically motivated network architectures, as they have been recently proposed in (Croce et al., 2017): Kernel-based Deep network architectures aim at integrating syntactic/semantic information derived from the adoption of Tree Kernels (Collins and Duffy,

Proceedings of the 2018 EMNLP Workshop BlackboxNLP: Analyzing and Interpreting Neural Networks for NLP, pages 16–24
Brussels, Belgium, November 1, 2018. ©2018 Association for Computational Linguistics

2001) within neural-based learning. Here, we show that the inferences of such architectures can be motivated by simply applying the LRP method, which allows to trace back causal associations between the semantic classification and the examples expressed by parse tree-based metrics. Evaluation of the LRP algorithm to the problem of explaining the system decisions allows to demonstrate the meaningful impact of LRP on semantic transparency: users faced with explanations are better oriented to accept or reject the system decisions, thus improving the impact on the overall application accuracy.

In the rest of the paper, section 2 reports related works. In section 3 we describe the Kernel-based Deep Architecture (KDA) while section 4 illustrates the details of LRP and how it connects to KDAs. In section 5 we propose both a novel model to generate explanations of a network prediction and an evaluation methodology. In section 6 we provide experimental evidences of the overall system's effectiveness against two semantic tasks, question classification and frame-based argument classification in the semantic role labeling chain. Lastly, in section 7 conclusions are derived.

2 Related Work

Linguistically motivated *explanatory methods* should provide semantically clear justifications about a neural network textual inferences.

Methods making the neural learning more *readable* are usually designed to trace back the portions of the network input that mostly contributed to the output decision. Network propagation techniques are used to identify the patterns of a given input item (e.g., an image) that are linked to the particular deep neural network prediction as in (Erhan et al., 2010; Zeiler and Fergus, 2013). Usually, these are based on backward algorithms that layer-wise reuse arc weights to propagate the prediction from the output down to the input, thus leading to the re-creation of *meaningful* patterns in the input space. Typical examples are deconvolution heatmaps, used to approximate through Taylor series the partial derivatives at each layer (Simonyan et al., 2013), or the so-called Layer-wise Relevance Propagation (LRP), that redistributes back positive and negative evidence across the layers (Bach et al., 2015).

Several efforts have been made in the perspective of providing explanations of a neural classifier, often by focusing into highlighting an handful of crucial features (Baehrens et al., 2010) or deriving simpler, more readable models from a complex one, e.g. a binary decision tree (Frosst and Hinton, 2017), or by local approximation with linear models (Ribeiro et al., 2016). However, although they can explicitly show the representations learned in the specific hidden neurons (Frosst and Hinton, 2017), these approaches base their effectiveness on the user ability to study the quality of the reasoning and of the accountability as a side effect of the quality of the selected features: this can be very hard in tasks where boundaries between classes are not well defined. Sometimes, explanations are associated to vector representations as in (Ribeiro et al., 2016), i.e. bag-of-word in case of text classification, which is clearly weak at capturing significant linguistic abstractions, such as the involved syntactic relations. In this work, we propose a model which allows to provide explanations that are easily interpretable even by non-expert users, as they are expressed in natural language and are hence a more natural solution. It implicitly captures lexical, semantic and syntactic generalizations through the generation of a linguistically fluent explanation of predictions: as this is exploit linguistic analogies it provides a more transparent and epistemologically coherent view on the system's decision.

3 A Kernel-based Deep Architecture

In this section, we will first describe the Nyström method for generating low dimensional embeddings that approximate high dimensional kernel spaces. Then we will review the Kernel-based Deep Architecture discussed in (Croce et al., 2017), that efficiently combines kernel methods and deep learning by using a Nyström layer into a neural architecture.

Given an input dataset $\mathcal{D}$, a kernel $K(o_i, o_j)$ is a similarity function over $\mathcal{D}^2$ that corresponds to a dot product in the implicit kernel space, i.e., $K(o_i, o_j) = \Phi(o_i) \cdot \Phi(o_j)$. Kernel functions are used by learning algorithms, such as Support Vector Machines (Shawe-Taylor and Cristianini, 2004), to operate only implicitly on instances in the kernel space, by never accessing their explicit definition. Let us apply the projection function Φ over all examples from $\mathcal{D}$ to derive representations, $\vec{x}$ denoting the rows of the matrix

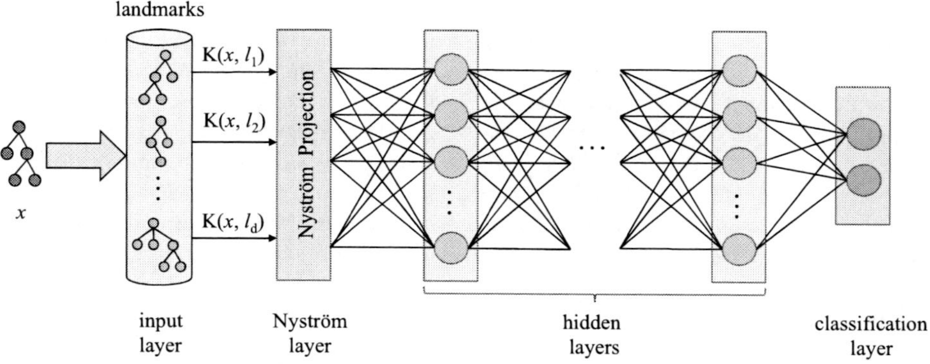

Figure 1: Kernel-based Deep Architecture.

X. The Gram matrix can always be computed as $G = XX^\top$, with each single element corresponding to $G_{ij} = \Phi(o_i)\Phi(o_j) = K(o_i, o_j)$. The aim of the Nyström method is to derive a new low-dimensional embedding $\tilde{x}$ in a l-dimensional space, with $l \ll n$ so that $\tilde{G} = \tilde{X}\tilde{X}^\top$ and $\tilde{G} \approx G$. This is obtained by generating an approximation $\tilde{G}$ of G using a subset of l columns of the matrix, i.e., a selection of a subset $L \subset \mathcal{D}$ of the available examples, called *landmarks*. Suppose we randomly sample l columns of G, and let $C \in \mathbb{R}^{|D| \times l}$ be the matrix of these sampled columns. Then, we can rearrange the columns and rows of G and define $X = [X_1 \ X_2]$ such that:

$$G = XX^\top = \begin{bmatrix} W & X_1^\top X_2 \\ X_2^\top X_1 & X_2^\top X_2 \end{bmatrix}$$
$$\text{and} \quad C = \begin{bmatrix} W \\ X_2^\top X_1 \end{bmatrix}$$

where $W = X_1^\top X_1$, i.e., the subset of G that contains only landmarks. The Nyström approximation can be defined as:

$$G \approx \tilde{G} = CW^\dagger C^\top \tag{1}$$

where $W^\dagger$ denotes the Moore-Penrose inverse of W. The Singular Value Decomposition (SVD) is used to obtain $W^\dagger$ as it follows. First, W is decomposed so that $W = USV^\top$, where U and V are both orthogonal matrices, and S is a diagonal matrix containing the (non-zero) singular values of W on its diagonal. Since W is symmetric and positive definite, $W = USU^\top$. Then $W^\dagger = US^{-1}U^\top = US^{-\frac{1}{2}}S^{-\frac{1}{2}}U^\top$ and the Equa-

tion 1 can be rewritten as

$$G \approx \tilde{G} = CUS^{-\frac{1}{2}}S^{-\frac{1}{2}}U^\top C^\top$$
$$= (CUS^{-\frac{1}{2}})(CUS^{-\frac{1}{2}})^\top = \tilde{X}\tilde{X}^\top$$

Given an input example $o \in \mathcal{D}$, a new low-dimensional representation $\tilde{\tilde{x}}$ can be thus determined by considering the corresponding item of C as

$$\tilde{\tilde{x}} = \vec{c}\,US^{-\frac{1}{2}} \tag{2}$$

where $\vec{c}$ is the vector whose dimensions contain the evaluations of the kernel function between o and each landmark $o_j \in L$. Therefore, the method produces l-dimensional vectors.

Notice that an optimal selection of landmarks can be expected to reduce the Gram Matrix approximation error. However, the uniform sampling without replacement policy is adopted: it is in fact theoretically and empirically shown in Kumar et al. (2012) to achieve results comparable with alternative but (more complex) selection policies.

In (Croce et al., 2017), the Nyström representation $\tilde{\tilde{x}}$ has been used as input within neural network architectures. In fact, given a labeled dataset $\mathcal{L} = \{(o, y) \mid o \in \mathcal{D}, \ y \in Y\}$, where o refers to a generic instance and y is its associated class, a Multi-Layer Perceptron (MLP) architecture can be defined, with a specific Nyström layer based on the Nyström embeddings of Eq. 2. Such Kernel-based Deep Architecture (KDA) has an *input layer*, a *Nyström layer*, a possibly empty sequence of non-linear *hidden layers* and a final *classification layer*, which produces the output, as shown in Figure 1.

The *input* layer corresponds to the input vector $\vec{c}$, i.e., the row of the C matrix associated to an example o. The input layer is mapped to the *Nyström* layer, through the projection in Equation 2. Notice that the embedding provides also the proper weights, defined by $US^{-\frac{1}{2}}$, so that the mapping can be expressed through the Nyström matrix $H_{Ny} = US^{-\frac{1}{2}}$: it corresponds to a pre-trained stage derived through SVD. Formally, the low-dimensional embedding of an input example o, is $\tilde{x} = \vec{c}\,H_{Ny} = \vec{c}\,US^{-\frac{1}{2}}$.

The resulting outcome $\tilde{x}$ is the input to one or more non-linear *hidden* layers. Each t-th hidden layer is realized through a matrix $H_t \in \mathbb{R}^{h_{t-1} \times h_t}$ and a bias vector $\vec{b}_t \in \mathbb{R}^{1 \times h_t}$, where h_t denotes the desired hidden layer dimensionality. Clearly, given that $H_{Ny} \in \mathbb{R}^{l \times l}$, $h_0 = l$. The first hidden layer in fact receives in input $\tilde{x} = \vec{c}H_{Ny}$, that corresponds to the $t = 0$ layer input $\vec{x}_0 = \tilde{x}$ and its computation is formally expressed by $\vec{x}_1 = f(\vec{x}_0 H_1 + \vec{b}_1)$, where f is a non-linear activation function. In general, the generic t-th layer is modeled as:

$$\vec{x}_t = f(\vec{x}_{t-1}H_t + \vec{b}_t) \tag{3}$$

The final layer of KDA is the *classification layer*, realized through the output matrix H_O and the output bias vector $\vec{b}_O$. Their dimensionality depends on the dimensionality of the last hidden layer (called O_{-1}) and the number $|Y|$ of different classes, i.e., $H_O \in \mathbb{R}^{h_{O_{-1}} \times |Y|}$ and $\vec{b}_O \in \mathbb{R}^{1 \times |Y|}$, respectively. In particular, this layer computes a linear classification function with a softmax operator so that $\hat{y} = softmax(\vec{x}_{O_{-1}} H_O + \vec{b}_O)$.

In addition to standard dropout, a L_2 regularization is applied to the norm of each layer.

Finally, the KDA is trained by optimizing a loss function made of the sum of two factors: first, the cross-entropy function between the gold classes and the predicted ones; second the L_2 regularization, whose importance is regulated by a meta-parameter λ. The final loss function is thus

$$L(y, \hat{y}) = \sum_{(o,y) \in \mathcal{L}} y\,log(\hat{y}) + \lambda \sum_{H \in \{H_t\} \cup \{H_O\}} ||H||^2$$

where $\hat{y}$ are the softmax values computed by the network and y are the true one-hot encoding values associated with the example from the labeled training dataset $\mathcal{L}$.

As shown in Figure 1, it is worth noticing that the network is stimulated with an input vector c which contains the kernel evaluations $K(s, l_i)$ between each example and the landmarks. When using linguistic kernels (such as Semantic Tree Kernels) this measure corresponds to a syntactic/semantic similarity between the x and the subset of examples used for the space reconstruction (made available through the Nyström method). Once stimulated, the network will provide an output. In order to give an explanation to a network decision, we will discuss in the following section how to revert the propagation process connecting output and input. As a side effect we will be able to determine those landmarks mostly affecting the final decision and which are more semantically related to the input instance.

4 Layer-wise Relevance Propagation in Kernel-based Deep Architectures

Layer-wise Relevance propagation (LRP, presented in (Bach et al., 2015)) is a framework which allows to decompose the prediction of a deep neural network computed over a sample, e.g. an image, down to relevance scores for the single input dimensions of the sample such as subpixels of an image.

More formally, let $f : \mathbb{R}^d \to \mathbb{R}^+$ be a positive real-valued function taking a vector $x \in \mathbb{R}^d$ as input. The function f can quantify, for example, the probability of x being in a certain class. The Layer-wise Relevance Propagation assigns to each dimension, or feature, x_d a relevance score $R_d^{(1)}$ such that:

$$f(x) \approx \sum_d R_d^{(1)} \tag{4}$$

Features whose score is $R_d^{(1)} > 0$ or $R_d^{(1)} < 0$ correspond to evidence in favor or against, respectively, the output classification. In other words, LRP allows to identify fragments of the input playing key roles in the decision, by propagating relevance backwards. Let us suppose to know the relevance score $R_j^{(l+1)}$ of a neuron j at network layer $l + 1$, then it can be decomposed into messages $R_{i \leftarrow j}^{(l,l+1)}$ sent to neurons i in layer l:

$$R_j^{(l+1)} = \sum_{i \in (l)} R_{i \leftarrow j}^{(l,l+1)} \tag{5}$$

Hence it derives that the relevance of a neuron i at layer l can be defined as:

$$R_i^{(l)} = \sum_{j \in (l+1)} R_{i \leftarrow j}^{(l,l+1)} \tag{6}$$

Note that 5 and 6 are such that 4 holds. In this work, we adopted the ϵ-rule defined in (Bach et al., 2015) to compute the messages $R^{(l,l+1)}_{i \leftarrow j}$:

$$R^{(l,l+1)}_{i \leftarrow j} = \frac{z_{ij}}{z_j + \epsilon \cdot \mathrm{sign}(z_j)} R^{(l+1)}_j$$

where $z_{ij} = x_i w_{ij}$ and $\epsilon > 0$ is a numerical stabilizing term and must be small. The informative value is justified by the fact that the weights z_{ij} are linked to the activation weights w_{ij} of the input neurons.

If we apply it to a KDA processing linguistic observations, then LRP implicitly traces back the syntactic, semantic and lexical relations between the example and the landmarks, thus it selects the landmarks whose presences were the most influential to identify the predicted structure in the sentence. Indeed, each landmark is uniquely associated to an entry of the input vector $\vec{c}$, as illustrated in Sec 3.

5 Explanatory Models

Justifications for the KDA emissions can be obtained by explaining the evidence in favour or against a class using landmarks $\{\ell\}$ as examples. The idea is to select those $\{\ell\}$ that the LRP method produces as the most active elements in layer 0. Once such active landmarks are detected, an *Explanatory Model* is a function in charge to compile the linguistically fluent explanation by using analogies or differences with the input case. The semantic expressiveness of such analogies makes the resulting explanation clear and increases the user confidence on the system reliability. When a sentence s is classified, LRP assigns activation scores r^s_ℓ to each individual landmark ℓ: let $\mathcal{L}^{(+)}$ (or $\mathcal{L}^{(-)}$) denote the set of landmarks with positive (or negative) activation score.

Formally, every explanation is characterized by a triple $e = \langle s, C, \tau \rangle$ where s is the input sentence, C is the predicted label and τ is the modality of the explanation: $\tau = +1$ for positive (i.e. acceptance) statements while $\tau = -1$ correspond to rejections of the decision C.

A landmark ℓ is *positively activated* for a given sentence s if there are not more than $k-1$ other active landmarks ℓ' whose activation value is higher than the one for ℓ, i.e.

$$|\{\ell' \in \mathcal{L}^{(+)} : \ell' \neq \ell \wedge r^s_{\ell'} \geq r^s_\ell > 0\}| < k$$

Similarly, a landmark is *negatively activated* when:

$$|\{\ell' \in \mathcal{L}^{(-)} : \ell' \neq \ell \wedge r^s_{\ell'} \leq r^s_\ell < 0\}| < k$$

where k is a parameter used to make explanation depending on not more than k landmarks, denoted by $\mathcal{L}_k$. Positively (or negative) active landmarks in $\mathcal{L}_k$ are assigned to an activation value $a(\ell, s) = +1 \, (-1)$, while $a(\ell, s) = 0$ for all other not activated landmarks.

Given the explanation $e = \langle s, C, \tau \rangle$, a landmark ℓ whose (known) class is C_ℓ is *consistent* (or *inconsistent*) with e according to the fact that the following function:

$$\delta(C_\ell, C) \cdot a(\ell, q) \cdot \tau$$

is positive (or negative, respectively), where $\delta(C', C) = 2\delta_{kron}(C' = C) - 1$ and δ_{kron} is the Kronecker delta.

An *explanatory model* is then a function $M(e, \mathcal{L}_k)$ which maps an explanation e, a sub set $\mathcal{L}_k$ of the active *and* consistent landmarks $\mathcal{L}$ for e into a sentence f in natural language. Of course several definitions for $M(e, \mathcal{L}_k)$ are possible. A general explanatory model would be:

$$M(e, \mathcal{L}_k) = \begin{cases} \text{'}s \text{ is } C \text{ since it is similar to } \ell\text{'} \\ \forall \ell \in \mathcal{L}_k^+ \quad \text{if } \tau > 0 \\[1em] \text{'}s \text{ is not } C \text{ since it is different} \\ \text{from } \ell \text{ which is } C\text{'} \\ \forall \ell \in \mathcal{L}_k^- \quad \text{if } \tau < 0 \\[1em] \text{'}s \text{ is } C \text{ but I don't know why'} \\ \text{if } \mathcal{L} \equiv \emptyset \end{cases}$$

where $\mathcal{L}_k^{\pm}$ are the partition of landmarks with positive and negative relevance scores in $\mathcal{L}_k$, respectively.

Here we introduce three explanatory models we used during experimental evaluation:

(Basic Model) The first model is the simplest. It returns an analogy only with the (unique) consistent landmark with the highest positive score if $\tau = 1$ and lowest negative score when $\tau = -1$. In case no active and consistent landmark can be found, the Basic Model returns a phrase stating only the predicted class, with no explanation. As an example the explanation of an accepted decision in an argument classification task, described by the triple $e_1 = \langle \text{'Put this plate in the center of the table'},$ $\text{THEME}_{\text{PLACING}}, 1\rangle$, would be mapped by the model into:

I think **"this plate"** *is* THEME *of* PLACING *in "Robot* PUT ***this plate*** *in the center of the table" since similar to* **"the soap"** *in "Can you* PUT ***the soap*** *in the washing machine?".*

(Multiplicative Model) In a second model, denoted as *multiplicative*, the system makes reference to up to $k_1 \leq k$ analogies with positively (or negatively) active and consistent landmarks. Given the above explanation e_1, and $k_1 = 2$, it would return:

I think **"this plate"** *is* THEME *of* PLACING *in "Robot* PUT ***this plate*** *in the center of the table" since similar to* **"the soap"** *in "Can you* PUT **"the soap"** *in the washing machine?" and it is also similar to* **"my coat"** *in "*HANG ***my coat*** *in the closet in the bedroom".*

(Contrastive Model) The last proposed model is more complex since it returns both a positive (whether $\tau = 1$) and a negative ($\tau = -1$) analogy by selecting, respectively, the most positively relevant and the most negatively relevant consistent landmark: For instance, given $e1$, it could return:

I think **"this plate"** *is the* THEME *of* PLACING *in "Robot* PUT ***this plate*** *in the center of the table" since similar to* **"the soap"** *which is in "Can you* PUT ***the soap*** *in the washing machine" and it is not the* GOAL *of* PLACING *since different from* **"on the counter"** *in "*PUT *the plate* **on** *the counter".*

5.1 Using information theory for validating explanations

Let $P(C|s)$ and $P(C|s,e)$ be, respectively, the prior probability of the classification of s being correct and the probability of the classification being correct given an explanation. Note that both indicate the level of confidence the user has in the classifier (i.e. the KDA) given the amount of available information, i.e. with and without explanation. Three explanations are possible:

- **Useful explanations:** these are explanations such that C is correct and $P(C|s,e) > P(C|s)$ or C is not correct and $P(C|s,e) < P(C|s)$

- **Useless explanations:** they are explanations such that $P(C|s,e) = P(C|s)$

- **Misleading explanations:** they are explanations such that C is correct and $P(C|s,e) < P(C|s)$ or C is not correct and $P(C|s,e) > P(C|s)$

The core idea is that semantically coherent and exhaustive explanations must indicate correct classifications whereas incoherent or non-existent explanations must hint towards wrong classifications.

Given the above probabilities, we can measure the quality of an explanation by computing the achieved *Information Gain* (Kononenko and Bratko, 1991): the *posterior* probability is expected to grow w.r.t. to the *prior* one for correct decisions when a good explanation is available against the input sentence, while decreasing for bad or confusing explanations. The intuition behind Information Gain is that it measures the amount of information (provided in number of bits) gained by the explanation about the user decision of accepting the system classification on an incoming sentence s. A positive gain indicates that the probability amplifies towards the right decisions, and declines with errors. We will let users to judge the quality of the explanation and assign them a posterior probability that increases along with better judgments. In this way we have a measure of how convincing the system is about its decisions as well as how weak it is to clarify erroneous cases. To compare the overall performance of the different explanatory models M, the Information Gain is measured against a collection of explanations generated by M and then normalized throughout the collection's entropy E as follows:

$$I_r = \frac{1}{E} \frac{1}{|\mathcal{T}_s|} \sum_{j=1}^{|\mathcal{T}_s|} I(j) = \frac{I_a}{E} \qquad (7)$$

where $\mathcal{T}_s$ is the explanations collection and $I(j)$ is the Information Gain of explanation j.

6 Experimental Evaluation

The effectiveness of the proposed approach has been measured against two different semantic processing tasks,i.e. question classification and argument classification in semantic role labeling. The Nystrom projection has been implemented in the KeLP framework (Filice et al., 2018)[1], the neural network and LRP have been implemented in Tensorflow[2], with 1 and 2 hidden layers, respectively, whose dimensionality corresponds to the number of involved Nystrom landmarks (500 and 200, re-

---

[1]http://www.kelp-ml.org
[2]https://www.tensorflow.org

Category	$P(C|s,e)$	$1 - P(C|s,e)$
V.Good	0.95	0.05
Good	0.8	0.2
Weak	0.5	0.5
Bad	0.2	0.8
Incoher.	0.05	0.95

Table 1: Posterior probabilities w.r.t. quality categories

Class	Incoher.	Bad	Weak	Good	V.Good
Incoher.	1.00	0.83	0.50	0.16	0.00
Bad	0.83	1.00	0.66	0.33	0.16
Weak	0.50	0.66	1.00	0.66	0.50
Good	0.16	0.33	0.66	1.00	0.83
V.Good	0.00	0.16	0.50	0.83	1.00

Table 2: Weights for the Cohen's Kappa κ_w statistics

	QC	SRL-AC
Basic	0.548	0.669
Multiplicative	0.514	0.662
Contrastive	0.576	0.667
κ_w	0.677	0.783
accuracy	0.926	0.961

Table 3: Information gains for the three Explanatory Models applied to the SRL-AC and QC datasets. k_w is the weighted Cohen's Kappa κ_w.

spectively, randomly selected[3]), and the adoption of dropout regularization in hidden and final layers. For both tasks, hyper-parameters have been optimized via grid-search. The Adam optimizer has been applied to minimize the cross-entropy loss function, with a multi-epoch (500) training, each fed with batches of size 256. We adopted an early stop strategy, where the best model was selected according to the performance over the development set.

For evaluating our explanation method, we defined five quality categories and associated them to values for the posteriori probability $P(C|s,e)$, as shown in Table 1. We gathered into explanation datasets hundreds of explanations from the three models for each task and presented them to a pool of annotators (further details in related subsections) for independent labeling; annotators had no information of the correctness of the system emissions but just knowledge about the dataset entropy. We addressed their consensus by measuring a weighted Cohen's Kappa.

6.1 Question Classification

In our first evaluation, we replicated the experiments reported by (Croce et al., 2017) with respect to the question classification task. We thus used the UIUC dataset (Li and Roth, 2006), including a training and test set of 5452 and 500 questions, respectively, organized in 6 coarse-grained classes (as ENTITY or HUMAN). We generated Nystrom representation of the Compositionally Smoothed Partial Tree Kernel (Annesi et al., 2014) function with default parameters $\mu = \lambda = 0.4$. Using 500

---

[3]More complex policies have been applied to select landmarks but statistically significant results have not been measured (not reported here due to space limitations).

landmarks, the KDA accuracy was 92.6%.

A group of 3 annotators evaluated an explanation dataset of 300 explanations (perfectly balanced between correct and not correct classification), composed of 100 explanations for each model. Performances are shown in Table 3.

All three explanatory models were able to gain more than half the required information in order to ascertain the correctness of the classification. Consider:

I think "What year did Oklahoma become a state ?" refers to a NUMBER *since similar to "The film Jaws was made in what year ?"*

The model provided an evidently coherent analogy, but this is a easy case due to the occurrence in both questions of very discriminative words, i.e *"what year"*. However, the system is also able to capture semantic similarities when both syntactic and lexical features are different. E.g.:

I think "Where is the Mall of the America ?" refers to a LOCATION *since similar to "What town was the setting for The Music Man ?".*

This is an high-quality explanation since the system provided an analogy with a landmark requesting the same fine-grained category but with little sharing of lexical and syntactic information (note, for example, the absence in the landmark of the very discriminative word *"where"*). Let us now consider the case of wrong classifications:

I think "Mexican pesos are worth what in U.S. dollars ?" refers to a DESCRIPTION *since similar to "What is the Bernoulli Principle ?"*

The system provided an explanation that is not possible to easily interpret: indeed it was labeled as [Incoherent] by all the annotators.

However, system effectiveness is limited in case of negative modality for correct classifications. In these cases explanations, albeit coherent, can be trivial and do not actually help in reducing uncertainty about the correct target class. The explanation

I think "What is angiotensin ?" does not refer to a NUM *since different from "What was Einstein 's IQ ?".*

is correct but obvious. As an alternative, a negative analogy with a very likely class, i.e. ENTITY or DESCRIPTION, would have provided more useful information for disambiguation. A second challenge is represented by inherently ambiguous questions. The following explanation

I think "What is the sales tax in Minnesota ?" refers to a NUMBER *since similar to "What is the population of Mozambique ?" and does not refer to a* ENTITY *since different from "What is a fear of slime ?".*

tells why NUMBER is a more likely class than ENTITY. Although seemingly correct, this is a mistake, as ENTITY is the proper decision. However, the explanation is perfectly fine, as it well expresses the decision's rationale: lack of contextual information in the question is here the main cause of the error.

6.2 Argument Classification

Semantic role labeling (SRL (Palmer et al., 2010)) consists in detecting the semantic arguments associated with the predicate of a sentence and their classification into their specific roles (Fillmore (1985)). For example, given the sentence *"Bring the fruit onto the dining table"*, the task would be to recognize the verb *"bring"* as evoking the BRINGING frame, with its roles, THEME for *"the fruit"* and GOAL for *"onto the dining table"*. Argument classification corresponds to the subtask of assigning labels to the sentence fragments spanning individual roles.

As proposed in (Moschitti et al., 2008), SRL can be modeled as a multi classification task over each parse tree node n, where argument spans reflect sub-sentences covered by the tree rooted at n. Consistently with (Croce et al., 2011), in our experiments the KDA has been empowered with a Smoothed Partial Tree Kernel, operating over Grammatical Relation Centered Tree (GRCT) derived from dependency grammar.

We used the HuRIC dataset (Bastianelli et al., 2014), including over 650 annotated transcriptions of spoken robotic commands, organized in 18 frames and about 60 arguments[4]. We extracted single arguments from each HuRIC example, for a total of $1,300$ instances. We run experiments with a methodology similar to the one described in Sec

---

[4] http://sag.art.uniroma2.it/lu4r.html

6.1, but due to the limited data size we performed extensive 10-fold cross-validation, optimizing network hyper-parameters via grid-search for each test set. We generated Nystrom representation of a equally-weighted linear combination of SPTK function with default parameters $\mu = \lambda = 0.4$ and of linear kernel function applied to sparse vector representing the instance frame. With these settings, the KDA accuracy was 96.1%. We sampled 692 explanations almost equally distributed among the 3 explanatory models. Two annotators were involved.

Results are shown in Tab 3. In this task, all models were able to gain more than two thirds of needed information. The alike scores of the three models are probably due to the narrow linguistic domain of the corpus and the well-defined semantic boundaries between the arguments. To show the capability of such models, let us consider:

I think "the washer" is the CONTAINING OBJECT *of* CLOSURE *in "Robot can you* OPEN *the washer?" since similar to "the jar" in "*CLOSE *the jar" and it is not the* THEME *of* BRINGING *since different from "the jar" in "*TAKE *the jar to the table of the kitchen".*

I think "me" is the BENEFICIARY *of* BRINGING *in "I would like some cutlery can you* GET *me some?" since similar to "me" in "*BRING *me a fork from the press." and it is not the* COTHEME *of* COTHEME *since different from "me" in "Would you please* FOLLOW *me to the kitchen?".*

The above commands have very limited lexical overlap with retrieved landmarks. Nevertheless, the analogies make explanations quite effective: explanatory models seems to successfully capture semantic and syntactic relations among input instances and closely related landmarks.

7 Conclusion

This paper investigated the effectiveness of a novel method to generate epistemologically transparent and linguistically fluid explanations for a neural predictor emissions. The proposed approach applies LRP to a KDA to backpropagate and redistribute the prediction to input entries. It then produces a sentence exploiting analogies with landmarks, according to different explanatory models. Moreover a novel evaluation methodology based on Information Theory is provided. Empirical investigations carried out against the QC and AC tasks confirm that the explanatory models contribute to increase the user confidence in the machine correct responses.

References

Paolo Annesi, Danilo Croce, and Roberto Basili. 2014. Semantic compositionality in tree kernels. In *Proceedings of CIKM 2014*. ACM.

Sebastian Bach, Alexander Binder, Gregoire Montavon, Frederick Klauschen, Klaus-Robert Mller, and Wojciech Samek. 2015. On pixel-wise explanations for non-linear classifier decisions by layer-wise relevance propagation. *PLOS ONE*, 10(7).

David Baehrens, Timon Schroeter, Stefan Harmeling, Motoaki Kawanabe, Katja Hansen, and Klaus-Robert Müller. 2010. How to explain individual classification decisions. *J. Mach. Learn. Res.*, 11:1803–1831.

Emanuele Bastianelli, Giuseppe Castellucci, Danilo Croce, Luca Iocchi, Roberto Basili, and Daniele Nardi. 2014. Huric: a human robot interaction corpus. In *LREC*, pages 4519–4526. European Language Resources Association (ELRA).

Michael Collins and Nigel Duffy. 2001. New ranking algorithms for parsing and tagging: Kernels over discrete structures, and the voted perceptron. In *Proceedings of the 40th Annual Meeting on Association for Computational Linguistics (ACL '02), July 7-12, 2002, Philadelphia, PA, USA*, pages 263–270. Association for Computational Linguistics, Morristown, NJ, USA.

Danilo Croce, Simone Filice, Giuseppe Castellucci, and Roberto Basili. 2017. Deep learning in semantic kernel spaces. In *Proceedings of the 55th Annual Meeting of the Association for Computational Linguistics (Volume 1: Long Papers)*, pages 345–354, Vancouver, Canada. Association for Computational Linguistics.

Danilo Croce, Alessandro Moschitti, and Roberto Basili. 2011. Structured lexical similarity via convolution kernels on dependency trees. In *Proceedings of EMNLP '11*, pages 1034–1046.

Dumitru Erhan, Aaron Courville, and Yoshua Bengio. 2010. Understanding representations learned in deep architectures. Technical Report 1355, Université de Montréal/DIRO.

Simone Filice, Giuseppe Castellucci, Giovanni Da San Martino, Alessandro Moschitti, Danilo Croce, and Roberto Basili. 2018. Kelp: a kernel-based learning platform. *Journal of Machine Learning Research*, 18(191):1–5.

Charles J. Fillmore. 1985. Frames and the semantics of understanding. *Quaderni di Semantica*, 6(2):222–254.

Nicholas Frosst and Geoffrey Hinton. 2017. Distilling a neural network into a soft decision. *CEUR Workshop Proceedings*, 2071.

Sepp Hochreiter and Jürgen Schmidhuber. 1997. Long short-term memory. *Neural Comput.*, 9(8):1735–1780.

Igor Kononenko and Ivan Bratko. 1991. Information-based evaluation criterion for classifier's performance. *Machine Learning*, 6(1):67–80.

Sanjiv Kumar, Mehryar Mohri, and Ameet Talwalkar. 2012. Sampling methods for the nyström method. *J. Mach. Learn. Res.*, 13:981–1006.

Hugo Larochelle and Geoffrey E. Hinton. 2010. Learning to combine foveal glimpses with a third-order boltzmann machine. In *Proceedings of Neural Information Processing Systems (NIPS)*, pages 1243–1251.

Xin Li and Dan Roth. 2006. Learning question classifiers: the role of semantic information. *Natural Language Engineering*, 12(3):229–249.

Alessandro Moschitti, Daniele Pighin, and Roberto Basili. 2008. Tree kernels for semantic role labeling. *Computational Linguistics*, 34.

M.S. Palmer, D. Gildea, and N. Xue. 2010. *Semantic Role Labeling*. Online access: IEEE (Institute of Electrical and Electronics Engineers) IEEE Morgan & Claypool Synthesis eBooks Library. Morgan & Claypool Publishers.

Marco Túlio Ribeiro, Sameer Singh, and Carlos Guestrin. 2016. "why should I trust you?": Explaining the predictions of any classifier. *CoRR*, abs/1602.04938.

John Shawe-Taylor and Nello Cristianini. 2004. *Kernel Methods for Pattern Analysis*. Cambridge University Press, Cambridge, UK.

Karen Simonyan, Andrea Vedaldi, and Andrew Zisserman. 2013. Deep inside convolutional networks: Visualising image classification models and saliency maps. *CoRR*, abs/1312.6034.

Matthew D. Zeiler and Rob Fergus. 2013. Visualizing and understanding convolutional networks. *CoRR*, abs/1311.2901.

Nightmare at test time:
How punctuation prevents parsers from generalizing

Anders Søgaard[1]   **Miryam de Lhoneux**[2]   **Isabelle Augenstein**[1]

[1]Dpt. of Computer Science
University of Copenhagen

[2] Dpt. of Linguistics and Philology
Uppsala University

Abstract

Punctuation is a strong indicator of syntactic structure, and parsers trained on text with punctuation often rely heavily on this signal. Punctuation is a diversion, however, since human language processing does not rely on punctuation to the same extent, and in informal texts, we therefore often leave out punctuation. We also use punctuation ungrammatically for emphatic or creative purposes, or simply by mistake. We show that (a) dependency parsers are sensitive to *both* absence of punctuation and to alternative uses; (b) neural parsers tend to be more sensitive than vintage parsers; (c) training neural parsers *without* punctuation outperforms all out-of-the-box parsers across all scenarios where punctuation departs from standard punctuation. Our main experiments are on synthetically corrupted data to study the effect of punctuation in isolation and avoid potential confounds, but we also show effects on out-of-domain data.

1 Introduction

We study the sensitivity of modern dependency parsers to punctuation. While punctuation was originally motivated by reading aloud, serving the purpose of "breath marks" (Baldwin and Coady, 1978), many modern-day punctuation systems are designed to facilitate grammatical disambiguation. This paper aims to show that for this reason, punctuation can significantly hurt the generalization ability of state-of-the-art syntactic parsers. In other words, syntactic parsers become too reliant on punctuation and therefore suffer from the absence or creative uses of punctuation. Such uses are abundant; see Table 1 for examples from Twitter. Such situations, where highly predictive features are absent or distorted at test time, were referred to in Globerson and Roweis (2006) as *nightmare at test time*. Human reading is very robust to variation in punctuation (Baldwin and Coady,

No punctuation	
(1)	i have so many questions i dont know where to start

Creative punctuation	
(2)	What. The. Fuck. Ever. Dot. Com
(3)	... and then , , , , i start to feel ~lonely~

Both	
(4)	I feel like ... idk ... idk ... idk man. Nvm I'm good.

Table 1: Examples of uses of punctuation

1978); so creative use of punctuation does not hurt human reading performance. In effect, sensitivity to punctuation is a major obstacle that prevents our syntactic parser from achieving human-level robustness.

The generalization ability of a dependency parser is usually measured by evaluating its accuracy on held-out data, our yardstick to prevent over-fitting, i.e. we define the degree to which a parser has over-fitted to the training data as the difference between performance on training data and performance on the held-out data. This practice is poor when data is not i.i.d., since the held-out data cannot be assumed to be representative; in such cases, little or no over-fitting does not guarantee our parsers have learned important linguistic generalizations: Rather, the parsers may have over-fitted to superficial cues that are present in *both* the training and test datasets (Jo and Bengio, 2017). We argue that punctuation signs are superficial cues preventing modern parsers from learning appropriately high-level abstractions from our datasets.

Contributions   We evaluate three neural dependency parsers for English, as well as two older alternatives, on a standard benchmark, before and after stripping punctuation, as well as after injecting more punctuation signs in the benchmark.

25

Proceedings of the 2018 EMNLP Workshop BlackboxNLP: Analyzing and Interpreting Neural Networks for NLP, pages 25–29
Brussels, Belgium, November 1, 2018. ©2018 Association for Computational Linguistics

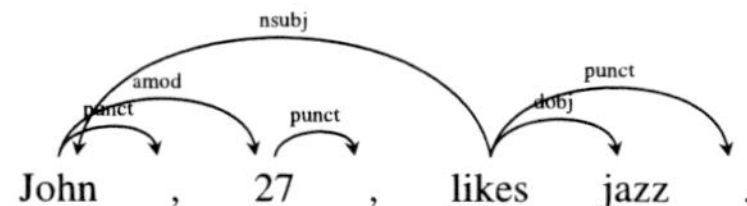

Figure 1: Punctuation in Stanford dependencies

We show that (a) projective parsers are, unsurprisingly, more sensitive to punctuation injection than non-projective ones, since punctuation injection may introduce crossing edges, and (b) neural parsers are more sensitive than vintage parsers. The latter is our main contribution, but we also show that training a neural parser *without* punctuation outperforms all parsers trained in a regular fashion across all punctuation scenarios. Our experiments are on semi-synthetic data to control for confounds, but we also show the parser trained without punctuation is superior on real data with non-standard punctuation.

2 Punctuation in Stanford dependencies

Dependency annotation Dependency annotation refers to the manual assignment of syntactic structures to sentences, following one of several sets of available annotation guidelines. This paper focuses exclusively on the Stanford dependencies annotation scheme (de Marneffe and Manning, 2008). This scheme restricts the set of possible syntactic structures to single-rooted, ordered, possibly non-projective trees whose edges are uniquely labeled by a single dependency label.

Punctuation Punctuation should be distinguished from diacritics and logographs. The two most frequently used punctuation signs are periods and commas. Periods ("."), however, are potentially ambiguous with other uses of dots, typically indicating omissions or pauses. When dots are used emphatically and creatively it is hard to maintain this distinction, and we will simply refer to *dots* and *commas* in this paper. We ignore other punctuation signs, including dashes, question and exclamation marks, and colons and semicolons.

Punctuation is, among other things, used to mark boundaries between constituents of written language. Space characters, for example, separate words, albeit sometimes inconsistently. Spacing is a fairly recent innovation in writing; classical Latin and Greek did not leave spaces between

words, and many Asian languages, e.g., Thai and Lao, still do not. A period is typically used to mark the end of a grammatical sentence, and commas are often used to separate clauses. Therefore, punctuation also correlates strongly with properties of syntactic structures and is therefore very predictive of dependency structures.

Variation in punctuation is often observed in informal texts, but variation may also be the result of errors. Punctuation errors are by far the most frequent error type in scientific writing, for example (Remse et al., 2016). Modern parsers should be robust to such variation, just like humans are (Baldwin and Coady, 1978).

Punctuation in Stanford dependencies In the Stanford dependencies (de Marneffe and Manning, 2008), periods attach to root tokens, and commas attach to their left neighbor or to root tokens; see Figure 1.

3 Experiments

This section describes how we remove and inject punctuation (our perturbation maps), and details of the parsers used in our experiments.

Perturbation maps Since dots consistently attach to the root token of the sentence, and commas attach to their left neighbour or to the root token, we can remove and inject additional punctuation in a sentence without affecting the rest of its syntactic structure and without violating the wellformedness of dependency trees. Note, however, that injecting a root-dominated dot or comma may lead to crossing edges, i.e., turn a projective dependency tree into a non-projective one. This may lead to cascading errors for projective dependency parsers (Ng and Curran, 2015). In our experiments, arc-eager MALTPARSER and STANFORD are the only projective parsers. We therefore propose two *perturbation maps* (Jo and Bengio, 2017): (a) simply removing punctuation, and (b) a simple injection scheme with two parameters χ and δ. Let a dependency structure be an ordered tree with n nodes decorated with words $w_1, \ldots, w_n$. At any node $1 \le i \le n$, we (a) inject a comma at position i with probability χ and move nodes $i \le j \le n$ to positions $j + 1$, increasing the size of the graph by 1; and (b) inject a dot at position $i+1$ with probability δ and move nodes $i < j \le n$ to positions $j + 1$, increasing the size of the graph by 1. If we follow standard methodology

Parser	Neural	Trans.-based	Projective
UUPARSER	✓	✓	
KGRAPHS	✓		
MALTPARSER		✓	✓
TURBOPARSER			
STANFORD	✓	✓	✓

Table 2: Our dependency parsers

and ignore punctuation when evaluating parsers, we can compare evaluations before and after applying the injection scheme. It is equally straightforward to remove punctuation without affecting the rest of the dependency tree. Each element w_i to the right of punctuation nodes w_j $(i > j)$ moves to the left $(j - 1)$ for every punctuation item, decreasing the length of the sentence by 1 each time.

Note that both removing punctuation and our injection scheme can be seen as perturbation maps (Jo and Bengio, 2017) of our dataset, with the following important properties: (a) grammatical structure recognizability, i.e., human ability to correctly process sentences, is preserved (Baldwin and Coady, 1978), (b) surface statistical regularities are qualitatively different, and (c) there exists a non-trivial generalization map between the original dataset and the perturbed version. These properties mean we can use our punctuation injection scheme to evaluate the sensitivity of neural dependency parsers to the surface statistical regularities involving dots and commas (Jo and Bengio, 2017). Since human reading is largely unaffected by erroneous punctuation, we may expect parsers to be robust to absence of punctuation and punctuation injection, as well. Our results clearly show this is not the case; in fact, recently proposed neural dependency parsers are *very* sensitive to differences in punctuation.

Our dependency parsers We use five parsers in our experiments: the Uppsala parser (UU-PARSER) (de Lhoneux et al., 2017a,b), the graph-based parser proposed in (Kiperwasser and Goldberg, 2016)(KGRAPHS) , the arc-eager MALT-PARSER (Nivre et al., 2007), the TURBOPARSER (Fernández-González and Martins, 2015), and the STANFORD parser (Chen and Manning, 2014). UUPARSER is a neural transition-based dependency parser, while KGRAPHS is a neural graph-based parser. MALTPARSER is a more traditional transition-based parser, and TURBOPARSER is a more traditional graph-based parser. Fi-

nally, the STANFORD parser is a projective, neural transition-based dependency parser. All parsers rely on predicted part-of-speech tags, except UU-PARSER (which does not rely on part-of-speech information at all). We use the TURBOTAGGER to obtain those. See Table 2 for an overview of our parsers.

Finally, we also evaluate three non-standard versions of the UUPARSER, namely, a parser trained with the same parameters as the off-the-shelf parser (de Lhoneux et al., 2017b), but which simply *ignores* dots and commas completely (NOPUNCT), and two heavily regularised versions of the parser trained in the standard fashion: (a) a version trained with the drop-out parameter set to 0.8 (zeros out 80% of activations); (b) a version with the gradient clipping parameter set to 0.075. We do so to answer the question of whether more heavily regularized dependency parsers are less sensitive to punctuation (they are not).

4   Results and analysis

We discuss the sensitivity of off-the-shelf dependency parsers to our perturbation maps, comparing to a parser trained after removing punctuation in the training data, as well as to heavily regularised versions of the same parser.

No punctuation We first test our parsers on a version of the validation set where we strip away all punctuation. The data thus consists of newswire (WSJ 22) with punctuation removed. This is similar to Example (1) in Table 1, but in-domain. The results are in the second results column in Table 3, with the relative increases in error listed in the third results column. The drop induced by removing punctuation is quite dramatic: The UUPARSER, for example, suffers an absolute drop of 5.4% LAS or an error increase of 67%. For every three mistakes, UUPARSER does, stripping away punctuation makes it introduce another two. Note that, generally, the relative increase in error is much higher for the three neural parsers, and that the regularisation strategies (drop-out and gradient clipping) do not seem to help much.

Comma and dot injection At medium injection rates, all parsers are sensitive to punctuation injection. With $\delta = 0.05, \gamma = 0.05$, for example, all parsers perform worse than in the absence of punctuation. Our main observation is, again, that neural parsers suffer higher relative increases in errors

	ENGLISH PENN TREEBANK (CORRUPTED)									OUT-OF-DOMAIN			
	δ=0	NO	Rel.err.	δ=0.01	δ=0.01	δ=0.05	δ=0.05	δ=0.1	Rel.err.	GWEB		FOSTER	
	χ=0	PUNCT	incr.	χ=0.01	χ=0.05	χ=0.01	χ=0.05	χ=0.1	incr.	ANSW	REV	FOOTBALL	TWITTER
UUPARSER	**0.918**	0.869	0.598	**0.901**	0.867	0.886	0.851	0.794	1.512	**0.676**	0.662	0.770	0.699
KGRAPHS	0.910	0.865	0.500	0.894	0.861	0.876	0.841	0.779	1.456	0.645	0.609	0.774	0.715
MALTPARSER	0.858	0.805	0.373	0.836	0.791	0.804	0.757	0.675	1.289	0.605	0.566	0.721	0.642
TURBOPARSER	0.894	0.852	0.396	0.883	0.858	0.875	0.851	0.802	0.868	0.640	0.595	0.766	**0.722**
STANFORD	0.870	0.816	0.415	0.845	0.808	0.806	0.772	0.688	1.400	0.640	0.608	0.735	0.689
NO PUNCT	0.898	**0.898**	0.000	0.898		**0.898**			0.000	0.670	**0.669**	**0.792**	0.701
DROPOUT α=0.8	0.904	0.847	0.594	0.884	0.845	0.858	0.820	0.748	1.625	0.661	0.652	0.761	0.682
CLIP t=0.075	0.917	0.871	0.554	0.900	0.864	0.887	0.851	0.793	1.494	0.672	0.657	**0.792**	0.676

Table 3: Labeled attachment scores with punctuation removed. All parsers suffer from absence of or additional punctuation. The relative increase in error ($\frac{1\text{-BL}}{1\text{-SYS}} - 1$; with BL performance on original text; SYS performance under NO PUNCT and $\delta = 0.1, \kappa = 0.1$, resp.) for neural parsers is higher than for non-neural parsers. GWEB and FOSTER scores are on development sentences (of at least five words) with no punctuation.

than vintage parsers. Note that the MALTPARSER is a projective parser and therefore has a higher relative increase in error; but TURBOPARSER is much more robust than the other parsers. That said, it still does much worse than the UUPARSER trained without punctuation.

Evaluation on informal text with non-standard punctuation We also evaluate the models on sentences with non-standard punctuation in the development sections in the Google Web Treebank with informal text (from Yahoo Answers and user reviews). Specifically, we evaluate the models on sentences with more than one dot. Again, we show that the neural dependency parser trained without punctuation is superior to the other parsers.

5   Related work

Punctuation in parsing Spitkovsky et al. (2011) introduced the idea of splitting sentences at punctuation and imposing parsing restrictions over the fragments and observed significant improvements in the context of unsupervised parsing. Ng and Curran (2015) aim to prevent cascading errors by enforcing correct punctuation arcs. They restrict themselves to projective dependency parsing; erroneous punctuation arcs do not lead to cascading errors in non-projective dependency parsing. Ma et al. (2014), motivated by the same observation, treat punctuation marks as properties of their neighboring words rather than as individual tokens, showing improvements on in-domain data.

Breaking NLP models Jia and Liang (2017) show how machine reading models can easily be broken with distractor sentences at test time

and propose an alternative evaluation scheme, and Belinkov and Bisk (2018) show how susceptible character-based machine translation models are to noise. Both papers are similar to ours in evaluating the performance of state-of-the-art models under corruptions of the data. There was recently a workshop dedicated to evaluation of NLP models under human adversarial example selection (Ettinger et al., 2017). Historically, NLP models were rarely evaluated on synthetic or otherwise adversarial data, but we believe this is a fruitful research direction. This is largely a philosophical question, and we believe a philosophical argument is in order. John Dewey (John Dewey, 1910), the American philosopher, distinguishes three modes of thinking: (i) common reasoning, which identifies pattern in available, historical data, (ii) empirical thinking, which collects new data to vary the experimental conditions, and (iii) experimental thinking, which actively modifies the conditions in controlled experiments to isolate the relevant variables. We believe recent work on breaking NLP models is an attempt to introduce experimental thinking into NLP, which has otherwise been limited – or *handicapped* in Dewey's words – by what data happens to be available.

6   Conclusions

We evaluate the sensitivity of five dependency parsers to variations in punctuation, showing that available neural parsers tend to be more sensitive to such variation. We also show, however, that training neural parsers without punctuation provides a robust model that is better than any off-the-shelf parsers.

Acknowledgments

We thank CSC in Helsinki and Sigma2 in Oslo for providing the computational resources used in the experiments, through NeIC-NLPL (www.nlpl.eu). The first author was supported by an ERC Starting Grant.

References

Scott Baldwin and James Coady. 1978. Psycholinguistic approaches to a theory of punctuation. *Journal of Literacy Research*, 10(4):363–376.

Yonatan Belinkov and Yonatan Bisk. 2018. Synthetic and Natural Noise Both Break Neural Machine Translation.

Danqi Chen and Christopher Manning. 2014. A fast and accurate dependency parser using neural networks. In *Proceedings of EMNLP*, pages 740–750. Association for Computational Linguistics.

Allyson Ettinger, Sudha Rao, Hal Daumé III, and Emily M. Bender. 2017. Towards Linguistically Generalizable NLP Systems: A Workshop and Shared Task. In *Proceedings of the First Workshop on Building Linguistically Generalizable NLP Systems*, pages 1–10, Copenhagen, Denmark. Association for Computational Linguistics.

Daniel Fernández-González and André F. T. Martins. 2015. Parsing as reduction. In *Proceedings of ACL*, pages 1523–1533. Association for Computational Linguistics.

Amir Globerson and Sam Roweis. 2006. Nightmare at test time: robust learning by feature deletion. In *ICML*.

Robin Jia and Percy Liang. 2017. Adversarial Examples for Evaluating Reading Comprehension Systems. In *Proceedings of EMNLP*.

Jason Jo and Yoshua Bengio. 2017. Measuring the tendency of CNNs to Learn Surface Statistical Regularities. *CoRR*, abs/1711.11561.

John Dewey. 1910. *How we think*. Dover.

Eliyahu Kiperwasser and Yoav Goldberg. 2016. Simple and accurate dependency parsing using bidirectional LSTM feature representations. 4:313–327.

Miryam de Lhoneux, Yan Shao, Ali Basirat, Eliyahu Kiperwasser, Sara Stymne, Yoav Goldberg, and Joakim Nivre. 2017a. From raw text to universal dependencies - look, no tags! pages 207–217, Vancouver, Canada.

Miryam de Lhoneux, Sara Stymne, and Joakim Nivre. 2017b. Arc-hybrid non-projective dependency parsing with a static-dynamic oracle. In *Proceedings of the 15th International Conference on Parsing Technologies*, pages 99–104, Pisa, Italy.

Ji Ma, Yue Zhang, and Jingbo Zhu. 2014. Punctuation processing for projective dependency parsing. In *ACL*.

Marie-Catherine de Marneffe and Chris Manning. 2008. The Stanford typed dependencies representation. In *Coling Workshop on Cross-Framework and Cross-Domain Parser Evaluation*.

Dominick Ng and James Curran. 2015. Identifying cascading errors using constraints in dependency parsing. In *ACL*.

Joakim Nivre, Johan Hall, Jens Nilsson, Atanas Chanev, Gülşen Eryiğit, Sandra Kübler, Svetoslav Marinov, and Erwin Marsi. 2007. MaltParser: A language-independent system for data-driven dependency parsing. *Natural Language Engineering*, 13(2):95–135.

Madeline Remse, Mohsen Mesgar, and Michael Strube. 2016. Feature-rich error detection in scientific writing using logistic regression. In *BEA*.

Valentin Spitkovsky, Hiyan Alshawi, and Dan Jurafsky. 2011. Punctuation: Making a point in unsupervised dependency parsing. In *CoNLL*.

Evaluating Textual Representations through Image Generation

Graham Spinks
Department of Computer Science
KU Leuven, Belgium
graham.spinks@cs.kuleuven.be

Marie-Francine Moens
Department of Computer Science
KU Leuven, Belgium
sien.moens@cs.kuleuven.be

Abstract

We present a methodology for determining the quality of textual representations through the ability to generate images from them. Continuous representations of textual input are ubiquitous in modern Natural Language Processing techniques either at the core of machine learning algorithms or as the by-product at any given layer of a neural network. While current techniques to evaluate such representations focus on their performance on particular tasks, they don't provide a clear understanding of the level of informational detail that is stored within them, especially their ability to represent spatial information. The central premise of this paper is that visual inspection or analysis is the most convenient method to quickly and accurately determine information content. Through the use of text-to-image neural networks, we propose a new technique to compare the quality of textual representations by visualizing their information content. The method is illustrated on a medical dataset where the correct representation of spatial information and shorthands are of particular importance. For four different well-known textual representations, we show with a quantitative analysis that some representations are consistently able to deliver higher quality visualizations of the information content. Additionally, we show that the quantitative analysis technique correlates with the judgment of a human expert evaluator in terms of alignment.

1 Introduction

In this paper, a method is proposed to evaluate the quality of a textual representation by conditioning an image generation network on it.

Neural networks implicitly construct representations of a textual input by learning which features are important for the task at hand. It is not immediately possible however to assess the level of detail and structure that is retained in such a representation. Many systems often complement or replace the input with pre-trained representations that have the advantage of being constructed with a larger unlabeled corpus. Depending on the task, this practice sometimes significantly improves the performance of the network (Turian et al., 2010). On the one hand, this is due to the use of a larger unlabeled corpus which reduces data sparsity and thus improves generalization accuracy. On the other hand, representations often contain higher-level features that are fundamental for the task they are trained for. A neural network in a separate task can thus rely on those features without having to discover them all over again.

As the field of Natural Language Processing advances and machine learning models expand to include multimodal information, the importance of understanding the level of detail and information that is retained in a textual representation only grows. Obtained representations can be employed in additional tasks (for example generation, translation, summarization, etc.) depending on their ability to capture certain types of information. The medical domain in particular might benefit from a better understanding of representations as the industry moves to adopt deep learning methods in increasingly intricate applications and researchers attempt to extract and utilize more complex information structures. An example is spatial information which is an important quantity in many natural language applications, yet no explicit methodology exists that indicates to what extent that information is present in textual representations. In many medical settings, a correct understanding and representation of such information is crucial. In thorax radiography, which is the focus of this paper, textual captions often include detailed findings which relate to specific areas in an X-Ray. Clinical texts in general, add an extra level of com-

Proceedings of the 2018 EMNLP Workshop BlackboxNLP: Analyzing and Interpreting Neural Networks for NLP, pages 30–39
Brussels, Belgium, November 1, 2018. ©2018 Association for Computational Linguistics

plexity as they often lack syntactic structure and employ many shorthands.

Images differ from texts in the sense that the retained information and generalization of a representation are immediately apparent for a human observer. It is not surprising that the 'human perceptual score' is a frequently used metric to evaluate image generation systems (Borji, 2018). In this paper we propose a novel method to assess the quality of textual representations. By creating images from different textual representations we show that some representations lack the necessary information to lead to detailed high-quality images. The textual representations are evaluated both by comparing the quality of the produced images compared to the images in the test data, as well as the alignment between images and captions. The outcome is determined both by a qualitative (human perceptual scores) as well as a quantitative (divergence scores) measure. To calculate the divergence scores, we rely on the methodology that estimates distance between two distributions as introduced by (Danihelka et al., 2017) and extend it to estimate how well image and text are aligned in the generated content.

As we show in the results, text-to-image architectures are indeed suitable to get an immediate visual estimate of the quality of the representation and the information contained within. We will evaluate several common textual representations that were constructed with unsupervised learning techniques on both a relatively straightforward conditional GAN as well as on a more advanced StackGan (Zhang et al., 2017) which uses several stages and a conditioning mechanism that augments the textual representation.

The contributions of this paper are:

- The formulation of a methodology to visualize and evaluate the information and quality of different textual representations.

- The extension of a GAN evaluation measure to evaluate alignment of output with conditional information.

2 Motivation and background

To understand the motivation of this paper, it is necessary to understand some background on the different types of textual representations and why better evaluation methods are necessary. As we use text-to-image models for evaluation purposes, we also discuss related research in that area.

2.1 Textual Representations

A textual representation is usually a vector associated with a piece of text, which may be a character, word, sentence, paragraph or document. In its simplest form, a representation can be a symbolic ID, such as in a one-hot vector where each dimension represents an ID. This is essentially a discrete, symbolic representation that is very sparse in information as by definition only one dimension is non-zero. They are also somewhat arbitrary in the sense that two texts that are near each other in the code space don't necessarily share a similar meaning or syntax.

More efficient methods assign particular hand-engineered or automatically extracted features to a lower-dimensional vector. One feature can be stored in exactly one dimension or it could be shared over many. In this paper we will focus on the latter, also referred to as distributed representations or word embeddings, which is the traditional method to represent sentences in recent neural network related research. They are dense, low-dimensional and real-valued (Turian et al., 2010). Texts that contain similar concepts or meaning for a typical task end up near each other in such a distributed representation space which serves as a proxy for generalized, semantic information storage. Word embeddings can be built with unsupervised training, for example by leveraging positional information of texts in a corpus; with weakly supervised training, for example in an adversarial setting; or with supervision of output labels. While this paper focuses on unsupervised and weakly supervised methods only, the methods that are described here are applicable to supervised representations as well.

Well-known methods of creating word embeddings are the word2vec algorithms, introduced by Mikolov et al. (2013a). Word embeddings are usually constructed with neural networks that predict the context of a word in a text document. They are able to scale to large training corpora, thus representing large amounts of information and features in a relatively small amount of dimensions. While word2vec word embeddings solely operate on the word level, extensions have been made that include information at the level of characters (e.g. char-CNN-RNN (Kim et al., 2016)), or at higher levels such as sentences, paragraphs or documents. (e.g. skipthought vectors (Kiros et al., 2015) or doc2vec (Le and Mikolov, 2014)).

While these methods usually are trained on tasks that reproduce the context of a textual component, autoencoders (AE) are trained to recreate the original text in its entirety while implicitly learning a compact, distributed representation as well of the input text along the way. A recent method that builds on the autoencoder approach is an Adversarially Regularized Autoencoder (ARAE) (Kim et al., 2017). Here, the representation is built explicitly from an encoder that is trained as part of an autoencoder as well as a conventional Generative Adversarial Network (GAN). Such representations contain semantic information about the sentence but also discriminative information that allows the adversarial network to distinguish real samples from fake ones. As a result, a smoother semantic transition is apparent while traversing the representation space when compared to an autoencoder. Spinks and Moens (2018) have applied this technique to create textual representations of X-Ray captions and generate textual output with low perplexity.

The quality of distributed vectors can be assessed with similarity tasks that give a rough measure of semantic and syntactic information (Mikolov et al., 2013a,c) but studies by Faruqui et al. (2016) and Linzen (2016) indeed suggest that the use of word similarity tasks for the evaluation of word vectors is problematic and may lead to incorrect inferences. Schnabel et al. (2015) have evaluated embeddings with a range of methods, both intrinsic, such as semantic and syntactic similarity, and extrinsic, such as noun phrase chunking and sentiment classification. For the extrinsic tasks, they found that different representations performed best for different tasks, suggesting that perhaps there isn't one optimal representation for all tasks. Such studies suggest that better methodologies and more research is needed into methods that accurately assess the value of different continuous representations. This paper addresses this by focusing on the evaluation of the information content of the representation rather than any task-oriented metric. Lazaridou et al. (2015) also worked towards a visualization method for text representations by averaging images of the nearest neighbors vectors after a cross-modal mapping. Contrary to this work, their approach did not include any evaluation mechanism of the outcome and only focused on individual words.

In this paper, we construct distributed representations of sentences with several *unsupervised methods* mentioned above. Subsequently, we propose a new methodology to evaluate the quality of the learned word embeddings by generating images from them, thus visualizing the level of detail and information retained in the different embeddings. To understand our methodology, it is useful to discuss some background on text-to-image models and, more in general, generative models.

2.2 Generative models

Recent text-to-image models rely on advances in generative models, which are probabilistic models that estimate a distribution given a certain input. Such generative systems have shown impressive progress in the creation of realistic data, most notably with Generative Adversarial Networks (GANs) (Goodfellow et al., 2014). In the original formulation, GANs are trained by alternately improving a generator network, G, which aims to create realistic samples and a discriminator network, D, which tries to distinguish real samples from generated ones. As training such an architecture tends to be unstable, several improvements have been proposed, for example the Wasserstein GAN (WGAN) (Arjovsky et al., 2017). In this formulation the discriminator is replaced by a critic, f, that is trained to approximate the Earth-Mover distance (EM). The EM is an estimate of the minimum amount of effort that is necessary to displace one distribution to another (Arjovsky et al., 2017). The loss function to train a GAN with the Wasserstein Distance is presented in Equation 1.

$$\min_G W(G) =$$
$$\min_G \max_f \mathbb{E}_{x \sim P_r}[f(x)] - \mathbb{E}_{\bar{x} \sim P_g}[f(\bar{x})] \quad (1)$$

where G is the generator, f is the critic, W is the Wasserstein distance, and P_r and P_g are the real and generated data distributions respectively. To ensure that the approximation to the earth mover distance is valid, the critic f should be enforced to be 1-Lipschitz continuous. (Arjovsky et al., 2017) achieve this by clipping the critic weights between $[-c, c]$, where c is typically smaller than 1.

Extensions to the GAN setup have been proposed, such as conditional adversarial networks (Odena et al., 2016), and progressively grown GANs (Zhang et al., 2017; Karras et al., 2017) which have made detailed high resolution category-dependent image generation possible. During the training of conditional GANs, the class or label is passed along to both generator and discriminator so that the networks implicitly learn relevant auxiliary information which leads to more detailed outputs. Progressively grown GANs rely on low-resolution outputs to learn outlines and structures of images that are refined into smooth visual output at higher resolutions. This approach is also the essence of cross-modal text-to-image architectures. Zhang et al. (2017), for example, have demonstrated how to produce realistic images conditioned on textual captions with a progressive GAN network called StackGAN.

In this paper, we use the StackGAN to visualize textual representations, as well as a simplified text-to-image architecture based on a GAN. The information and quality of the produced images allow us to evaluate the quality of the different textual representations. With that goal we will discuss some methods to evaluate the visual output of such text-to-image GANs.

2.3 Evaluation measures

As we produce images from text to determine the quality of the textual representations, accurate evaluation measures are needed to assess the generated images. We focus on evaluation measures for GANs as it is the only type of architecture that is used to create images in this paper.

Besides human perceptual scores, some recent advances have been made to assess the quality of the distribution of the generated output of GANs. Some of the most widely adopted measures are the Inception Score (IS) (Salimans et al., 2016) and the Fréchet Inception Distance (FID) (Heusel et al., 2017). Both measures have a reasonable correlation with image quality but also contain undesirable properties as explained by Borji (2018). One large problem is that both use a third-party network that was trained on a different dataset to measure the quality of the generated data. It therefore assumes that the distribution of the dataset used in the generation task is similar to the dataset that the third-party network was trained on. This assumption is often not fulfilled, particularly if specialized medical datasets are used.

To solve these issues, Danihelka et al. (2017) propose using divergence and distance functions that are normally used for training a GAN. Im et al. (2018) show that these metrics exhibit consistency across various models and find that they better reflect human perceptual scores than the IS and FID. To calculate how well the generated distribution has approached the data distribution, an independent critic is trained until convergence to distinguish between generated samples and samples from the validation set. The WGAN loss is used and the weights of the original generator are no longer updated. When applied to output images, the Wasserstein distance thus can give an estimate of the divergence between the generated and real images. This quantity is expressed as W_{qual_image} in Equation 2.

$$W_{qual\_image}(G, P_{r,v}) = \\ \max_{f_1}(\mathbb{E}_{x \sim P_{r,v}}[f_1(x)] - \mathbb{E}_{\bar{x} \sim P_g}[f_1(\bar{x})]) \quad (2)$$

where $P_{r,v}$ refers to the real distribution of the validation data.

Additionally, by evaluating the model that is trained in Equation 2 on the training and test set, Danihelka et al. (2017) suggest a method to estimate whether overfitting has occurred. Indeed, if the model generalizes well to the unseen examples in the testset, the expected values in Equation 3 should be roughly the same. In this equation $P_{r,te}$ and $P_{r,tr}$ refer to the real distributions of the test and training set respectively.

$$E[W_{qual\_image}(G, P_{r,te})] = \\ E[W_{qual\_image}(G, P_{r,tr})] \quad (3)$$

While this method allows us to judge the output quality of the images, and by extension the textual representations, in the following section we will explain how our methodology extends this approach in order to evaluate the alignment between image and text.

3 Method

This paper proposes a methodology that evaluates the quality of textual representations by visualizing them with text-to-image models. This is achieved in three separate stages as described in the following subsections.

3.1 Train and create a textual representation

In this paper 4 different textual representations are created by training on the captions of the

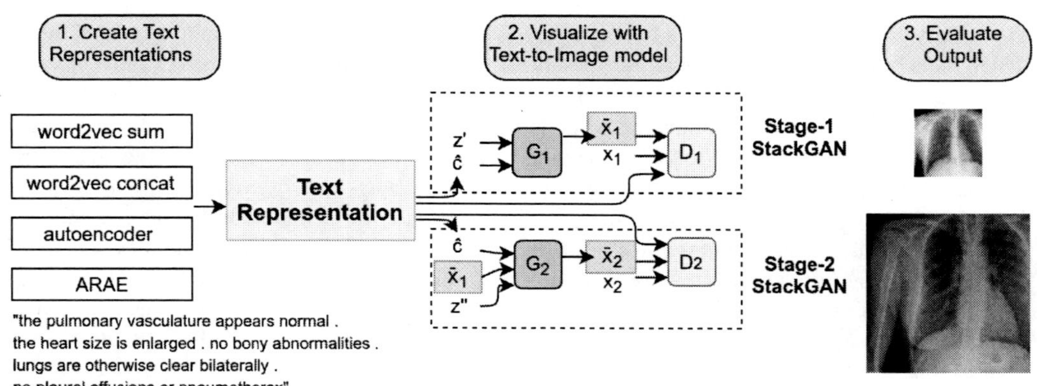

Figure 1. Overview of the methodology. A textual representation is first trained and then fed as a conditional input to a text-to-image model, in this figure a StackGAN. The textual representation is fed to both the first and second stage of an image StackGAN with the goal of creating low- and high-resolution images $\bar{x}_1$ and $\bar{x}_2$ respectively. From the representation, the augmented conditioning embedding $\hat{c}$ is formed. In a final step, the visual output is evaluated.

training set using unsupervised training methods. As these representations are compared afterwards, they each need to have the same, fixed dimension.

For the first 2 representations, the typical word2vec skip-gram word embeddings are used to build the vectors. A representation for a sentence is built by respectively summing and concatenating the individual word embeddings for the entire sequence. Such a comparison is interesting as summing (or averaging) word vectors allows to use high-dimensional word representations, yet sacrifices word order. Concatenating on the other hand, requires the use of low-dimensional word embeddings as the sentence dimension is fixed, but maintains word order and has been shown to work well at the input of convolutional networks (Kim, 2014), such as the text-to-image models used in this paper.

Additionally, the hidden state representation of an autoencoder is built. The autoencoder, that consists of a 1-layer LSTM encoder and a 1-layer LSTM decoder, is trained to recreate the input text with a cross-entropy loss at the word-level.

Finally, we also use the representation produced by an ARAE, as in section 2.1. The ARAE contains a 1-layer LSTM encoder and 1-layer LSTM decoder. The generator and discriminator consist of 3-layer feedforward networks.

3.2 Create images from text

From these representations, images are created with a text-to-image model, which can be a simple

conditional GAN or a more complex StackGAN. In the latter, a textual representation t is fed into a fully-connected net that creates a mean μ and a variance σ^2 from which augmented conditional representations $\hat{c}$ are generated. The Kullback-Leibler divergence (KL-loss) is used to coerce $\hat{c}$ to approach a normal distribution $\mathcal{N}(0, I)$. This ensures smoothness between different input texts and avoids overfitting when generating images from captions (Doersch, 2016; Larsen et al., 2015). The conditional vector $\hat{c}$ is then concatenated to a noise vector z', sampled from a normal distribution, and fed to the generator.

Such a StackGAN model is trained in two stages: at a first stage the features of real and generated images are matched to produce low-resolution images that lack detail. During the second stage, the generator produces larger images, conditioned on both the augmented conditional vector $\hat{c}$ as well as the image output of the first stage. The training is broken up into the maximization of the loss of D and the minimization of the loss of G as shown in Equations 4 and 5 for the first stage. Note that a traditional GAN formulation is used in the StackGAN model.

$$\max_{D_1} \mathcal{L}_{D_1} = \mathbb{E}_{x_1 \sim p_d}[log D_1(x_1, t)] +$$
$$\mathbb{E}_{z \sim p_z, t \sim p_d}[log(1 - D_1(G_1(z, \hat{c}), t))] \quad (4)$$

34

$$\min_{G_1} \mathcal{L}_{G_1} =$$

$$\mathbb{E}_{z \sim p_z, t \sim p_d}[log(1 - D_1(G_1(z, \hat{c}), t))] +$$
$$\lambda D_{KL}(\mathcal{N}(\mu_1(t), \Sigma_1(t)) \| \mathcal{N}(0, I)) \quad (5)$$

where p_z and p_d represent the random normal and data distribution respectively. t is the textual representation and λ is a regularization parameter to balance the loss between the two terms. Subfix 1 indicates that these equations relate to stage 1.

Note that the StackGAN model is distinct from more conventional text-to-image architectures not only in the sense that the former progressively constructs higher resolution images but also because of the conditioning augmentation. This mechanism is particularly important for this experiment, as it essentially augments the different textual representations. For the simple text-to-image GAN, which we refer to as TTI-GAN, we use a GAN architecture without separate stages that passes the textual representation to both the generator and discriminator without modifications.

Both generator and discriminator for all text-to-image architectures (i.e. the TTI-GAN and both stage-I and stage-II StackGAN) consist of a series of convolutional up- and down-sampling blocks respectively. As the text embedding t is passed to the discriminator it is compressed with a fully-connected network and replicated to match the dimensions of the image.

3.3 Evaluate the output quality

Evaluating the output quality will let us judge the textual representation quality. In order to do so, we can rely on Equation 2 to calculate W_{qual_image}. However, we would also like to have a rough idea of how well the conditional information is assimilated in the output. We therefore extend the previously mentioned setup to calculate the divergence between an additional pair of distributions. $W_{align\_im\_txt}$ in Equation 6 measures the distance between the aligned image-text distributions by also feeding the conditional information, in this case the textual representations, to the critic.

$$W_{align\_im\_txt}(G, P_{r,v}) =$$
$$\max_{f_2}(\mathbb{E}_{x \sim P_{r,v}}[f_2(x, c)] - \mathbb{E}_{\bar{x} \sim P_g}[f_2(\bar{x}, c)]) \quad (6)$$

where c is conditional information that corresponds to the current data sample. f_2 is distinct and independent from the critic f_1 in Equation 2

but is also trained until convergence on the validation set. The intuition behind Equation 6 is that $W_{align\_im\_txt}$ is a measure of the distance between the real and generated distributions with their conditional information. Thus, $W_{align\_im\_txt}$ should be smaller for models that take the conditional information into account when creating the output.

Note that the value of $W_{align\_im\_txt}$ also depends on the chosen textual representation and can therefore not be used to evaluate alignment of the TTI-GAN model across different representations. It can be used in the case of the StackGAN however as the representations are coerced to approach a normal distribution with the conditioning augmentation mechanism.

We would also like to get an estimate for the amount of overfitting that occurs for each textual representation. For this we rely on the insights of Equation 3. In Equations 7 and 8 we suggest a simple method to compare how much overfitting occurs on both the quality of the images itself, as well as on the alignment to the captions. By taking the quotient of the expected values of the evaluation of W_{qual_image} and $W_{align\_im\_txt}$, we can compare how much overfitting happened for each entity.

$$O_{qual\_image} = E[W_{qual\_image}(G, P_{r,te})] /$$
$$E[W_{qual\_image}(G, P_{r,tr})] - 1 \quad (7)$$

$$O_{align\_im\_txt} = E[W_{align\_im\_txt}(G, P_{r,te})] /$$
$$E[W_{align\_im\_txt}(G, P_{r,tr})] - 1 \quad (8)$$

The entire setup of the methodology is illustrated in Figure 1 where the StackGAN architecture is used as the text-to-image architecture.

4 Experiments

The used dataset is the chest X-Ray dataset of the National Library of Medicine, National Institutes of Health, Bethesda, MD, USA (Demner-Fushman et al., 2015). It contains the findings of the frontal and lateral X-Ray for 3851 patients. For this work only the frontal X-Rays are retained. Random crops are performed during training for data augmentation. As the content in the findings is invariant to the order of the sentences, up to 4 captions are created for each X-Ray by selecting different sentences or a different sentence order. Captions that contain less than 30

Representation	W_{qual_image}	σ
w2v sum	0.598	0.033
w2v concat	0.239	0.049
AE (*)	0.243	0.032
ARAE (*)	**0.219**	0.072

Table 1. Quantitative results of 10 runs for the TTI-GAN visualization method for each of the representations. A lower W_{qual_image} implies a better image quality. (*) For both the autoencoder and ARAE, an outlier was removed.

Representation	W_{qual_image}	$W_{align\_im\_txt}$
w2v sum	2.242	**2.239**
w2v concat	2.343	2.360
AE	2.360	2.344
ARAE	**2.229**	2.279

Table 2. Quantitative results for the trained Stage-2 StackGAN visualization method for each of the representations. A lower W_{qual_image} and $W_{align\_im\_txt}$ imply a better image quality and alignment respectively.

words are padded to equal length, with a maximum of 30 words. All words are lowercase and words with a frequency of less than 5 occurrences are removed and replaced by an out-of-vocabulary marker. While the dataset also contains diagnosis labels for each image, they are not used in this paper. The dataset is divided into training, validation and test set with 80%, 10% and 10% of the data respectively.

For the experiments we first create four different textual representations on the captions of the training set, as detailed in section 3.1. Those representations are referred to as word2vec (sum), word2vec (concat), autoencoder and ARAE. To illustrate the methodology, we set the fixed dimension of each representation to 300, which is a standard dimension for such embeddings, initially used by Mikolov et al. (2013b) in their analysis of distributed vectors. For the autoencoder and the ARAE, training is stopped when the validation error of the reconstruction is minimal.

To generate images from the text, the TTI-GAN and StackGAN models are used as explained in section 3.2. The latter produces images with higher resolution than the former approach. This is important as a higher resolution is required to make an accurate assessment about the alignment of the X-Ray images to the captions. The expected outcome is that a textual representation that maintains sequential information performs better than one that does not. Additionally we expect a code that lies on a regularized smooth space, such as the code produced by the ARAE, to be more useful than a code that does not.

Finally, we perform two types of experiments, for which the concrete setup is as follows.

1. As GAN training can be unstable, the TTI-GAN is trained 10 times for each representation. From the evaluation of each, we obtain measures for W_{qual_image}, O_{qual_image} and $O_{align\_im\_txt}$ which allow us to compare the value of the different representations. The TTI-GAN in our setup produces images with a resolution of 64x64 pixels.

2. For the StackGAN, we train one model for each representation, and train an independent critic 5 times for each model. As GAN training can be quite unstable, this experiment does not allow us to judge the value of the representations from just one run. However, we compare our estimates for W_{qual_image} and $W_{align\_im\_txt}$ to the evaluation of a trained clinician, to confirm that our methodology correlates with human judgment, both in terms of quality and alignment. For the first stage of the StackGAN we produce 64x64 pixel images, while the second stage outputs higher resolution 256x256 pixel images. For this experiment, λ was set to 0.05 and c was set to 0.01.

The text-to-image architectures are each trained during 120 epochs for each of the textual representations of the captions in the training set. The image quality is then assessed on the images that are generated from the captions of the validation and test set. This ensures that we check whether the learned representations can generalize well to captions that were never seen during their construction.

5 Results

In Table 1, the quality of the generated images of the TTI-GAN model are presented for each of the representations. Over the ten performed runs, the TTI-GAN training collapsed once for both the

Textual	Results	
Representation	#C/#N	#U
Ground Truth	20/1=20	4
w2v sum	15/4=**3.75**	6
w2v concat	12/8=1.5	5
AE	8/8=1.0	9
ARAE	11/7=1.57	7

Table 3. Qualitative assessment by clinicians for the produced images of the StackGAN Stage-2 model. Are the caption and the image congruent? (Congruent(C)/Not congruent(N)/Unclear(U). Higher values of the proportion #C/#N indicate better alignment.

ARAE and autoencoder representations. As those runs were clear outliers originating from the collapse of GAN training, they were removed from the results in Table 1. As expected, the ARAE results do appear to lead to the best overall image quality, followed by the word2vec (concat) and autoencoder models. The word2vec (sum) consistently leads to worse solutions. In terms of O_{qual_image}, the word2vec (concat) model experiences less overfitting in terms of image quality than the other representations (11.4% versus $15 - 50\%$), suggesting that such concatenated word2vec representations, that maintain word order, generalize well.

While the Stage-2 StackGAN results in Table 2 show that the ARAE representations achieve the highest image quality again, they don't entirely agree with the TTI-GAN results. This can be attributed to several causes: 1. The results for Stage-2 StackGAN only include results for 1 trained model as we would like to compare the metrics for such a model with the human judgment scores; 2. The Stage-2 StackGAN training produces more detailed images of higher resolution so consistent training is more difficult; 3. The augmented conditioning adds to the original representation, likely making the outcome for each representation more similar. With the exception of the autoencoder representation, the outcome of the Stage-2 model, which relies on the outcome of the first stage, exhibit a lot more overfitting in terms of both O_{qual_image} and $O_{align\_im\_txt}$ with values that range from 126% to 498%.

In order to assess the validity of the quantitative assessment, a trained clinician carries out a visual assessment of the produced image samples. We randomly pick 25 produced images of the StackGAN stage-2 models for each of the textual representations. We also selected 25 true caption-image pairs to compare the models to. The evaluator was asked to determine for each sample:

- Are the caption and the generated image congruent or conflicting? (Congruent/ Conflicting/ Unclear)

The evaluator was also asked for each image if it was clearly not a real but generated X-Ray, but didn't find that to be the case for any of the images. This reflects the fact that all W_{qual_image} appear to be quite similar in Table 2. Note that while our model produces an output of 256 by 256 pixels, a higher resolution is still desirable to make accurate judgments about the content of such X-Rays. In cases where the clinician found that additional information would be necessary to judge whether the alignment is correct, the clinician was able to respond with "unclear". Note that this does not mean that the quality of the image was bad.

The results are shown in Table 3. From the results, we find that indeed the word2vec summation model and the ARAE model, that obtained the best alignment scores $W_{align\_im\_txt}$ according to our quantitative measures, also appear to be the best aligned in the human judgment. While the word2vec concatenation model achieved a slightly worse $W_{align\_im\_txt}$ score, the clinician still judged its alignment to be better than the autoencoder model for the selected samples, perhaps reflecting its slightly improved W_{qual_image} over the autoencoder model.

In Figure 1, a generated image of stage-I and stage-II is presented along the architecture. While the Stage-I images capture the structure and main features of the X-Rays, there is a clear improvement in quality for the stage-II images.

6 Conclusion

In this paper, we have proposed a method to determine the quality of textual representations by visualizing them with text-to-image models. After testing our approach on four different unsupervised text-to-image models, it appears that textual representations that retain word order and lie on a smooth representation space, lead to the best quality of image output. We proposed a method to judge the alignment of the captions with the visual output which correlates with the judgment of a trained clinician. While only unsupervised representations were used in this paper, the methodology can be applied to other types of textual representations. The results in this paper constitute a new methodology to evaluate textual representations through visualization and offer an interesting path for future work. The application of the method to more complex sentences, different fields or topics as well as the development of alternative alignment measures are interesting possibilities for such research.

Acknowledgments

We thank Dr. Erwin Ströker from the UZ Brussel-VUB for sharing his expertise in the qualitative assessment of generated samples.

References

Martin Arjovsky, Soumith Chintala, and Léon Bottou. 2017. Wasserstein gan. *arXiv preprint arXiv:1701.07875*.

Ali Borji. 2018. Pros and cons of gan evaluation measures. *arXiv preprint arXiv:1802.03446*.

Ivo Danihelka, Balaji Lakshminarayanan, Benigno Uria, Daan Wierstra, and Peter Dayan. 2017. Comparison of maximum likelihood and gan-based training of real nvps. *arXiv preprint arXiv:1705.05263*.

Dina Demner-Fushman, Marc D Kohli, Marc B Rosenman, Sonya E Shooshan, Laritza Rodriguez, Sameer Antani, George R Thoma, and Clement J McDonald. 2015. Preparing a collection of radiology examinations for distribution and retrieval. *Journal of the American Medical Informatics Association*, 23(2):304–310.

Carl Doersch. 2016. Tutorial on variational autoencoders. *arXiv preprint arXiv:1606.05908*.

Manaal Faruqui, Yulia Tsvetkov, Pushpendre Rastogi, and Chris Dyer. 2016. Problems with evaluation of word embeddings using word similarity tasks. *arXiv preprint arXiv:1605.02276*.

Ian Goodfellow, Jean Pouget-Abadie, Mehdi Mirza, Bing Xu, David Warde-Farley, Sherjil Ozair, Aaron Courville, and Yoshua Bengio. 2014. Generative adversarial nets. In *Advances in Neural Information Processing Systems*, pages 2672–2680.

Martin Heusel, Hubert Ramsauer, Thomas Unterthiner, Bernhard Nessler, Günter Klambauer, and Sepp Hochreiter. 2017. Gans trained by a two time-scale update rule converge to a nash equilibrium. *arXiv preprint arXiv:1706.08500*.

Daniel Jiwoong Im, He Ma, Graham Taylor, and Kristin Branson. 2018. Quantitatively evaluating gans with divergences proposed for training. *arXiv preprint arXiv:1803.01045*.

Tero Karras, Timo Aila, Samuli Laine, and Jaakko Lehtinen. 2017. Progressive growing of gans for improved quality, stability, and variation. *arXiv preprint arXiv:1710.10196*.

Yoon Kim. 2014. Convolutional neural networks for sentence classification. *arXiv preprint arXiv:1408.5882*.

Yoon Kim, Yacine Jernite, David Sontag, and Alexander M Rush. 2016. Character-aware neural language models. In *AAAI*, pages 2741–2749.

Yoon Kim, Kelly Zhang, Alexander M Rush, Yann LeCun, et al. 2017. Adversarially regularized autoencoders for generating discrete structures. *arXiv preprint arXiv:1706.04223*.

Ryan Kiros, Yukun Zhu, Ruslan R Salakhutdinov, Richard Zemel, Raquel Urtasun, Antonio Torralba, and Sanja Fidler. 2015. Skip-thought vectors. In *Advances in Neural Information Processing Systems*, pages 3294–3302.

Anders Boesen Lindbo Larsen, Søren Kaae Sønderby, Hugo Larochelle, and Ole Winther. 2015. Autoencoding beyond pixels using a learned similarity metric. *arXiv preprint arXiv:1512.09300*.

Angeliki Lazaridou, Dat Tien Nguyen, and Marco Baroni. 2015. Do distributed semantic models dream of electric sheep? visualizing word representations through image synthesis. In *Proceedings of the Fourth Workshop on Vision and Language*, pages 81–86.

Quoc Le and Tomas Mikolov. 2014. Distributed representations of sentences and documents. In *International Conference on Machine Learning*, pages 1188–1196.

Tal Linzen. 2016. Issues in evaluating semantic spaces using word analogies. *arXiv preprint arXiv:1606.07736*.

Tomas Mikolov, Kai Chen, Greg Corrado, and Jeffrey Dean. 2013a. Efficient estimation of word representations in vector space. *arXiv preprint arXiv:1301.3781*.

Tomas Mikolov, Ilya Sutskever, Kai Chen, Greg S Corrado, and Jeff Dean. 2013b. Distributed representations of words and phrases and their compositionality. In *Advances in neural information processing systems*, pages 3111–3119.

Tomas Mikolov, Wen-tau Yih, and Geoffrey Zweig. 2013c. Linguistic regularities in continuous space word representations. In *Proceedings of the 2013 Conference of the North American Chapter of the Association for Computational Linguistics: Human Language Technologies*, pages 746–751.

Augustus Odena, Christopher Olah, and Jonathon Shlens. 2016. Conditional image synthesis with auxiliary classifier gans. *arXiv preprint arXiv:1610.09585*.

Tim Salimans, Ian Goodfellow, Wojciech Zaremba, Vicki Cheung, Alec Radford, and Xi Chen. 2016. Improved techniques for training gans. In *Advances in Neural Information Processing Systems*, pages 2234–2242.

Tobias Schnabel, Igor Labutov, David Mimno, and Thorsten Joachims. 2015. Evaluation methods for unsupervised word embeddings. In *Proceedings of the 2015 Conference on Empirical Methods in Natural Language Processing*, pages 298–307.

Graham Spinks and Marie-Francine Moens. 2018. Generating continuous representations of medical texts. *NAACL HLT 2018*, page 66.

Joseph Turian, Lev Ratinov, and Yoshua Bengio. 2010. Word representations: a simple and general method for semi-supervised learning. In *Proceedings of the 48th Annual Meeting of the Association for Computational Linguistics*, pages 384–394. Association for Computational Linguistics.

Han Zhang, Tao Xu, Hongsheng Li, Shaoting Zhang, Xiaolei Huang, Xiaogang Wang, and Dimitris Metaxas. 2017. Stackgan: Text to photo-realistic image synthesis with stacked generative adversarial networks. In *IEEE Int. Conf. Comput. Vision (ICCV)*, pages 5907–5915.

On the Role of Text Preprocessing in Neural Network Architectures: An Evaluation Study on Text Categorization and Sentiment Analysis

Jose Camacho-Collados
School of Computer Science
and Informatics
Cardiff University
camachocolladosj@cardiff.ac.uk

Mohammad Taher Pilehvar
School of Computer Engineering
Iran University of
Science and Technology
pilehvar@iust.ac.ir

Abstract

Text preprocessing is often the first step in the pipeline of a Natural Language Processing (NLP) system, with potential impact in its final performance. Despite its importance, text preprocessing has not received much attention in the deep learning literature. In this paper we investigate the impact of simple text preprocessing decisions (particularly tokenizing, lemmatizing, lowercasing and multiword grouping) on the performance of a standard neural text classifier. We perform an extensive evaluation on standard benchmarks from text categorization and sentiment analysis. While our experiments show that a simple tokenization of input text is generally adequate, they also highlight significant degrees of variability across preprocessing techniques. This reveals the importance of paying attention to this usually-overlooked step in the pipeline, particularly when comparing different models. Finally, our evaluation provides insights into the best preprocessing practices for training word embeddings.

1 Introduction

Words are often considered as the basic constituents of texts for many languages, including English.[1] The first module in an NLP pipeline is a tokenizer which transforms texts to sequences of words. However, in practise, other preprocessing techniques can be (and are) further used together with tokenization. These include lemmatization, lowercasing and multiword grouping, among others. Although these preprocessing decisions have

been studied in the context of conventional text classification techniques (Leopold and Kindermann, 2002; Uysal and Gunal, 2014), little attention has been paid to them in the more recent neural-based models. The most similar study to ours is Zhang and LeCun (2017), which analyzed different encoding levels for English and Asian languages such as Chinese, Japanese and Korean. As opposed to our work, their analysis was focused on UTF-8 bytes, characters, words, romanized characters and romanized words as encoding levels, rather than the preprocessing techniques analyzed in this paper.

Additionally, word embeddings have been shown to play an important role in boosting the generalization capabilities of neural systems (Goldberg, 2016; Camacho-Collados and Pilehvar, 2018). However, while some studies have focused on intrinsically analyzing the role of lemmatization in their underlying training corpus (Ebert et al., 2016; Kuznetsov and Gurevych, 2018), the impact on their extrinsic performance when integrated into a neural network architecture has remained understudied.[2]

In this paper we focus on the role of preprocessing the input text, particularly in how it is split into individual (meaning-bearing) tokens and how it affects the performance of standard neural text classification models based on Convolutional Neural Networks (LeCun et al., 2010; Kim, 2014, CNN). CNNs have proven to be effective in a wide range of NLP applications, including text classification tasks such as topic categorization (Johnson and Zhang, 2015; Tang et al., 2015; Xiao and Cho, 2016; Conneau et al., 2017) and polarity detection

---

[1]Note that although word-based models are mainstream in NLP in general and text classification in particular, recent work has also considered other linguistic units, such as characters (Kim et al., 2016; Xiao and Cho, 2016) or word senses (Li and Jurafsky, 2015; Flekova and Gurevych, 2016; Pilehvar et al., 2017). These techniques require a different kind of preprocessing and, while they have been shown effective in various settings, in this work we only focus on the mainstream word-based models.

[2]Not only the preprocessing of the corpus may play an important role but also its nature, domain, etc. Levy et al. (2015) also showed how small hyperparameter variations may have an impact on the performance of word embeddings. However, these considerations remain out of the scope of this paper.

Proceedings of the 2018 EMNLP Workshop BlackboxNLP: Analyzing and Interpreting Neural Networks for NLP, pages 40–46
Brussels, Belgium, November 1, 2018. ©2018 Association for Computational Linguistics

(Kalchbrenner et al., 2014; Kim, 2014; Dos Santos and Gatti, 2014; Yin et al., 2017), which are the tasks considered in this work. The goal of our evaluation study is to find answers to the following two questions:

1. Are neural network architectures (in particular CNNs) affected by seemingly small preprocessing decisions in the input text?

2. Does the preprocessing of the embeddings' underlying training corpus have an impact on the final performance of a state-of-the-art neural network text classifier?

According to our experiments in topic categorization and polarity detection, these decisions are important in certain cases. Moreover, we shed some light on the motivations of each preprocessing decision and provide some hints on how to normalize the input corpus to better suit each setting.

The accompanying materials of this submission can be downloaded at the following repository: https://github.com/pedrada88/preproc-textclassification.

2 Text Preprocessing

Given an input text, words are gathered as input units of classification models through tokenization. We refer to the corpus which is only tokenized as **vanilla**. For example, given the sentence "Apple is asking its manufacturers to move MacBook Air production to the United States." (running example), the vanilla tokenized text would be as follows (white spaces delimiting different word units):

Apple is asking its manufacturers to move MacBook Air production to the United States .

We additionally consider three simple preprocessing techniques to be applied to an input text: lowercasing (Section 2.1), lemmatizing (Section 2.2) and multiword grouping (Section 2.3).

2.1 Lowercasing

This is the simplest preprocessing technique which consists of lowercasing each single token of the input text:

apple is asking its manufacturers to move macbook air production to the united states .

Due to its simplicity, lowercasing has been a popular practice in modules of deep learning libraries and word embedding packages (Pennington et al., 2014; Faruqui et al., 2015). Despite its desirable property of reducing sparsity and vocabulary size, lowercasing may negatively impact system's performance by increasing ambiguity. For instance, the *Apple* company in our example and the *apple* fruit would be considered as identical entities.

2.2 Lemmatizing

The process of lemmatizing consists of replacing a given token with its corresponding lemma:

Apple be ask its manufacturer to move MacBook Air production to the United States .

Lemmatization has been traditionally a standard preprocessing technique for linear text classification systems (Mullen and Collier, 2004; Toman et al., 2006; Hassan et al., 2007). However, it is rarely used as a preprocessing stage in neural-based systems. The main idea behind lemmatization is to reduce sparsity, as different inflected forms of the same lemma may occur infrequently (or not at all) during training. However, this may come at the cost of neglecting important syntactic nuances.

2.3 Multiword grouping

This last preprocessing technique consists of grouping consecutive tokens together into a single token if found in a given inventory:

Apple is asking its manufacturers to move MacBook_Air production to the United_States .

The motivation behind this step lies in the idiosyncratic nature of multiword expressions (Sag et al., 2002), e.g. *United States* in the example. The meaning of these multiword expressions are often hardly traceable from their individual tokens. As a result, treating multiwords as single units may lead to better training of a given model. Because of this, word embedding toolkits such as Word2vec propose statistical approaches for extracting these multiwords, or directly include multiwords along with single words in their pretrained embedding spaces (Mikolov et al., 2013b).

3 Evaluation

We considered two tasks for our experiments: **topic categorization**, i.e. assigning a topic to a given document from a pre-defined set of topics, and **polarity detection**, i.e. detecting if the sentiment of a given piece of text is positive or negative (Dong et al., 2015). Two different settings were studied: (1) word embedding's training corpus and the evaluation dataset were preprocessed in a similar manner (Section 3.2); and (2) the two were preprocessed differently (Section 3.3). In what follows we describe the common experimental setting as well as the datasets and preprocessing used for the evaluation.

3.1 Experimental setup

We tried with two classification models. The first one is a standard CNN model similar to that of Kim (2014), using ReLU (Nair and Hinton, 2010) as non-linear activation function. In the second model, we add a recurrent layer (specifically an LSTM (Hochreiter and Schmidhuber, 1997)) before passing the pooled features directly to the fully connected softmax layer.[3] The inclusion of this LSTM layer has been shown to be able to effectively replace multiple layers of convolution and be beneficial particularly for large inputs (Xiao and Cho, 2016). These models were used for both topic categorization and polarity detection tasks, with slight hyperparameter variations given their different natures (mainly in their text size) which were fixed across all datasets. The embedding layer was initialized using 300-dimensional CBOW Word2vec embeddings (Mikolov et al., 2013a) trained on the 3B-word UMBC WebBase corpus (Han et al., 2013) with standard hyperparameters[4].

Evaluation datasets. For the topic categorization task we used the **BBC** news dataset[5] (Greene and Cunningham, 2006), **20News** (Lang, 1995), **Reuters**[6] (Lewis et al., 2004) and **Ohsumed**[7].

	Dataset	Type	Labels	# of docs	Eval.
TOPIC	BBC	News	5	2,225	10-cross
	20News	News	6	18,846	Train-test
	Reuters	News	8	9,178	10-cross
	Ohsumed	Medical	23	23,166	Train-test
POLARITY	RTC	Snippets	2	438,000	Train-test
	IMDB	Reviews	2	50,000	Train-test
	PL05	Snippets	2	10,662	10-cross
	PL04	Reviews	2	2,000	10-cross
	Stanford	Phrases	2	119,783	10-cross

Table 1: Evaluation datasets for topic categorization and polarity detection.

PL04 (Pang and Lee, 2004), **PL05**[8] (Pang and Lee, 2005), **RTC**[9], **IMDB** (Maas et al., 2011) and the Stanford sentiment dataset[10] (Socher et al., 2013, **SF**) were considered for polarity detection. Statistics of the versions of the datasets used are displayed in Table 1.[11] For both tasks the evaluation was carried out either by 10-fold cross-validation or using the train-test splits of the datasets, in case of availability.

Preprocessing. Four different techniques (see Section 2) were used to preprocess the datasets as well as the corpus which was used to train word embeddings (i.e. UMBC). For tokenization and lemmatization we relied on Stanford CoreNLP (Manning et al., 2014). As for multiwords, we used the phrases from the pre-trained Google News Word2vec vectors, which were obtained using a simple statistical approach (Mikolov et al., 2013b).[12]

3.2 Experiment 1: Preprocessing effect

Table 2 shows the accuracy[13] of the classification models using our four preprocessing techniques. We observe a certain variability of results depending on the preprocessing techniques used (aver-

---

[3]The code for this CNN implementation is the same as in (Pilehvar et al., 2017), which is available at https://github.com/pilehvar/sensecnn

[4]Context window of 5 words and hierarchical softmax.

[5]http://mlg.ucd.ie/datasets/bbc.html

[6]Due to the large number of labels in the original Reuters (i.e. 91) and to be consistent with the other datasets, we reduce the dataset to its 8 most frequent labels, a reduction already performed in previous works (Sebastiani, 2002).

[7]ftp://medir.ohsu.edu/pub/ohsumed

[8]Both PL04 and PL05 were downloaded from http://www.cs.cornell.edu/people/pabo/movie-review-data/

[9]http://www.rottentomatoes.com

[10]We mapped the numerical value of phrases to either negative (from 0 to 0.4) or positive (from 0.6 to 1), removing the neutral phrases according to the scale (from 0.4 to 0.6).

[11]For the datasets with train-test partitions, the sizes of the test sets are the following: 7,532 for 20News; 12,733 for Ohsumed; 25,000 for IMDb; and 1,000 for RTC.

[12]For future work it would be interesting to explore more complex methods to learn embeddings for multiword expressions (Yin and Schütze, 2014; Poliak et al., 2017).

[13]Computed by averaging accuracy of two different runs. The statistical significance was calculated according to an unpaired t-test at the 5% significance level.

	Preprocessing	Topic categorization				Polarity detection				
		BBC	20News	Reuters	Ohsumed	RTC	IMDB	PL05	PL04	SF
CNN	Vanilla	94.6	89.2	93.7	35.3	**83.2**	87.5	76.3	58.7†	**91.2**
	Lowercased	94.8	**89.8**	**94.2**	**36.0**	83.0	84.2†	76.1	59.6†	91.1
	Lemmatized	95.4	89.4	94.0	35.9	83.1	86.8†	75.8†	**64.2**	**91.2**
	Multiword	**95.5**	89.6	93.4†	34.3†	**83.2**	**87.9**	**77.0**	59.1†	**91.2**
CNN+LSTM	Vanilla	**97.0**	90.7	93.1	30.8†	**84.8**	**88.9**	79.1	71.4	87.1
	Lowercased	96.4	**90.9**	93.0	**37.5**	84.0	88.3†	**79.5**	**73.3**	87.1
	Lemmatized	95.8†	90.5	**93.2**	37.1	84.4	87.7†	78.7	72.6	86.8†
	Multiword	96.2	89.8†	92.7†	29.0†	84.0	**88.9**	79.2	67.0†	**87.3**

Table 2: Accuracy on the topic categorization and polarity detection tasks using various preprocessing techniques for the CNN and CNN+LSTM models. † indicates results that are statistically significant with respect to the top result.

age variability[14] of $\pm 2.4\%$ for the CNN+LSTM model, including a statistical significance gap in seven of the nine datasets), which proves the influence of preprocessing on the final results. It is perhaps not surprising that the lowest variance of results is seen in the datasets with the larger training data (i.e. RTC and Stanford). This suggests that the preprocessing decisions are not so important when the training data is large enough, but they are indeed relevant in benchmarks where the training data is limited.

As far as the individual preprocessing techniques are concerned, the vanilla setting (tokenization only) proves to be consistent across datasets and tasks, as it performs in the same ballpark as the best result in 8 of the 9 datasets for both models (with no noticeable differences between topic categorization and polarity detection). The only topic categorization dataset in which tokenization does not seem enough is Ohsumed, which, unlike the more general nature of other categorization datasets (news), belongs to a specialized domain (medical) for which fine-grained distinctions are required to classify cardiovascular diseases. In particular for this dataset, word embeddings trained on a general-domain corpus like UMBC may not accurately capture the specialized meaning of medical terms and hence, sparsity becomes an issue. In fact, lowercasing and lemmatizing, which are mainly aimed at reducing sparsity, outperform the vanilla setting by over six points in

the CNN+LSTM setting and clearly outperform the other preprocessing techniques on the single CNN model as well.

Nevertheless, the use of more complex preprocessing techniques such as lemmatization and multiword grouping does not help in general. Even though lemmatization has proved useful in conventional linear models as an effective way to deal with sparsity (Mullen and Collier, 2004; Toman et al., 2006), neural network architectures seem to be more capable of overcoming sparsity thanks to the generalization power of word embeddings.

3.3 Experiment 2: Cross-preprocessing

This experiment aims at studying the impact of using different word embeddings (with differently preprocessed training corpora) on tokenized datasets (vanilla setting). Table 3 shows the results for this experiment. In this experiment we observe a different trend, with multiword-enhanced vectors exhibiting a better performance both on the single CNN model (best overall performance in seven of the nine datasets) and on the CNN+LSTM model (best performance in four datasets and in the same ballpark as the best results in four of the remaining five datasets). In this case the same set of words is learnt but single tokens inside multiword expressions are not trained. Instead, these single tokens are considered in isolation only, without the added *noise* when considered inside the multiword expression as well. For instance, the word *Apple* has a clearly different meaning in isolation from the one inside

<hr>

[14]Average variability was the result of averaging the variability of each dataset, which was computed as the difference between the best and the worst preprocessing performances.

	Embedding Preprocessing	Topic categorization				Polarity detection				
		BBC	**20News**	**Reuters**	**Ohsumed**	**RTC**	**IMDB**	**PL05**	**PL04**	**SF**
CNN	Vanilla	94.6	89.2	93.7	35.3	83.2	$87.5^\dagger$	**76.3**	$58.7^\dagger$	**91.2**
	Lowercased	$93.9^\dagger$	$84.6^\dagger$	**93.9**	**36.2**	83.2	$85.4^\dagger$	**76.3**	$60.0^\dagger$	91.1
	Lemmatized	94.5	$88.7^\dagger$	93.8	35.4	83.0	$86.8^\dagger$	75.6	62.5	**91.2**
	Multiword	**95.6**	**89.7**	**93.9**	35.2	**83.3**	**88.1**	75.9	**63.1**	**91.2**
CNN+LSTM	Vanilla	97.0	$90.7^\dagger$	**93.1**	$30.8^\dagger$	**84.8**	**88.9**	79.1	71.4	$87.1^\dagger$
	Lowercased	96.4	**91.8**	$92.5^\dagger$	$30.2^\dagger$	84.5	$88.0^\dagger$	79.0	**74.2**	87.4
	Lemmatized	96.6	91.5	$92.5^\dagger$	$31.7^\dagger$	83.9	$86.6^\dagger$	$78.4^\dagger$	$67.7^\dagger$	87.3
	Multiword	**97.3**	91.3	92.8	**33.6**	84.3	$87.3^\dagger$	**79.5**	71.8	**87.5**

Table 3: Cross-preprocessing evaluation: accuracy on the topic categorization and polarity detection tasks using different sets of word embeddings to initialize the embedding layer of the two classifiers. All datasets were preprocessed similarly according to the vanilla setting. † indicates results that are statistically significant with respect to the top result.

the multiword expression *Big_Apple*, hence it can be seen as beneficial not to train the word *Apple* when part of this multiword expression. Interestingly, using multiword-wise embeddings on the vanilla setting leads to consistently better results than using them on the same multiword-grouped preprocessed dataset in eight of the nine datasets. This could provide hints on the excellent results provided by pre-trained Word2vec embeddings trained on the Google News corpus, which learns multiwords similarly to our setting.

Apart from this somewhat surprising finding, the use of the embeddings trained on a simple tokenized corpus (i.e. vanilla) proved again competitive, as different preprocessing techniques such as lowercasing and lemmatizing do not seem to help. In fact, the relatively weaker performance of lemmatization and lowercasing in this cross-processing experiment is somehow expected as the coverage of word embeddings in vanilla-tokenized datasets is limited, e.g., many entities which are capitalized in the datasets are not covered in the case of lowercasing, and inflected forms are missing in the case of lemmatizing.

4 Conclusions

In this paper we analyzed the impact of simple text preprocessing decisions on the performance of a standard word-based neural text classifier. Our evaluations highlight the importance of being careful in the choice of how to preprocess our data and to be consistent when comparing different systems. In general, a simple tokenization works equally or better than more complex pre-processing techniques such as lemmatization or multiword grouping, except for domain-specific datasets (such as the medical dataset in our experiments) in which sole tokenization performs poorly. Additionally, word embeddings trained on multiword-grouped corpora perform surprisingly well when applied to simple tokenized datasets. This property has often been overlooked and, to the best of our knowledge, we test the hypothesis for the first time. In fact, this finding could partially explain the long-lasting success of pre-trained Word2vec embeddings, which specifically learn multiword embeddings as part of their pipeline (Mikolov et al., 2013b).

Moreover, our analysis shows that there is a high variance in the results depending on the preprocessing choice ($\pm 2.4\%$ on average for the best performing model), especially when the training data is not large enough to generalize. Further analysis and experimentation would be required to fully understand the significance of these results; but, this work can be viewed as a starting point for studying the impact of text preprocessing in deep learning models. We hope that our findings will encourage future researchers to carefully select and report these preprocessing decisions when evaluating or comparing different models. Finally, as future work, we plan to extend our analysis to other tasks (e.g. question answering), languages (particularly morphologically rich languages for which these results may vary) and preprocessing techniques (e.g. stopword removal or part-of-speech tagging).

Acknowledgments

Jose Camacho-Collados is supported by the ERC Starting Grant 637277.

References

Jose Camacho-Collados and Mohammad Taher Pilehvar. 2018. From word to sense embeddings: A survey on vector representations of meaning. *Journal of Artificial Intelligence Research (JAIR)*.

Alexis Conneau, Holger Schwenk, Loïc Barrault, and Yann Lecun. 2017. Very deep convolutional networks for text classification. In *Proceedings of EACL*, pages 1107–1116, Valencia, Spain.

Li Dong, Furu Wei, Shujie Liu, Ming Zhou, and Ke Xu. 2015. A statistical parsing framework for sentiment classification. *Computational Linguistics*.

Cícero Nogueira Dos Santos and Maira Gatti. 2014. Deep convolutional neural networks for sentiment analysis of short texts. In *Proceedings of COLING*, pages 69–78.

Sebastian Ebert, Thomas Müller, and Hinrich Schütze. 2016. Lamb: A good shepherd of morphologically rich languages. In *Proceedings of the 2016 Conference on Empirical Methods in Natural Language Processing*, pages 742–752.

Manaal Faruqui, Jesse Dodge, Sujay K. Jauhar, Chris Dyer, Eduard Hovy, and Noah A. Smith. 2015. Retrofitting word vectors to semantic lexicons. In *Proceedings of NAACL*, pages 1606–1615.

Lucie Flekova and Iryna Gurevych. 2016. Supersense embeddings: A unified model for supersense interpretation, prediction, and utilization. In *Proceedings of ACL*, Berlin, Germany.

Yoav Goldberg. 2016. A primer on neural network models for natural language processing. *Journal of Artificial Intelligence Research*, 57:345–420.

Derek Greene and Pádraig Cunningham. 2006. Practical solutions to the problem of diagonal dominance in kernel document clustering. In *Proceedings of the 23rd International conference on Machine learning*, pages 377–384. ACM.

Lushan Han, Abhay Kashyap, Tim Finin, James Mayfield, and Jonathan Weese. 2013. UMBC ebiquitycore: Semantic textual similarity systems. In *Proceedings of the Second Joint Conference on Lexical and Computational Semantics*, volume 1, pages 44–52.

Samer Hassan, Rada Mihalcea, and Carmen Banea. 2007. Random walk term weighting for improved text classification. *International Journal of Semantic Computing*, 1(04):421–439.

Sepp Hochreiter and Jürgen Schmidhuber. 1997. Long short-term memory. *Neural computation*, 9(8):1735–1780.

Rie Johnson and Tong Zhang. 2015. Effective use of word order for text categorization with convolutional neural networks. In *Proceedings of NAACL*, pages 103–112, Denver, Colorado.

Nal Kalchbrenner, Edward Grefenstette, and Phil Blunsom. 2014. A convolutional neural network for modelling sentences. In *Proceedings of ACL*, pages 655–665.

Yoon Kim. 2014. Convolutional neural networks for sentence classification. In *Proceedings of EMNLP*.

Yoon Kim, Yacine Jernite, David Sontag, and Alexander M Rush. 2016. Character-aware neural language models. In *Proceedings of AAAI*.

Ilia Kuznetsov and Iryna Gurevych. 2018. From text to lexicon: Bridging the gap between word embeddings and lexical resources. In *Proceedings of the 27th International Conference on Computational Linguistics*, pages 233–244.

Ken Lang. 1995. Newsweeder: Learning to filter netnews. In *Proceedings of the 12th international conference on machine learning*, pages 331–339.

Yann LeCun, Koray Kavukcuoglu, and Clément Farabet. 2010. Convolutional networks and applications in vision. In *Circuits and Systems (ISCAS), Proceedings of 2010 IEEE International Symposium on*, pages 253–256. IEEE.

Edda Leopold and Jörg Kindermann. 2002. Text categorization with support vector machines. how to represent texts in input space? *Machine Learning*, 46(1-3):423–444.

Omer Levy, Yoav Goldberg, and Ido Dagan. 2015. Improving distributional similarity with lessons learned from word embeddings. *Transactions of the Association for Computational Linguistics*, 3:211–225.

David D. Lewis, Yiming Yang, Tony G Rose, and Fan Li. 2004. Rcv1: A new benchmark collection for text categorization research. *Journal of machine learning research*, 5(Apr):361–397.

Jiwei Li and Dan Jurafsky. 2015. Do multi-sense embeddings improve natural language understanding? In *Proceedings of EMNLP*, Lisbon, Portugal.

Andrew L. Maas, Raymond E. Daly, Peter T. Pham, Dan Huang, Andrew Y. Ng, and Christopher Potts. 2011. Learning word vectors for sentiment analysis. In *Proceedings of ACL-HLT*, pages 142–150, Portland, Oregon, USA.

Christopher D. Manning, Mihai Surdeanu, John Bauer, Jenny Finkel, Steven J. Bethard, and David McClosky. 2014. The Stanford CoreNLP natural language processing toolkit. In *Association for Computational Linguistics (ACL) System Demonstrations*, pages 55–60.

Tomas Mikolov, Kai Chen, Greg Corrado, and Jeffrey Dean. 2013a. Efficient estimation of word representations in vector space. *CoRR*, abs/1301.3781.

Tomas Mikolov, Ilya Sutskever, Kai Chen, Greg S Corrado, and Jeff Dean. 2013b. Distributed representations of words and phrases and their compositionality. In *Advances in neural information processing systems*, pages 3111–3119.

Tony Mullen and Nigel Collier. 2004. Sentiment analysis using support vector machines with diverse information sources. In *EMNLP*, volume 4, pages 412–418.

Vinod Nair and Geoffrey E. Hinton. 2010. Rectified linear units improve restricted boltzmann machines. In *Proceedings of the 27th International Conference on Machine Learning (ICML-10)*, pages 807–814. Omnipress.

Bo Pang and Lillian Lee. 2004. A sentimental education: Sentiment analysis using subjectivity summarization based on minimum cuts. In *Proceedings of the ACL*.

Bo Pang and Lillian Lee. 2005. Seeing stars: Exploiting class relationships for sentiment categorization with respect to rating scales. In *Proceedings of the ACL*.

Jeffrey Pennington, Richard Socher, and Christopher D Manning. 2014. GloVe: Global vectors for word representation. In *Proceedings of EMNLP*, pages 1532–1543.

Mohammad Taher Pilehvar, Jose Camacho-Collados, Roberto Navigli, and Nigel Collier. 2017. Towards a Seamless Integration of Word Senses into Downstream NLP Applications. In *Proceedings of ACL*, Vancouver, Canada.

Adam Poliak, Pushpendre Rastogi, M. Patrick Martin, and Benjamin Van Durme. 2017. Efficient, compositional, order-sensitive n-gram embeddings. In *Proceedings of EACL*.

Ivan A Sag, Timothy Baldwin, Francis Bond, Ann Copestake, and Dan Flickinger. 2002. Multiword expressions: A pain in the neck for nlp. In *International Conference on Intelligent Text Processing and Computational Linguistics*, pages 1–15. Springer.

Fabrizio Sebastiani. 2002. Machine learning in automated text categorization. *ACM computing surveys (CSUR)*, 34(1):1–47.

Richard Socher, Alex Perelygin, Jean Wu, Jason Chuang, Christopher Manning, Andrew Ng, and Christopher Potts. 2013. Parsing With Compositional Vector Grammars. In *Proceedings of EMNLP*.

Duyu Tang, Bing Qin, and Ting Liu. 2015. Document modeling with gated recurrent neural network for sentiment classification. In *EMNLP*, pages 1422–1432.

Michal Toman, Roman Tesar, and Karel Jezek. 2006. Influence of word normalization on text classification. *Proceedings of InSciT*, 4:354–358.

Alper Kursat Uysal and Serkan Gunal. 2014. The impact of preprocessing on text classification. *Information Processing & Management*, 50(1):104–112.

Yijun Xiao and Kyunghyun Cho. 2016. Efficient character-level document classification by combining convolution and recurrent layers. *CoRR*, abs/1602.00367.

Wenpeng Yin, Katharina Kann, Mo Yu, and Hinrich Schütze. 2017. Comparative study of cnn and rnn for natural language processing. *arXiv preprint arXiv:1702.01923*.

Wenpeng Yin and Hinrich Schütze. 2014. An exploration of embeddings for generalized phrases. In *ACL (Student Research Workshop)*, pages 41–47.

Xiang Zhang and Yann LeCun. 2017. Which encoding is the best for text classification in chinese, english, japanese and korean? *arXiv preprint arXiv:1708.02657*.

Jump to better conclusions: SCAN both left and right

Joost Bastings[1]   Marco Baroni[2]   Jason Weston[2]   Kyunghyun Cho[2,3,4]   Douwe Kiela[2]

[1]ILLC, University of Amsterdam
[2]Facebook AI Research
[3]New York University
[4]CIFAR Global Scholar

`bastings@uva.nl {mbaroni,jase,kyunghyuncho,dkiela}@fb.com`

Abstract

Lake and Baroni (2018) recently introduced the SCAN data set, which consists of simple commands paired with action sequences and is intended to test the strong generalization abilities of recurrent sequence-to-sequence models. Their initial experiments suggested that such models may fail because they lack the ability to extract systematic rules. Here, we take a closer look at SCAN and show that it does not always capture the kind of generalization that it was designed for. To mitigate this we propose a complementary dataset, which requires mapping actions back to the original commands, called NACS. We show that models that do well on SCAN do not necessarily do well on NACS, and that NACS exhibits properties more closely aligned with realistic use-cases for sequence-to-sequence models.

1   Introduction

In a recent paper, Lake and Baroni (2018) (L&B) investigate if recurrent sequence-to-sequence models can exhibit the same strong generalization that humans are capable of, by virtue of our capacity to infer the meaning of a phrase from its constituent parts (i.e., compositionality), providing empirical tests for this long-standing goal (Fodor and Pylyshyn, 1988). Compositional generalization might be a fundamental component in making models drastically less sample-thirsty than they currently are. L&B introduce the SCAN data set (§2), meant to study such generalization to novel examples. It consists of simple command-action pairs, in which more complex commands are composed of simpler ones (see Figure 1 for examples).

SCAN comprises several tests of generalization, namely with respect to (1) a random subset of the data ('simple'), (2) commands with action sequences longer than those seen during training ('length'), and (3) commands that compose a

jump
`JUMP`

turn around left
`LTURN LTURN LTURN LTURN`

jump thrice and turn left twice
`JUMP JUMP JUMP LTURN LTURN`

jump opposite left after walk twice
`WALK WALK LTURN LTURN JUMP`

Figure 1: SCAN maps commands to actions

primitive in novel ways that was only seen in isolation during training ('primitive'). In the latter case, the training set would for example only include the command 'jump', after which the test set includes all other commands containing 'jump', e.g. 'jump opposite left after walk twice'.

In this paper we take a closer look at SCAN. We start with the observation (§3) that there are few target-side dependencies in the data, a consequence of SCAN being generated from a phrase-structure grammar. We show (§6) that this allows simple sequence-to-sequence models (§5) to obtain good accuracies e.g. on tasks involving a new primitive, even without access to previous outputs. However, these simple models do not use composition in any interesting way, and their performance is therefore not a realistic indicator of their generalization capability. We hence propose NACS (§4) as a more realistic alternative: SCAN with commands and actions flipped, i.e., mapping actions back to their original commands. This is harder, because different commands may map to the same action sequence, and it introduces target-side dependencies, so that previous outputs need to be remembered. We show in particular that well-tuned attention-based models do achieve a certain degree of generalization on SCAN, and, as

Proceedings of the 2018 EMNLP Workshop BlackboxNLP: Analyzing and Interpreting Neural Networks for NLP, pages 47–55
Brussels, Belgium, November 1, 2018. ©2018 Association for Computational Linguistics

predicted, simpler models do better there. However, the models still struggle in the more demanding NACS setup, which we offer as a challenge for future work.

Our contributions can be summarized as follows:

1. we provide an analysis of SCAN and make the important observation that it does not test for target-side dependencies, allowing too simple models to do well;

2. we propose NACS to introduce target-side dependencies and remedy the problem;

3. we repeat all experiments in Lake and Baroni (2018) using early-stopping on validation sets created from the training data.

2 SCAN

SCAN stands for Simplified version of the CommAI Navigation tasks (Mikolov et al., 2016). Each example in SCAN is constructed by first sampling a command $X = (x_1, \ldots, x_T)$ from a finite phrase-structure grammar with start symbol C:

$C \rightarrow S$ and $S \mid S$ after $S \mid S$

$S \rightarrow V$ twice $\mid V$ thrice $\mid V$

$V \rightarrow D_{[1]}$ opposite $D_{[2]} \mid D_{[1]}$ around $D_{[2]} \mid D \mid U$

$D \rightarrow U$ left $\mid U$ right $\mid$ turn left $\mid$ turn right

$U \rightarrow$ walk $\mid$ look $\mid$ run $\mid$ jump

For each command, the corresponding target action sequence $Y = (y_1, \ldots, y_{T'})$ then follows by applying a set of *interpretation functions*, such as:

$$[\![\text{jump}]\!] = \text{JUMP}$$
$$[\![u \text{ around left}]\!] = \text{LTURN } [\![u]\!] \text{ LTURN } [\![u]\!]$$
$$\text{LTURN } [\![u]\!] \text{ LTURN } [\![u]\!]$$
$$[\![x_1 \text{ after } x_2]\!] = [\![x_2]\!] [\![x_1]\!]$$

of which only the last function requires global reordering, which occurs at most once per command. See the supplementary materials for the full set. Figure 1 shows examples of commands and their action sequences as obtained by the interpretation functions. The commands can be decoded compositionally by a learner by discovering the interpretation functions, enabling generalization to unseen commands. The total data set is finite but large (20910 unambiguous commands).

3 SCAN prefers simple models

We observe an important property of the data set generation process for SCAN: temporal dependencies of the action sequence are limited to the phrasal boundaries of each sub-phrase, which span at most 24 actions (e.g. jump around left thrice). Crucially, even rules that require repetition (such as 'thrice') as well as global reordering, can be resolved by simple counting and without remembering previously generated outputs, due to the limited depth of the phrase-structure grammar (see e.g. Rodriguez and Wiles (1998)).

This observation has two important implications. First, because SCAN is largely a phrase-to-phrase conversion problem, any machine learning method that aims at solving SCAN needs to have an *alignment mechanism* between the source and target sequences. Such an alignment mechanism could work fairly accurately by simply advancing a pointer. Somewhat contrary to the observation by Lake and Baroni (L&B), we therefore hypothesize that an attention mechanism (Bahdanau et al., 2015) always helps when a neural conditional sequence model (Sutskever et al., 2014; Cho et al., 2014) is used to tackle any variant of SCAN. Second, we speculate that any algorithm with strong long-term dependency modeling capabilities can be *detrimental* in terms of generalization, because such an approach might inappropriately capture spurious target-side regularities in the training data. We thus hypothesize that *less powerful decoders generalize better* on to unseen action combinations on SCAN when equipped with an attention mechanism.

To summarize: good performance on SCAN does not necessarily indicate the capability of a model to strongly generalize. SCAN favors simpler models that need not capture target-side dependencies, which might not work well on more realistic sequence-to-sequence problems, such as machine translation, where strong auto-regressive models are needed for good results (Bahdanau et al., 2015; Kaiser and Bengio, 2016).

4 NACS: actions to commands

By simply flipping the source X and target Y of each example, we obtain a data-set that suddenly features strong target-side dependencies. Even when the mapping $p(Y|X)$ from the source to target is simple, the opposite $p(X|Y) \propto p(Y|X)p(X)$ is non-trivial due to the complexity

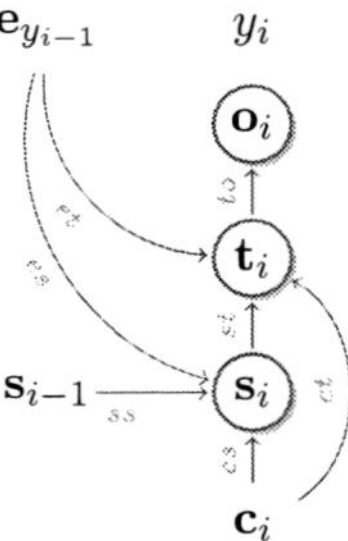

Figure 2: The decoder of Bahdanau et al. (2015)

of the prior $p(X)$. The inclusion of $p(X)$ naturally induces strong dependencies among the output tokens, while maintaining the original properties of SCAN that were intended to test various aspects of systematic generalization.

NACS naturally makes the mapping that needs to be learned stochastic and multi-modal (sensitive to both commands and actions). For instance, an action sequence of the form $[\![x_1]\!][\![x_2]\!]$ could be mapped to either $[\![x_1 \text{ and } x_2]\!]$ or $[\![x_2 \text{ after } x_1]\!]$, both of which are correct. In order for a model to decide whether to output "and" or "after", it is necessary for it to remember what has already been generated (i.e., $[\![x_1]\!]$ or $[\![x_2]\!]$).

Another example is LTURN LTURN LTURN LTURN, which can be translated into either "turn around left" or two repetitions of "turn opposite left". Deciding whether to output "and" after the first phrase requires the model to remember whether "around" was generated previously.

In §6 we experimentally evaluate the proposed NACS task using the same scenarios as SCAN (simple, length and primitive). We observe that NACS prefers more advanced models that could capture long-term dependencies in the output (now a command sequence) better. However, we notice that even these powerful models, equipped with GRUs and attention, cannot systematically generalize to this task, as was also observed by Lake and Baroni (2018). Based on this observation, we believe that NACS (or perhaps a combination of SCAN and NACS) is better suited for evaluating any future progress in this direction.

5   Sequence-to-sequence models

In this section, we describe the sequence-to-sequence models we use for evaluating on SCAN and its proposed sibling NACS.

We directly model the probability of a target sequence given a source sequence $p(Y|X)$.

Our encoder-decoder is modeled after Cho et al. (2014) and our attention-based encoder-decoder after Bahdanau et al. (2015). The attention-based decoder is a function that takes as input the previous target word embedding $\mathbf{e}_{y_{i-1}}$, the context vector $\mathbf{c}_i$, and the previous hidden state $\mathbf{s}_{i-1}$ (see also Figure 2): $\mathbf{s}_i = f(\mathbf{e}_{y_{i-1}}, \mathbf{c}_i, \mathbf{s}_{i-1})$.

The prediction for the current time step is then made from a pre-output layer $\mathbf{t}_i$: $\mathbf{t}_i = W_e\mathbf{e}_{y_{i-1}} + W_c\mathbf{c}_i + W_s\mathbf{s}_i$. We do not apply a max-out layer and directly obtain the output by $\mathbf{o}_i = W_o\mathbf{t}_i$. For the encoder-decoder without attention, the prediction is made directly from decoder state $\mathbf{s}_i$. We vary the recurrent cell, experimenting with simple RNN (Elman, 1990), GRU (Cho et al., 2014), and LSTM cells (Hochreiter and Schmidhuber, 1997). For conciseness we only report results with RNN and GRU cells in the main text, and LSTM results in the appendix.

In this paper, we investigate the properties of both SCAN and NACS using RNN-based sequence-to-sequence models for evaluation. We leave further investigation of alternative architectures (see, e.g., Vaswani et al., 2017; Gehring et al., 2017; Chen et al., 2018) for the future.

6   Experiments

6.1   Settings

Our models are implemented in PyTorch and trained using mini-batch SGD with an initial learning rate of 0.2, decayed by 0.96 each epoch. We use a batch size of 32, 256 hidden units (64 for embeddings), and a dropout rate of 0.2. We test on all SCAN/NACS tasks[1], as well as on the Fr-En Machine Translation (MT) task that L&B used. The reported results are averaged over three runs for each experiment. Models *with* attention are marked as such with *+Attn*, e.g. 'GRU +Attn'.

Validation Set.   L&B split each SCAN subtask into a training set (80%) and a test set (20%). They train for a fixed number of updates (100k) and evaluate on the test set. Because any training run without early stopping may have missed the optimal solution (Caruana et al., 2001), we believe their results may not reflect the reality as closely as they could. We thus augment each of the SCAN variants with a validation set that follows the training distribution but contains examples that are not contained in the corresponding training set. This

---

[1] github.com/facebookresearch/NACS

	Simple		Length		Turn left		Jump	
	SCAN	NACS	SCAN	NACS	SCAN	NACS	SCAN	NACS
GRU	$100.0_{\pm0.0}$	$99.0_{\pm0.1}$	$14.4_{\pm0.8}$	$12.9_{\pm1.2}$	$53.4_{\pm11.7}$	$47.5_{\pm4.7}$	$0.0_{\pm0.0}$	$0.0_{\pm0.0}$
RNN +Attn	$100.0_{\pm0.0}$	$99.8_{\pm0.1}$	$9.6_{\pm0.9}$	$19.4_{\pm0.7}$	$81.1_{\pm14.7}$	$44.1_{\pm0.9}$	$1.9_{\pm1.2}$	$0.3_{\pm0.3}$
RNN +Attn -Dep	$100.0_{\pm0.0}$	$61.1_{\pm0.3}$	$11.7_{\pm3.2}$	$0.5_{\pm0.2}$	$92.0_{\pm5.8}$	$18.6_{\pm1.0}$	$2.7_{\pm1.7}$	$0.0_{\pm0.0}$
GRU +Attn	$100.0_{\pm0.0}$	$99.8_{\pm0.1}$	$18.1_{\pm1.1}$	$17.2_{\pm1.9}$	$59.1_{\pm16.8}$	$55.9_{\pm3.5}$	$12.5_{\pm6.6}$	$0.0_{\pm0.0}$
GRU +Attn -Dep	$100.0_{\pm0.0}$	$51.2_{\pm1.2}$	$17.8_{\pm1.7}$	$2.0_{\pm1.4}$	$90.8_{\pm3.6}$	$16.9_{\pm1.2}$	$0.7_{\pm0.4}$	$0.0_{\pm0.0}$
L&B best	99.8	-	20.8	-	90.3	-	1.2	-
L&B best overall	99.7	-	13.8	-	90.0	-	0.1	-

Table 1: Test scores on the simple, length, and primitive (turn left, jump) tasks. *+Attn* marks attention, *-Dep* has the connections from the previous target word embedding removed (*es* and *et* in Figure 2). L&B$_{best}$ is the best reported score for each task by L&B, and L&B$_{best\ overall}$ is the score for their best-scoring model all tasks considered.

allows us to incorporate early stopping in our experiments so that they are better benchmarks for evaluating future progress. For each experiment we remove 10% of the training examples to be used as a validation set.

Accuracy. Following L&B we measure performance according to sequence-level accuracy, i.e., whether the generated sequence entirely matches the reference. This metric is also used for early stopping. For NACS, an output (command) is considered correct if its interpretation ('backmapping') produces the input action sequence.

Ablations. To validate our analysis, we remove the connections from the previous target word embedding $e_{y_{i-1}}$ to the decoder state and the pre-output layer (*es* and *et* in Figure 2), so that the current prediction is not informed by previous outputs. If our analysis in §3 is correct, then these simpler models should still be able to make the correct predictions on SCAN, but not on NACS.

6.2 Results and Analysis

Results on the three SCAN and NACS tasks are listed in Table 1. The full results including models with LSTM cells and MT experiments may be found in the supplementary materials. We will now discuss our observations.

SCAN is not enough. Table 1 shows that all model variants perform (near) perfectly on the SCAN simple task. While this is impressive, results for the severed models (+Attn -Dep) on the simple task for NACS show that it is possible to have a perfect accuracy on SCAN, while at the same time failing to do well on NACS.[2] Crucially, a (near) perfect score on SCAN does not imply strong generalization. A model can exploit the determinism and lack of target-side dependencies of SCAN by developing a simple translation strategy such as advancing a pointer and translating word by word, and the use of such a simple strategy is not revealed by SCAN.

NACS is harder. NACS is a harder problem to solve compared to SCAN, as evidenced by consistently lower accuracies in Table 1 for all tasks. The discrepancy between SCAN and NACS performance is the most extreme when we look at the primitive tasks (turn left and jump). For turn left, the severed models (+Attn -Dep) obtain the highest scores on SCAN, but are the worst on NACS.

The 'turn left' task benefits from TURNL occurring on the target-side in other contexts during training, which is not the case for 'jump'.[3] Since there is no evidence in the training data that 'jump' is a verb, Table 2 shows results where additional (composed) 'jump' commands were added for training. We see that performance quickly goes up when adding more commands.[4] Again here the simpler models (+Attn -Dep) perform better.

Machine Translation. We repeat L&Bs English-French MT experiment for both directions. Table 3 shows that models that perform well on NACS also perform well here, with the GRU outperforming the other cells (see appendix

---

[2] We made similar observations using LSTM cells, as we show in the appendix.

[3] See Lake and Baroni (2018) for a discussion.

[4] L&B performed this experiment without attention, which we show has a large positive impact.

		1	2	4	8	16	32
RNN $_{\text{+Attn}}$	SCAN	35.0 $_{\pm 2.8}$	48.6 $_{\pm 8.1}$	77.6 $_{\pm 2.6}$	89.2 $_{\pm 3.8}$	98.7 $_{\pm 1.3}$	99.8 $_{\pm 0.1}$
RNN $_{\text{+Attn -Dep}}$	SCAN	29.5 $_{\pm 10.5}$	53.3 $_{\pm 10.2}$	82.4 $_{\pm 4.7}$	98.8 $_{\pm 0.8}$	99.8 $_{\pm 0.1}$	100.0 $_{\pm 0.0}$
GRU $_{\text{+Attn}}$	SCAN	58.2 $_{\pm 12.0}$	67.8 $_{\pm 3.4}$	80.3 $_{\pm 7.0}$	88.0 $_{\pm 6.0}$	98.3 $_{\pm 1.8}$	99.6 $_{\pm 0.2}$
GRU $_{\text{+Attn -Dep}}$	SCAN	70.9 $_{\pm 11.5}$	61.3 $_{\pm 13.5}$	83.5 $_{\pm 6.1}$	99.0 $_{\pm 0.4}$	99.7 $_{\pm 0.2}$	100.0 $_{\pm 0.0}$
RNN $_{\text{+Attn}}$	NACS	2.8 $_{\pm 0.8}$	9.3 $_{\pm 7.3}$	24.7 $_{\pm 4.2}$	43.7 $_{\pm 4.4}$	57.1 $_{\pm 5.2}$	69.1 $_{\pm 2.1}$
RNN $_{\text{+Attn -Dep}}$	NACS	0.4 $_{\pm 0.1}$	0.9 $_{\pm 0.2}$	2.4 $_{\pm 0.3}$	3.9 $_{\pm 0.3}$	9.3 $_{\pm 0.3}$	15.9 $_{\pm 1.4}$
GRU $_{\text{+Attn}}$	NACS	5.5 $_{\pm 1.8}$	9.2 $_{\pm 2.8}$	11.0 $_{\pm 1.5}$	21.9 $_{\pm 2.4}$	23.5 $_{\pm 0.6}$	42.0 $_{\pm 1.5}$
GRU $_{\text{+Attn -Dep}}$	NACS	0.1 $_{\pm 0.1}$	0.6 $_{\pm 0.2}$	2.0 $_{\pm 0.2}$	3.2 $_{\pm 0.2}$	5.8 $_{\pm 1.1}$	10.9 $_{\pm 0.8}$
L&B	SCAN	0.1	0.1	4.1	15.3	70.2	89.9

Table 2: Test scores on the 'jump' task with additional commands. +Attn marks attention, -Dep has the *es* and *et* connections removed (Figure 2). The test set contains all jump commands except the 32 used for training. Columns indicate how many commands with 'jump' were added to the training set, such as 'jump around left thrice.'

	En-Fr	Fr-En
GRU $_{\text{+Attn}}$	32.1 $_{\pm 0.3}$	37.5 $_{\pm 0.6}$
GRU $_{\text{+Attn -Dep}}$	30.2 $_{\pm 0.3}$	35.9 $_{\pm 0.3}$

Table 3: Results (BLEU) on the Machine Translation experiment for both directions using a GRU. See appendix for results using SRN and LSTM cells.

for other cell types). In a setting similar to the jump task, the sentence pair 'I am daxy' ('je suis daxiste') was added to the training set. The goal is now to test if eight novel sentences that contain 'daxy' are correctly translated.

In our setting with mini-batching and early-stopping, the GRU gets 70.8% (En-Fr) and 54.2% (Fr-En) of the daxy-sentences right, which is surprisingly good compared to L&B (12.5%).

Other observations. As expected, Table 1 shows that attention always helps. Generalizing to longer sequences is generally hard, and this remains an open problem.

7 Related Work

Ever since Fodor and Pylyshyn (1988) conjectured that neural networks are unable to show strong generalization, many attempts were made to show that the opposite is true, leading to inconclusive evidence. For example, Phillips (1998) found that feed-forward nets and RNNs do not always generalize to novel 2-tuples on an auto-association task, while Wong and Wang (2007) and Brakel and Frank (2009) found that RNNs can show systematic behavior in a language modeling task.

In the context of analyzing RNNs, Rodriguez and Wiles (1998) found that simple RNNs can develop a symbol-sensitive counting strategy for accepting a simple (palindrome) context-free language. Weiss et al. (2018) show that LSTMs and simple RNNs with ReLU-activation can learn to count unboundedly, in contrast to GRUs.

Linzen et al. (2016) probed the sensitivity of LSTMs to hierarchical structure (not necessarily in novel constructions). Instead of a binary choice, with SCAN a sequence-to-sequence model productively generates an output string.

Liska et al. (2018) found that a small number of identical RNNs trained with different initializations show compositional behavior on a function composition task, suggesting that more specific architectures may not be necessary.

Finally, Lake and Baroni (2018) introduced the SCAN data set to study systematic compositionality in recurrent sequence-to-sequence models, including gating mechanisms and attention. This work is a direct response to that and aims to facilitate future progress by showing that SCAN does not necessarily test for strong generalization.

8 Conclusion

In the quest for strong generalization, benchmarks measuring progress are an important component. The existing SCAN benchmark allows too simple models to shine, without the need for compositional generalization. We proposed NACS to remedy this. NACS still requires systematicity, while introducing stochasticity and strong dependencies on the target side. We argue that a good benchmark needs at least those properties, in order not to fall prey to trivial solutions, which do not work on more realistic use-cases for sequence-to-sequence models such as machine translation.

Acknowledgments

We would like to thank Brenden Lake and Marc' Aurelio Ranzato for useful discussions and feedback.

References

Dzmitry Bahdanau, Kyunghyun Cho, and Yoshua Bengio. 2015. Neural Machine Translation by Jointly Learning to Align and Translate. In *Proceedings of the International Conference on Learning Representations (ICLR)*, San Diego, USA.

Philémon Brakel and Stefan Frank. 2009. Strong systematicity in sentence processing by simple recurrent networks. In *31th Annual Conference of the Cognitive Science Society (COGSCI-2009)*, pages 1599–1604. Cognitive Science Society.

Rich Caruana, Steve Lawrence, and C Lee Giles. 2001. Overfitting in neural nets: Backpropagation, conjugate gradient, and early stopping. In *Advances in neural information processing systems*, pages 402–408.

Mia Xu Chen, Orhan Firat, Ankur Bapna, Melvin Johnson, Wolfgang Macherey, George Foster, Llion Jones, Niki Parmar, Mike Schuster, Zhifeng Chen, et al. 2018. The best of both worlds: Combining recent advances in neural machine translation. *arXiv preprint arXiv:1804.09849*.

Kyunghyun Cho, Bart van Merrienboer, Caglar Gulcehre, Dzmitry Bahdanau, Fethi Bougares, Holger Schwenk, and Yoshua Bengio. 2014. Learning Phrase Representations using RNN Encoder–Decoder for Statistical Machine Translation. In *Proceedings of the 2014 Conference on Empirical Methods in Natural Language Processing (EMNLP)*, pages 1724–1734, Doha, Qatar. Association for Computational Linguistics.

Jeffrey L Elman. 1990. Finding structure in time. *Cognitive science*, 14(2):179–211.

Jerry A Fodor and Zenon W Pylyshyn. 1988. Connectionism and cognitive architecture: A critical analysis. *Cognition*, 28(1-2):3–71.

Jonas Gehring, Michael Auli, David Grangier, Denis Yarats, and Yann N Dauphin. 2017. Convolutional sequence to sequence learning. *arXiv preprint arXiv:1705.03122*.

Sepp Hochreiter and Jürgen Schmidhuber. 1997. Long Short-Term Memory. *Neural Computation*, 9(8):1735–1780.

Łukasz Kaiser and Samy Bengio. 2016. Can active memory replace attention? In *Advances in Neural Information Processing Systems*, pages 3781–3789.

Brenden M. Lake and Marco Baroni. 2018. Generalization without systematicity: On the compositional skills of sequence-to-sequence recurrent networks. *International Conference on Machine Learning (ICML)*.

Tal Linzen, Emmanuel Dupoux, and Yoav Goldberg. 2016. Assessing the ability of lstms to learn syntax-sensitive dependencies. *Transactions of the Association for Computational Linguistics*, 4:521–535.

Adam Liska, Germán Kruszewski, and Marco Baroni. 2018. Memorize or generalize? searching for a compositional RNN in a haystack. *CoRR*, abs/1802.06467.

Tomas Mikolov, Armand Joulin, and Marco Baroni. 2016. A roadmap towards machine intelligence. In *International Conference on Intelligent Text Processing and Computational Linguistics*, pages 29–61. Springer.

Steven Phillips. 1998. Are feedforward and recurrent networks systematic? analysis and implications for a connectionist cognitive architecture. *Connection Science*, 10(2):137–160.

Paul Rodriguez and Janet Wiles. 1998. Recurrent neural networks can learn to implement symbol-sensitive counting. In *Advances in Neural Information Processing Systems*, pages 87–93.

Ilya Sutskever, Oriol Vinyals, and Quoc V Le. 2014. Sequence to sequence learning with neural networks. In *Advances in neural information processing systems*, pages 3104–3112.

Ashish Vaswani, Noam Shazeer, Niki Parmar, Jakob Uszkoreit, Llion Jones, Aidan N Gomez, Łukasz Kaiser, and Illia Polosukhin. 2017. Attention is all you need. In *Advances in Neural Information Processing Systems*, pages 6000–6010.

Gail Weiss, Yoav Goldberg, and Eran Yahav. 2018. On the practical computational power of finite precision rnns for language recognition. In *Proceedings of the 56th Annual Meeting of the Association for Computational Linguistics (Volume 2: Short Papers)*, Melbourne, Australia. Association for Computational Linguistics.

Francis CK Wong and William SY Wang. 2007. Generalisation towards combinatorial productivity in language acquisition by simple recurrent networks. In *Integration of Knowledge Intensive Multi-Agent Systems, 2007. KIMAS 2007. International Conference on*, pages 139–144. IEEE.

Supplementary Materials

⟦walk ⟧ = WALK
⟦look⟧ = LOOK
⟦run⟧ = RUN
⟦jump⟧ = JUMP

⟦turn left⟧ = LTURN
⟦turn right⟧ = RTURN

⟦u left⟧ = LTURN ⟦u⟧
⟦u right⟧ = RTURN ⟦u⟧

⟦x twice⟧ = ⟦x⟧ ⟦x⟧
⟦x thrice⟧ = ⟦x⟧ ⟦x⟧ ⟦x⟧

⟦turn around left⟧ = LTURN LTURN LTURN LTURN
⟦turn around right⟧ = RTURN RTURN RTURN RTURN
⟦u around left⟧ = LTURN ⟦u⟧ LTURN ⟦u⟧ LTURN ⟦u⟧ LTURN ⟦u⟧
⟦u around right⟧ = RTURN ⟦u⟧ RTURN ⟦u⟧ RTURN ⟦u⟧ RTURN ⟦u⟧

⟦turn opposite left⟧ = LTURN LTURN
⟦turn opposite right⟧ = RTURN RTURN
⟦u opposite left⟧ = ⟦turn opposite left⟧ ⟦u⟧
⟦u opposite right⟧ = ⟦turn opposite right⟧ ⟦u⟧

⟦x_1 and x_2⟧ = ⟦x_1⟧ ⟦x_2⟧
⟦x_1 after x_2⟧ = ⟦x_2⟧ ⟦x_1⟧

Figure 3: The interpretation functions for translating SCAN commands to actions.

	Simple	Length	Turn left	Jump
RNN	75.6 ±5.4	0.2 ±0.0	26.7 ±12.8	0.0 ±0.0
GRU	100.0 ±0.0	14.4 ±0.8	53.4 ±11.7	0.0 ±0.0
LSTM	99.8 ±0.1	10.1 ±2.0	56.5 ±0.8	0.1 ±0.0
RNN +Attn	100.0 ±0.0	9.6 ±0.9	81.1 ±14.7	1.9 ±1.2
RNN +Attn-Dep	100.0 ±0.0	11.7 ±3.2	92.0 ±5.8	2.7 ±1.7
GRU +Attn	100.0 ±0.0	18.1 ±1.1	59.1 ±16.8	12.5 ±6.6
GRU +Attn-Dep	100.0 ±0.0	17.8 ±1.7	90.8 ±3.6	0.7 ±0.4
LSTM +Attn	100.0 ±0.0	15.6 ±1.6	83.8 ±16.8	9.7 ±2.9
LSTM +Attn-Dep	100.0 ±0.0	12.5 ±1.3	57.6 ±3.8	0.8 ±0.5
L&B best	99.8	20.8	90.3	1.2
L&B best overall	99.7	13.8	90.0	0.1

Table 4: SCAN test scores on the simple, length, and primitive (turn left and jump) tasks. For '+Attn-Dep' models we removed the connections from the previous target word embedding to the decoder state and the pre-output layer.

	Simple	Length	Turn left	Jump
RNN	26.9 $_{\pm0.2}$	0.2 $_{\pm0.1}$	26.4 $_{\pm12.0}$	0.0 $_{\pm0.0}$
GRU	99.0 $_{\pm0.1}$	12.9 $_{\pm1.2}$	47.5 $_{\pm4.7}$	0.0 $_{\pm0.0}$
LSTM	99.1 $_{\pm0.1}$	10.9 $_{\pm1.3}$	42.9 $_{\pm2.9}$	0.0 $_{\pm0.0}$
RNN +Attn	99.8 $_{\pm0.1}$	19.4 $_{\pm0.7}$	44.1 $_{\pm0.9}$	0.3 $_{\pm0.3}$
RNN +Attn-Dep	61.1 $_{\pm0.3}$	0.5 $_{\pm0.2}$	18.6 $_{\pm1.0}$	0.0 $_{\pm0.0}$
GRU +Attn	99.8 $_{\pm0.1}$	17.2 $_{\pm1.9}$	55.9 $_{\pm3.5}$	0.0 $_{\pm0.0}$
GRU +Attn-Dep	51.2 $_{\pm1.2}$	2.0 $_{\pm1.4}$	16.9 $_{\pm1.2}$	0.0 $_{\pm0.0}$
LSTM +Attn	99.1 $_{\pm0.2}$	17.1 $_{\pm2.0}$	48.3 $_{\pm1.7}$	0.0 $_{\pm0.0}$
LSTM +Attn-Dep	38.9 $_{\pm0.9}$	1.0 $_{\pm0.5}$	17.2 $_{\pm1.2}$	0.0 $_{\pm0.0}$

Table 5: NACS test scores on the simple, length, and primitive (turn left and jump) tasks. For '+Attn-Dep' models we removed the connections from the previous target word embedding to the decoder state and the pre-output layer.

	0	1	2	4	8	16	32
RNN	0.0 $_{\pm0.0}$	0.0 $_{\pm0.0}$	0.0 $_{\pm0.0}$	0.1 $_{\pm0.0}$	0.1 $_{\pm0.1}$	0.5 $_{\pm0.3}$	1.4 $_{\pm0.3}$
GRU	0.1 $_{\pm0.0}$	0.2 $_{\pm0.1}$	0.6 $_{\pm0.2}$	2.5 $_{\pm1.1}$	3.3 $_{\pm0.9}$	13.1 $_{\pm2.4}$	42.4 $_{\pm2.5}$
LSTM	0.1 $_{\pm0.0}$	0.3 $_{\pm0.2}$	1.3 $_{\pm0.2}$	3.8 $_{\pm1.8}$	2.5 $_{\pm1.1}$	6.5 $_{\pm2.7}$	21.3 $_{\pm1.4}$
RNN +Attn	3.5 $_{\pm3.0}$	35.0 $_{\pm2.8}$	48.6 $_{\pm8.1}$	77.6 $_{\pm2.6}$	89.2 $_{\pm3.8}$	98.7 $_{\pm1.3}$	99.8 $_{\pm0.1}$
RNN +Attn-Dep	2.7 $_{\pm1.7}$	29.5 $_{\pm10.5}$	53.3 $_{\pm10.2}$	82.4 $_{\pm4.7}$	98.8 $_{\pm0.8}$	99.8 $_{\pm0.1}$	100.0 $_{\pm0.0}$
GRU +Attn	12.5 $_{\pm6.6}$	58.2 $_{\pm12.0}$	67.8 $_{\pm3.4}$	80.3 $_{\pm7.0}$	88.0 $_{\pm6.0}$	98.3 $_{\pm1.8}$	99.6 $_{\pm0.2}$
GRU +Attn-Dep	0.7 $_{\pm0.4}$	70.9 $_{\pm11.5}$	61.3 $_{\pm13.5}$	83.5 $_{\pm6.1}$	99.0 $_{\pm0.4}$	99.7 $_{\pm0.2}$	100.0 $_{\pm0.0}$
LSTM +Attn	7.8 $_{\pm0.9}$	40.2 $_{\pm9.3}$	37.7 $_{\pm10.7}$	50.3 $_{\pm13.9}$	62.2 $_{\pm7.7}$	94.0 $_{\pm2.7}$	98.6 $_{\pm1.0}$
LSTM +Attn-Dep	0.8 $_{\pm0.6}$	39.0 $_{\pm6.5}$	43.6 $_{\pm17.6}$	66.0 $_{\pm1.6}$	86.1 $_{\pm2.3}$	98.7 $_{\pm1.6}$	99.8 $_{\pm0.2}$
L&B	0.1	0.1	0.1	4.1	15.3	70.2	89.9

Table 6: SCAN test scores for jump with additional composed commands.

	0	1	2	4	8	16	32
RNN	0.0 $_{\pm0.0}$	0.1 $_{\pm0.0}$	0.1 $_{\pm0.1}$	0.2 $_{\pm0.0}$	0.7 $_{\pm0.2}$	0.4 $_{\pm0.0}$	0.8 $_{\pm0.1}$
GRU	0.0 $_{\pm0.0}$	0.3 $_{\pm0.2}$	0.4 $_{\pm0.1}$	0.3 $_{\pm0.2}$	1.0 $_{\pm0.4}$	5.8 $_{\pm0.1}$	20.8 $_{\pm2.2}$
LSTM	0.0 $_{\pm0.0}$	0.6 $_{\pm0.4}$	0.5 $_{\pm0.3}$	0.7 $_{\pm0.0}$	1.0 $_{\pm0.3}$	3.7 $_{\pm0.4}$	11.4 $_{\pm1.2}$
RNN +Attn	0.3 $_{\pm0.3}$	2.8 $_{\pm0.8}$	9.3 $_{\pm7.3}$	24.7 $_{\pm4.2}$	43.7 $_{\pm4.4}$	57.1 $_{\pm5.2}$	69.1 $_{\pm2.1}$
RNN +Attn-Dep	0.0 $_{\pm0.0}$	0.4 $_{\pm0.1}$	0.9 $_{\pm0.2}$	2.4 $_{\pm0.3}$	3.9 $_{\pm0.3}$	9.3 $_{\pm0.3}$	15.9 $_{\pm1.4}$
GRU +Attn	0.0 $_{\pm0.0}$	5.5 $_{\pm1.8}$	9.2 $_{\pm2.8}$	11.0 $_{\pm1.5}$	21.9 $_{\pm2.4}$	23.5 $_{\pm0.6}$	42.0 $_{\pm1.5}$
GRU +Attn-Dep	0.0 $_{\pm0.0}$	0.1 $_{\pm0.1}$	0.6 $_{\pm0.2}$	2.0 $_{\pm0.2}$	3.2 $_{\pm0.2}$	5.8 $_{\pm1.1}$	10.9 $_{\pm0.8}$
LSTM +Attn	0.0 $_{\pm0.0}$	2.1 $_{\pm0.2}$	3.7 $_{\pm0.9}$	6.6 $_{\pm0.5}$	12.5 $_{\pm2.5}$	21.8 $_{\pm2.6}$	34.2 $_{\pm1.7}$
LSTM +Attn-Dep	0.0 $_{\pm0.0}$	0.4 $_{\pm0.2}$	0.9 $_{\pm0.1}$	1.5 $_{\pm0.2}$	1.9 $_{\pm0.3}$	3.2 $_{\pm0.6}$	7.4 $_{\pm0.9}$

Table 7: NACS test scores for jump with additional composed commands.

	En-Fr	Fr-En
RNN +Attn	$29.1_{\pm 0.4}$	$34.9_{\pm 0.8}$
RNN +Attn-Dep	$27.5_{\pm 0.7}$	$32.9_{\pm 0.8}$
GRU +Attn	$32.1_{\pm 0.3}$	$37.5_{\pm 0.6}$
GRU +Attn-Dep	$30.2_{\pm 0.3}$	$35.9_{\pm 0.3}$
LSTM +Attn	$31.5_{\pm 0.2}$	$36.9_{\pm 1.1}$
LSTM +Attn-Dep	$28.7_{\pm 0.2}$	$34.0_{\pm 0.1}$

Table 8: Results (BLEU) on the Machine Translation experiment for both directions.

	En-Fr	Fr-En
RNN +Attn	$79.2_{\pm 15.6}$	$41.7_{\pm 5.9}$
RNN +Attn-Dep	$66.7_{\pm 5.9}$	$41.7_{\pm 5.9}$
GRU +Attn	$70.8_{\pm 11.8}$	$54.2_{\pm 5.9}$
GRU +Attn-Dep	$58.3_{\pm 5.9}$	$45.8_{\pm 11.8}$
LSTM +Attn	$75.0_{\pm 10.2}$	$41.7_{\pm 15.6}$
LSTM +Attn-Dep	$50.0_{\pm 10.2}$	$41.7_{\pm 5.9}$

Table 9: Machine Translation: accuracy on eight novel sentences containing 'daxy' ('daxiste').

	En-Fr	Fr-En
RNN +Attn	$66.7_{\pm 5.9}$	$20.8_{\pm 5.9}$
RNN +Attn-Dep	$66.7_{\pm 5.9}$	$29.2_{\pm 15.6}$
GRU +Attn	$62.5_{\pm 0.0}$	$33.3_{\pm 5.9}$
GRU +Attn-Dep	$66.7_{\pm 5.9}$	$25.0_{\pm 20.4}$
LSTM +Attn	$66.7_{\pm 5.9}$	$25.0_{\pm 10.2}$
LSTM +Attn-Dep	$62.5_{\pm 0.0}$	$25.0_{\pm 17.7}$

Table 10: Machine Translation: accuracy on eight novel sentences containing 'tired' ('fatigué').

Understanding Convolutional Neural Networks for Text Classification

Alon Jacovi[1,2]   **Oren Sar Shalom**[2,3]   **Yoav Goldberg**[1,4]

[1] Computer Science Department, Bar Ilan Univesity, Israel
[2] IBM Research, Haifa, Israel
[3] Intuit, Hod HaSharon, Israel
[4] Allen Institute for Artificial Intelligence

`{alonjacovi,oren.sarshalom,yoav.goldberg}@gmail.com`

Abstract

We present an analysis into the inner workings of Convolutional Neural Networks (CNNs) for processing text. CNNs used for computer vision can be interpreted by projecting filters into image space, but for discrete sequence inputs CNNs remain a mystery. We aim to understand the method by which the networks process and classify text. We examine common hypotheses to this problem: that filters, accompanied by global max-pooling, serve as ngram detectors. We show that filters may capture several different semantic classes of ngrams by using different activation patterns, and that global max-pooling induces behavior which separates important ngrams from the rest. Finally, we show practical use cases derived from our findings in the form of model interpretability (explaining a trained model by deriving a concrete identity for each filter, bridging the gap between visualization tools in vision tasks and NLP) and prediction interpretability (explaining predictions).

1 Introduction

Convolutional Neural Networks (CNNs), originally invented for computer vision, have been shown to achieve strong performance on text classification tasks (Bai et al., 2018; Kalchbrenner et al., 2014; Wang et al., 2015; Zhang et al., 2015; Johnson and Zhang, 2015; Iyyer et al., 2015) as well as other traditional Natural Language Processing (NLP) tasks (Collobert et al., 2011), even when considering relatively simple one-layer models (Kim, 2014).

As with other architectures of neural networks, explaining the learned functionality of CNNs is still an active research area. The ability to interpret neural models can be used to increase trust in model predictions, analyze errors or improve the model (Ribeiro et al., 2016). The problem of interpretability in machine learning can be divided into two concrete tasks: Given a trained model, *model interpretability* aims to supply a structured *explanation* which captures what the model has learned. Given a trained model and a single example, *prediction interpretability* aims to explain how the model arrived at its prediction. These can be further divided into white-box and black-box techniques. While recent works have begun to supply the means of interpreting predictions (Alvarez-Melis and Jaakkola, 2017; Lei et al., 2016; Guo et al., 2018), interpreting neural NLP models remains an under-explored area.

Accompanying their rising popularity, CNNs have seen multiple advances in interpretability when used for computer vision tasks (Zeiler and Fergus, 2014). These techniques unfortunately do not trivially apply to discrete sequences, as they assume a continuous input space used to represent images. Intuitions about how CNNs work on an abstract level also may not carry over from image inputs to text—for example, pooling in CNNs has been used to induce deformation invariance (Le-Cun et al., 1998, 2015), which is likely different than the role it has when processing text.

In this work, we examine and attempt to understand how CNNs process text, and then use this information for the more practical goals of improving model-level and prediction-level explanations.

We identify and refine current intuitions as to how CNNs work. Specifically, current common wisdom suggests that CNNs classify text by working through the following steps (Goldberg, 2016):

1) 1-dimensional convolving filters are used as ngram detectors, each filter specializing in a closely-related family of ngrams.

2) Max-pooling over time extracts the relevant ngrams for making a decision.

3) The rest of the network classifies the text based on this information.

Proceedings of the 2018 EMNLP Workshop BlackboxNLP: Analyzing and Interpreting Neural Networks for NLP, pages 56–65
Brussels, Belgium, November 1, 2018. ©2018 Association for Computational Linguistics

We refine items 1 and 2 and show that:

- Max-pooling induces a thresholding behavior, and values below a given threshold are ignored when (i.e. irrelevant to) making a prediction. Specifically, we show an experiment for which 40% of the pooled ngrams on average can be dropped with no loss of performance (Section 4).

- Filters are not homogeneous, i.e. a single filter can, and often does, detect multiple distinctly different families of ngrams (Section 5.3).

- Filters also detect negative items in ngrams— they not only select for a family of ngrams but often actively suppress a related family of negated ngrams (Section 5.4).

We also show that the filters are trained to work with naturally-occurring ngrams, and can be easily misled (made to produce values substantially larger than their expected range) by selected non-natural ngrams.

These findings can be used for improving model-level and prediction-level interpretability (Section 6). Concretely: 1) We improve model interpretability by deriving a useful summary for each filter, highlighting the kinds of structures it is sensitive to. 2) We improve prediction interpretability by focusing on informative ngrams and taking into account also the negative cues.

2   Background: 1D Text Convolutions

We focus on the task of text classification. We consider the common architecture in which each word in a document is represented as an embedding vector, a single convolutional layer with m filters is applied, producing an m-dimensional vector for each document ngram. The vectors are combined using max-pooling followed by a ReLU activation. The result is then passed to a linear layer for the final classification.

For an n-words input text $w_1, ..., w_n$ we embed each symbol as d dimensional vector, resulting in word vectors $\mathbf{w}_1, ..., \mathbf{w}_n \in R^d$. The resulting $d \times n$ matrix is then fed into a convolutional layer where we pass a sliding window over the text. For each l-words ngram:

$$\mathbf{u_i} = [\mathbf{w}_i, ..., \mathbf{w}_{i+\ell-1}] \in R^{d \times \ell} \; ; \; 0 \leq i \leq n - \ell$$

And for each filter $\mathbf{f_j} \in R^{d \times \ell}$ we calculate $\langle \mathbf{u_i}, \mathbf{f_j} \rangle$. The convolution results in matrix $\mathbf{F} \in R^{n \times m}$. Applying max-pooling across the ngram dimension results in $\mathbf{p} \in R^m$ which is fed into ReLU non-linearity. Finally, a linear fully-connected layer $\mathbf{W} \in R^{c \times m}$ produces the distribution over classification classes from which the strongest class is outputted. Formally:

$$\mathbf{u}_i = [\mathbf{w}_i; ...; \mathbf{w}_{i+\ell-1}]$$
$$F_{ij} = \langle \mathbf{u}_i, \mathbf{f}_j \rangle$$
$$p_j = \mathrm{ReLU}(\max_i F_{ij})$$
$$\mathbf{o} = \mathrm{softmax}(\mathbf{W}\mathbf{p})$$

In practice, we use multiple window sizes $\ell \in L$, $L \subsetneq \mathbb{N}$ by using multiple convolution layers in parallel and concatenating the resulting $\mathbf{p}^\ell$ vectors. We note that the methods in this work are applicable for dilated convolutions as well.

3   Datasets and Hyperparameters

For our empirical experiments and results presented in this work we use three text classification datasets for Sentiment Analysis, which involves classifying the input text (user reviews in all cases) between positive and negative. The specific datasets were chosen for their relative variety in size and domain as well as for the relative simplicity and interpretability of the binary sentiment analysis task.

The three datasets are: a) **MR**: sentence polarity dataset v1.0 introduced by Pang and Lee (2005), containing 10k evenly split short (sentences or snippets) movie reviews. b) **Elec**: electronic product reviews for sentiment classification introduced by Johnson and Zhang (2015), assembled from the Amazon review dataset (McAuley and Leskovec, 2013; McAuley et al., 2015), containing 200k train and 25k test evenly split reviews. c) **Yelp Review Polarity**: introduced by Zhang et al. (2015) from the Yelp Dataset Challenge 2015, containing 560k train and 38k test evenly split business reviews.

For word embeddings, we use the pre-trained GloVe *Wikipedia 2014—Gigaword 5* embeddings (Pennington et al., 2014), which we fine-tune with the model.

We use embedding dimension of 50, filter sizes of $\ell \in \{2, 3, 4\}$ words, and $m \in \{10, 50\}$ filters. Models are implemented in PyTorch and trained with the Adam optimizer.

4 Identifying Important Features

Current common wisdom posits that filters serve as ngram detectors: each filter searches for a specific class of ngrams, which it marks by assigning them high scores. These highest-scoring detected ngrams survive the max-pooling operation. The final decision is then based on the set of ngrams in the max-pooled vector (represented by the set of corresponding filters). Intuitively, ngrams which any filter scores highly (relative to how it scores other ngrams) are ngrams which are highly relevant for the classification of the text.

In this section we refine this view by attempting to answer the questions: what information about ngrams is captured in the max-pooled vector, and how is it used for the final classification?[1]

4.1 Informative vs. Uninformative Ngrams

Consider the pooled vector $\mathbf{p} \in R^m$ on which the classification is based. Each value $p_j = \text{ReLU}(\max_i \langle \mathbf{u_i}, \mathbf{f_j} \rangle)$ stems from a filter-ngram interaction, and can be traced back to the ngram $\mathbf{u_i} = [\mathbf{w}_i, ..., \mathbf{w}_{i+\ell-1}]$ that triggered it. Denote the set of ngrams contributing to $\mathbf{p}$ as $S_{\mathbf{p}}$. Ngrams not in $S_{\mathbf{p}}$ do not influence the decision of the classifier. But what about the ngrams that are in $S_{\mathbf{p}}$? Previous attempts in prediction-based interpretation of CNNs for text highlight the ngrams in $S_{\mathbf{p}}$ and their scores as means of explaining the prediction. We take here a more refined view. Note that the final classification does not observe the ngram identities directly, but only through the scores assigned to them by the filters. Hence, the information in $\mathbf{p}$ must rely on the assigned scores.

Conceptually, we separate ngrams in $S_{\mathbf{p}}$ into two classes, *deliberate* and *accidental*.
Deliberate ngrams end up in $S_{\mathbf{p}}$ because they were scored high by their filter, likely because they are *informative* regarding the final decision. In contrast, **accidental** ngrams end up in $S_{\mathbf{p}}$ despite having a low score, because no other ngram scored higher than them. These ngrams are likely *not informative* for the classification decision. Can we tease apart the deliberate and accidental ngrams?

We assume that there is *threshold* for each filter, where values above the threshold signal informative information regarding the classification, while values below the threshold are uninformative and can be ignored for the purpose of classification. We thus search for the threshold that separate the two classes. However, as we cannot measure directly which values p_j influence the final decision, we opt instead for measuring *correlation* between p_j values and the predicted label for the vector $\mathbf{p}$.

The linearity of the decision function $\mathbf{Wp}$ allows to measure exactly how much p_j is weighted for the logit of label class k. The class which filter $\mathbf{f}_j$ contributes to is $c_j = \arg\max_k W_{kj}{}^2$. We refer to class c_j as the *class identity* of filter f_j.

By assigning each filter a class identity c_j and comparing it to the predicted label we arrive at a *correlation label*—whether the filter's identity class matches the final decision by the network. Concretely, we run the classifier over a set of texts, resulting in pooled vectors $\mathbf{p}^i$ and network predictions c^i. For each filter j we then consider the values $\mathbf{p}_j^i$ and whether $c^i = c_j$. For each filter, we obtain a dataset $(p_j^1, c^1 = c_j), ..., (p_j^D, c^D = c_j)$, and we look for a threshold t_j that separates p_j^i for which $c^i = c_j$ from those where $c^i \neq c_j$.

$$(X, Y)_j = \{(p_j^i, c^i = c_j) \mid j < m \ \& \ i < D\}$$

In an ideal case, the set is linearly separable and we can easily separate informative from uninformative values: if $p_j^i > t_j$ then the classifier's prediction agrees with the filter's label, and otherwise they disagree. In practice, the set is not separable. We instead work with the *purity* of a filter-threshold combination, defined as the percentage of informative (correlative) ngrams which were scored above the threshold[3]. Formally, given threshold dataset (X, Y):

$$purity(f, t) = \frac{|\{(x, y) \in (X, Y)_f \mid x \geq t \ \& \ y = true\}|}{|\{(x, y) \in (X, Y)_f \mid x \geq t\}|}$$

We heuristically set the threshold of a filter to the lowest value that achieves a sufficiently high

---

[1] Although this work focuses on text classification, the findings in this section apply to any neural architecture which utilizes global max pooling, for both discrete and continuous domains. To our knowledge this is the first work that examines the assumption that max-pooling induces classifying behavior. Previously, Ruderman et al. (2018) showed that other assumptions to the functionality of max-pooling as deformation stabilizers (relevant only in continuous domains) do not necessarily hold true.

[2] In the case of non-linear fully-connected layers, the question of how each feature contributes to each class is significantly harder to answer. Possible methods include saliency map methods or gradient-based methods. Recently, Guo et al. (2018) has attributed labels to filters using Bayesian inference and other image annotations.

[3] The purity metric can be considered as the precision metric for this task.

purity (we experimentally find that a purity value of 0.75 works well).

In Figure 2b,c we show examples for threshold datasets for a model trained on the MR sentiment analysis task.

Threshold Effectiveness We described a method for obtaining per-filter threshold values. But is the threshold assumption—that items below a given threshold do not participate in the decision—even correct? To assess the quality of threshold obtained by our proposal and validate the thresholding assumption, we discard values that do not pass the threshold for each filter and observe the performance of the model. Practically, we replace the ReLU non-linearity with a threshold function:

$$threshold(x, t) = \begin{cases} x, & \text{if } x \geq t \\ 0, & \text{otherwise} \end{cases}$$

Figure 1 presents the results on the MR dataset (we observed similar results on the Elec dataset). where the threshold is set for each filter separately, based on a shared purity value. If the thresholding assumption is correct and our way of deriving the threshold is effective, we expect to not see a drop in accuracy. Indeed, for purity value of 0.75, we observe that the model performance *improves* slightly when replacing the ReLU with a per-filter threshold, indicating that the thresholding model is indeed a good approximation for the feature behavior. The percentage of informative (non-accidental) values in $\mathbf{p}$ is roughly a linear function of the purity (Figure 1c). With a purity value of 0.75^4, we discard roughly 44% of the values in $\mathbf{p}$—and hence 44% of the ngrams in $S_\mathbf{p}$.

Not all filters behave in a similar way, however. In Figure 2 we show an example for a filter—#6 in the figure—which is especially uninformative: by applying the lowest threshold which satisfies a purity of 0.75, we discard 99.99% of activations. Therefore in the experiments in Figure 1, this filter is effectively unused, yet it does not cause loss in performance. In essence, the threshold classifier

---

[4]We note that empirically and intuitively, the more filters we utilize in the network, the less correlation there is between each filter's class and the final classification, as the decision is being made by a greater consensus. This means that demanding a higher purity will be accompanied by lower coverage, relative to other experiments, and more ngrams will be discarded. The "correct" purity level for a filter then is a function of the model and dataset used, and should be investigated using the train or validation datasets.

identified and effectively discarded a filter which is not useful to the model.

To summarize, we validated our assumptions and shown empirically that global max-pooling indeed induces a functionality of separating important and not important activation signals using a latent (presumably soft) threshold. For the rest of this work we will assume a known threshold value for every filter in the model which we can use to identify important ngrams.

5 What is captured by a filter?

Previous work looked at the top-k scoring ngrams for each filter. However, focusing on the top-k does not tell a complete story. We insead look at the set of deliberate ngrams: those that pass the filter's threshold value. Common intuition suggests that each filter is *homogeneous* and specializes in detecting a specific classes of ngrams. For example, a filter may specializing in detecting ngrams such as "had no issues", "had zero issues", and "had no problems". We challenge this view and show that filters often specialize in multiple distinctly different semantic classes by utilizing activation patterns which are not necessarily maximized. We also show that filters may not only identify good ngrams, but may also actively supress bad ones.

5.1 Slot Activation Vectors

As discussed in Section 2, for each ngram $\mathbf{u} = [\mathbf{w}_1, ..., \mathbf{w}_\ell]$ and for each filter $\mathbf{f}$ we calculate the score $\langle \mathbf{u}, \mathbf{f} \rangle$. The ngram score can be decomposed as a sum of individual word scores by considering the inner products between every word embedding $\mathbf{w}_i$ in $\mathbf{u}$ and every parallel slice in $\mathbf{f}$:

$$\langle \mathbf{u}, \mathbf{f} \rangle = \sum_{i=0}^{\ell-1} \langle \mathbf{w}_i, \mathbf{f}_{\mathbf{id}:\mathbf{i(d+1)}} \rangle$$

We refer to slice $\mathbf{f}_{\mathbf{id}:\mathbf{i(d+1)}}$ as *slot i* of the filter weights, denoted as $\mathbf{f(i)}$. Instead of taking the sum of these inner products, we can instead interpret them directly—saying that $\langle \mathbf{w}_i, \mathbf{f(i)} \rangle$ captures how much slot i in $\mathbf{f}$ is activated by the ith word in the ngram^5.

We can now move from examining the activation of an ngram-filter pair $\langle \mathbf{u} := [\mathbf{w}_1; ...; \mathbf{w}_\ell], \mathbf{f} \rangle$ to examining its *slot activation vector*: $(\langle \mathbf{w}_1, \mathbf{f(1)} \rangle, ..., \langle \mathbf{w}_\ell, \mathbf{f(\ell)} \rangle)$. The slot ac-

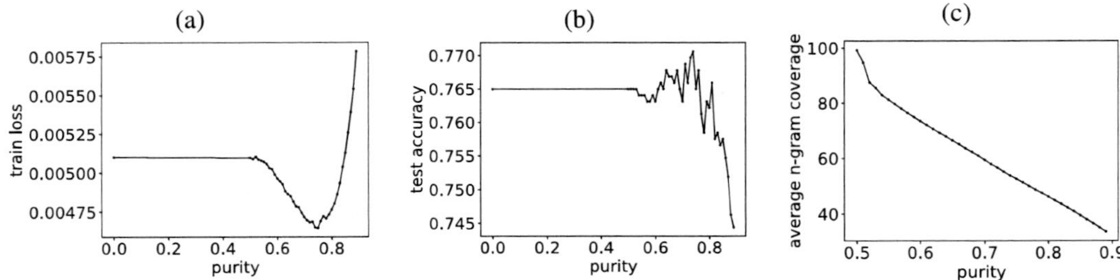

Figure 1: Evaluation results for identifying important ngrams on the MR model.

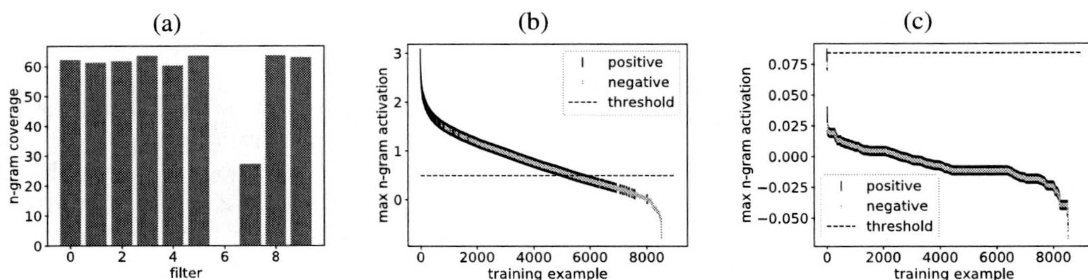

Figure 2: Visualization of informative and uninformative filters for the MR model and a universal purity of 0.75. In (a) we show the percentage of pooled ngrams which pass the threshold per filter. The threshold datasets of filters #0 and #6 are shown in (b) and (c) respectively.

tivation vector captures how much each word in the ngram contributes to its activation.

5.2 Naturally occurring vs. possible ngrams

We distinguish *naturally occurring* or *observed* ngrams, which are ngrams that are observed in a large corpus, from *possible* ngrams which are any combination of ℓ words from the vocabulary. The possible ngrams are a superset of the naturally occurring ones. Given a filter, we can find its top-scoring naturally occurring ngram by searching over all ngrams in a corpus. We can find its top-scoring possible ngram by maximizing each slot value individually. We observe there is a big and consistent gap in scores between the top-scoring natural ngrams and top-scoring possible ngrams. In our Elec model, when averaging over all filters, the top naturally-occurring ngrams score 30% less than the top possible ngrams. Interestingly, *the*

top-scoring natural ngrams almost never fully activate all slots in a filter.

Table 1 shows the top-scoring naturally occurring and possible ngrams for nine filters in the Elec model. In each of the top scoring natural ngrams, at least one slot receives a low activation. Table 2 zooms in on one of the filters and shows its top-7 naturally occurring ngrams and top-7 most activated words in each slot. Here, most top-scoring ngrams maximize slot #3 with words such as *invaluable* and *perfect*, however some ngrams such as "*works* as good" and "still *holding* strong" maximize slots #1 and #2 respectively, instead.

Additionally, most top-scoring words do not appear to be utilized in high-scoring ngrams at all. This can be explained with the following: if a word such as *crt* rarely or never appears in slot #1 alongside other high-scoring words in other slots, then *crt* can score highly with no consequence. Since an ngram containing *crt* at slot #1 will rarely pass the max-pooling layer, its score at that slot is essentially random.

On naturally occurring ngrams, the filters do not achieve maximum values in all slots but only on some of them. Why? We consider two hypotheses to explain this behavior:

---

[5] We note that this breakdown does not consider the filter's *bias*, if one is used. This bias is a single number (per filter) which is added to the sum of slot activations to arrive at the ngram activation which is passed to the max-pooling layer. Bias can be accommodated by appending an additional "bias word" with an embedding vector of $[1, ..., 1]$ to every ngram. Regardless, as this bias is identical for all ngrams for the filter in question, it has no role in identifying which ngrams the filter is most similar to, and we can ignore it in this context.

	top ngrams				top words by slot						
filter	ngram	score	slot scores			slot #1		slot #2		slot #3		sum
0	poorly designed junk	7.31	5.47	0.97	0.87	poorly	5.47	displaying	3.06	landfill	1.75	10.28
1	simply would not	5.75	2.16	1.28	2.3	chapters	2.31	avoid	3.07	impossible	3.06	8.44
2	a minor drawback	6.11	0.88	1.85	3.38	workstation	2.06	high-quality	3.82	drawback	3.39	9.27
3	still working perfect	6.42	1.58	1.22	3.62	saves	2.52	delight	2.29	invaluable	4.19	9.0
4	absolutely gorgeous .	5.36	1.09	3.84	0.42	complain	2.57	gorgeous	3.84	expect	1.22	7.63
5	one little hitch	5.72	0.98	3.43	1.31	path	2.81	delight	4.09	everyday	2.64	9.54
6	utterly useless .	6.33	2.03	3.49	0.81	stopped	2.77	refund	3.81	disabled	1.38	7.96
7	deserves four stars	5.56	0.44	1.69	3.44	excelente	1.89	crossover	1.93	incredible	3.96	7.78
8	a mediocre product	6.91	0.35	3.11	3.45	began	1.86	mediocre	3.11	product	3.45	8.42

Table 1: Top ngrams and words by filter from a sample of nine filters from the Elec model. The average difference between the top natural ngram activation and the top possible ngram activation for this model is 2.5, or a 30% average reduction.

	top ngrams					top words by slot					
rank	ngram	score	slot scores			slot #1		slot #2		slot #3	
1	still working **perfect**	6.42	1.58	1.22	**3.62**	saves	2.52	delight	2.29	**invaluable**	**4.19**
2	works - **perfect**	5.78	1.91	0.25	**3.62**	crt	2.1	**holding**	**1.81**	**perfect**	**3.62**
3	isolation proves **invaluable**	5.61	0.39	1.03	**4.19**	beginner	2.09	welcome	1.8	cm	3.61
4	still near **perfect**	5.6	1.58	0.4	**3.62**	mics	2.08	dhcp	1.72	pleasant	3.38
5	still working great	5.45	1.58	1.22	2.65	genius	2.07	completely	1.64	simplicity	3.14
6	**works** as good	5.44	**1.91**	1.45	2.08	final	2.01	cradle	1.56	england	3.09
7	still **holding** strong	5.37	1.58	**1.81**	1.98	**works**	**1.91**	well-made	1.51	daily	3.04

Table 2: Top-k words by slot scores and top-k ngrams by filter scores from the Elec model. In bold are words from the top-k ngrams which appear in the top-k slot words - i.e. words which maximize their slot.

(i) Each filter captures multiple semantic classes of ngrams, and each class has some dominating slots and some non-dominating slots (which we define as a *slot activation pattern*).

(ii) A slot may not be maximized because it's not used to detect word existence, but rather lack of existence—ensuring that specific words do not occur.

We investigate both hypotheses in Sections 5.3 and 5.4 respectively.

Adversarial potential We note in passing that this discrepancy in scores between naturally occurring and possible ngrams can be used to derive adversarial examples that cause a trained model to misclassify. By inserting a few seemingly random ngrams, we can cause filters to activate beyond their expected range, potentially driving the model to misclassification. We reserve this area of exploration for future work.

5.3 Clustering (Hypothesis (i))

We explore hypothesis (i) by clustering threshold-passing (naturally occurring) ngrams in each filter according to their activation vectors. We use Mean Shift Clustering (Fukunaga and Hostetler, 1975; Cheng, 1995), an algorithm that does not require specifying an a-priori number of clusters, and does not make assumptions about their shapes. Mean Shift considers the feature vectors as sampled from an underlying probability density function[6]. Each cluster captures a different slot activation pattern. We use the cluster's centroid as the prototypical slot activation for that cluster.

Table 3 shows a sample clustering output. The clustering algorithm identified two clusters: one primarily containing ngrams of the pattern *DET INTENSITY-ADVERB POSITIVE-WORD*, while the second contains ngrams that begin with phrases like *go wrong*.[7]

The centroids for these clusters capture the activation patterns well: low-medium-high and high-high-low for clusters 1 and 2 respectively.

To summarize, by discarding noisy ngrams which do not pass the filter's threshold and then clustering those that remain according to their slot activation patterns, we arrived at a clearer image

---

[6]Intuitively, we can think of the sampling noise as the ngram embeddings, and the probability distribution as defined by a function of the filter weights.

[7]In the Yelp dataset, *go wrong* overwhelmingly occurs in a negated context such as "can't go wrong" and "won't go wrong", which explains why it is detected by a positive filter.

ngram	slot #1	slot #2	slot #3	cluster
centroid	0.75	1.97	2.79	1
was super intriguing	1.01	3.16	5.84	1
am so grateful	2.59	3.27	4.07	1
overall very worth	3.84	1.86	4.22	1
also well worth	1.83	3.06	4.22	1
- super compassionate	0.51	3.17	5.01	1
a well oiled	0.75	3.06	4.84	1
centroid	2.87	2.17	0.12	2
go wrong bringing	3.97	4.12	1.81	2
go wrong pairing	3.97	4.12	1.65	2
go wrong when	3.97	4.12	-0.4	2

Table 3: Example clustering results on the Yelp dataset. After applying thresholds, the ngrams for this filter were split into two clusters of sizes 83% and 17% respectively. The table shows top-scoring ngrams for this filter with their clustering results, sorted by their activation strength.

of the semantic classes of ngrams that a given filter specializes in capturing. In particular, we reveal that filters are not necessarily homogeneous: a single filter may detect several different semantic patterns, each one of them relying on a different slot activation pattern.

5.4 Negative Ngrams (Hypothesis (ii))

Our second theory to explain the discrepancy between the activations of naturally occurring and possible ngrams is that certain filter slots are not used to detect a class of highly activating words, but rather to rule out a class of highly negative words. We refer to these as *negative ngrams*.

For example, Table 3 shows an ngram pattern for which slot #1 contains determiners and other "filler" tokens such as hyphens, periods and commas with relatively weak slot activations. Hypothesis (ii) suggests that this slot may receive a strong *negative* score for words such as *not* and *n't*, causing such negated patterns to drop below the threshold. Indeed, ngrams containing *not* or *n't* in slot #1 do not pass the threshold for this filter.

We are interested in a more systematic method of identifying these cases. Identifying negative slot activations would be very useful for understanding the semantics captured by a filter and the reasoning behind the dismissal of an ngram, as we discuss in Sections 6.1 and 6.2 respectively.

We achieve this by searching the below-threshold ngram space for ngrams which are "flipped versions" of above-threshold ngrams. Concretely: Given ngram u which was scored highly by filter f, we search for low-scoring ngrams u' such that the hamming distance between u and u' is low. By doing this for the top-k scoring ngrams per cluster, we arrive at a comprehensive set of negative ngrams. In Table 4 we show a sample output of this algorithm.

Furthermore, we can divide negative ngrams into two cases: 1) Lowering the ngram score below the threshold by replacing high-scoring words with low-scoring words. 2) Lowering the ngram score below the threshold by replacing words with a low positive score with words with a highly-negative score. Case 2 is more interesting because it embodies cases where hypothesis (ii) is relevant. Additionally, it highlights ngrams where a strongly positive word in one slot was negated with another strongly negative word in another slot. Table 4 shows examples in bold.

In order to identify "Case 2" negative ngrams, we heuristically test whether the "changed" words' scores directly influence the status of the activation relative to the threshold: given an already identified negative ngram, if the ngram score—sans the bottom-k negative slot activations (considering a hamming distance of k and given that there are k negative slot activations)—passes the threshold, yet it does not pass the threshold by including the negative slot activations, then the ngram is considered a "Case 2" negative ngram.

6 Interpretability

In this section we show two practical implications of the findings above: improvements in both model-level and prediction-level interpretability of 1D CNNs for text classification.

6.1 Model Interpretability

As in computer vision, we can now interpret a trained CNN model by "visualizing" its filters and interpreting the visible shapes—in other words, defining a high-level description of what the filter detects. We propose to associate each filter with the following items: 1) The class which this filter's strong signals contribute to (in the sentiment task: positive or negative); 2) The threshold value for the filter, together with its purity and coverages percentages (which essentially capture how informative this filter is); 3) A list of semantic patterns identified by this filter. Each list item corresponds to a slot-activations cluster. For each cluster we present the top-k ngrams activating it, and for each ngram we specify its total activation, its

ngram	slot #1	slot #2	slot #3	sum
'm really pleased	2.59	1.86	5.05	9.5
'm really not			-2.49	1.96
'm really upset			-1.14	3.31
'm not pleased		-3.4		4.24
is extremely useful	2.3	3.24	3.96	9.5
is extremely limited			-2.8	2.74
is extremely noisy			-2.77	2.8
is not useful		-3.4		2.86
is only useful		-2.82		3.44
is surprisingly good	2.3	4.32	2.8	9.42
is not good		-3.4		1.7
is only good		-2.82		2.28
is no good		-1.88		3.22
is probably good		-1.66		3.44
am very satisfied	2.01	2.17	5.09	9.26
am very dissatisfied			-1.9	2.27
am very disappointed			-1.87	2.3
am not satisfied		-3.4		3.69
not very satisfied	-2.6			4.66

Table 4: Top-scoring ngrams from one filter from a model trained on the Elec dataset, and their accompanying lowest-scoring negative ngrams. We selected a hamming distance of 1 word. Bold ngrams are Case 2 negative ngrams.

slot-activation vector, and its list of bottom-k negative ngrams with their activations and slot activations. In particular, by clustering the activated ngrams according to their slot activation patterns and showing the top-k in each clusters, we get a much more refined coverage of the linguistic patterns that are captured by the filter.

6.2 Prediction Interpretability

Previous prediction-based interpretation attempts traced back the ngrams from the max-pooling layer. Here we improve these previous attempts by considering only ngrams that pass the threshold for their filter. This results in a more concise and relevant explanation (Figure 1). Figure 3 shows two examples. Note that in example #1, many negative-class filters were "forced" to choose an ngram in max-pooling despite there not being strongly negative phrases—but those ngrams do not pass the threshold and are thus cleaned from the explanation.

Additionally we can use the individual slot activations to tease-apart the contribution of each word in the ngram. Finally, we can also mark cases of negative-ngrams (Section 5.4), where an ngram has high slot activations for some words, but these are negated by a highly-negative slot and

my **UNK fits perfectly . very well** made . nice looking and offers good protection

filter	f-class	ngram	slot scores		
0	pos	PAD PAD my	0.7	1.65	0.16
1	**pos**	**. very well**	**0.98**	**2.17**	**2.63**
2	neg	PAD my UNK	1.31	-0.07	0.21
3	neg	UNK fits perfectly	0.28	0.61	0.03
4	neg	looking and offers	0.6	0.12	0.5
5	neg	good protection PAD	0.52	1.6	-0.01
6	**pos**	**UNK fits perfectly**	**-0.06**	**2.36**	**1.82**
7	neg	fits perfectly .	1.34	-0.71	1.47
8	neg	. very well	-0.01	1.97	-0.55
9	**pos**	**perfectly . very**	**4.13**	**0.45**	**-0.01**

this product **sucked was not** loud at all lights **did n't work** *overall a bad* **product** that 's UNK taking up space

filter	f-class	ngram	slot scores		
0	pos	product sucked was	0.12	2.05	0.1
1	*pos*	*overall a bad*	*2.53*	*1.4*	*-1.16*
2	neg	lights did n't	-0.33	1.12	1.63
3	neg	PAD this product	-0.2	1.43	0.51
4	**neg**	**did n't work**	**1.21**	**0.97**	**2.65**
5	**neg**	**sucked was not**	**0.98**	**0.59**	**1.32**
6	pos	work overall a	-0.25	4.05	-0.21
7	neg	was not loud	-0.33	2.85	0.52
8	**neg**	**a bad product**	**-0.45**	**3.08**	**1.32**
9	pos	PAD PAD this	0.38	0.15	1.66

Figure 3: Examples predicted positive and negative respectively by a model trained on the Elec dataset, along with their explanations. Ngrams which passed the threshold are in bold, and case 2 negative ngrams are in italics. For clarity's sake we trained a small model which uses ten filters.

as a consequence are not selected by max-pooling, or are selected but do not pass the filter's threshold.

7 Conclusion

We have refined several common wisdom assumptions regarding the way in which CNNs process and classify text. First, we have shown that max-pooling over time induces a thresholding behavior on the convolution layer's output, essentially separating between features that are relevant to the final classification and features that are not. We used this information to identify which ngrams are important to the classification. We also associate each filter with the class it contributes to. We decompose the ngram score into word-level scores by treating the convolution of a filter as a sum of word-level convolutions, allowing us to examine the word-level composition of the activation. Specifically, by maximizing the word-level activations by iterating over the vocabulary, we observed that filters do not maximize activations at the word-level, but instead form slot activation patterns that give different types of ngrams similar activation strengths. This provides empirical evidence that filters are not homogeneous. By clustering high-scoring ngrams according to their slot-activation patterns we can identify the groups of linguistic patterns captured by a filter. We also show that filters sometimes opt to assign negative values to certain word activations in order to cause the ngrams which contain them to receive a low score despite having otherwise highly activating words. Finally, we use these findings to suggest improvements to model-based and prediction-based interpretability of CNNs for text.

References

David Alvarez-Melis and Tommi S. Jaakkola. 2017. A causal framework for explaining the predictions of black-box sequence-to-sequence models. In *Proceedings of the 2017 Conference on Empirical Methods in Natural Language Processing, EMNLP 2017, Copenhagen, Denmark, September 9-11, 2017*, pages 412–421. Association for Computational Linguistics.

Shaojie Bai, J. Zico Kolter, and Vladlen Koltun. 2018. An empirical evaluation of generic convolutional and recurrent networks for sequence modeling. *CoRR*, abs/1803.01271.

Yizong Cheng. 1995. Mean shift, mode seeking, and clustering. *IEEE Trans. Pattern Anal. Mach. Intell.*, 17(8):790–799.

Ronan Collobert, Jason Weston, Léon Bottou, Michael Karlen, Koray Kavukcuoglu, and Pavel P. Kuksa. 2011. Natural language processing (almost) from scratch. *Journal of Machine Learning Research*, 12:2493–2537.

Keinosuke Fukunaga and Larry D. Hostetler. 1975. The estimation of the gradient of a density function, with applications in pattern recognition. *IEEE Trans. Information Theory*, 21(1):32–40.

Yoav Goldberg. 2016. A primer on neural network models for natural language processing. *J. Artif. Intell. Res.*, 57:345–420.

Pei Guo, Connor Anderson, Kolten Pearson, and Ryan Farrell. 2018. Neural network interpretation via fine grained textual summarization. *CoRR*, abs/1805.08969.

Mohit Iyyer, Varun Manjunatha, Jordan L. Boyd-Graber, and Hal Daumé III. 2015. Deep unordered composition rivals syntactic methods for text classification. In *Proceedings of the 53rd Annual Meeting of the Association for Computational Linguistics and the 7th International Joint Conference on Natural Language Processing of the Asian Federation of Natural Language Processing, ACL 2015, July 26-31, 2015, Beijing, China, Volume 1: Long Papers*, pages 1681–1691. The Association for Computer Linguistics.

Rie Johnson and Tong Zhang. 2015. Effective use of word order for text categorization with convolutional neural networks. In *NAACL HLT 2015, The 2015 Conference of the North American Chapter of the Association for Computational Linguistics: Human Language Technologies, Denver, Colorado, USA, May 31 - June 5, 2015*, pages 103–112. The Association for Computational Linguistics.

Nal Kalchbrenner, Edward Grefenstette, and Phil Blunsom. 2014. A convolutional neural network for modelling sentences. In *Proceedings of the 52nd Annual Meeting of the Association for Computational Linguistics, ACL 2014, June 22-27, 2014, Baltimore, MD, USA, Volume 1: Long Papers*, pages 655–665. The Association for Computer Linguistics.

Yoon Kim. 2014. Convolutional neural networks for sentence classification. In *Proceedings of the 2014 Conference on Empirical Methods in Natural Language Processing, EMNLP 2014, October 25-29, 2014, Doha, Qatar, A meeting of SIGDAT, a Special Interest Group of the ACL*, pages 1746–1751. ACL.

Yann LeCun, Y Bengio, and Geoffrey Hinton. 2015. Deep learning. 521:436–44.

Yann LeCun, Leon Bottou, Y Bengio, and Patrick Haffner. 1998. Gradient-based learning applied to document recognition. 86:2278 – 2324.

Tao Lei, Regina Barzilay, and Tommi S. Jaakkola. 2016. Rationalizing neural predictions. In *Proceedings of the 2016 Conference on Empirical Methods in Natural Language Processing, EMNLP 2016, Austin, Texas, USA, November 1-4, 2016*, pages 107–117. The Association for Computational Linguistics.

Julian J. McAuley and Jure Leskovec. 2013. Hidden factors and hidden topics: understanding rating dimensions with review text. In *Seventh ACM Conference on Recommender Systems, RecSys '13, Hong Kong, China, October 12-16, 2013*, pages 165–172. ACM.

Julian J. McAuley, Christopher Targett, Qinfeng Shi, and Anton van den Hengel. 2015. Image-based recommendations on styles and substitutes. In *Proceedings of the 38th International ACM SIGIR Conference on Research and Development in Information Retrieval, Santiago, Chile, August 9-13, 2015*, pages 43–52. ACM.

Bo Pang and Lillian Lee. 2005. Seeing stars: Exploiting class relationships for sentiment categorization with respect to rating scales. *CoRR*, abs/cs/0506075.

Jeffrey Pennington, Richard Socher, and Christopher D. Manning. 2014. Glove: Global vectors for word representation. In *Empirical Methods in Natural Language Processing (EMNLP)*, pages 1532–1543.

Marco Túlio Ribeiro, Sameer Singh, and Carlos Guestrin. 2016. "why should I trust you?": Explaining the predictions of any classifier. In *Proceedings of the 22nd ACM SIGKDD International Conference on Knowledge Discovery and Data Mining, San Francisco, CA, USA, August 13-17, 2016*, pages 1135–1144. ACM.

Avraham Ruderman, Neil C. Rabinowitz, Ari S. Morcos, and Daniel Zoran. 2018. Learned deformation stability in convolutional neural networks. *CoRR*, abs/1804.04438.

Peng Wang, Jiaming Xu, Bo Xu, Cheng-Lin Liu, Heng Zhang, Fangyuan Wang, and Hongwei Hao. 2015. Semantic clustering and convolutional neural network for short text categorization. In *Proceedings of the 53rd Annual Meeting of the Association for Computational Linguistics and the 7th International Joint Conference on Natural Language Processing of the Asian Federation of Natural Language Processing, ACL 2015, July 26-31, 2015, Beijing, China, Volume 2: Short Papers*, pages 352–357. The Association for Computer Linguistics.

Matthew D. Zeiler and Rob Fergus. 2014. Visualizing and understanding convolutional networks. In *Computer Vision - ECCV 2014 - 13th European Conference, Zurich, Switzerland, September 6-12, 2014, Proceedings, Part I*, volume 8689 of *Lecture Notes in Computer Science*, pages 818–833. Springer.

Xiang Zhang, Junbo Jake Zhao, and Yann LeCun. 2015. Character-level convolutional networks for text classification. In *Advances in Neural Information Processing Systems 28: Annual Conference on Neural Information Processing Systems 2015, December 7-12, 2015, Montreal, Quebec, Canada*, pages 649–657.

Linguistic representations in multi-task neural networks for ellipsis resolution

Ola Rønning
Cobiro
ronning@pm.me

Daniel Hardt
Copenhagen Business School
dh.msc@cbs.dk

Anders Søgaard
University of Copenhagen
soegaard@di.ku.dk

Abstract

Sluicing resolution is the task of identifying the antecedent to a question ellipsis. Antecedents are often sentential constituents, and previous work has therefore relied on syntactic parsing, together with complex linguistic features. A recent model instead used partial parsing as an auxiliary task in sequential neural network architectures to inject syntactic information. We explore the linguistic information being brought to bear by such networks, both by defining subsets of the data exhibiting relevant linguistic characteristics, and by examining the internal representations of the network. Both perspectives provide evidence for substantial linguistic knowledge being deployed by the neural networks.

1 Introduction

Sluices are questions where material beyond the *wh*-word is missing and must be retrieved from context. Consider the following example from Rønning et al. (2018):

(1)   If [this is not practical], explain *why*.

Here, the antecedent is the complete sentential constituent, *this is not practical*.

Anand and Hardt (2016) present a sluice resolution system, in which candidate antecedents are required to be sentential constituents. Furthermore, each candidate is represented by features manually defined over syntactic dependency structures. Anand and Hardt report an accuracy of antecedent selection of 0.72, and a token-level F1 score 0.72, applied to a dataset based on news content (Anand and McCloskey, 2015). Rønning et al. (2018) show that neural network architectures with multi-task learning are able to achieve comparable results to Anand and Hardt, without relying on structured syntactic annotation or hand-crafted features. On a slightly different version of the news dataset, Rønning et al. report a token-level F1 score of 0.70, compared to 0.67 for Anand and Hardt's system. Furthermore, it is far superior to Anand and Hardt's system at adapting from the newswire to a dialogue dataset.

This is quite surprising as sluicing is traditionally understood to be constituent-based. Two explanations present themselves; first, the traditional view might simply be wrong – that is, linguistic structure is not actually needed for ellipsis resolution. The second, and perhaps more reasonable, explanation is that Rønning et al.'s multi-task neural network architectures have learned to extract and incorporate the relevant linguistic representations.

In this paper, we investigate the linguistic knowledge learned implicitly in the experiments in Rønning et al. (2018). We take two approaches to this:

1. We select linguistically-defined subsets of the data, and examine the output of different systems on these subsets; and

2. we examine activations of the networks, focusing in particular on the activations associated with the *wh*-word that identifies a sluice, to assess how well the network notices, remembers, and classifies them.

2 Systems

The two sluicing resolution systems we compare, are: The linguistic system (AH) by Anand and Hardt (2016) and the neural network architectures introduced by Rønning et al. (2018).

2.1 Linguistic System (AH)

The system presented in Anand and Hardt (2016) defines a set of linguistically motivated features over pre-parsed input to determine the most likely

66

Proceedings of the 2018 EMNLP Workshop BlackboxNLP: Analyzing and Interpreting Neural Networks for NLP, pages 66–73
Brussels, Belgium, November 1, 2018. ©2018 Association for Computational Linguistics

BI	KSG	RHS
		RHS
	KSG	Ant
BI	Ant	CCG
Ant	Chunk	Chunk
Plain	Comp	POS

Figure 1: Task hierarchy of the three networks considered; the tasks are (Ant)ecedent Selection, (Chunk)ing, Sentence (Comp)ression, (CCG) super-tagging and (POS) tagging. Plain denotes a RNN-layer with no associated task.

antecedent among a set of candidates. The candidate set consist of all sentential constituents within a predefined context window of the sluice. AH parameterizes a log-linear score akin to Denis and Baldridge (2008) using hill-climbing. Anand and Hardt (2016) evaluates AH by the accuracy of chosen constituents, but also report token-level F1 scores. We focus on token-F1 score in this paper to compare with the neural networks as these do not operate with predefined constituents.

2.2 Neural Network Architectures

We examine three neural network architectures, all defined in Rønning et al. (2018), and depicted in Figure 1. In all three systems, the input is a sequence of tokens without syntactic annotations. All our neural networks use 50 dimensional fixed GloVe embeddings, obtained by applying the model in Pennington et al. (2014) on Wikipedia and Gigaword 5. The sluice expression is not specifically marked in the text. Instead, a copy of the sluice expression is prefixed to the sequence. The networks assign either a begin, inside or outside (BIO) label to each token and the task is to align these with the span of the antecedent. The three networks are:

BI: This is a single-task, two-layered long-short-term memory (LSTM) network, with a projection layer and a softmax layer.

KSG: This is a cascading, three-layered LSTM, as described by Klerke et al. (2016). The KSG system is trained with the following auxiliary tasks:

> **Chunking**: a partial parsing task, in which we need to identify the boundaries of the phrases in a sentence; and

Sentence compression: the task of finding sentence parts that can be dropped without losing coherence or important information

During an epoch, k batches of size b are sampled from each of the three tasks such that kb is the number of examples in the antecedent selection task. We choose batches from each of the auxiliary tasks in the fixed order: sentence compression, chunking, antecedent selection.

RHS: This system also cascades the auxiliary tasks. However, it uses a different set of auxiliary tasks than KGS, computes label embeddings that are also passed on to subsequent layers, and has skip connections from the embedding layer to all layers in the network. RHS uses the auxiliary tasks described below:

> **CCG super-tagging:** another form of partial parsing, using a more fine-grained tagset.

> **Chunking**: same task as described for KSG.

> **POS tagging**: determining the syntactic category (part of speech) of a word in context.

RHS cycles through all data for each of the auxiliary tasks during a epoch, only layers up to and including the layer associated with the tasks currently being optimized is active during training of that task. Over the course of an epoch, the network trains on POS, Chunk, CCG-super tagging and, then, antecedent selection.

Table 1 gives the token-level F1 score for each system on the dataset used in Rønning et al. (2018). It also includes the baseline performance of choosing a random constituent within the two sentence window of the sluice site. This is the same window size AH uses to determine its candidate set.

System	Score
AH	0.67
Random	0.45
RHS	0.70
KSG	0.64
BI	0.54

Table 1: Token-F1 Score on complete test set.

3 Data Subsets

Below we introduce various linguistic dimensions of the ellipsis resolution data, which we can use to study the models' behavior on subsets of the data, indirectly probing what linguistic distinctions they make.

3.1 Adjacency

It is very common for the correct antecedents to be sentential constituent immediately preceding the ellipsis site. Call this constituent the *adjacent* candidate to the sluice. The antecedent in Example 1 is adjacent. However, adjacency is not ubiquitous. We refer to all other candidates as non-adjacent. Example 2 from Anand and Hardt (2016) is non-adjacent:

(2) [$_{S-3}$ Deliveries would increase as a result of the acquisition] , [$_{S-2}$ he predicted] , but [$_{S-1}$ he would not say by how much]

The sluice expression *how much* has S_2 as the adjacent constituent, while the correct antecedent is the non-adjacent S_3. Table 2 gives token-level F1 scores for all systems with the dataset partitioned by adjacency.

System	Adjacent	Non-Adjacent	Difference
AH	84.8	56.5	28.3
RHS	84.7	65.5	19.2
KSG	74.5	60.6	13.9
BI	62.3	51.0	11.3

Table 2: F1 score for Adjacent vs. Non-adjacent Sluice Antecedents

All systems score higher with adjacent candidates than with non-adjacent ones, i.e., when the true antecedent is adjacent. AH scores marginally higher on adjacent candidates than RHS, but has a significantly higher difference between adjacent and non-adjacent compared to the three neural systems. Since AH has explicit constituency information, it makes sense that it would have a high token-level F1 score, when the antecedent is adjacent. For the MTL systems, RHS and KSG, adjacency also makes a big difference in F1 scores, albeit less than for AH. The smallest performance drop is seen with BI, the single-task system.

This is somewhat comparable to the case of subject-verb agreement studied in Linzen et al. (2016), where it was found that an LSTM could learn structural information necessary to identify the subject, but that performance decreased when the subject was not the nearest noun phrase to the verb. In their case, the neural model had learned

a representation that was too dependent on adjacency information; in our case, it seems like the neural architectures have successfully learned a representation that makes them less dependent on adjacency than the baseline BI system.

3.2 Punctuation/Boundary Tokens

A major difference between AH and the neural models is that the neural models do not have explicit marking of the boundaries of candidate antecedents, as AH does. The neural models may, however, rely on specific tokens that signal these boundaries. We hypothesize that punctuation can play this role. Based on this, we would expect that the neural networks do better when antecedents are marked by punctuation, while this should matter less, if at all, to the AH system.

We define the following subsets of the data: first, we restrict ourselves to cases where the antecedent is adjacent. Then we define three subsets:

- (L) the correct antecedent has a punctuation token on its left edge

- (R) the correct antecedent has a punctuation token on its right edge

- (LR) the correct antecedent has a punctuation token on both its left edge and its right edge

System	LR	R	L
AH	85.0	84.9	85.8
RHS	85.6	85.5	80.7
KSG	75.2	74.1	71.1
BI	62.3	62.3	58.7

Table 3: F1 score for punctuation as boundary token for antecedent

The results, which are given in Table 3, partially support our hypothesis. Focusing on LR (where punctuation marks both edges of the adjacent antecedent), we observe that RHS and KSG see improvements of .9 and .7 respectively, while AH is improved only by .2. This confirms our expectation that punctuation marking would help the neural networks more than AH. However, BI is surprising here, since it is not helped at all. Furthermore, the pattern is much less clear when we look at the cases of R and L. For the R case, we see that RHS is helped quite a bit, while AH is not; this again supports our hypothesis. However, we are surprised to see that KSG is worse with R than adjacency overall, and the pattern with L does not at all support the hypothesis. Thus while our results are indeed suggestive that punctuation might play an important role here, the picture seems to be complicated by other factors.

3.3 Discontinuity

Since the sluicing antecedent is a constituent, it often consists of a continuous sequence of tokens, as in Example 1. This is not *always* true, however; it is well known that constituents are sometimes *discontinuous*, and this can in fact be observed in our sluicing data, as in the following example (Anand and Hardt, 2016):

> (3) $[_{S-2}$ A major part of the increase in coverage , $[_{S-1}$ though Mitchell 's aides could not say just **how much** ,] would come from a provision providing insurance for children and pregnant women .]

Here, the antecedent is *A major part of the increase in coverage would come from a provision providing insurance for children and pregnant women*; the tokens constituting S_1 are not included. However, such cases of discontinuous antecedents are rare in our data – the vast majority of sluice antecedents consist of a continuous sequence of tokens.

The AH system nearly always selects continuous antecedents, since the underlying syntactic parser is unable to predict discontinuous constituents. The other systems are under no such constraint; however, implicit linguistic knowledge might be expected to result in a higher degree of continuity, which we measure as follows:

$$1 - \frac{|\text{holes}|}{|\text{inner-span}|}$$

where the span is the subsequence starting with the first begin or inside tag and ending with the last begin or inside tag; the *inner-span* is the span without the boundary tags, and *holes* is the set of outside tags within the span.

System	Contiguity
RHS	84.5
KSG	82.0
BI	78.4

Table 4: Degree of token continuity

BI has a lower degree of token continuity than the multi-task systems, RHS and SG. This suggests that the multi-task architectures learn implicit knowledge about linguistic constituency.

3.4 Matching Content

Anand and Hardt (2016) point out that, in sluicing, "the wh-phrase must semantically cohere with the main predicate of the antecedent", which they illustrate with example 4. Here S-3 is a more likely antecedent than S-2 because *increase* is more likely to take an implicit extent than *predict*. In other words *increase* is a better match for *how much* than *predict* is.

> (4)   . $[_{S-3}$ Deliveries would increase as a result of the acquisition] , $[_{S-2}$ he predicted] , but $[_{S-1}$ he would not say by how much]

To capture this information, Anand and Hardt collect data on cooccurrences between wh-phrases and main predicates, and based on this they calculate a feature WHGOVNPMI, the Pointwise Mutual Information (PMI) of the wh-phrase and the main verb of each candidate. In general, the adjacent candidate S_2 would normally be preferred by the AH system. But this could be overruled by the fact that the non-adjacent candidate, S_3, has a higher value for the WHGOVNPMI feature.

We wish to explore whether the neural networks can also take advantage of this information. While the networks do not have access to the PMI information Anand and Hardt computed, they do have access to embeddings for each input word, and one might imagine that pairs with high PMI would also tend to be closer in embedding space. To see why we would expect that, consider that Anand and Hardt collected statistics on *overt* WH-constructions, where the WH-phrase and associated main predicate would co-occur in close proximity, as in cases like **how much** it **increased**, or **why** did they **attack**. Thus highly related such pairs would tend to cooccur frequently within a fairly small context window, while less related pairs would not. The distances of word embeddings (such as Glove, used here), tend to reflect such differences in cooccurence frequency.

To explore this, we examine cases where the correct antecedent receives a comparatively high WHGOVNPMI score, but where it is not adjacent to the sluice (since adjacent antecedents tend to be chosen as the default option). We define various thresholds for the WHGOVNPMI, and define the subset of only those examples where the correct antecedent receives a PMI score above that threshold. These should be examples where the PMI score provides a strong signal about the correct antecedent, although the antecedent is not adjacent to the sluice. We examine the F1 scores of the systems on these subsets. As we raise the threshold, we would expect F1 scores to increase, if the system is indeed making use of this information.

Figure 2 shows F1 scores as a function of PMI score thresholds. For RHS and BI, we do observe an increase of F1 scores as thresholds increase, but this is not consistently the case for either AH or KSG. It is difficult to draw any firm conclusions here. While the plot does not show a consistent pattern for the AH system, (Anand and Hardt, 2016) give feature ablation results that show that the WHGOVNPMI does make a positive, although modest, contribution. The plots here suggest that the word embedding comparisons of the neural networks might in fact contain more useful information than the PMI statistics.

4 Probing the Networks

We probe the networks by examining particular network states, posing three specific questions that are fundamental to the sluice resolution task:

- How well does the network distinguish *adjacent* from *non-adjacent* antecedents?

- How well does the network *notice* the sluice word?

- How well does the network *remember* the sluice word, when the antecedent is encountered?

4.1 Classification of Adjacent vs. Non-adjacent

We collect the final state activation for the network for each instance, and divide these states into two classes: in one class, the correct antecedent is adjacent to the sluice, and in the other class it is not. We perform logistic regression, using class balancing, with five-fold cross validation.

The MTL systems, RHS and KSG, score higher than chance, while the single-task baseline is a bit below chance. KSG performance significantly better than RHS; however, all networks are close to chance. From Table 2, we saw that

System	Adjacent
RHS	54.3
KSG	55.9
BI	48.0

Table 5: Accuracy of classifying adjacent antecedents from non-adjacent antecedents.

all networks perform substantially worse on non-adjacent sluices, which suggests the networks are treating non-adjacent antecedents as if they were adjacent.

4.2 Noticing the Sluice Word

The AH system uses input in which the sluice occurrence is explicitly marked. This is not the case for the neural networks. Instead, a copy of the sluice phrase is prefixed to the example. Ideally, the neural network would remember this phrase and locate its copy within the text. Then the system would search for the antecedent in proximity to the sluice phrase. The following example illustrates the representation for Example 1:

(5)   why If this is not practical , explain why .

We term the first occurrence of *why* a *prefixed* wh-word, and the second occurrence is an *in-situ* wh-word. Wh-word occurrences that are neither prefixed or in-situ, are termed *other*.

We collect all the activations associated with in-situ wh-words. This is the positive class in our classification task. Next we collect all activations associated with wh-words occurring in the data, when they are *not* sluice words. This constitutes the negative class. We perform logistic regression, again with class balancing. We want to see if the network activations clearly distinguish the sluice wh-words from other wh-words.

System	Sluiced Wh-word
RHS	78.0
KSG	80.2
BI	76.6

Table 6: Accuracy of classifying *wh*-words in sluiced and non-sluiced positions.

Results in Table 6 show that all three networks are doing substantially better than chance. This is interesting, since noticing the sluice wh-word would seem to be a crucial first step in the sluice

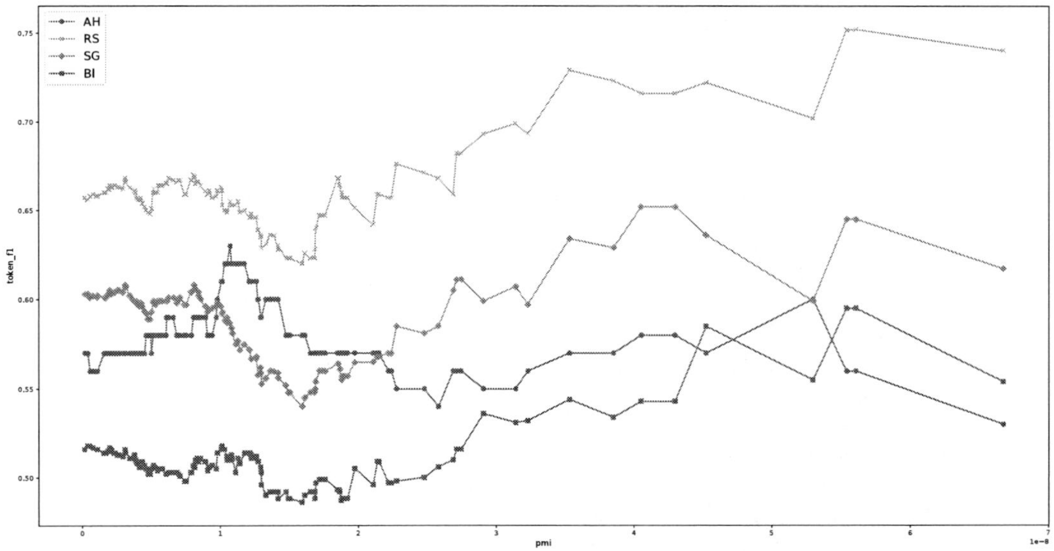

Figure 2: Minimum pointwise mutual information vs token-F1 score on those examples, only thresholds with at least one hundred examples included in plot.

resolution task. We note further that the activations from both multi-task systems (KSG and RHS) provide a better basis for classification than the baseline BI. We suggest that the linguistic auxiliary tasks might explain this difference, since distinguishing the sluice word is facilitated by knowledge of linguistic structure. It is, however, somewhat surprising that KSG performs better than RHS on this task, since RHS does better on the sluice resolution task, overall.

These classification results provide an indication that, in some sense, the networks are indeed noticing whether the wh-words appear in a sluice or not. We suggest further that this is reflected quite directly in network activations. In general, we suggest that the distance between a word embedding and its associated activation provides a measure of how much the network notices that word. Table 7 supports this idea; here, we compare embedding and activation distances for prefixed, in-situ and other wh-words. The results support the idea that in-situ wh-words are noticed the most, as they are crucial to task of determining the antecedent. The prefix wh-word has somewhat larger distances, while other wh-words, which play no role is sluicing, have the highest distances. Furthermore, we note that the distances suggest that the KSG system is "best" at noticing the in-situ wh-word, while BI is worst. In Table

6 the accuracy of in-situ sluice word classification follows the same ordering.

System	other-wh	in-situ	prefix	all
RHS	5.82	5.16	5.33	5.61
KSG	5.61	5.03	5.29	5.43
BI	6.32	5.31	5.61	6.11

Table 7: Average distance between embedding and activation for same token.

4.3 Remembering Sluice Word at Antecedent

We have shown that the networks are able to distinguish adjacent from non-adjacent antecedents, and they are also able to notice the sluice *wh*-word. The next question is: Can the network draw a connection between the sluice *wh*-word and the antecedent? This is fundamental to the task of sluice resolution – connecting the sluice occurrence with the antecedent.

To address this question, we propose to measure how well the sluice wh-word is "remembered" by the network when the edge of the antecedent is encountered. We compute the vector distance between the word embedding for the sluice wh-word and the state associated with the token appearing at the edge of the antecedent. We suggest that this distance provides a metric of how much the network remembers the wh-word, when the an-

System	Forward			Backward		
	WH-Ant Dist.	Avg. Dist.	Normalized	WH-Ant Dist.	Avg. Dist.	Normalized
RHS	6.34	10.72	0.59	6.22	11.52	0.54
KSG	5.07	9.47	0.54	5.33	11.08	0.48
BI	5.88	9.99	0.59	5.71	12.37	0.46

Table 8: Euclidean distance between the antecedent left boundary activation and avg. sluice word vector representation. Distances compared to average Euclidean norm distance between word representations and activations separated by the same number of tokens as the antecedent sluice pair.

tecedent is encountered. Table 8 shows the relevant measurements, both for the forward and backward directions of the each of the neural networks. The column *WH-Ant Dist* gives the average vector distance between the wh-word embedding and the state vector when the antecedent is encountered. The *Avg. Dist.* column gives a corresponding average over all token occurrences. Our intention is to provide a relevant comparison to see if the *wh*-word is remembered more than words are in general. So the Avg. Dist. column has a weighted average of the vector distances for all words, using the distribution of token distances seen for the WH-Ant Dist values. Finally, the Normalized column is the ratio, WH-Ant Dist/Avg.Dist.

Overall, we see a strong effect of the networks remembering the sluice word at the antecedent site, to a much higher degree than an average word is remembered. Furthermore, there is a difference with directionality. Avg Dist is higher in the Backwards direction – in general, words are remembered less when moving backwards. But WH-Ant Dist. is lower in Backward, which makes sense, since the system needs to keep track of the wh-word to help identify the antecedent. There are also modest differences among the three systems.

We would like to see how this develops over time. Our hypothesis is that the neural networks will remember the sluice word more at the point where it is within the antecedent, and less when it is outside the antecedent. We define four areas of interest:

1. **Between:** tokens between the sluice and the antecedent (Except the **Right** token)

2. **Right:** the token just to the right of the antecedent

3. **Ant:** tokens within the antecedent

4. **Left:** the token just to the left of the antecedent

In Figure 3, we can observe a modest effect of the sort we hypothesized: distances are indeed lower within the antecedent than in the other regions, suggesting that the neural networks do in fact have a stronger memory of the wh-word at that point in the computation.

5 Conclusion

Ellipsis resolution is widely believed to require sophisticated knowledge of linguistic structure. Thus, it is interesting that the neural architectures presented by Rønning et al. (2018), are able to match and even surpass systems like that of Anand and Hardt (2016), which rely on pre-parsed input and linguistically engineered features. In this paper, we investigated the linguistic knowledge implicit in the neural models. We have done so in two ways: (1) We have defined subsets of the data based on adjacency, boundary tokens, discontinuity, and matching content. In general, we have observed that these linguistic factors clearly play a role in the network performance, and there is further evidence that the systems with MTL have a higher degree of linguistic sophistication in their performance, compared to a single task baseline network. (2) We then examined the internal states of the networks. Focusing on the *wh*-word of the sluice, we have shown that the networks are sensitive to the occurrence of the sluice *wh*-word. Furthermore, we find some evidence that the networks remember the *wh*-word more at the point where the antecedent is encountered, compared to other points in the computation.

References

Pranav Anand and Daniel Hardt. 2016. Antecedent selection for sluicing: Structure and content. In *EMNLP*. pages 1234–1243.

Pranav Anand and Jim McCloskey. 2015. Annotating the implicit content of sluices. In *Proceedings*

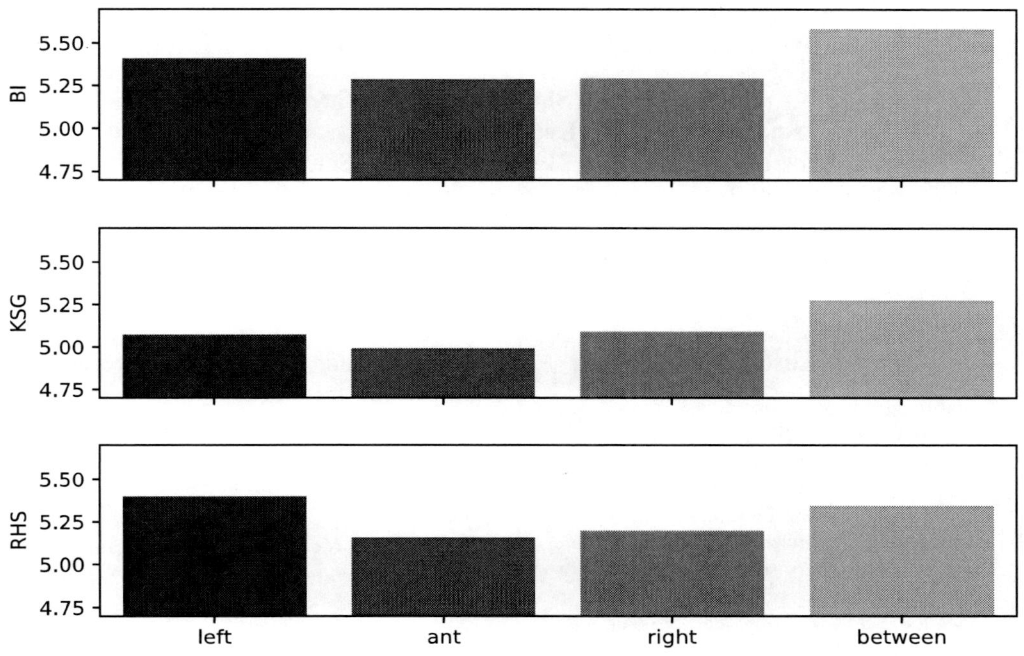

Figure 3: Euclidean distance over antecedent tokens.

of The 9th Linguistic Annotation Workshop. pages 178–187.

Pascal Denis and Jason Baldridge. 2008. Specialized models and ranking for coreference resolution. In *Proceedings of the Conference on Empirical Methods in Natural Language Processing*. Association for Computational Linguistics, pages 660–669.

Sigrid Klerke, Yoav Goldberg, and Anders Søgaard. 2016. Improving sentence compression by learning to predict gaze. *arXiv preprint arXiv:1604.03357* .

Tal Linzen, Emmanuel Dupoux, and Yoav Goldberg. 2016. Assessing the ability of lstms to learn syntax-sensitive dependencies. *arXiv preprint arXiv:1611.01368* .

Jeffrey Pennington, Richard Socher, and Christopher D. Manning. 2014. Glove: Global vectors for word representation. In *Empirical Methods in Natural Language Processing (EMNLP)*. pages 1532–1543.

Ola Rønning, Daniel Hardt, and Anders Søgaard. 2018. Sluice resolution without hand-crafted features over brittle syntax trees. In *Proceedings of the 2018 Conference of the North American Chapter of the Association for Computational Linguistics: Human Language Technologies, Volume 2 (Short Papers)*. Association for Computational Linguistics, pages 236–241. http://aclweb.org/anthology/N18-2038.

Unsupervised Token-wise Alignment to Improve Interpretation of Encoder-Decoder Models

Shun Kiyono[1*] **Sho Takase**[2] **Jun Suzuki**[1,2,4]
Naoaki Okazaki[3] **Kentaro Inui**[1,4] **Masaaki Nagata**[2]

[1] Tohoku University [2] NTT Communication Science Laboratories
[3] Tokyo Institute of Technology [4] RIKEN Center for Advanced Intelligence Project

{kiyono,jun.suzuki,inui}@ecei.tohoku.ac.jp,
{takase.sho, nagata.masaaki}@lab.ntt.co.jp,
okazaki@c.titech.ac.jp

Abstract

Developing a method for understanding the inner workings of black-box neural methods is an important research endeavor. Conventionally, many studies have used an attention matrix to interpret how Encoder-Decoder-based models translate a given source sentence to the corresponding target sentence. However, recent studies have empirically revealed that an attention matrix is not optimal for token-wise translation analyses. We propose a method that explicitly models the token-wise alignment between the source and target sequences to provide a better analysis. Experiments show that our method can acquire token-wise alignments that are superior to those of an attention mechanism[1].

1 Introduction

The Encoder-Decoder model with an attention mechanism (EncDec) (Sutskever et al., 2014; Cho et al., 2014; Bahdanau et al., 2015; Luong et al., 2015) has been an epoch-making development that has led to great progress in many natural language generation tasks, such as machine translation (Bahdanau et al., 2015), dialog generation (Shang et al., 2015), and headline generation (Rush et al., 2015). An enormous number of studies have attempted to enhance the ability of EncDec.

Furthermore, several intensive studies have also attempted to analyze and interpret the inside of black-box EncDec models, especially how they translate a given source sentence to the corresponding target sentence (Ding et al., 2017). One typical approach to this is to visualize an attention matrix, which is a collection of attention vectors (Bahdanau et al., 2015; Luong et al., 2015; Tu et al., 2016).

The assumption behind this interpretation is that the attention matrix has a "soft" token-wise alignment between the source and target sequences, and thus we can use EncDec models to skim which tokens in the source are converted to which tokens in the target.

However, recent studies have empirically revealed that an attention model can operate not only for token-wise alignment but also for other functionalities, such as reordering (Ghader and Monz, 2017; Liu et al., 2016). In addition, Luong et al. (2015) reported that the quality of attention matrix-based alignment is quantitatively inferior to that of the Berkeley aligner (Liang et al., 2006). Koehn and Knowles (2017) also reported that attention matrix-based alignment is significantly different from that acquired from an off-the-shelf aligner for English-German language pairs. From these recent findings, the goal of this paper is to provide a method that can offer a better interpretation of how EncDec models translate a given source sentence to the corresponding target sentence.

In this paper, we focus exclusively on the headline generation task, which is categorized as a *lossy-compression* generation (*lossy-gen*) task (Nallapati et al., 2016). Compared with a machine translation task, which is categorized as a *loss-less* generation (*lossless-gen*) task, the headline generation task additionally requires EncDec models to appropriately select salient ideas in given source sentences (Suzuki and Nagata, 2017). Therefore, the *lossy-gen* task seems to make modeling by EncDec much harder. In fact, our preliminary experiments revealed that the attention mechanism in EncDec models largely fails to capture token-wise alignments, e.g., less than 10 percent accuracy, even if we use one of the current state-of-the-art EncDec models (Table 3).

To obtain a better analysis of how EncDec models translate a given source sentence to the corre-

---

[*] This work is a product of collaborative research program of Tohoku University and NTT Communication Science Laboratories.

[1] Our code for reproducing the experiments is available at
https://github.com/butsugiri/UAM

Proceedings of the 2018 EMNLP Workshop BlackboxNLP: Analyzing and Interpreting Neural Networks for NLP, pages 74–81
Brussels, Belgium, November 1, 2018. ©2018 Association for Computational Linguistics

sponding target sentence in the headline generation task, this paper introduces the Unsupervised token-wise Alignment Module (UAM), a novel component that can be plugged into EncDec models. Unlike a conventional attention model, the proposed UAM explicitly captures token-wise alignments between the source and target sequences on the final hidden layer. One can plug the UAM into a EncDec model during a training phase and easily understand the EncDec model's behavior by analyzing the UAM's token-wise alignments. Moreover, the UAM does not require any gold alignment data.

To demonstrate the effectiveness of the UAM, we evaluate EncDec models with the UAM in the headline generation task (Rush et al., 2015), a widely used benchmark for EncDec models. Our experiments show that (i) EncDec models with a UAM achieve comparable (or even superior) performance to the current state-of-the-art headline generation model, and (ii) the produced token-wise alignment is practical regardless of the absence of gold alignment during its training phase.

2 Headline Generation Task

We address the headline generation task introduced in Rush et al. (2015). The source (input) is the first sentence of a news article, and the target (output) is the article's headline. We say I and J represent the numbers of tokens in the source and target, respectively. An important assumption in headline generation is that the target must be shorter than the source ($I > J$).

Here, we denote a source sequence as sequence X of one-hot vectors. Let $x_i \in \{0,1\}^{V_s}$ represent the one-hot vector of the i-th token in X, where V_s represents the number of tokens in the source-side vocabulary $\mathcal{V}_s$. We use $x_{1:I}$ to represent $(x_1, \ldots, x_I)$; namely, $X = x_{1:I}$. Similarly, let $y_j \in \{0,1\}^{V_t}$ represent the one-hot vector of the j-th token in target sequence Y, where V_t is the number of tokens in the target-side vocabulary $\mathcal{V}_t$. Here, we define Y as always containing two additional one-hot vectors of special tokens $\langle bos \rangle$ for y_0 and $\langle eos \rangle$ for y_{J+1}, namely, $Y = y_{0:J+1}$.

3 Encoder-Decoder Model with Attention Mechanism (EncDec)

This section briefly describes EncDec as the base model of our method[2].

<hr>

[2]Our EncDec configuration follows the model described in Luong et al. (2015).

3.1 Model Definition

EncDec models the following conditional probability:

$$p(Y|X) = \prod_{j=1}^{J+1} p(y_j|y_{0:j-1}, X). \qquad (1)$$

Encoder EncDec encodes the source one-hot vector sequence $x_{1:I}$ and generates the hidden state sequence $h_{1:I}$, where $h_i \in \mathbb{R}^H$ for all i and H is the size of the hidden state.

We employ bidirectional RNN (BiRNN) as the encoder of the base model. BiRNN is composed of two separate RNNs for the forward ($\overrightarrow{\mathrm{RNN}}_{\mathrm{src}}$) and backward ($\overleftarrow{\mathrm{RNN}}_{\mathrm{src}}$) directions. The forward RNN reads the source sequence X from left to right and constructs hidden states ($\vec{h}_{1:I}$). Similarly, the backward RNN reads the input in the reverse order to obtain another sequence of hidden states ($\overleftarrow{h}_{1:I}$). Finally, we take the summation of hidden states in each direction to construct the final representation of the source sequence ($h_{1:I}$).

Concretely, for a given time step i, the representation h_i is constructed as follows:

$$\vec{h}_i = \overrightarrow{\mathrm{RNN}}_{\mathrm{src}}(E_s x_i, \vec{h}_{i-1}), \qquad (2)$$

$$\overleftarrow{h}_i = \overleftarrow{\mathrm{RNN}}_{\mathrm{src}}(E_s x_i, \overleftarrow{h}_{i+1}), \qquad (3)$$

$$h_i = \vec{h}_i + \overleftarrow{h}_i \qquad (4)$$

where $E_s \in \mathbb{R}^{D \times V_s}$ denotes the word embedding matrix of the source-side and D denotes the size of word embedding.

Decoder The decoder is the unidirectional RNN in the input-feeding approach (Luong et al., 2015). Concretely, decoder RNN takes the output of the previous time step y_{j-1}, decoder hidden state $\vec{z}_{j-1}$ and final hidden state z_{j-1} to derive the hidden state of current time step z_j:

$$\vec{z}_j = \overrightarrow{\mathrm{RNN}}_{\mathrm{trg}}(E_t y_{j-1}, z_{j-1}, \vec{z}_{j-1}), \qquad (5)$$

$$\vec{z}_0 = \vec{h}_I + \overleftarrow{h}_1 \qquad (6)$$

where $E_t \in \mathbb{R}^{D \times V_t}$ denotes the word embedding matrix of the decoder. Here, z_0 is defined as a zero vector.

Attention Mechanism The attention architecture of the base model is the same as that of the *Global Attention* model proposed by Luong et al. (2015). Attention is responsible for constructing the final hidden state z_j from the decoder hidden state $\vec{z}_j$ and encoder hidden states $(h_{1:I})$.

First, the model computes the attention vector $\alpha_j \in \mathbb{R}^I$ from the decoder hidden state $\vec{z}_j$ and encoder hidden states $(h_{1:I})$. From among three attention scoring functions proposed in Luong et al. (2015), we employ a *general* function. This function calculates the attention score in bilinear form. Specifically, the attention score between the i-th source hidden state and the j-th decoder hidden state is computed by the following equation:

$$\alpha_j[i] = \frac{\exp(h_i^\top W_\alpha \vec{z}_j)}{\sum_{i=1}^I \exp(h_i^\top W_\alpha \vec{z}_j)} \quad (7)$$

where $W_\alpha \in \mathbb{R}^{H \times H}$ is a parameter matrix, and $\alpha_j[i]$ denotes the i-th element of α_j.

α_j is then used for collecting the source-side information that is relevant for predicting the target token. This is done by taking the weighted sum on the encoder hidden states:

$$c_j = \sum_{i=1}^I \alpha_j[i]h_i \quad (8)$$

Next, the source-side information is mixed with the decoder hidden state to derive final hidden state z_j. Concretely, the context vector c_j is concatenated with $\vec{z}_j$ to form vector $u_j \in \mathbb{R}^{2H}$. u_j is then fed into a single fully-connected layer with $\tanh$ nonlinearity:

$$z_j = \tanh(W_s u_j) \quad (9)$$

where $W_s \in \mathbb{R}^{H \times 2H}$ is a parameter matrix.

Finally, z_j is fed into the softmax layer. The model generates a target-side token based on the probability distribution $o_j \in \mathbb{R}^{V_t}$ as

$$o_j = \mathrm{softmax}(W_o z_j + b_o), \quad (10)$$

where $W_o \in \mathbb{R}^{V_t \times H}$ is a parameter matrix and $b_o \in \mathbb{R}^{V_t}$ is a bias term.

3.2 Training of EncDec

To train EncDec, let $\mathcal{D}$ be training data for headline generation, which consists of source-headline sentence pairs. Let θ represent all parameters in EncDec. Our goal is to find the optimal parameter set $\hat{\theta}$ that minimizes the following objective function $G_0(\theta)$ for the given training data $\mathcal{D}$:

$$G_0(\theta) = \frac{1}{|\mathcal{D}|} \sum_{(X,Y)\in\mathcal{D}} \ell_{\mathrm{trg}}(Y, X, \theta),$$

$$\ell_{\mathrm{trg}}(Y, X, \theta) = -\log\Big(p(Y|X,\theta)\Big). \quad (11)$$

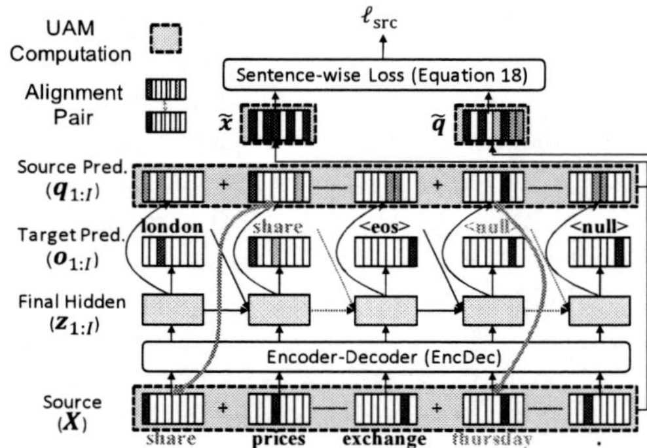

Figure 1: Overview of EncDec with UAM. UAM predicts the probability distribution over the source vocabulary q_j at each time step j. After predicting all the time steps, the SPM compares the sum of the predictions $\tilde{q}$ with the sum of the source-side tokens $\tilde{x}$ as an objective function ℓ_{src}.

Since o_j for each j is a vector representation of the probabilities of $p(\hat{y}|y_{0:j-1}, X, \theta)$ over the target vocabularies $\hat{y} \in \mathcal{V}_t$, we can calculate ℓ_{trg} as

$$\ell_{\mathrm{trg}}(Y, X, \theta) = -\sum_{j=1}^{J+1} y_j^\top \cdot \log\big(o_j\big). \quad (12)$$

3.3 Inference of EncDec

In the inference step, we use the trained parameters to search for the best target sequence. We use beam search to find the target sequence that maximizes the product of the conditional probabilities as described in Equation 1. From among several stopping criteria for beam search (Huang et al., 2017), we adopt the widely used "shrinking beam" implemented in RNNsearch (Bahdanau et al., 2015)[3].

4 Proposed Method: Unsupervised Alignment Module (UAM)

Figure 1 illustrates the proposed method, UAM. UAM is the module attached on top of the decoder output layer of an EncDec model, and it explicitly represents a token-wise alignment by predicting source tokens simultaneously with target tokens.

Specifically, during the training of EncDec, the decoder estimates the probability distribution over the source-side vocabulary, $q_j \in \mathbb{R}^{V_s}$, simultaneously with that of the target-side vocabulary,

---

[3]https://github.com/lisa-groundhog/GroundHog

$o_j \in \mathbb{R}^{V_t}$, for each time step j. In Figure 1, when the decoder predicts the target-side token "share", we want to predict its corresponding source-side token "share." If we can correctly predict the corresponding source-side token for each target-side token, we can obtain token-wise alignment. As shown below, we can train the model for this prediction without gold token-wise alignment signals.

This way of representing alignments can be extended to $\langle null \rangle$ alignments. We first expand a given target sequence with a sequence of $\langle null \rangle$s so that its length is the same as that of the source sequence (in Figure 1, we extend "london share... $\langle eos \rangle$" to "london share... $\langle eos \rangle \langle null \rangle ... \langle null \rangle$"). We then train the model so that it can predict a discarded source-side token (e.g., "thursday") when it predicts $\langle null \rangle$ for the target-side. Through the task of predicting source-side tokens corresponding to $\langle null \rangle$s, we expect the model to effectively learn to identify unimportant information in the source sequence.

4.1 Model Definition

EncDec with UAM jointly estimates the probability distributions over the source and target vocabularies. Specifically, UAM estimates a probability distribution over the source vocabulary $q_j \in \mathbb{R}^{V_s}$ at each time step j in the decoding process by:

$$q_j = \mathrm{softmax}(W_q z_j + b_q), \qquad (13)$$

where $W_q \in \mathbb{R}^{V_s \times H}$ is a parameter matrix, $z_j \in \mathbb{R}^H$ is a decoder's final hidden layer, and $b_q \in \mathbb{R}^{V_s}$ is a bias term. H is the size of the hidden state. EncDec also calculates a probability distribution over target vocabulary o_j from the same vector z_j.

Next, we define Y' as a concatenation of the one-hot vectors of the target-side sequence Y and those of the special token $\langle null \rangle$ of length $I - (J + 1)$. Here, y_{J+1} is a one-hot vector of $\langle eos \rangle$, and y_j for each $j \in \{J + 2, \ldots, I\}$ is a one-hot vector of $\langle null \rangle$. Note that the length of Y' is always no shorter than that of Y, that is, $|Y'| \geq |Y|$ because headline generation always assumes $I > J$.

Based on this setting, we train the model in an unsupervised manner without gold alignment signals. To this end, we consider a sentence-wise loss function instead of token-wise loss. Specifically, we define the sentence-wise loss as the degree of difference between the sum of all one-hot vectors in the source sequence and the sum of UAM predictions. Namely, we take the difference of $\tilde{x} = \sum_{i=1}^{I} x_i$

and $\tilde{q} = \sum_{j=1}^{I} q_j$. Note that $\tilde{x}$ is a vector representation of the occurrences (or bag-of-words representation) of the source-side tokens. To minimize sentence-wise loss, the model must predict the bag-of-words representation. Through this optimization, the model is expected to eventually find the token-wise alignment.

EncDec with UAM models the following conditional probability:

$$p(Y', \tilde{x}|X) = p(\tilde{x}|Y', X)p(Y'|X). \qquad (14)$$

We define $p(Y'|X)$ as follows:

$$p(Y'|X) = \prod_{j=1}^{I} p(y_j|y_{0:j-1}, X), \qquad (15)$$

which is identical to the conditional probability modeled by the base EncDec, except for considering $\langle null \rangle$ as part of the probability. Next, we define $p(\tilde{x}|Y', X)$ as follows:

$$p(\tilde{x}|Y', X) = \frac{1}{Z} \exp\left(\frac{-\|\tilde{q} - \tilde{x}\|_2^2}{C}\right), \qquad (16)$$

where Z is a normalization term and C is a hyperparameter that controls the sensitivity of the distribution.

4.2 Training of UAM

We optimize the UAM combined with EncDec by minimizing the negative log-likelihood of Equation 14 as a loss function. Let γ represent the parameter set of SPM Then, we define the UAM loss ℓ_{src} as follows;

$$\ell_{\mathrm{src}}(\tilde{x}, X, Y', \gamma, \theta) = -\log(p(\tilde{x}|Y', X, \gamma, \theta)) \qquad (17)$$

From Equation 16, we can derive ℓ_{src} as

$$\ell_{\mathrm{src}}(\tilde{x}, X, Y', \gamma, \theta) = \frac{1}{C}\|\tilde{q} - \tilde{x}\|_2^2 + \log(Z). \qquad (18)$$

We can discard $\log(Z)$ from the RHS, since it is independent of γ and θ.

Here, we regard the sum of ℓ_{src} and ℓ_{trg} as an objective loss function of multi-task training. Formally, we train EncDec with the UAM by minimizing the following objective function G_1:

$$G_1(\theta, \gamma) = \frac{1}{|\mathcal{D}|} \sum_{(X,Y)\in\mathcal{D}} \Big(\ell_{\mathrm{trg}}(Y', X, \theta)$$
$$+ \ell_{\mathrm{src}}(\tilde{x}, X, Y', \gamma, \theta)\Big), \qquad (19)$$

where $\mathcal{D}$ is training data for headline generation, which consists of source-headline sentence pairs.

4.3 Inference of UAM

In the inference time, the goal is only to search for the best target sequence. Thus, we do not need to compute the UAM during the inference. Similarly, it is unnecessary to produce $\langle null \rangle$ after generating $\langle eos \rangle$. Thus, we can utilize the beam search procedure described in Section 3.3, and as a result the actual computation cost for the inference remains unchanged from the base EncDec.

5 Experiment

5.1 Dataset

The origin of the headline generation dataset used in our experiments is identical to that used in Rush et al. (2015). The dataset consists of pairs of the first sentence of each article and its headline from the annotated English Gigaword corpus (Napoles et al., 2012). Rush et al. (2015) defined the training, validation and test splits, which contain approximately 3.8M, 200K and 400K source-headline pairs, respectively

We used the entire training split for training as in the previous studies. We randomly sampled 8K instances as validation data and 10K instances as test data from the validation split. Moreover, we experimented on the test data provided by Zhou et al. (2017) and Toutanova et al. (2016) for comparison with the reported state-of-the-art performance (Zhou et al., 2017). We refer to those test data sets as Test (Ours), Test (Zhou), and MSR-ATC respectively. Among these test sets, MSR-ATC is the only dataset created by a human worker.

5.2 Implementation Details

In the experiment, we selected the hyper-parameter settings commonly used in previous studies e.g., (Rush et al., 2015; Nallapati et al., 2016; Suzuki and Nagata, 2017) We constructed the vocabulary set using byte pair encoding[4] (BPE) (Sennrich et al., 2016) to handle low-frequency words, since this is now a common practice in the field of neural machine translation. The BPE merge operations are jointly learned from the source and the target. We set the number of BPE merge operations at $5,000$.

---

[4] https://github.com/rsennrich/
subword-nmt

Source Vocab. Size V_s	5131
Target Vocab. Size V_t	5131
Word Embed. Size D	200
Hidden State Size H	400

RNN Cell	Long Short-Term Memory (LSTM) (Hochreiter and Schmidhuber, 1997)
Encoder RNN Unit	2-layer bidirectional-LSTM
Decoder RNN Unit	2-layer LSTM with attention (Luong et al., 2015)

Optimizer	Adam (Kingma and Ba, 2015)
Initial Learning Rate	0.001
Learning Rate Decay	0.5 for each epoch (after epoch 9)
Weight C of ℓ_{src}	10
Mini-batch Size	256 (shuffled at each epoch)
Gradient Clipping	5
Stopping Criterion	Max 15 epochs with early stopping
Regularization	Dropout (rate 0.3)
Beam Search	Beam size 20 with the length normalization

Table 1: Configurations used in our experiments

5.3 Evaluation Metric

We evaluated the performance by ROUGE-1 (RG-1), ROUGE-2 (RG-2) and ROUGE-L (RG-L)[5]. We report the F1 value as given in a previous study[6]. We computed the ROUGE scores using the official ROUGE script (version 1.5.5).

5.4 Results

To investigate the effectiveness of the UAM quantitatively, we chose a very strong baseline, SEASS (Zhou et al., 2017), which is the current state-of-the-art model. We reimplemented SEASS, hereafter EncDec+sGate, and compared EncDec+sGate with the model incorporating UAM into EncDec+sGate.

Table 2 summarizes ROUGE-F1 results for all test data. The table shows that EncDec+sGate+UAM achieved a huge gain particularly for MSR-ATC and a performance comparable to EncDec+sGate in Test (Ours) and Test (Zhou). Considering that the MSR-ATC dataset was created by a human worker, we believe that the improvement in MSR-ATC is the most remarkable result among the three test sets, since it indicates that our model most closely fits the human-generated summary.

6 Discussion

We investigated whether the UAM improves token-wise alignment between the source and target se-

---

[5] We restored sub-words to the standard token split for the evaluation.

[6] ROUGE script option is: "-n2 -m -w 1.2"

Model	Test (Ours)			Test (Zhou)			MSR-ATC		
	RG-1	RG-2	RG-L	RG-1	RG-2	RG-L	RG-1	RG-2	RG-L
EncDec+sGate	46.80	24.48	43.74	46.79	24.75	43.62	29.73	15.45	27.30
EncDec+sGate+UAM[†]	**46.91**	**24.86**	**43.87**	**46.89**	**24.93**	**43.68**	**32.32**	**17.02**	**29.76**
SEASS (Zhou et al., 2017)	-	-	-	46.86	24.58	43.53	25.75	10.63	22.90

Table 2: Full-length ROUGE F1 evaluation results. † is the proposed model.

quences. We compared the alignments acquired by the UAM and the attention model, since attention has been implicitly considered as alignment (Bahdanau et al., 2015; Luong et al., 2015; Tu et al., 2016).

6.1 Visualizing UAM and Attention

We visualized UAM prediction and the attention matrix to see the acquired token-wise alignment between the source and target. Specifically, we fed the source-target pair (X, Y) to EncDec+sGate and EncDec+sGate+UAM, and then collected UAM predictions $(q_{1:I})$ of EncDec+sGate+UAM and the attention vectors $(\alpha_{1:J})$ of EncDec+sGate. We computed the attention vectors using Equation 7. For UAM prediction, we extracted the probability of each token $x_i \in X$ from $q_{1:I}$.

Figure 2 and 3 show an example of the heat map. We used Test (Ours) as the input. The brackets in the y-axis represent the source-side tokens that are aligned with target-side tokens. We obtained the aligned tokens as follows: For attention (Figure 2a, 3a), we select the token with the largest attention value. For the UAM (Figure 2b, 3b), we select the token with the largest probability over the vocabulary $\mathcal{V}_s$.

Figure 2a indicates that attention provides poor token-wise alignment. For example, the target-side token "kong" is incorrectly aligned with the source-side sentence period. In contrast, Figure 2b shows that the UAM captures reasonable alignments. Here, the source-side token "rose" is aligned with the target-side token "higher." UAM also correctly aligned unimportant tokens such as "##.##" with ⟨*null*⟩.

In Figure 3a, the attention model repeatedly pays attention to the source-side token "positive." As a result, the attention model aligned the target-side token "egyptian" to "positive." On the other hand, in 3b, the UAM correctly aligns "egyptian." In addition, the UAM aligned source-side token "foreign" with target-side token "fm."

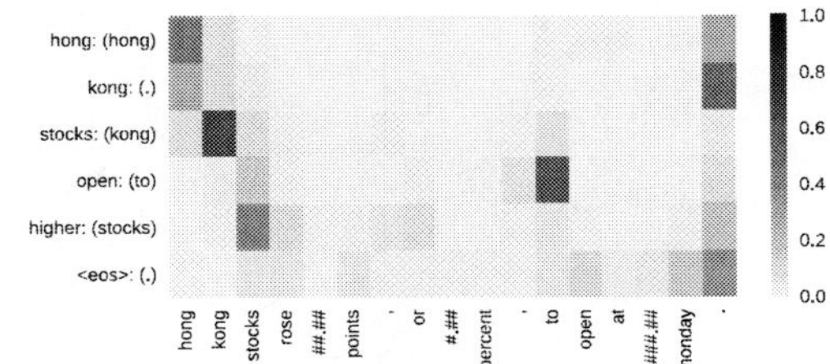

(a) Attention matrix of EncDec+sGate

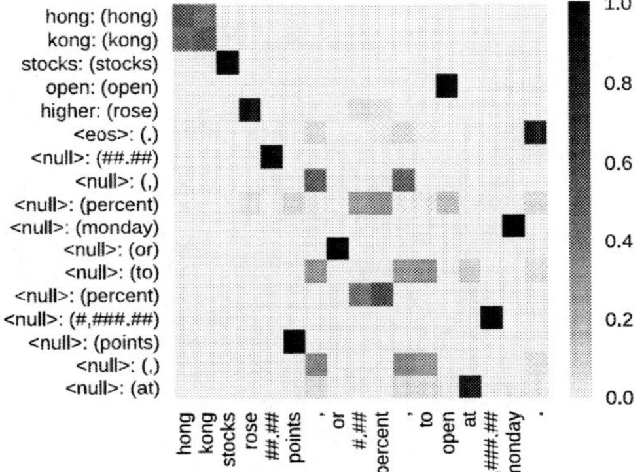

(b) UAM prediction of EncDec+sGate+UAM

Figure 2: Visualization of models. The x-axis and y-axis correspond to the source and the target sequence respectively. Tokens in the brackets are source-side tokens aligned at that time step.

6.2 Alignment Accuracy

In order to quantitatively investigate the quality of the alignment, we evaluated the alignment accuracy of both EncDec+sGate and EncDec+sGate+UAM.

We randomly sampled 40, 30 and 30 instances from Test (Ours), Test (Zhou) and MSR-ATC respectively. We acquired the alignment of the data by applying the UAM and the attention model, in the same manner as described in Section 6.1. A single annotator then evaluated the accuracy of the alignment by hand.

Table 3 summarizes the results. The alignment of the UAM is significantly more accurate than

Model	Test (Ours)	Test (Zhou)	MSR-ATC	Overall
EncDec+sGate	8.60	5.97	6.11	6.71
EncDec+sGate+UAM	52.52	50.91	51.07	51.41

Table 3: Alignment Macro Accuracy (%)

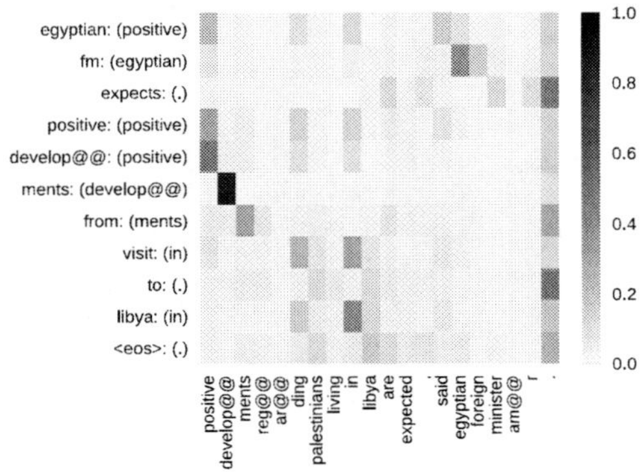

(a) Attention matrix of EncDec+sGate

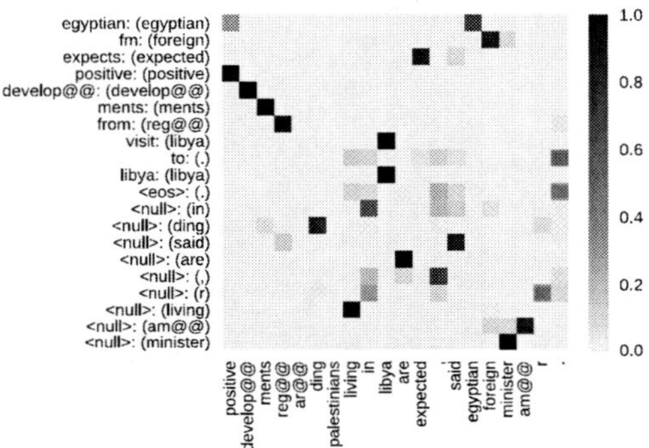

(b) UAM prediction of EncDec+sGate+UAM

Figure 3: Visualization of models. The x-axis and y-axis correspond to the source and the target sequence respectively. Tokens in the brackets are source-side tokens aligned at that time step.

that of the attention model. This result is consistent with the empirical results reported by Koehn and Knowles (2017) and Luong et al. (2015). The attention alignment mistakes are mostly due to paying attention to either the sentence period or to the token decoded in the previous time step. It is noteworthy that the accuracy of the UAM alignment exceeds 50% even though we trained the model in an unsupervised manner. The fact that the UAM prediction acquires reasonable alignment suggests that the UAM has the potential to provide us a better understanding of the model's behavior.

7 Conclusion

In this paper, we introduced the Unsupervised token-wise Alignment Module (UAM), which learns to predict the token-wise alignment of tokens in the source and the target. Experiments on the headline generation task showed that the UAM can achieve comparable performance to the current state-of-the-art sGate model. In addition, the UAM obtained token-wise alignment that is superior to that of the attention model. This finding suggests we can use the UAM as an alternative to the attention matrix to attain a better understanding of the token-wise alignment of EncDec-based model.

Acknowledgment

We are grateful to anonymous reviewers for their insightful comments. We thank Sosuke Kobayashi for providing helpful comments. We also thank Qingyu Zhou for providing a dataset and information for a fair comparison.

References

Dzmitry Bahdanau, Kyunghyun Cho, and Yoshua Bengio. 2015. Neural Machine Translation by Jointly Learning to Align and Translate. In *Proceedings of the 3rd International Conference on Learning Representations (ICLR 2015)*.

Kyunghyun Cho, Bart van Merrienboer, Caglar Gulcehre, Dzmitry Bahdanau, Fethi Bougares, Holger Schwenk, and Yoshua Bengio. 2014. Learning Phrase Representations using RNN Encoder–Decoder for Statistical Machine Translation. In *Proceedings of the 2014 Conference on Empirical Methods in Natural Language Processing (EMNLP 2014)*, pages 1724–1734.

Yanzhuo Ding, Yang Liu, Huanbo Luan, and Maosong Sun. 2017. Visualizing and Understanding Neural Machine Translation. In *Proceedings of the 55th Annual Meeting of the Association for Computational Linguistics (ACL 2017)*, pages 1150–1159.

Hamidreza Ghader and Christof Monz. 2017. What does Attention in Neural Machine Translation Pay Attention to? In *Proceedings of the Eighth International Joint Conference on Natural Language Processing (IJCNLP 2017)*, pages 30–39.

Sepp Hochreiter and Jürgen Schmidhuber. 1997. Long Short-Term Memory. *Neural Computation*, 9(8):1735–1780.

Liang Huang, Kai Zhao, and Mingbo Ma. 2017. When to Finish? Optimal Beam Search for Neural Text Generation (modulo beam size). In *Proceedings of the 2017 Conference on Empirical Methods in Natural Language Processing (EMNLP 2017)*, pages 2124–2129.

Diederik Kingma and Jimmy Ba. 2015. Adam: A Method for Stochastic Optimization. In *Proceedings of the 3rd International Conference on Learning Representations (ICLR 2015)*.

Philipp Koehn and Rebecca Knowles. 2017. Six Challenges for Neural Machine Translation. In *Proceedings of the First Workshop on Neural Machine Translation*, pages 28–39.

Percy Liang, Ben Taskar, and Dan Klein. 2006. Alignment by Agreement. In *Proceedings of the 2006 Conference of the North American Chapter of the Association for Computational Linguistics (NAACL 2006)*, pages 104–111.

Lemao Liu, Masao Utiyama, Andrew Finch, and Eiichiro Sumita. 2016. Neural Machine Translation with Supervised Attention. In *Proceedings of COLING 2016, the 26th International Conference on Computational Linguistics*, pages 3093–3102.

Thang Luong, Hieu Pham, and Christopher D. Manning. 2015. Effective Approaches to Attention-based Neural Machine Translation. In *Proceedings of the 2015 Conference on Empirical Methods in Natural Language Processing (EMNLP 2015)*, pages 1412–1421.

Ramesh Nallapati, Bowen Zhou, Cicero dos Santos, Caglar Gulcehre, and Bing Xiang. 2016. Abstractive Text Summarization Using Sequence-to-Sequence RNNs and Beyond. In *Proceedings of The 20th SIGNLL Conference on Computational Natural Language Learning*, pages 280–290.

Courtney Napoles, Matthew Gormley, and Benjamin Van Durme. 2012. Annotated Gigaword. In *Proceedings of the Joint Workshop on Automatic Knowledge Base Construction and Web-scale Knowledge Extraction*, AKBC-WEKEX '12, pages 95–100.

Alexander M. Rush, Sumit Chopra, and Jason Weston. 2015. A Neural Attention Model for Abstractive Sentence Summarization. In *Proceedings of the 2015 Conference on Empirical Methods in Natural Language Processing (EMNLP 2015)*, pages 379–389.

Rico Sennrich, Barry Haddow, and Alexandra Birch. 2016. Neural Machine Translation of Rare Words with Subword Units. In *Proceedings of the 54th Annual Meeting of the Association for Computational Linguistics (ACL 2016)*, pages 1715–1725.

Lifeng Shang, Zhengdong Lu, and Hang Li. 2015. Neural Responding Machine for Short-Text Conversation. In *Proceedings of the 53rd Annual Meeting of the Association for Computational Linguistics and the 7th International Joint Conference on Natural Language Processing (ACL & IJCNLP 2015)*, pages 1577–1586.

Ilya Sutskever, Oriol Vinyals, and Quoc V. Le. 2014. Sequence to Sequence Learning with Neural Networks. In *Advances in Neural Information Processing Systems 27 (NIPS 2014)*, pages 3104–3112.

Jun Suzuki and Masaaki Nagata. 2017. Cutting-off Redundant Repeating Generations for Neural Abstractive Summarization. In *Proceedings of the 15th Conference of the European Chapter of the Association for Computational Linguistics (EACL 2017)*, pages 291–297.

Kristina Toutanova, Chris Brockett, Ke M. Tran, and Saleema Amershi. 2016. A Dataset and Evaluation Metrics for Abstractive Compression of Sentences and Short Paragraphs. In *Proceedings of the 2016 Conference on Empirical Methods in Natural Language Processing (EMNLP 2016)*, pages 340–350.

Zhaopeng Tu, Zhengdong Lu, Yang Liu, Xiaohua Liu, and Hang Li. 2016. Modeling Coverage for Neural Machine Translation. In *Proceedings of the 54th Annual Meeting of the Association for Computational Linguistics (ACL 2016)*, pages 76–85.

Qingyu Zhou, Nan Yang, Furu Wei, and Ming Zhou. 2017. Selective Encoding for Abstractive Sentence Summarization. In *Proceedings of the 55th Annual Meeting of the Association for Computational Linguistics (ACL 2017)*, pages 1095–1104.

Rule induction for global explanation of trained models

Madhumita Sushil, Simon Šuster and **Walter Daelemans**
Computational Linguistics & Psycholinguistics Research Center,
University of Antwerp, Belgium
`firstname.lastname@uantwerpen.be`

Abstract

Understanding the behavior of a trained network and finding explanations for its outputs is important for improving the network's performance and generalization ability, and for ensuring trust in automated systems. Several approaches have previously been proposed to identify and visualize the most important features by analyzing a trained network. However, the relations between different features and classes are lost in most cases. We propose a technique to induce sets of if-then-else rules that capture these relations to globally explain the predictions of a network. We first calculate the importance of the features in the trained network. We then weigh the original inputs with these feature importance scores, simplify the transformed input space, and finally fit a rule induction model to explain the model predictions. We find that the output rule-sets can explain the predictions of a neural network trained for 4-class text classification from the 20 newsgroups dataset to a macro-averaged F-score of 0.80. We make the code available at `https://github.com/clips/interpret_with_rules`.

1 Introduction

Deep, non-linear neural networks are notorious for being black boxes, because the basis of a network's decision is unknown. Although sometimes we only care about better performance, understanding a trained model is important in many cases. For example, when a statistical system is used to take decisions regarding a patient's health, it is critical to know the underlying reasons. Caruana et al. (2015) have previously discussed a rule-based system that had associated the history of asthma in patients suffering from pneumonia with a lower risk of death due to it. Despite being counterintuitive, it was a predictive pattern in the data because the patients with asthma were admitted directly to the ICU and received more intensive care, which resulted in better outcomes. Model interpretability is also useful to understand the biases in the data that influence its decision. For example, explaining a trained model and its outputs can bring attention towards a potentially unfair outcome when a loan or a job opportunity is denied to an individual due to any societal bias present in the training data[1,2]. Another less discussed aspect of model interpretability is its utility for analyzing a model's strengths and weaknesses. This understanding can assist with improving the model's performance and generalization ability (Andrews et al., 1995).

Model interpretability techniques can either have a *global* or a *local* scope. A global explanation refers to the explanation of a complete model, as opposed to local explanations of individual predictions. Several existing model-agnostic interpretability techniques provide a list of important features as explanations. In such a list, the information about the interaction between different features and their correspondence to the class is lost. We propose a technique to understand the relations between the input features and the class labels that a trained supervised neural network captures. It is therefore a mechanism for global interpretability. We first weigh the input features with their importance in a trained network. We then select the best features according to the training set, and simplify them to discrete features that represent either a positive, a negative, or no correlation between a high feature value and a class label. We perform this step to limit the complexity of the output rules and make them easily understandable by

---

[1]`https://obamawhitehouse.archives.gov/sites/default/files/microsites/ostp/2016_0504_data_discrimination.pdf`
[2]`http://www.cs.toronto.edu/~madras/presentations/fairness-ml-uaig.pdf`

Proceedings of the 2018 EMNLP Workshop BlackboxNLP: Analyzing and Interpreting Neural Networks for NLP, pages 82–97
Brussels, Belgium, November 1, 2018. ©2018 Association for Computational Linguistics

humans. We use this smaller, transformed input space to induce rules that best explain the model's predictions. We evaluate the technique on a simple text categorization problem to clearly illustrate its operation and results. We find that the output rules have a macro-averaged F-score 0.80 when explaining the predictions of a feedforward neural network trained to classify a subset of documents from the 20 newsgroups dataset[3] into those about either 'Medicine', 'Space', 'Cryptography', or 'Electronics'.

2 Related Work

There has been a lot of recent interest in making machine learning models interpretable. Different approaches can be broadly grouped under two headings—1) the use of interpretable models, and 2) model-agnostic interpretability techniques. In the first case, the choice of machine learning methods is limited to the more interpretable models such as linear models and decision trees (Molnar; Caruana et al., 2015). The drawback of incorporating model interpretability through specific model choices is that these models may not perform well enough for a given task or a given dataset. To overcome this, the second set of approaches try to explain either a complete model, or an individual prediction by using the input data and the model output(s). Several approaches involve manipulation of the trained network to identify the most significant input features. In some cases, the input features are deleted one by one, and the corresponding effect on the output is recorded (Li et al., 2016b; Avati et al., 2017; Suresh et al., 2017). The features that cause the maximum change in the output are ranked the highest. Another computational approach uses gradient ascent to learn the input vector that maximizes a given output in a trained network (Erhan et al., 2009; Simonyan et al., 2013). In some other cases, the gradient of the output with respect to the input is computed, which corresponds to the effect of an infinitesimal change of the input on the output (Engelbrecht and Cloete, 1998; Simonyan et al., 2013; Aubakirova and Bansal, 2016; Sushil et al., 2018). Another approach computes feature importance using layerwise relevance propagation (LRP) (Bach et al., 2015; Montavon et al., 2017; Arras et al., 2017), which has been shown to be equivalent to the prod-

uct of the gradient value and the input (Kindermans et al., 2016). Sometimes the importance of a feature is analyzed by setting its value to a reference value, and then backpropagating the difference (DeepLIFT) (Shrikumar et al., 2017). In another approach, a separate 'explanation model' is trained to fit the predictions of the original model (Ribeiro et al., 2016; Lundberg and Lee, 2017; Lakkaraju et al., 2017). In an information theoretic approach, the mutual information between feature subsets and the model output is approximated to identify the most important features, similar to feature selection techniques (Chen et al., 2018). For recurrent neural networks with an attention mechanism, attention weights are often used as feature importance scores (Hermann et al., 2015; Yang et al., 2016; Choi et al., 2016). Poerner et al. (2018) have investigated several of the previously discussed techniques and have found LRP and DeepLIFT to be the most effective approaches for explaining deep neural networks in NLP.

Most of the above-mentioned techniques output a ranked list of the most significant features for a model. Several approaches, especially when the input is an image, visualize these features as image segments (Erhan et al., 2009; Simonyan et al., 2013; Olah et al., 2018). These act as visual cues about the salient objects in an image for the classifier. However, such visual understanding is limited when we use either structured or textual input. Heatmaps are often used to visualize interpretations of text-based models (Hermann et al., 2015; Li et al., 2016a,b; Yang et al., 2016; Aubakirova and Bansal, 2016; Arras et al., 2017). However, the interaction between different features and their relative contribution towards class labels remains unknown in this qualitative representation. To overcome this limitation, in the same vein as our work, rule induction for interpreting neural networks has been proposed (Andrews et al., 1995; Lakkaraju et al., 2017). Thrun (1993) have proposed a technique to find disjunctive rules by identifying valid intervals of input values for the correct classification. Intervals are expanded starting with the known values for instances. Lakkaraju et al. (2017) use the input data and the model predictions to learn decision sets that are optimized to jointly maximize the interpretability of the explanations and the extent to which the original model is explained.

In our approach, we aim to generate a set of if-

---

then-else rules that approximate the interaction between the most important features and classes for a trained model. As opposed to Lakkaraju et al. (2017), before learning an explanation model, we modify the input data based on the importance of the features in the trained network. In doing so, we already encode some information about the network's performance within these input features.

3 Methodology

We are interested in identifying the if-then-else rules between different input features and class labels that are captured by a trained network to analyze the features that are the most important for classification according to the model. The insight gained in this manner can facilitate model understanding and error analysis. These rules should reflect and mimic a network's behavior for generating its output and may not correspond to human intuitions about a task, or expectations about what a network would learn. We focus on learning the rules that explain an entire model, as opposed to a single prediction. Our proposed technique comprises of these main steps:

1. Input saliency computation (§ 3.1)

2. Input transformation and selection (§ 3.2)

3. Rule induction (§ 3.3)

The entire pipeline is depicted in Figure 1.

3.1 Input saliency computation

As the first step in the pipeline, we compute the contribution of the input features towards the predicted output in a trained network. This gives us the importance of different features in the network. For this, we record the change in the predicted output on modifying the input features infinitesimally; i.e., for every test instance j, we compute the gradient of the predicted output $o_m^{(j)}$ (where m is the predicted output class for that instance) w.r.t. all the K input features $i_k^{(j)}$, $k = 1...K$. We get a saliency map similar to Simonyan et al. (2013), where the saliency S of the kth input feature for the jth instance is defined as

$$S_k^{(j)} = \frac{\partial o_m^{(j)}}{\partial i_k^{(j)}}.$$

Here, m, which is the predicted output class for that instance among all possible n output classes, is computed as

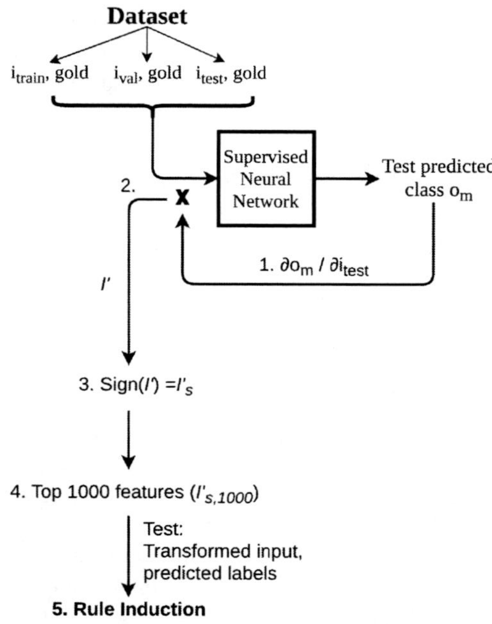

Figure 1: Pipeline for rule induction for global model interpretability.

$$m^{(j)} = \arg\max_n(o_n^{(j)}).$$

The higher the absolute value of the gradient $S_k^{(j)}$, the greater the importance of the feature k in the instance j for the predicted class. Here, a positive sign of the saliency score indicates that the feature is positively correlated with the probability of the output class, a negative sign shows an inverse correlation, and a value of 0 shows that there is no effect of the feature on the predicted output class for that instance.

3.2 Input transformation and selection

Once we have obtained the saliency scores S in § 3.1, we multiply these scores with the original inputs. Hence, we get transformed input data I', where the input values have been reweighed according to their importance in the trained network. This corresponds to step 2 in Figure 1.

We then reduce the transformed input data I' to their sign. This is the 3rd step in the figure. This gives us a set of discrete features $I'_s \in \{-1, 0, 1\}$. The value -1 indicates that the feature is highly negatively correlated with the class, i.e., a higher feature value decreases the probability of the output class. The value 1 indicates that the feature is highly positively correlated with the class, i.e., a higher value of that feature increases the probability of the output class. 0 may mean either that the feature is absent for the document, or that it is not important for the output class[4]. We perform this sign reduction step because the rule conditions with these discrete feature values are more interpretable and readable than those containing continuous reweighed vector values.

We then keep only the top 1000 features in the trained network, represented by step 4 in the figure. We restrict the feature space to reduce the complexity of the rule induction step. We use either an unsupervised technique—sensitivity analysis, or the mutual information between the inputs I'_s and the corresponding training labels. The first technique uses only the gradient values to find the most important features, whereas the second supervised technique makes use of both the transformed inputs I'_s and the labels for this purpose.

- **Sensitivity analysis**

  For feature selection using sensitivity analysis (Engelbrecht and Cloete, 1998), we first compute the gradients of all the output nodes with respect to all the input features for all the instances. We then aggregate these gradient values across the instances by taking a root mean square value. The squaring ensures that negative and positive effects of a feature are treated in an equivalent manner. Hence, we obtain the overall importance scores of all the features for every output node in the network. Now, we use the maximum importance of the features across all the output nodes as the significance of the features in the trained network. The features with the highest significance scores are then selected as the top features. Hence, the method uses only the trained network weights and the original input data for feature selection. It does not make use of the labels for the instances and is hence an unsupervised technique for selecting the most important features in a trained neural network.

- **Mutual information**

  In this step, we identify the top features using

mutual information between the reweighed features I'_s (computed as the product of gradients and the original inputs, and then reduced to the corresponding sign), and the labels in the training data.

3.3 Rule induction

We train a rule induction model on the transformed features I'_s obtained as a result of the previous step (§ 3.2) to fit the output predictions of the original model. For multi-class problems, we induce the rules in a one-vs-rest manner where the rules for explaining every individual class are found one at a time. This gives us separate discriminatory rules for all the classes. Separate rule-sets for individual classes are more interpretable compared to an ordered set of rules for multiple classes at once. In the latter case, we often need to take into account the rules that have been first learned for other classes to interpret the rules for the class we are interested in, which increases its complexity, especially when we have a large number of classes.

RIPPER-k

We use the implementation of the rule induction algorithm RIPPER-k (Cohen, 1995) in Weka (Hall et al., 2009) (JRIP). The algorithm generates a set of if-then-else rule by first overfitting the conditions on a *growing set*, and then pruning them based on their performance on a *pruning set*. These rules are learned in one-vs-rest manner in order of increasing class prevalence, where the final else condition covers the majority class.

In the growing phase, starting with an empty set, the algorithm adds conditions that test the values of discrete and continuous features in the dataset to attribute them to the corresponding class. For example, given two input features f_1 and f_2, the algorithm checks if the concerned class is covered by the rules $f_1 = d_1$, $f_2 \leq c_1$ or $f_2 \geq c_1$, where d_1 is a valid value of the nominal feature f_1, and c_1 is the value of a continuous feature f_2 that occurs in the training data. The conditions are added repeatedly to maximize an information gain criterion. Next, the final sequence of the obtained conditions are removed one at a time to increase the generalization of the rule on the pruning set. When deleting conditions does not improve the error rate any more, pruning is terminated. Thereby, the instances covered by the rule are removed, and the process is repeated for the rest of the instances,

---

[4]We have two interpretations for 0 because we take a product of the gradients and the input feature values. 0 value of either of these two terms could transform the final value to 0.

until more than half of the instances covered by a rule in the pruning data are incorrect.

4 Experimental Details

4.1 Data

We use the documents related to 'Space', 'Medicine', 'Electronics' and 'Cryptography' from the 20-newsgroups dataset for text classification. We limit ourselves to 4 classes under the 'Science' category to reduce experimental complexity. There are approximately 535 training instances, 60 development instances, and 395 test instances for every category. The development set is used for optimizing the model we want to explain. We featurize the data as a bag-of-words with TF-IDF values after removing headers, signature blocks, quotation blocks and stopwords. We get 30,346 input features in this manner.

4.2 Model to be explained

We explain a feedforward neural network that has been trained for 4-class text classification. The neural network has 2 hidden layers with 100 units each, ReLU activation function for these layers, and a softmax output layer. It has been optimized using the Adam optimizer (Kingma and Ba, 2014) for 50 epochs to minimize the cross entropy loss. We get a macro-averaged F-score of 0.82 on the test set.

4.3 Metrics

Fidelity refers to the extent to which an interpretability technique explains the original model. It can be expressed using many different metrics. We quantify fidelity as the macro-averaged F-score of predicting the output of the model that is being explained using the rules that are induced by the explanation technique. The F-scores for the individual classes obtained in the one-vs-rest manner are averaged to compute this overall fidelity.

4.4 Hyperparameter optimization

We found that the rules induced using RIPPER-k are sensitive to its hyperparameters, especially to the minimum number of correctly covered instances and the seed value chosen for randomizing the instances, particularly when the dataset is small. To account for the variation, we run RIPPER-k with 50 different seed values, and the value of the minimum number of instances positively covered by a rule ranging between 2 and the number of instances of the class being explained. For each run, we compute the macro-averaged F-score for explaining the predictions of the neural network. In doing so, we obtain a standard deviation of around 10%, 18%, 17% and 14% for the classes 'Space', 'Medicine', 'Electronics', and 'Cryptography' respectively. This shows that it is important to find an optimum performance over several runs.

We select the rule-set that results in the maximum score, and hence is the one that explains the original model predictions the best among the possible alternatives. We select the rule-set with the maximum score instead of the most generalizable RIPPER-k model because we are not interested in transferring the rules to unknown tasks. If we do not ensure that the learned rules approximate the patterns in the original model to the best possible extent, it remains unclear whether an unintuitive rule-set is obtained because of the parameters of RIPPER-k, or because our neural network has poor explanations. We compare different rule-sets with high F-scores to verify their consistency, which has been discussed in § 5.2.

5 Results and Discussion

5.1 Rules as explanations

We obtain a fidelity score of 0.80 using the proposed technique when the features are pre-selected using the mutual information (MI) score between the transformed inputs and the output labels. Hence, the learned set of if-then-else rules can explain the output of our neural network for 4-class text classification to an F-score of 0.80. The precision, recall, and F-scores for individual classes is presented in Table 1. The precision of the rules is high, which shows that the rules, if induced, are reliable. The largest F-score of 0.90 is obtained for the class *space*, and the lowest F-score of 0.75 is obtained for the classes *electronics* and *cryptography*. On analyzing the rule-sets obtained for different classes, we see that the complexity of the rules for the *space* class is lower than that of *electronics*. For *space* classification, single terms are often indicative of the correct class. On the other hand, for *electronics* and *cryptography* classes, the rules often consist of multiple words, which are jointly used to discriminate between different classes. This suggests that *cryptography* and *electronics* are more confusable classes, which is also reflected in their lower F-scores.

Text class	MI			SA		
	P	**R**	**F**	**P**	**R**	**F**
Space	0.99	0.82	0.90	0.99	0.76	0.86
Medicine	0.94	0.68	0.79	0.92	0.70	0.79
Electronics	0.89	0.64	0.75	0.92	0.63	0.75
Cryptography	0.97	0.61	0.75	0.99	0.61	0.75
Macro-average	0.95	0.69	0.80	0.96	0.68	0.79

Table 1: Precision (P), Recall (R), and F-score (F) when explaining neural network predictions using the induced rules with features selected using mutual information (MI) and sensitivity analysis (SA).

The results with MI feature selection are comparable to those obtained using sensitivity analysis feature selection, presented in Table 1 as well. The observed patterns in the corresponding rule sets are also very similar. Hence, we only present the rules induced using MI feature selection, and those using sensitivity analysis can be found in the Appendix.

Now, in Figure 2, we present the rules that explain the predictions of the neural network for the *electronics* class. The coverage of the individual rules in these sets is also reported in the format a/b, which means that the rule covers b instances in the dataset, out of which a instances are correctly covered. A higher value of b suggests that a rule is more generalized, especially if it is higher up in the hierarchy where it has more instances of the correct class to its disposal. The value of a/b should be used to assess how trustworthy a rule is, with lower values indicating less trustworthiness. On inspecting the gradients, we found that the gradient value was 0 only for one feature for one instance in the test set. This feature is not present in the induced rules. Hence, in these rules, the feature value of 0 has only one interpretation—the absence of the feature. The rules for the other classes can be found in the Appendix.

There are several rules which associate class-specific content words with the corresponding class. In complex rules, we find several terms that are used to identify the *electronics* class by excluding the likelihood of the other classes. For example, in the rule:

(1)   *(people = 0) and (used = 1) and (key = 0)*
   and (don = 0) and (use = 0) and (edu =
   0) and (medication = 0) and (concept = 0)
   and (did = 0) $\implies$ *electronics*

the absence of the term *medication* is used to rule

out the possibility of the *medicine* class, the absence of the term *key* is used to rule out the possibility of the class *cryptography*. Hence, the model uses an elimination strategy in combination with class-relevant features for its predictions.

One of the rules learned for the class *space* is:

(2)   *(idea = 1) and (probably = -1)* $\implies$ *space*

This rule, which is matched after some other rules[5] with higher coverage, covers 3 correct and 0 incorrect instances. The value of -1 associated with *probably* in conjunction with 1 for *idea* shows that a low score of probably, combined with a high score of idea corresponds to the class space. Similarly, in Figure 2, we often see that the presence of the word *just* reduces the probability of *electronics* class. Similar associations can be observed in the rule:

(3)   *(don = -1) and (just = -1)* $\implies$ *medicine*

where the presence of *don't*[6] and *just* reduces the probability of the *medicine* class. This rule covers 4 positive and 0 negative examples. These rules show that function words, which may hint towards terms related to modality, are often important for the network to classify the class of the text documents.

In Figure 3, we present the most important features for the same model, as generated by SHAP (Lundberg and Lee, 2017). This is a state-of-the-art tool that unifies several popular approaches for model interpretability. The top features presented here overlap with the features we identify using our technique. However, the interaction between these features is not obvious from the figure. It is possible to generate an interac-

---

[5]The complete rule set can be found in the Appendix.

[6]*don't* is tokenized as *don* and *'t*, and the mention of *don* is found in the rule.

```
if (just = -1) and (use = 1)  ⟹  electronics (24/24)
elif (circuit = 1)  ⟹  electronics (32/32)
elif (just = -1) and (don = 1)  ⟹  electronics (11/11)
elif (people = 0) and (used = 1) and (key = 0) and (don = 0) and (use = 0) and (edu = 0) and (medication
= 0) and (concept = 0) and (did = 0)  ⟹  electronics (36/43)
elif (electronics = 1)  ⟹  electronics (17/18)
elif (battery = 1)  ⟹  electronics (23/23)
elif (radio = 1) and (shack = 1)  ⟹  electronics (9/9)
elif (people = 0) and (thanks = 1) and (advance = 1)  ⟹  electronics (12/14)
elif (signal = 1)  ⟹  electronics (13/15)
elif (people = 0) and (company = 1) and (just = 0)  ⟹  electronics (13/18)
elif (pc = 1)  ⟹  electronics (16/19)
elif (people = 0) and (use = 1) and (just = 0) and (good = 0) and (clipper = 0) and (probably = 0) and
(center = 0) and (unless = 0) and (18084tm = 0) and (algorithms = 0)  ⟹  electronics (29/33)
elif (appreciated = 1) and (time = 0)  ⟹  electronics (11/16)
elif (voltage = 1)  ⟹  electronics (8/8)
elif (program = -1)  ⟹  electronics (10/15)
else: others (1134/1281)
```

Figure 2: Set of if-then-else rules that explain the predictions of the neural network for the 'electronics' class when using mutual information feature selection. Here the discrete test value 1 means a positive correlation between a feature value (which we can approximate to relative frequency due to the use of TF-IDF vectors) and the probability of the class, -1 means a negative correlation, and 0 shows an absence of a feature. The values (a/b) mean that a of b instances covered by the rule are correct. The rules with lower values of a/b are less trustworthy, and the rules with lower value of b, especially in the first few conditions, are less generalized.

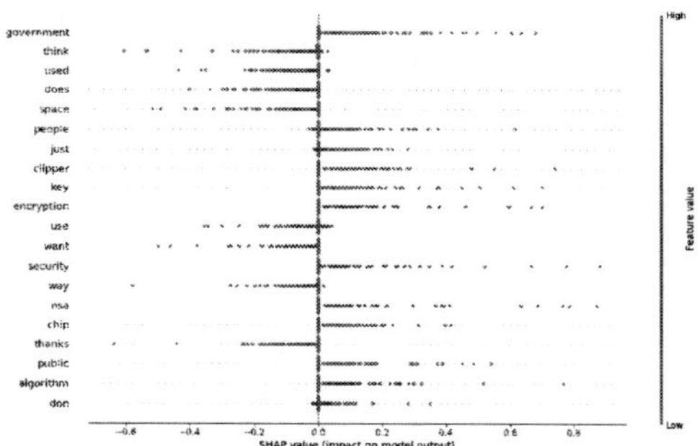

Figure 3: Feature importance estimation using SHAP for model interpretability.

tion plot in SHAP, where the interaction between different features is visualized. However, only a few features can be compared against each other in this manner without making the process expensive. These interactions are not understandable without extensive analysis. The technique we propose instead manages to capture the associations between features and classes, alleviating the need for these complex visualizations to understand the model.

Next, in Figure 4a, we present the if-then-else rules that have been induced from the training data using the original input and the gold labels, to give an idea about the relations between features and classes that we would expect the model to pick up from the data. In Figure 4b, we compare them with the feature-class associations that are instead captured by the trained network. These have been identified by using the transformed input space for rule induction, also to explain gold labels. Although the rules in these ordered sets are not directly comparable, we see that there are three exactly matching rules in the two sets (ignoring the order) and several common feature conditions. In these cases, the patterns in the training data are approximated by the network. We find that the rules fit on the network-transformed training data have a 2% higher macro averaged F-score compared to those on the original data. This suggests that the generalization brought about by the network assists in rule induction for this dataset on these tasks.

```
if (circuit = 1) ⟹ electronics (53/55)
elif (people = 0) and (electronics = 1) ⟹ electronics (31/34)
elif (people = 0) and (power = 1) and (time = 0) and (research = 0) and (years = 0) ⟹ electronics (43/55)
elif (people = 0) and (thanks = 1) and (used = 1) and (particular = 0) ⟹ electronics (12/14)
elif (people = 0) and (space = 0) and (voltage = 1) ⟹ electronics (22/22)
elif (people = 0) and (motorola = 1) ⟹ electronics (16/19)
elif (people = 0) and (space = 0) and (line = 1) and (encryption = 0) and (med = 0) and (doesn = 0) and (case = 0) ⟹ electronics (28/39)
elif (people = 0) and (space = 0) and (wire = 1) ⟹ electronics (14/18)
elif (space = 0) and (people = 0) and (1174 = 1) ⟹ electronics (9/9)
elif (amp = 1) ⟹ electronics (13/14)
elif (just = 0) and (space = 0) and (8051 = 1) ⟹ electronics (8/8)
else: others (1565/1848)
```

(a) The rules induced on the **original training data** that point towards the associations in the data that we would expect the neural network to capture.

```
if (circuit = 1) ⟹ electronics (53/53)
elif (people = 0) and (power = 1) and (time = 0) and (national = 0) ⟹ electronics (48/63)
elif (people = 0) and (electronics = 1) ⟹ electronics (27/28)
elif (people = 0) and (voltage = 1) ⟹ electronics (22/23)
elif (people = 0) and (space = 0) and (line = 1) and (want = 0) and (government = 0) and (block = 0) and (years = 0) and (amateur = 0) and (cell = 0) ⟹ electronics (28/33)
elif (people = 0) and (space = 0) and (advance = 1) ⟹ electronics (18/26)
elif (people = 0) and (motorola = 1) ⟹ electronics (16/16)
elif (people = 0) and (space = 0) and (wire = 1) and (digital = 0) ⟹ electronics (14/14)
elif (think = 0) and (buy = 1) and (government = 0) ⟹ electronics (14/21)
elif (people = 0) and (space = 0) and (uucp = 1) ⟹ electronics (10/12)
elif (space = 0) and (government = 0) and (amp = 1) ⟹ electronics (13/15)
elif (people = 0) and (space = 0) and (8051 = 1) ⟹ electronics (8/8)
else: others (1562/1823)
```

(b) The rules induced on the **training data transformed according to the network weights**. These point towards the associations that the network actually captures, as opposed to those we expect it to capture. To find these rules, we compute the gradients of the output of the corresponding gold label class w.r.t. the input features, instead of taking the gradients of the output predictions.

Figure 4: The rules induced on the training data to fit the gold labels.

5.2 Consistency of the induced rule-sets

As we discussed in § 4.4, it is important to optimize the hyperparameters of RIPPER-k to find an optimum set of rules because we obtain high standard deviations of the fidelity scores of explanations across different hyperparameters. Additionally, if several sets of explanations have high fidelity scores, they should also be consistent with each other. To this end, we analyze multiple rule-sets with high fidelity scores to check whether they are similar to each other. For this comparison, we identify all the sets of rules whose F-scores lie within 1% of the F-score of the best model. However, a comparison between different sets of ordered rules is not trivial. We calculate the mean percentage of the exactly matching rules between the well-performing models and the final selected set of rules, when these sets are assumed to be unordered. This score penalizes the rules that match partially as being a mismatch, which makes it a strict metric for sets with longer rules. In this process, we get the scores in the range 50%–79% using MI, and 48%–90% using sensitivity analysis feature selection techniques. We find that the classes with high fidelity scores also have high rule overlap, and vice versa. This suggests that different models that explain less confusable classes are also more consistent across different parameters.

We additionally calculate the mean percentage of the instances that have been classified identically by the well-performing models and the final selected model to facilitate a semantic comparison. We find that the classification overlap between different models ranges from 94%–97% when using MI feature selection, and 93%–98% with sensitivity analysis feature selection. The exact numbers can be found in the Appendix.

6   Limitations

While the advantage of using a rule inducer like RIPPER-k lies in gaining insight into feature-class associations, the approach has its own drawbacks. RIPPER-k outputs rules according to class prevalence. Hence, the majority class only has an 'else' clause associated with it. Furthermore, only the default rule is fired when there is just one class in the dataset. Hence, this technique is unsuitable for one-class problems, and when the class we are interested in is the majority class in the one-vs-rest binary setup. Moreover, if several features frequently co-occur and infrequently occur without each other, this technique may find only one of them.

Next, the proposed technique is a global explanation technique that can be used to identify the if-then-else rules that explain a model as a whole. However, using this technique, we can not obtain such rules for explaining only a single instance.

Finally, the learned rules are sensitive to some parameters in RIPPER-k. As discussed earlier, we overcome this limitation by optimizing the performance over different parameters. However, this step reduces the speed of finding explanations.

7   Conclusions and Future work

In this paper, we have proposed a technique to learn if-then-else rules to explain the predictions of supervised models. We have first computed the gradients of the output predictions with respect to the input features for every instance. We have then rescaled these gradients to feature weights, and have multiplied them with the original inputs to learn reweighed inputs for every instance. We have then simplified them to a set of 1000 transformed features with discrete values. Finally, we have induced rules that combine these features into rule conditions for every class in the data separately. We have found that the induced rules can explain the predictions of our classifier to a macro-

averaged F-score of 0.80. We have shown that these rules can be used to understand a model's behavior and output predictions.

In future, we plan to evaluate the proposed technique on different datasets to compare the fidelity scores of the explanations across datasets with different complexities. We would also like to compare our work with other techniques for inducing rules as explanations. It would also be interesting to investigate other rule induction algorithms that can support one-class problems, and that are less sensitive to parameters such as shuffling of data to overcome the limitations present due to the use of RIPPER-k.

Acknowledgments

We would like to thank the anonymous reviewers for their useful comments. This research was carried out within the Accumulate strategic basic research project, funded by the government agency Flanders Innovation & Entrepreneurship (VLAIO) [grant number 150056].

References

Robert Andrews, Joachim Diederich, and Alan B Tickle. 1995. Survey and critique of techniques for extracting rules from trained artificial neural networks. *Knowledge-based systems*, 8(6):373–389.

Leila Arras, Franziska Horn, Grégoire Montavon, Klaus-Robert Müller, and Wojciech Samek. 2017. "What is relevant in a text document?": An interpretable machine learning approach. In *PloS one*.

Malika Aubakirova and Mohit Bansal. 2016. Interpreting neural networks to improve politeness comprehension. In *Proceedings of the 2016 Conference on Empirical Methods in Natural Language Processing, EMNLP 2016, Austin, Texas, USA, November 1-4, 2016*, pages 2035–2041.

Anand Avati, Kenneth Jung, Stephanie Harman, Lance Downing, Andrew Ng, and Nigam H Shah. 2017. Improving palliative care with deep learning. *Computing Research Repository*, arXiv:1711.06402.

Sebastian Bach, Alexander Binder, Grégoire Montavon, Frederick Klauschen, Klaus-Robert Müller, and Wojciech Samek. 2015. On pixel-wise explanations for non-linear classifier decisions by layer-wise relevance propagation. *PloS one*, 10(7):e0130140.

Rich Caruana, Yin Lou, Johannes Gehrke, Paul Koch, Marc Sturm, and Noemie Elhadad. 2015. Intelligible models for healthcare: Predicting pneumonia risk and hospital 30-day readmission. In *Proceedings of the 21th ACM SIGKDD International Conference on Knowledge Discovery and Data Mining*, pages 1721–1730. ACM.

Jianbo Chen, Le Song, Martin J Wainwright, and Michael I Jordan. 2018. Learning to explain: An information-theoretic perspective on model interpretation. *Computing Research Repository*, arXiv:1802.07814.

Edward Choi, Mohammad Taha Bahadori, Jimeng Sun, Joshua Kulas, Andy Schuetz, and Walter Stewart. 2016. RETAIN: An interpretable predictive model for healthcare using reverse time attention mechanism. In *Advances in Neural Information Processing Systems*, pages 3504–3512.

William W Cohen. 1995. Fast effective rule induction. In *Machine Learning Proceedings 1995*, pages 115–123. Elsevier.

A Engelbrecht and I Cloete. 1998. Feature extraction from feedforward neural networks using sensitivity analysis. In *Proceedings of the International Conference on Systems, Signals, Control, Computers*, pages 221–225.

Dumitru Erhan, Yoshua Bengio, Aaron Courville, and Pascal Vincent. 2009. Visualizing higher-layer features of a deep network. *University of Montreal*, 1341(3):1.

Mark Hall, Eibe Frank, Geoffrey Holmes, Bernhard Pfahringer, Peter Reutemann, and Ian H Witten. 2009. The weka data mining software: an update. *ACM SIGKDD explorations newsletter*, 11(1):10–18.

Karl Moritz Hermann, Tomás Kociský, Edward Grefenstette, Lasse Espeholt, Will Kay, Mustafa Suleyman, and Phil Blunsom. 2015. Teaching machines to read and comprehend. In *Advances in Neural Information Processing Systems 28: Annual Conference on Neural Information Processing Systems 2015, December 7-12, 2015, Montreal, Quebec, Canada*, pages 1693–1701.

Pieter-Jan Kindermans, Kristof Schütt, Klaus-Robert Müller, and Sven Dähne. 2016. Investigating the influence of noise and distractors on the interpretation of neural networks. *Computing Research Repository*, arXiv:1611.07270.

Diederik P Kingma and Jimmy Ba. 2014. Adam: A method for stochastic optimization. *Computing Research Repository*, arXiv:1412.6980.

Himabindu Lakkaraju, Ece Kamar, Rich Caruana, and Jure Leskovec. 2017. Interpretable & explorable approximations of black box models. *Workshop on Fairness, Accountability, and Transparency in Machine Learning, KDD*, arXiv:1707.01154.

Jiwei Li, Xinlei Chen, Eduard H. Hovy, and Dan Jurafsky. 2016a. Visualizing and understanding neural models in NLP. In *NAACL HLT 2016, The 2016 Conference of the North American Chapter of the Association for Computational Linguistics: Human Language Technologies, San Diego California, USA, June 12-17, 2016*, pages 681–691.

Jiwei Li, Will Monroe, and Dan Jurafsky. 2016b. Understanding neural networks through representation erasure. *Computing Research Repository*, arXiv:1612.08220.

Scott M Lundberg and Su-In Lee. 2017. A unified approach to interpreting model predictions. In *Advances in Neural Information Processing Systems*, pages 4768–4777.

Christoph Molnar. Interpretable machine learning. Available at `https://christophm.github.io/interpretable-ml-book/` (2018-06-25).

Grégoire Montavon, Sebastian Lapuschkin, Alexander Binder, Wojciech Samek, and Klaus-Robert Müller. 2017. Explaining nonlinear classification decisions with deep taylor decomposition. *Pattern Recognition*, 65:211–222.

Chris Olah, Arvind Satyanarayan, Ian Johnson, Shan Carter, Ludwig Schubert, Katherine Ye, and Alexander Mordvintsev. 2018. The building blocks of interpretability. *Distill*, 3(3):e10.

Nina Poerner, Hinrich Schütze, and Benjamin Roth. 2018. Evaluating neural network explanation methods using hybrid documents and morphosyntactic agreement. In *Proceedings of the 56th Annual Meeting of the Association for Computational Linguistics (Volume 1: Long Papers)*, pages 340–350. Association for Computational Linguistics.

Marco Tulio Ribeiro, Sameer Singh, and Carlos Guestrin. 2016. Why should I trust you?: Explaining the predictions of any classifier. In *Proceedings of the 22nd ACM SIGKDD International Conference on Knowledge Discovery and Data Mining*, pages 1135–1144. ACM.

Avanti Shrikumar, Peyton Greenside, and Anshul Kundaje. 2017. Learning important features through propagating activation differences. In *Proceedings of the 34th International Conference on Machine Learning*, volume 70 of *Proceedings of Machine Learning Research*, pages 3145–3153, International Convention Centre, Sydney, Australia. PMLR.

Karen Simonyan, Andrea Vedaldi, and Andrew Zisserman. 2013. Deep inside convolutional networks: Visualising image classification models and saliency maps. *Computing Research Repository*, arXiv:1312.6034.

Harini Suresh, Nathan Hunt, Alistair E. W. Johnson, Leo Anthony Celi, Peter Szolovits, and Marzyeh Ghassemi. 2017. Clinical intervention prediction and understanding using deep networks. *Proceedings of Machine Learning for Healthcare, JMLR W&C Track Volume 68*, arXiv:1705.08498.

Madhumita Sushil, Simon Šuster, Kim Luyckx, and Walter Daelemans. 2018. Patient representation learning and interpretable evaluation using clinical notes. *Journal of Biomedical Informatics*, 84:103 – 113.

Sebastian B. Thrun. 1993. Extracting provably correct rules from artificial neural networks. Technical report, University of Bonn.

Zichao Yang, Diyi Yang, Chris Dyer, Xiaodong He, Alexander J. Smola, and Eduard H. Hovy. 2016. Hierarchical attention networks for document classification. In *NAACL HLT 2016, The 2016 Conference of the North American Chapter of the Association for Computational Linguistics: Human Language Technologies, San Diego California, USA, June 12-17, 2016*, pages 1480–1489.

A Appendix

In Table 2, we present the mean percentage of the exact match between different rule-sets output by several good models obtained with different RIPPER-k parameters, compared to the rule-set we finally selected. In the same table, we also present the mean percentage of instances that have been classified by different models identically as the model we finally selected. Furthermore, in Figure 5, we present the rules induced after performing feature selection using sensitivity analysis to explain the predictions of the neural network on the test data. In Figure 6, we present the rules induced when we instead use mutual information for feature selection to explain the same predictions.

Text class	MI		SA	
	Rule match	**Classification match**	**Rule match**	**Classification match**
Space	79%	97%	90%	98%
Medicine	63%	96%	68%	94%
Electronics	52%	94%	57%	93%
Cryptography	50%	97%	48%	97%

Table 2:   Mean exact match between unordered set of rules from several good models obtained with different parameters of RIPPER-k and the selected model for every class, and the mean classification overlap between them.

```
if (just = -1) and (use = 1) ⟹ electronics (24/24)
elif (just = -1) and (like = 1) ⟹ electronics (14/14)
elif (circuit = 1) ⟹ electronics (32/32)
elif (electronics = 1) ⟹ electronics (24/25)
elif (battery = 1) ⟹ electronics (22/22)
elif (people = 0) and (used = 1) and (way = 0) and (clipper = 0) and (space = 0) and (good = 0) and
(fairly = 0) and (drug = 0) ⟹ electronics (38/48)
elif (line = 1) and (space = 0) and (encryption = 0) and (clipper = 0) and elif (medical = 0) and (doctor
= 0) ⟹ electronics (20/20)
elif (people = 0) and (thanks = 1) and (advance = 1) and (long = 0) ⟹ electronics (10/10)
elif (people = 0) and (voltage = 1) ⟹ electronics (10/11)
elif (company = 1) and (medical = 0) and (order = 0) and (minutes = 0) and elif (clipper = 0) ⟹
electronics (19/23)
elif (pc = 1) and (security = 0) ⟹ electronics (12/12)
elif (think = -1) and (didn = -1) ⟹ electronics (5/5)
elif (people = 0) and (cheap = 1) ⟹ electronics (10/14)
elif (just = 0) and (motorola = 1) ⟹ electronics (6/6)
elif (just = 0) and (tape = 1) ⟹ electronics (6/7)
elif (end = -1) ⟹ electronics (7/10)
else: others (1144/1296)
```

(a) Rules for the electronics class

if *(medical = 1)* $\implies$ *medicine* (55/55)
elif *(doctor = 1)* $\implies$ *medicine* (38/38)
elif *(cause = 1) and (time = 0)* $\implies$ *medicine* (30/35)
elif *(disease = 1)* $\implies$ *medicine* (17/17)
elif *(body = 1)* $\implies$ *medicine* (25/31)
elif *(med = 1)* $\implies$ *medicine* (14/14)
elif *(effects = 1) and (space = 0)* $\implies$ *medicine* (17/21)
elif *(like = -1) and (time = 1)* $\implies$ *medicine* (7/7)
elif *(don = 0) and (skin = 1)* $\implies$ *medicine* (7/7)
elif *(photography = 1)* $\implies$ *medicine* (13/13)
elif *(cancer = 1)* $\implies$ *medicine* (8/8)
elif *(surgery = 1)* $\implies$ *medicine* (8/8)
elif *(pain = 1)* $\implies$ *medicine* (6/8)
elif *(allergic = 1)* $\implies$ *medicine* (7/7)
elif *(water = 1) and (make = 0)* $\implies$ *medicine* (9/13)
elif *(left = 1) and (use = 0)* $\implies$ *medicine* (7/9)
elif *(don = 0) and (blood = 1)* $\implies$ *medicine* (5/5)
elif *(don = 0) and (experience = 1)* $\implies$ *medicine* (7/9)
elif *(therapy = 1)* $\implies$ *medicine* (4/4)
else: others (1147/1270)

(b) Rules for the medicine class

if *(space = 1)* $\implies$ *space* (116/118)
elif *(orbit = 1)* $\implies$ *space* (29/29)
elif *(earth = 1)* $\implies$ *space* (23/24)
elif *(sky = 1)* $\implies$ *space* (17/17)
elif *(nasa = 1)* $\implies$ *space* (12/12)
elif *(launch = 1)* $\implies$ *space* (14/14)
elif *(solar = 1)* $\implies$ *space* (9/9)
elif *(moon = 1)* $\implies$ *space* (7/7)
elif *(shuttle = 1)* $\implies$ *space* (6/6)
elif *(spacecraft = 1)* $\implies$ *space* (6/6)
elif *(ground = -1) and (secret = 0)* $\implies$ *space* (4/4)
elif *(plane = 1)* $\implies$ *space* (3/3)
elif *(materials = 1) and (st = 0)* $\implies$ *space* (4/4)
else: others (1245/1326)

(c) Rules for the space class

if *(clipper = 1) and (moon = 0)* $\Longrightarrow$ *cryptography* (90/90)
elif *(key = 1) and (care = 0) and (like = 0)* $\Longrightarrow$ *cryptography* (37/38)
elif *(government = 1) and (launch = 0) and (medical = 0) and (nasa = 0)* $\Longrightarrow$ *cryptography* (45/46)
elif *(encryption = 1)* $\Longrightarrow$ *cryptography* (25/25)
elif *(nsa = 1)* $\Longrightarrow$ *cryptography* (13/13)
elif *(just = 0) and (david = 1) and (want = 0) and (disease = 0)* $\Longrightarrow$ *cryptography* (13/15)
elif *(time = 0) and (algorithm = 1)* $\Longrightarrow$ *cryptography* (8/8)
elif *(com = 1) and (metzger = 1)* $\Longrightarrow$ *cryptography* (9/9)
elif *(good = 0) and (modem = 1)* $\Longrightarrow$ *cryptography* (6/6)
elif *(does = 0) and (crypto = 1)* $\Longrightarrow$ *cryptography* (8/8)
elif *(just = 0) and (don = 0) and (security = 1)* $\Longrightarrow$ *cryptography* (7/7)
else: others (1145/1314)

(d) Rules for the cryptography class

Figure 5: Set of if-then-else rules that **explain the test predictions** of the neural network for the all the classes when **using sensitivity analysis for feature selection**. Here the discrete test value 1 means a positive correlation between a feature value (which we can approximate to relative frequency due to the use of TF-IDF vectors) and the probability of the class, -1 means a negative correlation, and 0 shows the absence of a feature. The values (a/b) mean that a of b instances covered by the rule are correct. The rules with lower values of a/b are less trustworthy, and the rules with lower value of b, especially in the first few conditions, are less generalized.

if *(just = -1) and (use = 1)* $\Longrightarrow$ *electronics* $(24/24)$
elif *(circuit = 1)* $\Longrightarrow$ *electronics* $(32/32)$
elif *(just = -1) and (don = 1)* $\Longrightarrow$ *electronics* $(11/11)$
elif *(people = 0) and (used = 1) and (key = 0) and (don = 0) and (use = 0) and (edu = 0) and (medication = 0) and (concept = 0) and (did = 0)* $\Longrightarrow$ *electronics* $(36/43)$
elif *(electronics = 1)* $\Longrightarrow$ *electronics* $(17/18)$
elif *(battery = 1)* $\Longrightarrow$ *electronics* $(23/23)$
elif *(radio = 1) and (shack = 1)* $\Longrightarrow$ *electronics* $(9/9)$
elif *(people = 0) and (thanks = 1) and (advance = 1)* $\Longrightarrow$ *electronics* $(12/14)$
elif *(signal = 1)* $\Longrightarrow$ *electronics* $(13/15)$
elif *(people = 0) and (company = 1) and (just = 0)* $\Longrightarrow$ *electronics* $(13/18)$
elif *(pc = 1)* $\Longrightarrow$ *electronics* $(16/19)$
elif *(people = 0) and (use = 1) and (just = 0) and (good = 0) and (clipper = 0) and (probably = 0) and (center = 0) and (unless = 0) and (18084tm = 0) and (algorithms = 0)* $\Longrightarrow$ *electronics* $(29/33)$
elif *(appreciated = 1) and (time = 0)* $\Longrightarrow$ *electronics* $(11/16)$
elif *(voltage = 1)* $\Longrightarrow$ *electronics* $(8/8)$
elif *(program = -1)* $\Longrightarrow$ *electronics* $(10/15)$
else: others (1134/1281)

(a) Rules for the electronics class

if *(medical = 1)* $\implies$ *medicine* (55/55)
elif *(doctor = 1)* $\implies$ *medicine* (38/38)
elif *(body = 1)* $\implies$ *medicine* (28/34)
elif *(effects = 1) and (don = 0) and (earth = 0)* $\implies$ *medicine*(18/19)
elif *(disease = 1)* $\implies$ *medicine* (19/19)
elif *(photography = 1)* $\implies$ *medicine* (13/13)
elif *(med = 1)* $\implies$ *medicine* (15/15)
elif *(cause = 1) and (station = 0) and (enforcement = 0) and (antennas = 0) and (attacks = 0) and (battery = 0)* $\implies$ *medicine* (24/26)
elif *(allergic = 1)* $\implies$ *medicine* (7/7)
elif *(experience = 1) and (data = 0)* $\implies$ *medicine* (9/13)
elif *(surgery = 1)* $\implies$ *medicine* (10/10)
elif *(skin = 1)* $\implies$ *medicine* (7/7)
elif *(blood = 1)* $\implies$ *medicine* (6/7)
elif *(pain = 1)* $\implies$ *medicine* (6/8)
elif *(therapy = 1)* $\implies$ *medicine* (4/4)
elif *(cancer = 1)* $\implies$ *medicine* (5/5)
elif *(food = 1)* $\implies$ *medicine* (4/4)
elif *(just = -1) and (don = -1)* $\implies$ *medicine* (4/4)
elif *(cells = 1)* $\implies$ *medicine* (5/7)
else: others (1154/1284)

(b) Rules for the medicine class

if *(space = 1)* $\implies$ *space* (116/118)
elif *(orbit = 1)* $\implies$ *space* (29/29)
elif *(earth = 1)* $\implies$ *space* (23/24)
elif *(sky = 1)* $\implies$ *space* (17/17)
elif *(nasa = 1)* $\implies$ *space* (12/12)
elif *(launch = 1)* $\implies$ *space* (14/14)
elif *(moon = 1)* $\implies$ *space* (7/7)
elif *(solar = 1)* $\implies$ *space* (9/9)
elif *(shuttle = 1)* $\implies$ *space* (6/6)
elif *(spacecraft = 1)* $\implies$ *space* (6/6)
elif *(atmosphere = 1)* $\implies$ *space* (4/4)
elif *(idea = 1) and (probably = -1)* $\implies$ *space* (3/3)
elif *(18084tm = 1)* $\implies$ *space* (4/4)
elif *(gamma = 1)* $\implies$ *space* (3/3)
elif *(exploration = 1)* $\implies$ *space* (3/3)
elif *(landing = 1)* $\implies$ *space* (3/3)
elif *(aircraft = 1)* $\implies$ *space* (3/3)
elif *(ground = -1) and (accepted = 0)* $\implies$ *space* (4/4)
elif *(materials = 1) and (aids = 0)* $\implies$ *space* (3/3)
elif *(rocket = 1)* $\implies$ *space* (2/2)
else: others (1245/1305)

(c) Rules for the space class

```
if (clipper = 1) and (delta = 0)  ⟹  cryptography (90/90)
elif (key = 1) and (care = 0)  ⟹  cryptography (49/54)
elif (government = 1) and (money = 0) and (develop = 0)  ⟹  cryptography (37/39)
elif (encryption = 1)  ⟹  cryptography (23/23)
elif (nsa = 1)  ⟹  cryptography (14/14)
elif (com = 1) and (metzger = 1)  ⟹  cryptography (9/9)
elif (crypto = 1)  ⟹  cryptography (11/11)
elif (time = 0) and (algorithm = 1)  ⟹  cryptography (8/8)
elif (used = 0) and (court = 1)  ⟹  cryptography (6/6)
elif (security = 1)  ⟹  cryptography (8/9)
elif (used = 0) and (modem = 1)  ⟹  cryptography (5/5)
else: others (1141/1311)
```

(d) Rules for the cryptography class

Figure 6: Set of if-then-else rules that **explain the test predictions** of the neural network for the all the classes when **using mutual information for feature selection**. Here the discrete test value 1 means a positive correlation between a feature value (which we can approximate to relative frequency due to the use of TF-IDF vectors) and the probability of the class, -1 means a negative correlation, and 0 shows the absence of a feature. The values (a/b) mean that a of b instances covered by the rule are correct. The rules with lower values of a/b are less trustworthy, and the rules with lower value of b, especially in the first few conditions, are less generalized.

Can LSTM Learn to Capture Agreement? The Case of Basque

Shauli Ravfogel[1] and **Francis M. Tyers**[2,3] and **Yoav Goldberg**[1,4]
[1] Computer Science Department, Bar Ilan University
[2] School of Linguistics, Higher School of Economics
[3] Department of Linguistics, Indiana University
[4] Allen Institute for Artificial Intelligence
`{shauli.ravfogel, yoav.goldberg}@gmail.com, ftyers@prompsit.com`

Abstract

Sequential neural networks models are powerful tools in a variety of Natural Language Processing (NLP) tasks. The sequential nature of these models raises the questions: to what extent can these models implicitly learn hierarchical structures typical to human language, and what kind of grammatical phenomena can they acquire?

We focus on the task of agreement prediction in Basque, as a case study for a task that requires implicit understanding of sentence structure and the acquisition of a complex but consistent morphological system. Analyzing experimental results from two syntactic prediction tasks – verb number prediction and suffix recovery – we find that sequential models perform worse on agreement prediction in Basque than one might expect on the basis of a previous agreement prediction work in English. Tentative findings based on diagnostic classifiers suggest the network makes use of local heuristics as a proxy for the hierarchical structure of the sentence. We propose the Basque agreement prediction task as challenging benchmark for models that attempt to learn regularities in human language.

1 Introduction

In recent years, recurrent neural network (RNN) models have emerged as a powerful architecture for a variety of NLP tasks (Goldberg, 2017). In particular, gated versions, such as Long Short-Term Networks (LSTMs) (Hochreiter and Schmidhuber, 1997) and Gated Recurrent Units (GRU) (Cho et al., 2014; Chung et al., 2014) achieve state-of-the-art results in tasks such as language modeling, parsing, and machine translation.

RNNs were shown to be able to capture long-term dependencies and statistical regularities in input sequences (Karpathy et al., 2015; Linzen et al., 2016; Shi et al., 2016; Jurafsky et al., 2018; Gulordava et al., 2018). An adequate evaluation of the ability of RNNs to capture syntactic structure requires a use of established benchmarks. A common approach is the use of an annotated corpus to learn an explicit syntax-oriented task, such as parsing or shallow parsing (Dyer et al., 2015; Kiperwasser and Goldberg, 2016; Dozat and Manning, 2016) . While such an approach does evaluate the ability of the model to learn syntax, it has several drawbacks. First, the annotation process relies on human experts and is thus demanding in term of resources. Second, by its very nature, training a model on such a corpus evaluates it on a human-dictated notion of grammatical structure, and is tightly coupled to a linguistic theory. Lastly, the supervised training process on such a corpus provides the network with explicit grammatical labels (e.g. a parse tree). While this is sometimes desirable, in some instances we would like to evaluate the ability of the model to implicitly acquire hierarchical representations.

Alternatively, one can train language model (LM) (Graves, 2013; Józefowicz et al., 2016; Melis et al., 2017; Yogatama et al., 2018) to model the probability distribution of a language, and use common measures for quality such as perplexity as an indication of the model's ability to capture regularities in language. While this approach does not suffer from the above discussed drawbacks, it conflates syntactical capacity with other factors such as world knowledge and frequency of lexical items. Furthermore, the LM task does not provide one clear answer: one cannot be "right" or "wrong" in language modeling, only softly worse or better than other systems.

A different approach is testing the model on a grammatical task that does not require an extensive grammatical annotation, but is yet indicative of syntax comprehension. Specifically, previous works (Linzen et al., 2016; Bernardy and Lappin, 2017; Gulordava et al., 2018) used the task of predicting agreement, which requires detecting

Proceedings of the 2018 EMNLP Workshop BlackboxNLP: Analyzing and Interpreting Neural Networks for NLP, pages 98–107
Brussels, Belgium, November 1, 2018. ©2018 Association for Computational Linguistics

hierarchal relations between sentence constituents. Labeled data for such a task requires only the collection of sentences that exhibit agreement from an unannotated corpora. However, those works have focused on relatively small set of languages: several Indo-European languages and a Semitic language (Hebrew). As we show, drawing conclusions on the model's abilities from a relatively small subset of languages can be misleading.

In this work, we test agreement prediction in a substantially different language, Basque, which is a language with ergative–absolutive alignment, rich morphology, relatively free word order, and polypersonal agreement (see Section 3). We propose two tasks, verb-number prediction (Section 6) and suffix prediction (Section 7), and show that agreement prediction in Basque is indeed harder for RNNs. We thus propose Basque agreement as a challenging benchmark for the ability of models to capture regularities in human language.

2   Background and Previous Work

To shed light on the question of hierarchical structure learning, a previous work on English (Linzen et al., 2016) has focused on subject-verb agreement: The form of third-person present-tense verbs in English is dependent upon the number of their subject ("They walk" vs. "She walks"). Agreement prediction is an interesting case study for implicit learning of the tree structure of the input, as once the arguments of each present-tense verb in the sentence are found and their grammatical relation to the verb is established, predicting the verb form is straightforward.

Linzen et al. (2016) tested different variants of the agreement prediction task: categorical prediction of the verb form based on the left context; grammatical assessment of the validity of the agreement present in a given sentence; and language modeling. Since in many cases the verb form can be predicted according to number of the preceding noun, they focused on agreement attractors: sentences in which the preceding nouns have the opposite number of the grammatical subject. Their model achieved very good overall performance in the first two tasks of number prediction and grammatical judgment, while in the third task of language modeling, weak supervision did not suffice to learn structural dependencies. With regard to the presence of agreement attractors, they have shown the performance decays with their number, to the point of worse-than-random accuracy in the presence of 4 attractors; this suggests

the network relies, at least to a certain degree, on local cues. Bernardy and Lappin (2017) evaluated agreement prediction on a larger dataset, and argued that a large vocabulary aids the learning of structural patterns. Gulordava et al. (2018) focused on the ability of LM's to capture agreement as a marker of syntactic ability, and used nonsensical sentences to control for semantic clues. They have shown positive results in four languages, as well as some similarities between their models' performance and human judgment of grammaticality.

3   Properties of the Basque Language

Basque agreement patterns are ostensibly more complex and very different from those of English. In particular, nouns inflect for case, and the verb agrees with all of its core arguments. How well can a RNN learn such agreement patterns?

We first outline key properties of Basque relevant to this work. We have used the following two grammars written in English for reference (Laka, 1996; de Rijk, 2007).

Morphological marking of case and number on NPs   The grammatical role of noun phrases is explicitly marked by nuclear case suffixes that attach after the determiner in a noun phrase — this is typically the last element in the phrase.

The nuclear cases are the *ergative* (ERG), the *absolutive* (ABS) and the *dative* (DAT).[1] In addition to case, the same suffixes also encode for number (singular or plural) as seen in Table 1.

Ergative-absolutive case system   Unlike English and most other Indo-European languages that have *nominative–accusative* morphosyntactic alignment in which the single argument of intransitive verbs and the agent of transitive verbs behave similarly to each other ("subjects") but differently from the object of transitive verbs, Basque has *ergative–absolutive* alignment. This means that the "subject" of an intransitive verb and the "object" of a transitive verbs behave similarly to each other and receive the absolutive case, while the "subject" of a transitive verb receives the ergative case. To illustrate the difference, while in English we say "she sleeps" and "she sees them" (treating *she* the same in both sentences), in an

---

[1] Additional cases encode different aspects of the role of the noun phrase in the sentence. For example, local cases indicate aspects such as destination and place of occurrence, possessive/genitive cases indicate possession, causal cases indicate causation, etc. In this work we focus only on the three mentioned.

Case	Function	Suffix Forms		
		Sg	**Pl**	**No det**
Absolutive	S, O	*-a*	*-ak*	-
Ergative	A	*-ak*	*-ek*	*-(e)k*
Dative	IO	*-ari*	*-ei*	*-(r)i*

Table 1: Basque case and their corresponding determined nuclear case suffixes. Note the case syncretism, resulting in structural ambiguity between the plural absolutive and the ergative singular. Under function, S refers to the single argument of a prototypical intransitive verb, O refers to the most patient-like argument of a prototypical transitive verb, and A refers to the most agent-like argument of a prototypical transitive verb. Subsequently IO refers to the indirect object, often filling the recipient or experiencer role.

imaginary ergative-absolutive version of English we would say "she sleeps" and "her sees they", inflecting "she" and "they" similarly (the absolutive), and different from "her" (the ergative).

Examples The following sentence (1) demonstrates the use of case suffixes to encode grammatical function.

(1) *Kutxazain-ek   bezeroa-ri*
cashier-PL.ERG customer-SG.DAT
liburu-ak   eman dizkiote
book-PL.ABS gave they-them-to-her/him

The cashiers gave the books to the customer.

In (1), the verb *eman* 'give' is transitive, the ergative corresponds to English grammatical subject and the absolutive corresponds to English grammatical object. However, Basque is absolutive–ergative, namely, the subject of an intransitive verb is marked for case like the object of a transitive verb, and differently from the subject of a transitive verb (2).

(2) *Kutxazain-ak   hemen daude*
cashier-PL-ABS here   they are-PL.ABS3

The cashiers are here.

Since the verb *daude* 'are' is intransitive, the word *kutxazain-* 'cashier' accepts the plural absolutive suffix *-ak*, and not the plural ergative suffix *-ek*.

Interestingly, Basque exhibits case syncretism, namely, nuclear case suffixes are ambiguous: the suffix *-ak* marks both plural absolutive and singular ergative. Compare Example (3) with Example (4).

(3) *Pertson-ak   zuhaitz-ak*
person-SG.ERG tree-PL.ABS
ikusten ditu
he/she-sees-them

The person sees the trees.

(4) *Zuhaitz-ak   pertson-ak*
tree-SG.ERG person-PL.ABS
ikusten ditu
seeing it-is-them

The tree sees the people.

Word-order and Polypersonal Agreement
Basque is often said to have a SOV word order, although the rules governing word order are rather complex, and word order is dependent on the focus and topic of the sentence. While the case marking system handles most of the word-order variation, the ambiguity between the single ergative and plural absolutive — which are both marked with *-ak* — results in sentence-level ambiguity. For instance, Example (3) can also be interpreted as "it is the tree [SG] that sees the people [PL]" (with a focus on "the tree"). Disambiguation in such cases depends on context and world knowledge.

Unlike English verbs that only agree in number with their grammatical subject, Basque verbs agree in number *with all* their nuclear arguments: the ergative, the absolutive and the dative (roughly corresponding to the subject, the object and the indirect object).[2] Verbs are formed in two ways: *aditz trinkoak* 'synthetic verbs' — such as *jakin* 'to know' — are conjugated according to the aspect, tense and agreement patterns, e.g. *dakigu* 'We know it' and *genekien* 'We knew it'. There are only about two dozen such verbs; all other verbs are composed of a non-finite stem, indicating the tense or aspect, and an auxiliary verb, that is conjugated according to the number of its arguments — such as *ikusi* 'to see' — e.g. *ikusten dugu* 'We see it' and *ikusi genuen* 'We saw it'. There are several auxiliary verbs, including *izan* 'to be' and *ukan* 'to have'. The form of an auxiliary verb used in a sentence also is also dependent on the transitivity of the verb, with *izan* being the intransitive auxiliary and *ukan* being the transitive auxiliary.

To summarize Noun phrases are marked for case (ergative, absolutive or dative) and number (singular or plural), and appear in relatively-free word order relative to the verb to which they are arguments. The verbs (or their auxiliaries) inflect for tense, time and number-agreement, and agree with all their arguments on number. Case syn-

---

[2]Note that some arguments, in particular proper-nouns, are not marked for number. Other arguments, in particular the ergative, can be omitted and not spelled out. The verb form still needs to mark the correct number for these arguments.

cretism results in ambiguity between the singular ergative and the plural absolutive suffixes.

4 Learning Basque Agreement

To assess the ability of RNNs to learn Basque agreement we perform two sets of experiments. In the first set (Section 6), we focus on the ability to learn to predict the number inflections of verbs, namely, the number of each of their arguments, where the model reads the sentence, with one of the verbs randomly replaced with a ⟨verb⟩ token. This is analogous to the agreement task explored in previous work on English (Linzen et al., 2016) and other languages (Gulordava et al., 2018), but in an arguably more challenging settings, as the Basque task requires the model: (a) to identify all the verb's arguments; (b) to learn the ergative–absolutive distinction; and (c) to cope with a relatively free word order and a rich morphological inflection system. As we show, the task is indeed substantially harder than in English, resulting in much lower accuracies than in Linzen et al. (2016) while not focusing on the hard cases.

However, we also identify some problems with the verb number prediction task. The presence of case suffixes presumably makes the task easier, in some sense, than in English: the grammatical role of arguments with respect to the verb is encoded in grammatical suffixes, potentially making it easier to capture surface heuristics that do not require the understanding of the hierarchical structure of the sentence. In addition, the ergative—whose number is encoded in the verb form—is often omitted from sentences, making the task of ergative number prediction impossible without relying on context or world knowledge. We thus propose an alternative setup (Section 7), in which, rather than predicting the agreement pattern of the verb, we remove all nuclear case suffixes from words and ask the model to recover them (or predict the absence of a suffix, for unsuffixed words). We argue that this setup is a better one for assessing models' ability to capture Basque sentence structure and agreement system: it requires the model to accurately identify the role of NPs with respect to a verb in order to assign them the correct case suffix (as marked on the verb), while not requiring the model to make-up information that is not encoded in the sentence.

5 Experimental Setup

In contrast to more explicit grammatical tasks (e.g. tagging, parsing), the data needed for training a model on agreement prediction task does not require annotated data and can be derived relatively easily from unannotated sentences. We have used the text of the Basque Wikipedia. A considerable number of the articles in Basque Wikipedia appear to be bot-generated; we have tried to filter these from the data according to keywords. The data consists of 1,896,371 sentences; we have used 935,730 sentences for training, 129,375 for validation and 259,215 for evaluation. We make the data publicly available[3].

We use the Apertium morphological analyzer (Forcada et al., 2011; Ginest-Rosell et al., 2009) to extract the parts-of-speech (POS) and morphological marking of all words.[4] The POS information was used to detect verbs, nouns and adjectives, but was not incorporated in the word embeddings.

For section 7.1, grammatical generalization, we used the Basque Universal Dependencies treebank (Aranzabe et al., 2015) to extract human-annotated POS, case, number and dependency edge labels. We have used their train:dev:test division, resulting in 5,173 training sentences, 1,719 development sentences and 1,719 test sentences.

Word Representation We represent each word with an embedding vector. To account for the rich morphology of Basque, our word embeddings combine the word identity, its lemma[5] as determined by the morphological analyzer, and character ngrams of lengths 1 to 5. Let E_t, E_l and E_{ng} be token, lemma and n-gram embedding matrices, and let t_w, l_w and $\{ng_w\}$ be the word token, the lemma and the set of all n-grams of lengths 1 to 5, for a given word w. The final vector representation of w, e_w, is given by $e_w = E_t[t] + E_l[l] + \sum_{ng \in \{ng_w\}} E_{ng}[ng]$. We use embedding vectors of size 150. We recorded the 100,000 most common words, n-grams and lemmas, and used them to calculate the vector representation of words. Out-of-vocabulary words, ngrams and lemmas are replaced by a ⟨unk⟩ token.

Model In previous studies, the agreement was between two elements, and the model was tasked with predicting a morphological property of the second one, based on a property encoded on the

---

[3] http://nlp.biu.ac.il/data/basque/

[4] We use the Apertium analyzer instead of other options as it is freely available online under a free/open-source licence covering both the lexicon and the source code.

[5] Most words admit to a single interpretation by the morphological analyzer. For words that had several optional lemmas, we chose the first one, after the exclusion of colloquial or familiar verb forms, which are infrequent in Wikipedia.

Suffix	Closest verb is incorrect			Closest verb is correct		
	Rec	Prec	F1	Rec	Prec	F1
-ak	70.2 (2961)	85.2 (2438)	76.9	80.5 (8312)	88.2 (4954)	84.1
-ek	60.8 (758)	98.2 (469)	75.1	64.7 (1976)	95.9 (1333)	77.2

Table 2: Model performance according to closest-verb grammatical connection to the verb, for sentences that contain the verb *da* 'it is'. The number of sentences appears in parentheses.

Verb form	Diagnostic classifier	Accuracy (%)			Majority (%)
		Total	BiLSTM wrong	BiLSTM correct	
da 'is'	Linear model	67.7	56.2	70.2	62.4
	1-layer MLP	74.7	69.3	75.6	
zen 'was'	Linear model	64.4	52.8	66.5	61.9
	1-layer MLP	74.8	71.5	75.4	
ziren 'were'	Linear model	67.4	57.8	70.1	59.8
	1-layer MLP	76.6	72.3	77.8	

Table 3: Diagnostic classifier accuracy in predicting whether or not the closest verb is grammatically connected to a word, according to BiLSTM suffix prediction success on that word. "BiLSTM correct": success rate on instances in which the BiLSTM correctly predicted the case suffix. "BiLSTM wrong": success rate on instances in which the BiLSTM failed. "Majority" signifies the success of majority-classifier.

first. Thus, a uni-directional RNN sufficed. Here, due to a single verb having to agree with several arguments, while following a relatively free word order, we cannot use a uni-directional model. We opted instead for a bi-directional RNN.[6] In all tasks, we use a one-layer BiLSTM network with 150 hidden units, compared with 50 units in (Linzen et al., 2016)[7]. In the verb prediction task, the BiLSTM encodes the verb in the context of the entire sentence, and the numbers of the ergative, absolute and datives are predicted by 3 independent multilayer perceptrons (MLPs) with a single hidden layer of size 128, that receive as an input the hidden state of the BiLSTM over the ⟨verb⟩ token.

In the suffix prediction task, the prediction of the case suffix is performed by a MLP of size 128, that receives as an input the hidden state of the BiLSTM over each word in the sentence.

The whole model, including the embedding, is trained end-to-end with the Adam optimizer (Kingma and Ba, 2014).

6 Verb Argument Number Prediction

In this task, the model sees the sentence with one of the auxiliary verbs replaced by a ⟨verb⟩ token, and predicts the number of its ergative, absolute and dative. For example, in (1) above, the network sees the embeddings of the words in the sentence:[8]

Kutxazain-ek bezeroa-ri liburu-ak eman ⟨verb⟩

It is then expected to predict the number of the arguments of the missing verb, *dizkiote*: ergative:plural, dative:singular and absolutive:plural. Each argument can take one of three values, *singular*, *plural* or *none*. In order to succeed in this task, the model has to identify the arguments of the omitted verb, and detect their plurality status as well as their grammatical relation to the verb. Note that as discussed above, these relations do not overlap with the notions of "subject" and "object" in English, as the grammatical case is also dependent on the transitivity of the verb. Since the model is exposed to the lemma of the auxiliary verb and the stem that precedes it, it can, in principle, learn dividing verbs into transitive and intransitive.

6.1 Results and Analysis

We conducted a series of experiments, as detailed below. A summary of all the results in available in Table 4.

Main results The model achieved moderate success in this task, with accuracy of 87.1% and 93.8% and recall of 80.0% and 100%[9] in ergative and absolutive prediction, respectively. Dative accuracy was 98.0%, but the recall is low

---

[6]A unidirectional LSTM baseline achieved accuracy scores of 86.6%, 91.7% and 98.2% and recall values of 78.9%, 100% and 60.1% for ergative, absolutive and dative verb arguments prediction, respectively.

[7]Network size was chosen based on development set performance.

[8]See:

(1) *Kutxazain-ek   bezeroa-ri   liburu-ak*
     cashier-PL.ERG customer-PL.DAT book-SG.ABS
     eman   ⟨verb⟩
     give-PTCP ⟨aux⟩
     'The cashiers gave the books to the customers'

[9]This reflects the fact the absolutive is almost always present.

Condition	Ergative A / R	Absolutive A / R	Dative A / R
Base	87.1 / 80.0	93.8 / 100	98.0 / 54.9
Suffixes only	69.0 / 40.3	83.7 / 100	97.0 / 26.0
No suffixes	83.8 / 80.0	87.8 / 100	97.3 / 34.7
Neutralized case	86.0 / 79.3	93.3 / 100	97.3 / 38.1
Single verb	90.6 / 89.0	96.04 / 100	98.9 / 74.7
No -*ak*	90.9 / 81.1	96.6 / 100	98.6 / 67.7
Sing. verb, no -*ak*	92.6 / 83.4	97.2 / 100	99.1 / 75.4

Table 4: Summary of verb number prediction results for accuracy (A) and recall (R).

(54.9%), perhaps due to the relative rarity of dative nouns in the corpus (only around 3.5% of the sentences contain dative). These relatively low numbers are in sharp contrast to previous results on English in which the accuracy scores on general sentences was above 99%. While English agreement results drop when considering hard cases where agreement distractors or intervening constructions intervene between the verb and its argument, in Basque the numbers are low already for the common cases.

This suggests that agreement prediction in Basque can serve as a valuable benchmark for evaluating the syntactic abilities of sequential models such as LSTMs in a relatively challenging grammatical environment, as well as for assessing the generality of results across language families.

Ablations: case suffixes vs. word forms The presence of nuclear case suffixes in Basque can, in principle, make the task of agreement prediction easier, as (ambiguous) grammatical annotation is explicit in the form of the nuclear case suffixes, that encode the type of grammatical connection to the verb. How much of the relevant information is encoded in the case suffixes? To investigate the relative importance of these suffixes, we considered a baseline in which the model is exposed only to the nuclear suffixes, ignoring the identities of the words and the character n-grams (Table 4, Suffixes only). This model achieved accuracy scores of 69.0%, 83.7% and 97.0% and recall values of 40.3%, 100% and 26% for ergative, absolutive and dative prediction, respectively. While substantially lower than when considering the word forms, the absolute numbers are not random, suggesting that agreement can in large part be predicted based on the presence of the different suffixes and their linear order in the sentence, without paying attention to specific words.

In a complementary setting the model is ex-

posed to the sentence after the removal of all nuclear case suffixes (according to the morphological analyzer output). This setting (Table 4, No suffixes) yields accuracies of 83.8%, 87.8% and 97.3% and recall scores of 80.0%, 100% and 34.7% for ergative, absolutive and dative, respectively. Interestingly, in the last setting the model succeeds to some extent to predict the verb arguments number although the number is not marked on the arguments. This suggests the model uses cues such as the existence of certain function words that imply a number, and the forms of non-nuclear suffixes to infer the number of the arguments.

Importance of explicit case marking The verb numbers prediction task requires the model to identify the arguments, and hence the hierarchical structure of the sentence. However, the Basque suffixes encode not only the number but also the explicit grammatical function of the argument. This makes the model's task potentially easier, as it may make use of the explicit case information as an effective heuristic instead of modeling the sentence's syntactic structure. To control for this, we consider a neutralized version (Table 4, Neutralized case) in which we removed case information and kept only the number information: suffixes were replaced by their number, or were marked as "ambiguous" in case of -*ak*. For example, the word kutxazainek was replaced with kutxazain⟨plural⟩, since the suffix -*ek* encodes plural ergative. Interestingly, in this settings the performance was only slightly decreased, with accuracy scores of 86.0%, 93.3% and 97.3% and recall values of 79.3%, 100% and 38.1% for ergative, absolutive and dative, respectively. These results suggest that the network either makes little use of explicit grammatical marking in the suffixes, or compensates for the absence of grammatical annotation using other information present in the sentence.

Performance on simple sentences The presence of multiple verbs, along with the inherent ambiguity of the suffix system, can both complicate the task of number prediction. To assess the relative importance of these factors, we considered modified training and test sets that contain only sentences with a single verb (Table 4, Single verb). This resulted in a significant improvement, with accuracy scores of 90.61%, 96.04% and 98.9% and recall values of 89.0%, 100% and 74.7% for ergative, absolutive, and dative, respectively; note that sentences with a single verb also tend to be shorter and simpler in their grammatical structure. To evaluate the influence of the ambiguous suffix, we removed all sentences that contain the ambiguous suffix *-ak* from the dataset (Table 4, No *-ak*). This resulted in a more moderate improvement to accuracy values of 90.9%, 96.6% and 98.6% and recall of 81.1%, 100% and 67.7% for ergative, absolutive and dative. Limiting the dataset to unambiguous sentences with a single verb (Table 4, Sing. verb, no *-ak*) yields an additional improvement, with accuracies of 92.6%, 97.2% and 99.1% and recall values of 83.4%, 100% and 75.4% for ergative, absolutive and dative, respectively.

7 NP Suffix Prediction

The general trend in the experiments above is a significantly higher success in absolutive number prediction, compared with ergative number prediction. This highlights a shortcoming in the verb-number prediction task: as Basque encodes the number of the verb arguments in the verb forms, the subject can — and often is — be omitted from the sentence. Additionally, the number of proper nouns is often not marked. These cases are common for the ergative: 55% of the sentences marked for ERG.PL3 agreement do not contain words suffixed with *-ek*. This requires the model to predict the number of the verb based on information which is not directly encoded in the sentence.

To counter these limitations, we propose an alternative prediction task that also takes advantage of the presence of case suffixes, while not requiring the model to guess based on unavailable information. In this task, the network reads the input sentence with all nuclear case suffixes removed, and has to predict the suffix (or the absence of thereof) for each word in the sentence. For example, in (1) above, the model reads (5).

(5) Kutxazaina   bezeroa   liburua   eman
     dizkiote.

It is then expected to predict the omitted case and determiner suffixes (*-ek*, *-ak*, *-ari*, none, none). We note that we remove the suffixes only from NPs, keeping the verbs in their original forms. As the verbs encode the numbers of its argument as well as their roles, the network is exposed to all relevant information required for predicting the missing suffixes, assuming it can recover the sentence structure. In order to succeed in this task, the model should link each argument to its verb, evaluate its grammatical re-

Suffix	Prec	Rec	F1
-ek [ergative plural]	82.0	74.7	78.2
-a [absolutive singular]	88.0	83.2	85.5
-ak [abs. pl / erg. sg]	83.2	83.1	83.2
-ari [dative singular]	80.2	77.5	78.8
-ei [dative plural]	65.5	64.5	65.0
Any	95.1	91.7	93.4

Table 5: nuclear case prediction results.

lation to the verb, and choose the case suffix accordingly. Case suffixes are appended at the end of the NP. As a result, suffix recovery also requires some degree of POS tagging and NP chunking, and thus shares some similarities with shallow parsing in languages such as English. This suggests that the task of case suffix recovery in languages with complex case system such as Basque can serve as a proxy task for full parsing, while requiring a minimal amount of annotated data.

The singular absolutive determiner suffix, *-a*, also appears in the base form of some words. Therefore, for *-a* suffixed words, we have used the morphological analyzer to detect whether not the *-a* suffix is a part of the lemma. Consider the examples *ur* 'water'—*ura* 'the water-ABS' and *uda* 'summer'—*uda* 'the summer-ABS'. *-a* suffixed words not known to the analyzer were excluded from the experiment.

7.1 Results and Analysis

The results for the suffix prediction task are presented in Table 5 and Table 6. The model achieves F1 scores of 78.2 and 83.2% for the erg. plural *-ek* and absolutive singular/ergative singular *-ak* suffixes, respectively. The F1 score for the ABS singular suffix *-a* is higher — 85.5%; This might be due to the fact this suffix is unambiguous (unlike *-ak*), and the fact the absolutive is rarely omitted (unlike words suffixed with *-ek*), which implies that verb forms indicating verb-absolutive singular agreement also reliably predicts the presence of a word suffixed with -a in the sentence. Similarly to the trend in the first task, the model achieved relatively low F1 scores in the prediction of dative suffixes, *-ari* and *-ei*: 78.8% and 65.0%, respectively.

Importance of verb form Once the grammatical connection between verbs and their arguments is established, the nuclear suffix of each of the verb's arguments is deterministically determined by the form of the verb. As such, verb forms

	-ak	*-ek*	*-a*	*-ari*	*-ei*
Base	83.2	78.2	85.5	78.8	65.0
Word-only	56.0	49.5	55.2	56.5	24.2
No verb	72.0	65.4	78.1	67.5	47.3

Table 6: Summary of F1 scores for suffix prediction.

are expected to be of importance for suffix prediction. To assess this importance, we have evaluated the model in a setting in which the original verb forms are replaced by a ⟨verb⟩ token. In this setting, the model achieved F1 scores of 72.0%, 65.4%, 78.1%, 67.5%, 47.3% and 92.0% for *-ak*, *-ek*, *-a*, *-ari*, *-ei*, and the prediction of the presence of any nuclear suffix, respectively (Table 6, No verb). These results, that are far from random, indicate that factors such as the order of words in the sentence, the identity of the words (as certain words tend to accept certain cases irrespective of context), and the non-nuclear case suffixes (which are not omitted), all aid the task of nuclear-suffix prediction.

Word-only baseline Some words tend to appear more frequently in certain grammatical positions, regardless of their context. We therefore compared the model performance with a baseline of a 1-layer MLP that predicts the case suffix of each word based only its embedding vector. As expected, this baseline achieved lower F1 scores of 56.0%, 49.5%, 55.2%, 56.5%, 24.2% and 69.8% for *-ak*, *-ek*, *-a*, *-ari*, *-ei*, and the prediction of the presence of any suffix, respectively (Table 6, Words only).

Focusing on the harder cases An essential step in the process of suffix prediction is identifying the arguments of each verb. To what extent does the model rely on local cues as a proxy for this task? A simple heuristics is relating each word to its closest verb. We compared the model's performance on "easier" instances where the closest verb is grammatically connected to the word, versus "harder" instances in which the closest verb is not grammatically connected to the word.

This evaluation requires automatically judging the grammatical connection between words and verbs in the input sentence. Due to the ambiguous case suffixes, this is generally not possible in unparsed corpora. However, we focus on several special cases of sentences containing exactly 2 verbs of specific types, in which it is possible to unambiguously link certain words in the sentences to certain verbs. Since these instances consists only a fraction of the dataset, for this evaluation we have used a larger test set containing 50% of the data.

Table 2 depicts the results for sentences that contain the verb *da* 'is'. The general trend, for *da* and for several other verbs (not presented here) , is higher F1 scores in the "easier" instances. We note, however, that in these instances there is also larger absolute distance between the verb and its argument, which prevents us from drawing causal conclusions.

Diagnostic classifiers To overcome this difficulty and understand if the model encodes the grammatical connection between a word to its closest verb in the BiLSTM hidden state over a given word, we have trained a diagnostic classifier (Adi et al., 2016; Hupkes and Zuidema, 2018) that receives as an input the hidden state of a BiLSTM over a word, and predicts whether or not the closest verb (which is unseen by the diagnostic classifier) was grammatically connected to the word.

We have compared two diagnostic classifiers: a linear model, and a 1-layer MLP. A training set was created by collecting hidden states of the BiLSTM over words, and labeling each training example according to the existence of a verb-argument connection between the word over which the state was collected and its closest verb (a binary classification task). We then compared the success rate of the diagnostic classifier on instances in which the BiLSTM correctly predicted a case suffix (Table 3, BiLSTM correct), versus the instances on which the BiLSTM predicted incorrectly (Table 3, BiLSTM wrong). The results, depicted in Table 3, demonstrate that in instances in which the model predicts a wrong case suffix, the diagnostic classifier tends to inaccurately predict the connection between the closest verb and the word. For example, for sentences that contain the verb form *da*, the success rate of the linear model increases from 56.2% to 70.2% in the instances in which the BiLSTM predicted correctly. This differential success may imply a causal relation between the inference of the closest-verb grammatical connection to the word and the success in suffix prediction.

Grammatical generalization Does training on suffix recovery induce learning of grammatical generalizations such as morphosyntactic alignment (ergative, absolutive or dative), number agreement (sg / pl) and POS? To test this question, We have collected the states of our trained model over the words in sentences from the Basque Universal Dependencies dataset. Different diagnostic classifiers were then trained to predict case, number, POS and the type of the dependency edge to the head of the word. All diagnostic classifiers are MLPs with two hidden layers of sizes 100 and 50. For each task, we trained 5 models with different initializations and report those that achieved highest development set accuracy.

For nuclear case and number prediction, we limit the dataset to words suffixed with a nuclear case. In this setting, for words on which the BiLSTM predicted correctly, the MLPs perform well, predicting the correct number with an accuracy of 95.0% (majority classifier: 67.3%) and the correct case with an accuracy of 93.5% (majority: 61.7%). Even when the dataset is limited to words suffixed with the ambiguous suffix -ak, the MLP correctly distinguishes ergative and absolutive with 91.2% accuracy (majority: 65.4%). Interestingly, in a complementary setting on which the dataset is limited to words on which the BiLSTM failed in nuclear case suffix recovery, a diagnostic classifier can still be trained to achieve 74.7% accuracy in number prediction and 69.7% accuracy in case prediction. This indicates that to a large degree, the required information for correct prediction is encoded by the state of the model even when it predicts a wrong suffix.

For the prediction of POS, dependency edge to the head and any case (not just nuclear cases — 16 cases in total, including the option of an absence of case), the dataset was not limited to words suffixed with nuclear cases or to words on which the BiL-STM predicted correctly. The classifier achieves accuracies of 87.5% In POS prediction (majority: 23.2%), 85.7% in the prediction of any case (majority: 64.7%), and 69.0% for the prediction of dependency edge to the head (majority: 19.0%).

These results indicate that during training on suffix recovery, the model indeed learns, to some degree, the generalizations of number, alignment and POS, as well as some structural information (connection to the head in the dependency tree). These findings support our hypothesis that a success in case recovery entails the acquiring of some grammatical information.

8   Conclusion

In this work, we have performed of series of controlled experiments to evaluate the performance of LSTMs in agreement prediction, a task that requires implicit understanding of syntactic structure. We have focused on Basque, a language that is characterized by a very different grammar compared with the languages studied for this task so far. We have proposed two tasks for the evaluation of agreement prediction: verb number prediction and suffix recovery.

Both tasks were found to be more challenging than agreement prediction in other languages studied so far. We have evaluated different contributing factors to that difficulty, such as the presence of ambiguous case suffixes. We have used diagnostic classifiers to test hypotheses on the inner representation the model had acquired, and found tentative evidence for the use of shallow heuristics as a proxy of hierarchical structure, as well as for the acquisition of grammatical information during case recovery training.

These results suggest that agreement prediction in Basque could be a challenging benchmark for the evaluation of the syntactic capabilities of neural sequence models. The task of case-recovery can be utilized in other languages with a case system, and provide a readily-available benchmark for the evaluation of implicit learning of syntactic structure, that does not require the creation of expert-annotated corpora. A future line of work we suggest is investigating what syntactic representations are shared between case recovery and full parsing, i.e., to what extent does a model trained on case recovery learn the parse tree of the sentence, and whether transfer learning from case-recovery would improve parsing performance.

Acknowledgements

We would like to thank Mikel L. Forcada and Mikel Artetxe for discussions regarding Basque grammar and the anonymous reviewers for their helpful comments.

References

Yossi Adi, Einat Kermany, Yonatan Belinkov, Ofer Lavi, and Yoav Goldberg. 2016. Fine-grained analysis of sentence embeddings using auxiliary prediction tasks. *CoRR*, abs/1608.04207.

M. Aranzabe, A. Atutxa, K. Bengoetxea, A. Daz de Ilarraza, I. Goenaga, K. Gojenola, and L. Uria. 2015. Automatic conversion of the basque dependency treebank to universal dependencies. In *Proceedings of the 14th International Workshop on Treebanks and Linguistic Theories, TLT 2015*.

Jean-Philippe Bernardy and Shalom Lappin. 2017. Using deep neural networks to learn syntactic agreement. *LiLT (Linguistic Issues in Language Technology)*, 15.

Kyunghyun Cho, Bart van Merrienboer, Caglar Gulcehre, Dzmitry Bahdanau, Fethi Bougares,

Holger Schwenk, and Yoshua Bengio. 2014. Learning Phrase Representations using RNN Encoder–Decoder for Statistical Machine Translation. In *Proceedings of the 2014 Conference on Empirical Methods in Natural Language Processing (EMNLP)*, pages 1724–1734, Doha, Qatar. Association for Computational Linguistics.

Junyoung Chung, Caglar Gulcehre, KyungHyun Cho, and Yoshua Bengio. 2014. Empirical Evaluation of Gated Recurrent Neural Networks on Sequence Modeling. *arXiv:1412.3555 [cs]*.

Rudolf P. G. de Rijk. 2007. *Standard Basque: A Progressive Grammar*. MIT Press.

Timothy Dozat and Christopher D. Manning. 2016. Deep biaffine attention for neural dependency parsing. *CoRR*, abs/1611.01734.

Chris Dyer, Miguel Ballesteros, Wang Ling, Austin Matthews, and Noah A. Smith. 2015. Transition-based dependency parsing with stack long short-term memory. In *Proceedings of the 53rd Annual Meeting of the Association for Computational Linguistics and the 7th International Joint Conference on Natural Language Processing of the Asian Federation of Natural Language Processing, ACL 2015, July 26-31, 2015, Beijing, China, Volume 1: Long Papers*, pages 334–343.

M. L. Forcada, M. Ginest-Rosell, J. Nordfalk, J. O'Regan, S. Ortiz-Rojas, J. A. Pérez-Ortiz, F. Sánchez-Martínez, G. Ramrez-Sánchez, and F. M. Tyers. 2011. Apertium: a free/open-source platform for rule-based machine translation. *Machine Translation*, 25(2):127–144.

Mireia Ginest-Rosell, Gema Ramrez-Sánchez, Sergio Ortiz-Rojas, Francis M Tyers, and Mikel L Forcada. 2009. Development of a free Basque to Spanish machine translation system. *Procesamiento del Lenguaje Natural*, 43:187–195.

Yoav Goldberg. 2017. *Neural Network Methods for Natural Language Processing*. Synthesis Lectures on Human Language Technologies. Morgan & Claypool Publishers.

Alex Graves. 2013. Generating sequences with recurrent neural networks. *CoRR*, abs/1308.0850.

Kristina Gulordava, Piotr Bojanowski, Edouard Grave, Tal Linzen, and Marco Baroni. 2018. Colorless green recurrent networks dream hierarchically. In *Proceedings of the 2018 Conference of the North American Chapter of the Association for Computational Linguistics: Human Language Technologies, NAACL-HLT 2018, New Orleans, Louisiana, USA, June 1-6, 2018, Volume 1 (Long Papers)*, pages 1195–1205.

Sepp Hochreiter and Jürgen Schmidhuber. 1997. Long short-term memory. *Neural computation*, 9(8):1735–1780.

Dieuwke Hupkes and Willem H. Zuidema. 2018. Visualisation and 'diagnostic classifiers' reveal how recurrent and recursive neural networks process hierarchical structure (extended abstract). In *Proceedings of the Twenty-Seventh International Joint Conference on Artificial Intelligence, IJCAI 2018, July 13-19, 2018, Stockholm, Sweden.*, pages 5617–5621.

Rafal Józefowicz, Oriol Vinyals, Mike Schuster, Noam Shazeer, and Yonghui Wu. 2016. Exploring the limits of language modeling. *CoRR*, abs/1602.02410.

Dan Jurafsky, He He, Peng Qi, and Urvashi Khandelwal. 2018. Sharp nearby, fuzzy far away: How neural language models use context. In *Proceedings of the 56th Annual Meeting of the Association for Computational Linguistics, ACL 2018, Melbourne, Australia, July 15-20, 2018, Volume 1: Long Papers*, pages 284–294.

Andrej Karpathy, Justin Johnson, and Fei-Fei Li. 2015. Visualizing and understanding recurrent networks. *CoRR*, abs/1506.02078.

Diederik P. Kingma and Jimmy Ba. 2014. Adam: A method for stochastic optimization. *CoRR*, abs/1412.6980.

Eliyahu Kiperwasser and Yoav Goldberg. 2016. Simple and accurate dependency parsing using bidirectional LSTM feature representations. *TACL*, 4:313–327.

Itziar Laka. 1996. *A brief grammar of Euskara – the Basque language*. EHU Euskararako Errektoreordetza.

Tal Linzen, Emmanuel Dupoux, and Yoav Goldberg. 2016. Assessing the ability of LSTMs to learn syntax-sensitive dependencies. *Transactions of the Association for Computational Linguistics*, 4:521–535.

Gábor Melis, Chris Dyer, and Phil Blunsom. 2017. On the state of the art of evaluation in neural language models. *CoRR*, abs/1707.05589.

Xing Shi, Inkit Padhi, and Kevin Knight. 2016. Does string-based neural MT learn source syntax? In *Proceedings of the 2016 Conference on Empirical Methods in Natural Language Processing, EMNLP 2016, Austin, Texas, USA, November 1-4, 2016*, pages 1526–1534.

Dani Yogatama, Yishu Miao, Gabor Melis, Wang Ling, Adhiguna Kuncoro, Chris Dyer, and Phil Blunsom. 2018. Memory architectures in recurrent neural network language models. In *International Conference on Learning Representations*.

Rearranging the Familiar: Testing Compositional Generalization in Recurrent Networks

João Loula
École Polytechnique
Facebook AI Research
joaoloula@fb.com

Marco Baroni
Facebook AI Research
mbaroni@fb.com

Brenden M. Lake
New York University
Facebook AI Research
brenden@nyu.edu

Abstract

Systematic compositionality is the ability to recombine meaningful units with regular and predictable outcomes, and it's seen as key to the human capacity for generalization in language. Recent work (Lake and Baroni, 2018) has studied systematic compositionality in modern seq2seq models using generalization to novel navigation instructions in a grounded environment as a probing tool. Lake and Baroni's main experiment required the models to quickly bootstrap the meaning of new words. We extend this framework here to settings where the model needs only to recombine well-trained functional words (such as "*around*" and "*right*") in novel contexts. Our findings confirm and strengthen the earlier ones: seq2seq models can be impressively good at generalizing to novel combinations of previously-seen input, but only when they receive extensive training on the specific pattern to be generalized (e.g., generalizing from many examples of "X *around right*" to "*jump around right*"), while failing when generalization requires novel application of compositional rules (e.g., inferring the meaning of "*around right*" from those of "*right*" and "*around*").

1 Introduction

Human language learning enjoys a good kind of combinatorial explosion — if a person knows the meaning of "*to run*" and that of "*slowly*", she can immediately understand what it means "*to run slowly*", even if she has never uttered or heard this expression before. This is an example of *compositionality*, the algebraic capacity to understand and produce novel combinations from known components (Montague, 1970). This principle helps to explain how, when acquiring a language, we can quickly bootstrap to a potentially infinite number of expressions from very limited training data (Chomsky, 1957).

Neural networks have recently been successfully applied to many tasks requiring considerable generalization abilities (LeCun et al., 2015), including applications in the domain of natural language (Goldberg, 2017). However, it has also been observed that they require a very large number of training examples to succeed, which suggests that they lack compositional abilities (Lake et al., 2017). There has been a substantial earlier debate on the extent to which neural networks display some degree of compositional generalization (e.g., Fodor and Pylyshyn, 1988; Christiansen and Chater, 1994; Marcus, 1998; Phillips, 1998; Chang, 2002; Marcus, 2003; van der Velde et al., 2004; Bowers et al., 2009; Botvinick and Plaut, 2009; Brakel and Frank, 2009; Frank, 2014). Recently, Lake and Baroni (2018) revisited these issues in light of the latest advances in deep neural networks for natural language processing.

The authors introduced the SCAN dataset for studying compositionality in sequence-to-sequence (seq2seq) neural network models (Sutskever et al., 2014). SCAN is a simple language-driven navigation environment that supports one-shot learning experiments, where the trained agent must execute test commands that it has never encountered in training, but are assembled from the same components as the training commands.

Lake and Baroni found that state-of-the-art recurrent neural networks (RNNs) showed impressive zero-shot generalization capabilities when commands were arbitrarily split between train and test set, but they failed in cases that required *systematic* compositionality, that is, to extract algebraic composition rules from the training examples. To begin with, RNNs failed when they had to generalize to commands requiring longer action sequences to be executed. This is not too surprising, as longer sequences are notoriously challeng-

Proceedings of the 2018 EMNLP Workshop BlackboxNLP: Analyzing and Interpreting Neural Networks for NLP, pages 108–114
Brussels, Belgium, November 1, 2018. ©2018 Association for Computational Linguistics

ing for seq2seq models (Cho et al., 2014). More interestingly, Lake and Baroni found that RNNs do not correctly generalize the usage of a new action verb (shown in isolation during training) to contexts that are familiar from other verbs. In other words, RNNs fail the following basic compositionality test: Even after they acquired the meaning of *"to run again"* and *"to dax"*, they do not understand *"to dax again"* on first encounter.

As Lake and Baroni show, the generalization problem is linked to the fact that RNNs fail to learn a representation (an embedding) for the new verb (*"to dax"*) that is similar to those of known verbs (*"to run"*, *"to look"*), and consequently it cannot rely on similarity information to correctly generalize verb usage. This is arguably more of an instance of the problem of quickly learning meaningful new-word embeddings (Herbelot and Baroni, 2017; Lampinen and McClelland, 2017), than strictly a failure of compositionality.

In this paper, we repurpose SCAN to test another kind of compositionality, namely one that requires combining highly familiar words in new ways to create novel meaning. As illustrated above, this is what we do when we combine a functional term such as *"slowly"* with the verb *"to run"* to obtain the phrase *"to run slowly"*. Or, in terms of the SCAN commands that we test here, this is what is required to understand an expression such as *"jump around right"* when the meanings of *"jump"*, *"right"* and *"around"* are known.

Our results confirm and strengthen the conclusions of Lake and Baroni. On the one hand, RNNs do show a considerable degree of generalization in our experiments as well. However, their performance dramatically decreases as the difference between training and testing becomes more systematic, even though all test examples could be correctly processed by relying on simple composition rules amply illustrated in the training data.

2 Generalizing functional terms with SCAN

The SCAN dataset (Lake and Baroni, 2018) presents the problem of translating commands from a simplified natural language to a sequence of actions, framed as a seq2seq task (Sutskever et al., 2014). The commands are generated by a phrase-structure grammar and then converted into actions by a semantic interpretation function.

By way of illustration, let us take a prototypical SCAN command like *"turn right twice and jump around left"*. This command's building blocks are *"turn right"* and "Primitive *around left"*, which are part of SCAN's 12 *templates*, a collection of base expressions that present a great deal of symmetry over actions, spatial terms, and manner adverbs (Table 1). Some of these templates can operate over different Primitives (*"jump"*, *"walk"*, *"run"*, or *"look"*), mapping them systematically to their correspondent output [Primitive] ("JUMP", "WALK", "RUN", and "LOOK"). The templates can in turn be combined using the conjunctions *"and"* and *"after"* and quantified by *"twice"* and *"thrice"* for a total of 20,910 commands: these include things like *"walk left after look opposite left"*, *"turn around right thrice"*, *"jump right and run left"* etc.

Lake and Baroni (2018) present three experiments based on different train-test splits: a random split, a split where the test set contains commands requiring longer action sequences than the training set, and a split where the test set contains commands with compositions of primitives of which few examples exist in the training set (in the limit, the primitives are only presented in isolation). Their main conclusion is that neural networks, though surprisingly good at zero-shot generalization to novel commands, are still far from systematic compositionality. In the first split, networks are able to achieve high accuracy with relatively few training examples. In the second and third ones, where the training/testing gap is larger yet there exist systematic rules linking the training and test sets, the same models fail.

The main contribution of this paper is showing how the SCAN dataset can be repurposed to analyze compositionality with known functional terms used in new contexts, where it is not a matter of quickly learning a new embedding as in the original primitive generalization experiment, but rather of adequately recombining familiar words. The key insight is that manner adverbs in the dataset, such as *"around"* and *"opposite"*, act as second-order modifiers, operating over the spatial modifiers *"left"* and *"right"* and the primitives *"look"*, *"walk"*, *"run"* and *"jump"*. This opens up the possibility of splitting the dataset such that examples like *"walk left"*, *"walk right"*, and *"jump around left"* are seen in the training set, and at test time the network must piece these together to interpret commands like *"jump around right"*, which

Template	Command	Target
1	*"turn left"*	LTURN
2	*"turn right"*	RTURN
3	*"Primitive left"*	LTURN [Primitive]
4	*"Primitive right"*	RTURN [Primitive]
5	*"turn opposite left"*	LTURN LTURN
6	*"turn opposite right"*	RTURN RTURN
7	*"Primitive opposite left"*	LTURN LTURN [Primitive]
8	*"Primitive opposite right"*	RTURN RTURN [Primitive]
9	*"turn around left"*	LTURN LTURN LTURN LTURN
10	*"turn around right"*	RTURN RTURN RTURN RTURN
11	*"Primitive around left"*	LTURN [Primitive] LTURN [Primitive] LTURN [Primitive] LTURN [Primitive]
12	*"Primitive around right"*	RTURN [Primitive] RTURN [Primitive] RTURN [Primitive] RTURN [Primitive]

Table 1: All command templates in the SCAN dataset, along with the target output. Here, "Primitive" can stand for *"jump"*, *"walk"*, *"run"*, or *"look"*, with the corresponding output [Primitive] being "JUMP", "WALK", "RUN", or "LOOK".

contain only extensively seen words, but presented in a new context. In other words, the network must internalize the symmetry between the terms *"left"* and *"right"* that is evident across SCAN (by comparing templates 1 and 2, templates 3 and 4, etc. in Table 1), and use it to learn abstract rules for higher-order modifiers such as *"opposite"*.

3   Experiments

All reported accuracies correspond to the percentage of instances where the model successfully predicted the entire output sequence. All experiments were run using the overall best neural network from Lake and Baroni (2018): a seq2seq 2-layer, 200-unit LSTM with 50% dropout (Figure 1). The values of all other hyperparameters were those specified by Lake and Baroni. This model was very successful in their basic, random-split experiment, where it achieved 99.8% accuracy. We also tried the best attention-augmented model from Lake and Baroni, but it was outperformed by the overall-best in all experiments, and is thus omitted here. All test-set accuracies are reported with mean and standard deviation across 5 runs: in experiments where the splits were created by random sampling, each run corresponds to a different sample. Though the size of the training set varies across conditions, the training regime is always fixed at 100k presentations (approximately 5 epochs for the condition with the largest training set): in practice, this was sufficient for near-

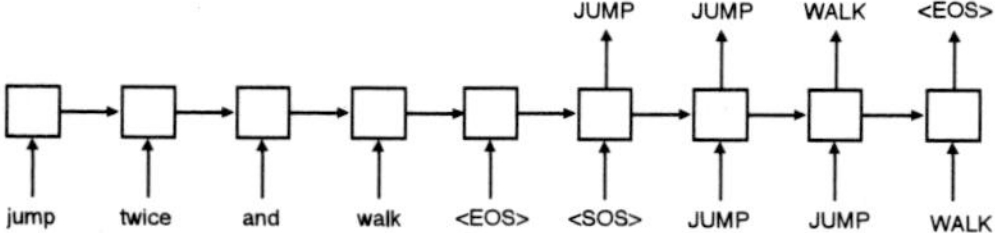

Figure 1: Illustration of the sequence-to-sequence model operating on the SCAN dataset. The network takes a command such as *"jump twice and walk"* and must convert it to a sequence of actions, in this case "JUMP", "JUMP", "WALK". Reproduced from Lake and Baroni (2018) with permission.

perfect training set accuracy in all conditions[1].

Experiment 1: Generalizing to novel templates

In order to probe the network's ability to recombine well-trained words as well as to assess the factors that render that task easier or harder, we compared performance across 4 different train-test splits. In the first one we leave out examples containing the subcommand *"jump around right"* (a specific instance of Template 12) whereas in the other 3 we leave out all instances of different templates described in-depth in Table 1. In all of the splits, the network is tasked with generalizing to novel commands involving *"right"* by exploiting the *"left"*/*"right"* symmetry in the training set and/or the distributional similarity among primitives. We present the splits in order of conjectured increasing complexity, in terms of systematic gaps

---

[1]All train-test splits are available along with the original SCAN dataset at: https://github.com/brendenlake/SCAN.

between training and test sets. Table 2 shows examples of commands in the training and test set for the different conditions.

- **jump around right**: The test set consists of all commands containing the phrase "*jump around right*", while all remaining commands are in the training set, including uses of "*jump around left*" and "Primitive *around right*" for the other primitives. The network is thus exposed to plenty of evidence that "*jump*" has the same distribution as the other primitives (thus, it should easily discover the similarity of "*jump*" to the other primitives), and it sees many instances of the "Primitive *around right*" template with all other primitive fillers but "*jump*".

- **Primitive *right***: The test set consists of all commands containing "Primitive *right*" (Template 4 in Table 1), with all remaining templates (and their conjunctions and quantifications) in the training set. In this case, the network is exposed to "Primitive *left*" and many examples illustrating the "*left*"/"*right*" symmetry during training, and it must bootstrap to the *simplest* usage of "*right*" at test time.

- **Primitive *opposite right***: The test set consists of all commands containing templates of the form "Primitive *opposite right*" (Template 8), with the remaining templates (and their conjunctions and quantifications) in the training set. Here, the network is never exposed to the "Primitive *opposite right*" template with *any* primitive filler, and it has to bootstrap the combined effect of "*opposite*" and "*right*" based on seeing them applied independently, plus the "*left*"/"*right*" symmetry.

- **Primitive *around right***: The test set consists of all commands containing templates of the form "Primitive *around right*" (Template 12), with the remaining templates in the training set. This is analogous to "Primitive *opposite right*", but requires executing a longer action sequence due to the different SCAN semantics of "*opposite*" (two turning+Primitive steps to turn in the opposite direction) vs. "*around*" (four turn-

ing+Primitive steps to perform a full roundabout, refer to Table 1).

Observe that "*turn*" in SCAN has a different semantics from the other actions verbs (see Table 1). We found that removing all commands where "*turn*" appeared in the target expression (e.g. "*turn around right*" in the "Primitive *around right*" condition, "*turn opposite right*" in the "Primitive *opposite right*" condition etc.) from both training and test sets systematically increased accuracy, and we thus report results in this setup.

Results: A summary of the results is presented in Table 3. We see that the network had no problem generalizing to "*jump around right*" when being exposed to all commands containing this template with all other possible fillers. This confirms Lake and Baroni's result that modern RNNs do to some extent generalize to new combinations. However, the remaining results also confirm their finding of a lack of systematicity in generalization.

Interestingly, the poor performance in the "Primitive *right*" condition shows that generalization is problematic for RNNs not only when they have to bootstrap to *longer* constructions, but also when they have to systematically generalize to *shorter* ones (a network exposed to "*run left*", "*run opposite right*", "*jump left*", "*jump around right*" etc. fails to execute "*run right*" or "*jump right*").

The dramatic difference in accuracy between training without "*around right*" commands vs. training on all templates except "*jump around right*" commands (2.46% vs. 98.43%) points to the network being able to generalize the application of "*around right*" across primitives, but not being able to directly apply "*right*" and "*around*" to a primitive, without having seen them presented together. The failure modes in the "Primitive *around right*" condition further showcase, qualitatively, the lack of systematicity. For instance, though the network correctly interprets the complex expression "*jump right after walk around right*", it fails to do so for the subcommand "*walk around right*", where it flips one of the four "*right*" turns for a "*left*" one.

Surprisingly, the network, while still far from perfect, has considerably higher accuracy (47.62%) when generalizing to "*opposite right*", a simpler command of the same nature as "*around right*". This suggests that memory factors (learning to repeat the relevant steps 4 times instead of

Condition	Example train commands	Example test commands
jump around right	*"jump left"*, *"jump around left"*, *"walk around right"*	*"jump around right"*, *"jump around right and walk"*
Primitive *right*	*"jump left"*, *"walk around right"*	*"jump right"*, *"walk right"*
Primitive *opposite right*	*"jump left"*, *"jump opposite left"*, *"walk right"*	*"jump opposite right"*, *"walk opposite right"*
Primitive *around right*	*"jump left"*, *"jump around left"*, *"walk right"*	*"jump around right"*, *"walk around right"*

Table 2: Example train and test commands for different conditions of Experiment 1. Note that the train commands are meant to illustrate relevant constructions, but the training set always contains all possible commands not in the test set.

Condition	Acc. ± s.d.	Test size
jump around right	98.43% ±0.54%	1,173
Primitive *right*	23.49% ±8.09%	4,476
Primitive *opposite right*	47.62% ±17.72%	4,476
Primitive *around right*	2.46% ±2.68%	4,476

Table 3: Experiment 1: test set accuracy mean and standard deviation for different train-test splits on the SCAN dataset. Test set sizes are also reported.

2) interact with the network ability to extract the right patterns.

Experiment 2: Impact of filler variety in learning a complex template

One interesting result of Experiment 1 is that the number of distinct primitive fillers of a template that the network sees in training affects its ability to generalize the template, as shown by the striking performance difference between the "Primitive *around right*" (0 fillers of the relevant template seen in training, very low accuracy) and "*jump around right*" conditions (3 fillers seen in training, near-perfect generalization). In Experiment 2, we take a detailed look at this phenomenon by varying the number of primitive fillers for this template (Template 12 in Table 1) that the model observes during training, with the goal of learning the full abstract template. We fix the test set across all conditions by making it consist only of the commands containing the expression "*jump around right*" — this allows for more direct comparison across the conditions. Again, commands containing the expression "*turn around right*" were removed to avoid interference. The different conditions for this experiment are, in order of decreasing difficulty:

- *0 fillers*: The training set contains **no** examples of Template 12, e.g., no command of the form "Primitive *around right*". It does contain all other complete templates (1-11) in Table 1.

- *1 filler*: The training set has commands containing "*look around right*" for Template 12 as well as all other complete templates in Table 1.[2]

- *2 fillers*: The training set has commands containing "*look around right*" and "*walk around right*" for Template 12 as well as all other complete templates in Table 1.

- *3 fillers*: The training set has commands containing the templates "*look around right*", "*walk around right*" and "*run around right*" for Template 12 as well as all other complete templates in Table 1.

Each new template corresponds to roughly an additional 1,100 distinct examples in the training set.[3] Note that the actual primitives chosen for each condition do not matter, as their distribution is identical.

Results: A summary of the results is shown in Figure 2. We observe that the network only needs examples of 1 primitive filler to start generalizing

---

[2]If a command contains both "look around right" and "Primitive + *around right*" for another primitive, then that command is held out. This is true of the other conditions as well.

[3]We remind the reader that, though the number of distinct examples in the training set varies across conditions, the total number of presentations seen during the training regime is fixed at 100k

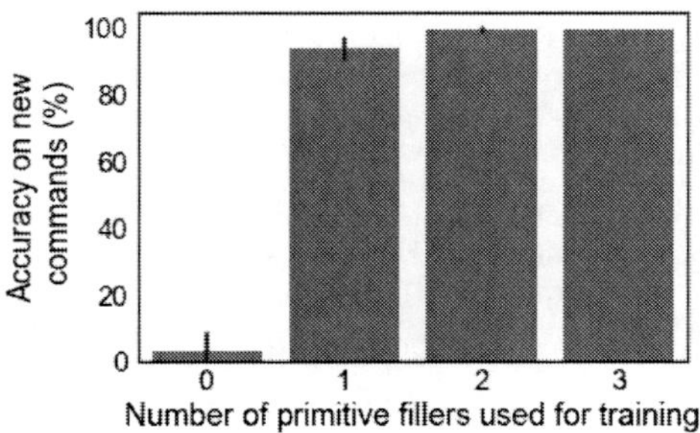

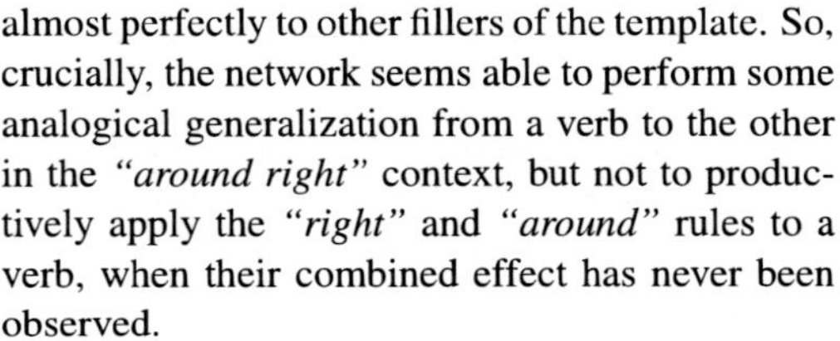

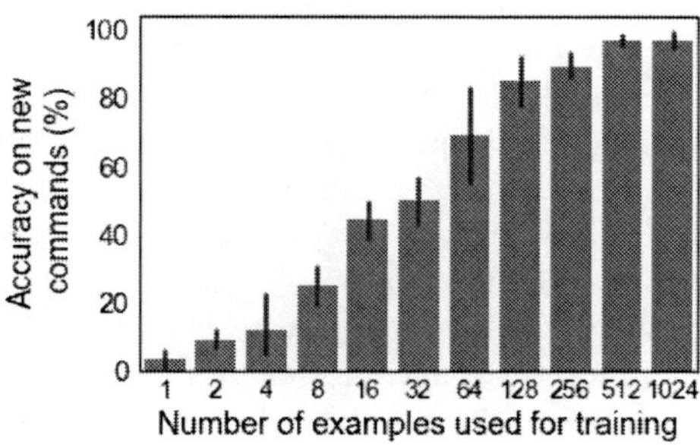

Figure 2: Experiment 2: accuracy on held-out commands containing "*jump around right*" after training on sets including a different number of commands of the form "Primitive *around right*". Error bars are bootstrapped 95% confidence intervals.

Figure 3: Experiment 3: accuracy on held-out commands containing "*jump around right*" after training on sets including a different number of commands containing "*walk around right*". Error bars are bootstrapped 95% confidence intervals.

almost perfectly to other fillers of the template. So, crucially, the network seems able to perform some analogical generalization from a verb to the other in the *"around right"* context, but not to productively apply the *"right"* and *"around"* rules to a verb, when their combined effect has never been observed.

Experiment 3: Impact of number of distinct training examples in learning a complex template

We consider here a further level of granularity. Adding one additional primitive filler, as we did in Experiment 2, corresponds to about 1,100 additional distinct training examples. Are they all needed, or is it sufficient to observe the target complex template in a smaller number of examples? This question is the subject of Experiment 3. In order to analyze the sample complexity of the model's generalizations, we now take the *0 filler* condition from Experiment 2 and progressively add examples from the *1 filler* condition. More precisely, we randomly add 1, 2, 4, 8, 16, 32, 64, 128, 256, 512, or 1,024 commands containing "*look around right*", but no other command of the form "Primitive *around right*", to the training set of the *0 filler* condition. As before, all other templates (1-11) and their conjunctions and quantifications are also provided during training. Note that 1,024 is approximately the difference in distinct examples between the *0* and *1 filler* conditions, such that this experiment spans the entire range from one to the other.

Results: A summary of the results is shown in

Figure 3. On the one hand, the sample complexity with which performance ramps up is quite impressive, being at a respectable 70% with 64 additional examples and peaking at 512 examples. On the other hand, the very fact that performance increases gradually, and that it takes so long for the network to peak points to a failure to generalize systematically: instead of piecing together the general rule, the network seems to be rather accumulating evidence for some specific cases.

4 Conclusion

Our findings complement those of Lake and Baroni (2018) now in a setting where, instead of having to learn a new embedding, the network needs only to recombine well-trained functional words, such as *"right"* and *"around"*. The results show the impressive generalization capabilities of seq2seq models, correctly interpreting complex new combinations of previously seen commands, but also their lack of systematicity. On the one hand, as shown in Experiment 2, the fact that the network is able to correctly generalize to new constructions of the form "Primitive *around right*" after only seeing this template with one filler primitive is quite impressive. On the other hand, Experiment 1 suggests that this generalization is not based on the network being able to combine systematic composition rules associated to the functional terms *"right"* and *"around"*. Experiment 3 further confirms that generalization is not systematic in nature, and that the network still needs to be shown a wealth of additional examples in the same context as the test set in order to achieve it, even though it has already observed ample evidence for all the test words in the training set.

Future directions include probing what kind of training set evidence is crucial for systematic generalization, and how the ability to generalize in this manner differs across different kinds of commands (primitives, manner adverbs, spatial expressions, etc.). Further empirical investigations might focus on generalization of functional terms in real-life seq2seq tasks, such as machine translation. On the modeling side, we need to study what are the right priors to encode in seq2seq models to endow them with the ability of systematic generalization without losing their generality.

Acknowledgments

We'd like to thank Joost Bastings, Kyunghyun Cho and Jason Weston for helpful comments and conversations.

References

Matthew Botvinick and David Plaut. 2009. Empirical and computational support for context-dependent representations of serial order: Reply to Bowers, Damian, and Davis (2009). *Psychological Review*, 116(4):998–1002.

Jeffrey Bowers, Markus Damian, and Colin David. 2009. A fundamental limitation of the conjunctive codes learned in PDP models of cognition: Comment on Botvinick and Plaut (2006). *Psychological Review*, 116(4):986–997.

Philémon Brakel and Stefan Frank. 2009. Strong systematicity in sentence processing by simple recurrent networks. In *Proceedings of CogSci*, pages 1599–1604, Amsterdam, the Netherlands.

Frankilin Chang. 2002. Symbolically speaking: a connectionist model of sentence production. *Cognitive Science*, 26:609–651.

Kyunghyun Cho, Bart Van Merriënboer, Dzmitry Bahdanau, and Yoshua Bengio. 2014. On the properties of neural machine translation: Encoder-decoder approaches. *arXiv preprint arXiv:1409.1259*.

Noam Chomsky. 1957. *Syntactic structures*. Walter de Gruyter.

Morten Christiansen and Nick Chater. 1994. Generalization and connectionist language learning. *Mind & Language*, 9(3):273–287.

Jerry A Fodor and Zenon W Pylyshyn. 1988. Connectionism and cognitive architecture: A critical analysis. *Cognition*, 28:3–71.

Stefan Frank. 2014. Getting real about systematicity. In Paco Calvo and John Symons, editors, *The architecture of cognition: Rethinking Fodor and Pylyshyn's systematicity challenge*, pages 147–164. MIT Press, Cambridge, MA.

Yoav Goldberg. 2017. *Neural Network Methods in Natural Language Processing*. Morgan & Claypool Publishers.

Aurélie Herbelot and Marco Baroni. 2017. High-risk learning: acquiring new word vectors from tiny data. In *Proceedings of EMNLP*, pages 304–309, Copenhagen, Denmark.

Brenden Lake and Marco Baroni. 2018. Generalization without systematicity: On the compositional skills of sequence-to-sequence recurrent networks. In *Proceedings of ICML*, pages 2879–2888, Stockholm, Sweden.

Brenden M Lake, Tomer D Ullman, Joshua B Tenenbaum, and Samuel J Gershman. 2017. Building machines that learn and think like people. *Behavioral and Brain Sciences*.

Andrew Kyle Lampinen and James L McClelland. 2017. One-shot and few-shot learning of word embeddings. *CoRR*.

Yann LeCun, Yoshua Bengio, and Geoffrey Hinton. 2015. Deep learning. *Nature*, 521:436–444.

Gary F Marcus. 1998. Rethinking Eliminative Connectionism. *Cognitive Psychology*, 282(37):243–282.

Gary F Marcus. 2003. *The Algebraic Mind: Integrating Connectionism and Cognitive Science*. MIT Press, Cambridge, MA.

Richard Montague. 1970. Universal grammar. *Theoria*, 36(3):373–398.

Steven Phillips. 1998. Are feedforward and recurrent networks systematic? analysis and implications for a connectionist cognitive architecture. *Connection Science*, 10:137–160.

Ilya Sutskever, Oriol Vinyals, and Quoc V Le. 2014. Sequence to sequence learning with neural networks. In *Advances in neural information processing systems*, pages 3104–3112.

Frank van der Velde, Gwendid van der Voort van der Kleij, and Marc de Kamps. 2004. Lack of combinatorial productivity in language processing with simple recurrent networks. *Connection Science*, 16(1):21–46.

Evaluating the Ability of LSTMs to Learn Context-Free Grammars

Luzi Sennhauser
Federal Institute of Technology
Zurich, Switzerland
Massachusetts Institute of Technology
Cambridge, MA, USA
`luzis@student.ethz.ch`

Robert C. Berwick
LIDS, Room 32-D728
Massachusetts Institute of Technology
Cambridge, MA, USA
`berwick@csail.mit.edu`

Abstract

While long short-term memory (LSTM) neural net architectures are designed to capture sequence information, human language is generally composed of hierarchical structures. This raises the question as to whether LSTMs can learn hierarchical structures. We explore this question with a well-formed bracket prediction task using two types of brackets modeled by an LSTM.

Demonstrating that such a system is learnable by an LSTM is the first step in demonstrating that the entire class of CFLs is also learnable. We observe that the model requires exponential memory in terms of the number of characters and embedded depth, where a sub-linear memory should suffice.

Still, the model does more than memorize the training input. It learns how to distinguish between relevant and irrelevant information. On the other hand, we also observe that the model does not generalize well.

We conclude that LSTMs do not learn the relevant underlying context-free rules, suggesting the good overall performance is attained rather by an efficient way of evaluating nuisance variables. LSTMs are a way to quickly reach good results for many natural language tasks, but to understand and generate natural language one has to investigate other concepts that can make more direct use of natural language's structural nature.

1 Introduction

Composing hierarchical structure for natural language is an extremely powerful tool for human language generation. These structures are of great importance in order to extract semantic interpretation (Berwick and Chomsky, 2016) and enable us to produce a vast repertoire of sentences via a very small set of rules. Having acquired such a set of rules, it is easy to construct new structures without having previously seen similar examples.

For purposes of external communication, the syntactic structures generated by grammars must be "flattened" or linearized into a sequential output form (e.g. written, signed, or spoken). When reading such a (linearized) text, hearing a spoken sentence or observing a signed language, the structure has to be recovered implicitly to recover the original meaning (i.e., parsing).

In this study, we investigate whether Long Short-Term Memory (LSTM) models (Hochreiter and Schmidhuber, 1997) possess this same ability as humans do: inferring rule-based structure from a linear representation. Everaert et al. (2015) show clearly that there are phenomena in human language that can only be understood by taking the underlying hierarchical structure into account. For neural networks to do the same, it is therefore essential to acquire the underlying structure of sentences.

Recurrent neural networks are often used for tasks like language modeling (Mikolov et al., 2010; Sundermeyer et al., 2012), parsing (Vinyals et al., 2015; Kiperwasser and Goldberg, 2016; Dyer et al., 2016), machine translation (Bahdanau et al., 2014), and morphological compositions (Kim et al., 2016). LSTMs are inherently sequential models. Since the hierarchical structures appearing in natural language often correlate with sequential statistical features, it can be difficult to evaluate whether an LSTM learns the underlying rules of the sentence's syntax or alternatively simply learns sequential statistical correlations. In this paper we carry out experiments to determine this.

We set up our experiments by posing the LSTM with a bracket completion problem having two possible bracket types, a so-called Dyck Language. A model which recognizes this language has to infer rules of the underlying structure.

Proceedings of the 2018 EMNLP Workshop BlackboxNLP: Analyzing and Interpreting Neural Networks for NLP, pages 115–124
Brussels, Belgium, November 1, 2018. ©2018 Association for Computational Linguistics

Furthermore, a system that can solve this task is able to recognize every context-free grammar (see section 3 regarding Dyck Languages via the Chomsky-Schützenberger theorem for why this is so).

By analyzing the intermediate states of the corresponding LSTM networks, observing generalization behaviours, and evaluating the memory demands of the model we investigate whether LSTMs acquire rules as opposed to statistical regularities.

2 Related work

It has been shown that LSTMs are able to count and partly acquire for context-free languages like $a^n b^n$ and simple context-sensitive languages (Gers and Schmidhuber, 2001; Rodriguez, 2001). We note that in contrast to the language we investigate here, $a^n b^n$ may be considered the "simplest" context-free language, since it can be generated by a grammar with just one transition.

The question as to whether LSTMs can infer rules on a natural language corpus, e.g., for subject-verb agreement, was initially explored by others such as (Linzen et al., 2016). Liska et al. (2018) investigated the memorization vs. generalization issue for LSTMs for function composition: they showed that if an LSTM learns the mapping from a string-set A to B and from B to C, then the direct mapping from A to C can partly be learned. We use the same method and model for a different task – instead of function composition we evaluate it for bracket matching.

Since most of the time it is challenging to determine what is actually going on with respect to the neural network's internal state, several attempts have been made to visualize a neural network's intermediate states with the goal of making them interpretable (Rauber et al., 2017; Karpathy et al., 2015; Krakovna and Doshi-Velez, 2016). For several simple copy and palindrome language tasks, it has been shown that RNNs learn a fractal encoding similar to a binary expansion of the input (Tabor, 2000; Grüning, 2006; Kirov and Frank, 2012). With the same objective we use another, recently introduced method to investigate the internal states.

While here we investigate the ability of how well structural information can be stored in originally sequential models, other approaches are currently being taken to move from sequential models to structural ones, e.g. to hardwire structural properties into the model's architecture (Tai et al., 2015; Kiperwasser and Goldberg, 2016; Joulin and Mikolov, 2015); to make a larger external memory available to the network (Graves et al., 2014; Sukhbaatar et al., 2015); or to make the network architecture dynamic (Looks et al., 2017).

Finally, we note that thanks to careful reviewing, we were made aware of Bernardy's work (2018), that addresses essentially the same task as the one we tackle: He investigated also the generalization behaviour of LSTMs for a Dyck-language corpus with several bracket types. He investigated generalization for sentences by concatenating several training sentences; or embedding training sentences in a centrally embedded bracket string. In contrast, we evaluate generalization by training sentences on a certain feature (number of characters, embedded depth) and testing the resulting model on the out-of-sample sentences. By this method, we strive to reduce the probability of similar sub-strings in the training versus the test set.

3 Corpus

When dealing with natural language, there are many side effects or nuisance variables – e.g. words occurring more often in certain correlative contexts or clusters than others. These can influence any classification and experimental result. To minimize such effects, we conducted all experiments on artificial corpora.

The Chomsky-Schützenberger theorem (Chomsky and Schützenberger, 1963; Autebert et al., 1997) about representing context-free language (CFL) states the following: "For each context-free language L, there is a positive integer n, a regular language R, and a homomorphism h such that $L = h(D_n \cup R)$." where D_n is a Dyck language with n different bracket pairs. As described by Forišek (2018), it follows that the Dyck language D_2 essentially covers the entire class of CFLs. Every model which recognizes or generates well-formed Dyck words with two types of brackets should be powerful enough to handle any CFL when intersected with a relabeling (homomorphism of a constructed regular language).

The synthetic corpus we use consists of such a Dyck language with two types of brackets ([ ] and { }). Sentences are generated according to the following grammar:

```
S   -> S1 S | S1
S1  -> B | T
B   -> [ S ] | { S }
T   -> [ ] | { }
```

The probabilities of the rules are defined in a way that the entropy – in terms of the number of characters between an opening and its corresponding closing bracket and the depth of embedding at which a bracket appears – is larger than if the rules had all equal probabilities. Formally, the branching probability $P_b = P[\text{S1} \rightarrow \text{B}]$ and the concatenation probability $P_c = P[\text{S} \rightarrow \text{S1 S}]$ are defined as follows:

$$s(l) = min(1, -3 \cdot \frac{l}{n} + 3)$$
$$P_b = r_b \cdot s(l) \quad \text{where} \quad r_b \sim \mathcal{U}(0.4, 0.8) \quad (1)$$
$$P_c = r_c \cdot s(l) \quad \text{where} \quad r_c \sim \mathcal{U}(0.4, 0.8)$$

where r_b and r_c are sampled once per sentence and l is the number of already generated characters in the sentence. All 1M generated sentences have a length n of 100 characters.

In this paper, we check whether an LSTM can be trained to recognize this grammar.

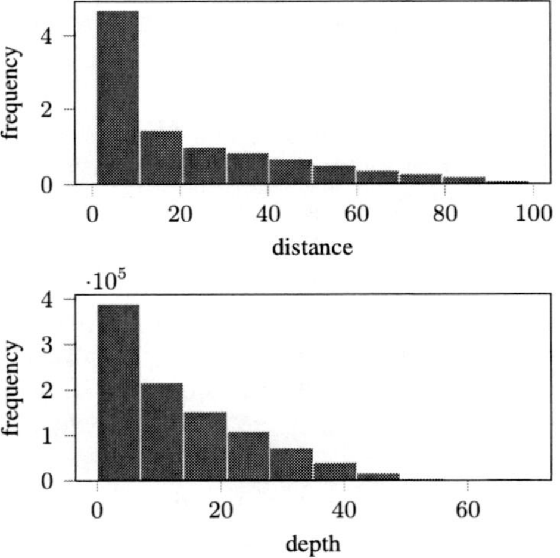

Figure 1: Corpus frequencies

4   Model

To check if we can train a neural network to accept the language generated by the grammar above, an LSTM is used.

4.1   Long Short-Term Memory

Long-Short-Term-Memory networks (LSTM) (Hochreiter and Schmidhuber, 1997) are a variant of recurrent neural networks (RNNs). Both of them possess a memory state that is updated in the process of reading a time series. Many RNNs suffer from the problem of vanishing gradients (Hochreiter and Schmidhuber, 1997): The recurrent activation functions of RNNs are often set to be $tanh$ or the sigmoid function. Since their gradients are most of the times smaller than 1 (for $tanh$ it is upper bounded by 1, and for the sigmoid function even by 0.25), the gradient cannot be conserved during extense backpropagation and approaches 0. LSTMs deal with this issue by containing three multiplicative gates controlling what proportion of the input to pass to the memory cell (input gate), what proportion of the previous memory cell information to discard (forget gate) and what proportion of the memory cell to output (output gate). In the recurrency of the LSTM the activation function is the identity function, which has gradient 1.0. This means that if the forget gate is open, the gradient is fully passed on to previous time steps, and long term dependencies can be learned.

The LSTM reads each input x_i consecutively and updates its memory state c_i accordingly. After each step, an output h_i is generated based on the updated memory state. More specifically, the LSTM solves the following equations in a forward pass:

$$\mathbf{i}_t = \sigma(\mathbf{W}_{ix}\mathbf{x}_t + \mathbf{W}_{ih}\mathbf{h}_{t-1} + \mathbf{b}_i)$$
$$\mathbf{f}_t = \sigma(\mathbf{W}_{fx}\mathbf{x}_t + \mathbf{W}_{fh}\mathbf{h}_{t-1} + \mathbf{b}_f)$$
$$\mathbf{c}_t = \mathbf{f}_t \odot \mathbf{c}_{t-1}$$
$$\qquad + \mathbf{i}_t \odot tanh(\mathbf{W}_{cx}\mathbf{x}_t + \mathbf{W}_{ch}\mathbf{h}_{t-1} + \mathbf{b}_c)$$
$$\mathbf{o}_t = \sigma(\mathbf{W}_{ox}\mathbf{x}_t + \mathbf{W}_{oh}\mathbf{h}_{t-1} + \mathbf{b}_o)$$
$$\mathbf{h}_t = \mathbf{o}_t \odot tanh(\mathbf{c}_t)$$
$$(2)$$

4.2   Basic Model

Now let us turn to the details of the model implementation. We begin with the basic formulation.

Let B_{open} and B_{close} be the sets of opening and closing brackets and $B = B_{open} \cup B_{close}$ the set of all brackets. Given the beginning of a sentence $w_1, w_2, ..., w_{k-1}, w_k$ with $w_1, ..., w_{k-1} \in B$ and $w_k \in B_{close}$, the LSTMs tries approximate the

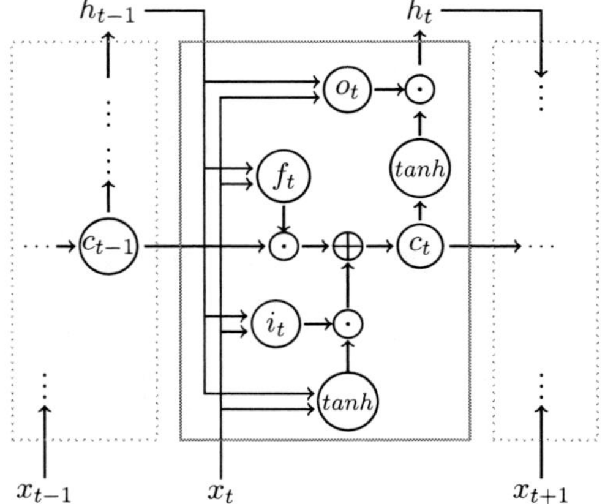

Figure 2: schematic model of an LSTM-cell. $\odot$ stands for element-wise multiplication and $\oplus$ for vector addition.

function:

$$F: B^{k-1} \rightarrow B_{close}$$

$$w_1, w_2, ..., w_{k-1} \mapsto w_k.$$

The substring (clause) between the corresponding opening bracket of w_i and w_i will be referred to as the *relevant clause* in the remainder of this paper. Likewise, by *distance* we denote the number of characters of the relevant clause. Note that this distance is always a multiple of 2, since the relevant clause is well-balanced. The *depth* at a certain position i is the number of unclosed brackets in the first i characters. The *embedded depth* of a sentence is the maximum *depth* when processing the relevant clause.

To read the input characters, an embedding layer with 5 output dimensions precedes the LSTM. Together they build the encoder, which will read the input sequentially. The decoder, mapping the internal representation to a probability of predicting } or] is a dense layer with one output variable.

We have compared different initialization methods. It turns out that the initialization of the model is crucial to avoid bad local minima. The following initialization method results in consistently good solutions: To initialize the weights, the model is trained with sentences of length 50 and only afterwards on the actual corpus with sentence length 100.

For backpropagation, the Adam (Kingma and Ba, 2014) optimizer was used. Furthermore, to en-sure faster and more consistent convergence, at the beginning of the training, the batch size is gradually increased, which has a similar effect as reducing the learning rate (Smith et al., 2017). In all experiments (and for all models), the corpus is split into 50% training sentences and 50% test sentences. The reported results always refer to the results on the test set.

4.3 Analysis Model

The analysis model is used to analyze what information is stored in the internal representation of the LSTM. In a Push-Down-Automaton model, this internal representation would conceptually correspond to the entire stack.

To analyze the internal representation $[h_i, c_i]$ of the LSTM after having read the input or part of it, we use a method already developed by Shi et al. (2016) and Belinkov et al. (2017): After having trained the basic model, the weights of the encoder are fixed and the labels (previously y) are replaced by some feature z_i of the input $x_1, \ldots, x_i$.

This feature z_i can either be a scalar or a vector. If z_i is a scalar, a dense layer (scalar analysis decoder) is trained to predict z_i. On the other hand, if z_i is a vector (sequence analysis decoder), another LSTM is trained to predict $z_{i,1}, \ldots, z_{i,j}$.

Analyzing the performance of the analysis network shows us how accurately a feature z_i is preserved in $[h_i, c_i]$. One can assume that the LSTM uses its limited memory "efficiently" and therefore discards irrelevant information. Hence, the performance of the analysis decoder shows whether z_i is contained in the information that is relevant for the original classification task.

To begin, two of the experiments which were conducted are presented in the following section to test the trained model performance. For the first experiment z_i is the *depth* (nesting level) after i characters.

Example: For the sequence { [{ } [[ ], z is $(1, 2, 3, 2, 3, 4, 3)$.

For the second experiment we note that theoretically, at any time t, no information about a closed clause in $w_1, \ldots, w_t$ has to be stored, since it is irrelevant for any eventual future prediction of $w_{t+1}, w_{t+2}, \ldots$. When reading from left to right, as soon as a closing bracket is processed, the corresponding clause becomes irrelevant. There-

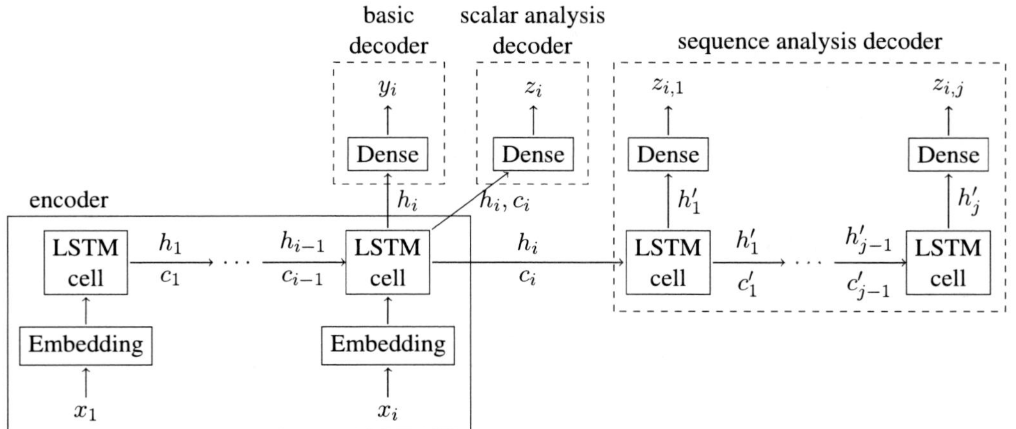

Figure 3: Network architecture of the model. The basic end-to-end model consists of the encoder and the basic decoder. The analysis model fixes the weights for the encoder and uses the scalar (if z_i is a scalar) or sequence analysis decoder (if z_i is a sequence).

fore, the relevant information is simply the list of bracket types of unclosed clauses. In this experiment we investigate how well the previous characters are preserved in the intermediate representation and evaluate if this correlates with the recovered characters being relevant or not.

Example: after having processed { [{ }] [, only the first and the last characters are relevant, since they are the only ones that could matter for a future classification task. On the other hand, the sub-string [{ }] is irrelevant. In this example we would evaluate whether the first and last character are better preserved in the intermediate state than the irrelevant sub-string.

To set up the experiment, we set $z_{i,k}$ to be equal to x_{i-k+1}, corresponding to predicting the previous characters of a given intermediate state.

4.4 Varying hidden units

The basic model is evaluated with $2, 4, 6, ..., 50$ hidden units. The error rate with 50 hidden units is 0.38% and an error rate of 1% is reached around 20 hidden units. Thus, the error seems to converge with increasing hidden units to a fairly small value. As a result, in all further experiments, the maximum number of hidden units the models are tested against was set to 50.

4.5 Memory demand

In this section we evaluate how "difficult" sentences can be with respect to the memory demand of the model, while still reaching an error toler-

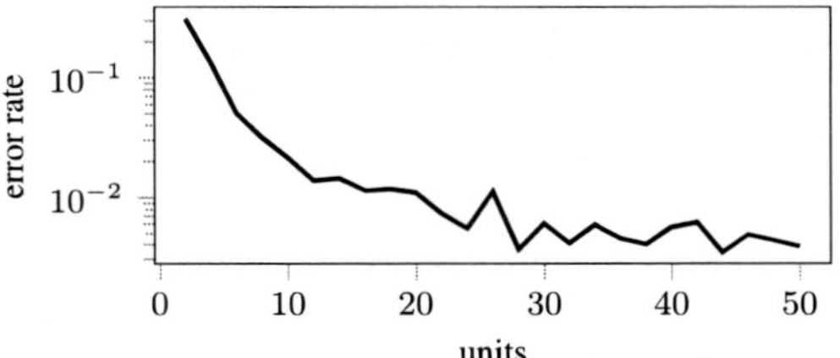

Figure 4: Overall error rate of the basic model with respect to the number of hidden units of the LSTM.

ance of 5%. We have to work with tolerances, because 100% accuracy is not reached. Since it can be challenging measuring how difficult a sentence is to predict, we use the *distance* and the *embedded depth* of a sentence as defined above as metrics.

The resulting values (figure 5) demonstrate that memory demand grows exponentially with respect to the *distance* of sentences that can be predicted. The same behaviour can be observed with respect to the *embedded depth*.

4.6 Generalization

To evaluate the model's generalization performance, training was done only on a systematically chosen subset of sentences (in-sample). To avoid adding additional nuisance variables in this selection, the training sentences are selected according

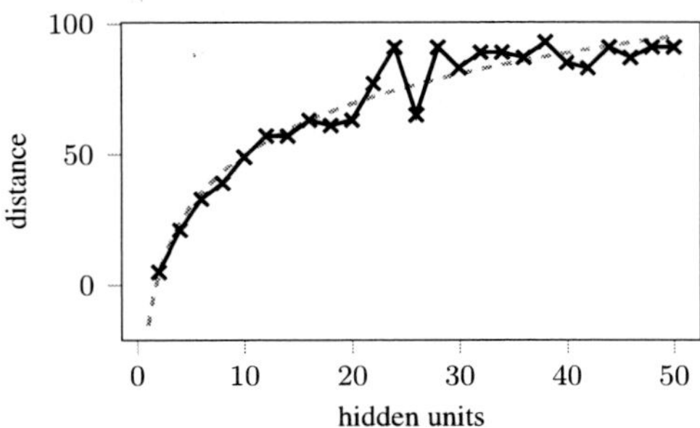
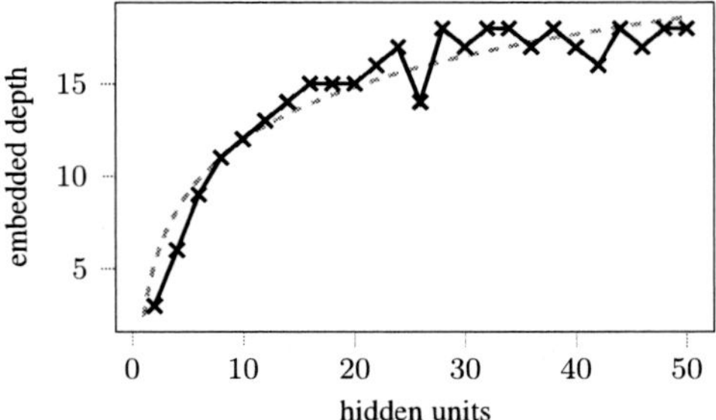

Figure 5: *Distances* (left figure) and *embedded depth* (right figure) that can be predicted with a given number of hidden units and 5% error tolerance. The dashed line is a logarithmic approximation.

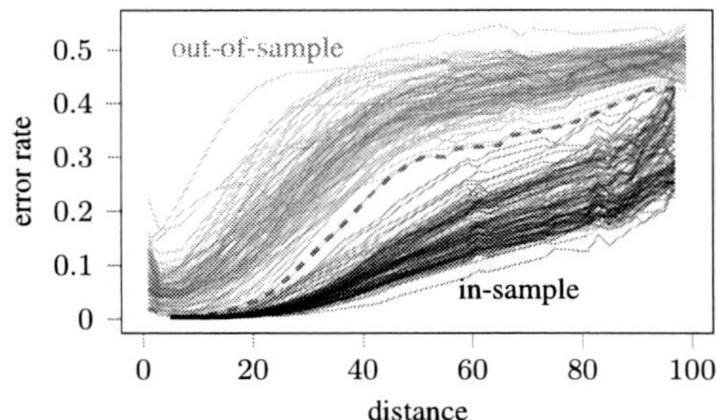

Figure 6: Generalization behaviour of a model with 10 hidden units with respect to the *distance* for 100 runs. Half of the corpus is systematically selected for training (in-sample) – for testing also the left out *distances* are considered (out-of-sample). The bold dashed line is the minimal out-of-sample error out of all 100 runs.

to one of the following rules:

regular interpolation: the sentence has *distance* 2, 6, 10, 14, . . . / odd *embedded depth*.

random interpolation: the *distance / embedded depth* of the relevant clause belongs to a set D. D is a random subset consisting of half of all *distances / embedded depths* present in the corpus.

extrapolation: the *distance / embedded depth* of the relevant clause is smaller than a certain threshold (11 for *distance* and 13 for *embedded depth*).

Running the experiment 100 times – each one with a different random weight initialization – has shown (figure 6) that the results are consistent with respect to the weight initialization. The best out-of-sample accuracy is still worse than almost all in-sample accuracies.

The results (figure 7) demonstrate a large discrepancy between the performance on in-sample (training) and the out-of-sample (testing) accuracy. The experiment was evaluated for different numbers of hidden units. On the one hand, with a large number of hidden units, the generalization error is similarly large (the out-of-sample error rate for interpolation was already between 8.1 and 14.3 times larger than the in-sample error). On the other hand, models with a small number of hidden units did not even converge. The reason for no convergence can be reasonably be explained by the sparse data set, that might lead to more local minima. The maximum generality – especially for smaller *distances* – is observed at around 10 hidden units.

Generalization was evaluated with respect to *distance* and with respect to the *embedded depth*.

For regular interpolation the out-of-sample error for 10 hidden units was on average 5.4 (*distance*) and 5.9 (*embedded depth*) times higher than the in-sample error. Figure 7 shows also that for random interpolation and extrapolation, the model generalizes much worse or not at all.

4.7 Intermediate State Analysis

For the first experiment analyzing intermediate states, recovering the *depth* as defined in section 4.2 from intermediate states shows that the *depth* is only marginally conserved in the intermediate state (figure 8). For a small number of units, the model is only able to distinguish whether a *depth* is either close to 0 or close to the mean *depth* (see figure 8 with two hidden units). When increasing the number of hidden units, the distribution of

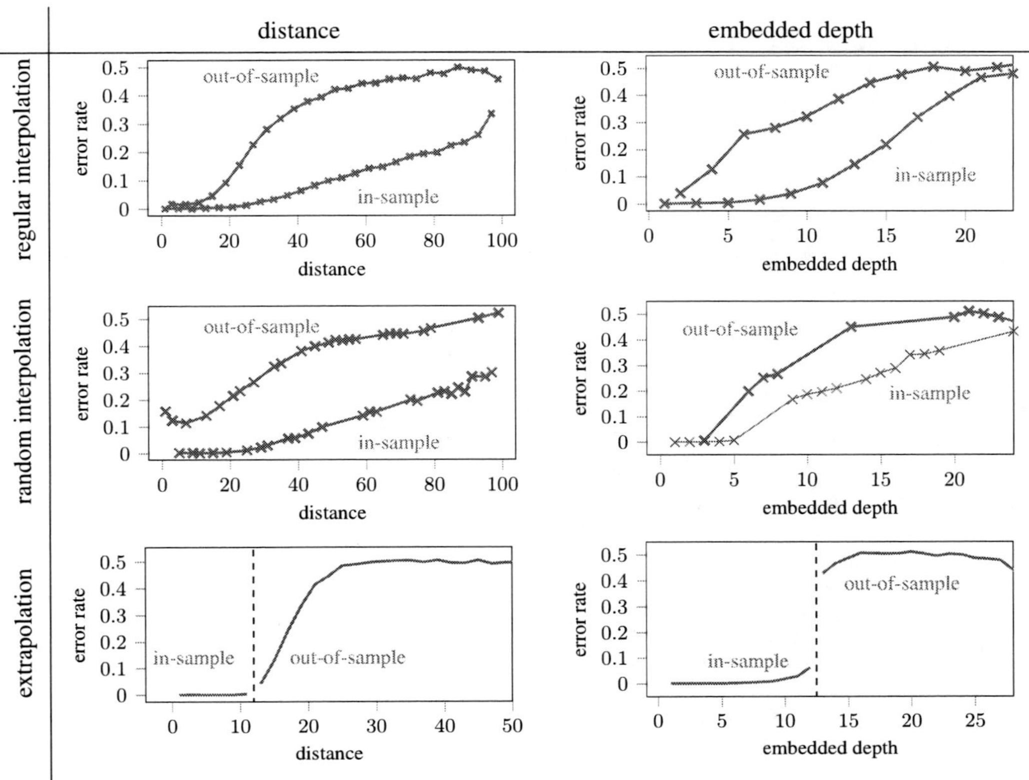

Figure 7: Test for generalization: The error rate of the model with 10 hidden units if only half of the corpus is systematically selected for training (in-sample), while during testing also the left out *distances / embedded depths* were considered (out-of-sample).

predictions gets closer to the real distribution of *depths*.

While for two hidden units the prediction of the *depth* is on average off by 7.04, it decreases until it reaches a value of 1.34 for 50 hidden units.

Figure 9 shows how accurately a past character can be recovered from an intermediate state. There is a large discrepancy between the accuracy of relevant and irrelevant characters: If the 4th-to-last character is an irrelevant one, the model is only able to recover the type of bracket with a 33% error rate; whereas if it is a relevant character, it reaches an error below 1.8%. As the number of past characters k approaches 10, the irrelevant information cannot be recovered anymore. Note that an error rate of 0.5 amounts to a random guess, since we evaluate only if it can predict the type of bracket (square or curly) correctly, and not whether it was an opening or a closing one.

5 Discussion

We now consider the results of the various experiments, some of which might be considered as controversial on first sight. On the one hand, we see that the LSTM exhibits an exponential memory demand as sentences grow longer, while theoretically, a sub-linear memory ought to be sufficient (Magniez et al., 2014). On the other hand, we see that the model has successfully sorted out irrelevant information: the intermediate state analysis shows that irrelevant characters are very quickly forgotten. So, the exponential memory space is not needed for storing irrelevant information for the original classification task.

The strength of structural rules is that they generalize well. In human language this enables humans to create new sentences which have never been heard before. But also for the Dyck language being used, the 4 rules defining the language are enough to generate sentences of arbitrary *dis-*

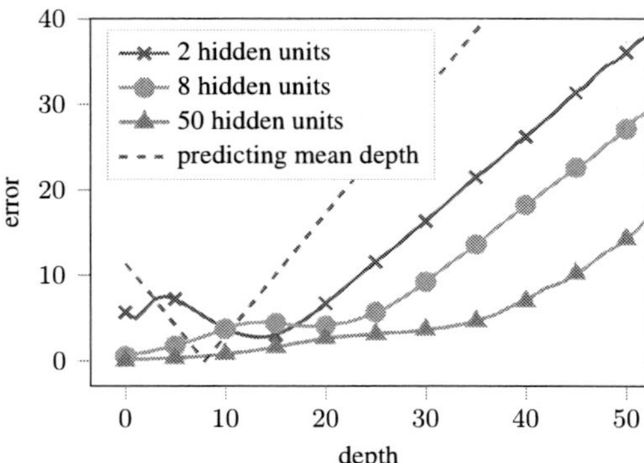

Figure 8: Error rates of predicting the *depth* given an intermediate state of the basic model. It is evaluated for $2, 8, 50$ hidden units. The dashed line indicates the baseline always predicting the mean *depth*. The error indicates how far the prediction is off from the true *depth*.

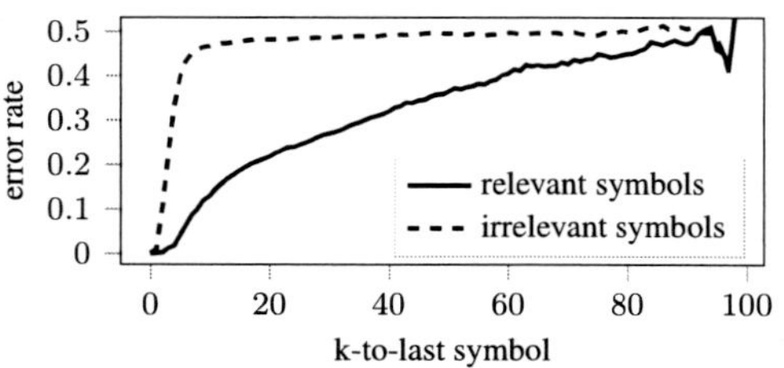

Figure 9: Error rate of predicting the previous characters given an intermediate state of the basic model with 20 hidden units. Characters are grouped as being either relevant or irrelevant for the basic classification task.

tance and *(embedded) depth*. The only constraint is the memory to store intermediate results while streaming the input. Assuming the model had in fact learned the underlying grammatical rules correctly, an upper bound for the memory required is 50 bits. The model we are using has up to 50 hidden units which corresponds to 11,200 trainable parameters. Collins et al. (2016) showed that LSTMs can store up to 5 bits of information per parameter and one real number per hidden unit. So we can assume that memory to store the values to process the corpus-defining rules sequentially is not an issue. To partially answer the question of whether LSTM can learn rules we follow a proof by contradiction: if the LSTM learns rules and if these rules are the correct ones, the model would generalize. What we observe is that the LSTM generalizes poorly. Therefore we conclude that the model is not able to learn the right rules.

Combining the generalization results and the intermediate state analysis reveals that the model determines each character's relevance – but it has learned this without resorting to hierarchical rules. As LSTMs are known to have the ability to capture statistical contingencies, it suggests instead that rather than the "perfect" rule-based solution, what the LSTM has in fact acquired is a sequential statistical approximation to this solution.

The large effect of initialization to a good local minimum suggests that the underlying function may well have many local minima as on reviewers noted. Indeed, Collins et al. (2016) has already concluded that the memory in LSTMs is mainly used for training effectiveness rather than to increase the storage capacity. Therefore, the large memory demand in our experiments suggests that the LSTM memory is needed to avoid such local minima.

6 Conclusion

At heart, neural networks are statistical models, performing well at capturing and combining correlations of the output variable values and the corresponding component values in the training input. In particular, LSTMs are constructed such that they capture sequential information. Hence, due to the design of their architecture, LSTMs perform very well on statistically-oriented, sequential tasks.

As a result, in experiments like this one that examine whether LSTMs can acquire hierarchical knowledge, one has to pay close attention to nuisance variables like sequential statistical correlations that might be hard to detect and confounded with true hierarchical information.

The bottom line that emerges from this experiment is that the range of rules that an LSTM can learn is very restricted: even a context-free grammar with four simple rules apparently cannot be appropriately learned by an LSTM.

According to most linguistic accounts, natural language syntax relies heavily on hierarchical rules. It enables humans to compose new sentences with relatively little memory capacity and training data. Furthermore, there are sentences that have the same linear representation but differ in structure – syntactically ambiguous sentences. From this perspective, it seems not only more efficient to directly infer structures and rules, but also useful to use rules to understand sentences correctly. The bracket completion task presented here can be understood by a human after only a few training sentences, though online processing of the rules themselves may be difficult. This result invites the conclusion that it will be very challenging for LSTMs to understand natural language as humans do. While LSTMs remain good engineering tools to approximate certain language features based on statistical correlations, the exploration of fundamentally new models and architectures seems a valuable direction to explore on the way to developing methods for understanding human language in the way that people do.

Acknowledgments

We want to thank Beracah Yankama for his help, valuable discussions and the machines to run the experiments on. We thank Prof. Thomas Hofmann for the fast and easy administrative process at ETH Zurich and also for granting access to high-computing clusters. Additionally we are very grateful for the financial support provided by the Zeno Karl Schindler Foundation.

References

Jean-Michel Autebert, Jean Berstel, and Luc Boasson. 1997. Context-free languages and pushdown automata. In *Handbook of formal languages*, pages 111–174. Springer.

Dzmitry Bahdanau, Kyunghyun Cho, and Yoshua Bengio. 2014. Neural machine translation by jointly learning to align and translate. *arXiv preprint arXiv:1409.0473*.

Yonatan Belinkov, Nadir Durrani, Fahim Dalvi, Hassan Sajjad, and James Glass. 2017. What do neural machine translation models learn about morphology? *arXiv preprint arXiv:1704.03471*.

Jean-Philippe Bernardy. 2018. Can recurrent neural networks learn nested recursion? *LiLT (Linguistic Issues in Language Technology)*, 16(1).

Robert C Berwick and Noam Chomsky. 2016. *Why only us: Language and evolution*. MIT press.

Noam Chomsky and Marcel P Schützenberger. 1963. The algebraic theory of context-free languages. In *Studies in Logic and the Foundations of Mathematics*, volume 35, pages 118–161. Elsevier.

Jasmine Collins, Jascha Sohl-Dickstein, and David Sussillo. 2016. Capacity and trainability in recurrent neural networks. *arXiv preprint arXiv:1611.09913*.

Chris Dyer, Adhiguna Kuncoro, Miguel Ballesteros, and Noah A Smith. 2016. Recurrent neural network grammars. *arXiv preprint arXiv:1602.07776*.

Martin BH Everaert, Marinus AC Huybregts, Noam Chomsky, Robert C Berwick, and Johan J Bolhuis. 2015. Structures, not strings: linguistics as part of the cognitive sciences. *Trends in cognitive sciences*, 19(12):729–743.

Michal Forišek. 2018. What is the significance of the chomsky-schützenberger theorem about representing context-free languages?

Felix A Gers and E Schmidhuber. 2001. Lstm recurrent networks learn simple context-free and context-sensitive languages. *IEEE Transactions on Neural Networks*, 12(6):1333–1340.

Alex Graves, Greg Wayne, and Ivo Danihelka. 2014. Neural turing machines. *CoRR*, abs/1410.5401.

André Grüning. 2006. Stack-like and queue-like dynamics in recurrent neural networks. *Connection Science*, 18(1):23–42.

Sepp Hochreiter and Jürgen Schmidhuber. 1997. Long short-term memory. *Neural computation*, 9(8):1735–1780.

Armand Joulin and Tomas Mikolov. 2015. Inferring algorithmic patterns with stack-augmented recurrent nets. In *Advances in neural information processing systems*, pages 190–198.

Andrej Karpathy, Justin Johnson, and Fei-Fei Li. 2015. Visualizing and understanding recurrent networks. *CoRR*, abs/1506.02078.

Yoon Kim, Yacine Jernite, David Sontag, and Alexander M Rush. 2016. Character-aware neural language models. In *AAAI*, pages 2741–2749.

Diederik P Kingma and Jimmy Ba. 2014. Adam: A method for stochastic optimization. *arXiv preprint arXiv:1412.6980*.

Eliyahu Kiperwasser and Yoav Goldberg. 2016. Simple and accurate dependency parsing using bidirectional lstm feature representations. *arXiv preprint arXiv:1603.04351*.

Christo Kirov and Robert Frank. 2012. Processing of nested and cross-serial dependencies: an automaton perspective on srn behaviour. *Connection Science*, 24(1):1–24.

Viktoriya Krakovna and Finale Doshi-Velez. 2016. Increasing the interpretability of recurrent neural networks using hidden markov models. *arXiv preprint arXiv:1606.05320*.

Tal Linzen, Emmanuel Dupoux, and Yoav Goldberg. 2016. Assessing the ability of lstms to learn syntax-sensitive dependencies. *arXiv preprint arXiv:1611.01368*.

Adam Liska, Germán Kruszewski, and Marco Baroni. 2018. Memorize or generalize? searching for a compositional RNN in a haystack. *CoRR*, abs/1802.06467.

Moshe Looks, Marcello Herreshoff, DeLesley Hutchins, and Peter Norvig. 2017. Deep learning with dynamic computation graphs. *CoRR*, abs/1702.02181.

F. Magniez, C. Mathieu, and A. Nayak. 2014. Recognizing well-parenthesized expressions in the streaming model. *SIAM Journal on Computing*, 43(6):1880–1905.

Tomáš Mikolov, Martin Karafiát, Lukáš Burget, Jan Černocký, and Sanjeev Khudanpur. 2010. Recurrent neural network based language model. In *Eleventh Annual Conference of the International Speech Communication Association*.

P. E. Rauber, S. G. Fadel, A. X. Falcão, and A. C. Telea. 2017. Visualizing the hidden activity of artificial neural networks. *IEEE Transactions on Visualization and Computer Graphics*, 23(1):101–110.

Paul Rodriguez. 2001. Simple recurrent networks learn context-free and context-sensitive languages by counting. *Neural Computation*, 13(9):2093–2118.

Xing Shi, Inkit Padhi, and Kevin Knight. 2016. Does string-based neural mt learn source syntax? In *Proceedings of the 2016 Conference on Empirical Methods in Natural Language Processing*, pages 1526–1534.

Samuel L Smith, Pieter-Jan Kindermans, and Quoc V Le. 2017. Don't decay the learning rate, increase the batch size. *arXiv preprint arXiv:1711.00489*.

Sainbayar Sukhbaatar, arthur szlam, Jason Weston, and Rob Fergus. 2015. End-to-end memory networks. In C. Cortes, N. D. Lawrence, D. D. Lee, M. Sugiyama, and R. Garnett, editors, *Advances in Neural Information Processing Systems 28*, pages 2440–2448. Curran Associates, Inc.

Martin Sundermeyer, Ralf Schlüter, and Hermann Ney. 2012. Lstm neural networks for language modeling. In *Thirteenth Annual Conference of the International Speech Communication Association*.

Whitney Tabor. 2000. Fractal encoding of context-free grammars in connectionist networks. *Expert Systems*, 17(1):41–56.

Kai Sheng Tai, Richard Socher, and Christopher D. Manning. 2015. Improved semantic representations from tree-structured long short-term memory networks. *CoRR*, abs/1503.00075.

Oriol Vinyals, Łukasz Kaiser, Terry Koo, Slav Petrov, Ilya Sutskever, and Geoffrey Hinton. 2015. Grammar as a foreign language. In *Advances in Neural Information Processing Systems*, pages 2773–2781.

Interpretable Neural Architectures
for Attributing an Ad's Performance to its Writing Style

Reid Pryzant*

Stanford University

rpryzant@stanford.edu

Kazoo Sone

Google

sone@google.com

Sugato Basu

Google

sugato@google.com

Abstract

How much does "free shipping!" help an advertisement's ability to persuade? This paper presents two methods for *performance attribution*: finding the degree to which an outcome can be attributed to parts of a text while controlling for potential confounders[1]. Both algorithms are based on interpreting the behaviors and parameters of trained neural networks. One method uses a CNN to encode the text, an adversarial objective function to control for confounders, and projects its weights onto its activations to interpret the importance of each phrase towards each output class. The other method leverages residualization to control for confounds and performs interpretation by aggregating over learned word vectors. We demonstrate these algorithms' efficacy on 118,000 internet search advertisements and outcomes, finding language indicative of high and low click through rate (CTR) regardless of who the ad is by or what it is for. Our results suggest the proposed algorithms are high performance and data efficient, able to glean actionable insights from fewer than 10,000 data points. We find that quick, easy, and authoritative language is associated with success, while lackluster embellishment is related to failure. These findings agree with the advertising industry's emperical wisdom, automatically revealing insights which previously required manual A/B testing to discover.

1 Introduction

A text's style can affect our cognitive responses and attitudes, thereby influencing behavior (Spence, 1983; Van Laer et al., 2013). The predictive relationship between language and behavior has been well studied in applications of NLP to tasks like linking text to sales figures (Ho and Wu, 1999; Pryzant et al., 2017) and voter preference (Luntz, 2007; Ansolabehere and Iyengar, 1995).

In this paper, we are interested in interpreting rather than predicting the relationship between language and behavior. We focus on a specific instance: the relationship between the way a search advertisement is written and internet user behavior as measured by click through rate (CTR). In this study CTR is the ratio of clicks to impressions over a 90-day period, i.e. the probability of a click, given the person saw the ad. Our goal is to develop a method for *performance attribution* in textual advertisements: identifying lexical features (words, phrases, etc.) to which we can attribute the success (or failure) of a search ad, regardless of who created the advertisement or what it is selling.

Identifying linguistic features that are associated with various outcomes is a common activity among machine learning scientists and practitioners. Indeed, it is essential for developing transparent and interpretable machine learning NLP models (Yamamoto, 2012). However, the various forms of regression and association quantifiers like mutual information or log-odds ratio that are the de-facto standard for feature weighting and text attribution all have known drawbacks, largely related to problems of multicollinearity (Imai and Kim, 2016; Gelman and Loken, 2014; Wurm and Fisicaro, 2014; Estévez et al., 2009; Szumilas, 2010).

Furthermore, these prior methods of text attribution critically fail to disentangle the explanatory power of the text from that of confounding information which could also explain the outcome. For example, in movie reviews, the actors who star in a film are the most powerful predictors of box office success (Joshi et al., 2010). However, these are words that the film's marketers can't change.

---

*This work was conducted while the first author was doing internship at Google.

[1]Our code is available at github.com/rpryzant/
deconfounded_lexicon_induction/tree/
master/text-performance-attribution

Proceedings of the 2018 EMNLP Workshop BlackboxNLP: Analyzing and Interpreting Neural Networks for NLP, pages 125–135
Brussels, Belgium, November 1, 2018. ©2018 Association for Computational Linguistics

Likewise, the name of a well-known brand in an ad for shoes might boost its effectiveness, but if we attribute the ad's success to the brand terms, we are actually crediting the power of the brand, not necessarily an actionable writing strategy (Ghose and Sundararajan, 2006).

There is an emerging line of work on text understanding for confound-controlled settings (Johansson et al., 2016; Egami et al., 2017; Pryzant et al., 2018; Li et al., 2018), but these methods are usually concerned with making causal inferences using text. They are limited to word-features and can only tell you whether a word is discriminative. Attribution involves the more fine-grained problem of identifying discriminative subsequences of the text *and* being able to explain which level of the outcome these subsequences support.

We present a pair of new algorithms for solving this problem. Based on the Adversarial and Residualizing models of (Pryzant et al., 2018), these algorithms first train a machine learning model and then analyze the trained parameters on strategically chosen inputs to infer the most important features for each output class. Our first algorithm encodes the text with a convolutional neural network (CNN) and proceeds to predict the outcome and adversarially predict the confounders. We select attributional n-grams by projecting back the weights of the output layer onto the encoder's convolutional feature maps. Our second algorithm uses a bag-of-words text representation and is trained to learn the part of the text's effect that the confounds cannot explain. We get n-grams from this method by tracing back the contribution of each feature towards each outcome class.

We demonstrate these algorithms' efficacy by conducting attribution studies on high- and low-performing search advertisements across three domains: real estate, job listings, and apparel. We find the proposed algorithms lend importance to words that are more predictive and less confound-related than a variety of strong baselines.

2 Text Attribution

We begin by proposing a methodological framework for text attribution and formalizing the activity into a concrete task.

We have access to a vocabulary $V = \{v_1, ..., v_m\}$, text $T = (w_1, ..., w_t)$ that is represented as a sequence of tokens, where each w is an element of V, outcome variable $Y \in \{1, ..., k\}$,

and confounding variable(s) C. The data consists of (T^i, Y^i, C^i) triples, where the ith data point includes a passage of text, an outcome, and confounding information that could also explain the outcome. Note that parts of T and C are related because language reflects circumstance (the text T is usually authored within a broader pragmatic context, for example the intent to promote a certain product at a certain price); T and Y are related because language influences behavior; C and Y are related because circumstance also influences behavior. We are interested in isolating the T-Y relationship and finding out which parts of the text act towards each possible outcome. We do so by choosing a lexicon $L_1, ..., L_k \subset V$ for each each outcome class Y_i such that the outcome x in observation $(T^i, Y^i = x, C^i)$ can be credited to $T^i \cap L_x$, regardless of C. In other words, observing $Y^i = x$ can always be attributed to the tokens in L_x no matter the circumstances.

Saying that $Y^i = x$ can be attributed to L_x means (1) the words in L_x have a causal effect on Y and (2) that these words push Y towards class x, i.e., L_x is associated with class x. Based on the potential outcomes model of (Holland et al., 1985; Splawa-Neyman et al., 1990; Rubin, 1974; Pearl, 1999), Pryzant et al. (2018) developed a *causal informativeness coefficient* which measures the causal effects of a lexicon L on Y:

$$\mathcal{I}(L) = \mathbb{E}\left[\left(Y - \mathbb{E}\left[Y|C, T \cap L\right]\right)^2\right] \\ - \mathbb{E}\left[\left(Y - \mathbb{E}\left[Y|C\right]\right)^2\right], \tag{1}$$

$\mathcal{I}(L)$ measures the ability of $T \cap L$ to explain Y's variability beyond the information already contained in the confounders. One computes $\mathcal{I}(L)$ by (1) regressing C on Y, (2) regressing $C + L \cap T$ on Y, and (3) measuring the difference in cross-entropy error between these models over a test set.

So $\mathcal{I}(L_x)$ measures the degree to which L_x influences Y, but it can't describe the degree to which L_x influences Y *towards* the specific outcome x. We propose circumventing this issue with a new *directed* informativeness coefficient $\mathcal{I}'(L, x) = \bar{lo}(L, x) \cdot \mathcal{I}(L)$, where $\bar{lo}$ is the average strength of association between the tokens in L_x and outcome x, as measured by log-odds:

$$\bar{lo}(L, x) = \frac{\sum_{v \in L} \log p_v^x - \log\left(1 - p_v^x\right)}{|L|} \tag{2}$$

$$p_v^x = \frac{\text{count}(Y = x \wedge v \in T)}{\text{count}(v \in T)} \tag{3}$$

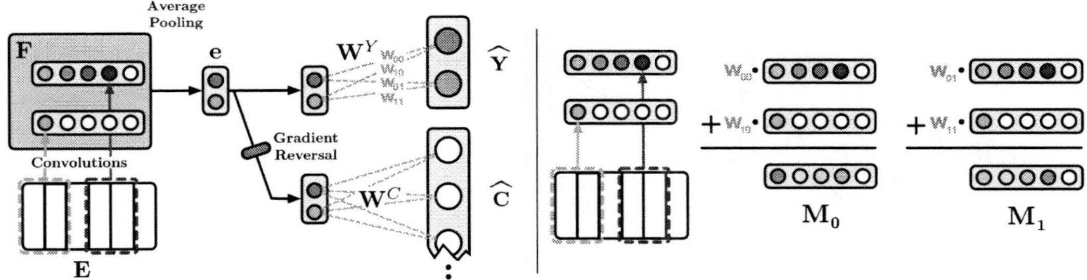

Figure 1: A Convolutional Adversarial Selector with $f = 2$ filters (both of size $n = 2$). Having filters of size 2 restricts this model to bigram attribution. Best viewed in color. **Left:** training phase. **Right:** interpretation phase.

Intuitively, if $\mathcal{I}'(L_x, x)$ is high, then L_x is both highly influential on Y and strongly associated with outcome x.

3 Proposed Algorithms

We continue by describing the pair of novel algorithms we are proposing to use for text attribution. Each algorithm consists of two phases: *training*, where we use T, Y, and C to train a machine learning model, and *interpretation*, where we analyze the learned parameters to identify attributional language.

3.1 Convolutional Adversarial Selector (CA)

Training. We begin by observing that the language we want to attribute should be able to explain the variation in Y and should also be decorrelated from the confounders C. This implies that the features we want to select should be predictive of Y, but not C (*e.g.* brand name). The Convolutional Adversarial Selector (CA) draws inspiration from this. It adversarially learns encodings of T which are useful for predicting Y but are *not* useful for predicting C. The model is depicted on the left-hand side of Figure 1.

First, we encode T into $e \in \mathcal{R}^f$ with the following steps:

1. Embed the tokens of T with word vectors of dimension e. If the input text sequence has length t, the embedded input is a matrix $\mathbf{E} \in \mathcal{R}^{e \times t}$.

2. Slide convolutional filters of size $f \times n$ along the *time* axis of $\mathbf{E}$, where n are the n-gram size(s) we are interested in attributing during the interpretation stage. This process transforms text T into a set of n-gram features of various sizes, n. The input are now transformed into $\mathbf{F^n} \in \mathcal{R}^{f \times (t-n+1)}$, aka f one-dimensional feature maps of length $t - (n-1)$ for each n-gram size n.

3. Perform *global average pooling* (Lin et al., 2014) on $\mathbf{F^n}$. We now have our encoding $\mathbf{e^n} \in \mathcal{R}^f$, where each $e_j^n = \sum_i F^n_{j,i}$.

4. Concatenate all $\mathbf{e^n}$'s from every filter width n. This produces the final encoding, e.

Armed with e, we proceed to predict Y and C with a single linear transformation:

$$\hat{\mathbf{Y}} = \mathbf{e}\mathbf{W}^Y$$
$$\hat{\mathbf{C}} = \mathbf{e}\mathbf{W}^C$$

The model receives error signals from both of these "prediction heads" via a cross-entropy loss term:

$$\mathcal{L} = \sum_i -p_i \log \hat{p}_i \qquad (4)$$

Where p_i and $\hat{p}_i$ correspond to the ground truth and predicted probabilities for class i, respectively.

Last, as gradients backpropagate from the C-prediction head to the encoder, we pass them through a *gradient reversal layer* in the style of (Ganin et al., 2016; Britz et al., 2017), which multiplies gradients by -1. If the loss of the Y-prediction head is $\mathcal{L}_Y$, and that of the confounders is $\mathcal{L}_C$, then the loss which is implicitly used to train the encoder is $L_e = L_Y - L_C$. This encourages the encoder to match e's distributions, regardless of C, thereby learning representations of the text which are invariant to the confounders (Xie et al., 2017).

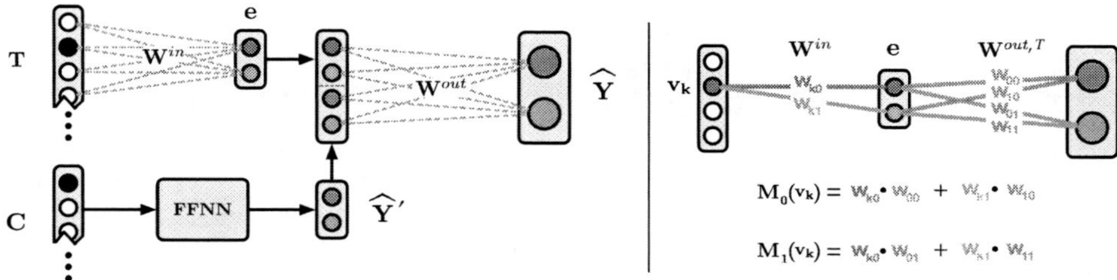

Figure 2: A Directed Residualization Selector with input embeddings of size $f = 2$. Best viewed in color. **Left:** training phase. **Right:** interpretation phase.

Interpretation. Once we've trained a CA model, we interpret its behavior in order to determine the most important n-grams for each level of the outcome. This stage is depicted in the right-hand side of Figure 1.

Inspired by the *class activation mapping* technique for computer vision (Zhou et al., 2016), we project the weights of $\mathbf{W}^Y$, the output layer, onto $\mathbf{F^n}$, the convolutional feature maps. Since $\hat{Y}_k = \sum_i e_i W^Y_{i,k}$, each $W^Y_{i,k}$ indicates the importance of e_i for class k. The elements of $\mathbf{e}$ are averages of each feature map, so $W^Y_{i,k}$ also indicates the importance of the ith feature map for class k. Each feature map contains one activation per n-gram feature. This means we can quantify the importance of the jth n-gram feature v^n_j towards each output class k by summing over all feature maps:

$$M_k(v^n_j) = \sum_i F^n_{i,j} W^Y_{i,k} \qquad (5)$$

M_k is a mapping between input features and their importance towards class k.

In order to draw lexicons L_i from our vocabulary V, we perform interpretation over a dataset and map each (n-gram, outcome class) tuple to all of the importance values it was assigned. We then compute the average importance for each n-gram and select the top k for inclusion in the outgoing lexicon.

Note that this algorithm is only interpretable to the extent that there is a single linear combination relating $\mathbf{e}$ to $\hat{Y}$. With multiple layers at the "decision" stage of the network, the relationship between each dimension of $\mathbf{e}$ (and by extension, the rows of $\mathbf{F}$) and each output class becomes obfuscated.

3.2   Directed Residualization Selector (DR)

Training. Recall from Section 2 that $\mathcal{I}'(L, x)$ measures two quantities: (1) the amount by which L can further improve predictions of Y compared to the prediction only made from the confounders C, and (2) the strength of association between members of L and outcome class x. The Directed Residualization method is directly motivated by this setup. It first predicts Y directly from C as well as possible, and then seeks to fine-tune these predictions using T. This two-stage prediction process lets us control for the confounders C, because T is being used to predict the part of Y that the confounders can't explain. This model is depicted in the left-hand side of Figure 2.

First, the confounders C are converted into one-hot feature vectors that are passed through a feedforward neural network (FFNN) to obtain a vector of preliminary predictions $\hat{\mathbf{Y}}'$. We then re-predict the outcome with the following steps:

$$\mathbf{e} = \mathbf{t}\, \mathbf{W}^{in} \qquad (6)$$
$$\hat{\mathbf{Y}} = \left[\, \mathbf{e} \mid \hat{\mathbf{Y}}' \,\right] \mathbf{W}^{out} \qquad (7)$$

Where $\mathbf{t} = \{0, 1\}^{|V|}$ is a bag-of-words representation of T, $\mathbf{W}^{in} \in \mathcal{R}^{|V| \times f}$, $\mathbf{e} \in \mathcal{R}^f$, $\mathbf{W}^{out} \in \mathcal{R}^{(f+k) \times k}$, and k is the number of classes in Y. The model receives supervision from both $\hat{\mathbf{Y}}'$ and $\hat{\mathbf{Y}}$. We use the same cross-entropy loss function as the Convolutional Adversarial Selector of Section 3.1.

Note the similarities between this approach and the popular residualizing regression (RR) attribution technique (Jaeger et al., 2009; Baayen et al., 2010, inter alia). Both use the text to improve an estimate generated from the confounds. RR treats this as two separate regression tasks (using C to predict Y, then T to predict the first model's residuals). We introduce the capacity for nonlinear interactions by backpropagating between RR's steps.

Interpretation. This stage is depicted in the right-hand side of Figure 2. Once we've trained a DR model, we determine the importance of each feature v_j for each class Y_k by tracing all possible paths between v_j and Y_k, multiplying the weights along those paths, then summing across paths. The resulting importance value, $M_k(v_j)$, is how much Y_k's log-likelihood increases if v_j is added to a text according to the trained model (and thus irrespective of the confounders).

We can derive this procedure by considering the models' parameters. In equation 7, we produce log-likelihood estimates for $\mathbf{Y}$ by concatenating e and $\hat{\mathbf{Y}}'$ and multiplying the result with $\mathbf{W}^{out}$. This means the first $|\mathbf{e}| = f$ rows of $\mathbf{W}^{out}$ (written as $\mathbf{W}^{out,T}$) are an *output projection* transforming e into $\hat{\mathbf{Y}}^T$, the text's contribution towards $\hat{\mathbf{Y}}$. So $W_{i,k}^{out}$ indicates the importance of e_i for output class k. As per equation 6, e is the sum of all of the rows of $\mathbf{W}^{in}$ that correspond to features in the text. So we can decompose $\hat{\mathbf{Y}}^T$ into a sum of contributions from each text feature v_j:

$$\hat{\mathbf{Y}} = \left[\ \mathbf{e}\ \middle|\ \hat{\mathbf{Y}}'\ \right] \left[\frac{\mathbf{W}^{out,T}}{\mathbf{W}^{out,C}}\right]$$

$$\hat{\mathbf{Y}}^T = \mathbf{t}\, \mathbf{W}^{in} \cdot \mathbf{W}^{out,T}$$

$$\hat{Y}_k^T = \sum_j^{|V|} \sum_i^f \mathbb{1}_T(v_j) W_{j,i}^{in}\, W_{i,k}^{out,T}$$

And the estimated log-likelihood contribution of of any v_j towards class k is

$$M_k(v_j) = \sum_i^f W_{j,i}^{in}\, W_{i,k}^{out,T} \tag{8}$$

For this algorithm, there is no need to run the model over any data in order to retrieve importance values – we can directly obtain these values from the trained parameters. This procedure is depicted in the right-hand side of Figure 2.

Last, like the CA algorithm, DR is only interpretable to the extent that there is a single linear combination between e and $\hat{Y}$.

4 Experiments

We demonstrate the efficacy of the proposed algorithms on a dataset of internet advertisements.

4.1 Experimental Set-Up

Data. In this setting our (T, Y, C) data triples consist of

- T: the header text of sponsored search results in an internet search engine.

- Y: a binary categorical variable which indicates whether the corresponding advertisement was high-performing or low-performing.

- C: a categorical variable which indicates the *brand* of the ad. We use customer id and the hostname of the landing page the ad points to as a proxy for this.

We collect advertisements across three domains: apparel (16,000 advertisements), job listings (70,000), and real estate (32,000). See section A for more details on these data. We selected pairs of ads where both had the same landing page and targeting, but where one ad was in the 97.5^{th} CTR percentile (high-performing) and its counterpart was in the 2.5^{th} percentile (low-performing). This implies that any performance differences may be attributed to differences in their text.

We tokenized these data with Moses (Koehn et al., 2007) and joined word-tokens into n-grams of size 1, 2, 3, and 4 for the n-gram portion of the study.

Implementation. We implemented nonlinear models with the Tensorflow framework (Abadi et al., 2016) and optimized using Adam (Kingma and Ba, 2014) with a learning rate of 0.001. We implemented linear models with the scikit learn package (Pedregosa et al., 2011). We evaluate each algorithm by selecting lexicons of size $|L_i| = 50$. We optimized the hyperparameters of all algorithms for each dataset. Complete hyperparameter specifications are provided in the online supplementary materials; for the proposed **DR** and **CA** algorithms we set $|e|$ to 8, 32, and 32 for the apparel, job listing, and real estate data, respectively.

Baselines. Along with the Convolutional Adversarial Selector (**CA**) and Directed Residualization Selector (**DR**) of Section 3, we compare the following methods: Regression (**R**), Residualized Regressions (**RR**), Regression with Confound features (**RC**), and the Adversarial Selection (**AS**) algorithm of (Pryzant et al., 2018), which selects words that are important for a confound-controlled prediction task by considering the attentional scores of an adversarially-trained RNN.

4.2 Experimental results

We begin by investigating whether the proposed methods successfully discovered features that are simultaneously indicative of each CTR status and untangled from the confounding effects of brand (Tables 1, 2, 3).

| | **High CTR** | | | | | |
| | **Unigrams** | | | **N−grams** | | |
	lo	$\mathcal{I}$	$\mathcal{I}'$	lo	$\mathcal{I}$	$\mathcal{I}'$
DR	0.84	1.19	1.01	2.09	0.81	**1.68**
CA	1.28	1.19	**1.53**	1.99	0.78	1.55
AS	0.59	0.35	0.21	0.58	0.61	0.36
R	0.91	0.83	0.76	0.68	0.63	0.43
RC	0.92	0.99	0.90	0.55	0.78	0.43
RR	0.23	0.36	0.08	0.01	0.21	0.00

| | **Low CTR** | | | | | |
| | **Unigrams** | | | **N−grams** | | |
	lo	$\mathcal{I}$	$\mathcal{I}'$	lo	$\mathcal{I}$	$\mathcal{I}'$
DR	0.73	0.78	0.58	1.12	0.88	0.99
CA	1.17	0.81	**0.96**	1.42	0.88	**1.26**
AS	0.58	0.20	0.11	0.56	0.42	0.24
R	0.79	0.46	0.37	0.83	0.52	0.43
RC	1.05	0.29	0.31	1.42	0.49	0.70
RR	0.24	0.34	0.08	0.20	0.14	0.03

Table 1: Comparative performance over apparel advertisements. $\mathcal{I}$ and $\mathcal{I}'$ are inflated by an order of magnitude for readability.

On the apparel data (Table 1), we find that the proposed algorithms select words that are often both the most influential on CTR (highest $\mathcal{I}$) and are also the most strongly associated with their target outcome classes (highest $\overline{lo}$). It is not surprising that the Adversarial Selector of (Pryzant et al., 2018) (**AS**) had low $\overline{lo}$ because the method is only capable of identifying discriminative features while controlling for confounds. **AS** was also inconsistent in its ability to select words that are predictive of CTR while being unrelated to brand. This may be due to the instability of adversarial learning (Shrivastava et al., 2017) or the complex nonlinear relationship between the model's attention scores and final predictions.

On the job advertisements (Table 2), the proposed **DR** algorithm performed the best, selecting words that were both more influential on CTR and more strongly associated with its target than

| | **High CTR** | | | | | |
| | **Unigrams** | | | **N−grams** | | |
	lo	$\mathcal{I}$	$\mathcal{I}'$	lo	$\mathcal{I}$	$\mathcal{I}'$
DR	0.67	0.61	**0.41**	3.63	0.25	**0.91**
CA	1.33	0.17	0.22	3.35	0.17	0.57
AS	0.43	0.33	0.14	2.42	0.25	0.60
R	0.65	0.13	0.08	2.98	0.17	0.51
RC	0.35	0.71	0.24	3.04	0.16	0.51
RR	0.26	0.40	0.10	1.81	0.18	0.33

| | **Low CTR** | | | | | |
| | **Unigrams** | | | **N−grams** | | |
	lo	$\mathcal{I}$	$\mathcal{I}'$	lo	$\mathcal{I}$	$\mathcal{I}'$
DR	0.89	1.04	0.93	3.43	0.20	**0.69**
CA	1.20	0.86	**1.02**	4.62	0.13	0.62
AS	0.12	0.54	0.07	3.12	0.18	0.56
R	0.76	0.85	0.65	1.95	0.13	0.26
RC	0.48	0.97	0.47	1.90	0.13	0.24
RR	0.36	0.82	0.03	0.90	0.12	0.11

Table 2: Comparative performance over job postings. $\mathcal{I}$ and $\mathcal{I}'$ are inflated by an order of magnitude for the *unigram results only.*

any other algorithm. In general, $\mathcal{I}$ values were an order of magnitude larger for n-grams than unigrams, indicating that for job postings on the internet, *phrases* are more important than the individual words they are composed of. This suggests job seekers may read advertisements more closely than internet shoppers, who are known to "skim" content and are thus more attuned to individual keywords (Campbell and Maglio, 2013; Seda, 2004).

For real estate, Table 3 indicates that except for the case of weak unigrams, the proposed **DR** and **CA** algorithms can perform best. In many cases, the regression-based approaches successfully selected words that are strongly related to each target outcome class ($\overline{lo}$ was relatively high), but failed to choose words whose explanatory power exceeds that of the confounds ($\mathcal{I}$ was relatively low). For a plain regression (**R**) this makes sense; there is no mechanism to control for confounders. For the other regression-based approaches (**RC & RR**), this may be due to the multicolinearity of confounders and text which is described in (Gelman and Loken, 2014; Wurm and Fisicaro, 2014) as a fundamental weakness of these attribution algorithms. Again, n-grams performed drastically better than unigrams, implying that phraseology may matter more than vocabulary to prospective home-

High CTR					
	Unigrams			$N-grams$		
	lo	$\mathcal{I}$	$\mathcal{I}'$	lo	$\mathcal{I}$	$\mathcal{I}'$
DR	0.75	0.32	**0.25**	2.16	0.05	**0.12**
CA	1.00	0.24	0.24	2.63	0.04	0.11
AS	0.33	0.13	0.04	1.20	0.03	0.03
R	0.56	0.06	0.03	2.32	0.05	0.11
RC	0.68	0.05	0.03	1.76	0.04	0.08
RR	0.21	0.20	0.04	0.74	0.03	0.02

Low CTR					
	Unigrams			$N-grams$		
	lo	$\mathcal{I}$	$\mathcal{I}'$	lo	$\mathcal{I}$	$\mathcal{I}'$
DR	0.60	0.12	0.07	1.80	0.18	0.32
CA	0.80	0.09	0.08	2.05	0.16	**0.33**
AS	0.12	0.14	0.01	0.18	0.25	0.04
R	0.63	0.07	0.05	0.49	0.33	0.16
RC	1.39	0.07	**0.10**	0.57	0.17	0.10
RR	0.22	0.05	0.01	0.14	0.08	0.01

Table 3: Comparative performance over real estate advertisements. $\mathcal{I}$ and $\mathcal{I}'$ are inflated by an order of magnitude for the *unigram results only*.

owners.

4.3 Algorithmic Analysis

Ablation Study. We proceed to ablate the mechanism by which each proposed algorithm controls for the confounds. First we toggled the gradient reversal layer of the Convolutional Adversarial Selector (**CA**). Doing so reduced the algorithm's performance by an average of 0.03 $\bar{lo}$ and 0.24 $\mathcal{I}$. For the Directed Residualization Selector (**DR**), we removed the part of the model that uses the confounds to generate preliminary predictions. Doing so resulted in an average increase of 0.02 $\bar{lo}$ and a decrease of 0.21 $\mathcal{I}$. For both algorithms, only the average difference in $\mathcal{I}$ was significant ($p < 0.05$). From these results, we conclude that these confound-controlling mechanisms bear little impact on the degree to which the selected words are associated with their corresponding outcome classes. However, the mechanisms are important for getting the models to avoid confound-related features.

Visualization. We visualize $M_{\text{high}-\text{CTR}}$ and $M_{\text{low}-\text{CTR}}$ as computed by a proposed and baseline method (Figure 3). We see that the regression lends high-CTR importance to the name of a popular real estate company, and low-CTR importance to an unpopular location (which that company

happens to specialize in). The Adversarial Selector gives confound-related features less importance. By disabling the reversal layer, we recover some of the regression's confound-relatedness.

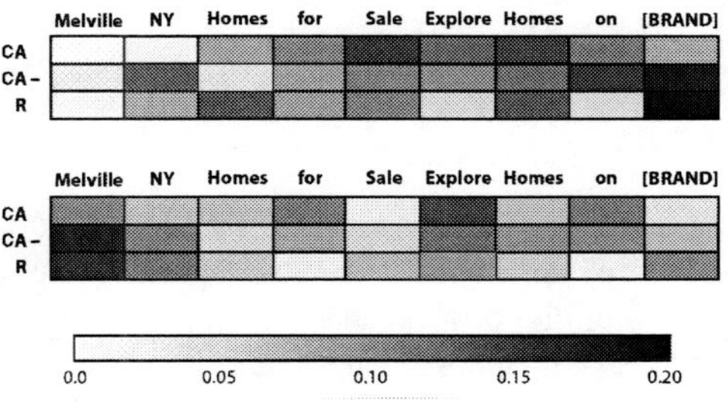

Figure 3: Feature importance maps for a real estate ad. high-CTR (top) and low-CTR (bottom) are the outcome classes. These maps are computed by the Convolutional Adversarial Selector with and without gradient flipping (CA, CA-) and a regression (R). Note that the Convolutional Adversarial Selector without gradient flipping (CA-) has similar weights to a regression model (R) while CA moves weight away from the brand-related words.

4.4 Language Analysis

We continue by studying high-scoring words and phrases from the models we experimented with in order to glean useful insights about internet advertising. Please note that this is an illustration of the present algorithm and this study is limited in scope. These are experimental results, not suggestions for real online advertising campaigns.

When comparing the words selected by the proposed and baseline methods, we observe that many of the regression-based methods selected brand names or words that are closely associated with brands, like locations (areas where real estate and staffing agencies specialize) or proper nouns (fashion designers, real estate agents, and so on). Indeed, for apparel, the percent of selected words and phrases which contained the name of a fashion retailer was less for DR and CA (6.5% and 8.5%) than AS (9%), R (23%) RC (19%) and RR (13%).

After clustering words and phrases based on the cosine similarity of their GloVe embeddings (Pennington et al., 2014), the authors found semantic classes that include industry best practices (e.g., Schwab, 2013). For example:

- **Involvement.** This includes language which

creates a dialogue with the reader ("your", "you", "we") and portrays a personal experience ("personalized") at the reader's discretion ("compare", "view"). This aligns with growing demand for personalized internet services (Meeker, 2018).

- **Authority.** This includes appeals to the rhetorical device of ethos, in the form of authoritative framing, such as "official site" and "®".

- **Logos.** These expressions appeal to the sensibilities of the reader, framing the product as easy ("simple", "any budget"), cheap ("outlet", "xx% off", "plus free shipping"), or available ("available", "shop them at").

We also find some semantic classes among weakly performing words and phrases. One notable class includes "filler words" consisting of lackluster embellishment. This aligns with prior psychological research suggesting that words that don't contribute to a topic can have a slightly negative effect on attitude (Fazio et al., 1986; Grush, 1976).

Finally, we note that popular items or categories of items were frequently high-scoring. This comes as no surprise and reflects an important aspect of the proposed methodology: it only controls for the confounders it is given, and we controlled for the *brand* of an ad, not its *content*. There are innumerable factors which influence clicking behavior (position, demographics, etc.) that we did not model explicitly in this study; we leave this to future work.

5 Related Work

Neural Network Interpretability. A variety of work has been done on understanding the relationship between input features and the network's behavior. Attention mechanisms (Bahdanau et al., 2015; Luong et al., 2015) are a popular method for highlighting parts of the input, but the nonlinear relationship between attention scores and ouputs makes it a poor tool for attribution on a per-class basis (as our Adversarial Selector (AS) baseline demonstrates). Dosovitskiy and Brox (2015) and Mahendran and Vedaldi (2015) invert the layers of a neural network to show which input features are being used. Zhou et al. (2016) extends this work to show exactly which parts of the input are being used. Parts of our Convolutional Adversarial

Selector draw on this, and as far as these authors know, we are the first to adapt class activation maps to language data. Sundararajan et al. (2017) also highlight important parts of the input with a method that is similar to our Directed Residualization Selector. Their method uses gradients to trace influence. Because our models' gradients are a composite of signals, only some of which we want to consider while attributing, the method can't be applied directly to our setting. Ribeiro et al. (2016), Biran and McKeown (2017), and Lei et al. (2016) also use "importance scores" to explain the predictions of neural network-based classifiers.

Causal Inference. Our methods have connections to recent advances in the causal inference literature. Johansson et al. (2016) and Shalit et al. (2016) propose an algorithm for causal inference which bears similarity to our Convolutional Adversarial Selector (CA). Imai et al. (2013) advocate a lasso-based method similar to our Directed Residualization (DR), and Egami et al. (2018) explore how to make causal inferences from texts through careful data splitting. Unlike the present study, these papaers are largely unconcerned with the underlying interpretability. Pryzant et al. (2018) makes a foray into causal interpretability, developing the *informativeness coefficient* metric we use in our evaluations. This work also proposed two algorithms for deconfounded lexicon induction which inspired our proposed CA and DR algorithms.

6 Conclusion

In this paper, we presented two new algorithms for the analysis of persuasive text. These algorithms are based on interpreting the behaviors and parameters of trained machine learning models. They perform *performance attribution*, the practice of finding words that are indicative of particular outcomes and are unrelated to confounding information. We used these algorithms to conduct the first public investigation into successful writing styles for internet search advertisements. We find that the proposed method can automatically identify successful (and unsuccessful) writing styles of advertising. These findings are inline with industry practices built on manual A/B testing and also previous psychological studies. This is an exciting new direction for NLP research. There are many directions for future work, including core algorithmic innovation and applying the proposed algorithms to new and rich social questions.

7 Acknowledgments

We are grateful to Emanuel Schorsch, Kristen LeFevre and Jason Baldridge for their helpful comments and suggestions.

A Corpus Statistics

Table 4 shows general statistics of the corpus used in the present study.

Category	N	$|V|$	$\bar{t}$	$\bar{l}$
Apparel	16,242	4,635	9.3	53.9
Job Postings	70,016	7,312	10.1	54.4
Real Estate	32,398	6,952	9.1	54.2

Table 4: Corpus statistics of advertising text used in this study. N is the number of documents (advertising headlines) used in the study. $|V|$ is the vocabulary size (number of unique tokens in the category corpus). $\bar{t}$ and $\bar{l}$ are average number of tokens and average length per ad respectively.

References

Martin Abadi, Paul Barham, Jianmin Chen, Zhifeng Chen, Andy Davis, Jeffrey Dean, Matthieu Devin, Sanjay Ghemawat, Geoffrey Irving, Michael Isard, Manjunath Kudlur, Josh Levenberg, Rajat Monga, Sherry Moore, Derek G. Murray, Benoit Steiner, Paul Tucker, Vijay Vasudevan, Pete Warden, Martin Wicke, Yuan Yu, and Xiaoqiang Zheng. 2016. Tensorflow: A system for large-scale machine learning. In *12th USENIX Symposium on Operating Systems Design and Implementation (OSDI 16)*, pages 265–283.

Stephen Ansolabehere and Shanto Iyengar. 1995. *Going Negative: How Attack Ads Shrinks and Polarize the Electorate*. New York: Free Press.

R. Harald Baayen, Victor Kuperman, and Raymond Bertram. 2010. Frequency effects in compound processing. In *Compounding*, pages 257–270. Benjamins.

Dzmitry Bahdanau, Kyunghyun Cho, and Yoshua Bengio. 2015. Neural machine translation by jointly learning to align and translate. *International Conference on Learning Representations (ICLR)*.

Or Biran and Kathleen R McKeown. 2017. Human-centric justification of machine learning predictions. In *IJCAI*, pages 1461–1467.

Denny Britz, Reid Pryzant, and Quoc V. Le. 2017. Effective domain mixing for neural machine translation. In *Second Conference on Machine Translation (WMT)*.

Christopher S Campbell and Paul Philip Maglio. 2013. Method of rewarding the viewing of advertisements based on eye-gaze patterns. US Patent 8,538,816.

Alexey Dosovitskiy and Thomas Brox. 2015. Inverting convolutional networks with convolutional networks. *CoRR abs/1506.02753*.

Naoki Egami, Christian J. Fong, Justin Grimmer, Margaret E. Roberts, and Brandon M. Stewart. 2017. How to make causal inferences using texts.

Naoki Egami, Christian J Fong, Justin Grimmer, Margaret E Roberts, and Brandon M Stewart. 2018. How to make causal inferences using texts. *arXiv preprint arXiv:1802.02163*.

Pablo A. Estévez, Michel Tesmer, Claudio A. Perez, and Jacek M. Zurada. 2009. Normalized mutual information feature selection. *IEEE Transactions on Neural Networks*, 20(2):189–201.

Russell H Fazio, David M Sanbonmatsu, Martha C Powell, and Frank R Kardes. 1986. On the automatic activation of attitudes. *Journal of personality and social psychology*, 50(2):229.

Yaroslav Ganin, Evgeniya Ustinova, Hana Ajakan, Pascal Germain, Hugo Larochelle, François Laviolette, Mario Marchand, and Victor Lempitsky. 2016. Domain-adversarial training of neural networks. *Journal of Machine Learning Research*, 17(59):1–35.

Andrew Gelman and Eric Loken. 2014. The statistical crisis in science data-dependent analysisa garden of forking pathsexplains why many statistically significant comparisons don't hold up. *American Scientist*, 102(6):460.

Anindya Ghose and Arun Sundararajan. 2006. Evaluating pricing strategy using e-commerce data: Evidence and estimation challenges. *Statistical Science*, pages 131–142.

Joseph E Grush. 1976. Attitude formation and mere exposure phenomena: A nonartifactual explanation of empirical findings. *Journal of Personality and Social Psychology*, 33(3):281.

Chin-Fu Ho and Wen-Hsiung Wu. 1999. Antecedents of customer satisfaction on the internet: An empirical study of online shopping. In *Systems Sciences, 1999. HICSS-32. Proceedings of the 32nd Annual Hawaii International Conference on*, pages 9–pp. IEEE.

Paul W Holland, Clark Glymour, and Clive Granger. 1985. Statistics and causal inference. *ETS Research Report Series*, 1985(2).

Kosuke Imai and In Song Kim. 2016. *When Should We Use Linear Fixed Effects Regression Models for Causal Inference with Longitudinal Data?* Ph.D. thesis, Working paper, Princeton University, Princeton, NJ.

Kosuke Imai, Marc Ratkovic, et al. 2013. Estimating treatment effect heterogeneity in randomized program evaluation. *The Annals of Applied Statistics*, 7(1):443–470.

T. Florian Jaeger, Victor Kuperman, and Austin Frank. 2009. Issues and solutions in fitting, evaluating, and interpreting regression models. In *Talk given at WOMM presession to the 22nd CUNY Conference on Sentence Processing*.

Fredrik Johansson, Uri Shalit, and David Sontag. 2016. Learning representations for counterfactual inference. In *International Conference on Machine Learning*, pages 3020–3029.

Mahesh Joshi, Dipanjan Das, Kevin Gimpel, and Noah A. Smith. 2010. Movie reviews and revenues: An experiment in text regression. In *Human Language Technologies: The 2010 Annual Conference of the North American Chapter of the Association for Computational Linguistics*, HLT '10, pages 293–296, Stroudsburg, PA, USA. Association for Computational Linguistics.

Diederik Kingma and Jimmy Ba. 2014. Adam: A method for stochastic optimization. *3rd International Conference for Learning Representations (ICLR)*.

Philipp Koehn, Hieu Hoang, Alexandra Birch, Chris Callison-Burch, Marcello Federico, Nicola Bertoldi, Brooke Cowan, Wade Shen, Christine Moran, Richard Zens, et al. 2007. Moses: Open source toolkit for statistical machine translation. In *Proceedings of the 45th annual meeting of the ACL on interactive poster and demonstration sessions*, pages 177–180. Association for Computational Linguistics.

Tao Lei, Regina Barzilay, and Tommi Jaakkola. 2016. Rationalizing neural predictions. *EMNLP*.

Yitong Li, Timothy Baldwin, and Trevor Cohn. 2018. Towards robust and privacy-preserving text representations. *arXiv preprint arXiv:1805.06093*.

Min Lin, Qiang Chen, and Shuicheng Yan. 2014. Network in network. *International Conference on Learning Representations*.

Frank Luntz. 2007. *Words that work: It's not what you say, it's what people hear.* Hachette Books.

Minh-Thang Luong, Hieu Pham, and Christopher D Manning. 2015. Effective approaches to attention-based neural machine translation. *EMNLP*.

Aravindh Mahendran and Andrea Vedaldi. 2015. Understanding deep image representations by inverting them. *Computer Vision and Pattern Recognition (CVPR)*.

Mary Meeker. 2018. Internet trends 2018. page 192.

Judea Pearl. 1999. Probabilities of causation: three counterfactual interpretations and their identification. *Synthese*, 121(1-2):93–149.

Fabian Pedregosa, Gaël Varoquaux, Alexandre Gramfort, Vincent Michel, Bertrand Thirion, Olivier Grisel, Mathieu Blondel, Peter Prettenhofer, Ron Weiss, Vincent Dubourg, et al. 2011. Scikit-learn: Machine learning in Python. *Journal of Machine Learning Research*, 12(Oct):2825–2830.

Jeffrey Pennington, Richard Socher, and Christopher Manning. 2014. Glove: Global vectors for word representation. In *Proceedings of the 2014 conference on empirical methods in natural language processing (EMNLP)*, pages 1532–1543.

Reid Pryzant, Young-joo Chung, and Dan Jurafsky. 2017. Predicting sales from the language of product descriptions. In *Special Interest Group on Information Retrieval (SIGIR) eCommerce Workshop*.

Reid Pryzant, Kelly Shen, Dan Jurafsky, and Stefan Wagner. 2018. Deconfounded lexicon induction for interpretable social science. In *16th Annual Conference of the North American Chapter of the Association for Computational Linguistics (NAACL)*.

Marco Tulio Ribeiro, Sameer Singh, and Carlos Guestrin. 2016. Why should i trust you?: Explaining the predictions of any classifier. In *Proceedings of the 22nd ACM SIGKDD international conference on knowledge discovery and data mining*, pages 1135–1144. ACM.

Donald B Rubin. 1974. Estimating causal effects of treatments in randomized and nonrandomized studies. *Journal of educational Psychology*, 66(5):688.

Victor O. Schwab. 2013. *How to Write a Good Advertisement: A Short Course in Copywriting.* Echo Point Books Media.

Catherine Seda. 2004. *Search Engine Advertising: Buying your way to the top to increase sales.* New Riders.

Uri Shalit, Fredrik Johansson, and David Sontag. 2016. Estimating individual treatment effect: generalization bounds and algorithms. *arXiv preprint arXiv:1606.03976*.

Ashish Shrivastava, Tomas Pfister, Oncel Tuzel, Josh Susskind, Wenda Wang, and Russ Webb. 2017. Learning from simulated and unsupervised images through adversarial training. In *The IEEE Conference on Computer Vision and Pattern Recognition (CVPR)*, volume 3, page 6.

Donald P. Spence. 1983. Narrative persuasion. *Psychoanalysis & Contemporary Thought*.

Jerzy Splawa-Neyman, Dorota M Dabrowska, and TP Speed. 1990. On the application of probability theory to agricultural experiments. essay on principles. section 9. *Statistical Science*, pages 465–472.

Mukund Sundararajan, Ankur Taly, and Qiqi Yan. 2017. Axiomatic attribution for deep networks. *arXiv preprint arXiv:1703.01365*.

Magdalena Szumilas. 2010. Explaining odds ratios. *Journal of the Canadian Academy of Child and Adolescent Psychiatry*, 19(3):227.

Tom Van Laer, Ko De Ruyter, Luca M. Visconti, and Martin Wetzels. 2013. The extended transportation-imagery model: A meta-analysis of the antecedents and consequences of consumers' narrative transportation. *Journal of Consumer research*, 40(5):797–817.

Lee H. Wurm and Sebastiano A. Fisicaro. 2014. What residualizing predictors in regression analyses does (and what it does not do). *Journal of Memory and Language*, 72:37–48.

Qizhe Xie, Zihang Dai, Yulun Du, Eduard Hovy, and Graham Neubig. 2017. Controllable invariance through adversarial feature learning. In *Conference on Neural Information Processing Systems (NIPS)*, Long Beach, California, USA.

Teppei Yamamoto. 2012. Understanding the past: Statistical analysis of causal attribution. *American Journal of Political Science*, 56(1):237–256.

Bolei Zhou, Aditya Khosla, Agata Lapedriza, Aude Oliva, and Antonio Torralba. 2016. Learning deep features for discriminative localization. In *Computer Vision and Pattern Recognition (CVPR), 2016 IEEE Conference on*, pages 2921–2929. IEEE.

Interpreting Neural Networks with Nearest Neighbors

Eric Wallace*, Shi Feng*, Jordan Boyd-Graber
University of Maryland
{ewallac2,shifeng,jbg}@umiacs.umd.edu

Abstract

Local model interpretation methods explain individual predictions by assigning an importance value to each input feature. This value is often determined by measuring the change in confidence when a feature is removed. However, the confidence of neural networks is not a robust measure of model uncertainty. This issue makes reliably judging the importance of the input features difficult. We address this by changing the test-time behavior of neural networks using Deep k-Nearest Neighbors. Without harming text classification accuracy, this algorithm provides a more robust uncertainty metric which we use to generate feature importance values. The resulting interpretations better align with human perception than baseline methods. Finally, we use our interpretation method to analyze model predictions on dataset annotation artifacts.

1 Introduction

The growing use of neural networks in sensitive domains such as medicine, finance, and security raises concerns about human trust in these machine learning systems. A central question is test-time *interpretability*: how can humans understand the reasoning behind model predictions?

A common way to interpret neural network predictions is to identify the most important input features. For instance, a visual saliency map that highlights important pixels in an image (Sundararajan et al., 2017) or words in a sentence (Li et al., 2016). Given a model's test prediction, the *importance* of each input feature is the change in model confidence when that feature is removed.

However, neural network confidence is not a proper measure of model uncertainty (Guo et al., 2017). This issue is emphasized when models make highly confident predictions on inputs that are completely void of information, for example, images of pure noise (Goodfellow et al., 2015) or meaningless text snippets (Feng et al., 2018). Consequently, a model's confidence may not properly reflect whether discriminative input features are present. This issue makes it difficult to reliably judge the importance of each input feature using common confidence-based interpretation methods (Feng et al., 2018).

To address this, we apply Deep k-Nearest Neighbors (DKNN) (Papernot and McDaniel, 2018) to neural models for text classification. Concretely, predictions are no longer made with a softmax classifier, but using the labels of the *training examples* whose representations are most similar to the test example (Section 3). This provides an alternative metric for model uncertainty, *conformity*, which measures how much support a test prediction has by comparing its hidden representations to the training data. This representation-based uncertainty measurement can be used in combination with existing interpretation methods, such as leave-one-out (Li et al., 2016), to better identify important input features.

We combine DKNN with CNN and LSTM models on six NLP text classification tasks, including sentiment analysis and textual entailment, with no loss in classification accuracy (Section 4). We compare interpretations generated using DKNN conformity to baseline interpretation methods, finding DKNN interpretations rarely assign importance to extraneous words that do not align with human perception (Section 5). Finally, we generate interpretations using DKNN conformity for a dataset with known artifacts (SNLI), helping to indicate whether a model has learned superficial patterns. We open source the code for DKNN and our results.[1]

---

*Equal contribution

[1] https://github.com/Eric-Wallace/deep-knn

Proceedings of the 2018 EMNLP Workshop BlackboxNLP: Analyzing and Interpreting Neural Networks for NLP, pages 136–144
Brussels, Belgium, November 1, 2018. ©2018 Association for Computational Linguistics

2 Interpretation Through Feature Attribution

Feature attribution methods explain a test prediction by assigning an importance value to each input feature (typically pixels or words).

In the case of text classification, we have an input sequence of n words $\mathbf{x} = \langle w_1, w_2, \ldots w_n \rangle$, represented as one-hot vectors. The word sequence is then converted to a sequence of word embeddings $\mathbf{e} = \langle v_1, v_2, \ldots v_n \rangle$. A classifier f outputs a probability distribution over classes. The class with the highest probability is selected as the prediction y, with its probability serving as the model confidence. To create an interpretation, each input word is assigned an importance value, $g(w_i \mid \mathbf{x}, y)$, which indicates the word's contribution to the prediction. A saliency map (or heat map) visually highlights words in a sentence.

2.1 Leave-one-out Attribution

A simple way to define the importance g is via leave-one-out (Li et al., 2016): individually remove a word from the input and see how the confidence changes. The importance of word w_i is the decrease in confidence[2] when word i is removed:

$$g(w_i \mid \mathbf{x}, y) = f(y \mid \mathbf{x}) - f(y \mid \mathbf{x}_{-i}), \quad (1)$$

where $\mathbf{x}_{-i}$ is the input sequence with the ith word removed and $f(y \mid \mathbf{x})$ is the model confidence for class y. This can be repeated for all words in the input. Under this definition, the sign of the importance value is opposite the sign of the confidence change: if a word's removal causes a decrease in the confidence, it gets a positive importance value. We refer to this interpretation method as *Confidence* leave-one-out in our experiments.

2.2 Gradient-Based Feature Attribution

In the case of neural networks, the model $f(\mathbf{x})$ as a function of word w_i is a highly non-linear, differentiable function. Rather than leaving one word out at a time, we can simulate a word's removal by approximating f with a function that is linear in w_i through the first-order Taylor expansion. The importance of w_i is computed as the derivative of f with respect to the one-hot vector:

$$\frac{\partial f}{\partial w_i} = \frac{\partial f}{\partial v_i} \frac{\partial v_i}{\partial w_i} = \frac{\partial f}{\partial v_i} \cdot v_i \quad (2)$$

[2]equivalently the change in class score or cross entropy loss

Thus, a word's importance is the dot product between the gradient of the class prediction with respect to the embedding and the word embedding itself. This gradient approximation simulates the change in confidence when an input word is removed and has been used in various interpretation methods for NLP (Arras et al., 2016; Ebrahimi et al., 2017). We refer to this interpretation approach as *Gradient* in our experiments.

2.3 Interpretation Method Failures

Interpreting neural networks can have unexpected negative results. Ghorbani et al. (2017) and Kindermans et al. (2017) show how a lack of model robustness and stability can cause egregious interpretation failures in computer vision settings. Feng et al. (2018) extend this to NLP and draw connections between interpretation failures and adversarial examples (Szegedy et al., 2014). To counteract this, new interpretation methods alone are not enough—models must be improved. For instance, Feng et al. (2018) argues that interpretation methods should not rely on prediction confidence as it does not reflect a model's uncertainty.

Following this, we improve interpretations by replacing neural network confidence with a robust uncertainty estimate using DKNN (Papernot and McDaniel, 2018). This algorithm achieves comparable accuracy on image classification tasks while providing a better uncertainty metric capable of defending against adversarial examples.

3 Deep k-Nearest Neighbors for Sequential Inputs

This section describes Deep k-Nearest Neighbors, its application to sequential inputs, and how we use it to determine word importance values.

3.1 Deep k-Nearest Neighbors

Papernot and McDaniel (2018) propose Deep k-Nearest Neighbors (DKNN), a modification to the test-time behavior of neural networks.

After training completes, the DKNN algorithm passes every training example through the model and saves each of the layer's representations. This creates a new dataset, whose features are the representations and whose labels are the model predictions. Test-time predictions are made by passing an example through the model and performing k-nearest neighbors classification on the resulting representations. This modification does not degrade the accuracy of image classifiers on several standard datasets (Papernot and McDaniel, 2018).

For our purposes, the benefit of DKNN is the algorithm's uncertainty metric, the *conformity* score. This score is the percentage of nearest neighbors belonging to the predicted class. Conformity follows from the framework of conformal prediction (Shafer and Vovk, 2008) and estimates how much the training data supports a classification decision.

The conformity score is based on the representations of every layer in the model, and therefore, a prediction only receives high conformity if it largely agrees with neighboring examples at all representation levels. This mechanism defends against adversarial examples (Szegedy et al., 2014), as it is difficult to construct a perturbation which changes the neighbors at every layer. Consequently, conformity is a better uncertainty metric for both regular examples and adversarial ones, making it suitable for generating interpretations.

3.2 Handling Sequences

The DKNN algorithm requires fixed-size vector representations. To reach a fixed-size representation for text classification, we can take the final hidden state of a recurrent neural network or use a form of max pooling across time (Collobert and Weston, 2008). We consider deep architectures of these two forms, using each of the layers' representations as the features.

3.3 Conformity leave-one-out

Using conformity, we generate interpretations through a modified version of leave-one-out (Li et al., 2016). After removing a word, rather than observing the drop in confidence, we instead measure the drop in conformity. Formally, we modify classifier f in Equation 1 to output probabilities based on conformity scores. We refer to this as *conformity leave-one-out* in our experiments.

4 DKNN Maintains Classification Accuracy

Interpretability should not come at the cost of performance—before investigating how interpretable DKNN is, we first evaluate its accuracy. We experiment with six text classification tasks and two models, verifying that DKNN achieves accuracy comparable to regular classifiers.

4.1 Datasets and Models

We consider six common text classification tasks: binary sentiment analysis using Stanford Sentiment Treebank (Socher et al., 2013, SST) and Customer Reviews (Hu and Liu, 2004, CR), topic classification using *TREC* (Li and Roth, 2002), opinion polarity (Wiebe et al., 2005, MPQA), and subjectivity/objectivity (Pang and Lee, 2004, SUBJ). Additionally, we consider natural language inference with SNLI (Bowman et al., 2015). We experiment with BiLSTM and CNN models.

CNN Our CNN architecture resembles Kim (2014). We use convolutional filters of size three, four, and five, with max-pooling over time (Collobert and Weston, 2008). The filters are followed by three fully-connected layers. We fine-tune GLOVE embeddings (Pennington et al., 2014) of each word. For DKNN, we use the activations from the convolution layer and the three fully-connected layers.

BiLSTM Our architecture uses a bidirectional LSTM (Graves and Schmidhuber, 2005), with the final hidden state forming the fixed-size representation. We use three LSTM layers, followed by two fully-connected layers. We fine-tune GLOVE embeddings of each word. For DKNN, we use the final activations of the three recurrent layers and the two fully-connected layers.

SNLI Classifier Unlike other tasks with a single input sentence, SNLI has two inputs, a premise and hypothesis. Following Conneau et al. (2017), we use the same model to encode the two inputs, generating representations u for the premise and v for the hypothesis. We concatenate the two representations along with their dot-product and element-wise absolute difference, arriving at a final representation $[u; v; u * v; |u - v|]$. This vector passes through two fully-connected layers for classification. For DKNN, we use the activations of the two fully-connected layers.

Nearest Neighbor Search For accurate interpretations, we trade efficiency for accuracy and replace locally sensitive hashing (Gionis et al., 1999) used by Papernot and McDaniel (2018) with a k-d tree (Bentley, 1975). We use $k = 75$ nearest neighbors at each layer. The empirical results are robust to the choice of k.

4.2 Classification Results

DKNN achieves comparable accuracy on the five classification tasks (Table 1). On SNLI, the BiL-STM achieves an accuracy of 81.2% with a soft-max classifier and 81.0% with DKNN.

5 DKNN is Interpretable

Following past work (Li et al., 2016; Murdoch et al., 2018), we focus on the SST dataset for generating interpretations. Due to the lack of standard interpretation evaluation metrics (Doshi-Velez and Kim, 2017), we use qualitative interpretation evaluations (Smilkov et al., 2017; Sundararajan et al., 2017; Li et al., 2016), performing quantitative experiments where possible to examine the distinction between the interpretation methods.

5.1 Interpretation Analysis

We compare our method (*Conformity leave-one-out*) against two baselines: leave-one-out using regular confidence (*Confidence leave-one-out*, see Section 2.1), and the gradient with respect to the input (*Gradient*, see Section 2.2). To create saliency maps, we normalize each word's importance by dividing it by the total importance of the words in the sentence. We display unknown words in angle brackets <>. Table 2 shows SST interpretation examples for the BiLSTM model. Further examples are on a supplementary website.[3]

Conformity leave-one-out assigns concentrated importance values to a small number of input words. In contrast, the baseline methods assign non-zero importance values to numerous words, many of which are irrelevant. For instance, in all three examples of Table 2, both baselines highlight almost half of the input, including words such as "about" and "movie". We suspect model confidence is oversensitive to these unimportant input changes, causing the baseline interpretations to highlight unimportant words. On the other hand, the conformity score better separates word importance, generating clearer interpretations.

The tendency for confidence-based approaches to assign importance to many words holds for the entire test set. We compute the average number of highlighted words using a threshold of 0.05 (a normalized importance value corresponding to a light blue or light red highlight). Out of the average 20.23 words in SST test set, gradient high-

lights 5.32 words, confidence leave-one-out highlights 5.79 words, and conformity leave-one-out highlights 3.65 words.

The second, and related, observation for confidence-based approaches is a bias towards selecting word importance based on the inherent sentiment, rather than a word's meaning in context. For example, see "clash", "terribly", and "unfaithful" in Table 2. The removal of these words causes a small change in the model confidence. When using DKNN, the conformity score indicates that the model's uncertainty has not risen without these input words and leave-one-out does not assign them any importance.

We characterize our interpretation method as significantly higher precision, but slightly lower recall than confidence-based methods. Conformity leave-one-out rarely assigns high importance to words that do not align with human perception of sentiment. However, there are cases when our method does not assign significant importance to any word. This occurs when the input has a high redundancy. For example, a positive movie review that describes the sentiment in four distinct ways. In these cases, leaving out a single sentiment word has little effect on the conformity as the model's representation remains supported by the other redundant features. Confidence-based interpretations, which interpret models using the linear units that produce class scores, achieve higher recall by responding to every change in the input for a certain direction but may have lower precision.

In the second example of Table 2, the word "terribly" is assigned a negative importance value, disregarding its positive meaning in context. To examine if this is a stand-alone example or a more general pattern of uninterpretable behavior, we calculate the importance value of the word "terribly" in other positive examples. For each occurrence of the word "great" in positive validation examples, we paraphrase it to "awesome", "wonderful", or "impressive", and add the word "terribly" in front of it. This process yields 66 examples. For each of these examples, we compute the importance value of each input word and rank them from most negative to most positive (the most negative word has a rank of 1). We compare the average ranking of "terribly" from the three methods: 7.9 from conformity leave-one-out, 1.68 from confidence leave-one-out, and 1.1 from gradient. The baseline methods consistently rank "terribly"

---

[3]https://sites.google.com/view/language-dknn/

	SST	CR	TREC	MPQA	SUBJ
LSTM	86.7	82.7	91.5	88.9	94.8
LSTM DKNN	86.6	82.5	91.3	88.6	94.9
CNN	85.7	83.3	92.8	89.1	93.5
CNN DKNN	85.8	83.4	92.4	88.7	93.1

Table 1: Replacing a neural network's softmax classifier with DKNN maintains classification accuracy on standard text classification tasks.

Method	Saliency Map
Conformity	an intelligent fiction about learning through cultural clash.
Confidence	an intelligent fiction about learning through cultural clash.
Gradient	an intelligent fiction about learning through cultural clash.
Conformity	<Schweiger> is talented and terribly charismatic.
Confidence	<Schweiger> is talented and terribly charismatic.
Gradient	<Schweiger> is talented and terribly charismatic.
Conformity	Diane Lane shines in unfaithful.
Confidence	Diane Lane shines in unfaithful.
Gradient	Diane Lane shines in unfaithful.
Color Legend	Positive Impact Negative Impact

Table 2: Comparison of interpretation approaches on SST test examples for the LSTM model. Blue indicates positive impact and red indicates negative impact. Our method (*Conformity* leave-one-out) has higher precision, rarely assigning importance to extraneous words such as "about" or "movie".

as the most negative word, ignoring its meaning in context. This echoes our suspicion: DKNN generates interpretations with higher precision because conformity is robust to irrelevant changes.

5.2 Analyzing Dataset Annotation Artifacts

Through DKNN, we get a new uncertainty measurement, conformity, that measures how a test example's representation is positioned relative to the training data representations. In this section, we use conformity leave-one-out to interpret a model trained on SNLI. This dataset is known to contain annotation artifacts and we demonstrate that our interpretation method can help identify when models exploit these dataset biases.

Recent studies (Gururangan et al., 2018; Poliak et al., 2018) identified annotation artifacts in the SNLI dataset. These works identified that superficial patterns exist in the input which strongly correlate with certain labels, making it possible for models to "game" the task: obtain high accuracy without true understanding. For instance, the hypothesis of an entailment example is often a more general paraphrase of the premise, using words such as "outside" instead of "playing soccer in a park". Contradiction examples often contain negation words or non-action verbs like "sleeping". Models trained solely on the hypothesis can learn these patterns to achieve an accuracy considerably higher than the majority baseline.

These studies indicate that the SNLI task can be gamed. We look to confirm that some artifacts are indeed exploited by normally trained models that use full input pairs. We create saliency maps for examples in the validation set using conformity leave-one-out. Table 3 shows samples and more can be found on the supplementary website.[4] We use the blue highlights to indicate words which positively support the model's predicted class, and the color red to indicate words that support a different class. The first example is a randomly sampled baseline, showing how the words "swims" and "pool" support the model's prediction of contradiction. The other examples are selected be-

---

[4] https://sites.google.com/view/language-dknn/

140

cause they contain terms identified as artifacts. In the second example, conformity leave-one-out assigns extremely high word importance to "sleeping", disregarding other words necessary to predict Contradiction (i.e., the Neutral class is still possible if "pets" is replaced with "people"). In the final two hypothesis, the interpretation method diagnoses the model failure, assigning high importance to "wearing", rather than focusing positively on the shirt color.

To explore this further, we compute the average importance rank using conformity and confidence leave-one-out for the top five artifacts in each SNLI class identified by Gururangan et al. (2018). Table 4 compares the average rank assigned by the two methods, sorting the words by Pointwise Mutual Information as provided by Gururangan et al. (2018). The word "nobody" particularly stands out: it is the most important input word every time it appears in a contradiction example.

For most of the artifacts, conformity leave-one-out assigns them a high importance, often ranking the artifacts as the most important input word. Confidence leave-one-out correlates less strongly with the known artifacts, frequently assigning importance values as low as fifth or sixth most important. Given the high correlation between conformity leave-one-out and the manually identified artifacts, this interpretation method may serve as a technique to identify undesirable biases a model may have learned.

6 Discussion and Related Work

We connect the improvements made by conformity leave-one-out to model confidence issues, compare alternative interpretation improvements, and discuss further features of DKNN.

6.1 Issues in Neural Network Confidence

Gradient and leave-one-out both interpret a model by determining the importance value for each input word. This effectively reduces the problem of interpretation to one of determining model uncertainty. Past work relies on model confidence as a measure of uncertainty. However, a neural network's confidence is unreasonably high: on held-out examples, it far exceeds empirical error rates (Guo et al., 2017). This is further exemplified by the high confidence predictions produced on inputs that are adversarial (Szegedy et al., 2014) or contain solely noise (Goodfellow et al.,

2015). Most importantly for interpretation, the change in confidence often will not properly reflect whether discriminative input features have been removed (Feng et al., 2018).

6.2 Confidence Calibration is Insufficient

We attribute one interpretation failure to neural network confidence issues. Guo et al. (2017) study overconfidence and propose a calibration procedure using Platt scaling. This adds a temperature to the softmax function to align confidence with accuracy. However, this is not input dependent. The confidence is lower for both full-length examples and ones with words left out. Hence, selecting influential words will remain difficult.

To verify this, we create an interpretation baseline using temperature scaling. The results corroborate the intuition: a calibrated leave-one-out does not fix the interpretation issues. Qualitatively, the calibrated interpretations are comparable to *confidence* leave-one-out. Furthermore, calibrating the DKNN conformity score followingPapernot and McDaniel (2018) does not improve interpretability compared to the uncalibrated conformity score.

6.3 Alternative Interpretation Improvements

Recent work improves interpretation methods through other means. Smilkov et al. (2017) and Sundararajan et al. (2017) both aggregate gradient values over multiple backpropagation passes to eliminate local noise or satisfy interpretation axioms. This work does not address model confidence and is orthogonal to our DKNN approach.

6.4 Interpretation Through Data Selection

Retrieval-Augmented Neural Networks (Zhao and Cho, 2018) are similar to DKNN: they augment model predictions with an information retrieval system that searches over network activations from the training data.

Retrieval-Augmented models and DKNN can both select influential training examples for a test prediction. In particular, the training data activations which are closest to the test point's activations are influential according to the model. These training examples can provide interpretations as a form of analogy (Caruana et al., 1999), an intuitive explanation for both machine learning experts and non-experts (Klein, 1989; Kim et al., 2014; Koh and Liang, 2017; Wallace and Boyd-Graber, 2018). However, unlike in computer vision where training data selection using DKNN

Prediction	Input	Saliency Map
Contradiction	Premise	a young boy reaches for and touches the propeller of a vintage aircraft.
	Hypothesis	a young boy swims in his pool.
Entailment	Premise	a brown a dog and a black dog in the edge of the ocean with a wave under them boats are on the water in the background.
	Hypothesis	the pets are sleeping on the grass..
	Premise	man in a blue shirt standing in front of a structure painted with geometric designs.
Entailment	Hypothesis	a man is wearing a blue shirt.
Entailment	Hypothesis	a man is wearing a black shirt.
Color Legend		Positive Impact Negative Impact

Table 3: Interpretations generated with conformity leave-one-out align with annotation biases identified in SNLI. In the second example, the model puts emphasis on the word "sleeping", disregarding other words that could indicate the Neutral class. The final example diagnoses a model's incorrect Entailment prediction (shown in red). Green highlights indicate words that support the classification decision made (shown in parenthesis), pink highlights indicate words that support a different class.

Label	Artifact	Conformity	Confidence
	outdoors	2.93	3.26
	least	2.22	4.41
Entailment	instrument	3.57	4.47
	outside	4.08	4.80
	animal	2.00	4.73
	tall	1.09	2.61
	first	2.14	2.99
Neutral	competition	2.33	5.56
	sad	1.39	1.79
	favorite	1.69	3.89
	nobody	1.00	1.00
	sleeping	1.64	2.34
Contradiction	no	2.53	5.74
	tv	1.92	3.74
	cat	1.42	3.62

Table 4: The top SNLI artifacts identified by Gururangan et al. (2018) are shown on the left. For each word, we compute the average importance rank over the validation set using either *Conformity* or *Confidence* leave-one-out. A score of 1.0 indicates that a word is always ranked as the most important word in the input. *Conformity* leave-one-out assigns stronger importance to artifacts, suggesting it better diagnoses model biases.

yielded interpretable examples (Papernot and McDaniel, 2018), our experiments did not find human interpretable data points for SST or SNLI.

6.5 Trust in Model Predictions

Model confidence is important for real-world applications: it signals how much one should trust a neural network's predictions. Unfortunately, users may be misled when a model outputs highly confident predictions on rubbish examples (Goodfellow et al., 2015; Nguyen et al., 2015) or adversarial examples (Szegedy et al., 2014). Recent work decides when to trust a neural network model (Ribeiro et al., 2016; Doshi-Velez and Kim, 2017; Jiang et al., 2018). For instance, analyzing local linear model approximations (Ribeiro et al., 2016) or flagging rare network activations using kernel density estimation (Jiang et al., 2018). The DKNN conformity score is a trust metric that helps defend against image adversarial examples (Papernot and McDaniel, 2018). Future work should study if this robustness extends to interpretations.

7 Future Work and Conclusion

A robust model uncertainty estimate is critical to determine feature importance. The DKNN conformity score is one such uncertainty metric which leads to higher precision interpretations. Although DKNN is only a test-time improvement—

the model is still trained with maximum likelihood. Combining nearest neighbor and maximum likelihood objectives during training may further improve model accuracy and interpretability. Moreover, other uncertainty estimators do not require test-time modifications. For example, modeling $p(x)$ and $p(y \mid \mathbf{x})$ using Bayesian Neural Networks (Gal et al., 2016).

Similar to other NLP interpretation methods (Sundararajan et al., 2017; Li et al., 2016), conformity leave-one-out works when a model's representation is fixed-sized. For other NLP tasks, such as structured prediction (e.g., translation and parsing) or span prediction (e.g., extractive summarization and reading comprehension), models output a variable number of predictions and our interpretation approach will not suffice. Developing interpretation techniques for these types of models is a necessary area for future work.

We apply DKNN to neural models for text classification. This provides a better estimate of model uncertainty—conformity—which we combine with leave-one-out. This overcomes issues stemming from neural network confidence, leading to higher precision interpretations. Most interestingly, our interpretations are supported by the training data, providing insights into the representations learned by a model.

Acknowledgments

Feng was supported under subcontract to Raytheon BBN Technologies by DARPA award HR0011-15-C-0113. JBG is supported by NSF Grant IIS1652666. Any opinions, findings, conclusions, or recommendations expressed here are those of the authors and do not necessarily reflect the view of the sponsor. The authors would like to thank the members of the CLIP lab at the University of Maryland and the anonymous reviewers for their feedback.

References

Leila Arras, Franziska Horn, Grégoire Montavon, Klaus-Robert Müller, and Wojciech Samek. 2016. Explaining predictions of non-linear classifiers in NLP. In *Workshop on Representation Learning for NLP*.

Jon Louis Bentley. 1975. Multidimensional binary search trees used for associative searching. *Communications of the ACM* .

Samuel R. Bowman, Gabor Angeli, Christopher Potts, and Christopher D. Manning. 2015. A large annotated corpus for learning natural language inference. In *EMNLP*.

Rich Caruana, Hooshang Kangarloo, John David N. Dionisio, Usha S. Sinha, and David B. Johnson. 1999. Case-based explanation of non-case-based learning methods. *Proceedings of AMIA Symposium* .

Ronan Collobert and Jason Weston. 2008. A unified architecture for natural language processing: Deep neural networks with multitask learning. In *ICML*.

Alexis Conneau, Douwe Kiela, Holger Schwenk, Loic Barrault, and Antoine Bordes. 2017. Supervised learning of universal sentence representations from natural language inference data. In *EMNLP*.

Finale Doshi-Velez and Been Kim. 2017. Towards a rigorous science of interpretable machine learning. *arXiv preprint arXiv: 1702.08608* .

Javid Ebrahimi, Anyi Rao, Daniel Lowd, and Dejing Dou. 2017. HotFlip: White-box adversarial examples for text classification. In *ACL*.

Shi Feng, Eric Wallace, Alvin Grissom II, Mohit Iyyer, Pedro Rodriguez, and Jordan Boyd-Graber. 2018. Pathologies of neural models make interpretations difficult. In *EMNLP*.

Yarin Gal, Yutian Chen, Roger Frigola, S. Gu, Alex Kendall, Yingzhen Li, Rowan McAllister, Carl Rasmussen, Ilya Sutskever, Gabriel Synnaeve, Nilesh Tripuraneni, Richard Turner, Oriol Vinyals, Adrian Weller, Mark van der Wilk, and Yan Wu. 2016. *Uncertainty in Deep Learning*. Ph.D. thesis, University of Oxford.

Amirata Ghorbani, Abubakar Abid, and James Y. Zou. 2017. Interpretation of neural networks is fragile. *arXiv preprint arXiv: 1710.10547* .

Aristides Gionis, Piotr Indyk, and Rajeev Motwani. 1999. Similarity search in high dimensions via hashing. In *VLDB*.

Ian J. Goodfellow, Jonathon Shlens, and Christian Szegedy. 2015. Explaining and harnessing adversarial examples. In *ICLR*.

Alex Graves and Jürgen Schmidhuber. 2005. Framewise phoneme classification with bidirectional LSTM and other neural network architectures. *Neural networks : the official journal of the International Neural Network Society* .

Chuan Guo, Geoff Pleiss, Yu Sun, and Kilian Q. Weinberger. 2017. On calibration of modern neural networks. In *ICML*.

Suchin Gururangan, Swabha Swayamdipta, Omer Levy, Roy Schwartz, Samuel R. Bowman, and Noah A. Smith. 2018. Annotation artifacts in natural language inference data. In *NAACL*.

Minqing Hu and Bing Liu. 2004. Mining and summarizing customer reviews. In *KDD*.

Heinrich Jiang, Been Kim, and Maya R. Gupta. 2018. To trust or not to trust a classifier. *arXiv preprint arXiv: 1805.11783* .

Been Kim, Cynthia Rudin, and Julie A. Shah. 2014. The bayesian case model: A generative approach for casebased reasoning and prototype classification. In *NIPS*.

Yoon Kim. 2014. Convolutional neural networks for sentence classification. *EMNLP* .

Pieter-Jan Kindermans, Sara Hooker, Julius Adebayo, Maximilian Alber, Kristof T. Schütt, Sven Dähne, Dumitru Erhan, and Been Kim. 2017. The (un)reliability of saliency methods. *arXiv preprint arXiv: 1711.00867* .

Gary A. Klein. 1989. Do decision biases explain too much. In *Proceedings of the Human Factors and Ergonomics Society*.

Pang Wei Koh and Percy Liang. 2017. Understanding black-box predictions via influence functions. In *ICML*.

Jiwei Li, Will Monroe, and Daniel Jurafsky. 2016. Understanding neural networks through representation erasure. *arXiv preprint arXiv: 1612.08220* .

Xin Li and Dan Roth. 2002. Learning question classifiers. In *COLT*.

W. James Murdoch, Peter J. Liu, and Bin Yu. 2018. Beyond word importance: Contextual decomposition to extract interactions from lstms. In *ICLR*.

Anh Mai Nguyen, Jason Yosinski, and Jeff Clune. 2015. Deep neural networks are easily fooled: High confidence predictions for unrecognizable images. In *CVPR*.

Bo Pang and Lillian Lee. 2004. A sentimental education: Sentiment analysis using subjectivity summarization based on minimum cuts. In *ACL*.

Nicolas Papernot and Patrick D. McDaniel. 2018. Deep k-nearest neighbors: Towards confident, interpretable and robust deep learning. *arXiv preprint arXiv: 1803.04765* .

Jeffrey Pennington, Richard Socher, and Christopher D. Manning. 2014. GloVe: Global vectors for word representation. In *EMNLP*.

Adam Poliak, Jason Naradowsky, Aparajita Haldar, Rachel Rudinger, and Benjamin Van Durme. 2018. Hypothesis only baselines in natural language inference. In **SEM@NAACL-HLT* .

Marco Túlio Ribeiro, Sameer Singh, and Carlos Guestrin. 2016. Why should i trust you?": Explaining the predictions of any classifier. In *KDD*.

Glenn Shafer and Vladimir Vovk. 2008. A tutorial on conformal prediction. *JMLR* .

Daniel Smilkov, Nikhil Thorat, Been Kim, Fernanda B. Viégas, and Martin Wattenberg. 2017. SmoothGrad: removing noise by adding noise. *arXiv preprint arXiv: 1706.03825* .

Richard Socher, A. V. Perelygin, Jean Wu, Jason Chuang, Christopher D. Manning, Andrew Ng, and Christopher Potts. 2013. Recursive deep models for semantic compositionality over a sentiment treebank. In *EMNLP*.

Mukund Sundararajan, Ankur Taly, and Qiqi Yan. 2017. Axiomatic attribution for deep networks. In *ICML*.

Christian Szegedy, Wojciech Zaremba, Ilya Sutskever, Joan Bruna, Dumitru Erhan, Ian J. Goodfellow, and Rob Fergus. 2014. Intriguing properties of neural networks. In *ICLR*.

Eric Wallace and Jordan Boyd-Graber. 2018. Trick me if you can: Adversarial writing of trivia challenge questions. In *Proceedings of ACL 2018 Student Research Workshop*.

Janyce Wiebe, Theresa Wilson, and Claire Cardie. 2005. Annotating expressions of opinions and emotions in language. In *LREC*.

Jake Zhao and Kyunghyun Cho. 2018. Retrievalaugmented convolutional neural networks for improved robustness against adversarial examples. *arXiv preprint arXiv: 1802.09502* .

Indicatements that character language models learn English morpho-syntactic units and regularities

Yova Kementchedjhieva
University of Copenhagen
yova@di.ku.dk

Adam Lopez
University of Edinburgh
alopez@inf.ed.ac.uk

Abstract

Character language models have access to surface morphological patterns, but it is not clear whether or *how* they learn abstract morphological regularities. We instrument a character language model with several probes, finding that it can develop a specific unit to identify word boundaries and, by extension, morpheme boundaries, which allows it to capture linguistic properties and regularities of these units. Our language model proves surprisingly good at identifying the selectional restrictions of English derivational morphemes, a task that requires both morphological and syntactic awareness. Thus we conclude that, when morphemes overlap extensively with the words of a language, a character language model can perform morphological abstraction.

1 Introduction

Character-level language models (Sutskever et al., 2011) are appealing because they enable open-vocabulary generation of language, and *conditional* character language models have now been convincingly used in speech recognition (Chan et al., 2016) and machine translation (Weiss et al., 2017; Lee et al., 2016; Chung et al., 2016). They succeed due to parameter-sharing between frequent, rare, and even unobserved training words, prompting claims that they learn morphosyntactic properties of words. For example, Chung et al. (2016) claim that character language models yield "better modelling [of] rare morphological variants" while Kim et al. (2016) claim that "Character-level models obviate the need for morphological tagging or manual feature engineering." But these claims of morphological awareness are backed more by intuition than direct empirical evidence. What do these models really learn about morphology? And, to the extent that they learn about morphology, *how* do they learn it?

Our goal is to shed light on these questions, and to that end, we study the behavior of a character-level language model (hereafter LM) applied to English. We observe that, when generating text, the LM applies certain morphological processes of English productively, i.e. in novel contexts (§3). This rather surprising finding suggests that the model can identify the morphemes relevant to these processes. An analysis of the LM's hidden units presents a possible explanation: there appears to be one particular unit that fires at morpheme and word boundaries (§4). Further experiments reveal that the LM learns morpheme boundaries through extrapolation from word boundaries (§5). In addition to morphology, the LM appears to encode syntactic information about words, i.e. their part of speech (§6). With access to both morphology and syntax, the model should also be able to learn linguistic phenomena at the intersection of the two domains, which we indeed find to be the case: the LM captures the (syntactic) selectional restrictions of English derivational morphemes, albeit with some incorrect generalizations (§7). The conclusions of this work can thus be summarized in two main points—a character-level language model can:

1. learn to identify linguistic units of higher order, such as morphemes and words.

2. learn some underlying linguistic properties and regularities of said units.

2 Language Modeling

The LM explored in this work is a 'wordless' character RNN with LSTM units (Karpathy, 2015).[1]

---

[1] Karpathy (2015) is a blog post that discusses exactly this model. We are unaware of scholarly publications that use this model in isolation, though it is used in several conditional models (Chan et al., 2016; Weiss et al., 2017; Lee et al., 2016; Chung et al., 2016), and it is similar to the character RNN

Proceedings of the 2018 EMNLP Workshop BlackboxNLP: Analyzing and Interpreting Neural Networks for NLP, pages 145–153
Brussels, Belgium, November 1, 2018. ©2018 Association for Computational Linguistics

It is 'wordless' in the sense that input is not segmented into words, and spaces are treated just like any other character. This architecture allows for experiments on a subword, i.e. morphological level: we can feed a partial word and ask the model to complete it or record the probability the model assigns to an ending of our choice.

2.1 Formulation

At each timestep t, character c_t is projected into a high-dimensional space by a character embedding matrix $\mathbf{E} \in \mathbb{R}^{|V| \times d}$: $\mathbf{x}_{c_t} = \mathbf{E}^T \mathbf{v}_{c_t}$, where $|V|$ is the vocabulary of characters encountered in the training data, d is the dimension of the character embeddings and $\mathbf{v}_{c_t} \in \mathbb{R}^{|V|}$ is a one-hot vector with c_tth element set to 1 and all other elements set to zero.

The hidden state of the neural network is obtained as: $\mathbf{h}_t = \mathrm{LSTM}(\mathbf{x}_{c_t}; \mathbf{h}_{t-1})$. This hidden state is followed by a linear transformation and a softmax function over all elements of V, which results in a probability distribution.

$$p(c_{t+1} = c \mid \mathbf{h}_t) = \mathrm{softmax}(\mathbf{W}_o \mathbf{h}_t + \mathbf{b}_o)_i \quad \forall c \in V$$

where i is the index of c in V.

2.2 Training

The model was trained on a continuous stream of the first 7M character tokens from the English Wikipedia corpus. Data was not lowercased and it was randomly split into training (90%) and development (10%). Following a grid search over hyperparameters on a subset of the training data, we chose to use one layer with a hidden unit size of 256, a learning rate of 0.003, minibatch size of 50, and dropout rate of 0.2, applied to the input of the hidden layer.

3 The English dialect of a character LM

In an initial analysis of the learned model we studied text generated with the LM and found that it closely resembled English on the word level and, to some degree, on the level of syntax.

3.1 Words

When sampled, the LM generates real English words most of the time, and only about 1 in every 20 tokens is a nonce word.[2] Regular morpho-

---

of Sutskever et al. (2011), which uses a multiplicative RNN rather than an LSTM unit.

[2] As measured by checking whether the word appeared in the training data or in the *pyenchant* UK or US English dictionaries.

| sinding, fatities, complessed |
| breaked, indicatement |
| applie, therapie |
| knwotator, mindt, ouctromor |

Table 1: Nonce words generated with the LM through sampling.

| The novel regarded the modern Laboratory has a weaken-little director and many of them in 2012 to defeat in 1973 - or eviven of Artitagements. |

Table 2: A sentence generated with the LM through sampling.

logical patterns can be observed within some of these nonce words (Table 1). The words *sinding*, *fatities* and *complessed* all seem like well-formed inflected variants of English-looking words. The forms *breaked* and *indicatement* show productive morphological patterns of inflection and derivation being applied to bases of the correct syntactic class, namely verbs. It happens that *break* is an irregular verb and *indicate* forms a noun with suffix *-ion* rather than *-ment*, but these are lexical rules that block the more regular inflectional and derivational rules the LM has applied. In addition to composing morphologically complex words, the LM also attempts to decompose them, as can be seen with the forms *therapie* and *applie*. Here the inflectional suffix *-s* has been dropped, but the orthographic change associated with it has not been successfully reversed. Not all nonce words generated by the LM can be explained in terms of morphological productivity, however: *knwotator, mindt,* and *ouctromor* don't resemble any real morphemes and don't follow English phonotactics. These forms may be highly improbable accidents of the sampling process.

3.2 Sentences

Consider the sentence in Table 2 generated with the LM through sampling. The sentence could not be considered fluent or grammatical: there are no clear dependencies between verbs, subjects, and objects; it contains the nonce word *eviven* and the novel and unlikely compound *weaken-little*. Yet, some short-distance syntactic regularities can be observed. Articles precede adjectives and nouns but not verbs, prepositions precede nouns, and particle *to* precedes a verb. On an even larger scale, the clause *the novel regarded the modern Labora-*

Unit	t_{-13}	$\ldots$	t
Punctuation	r (1936-1939)		
	chool in 1921.		
	il 13 , 1813 .		
	ified in 1901.		
	_(1993-1998)		
Word	's predictions		
	ral relativism		
	_contributions		
	_were contract		
	at connections		
Latinate suffix	ered in inform		
	_the concentra		
	ultural recrea		
	_was accommoda		
	_Reyes introdu		

Table 3: Top 5 Contexts for Three Units in the Network of the LM. The last character in each string marks the peak in activation.

tory has a weaken-little director is grammatical in terms of the order between parts of speech[3]. The sentence appears unnatural due to its odd semantics, but consider the following alternative choice of words for the same syntactic structure: *the man thought the modern laboratory has a weaken-little director*. This sentence sounds only marginally anomalous.

The predominantly well-formed output of the LM suggests that it is appropriate to further study the linguistic regularities learned by it.

4 Meaningful hidden units in the LM

The hidden units of the LM were analyzed by feeding the training data back into the system and tracking unit activations on each timestep, i.e. after every character. For each unit, the five inputs which triggered highest activation (highest absolute value) were recorded (Kadar et al., 2016). About 40 units exhibited patterns of activation that could be identified as meaningful with the human eye. We selected three of the more interesting units to briefly discuss here. Table 3 shows a list of the top five triggers for each of these units, together with up to 13 characters that preceded them, to put them in context. One unit, which we'll dub the *punctuation* unit, seems to respond to closing punctuation marks. Another, dubbed the *Latinate suffix* unit, appears to recognize contexts that are likely to precede suffix *-ion* and its variants, *-ation*, *-ction* and *-tion*.

---

[3]That is, assuming that *novel* is a noun in this context and *weaken-little* is an adjective, by analogy with its second base.

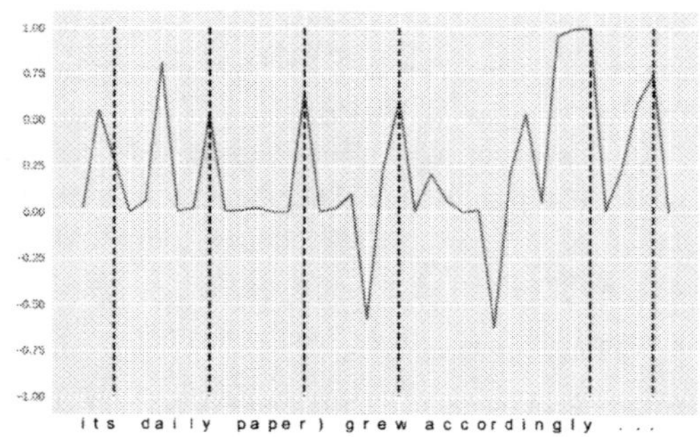

Figure 1: Activation of the *word* unit. Query: *its daily paper) grew accordingly*

4.1 The *word* unit

The most interesting unit, the *word* unit, appears to recognize complete words and sub-word units within them. Figure 1 shows the activation pattern of the *word* unit over a partial sentence from the training data. The dotted lines, which mark the end of tokens, often coincide with the peaks in activation. The unit also recognizes the base *it* within *its* and *according* within *accordingly*. The behavior of the unit could be explained either as a signal for the end of a familiar, repeated pattern, or as a predictor of a following space. The fact that we don't see a peak in activation at the right bracket symbol (which should be a cue for a following space) suggests that the former explanation is more plausible. Support for this idea comes from the low correlation coefficient between the activation of the unit and the probability the model assigns to a following space: only 0.08 across the entire training set. It appears that the LM knows that linguistic units need not occur on their own, i.e. that in a lot of cases a suffix is very likely to follow.

5 Morphemes encoded by the LM

Morphological segmentation aims to identify the boundaries in morphologically complex words, i.e. words consisting of multiple morphemes. A morpheme boundary could separate a base from an inflectional morpheme, e.g. *like+s* and *carrie+s*, a base from a derivational morpheme, e.g. *consider+able*, or two bases, e.g. *air+plane*. One approach to morphological segmentation is to see it as a sequence-labeling task, where words are processed one character at a time and every between-character position is considered a potential boundary. RNNs are particularly suitable for sequence labeling and recent work on supervised morphological segmentation with RNNs shows promising results (Wang et al., 2016).

In this experiment we probe the LM using a model for morphological segmentation to test the extent to which the LM captures morphological regularities.

5.1 Formulation

At each timestep t, character c_t is projected into high-dimensional space:

$$\mathbf{x}_{c_t} = \mathbf{E}^T \mathbf{v}_i \qquad \mathbf{E} \in \mathbb{R}^{|V_{char}| \times d_{char}}$$

The hidden state of the encoder is obtained as before: $\mathbf{h}_t^{enc} = LSTM^{enc}(\mathbf{x}_{c_t}; \mathbf{h}_{t-1}^{enc})$. The hidden state of the decoder is then obtained as: $\mathbf{h}_t^{dec} = LSTM^{dec}(\mathbf{h}_t^{enc}; \mathbf{h}_{t-1}^{dec})$ and followed by a linear transformation and a softmax function over all elements in V_{lab}, which results in a probability distribution over labels.

$$p(l_t = l \mid \mathbf{c}, \mathbf{l}_{word}) = \mathrm{softmax}(\mathbf{W}_o^{dec}\mathbf{h}_t^{dec} + \mathbf{b}_o^{dec})_i$$
$$\forall \quad l \in V_{lab}$$

where $\mathbf{l}_{word}$ refers to all previous labels for the current word and i refers to the index of l in V_{lab}.

The embedding matrix, $\mathbf{E}$ and $LSTM^{enc}$ weights are taken from the LM. Decoder weights and bias terms are learned during training.

5.2 Data

The model (hereafter referred to as C2M, character-to-morpheme) was trained on a combined set of gold standard (GS) segmentations from MorphoChallenge 2010 and Hutmegs 1.0 (free data). The data consisted of 2275 word forms; 90% were used for training and 10% for testing. For the purposes of meaningful LM embeddings, which are highly contextual, a past context is necessary. Since GS segmentations are available for words in isolation only, we extract contexts for every word from the Wiki data, taking the 15 word tokens that preceded the word on up to 15 of its appearances in the dump. The occurrence of a word in each of its contexts was then treated as a separate training instance.

5.3 Performance

The system achieved a rather low F1 score: 53.3. Compared to Ruokolainen et al. (2013), who obtain F1 score 86.5 with a bidirectional CRF model, C2M is clearly inferior. This is not particularly

Model	Precision	Recall	F1
C2M - WE	76.6	62.6	68.9
C2M - ¬WE	23.1	34.2	27.6
C2M - EOW	98.5	84.4	90.90
C2M - ¬PREF	53.6	59.2	56.3

Table 4: C2M Performance. WE stand for word edge, EOW for end of word, and PREF for prefix.

surprising given that the CRF makes predictions conditioned on past and future context, while C2M only has access to the past context. Recall also that the encoder of C2M shares the weights of the LM and is not fine-tuned for morphological segmentation. But taken as a probe of the LM's encoding, the F1 score of 53.3 suggests that this encoding still contains some information about morpheme boundaries. A breakdown of morphemic boundaries by type provides insights into the source of performance and limitations of C2M.

Potential word endings as cues for morpheme boundaries The results labeled *C2M - WE* and *C2M - ¬WE* in Table 4 refer to two types of morpheme boundaries: boundaries that could also be a word ending (WE), e.g. *drink+ing, agree+ment*, and boundaries that could not be a word ending (¬ WE), e.g. *dis+like, intens+ify*. It becomes apparent that a large portion of the correct segmentations produced by C2M can be attributed to an ability to recognize word endings. Earlier findings relating to the *word* unit of the LM (section 4.1) align with this line of argument: the unit indeed detects words, and those morphemes that resemble words. The sample segmentations in A and C of Table 5 can be straightforwardly explained in terms of transfer knowledge on word endings: *act, action* and *ant* are all words the LM has encountered during training. Notice that the morpheme *ant* has not been observed by C2M, i.e. it is not in the training data, but its status as a word is encoded by the LM.

Actual word endings An interesting result emerges when C2M's performance is tested on word-final characters, which by default should all be labeled as a morpheme boundary (*C2M - EOW* in Table 4). Recall that the rest of the results exclude these predictions, since morphological segmentation concerns word-internal morpheme boundaries. C2M performs extremely well at identifying actual word endings. The margin between *C2M - WE* results and *C2M - EOW* results is

	Input	True Segmentation	Predicted Segmentation	Correct
A.	actions	act+ion+s	act+ion+s	✓
B.	acquisition	acquisit+ion	acquisit+ion	✓
C.	antenna	antenna	ant+enna	
D.	included	in+clud+ed	in+clude+d	✓
E.	intensely	in+tense+ly	intense+ly	
F.	misunderstanding	mis+under+stand+ing	misunder+stand+ing	
G.	woodwork	wood+work	wood+work	✓

Table 5: Sample predictions of morphological segmentations.

substantial, even though both look at units of the same type, namely words. The higher accuracy in the EOW setting shows that the LM prefers to ends word where they actually end, rather than at earlier points that would have also allowed it. The LM thus appears to take into consideration context and what words would syntactically fit in it. Consider example E in Table 5. This instance of the word *in+tense+ly* occurred in the context of *the Himalayan regions of*. In this context C2M fails to predict a morpheme boundary, even though *in* is a very frequent word on its own. The LM may be aware that preposition *in* would not fit syntactically in the context, i.e. that the sequence *regions of in* is ungrammatical. It thus waits to see a longer sequence that would better fit the context, such as *intense* or *intensely*. Example D shows that C2M is indeed capable of segmenting prefix *in* in other contexts. The word *included* is preceded by the context *the English term propaganda*. This context allows a following preposition: *the English term propaganda in*, so the LM predicted that the word may end after just *in*, which allowed C2M to correctly predict a boundary after the prefix.

6 Parts of speech encoded by the LM

Part-of-speech (POS) tagging is also seen as a sequence labeling task because words can take on different parts of speech in different contexts. Access to the subword level can be highly beneficial to POS tagging, since the shape of words often reveals their syntax: words ending in *-ed*, for example, are much more often verbs or adjectives than nouns. Recent studies in the area of POS tagging demonstrate that processing input on a subword-level indeed boosts the performance of such systems (dos Santos and Zadrozny, 2014). Here we probe the LM with a POS-tagging model, hereafter C2T (character-to-tag). Its formulation is identical to that of C2M.

6.1 Data

We used the English UD corpus (with UD POS tags) with an 80-10-10 train-dev-test split. Training data for character-level prediction was created by pairing each character of a word with the POS tag of that word, e.g. 'like$_{VERB}$' was labeled as as $\langle VERB\ VERB\ VERB\ VERB \rangle$. UD doesn't specify a POS tag for the space character, so we used the generic X tag for it. Similarly to C2M, encodings for C2T were obtained for words in context.

6.2 Performance

C2T obtained an accuracy score of 78.85% on the character level and 87.06% on the word level, where word-level accuracy was measured by comparing the tag predicted for the last character of a word to the gold standard tag. The per-character score is naturally lower by a large margin, as predictions early on in the word are based on very little information about the identity of the word. Notice that the per-word score for C2T falls short of the state-of-the-art in POS tagging due a structural limitation: the tagger assigns tags based on just past and present information. The high accuracy of C2T in spite of this limitation suggests that the majority of the information concerning the POS tag of a word is contained within that word and its past context, and that the LM is particularly good at encoding this information.

Evolution of Tag Predictions over Time Figure 6.2 illustrates the evolution of POS tag predictions over the string *and I have already overheard youngsters* (extract from the UD data) as processed by C2T. Early into the word *already*, for example, C2T identifies the word, recognizes it as an adverb and maintains this hypothesis throughout. With respect to the morphologically complex word *youngsters* we see C2T making reasonable predictions, predicting PRON for *you-*, ADJ for the next two characters and NOUN for *youngster-* and *youngsters*.

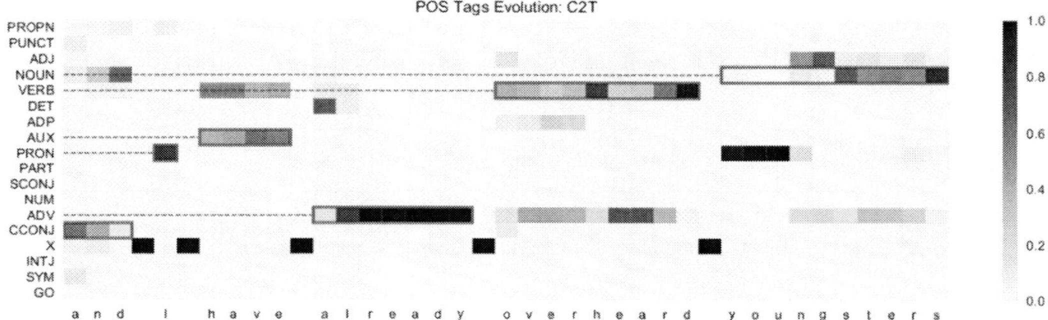

Figure 2: C2T Evolution of POS Tag Predictions. Red rectangles point to the correct tags of words.

7 Selectional restrictions in the LM

English derivational suffixes have **selectional restrictions** with respect to the syntactic category of the base they would attach to. Suffixes *-al, -ment* and *-ance*, for example, only attach to verbs, e.g. *betrayal, annoyance, containment*, while *-hood, -ous*, and *-ic* only attach to nouns, as in *nationhood, spacious and metallic*.[4] The former are thus known as **deverbal**, and the latter as **denominal**. Certain suffixes are members of more than one class, e.g. *-ful* attaches to both verbs and nouns, as in *forgetful* and *peaceful*, respectively. Since our LM appears to encode information about (some) morphological units and part of speech, it is natural to wonder whether it also encodes information about selectional restrictions of derivational suffixes. If it does, then the probability of a deverbal suffix should be significantly higher after a verbal base than after other bases, likewise with denominal suffixes and nominal bases. Our next experiment tests whether this is so.

7.1 Method

Our experiment measures and compares the probability of suffixes with different selectional restrictions across subsets of nominal, verbal, and adjectival bases, as processed by the LM. We use carefully chosen nonce words as bases in order to abstract away from previously seen base-suffix combinations, which the model may have simply memorized.

Probability We compute the probability of a suffix given a base as the joint probability of its characters. For example, the probability of suffix

---

[4] All examples are from Fabb (1988).

-ion attaching to base *edit* is:

$$p(ion \mid edit) = p(i \mid edit) \times p(o \mid editi) \times p(n \mid editio)$$

Since the LM is a wordless language model, $p(\cdot \mid base)$ is approximated from $p(\cdot \mid c)$ where c is the entire past. The probability of a suffix in the context of a particular syntactic category was computed as the average probability over all bases belonging to that category.

Nonce Bases Nonce bases were obtained by sampling complete words from the LM—that is, sequences delimited by a space or punctuation on both sides. We discarded all words that appeared in an English dictionary, and imposed several restrictions on the remaining candidates: their probability had to be at most one standard deviation below the mean for real words (to ensure they weren't highly unlikely accidents of the sampling procedure), and the probability of a following space character had to be at most one standard deviation below the mean for real words (to avoid prematurely finished words, such as *measu* and *experimen*). In addition, nonce words had to be composed entirely of lowercase characters and couldn't end in a suffix (as certain suffixes included in the experiment only attach to base stems). The candidates that met these conditions were labeled for POS using C2T. The final nonce bases used were the ones whose POS tag confidence was at most one standard deviation below the mean confidence with which tags of real words were assigned. Some examples of nonce words from the final selection are shown in Table 6. An embedding was recorded for every nonce word that met these conditions by taking the hid-

Noun	crystale, algorithm, cosmony, landlough
Verb	underspire, restruct, actrace
Adjective	nucleent, transplet, orthouble

Table 6: Sample Nonce Bases

Noun	-ous, -an, -ic, -ate, -ary, -hood, -less, -ish
Verb	-ance, -ment, -ant, -ory, -ive, -ion, -able, -ably
Adjective	-ness, -ity, -en

Table 7: Syntactically unambiguous derivational suffixes

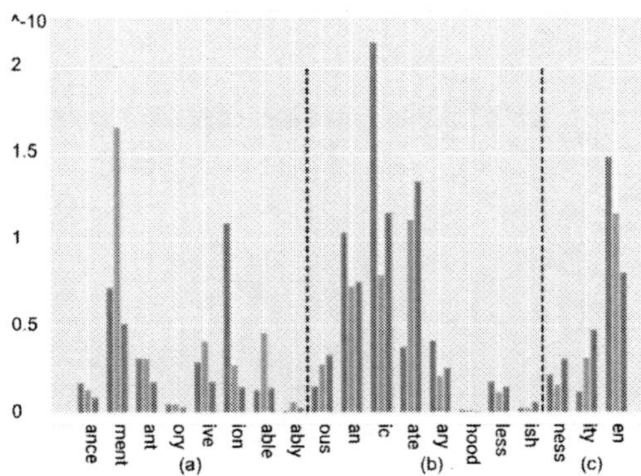

Figure 3: Suffix Probability Following Nominal (blue), Verbal (green) and Adjectival (red) Bases. Suffixes are grouped according to their selectional restrictions: (a) deverbal, (b) denominal and (c) deadjectival. Eleven out of nineteen suffixes obtained highest probability following the syntactic category that matched their selectional restrictions.

den state of the language model at the end of the word in context.

Suffixes The suffixes included in this experiment (listed in Table 7) were taken from Fabb (1988), one of the most extensive studies of the selectional restrictions of English derivational suffixes. Fabb discussed 43 suffixes, many of which attach to a base of two out of three available syntactic categories, e.g. *-ize* attaches to both nouns, as in *symbolize*, and adjectives, as in *specialize*. The analysis of such syntactically ambiguous suffixes is complex since the frequency with which they attach to each base type should be taken into consideration, but such statistics are not readily available and require morphological parsing. For the purposes of the present study ambiguous suffixes were thus excluded and only the remaining nineteen suffixes were used.

7.2 Results

Figure 3 shows the results from the experiment. Eleven out of nineteen suffixes exhibit the expected behavior: suffixes *-ment, -ive, -able, -ably, -an, -ic, -ary, -hood, -less, ness* and *-ity* are more probable in the context of their corresponding syntactic base than in other contexts. Suffix *-ment*, for instance, is more than twice as probable in the context of a verbal base than in the context of a nominal or an adjectival base. The fact that almost 70% of suffixes 'select' their correct bases, points to a linguistic awareness within the LM with respect to the selectional restrictions of suffixes.

Despite the overall success of the LM in this respect, some suffixes show a definitive preference for the wrong base. A further analysis of some of these cases shows that they don't necessarily counter the evidence for syntactic awareness within the LM.

7.3 Suffix *-ion*

Deverbal suffix *-ion* should be most probable following verbs, but prefers nominal bases. Notice that *-ion* is a noun-forming suffix: $communicate_{VERB} \rightarrow communication_{NOUN}$, $regress_{VERB} \rightarrow regression_{NOUN}$. It appears that from the perspective of the LM, the syntactic category of such morphologically complex forms extends to their bases, e.g. the LM perceives the *populat* substring in *population* as nominal. This observation can be explained precisely with reference to the high frequency of suffix *-ion*: the suffix itself occurred in 18,945 words in the dataset, while the frequency of its various bases in isolation, e.g. of *populate, regress*, etc., was estimated to be only 9,755[5]. This shows that bases that can take suffix *-ion* were seen more often with it than without it. As a consequence, the LM is biased to expect a noun when seeing one of these character sequences and may thus perceive the base itself as a nominal one.

The tag prediction evolution over *population* and *renewable* in Figure 4, show that this is indeed the case, by comparing a base suffixed with *-ion* to a base suffixed with *-able* (whose selectional restrictions, we know, were learned correctly). For both words C2T starts off predicting NOUN. For

---

[5]To estimate this, we removed the suffix of each word and then searched for the remainder in isolation, followed by *e* and followed by *s/ es*—e.g. for *population* we counted the occurrences of *populat, populate, populates* and *populated*.

151

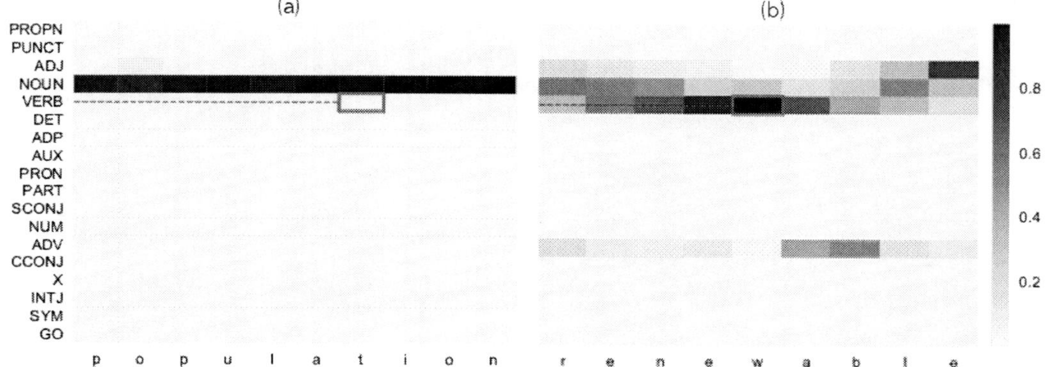

Figure 4: C2T Evolution: (a) *population* and (b) *renewable*. The red square points to the syntactic category of the base.

renew it switches to VERB, which is the correct tag for this base, and only upon seeing the suffix, progresses to the conclusive ADJ tag for *renewable*. For *population*, in contrast the prediction remains constant at NOUN, which is indeed the category of the word, as determined by the suffix.

8 Conclusion

This work presented an exploratory analysis of a 'wordless' character language model, aiming to identify the morpho-syntactic regularities captured by the model.

The first conclusion of this work is that morpheme boundaries are mainly learned by the LM through analogy with syntactic boundaries. Findings relating to the extremely frequent suffix *-ion* illustrate that the LM was able to learn to identify purely morphological boundaries through generalization. But a prerequisite for this generalization is that a morpho-syntactic boundary was also seen in the relevant position during training.

The second conclusion is that having recognized certain boundaries and by extension, the units that lie between them, the model could also learn the regularities that concern these units, e.g. the selectional restrictions of most derivational suffixes included in the study could be captured accurately.

9 Implications for future research

The above conclusions have strong implications with respect to the use of character-level LMs for languages other than English.

English is the perfect candidate for character-level language modeling, due to its fairly poor inflectional morphology. The nature of English is such that the boundary between a base and a suffix is often also a potential word boundary, which makes suffixes easily segmentable. This is not the case for many languages with richer and more complex morphology. Without access to the units of verbal morphology, it is less clear how the model would learn these types of regularities. This shortcoming should hold not just for the LM but for any character-level language model that processes input as a stream of characters without segmentation on the subword level.

This implication is in line with the results of Vania and Lopez (2017) showing that for many languages, language modeling accuracy improves when the model is provided with explicit morphological annotations during training, with English showing relatively small improvements. Our analysis might explain why this is so; we expect analyses of other languages to yield further insight.

Finally, we should point out that it may not be the case that a single, highly-specified *word* unit should exist in every character-level LM. Qian et al. (2016) find that different levels of linguistic knowledge are encoded with different model architectures, and Kádár et al. (2018) find that even a different initialization of an otherwise identical model can results in very different hierarchical processing of the input. We consider ourselves lucky for coming across this particular setup that produced a model with very interpretable behavior, but we also acknowledge the importance of evaluating the reliability of the *word* unit finding in future work.

Acknowledgements

We thank Sorcha Gilroy, Joana Ribeiro, Clara Vania, and the anonymous reviewers for comments on previous drafts of this paper.

References

William Chan, Navdeep Jaitly, Quoc Le, and Oriol Vinyals. 2016. Listen, attend and spell: A neural network for large vocabulary conversational speech recognition. In *Acoustics, Speech and Signal Processing (ICASSP), 2016 IEEE International Conference on*, pages 4960–4964. IEEE.

Junyoung Chung, Kyunghyun Cho, and Yoshua Bengio. 2016. A character-level decoder without explicit segmentation for neural machine translation. *arXiv preprint arXiv:1603.06147*.

Nigel Fabb. 1988. English suffixation is constrained only by selectional restrictions. *Natural Language and Linguistic Theory*, 6(4):527–539.

Akos Kadar, Grzegorz Chrupala, and Afra Alishahi. 2016. Representation of linguistic form and function in recurrent neural networks.

Ákos Kádár, Marc-Alexandre Côté, Grzegorz Chrupała, and Afra Alishahi. 2018. Revisiting the hierarchical multiscale lstm. *arXiv preprint arXiv:1807.03595*.

Andrej Karpathy. 2015. The unreasonable effectiveness of recurrent neural networks. *Andrej Karpathy blog*.

Yoon Kim, Yacine Jernite, David Sontag, and Alexander M Rush. 2016. Character-aware neural language models. In *Proceedings of AAAI*, pages 2741–2749.

Jason Lee, Kyunghyun Cho, and Thomas Hofmann. 2016. Fully Character-Level Neural Machine Translation without Explicit Segmentation. *Acl-2016*, pages 1693–1703.

Peng Qian, Xipeng Qiu, and Xuanjing Huang. 2016. Analyzing linguistic knowledge in sequential model of sentence. In *Proceedings of the 2016 Conference on Empirical Methods in Natural Language Processing*, pages 826–835.

Teemu Ruokolainen, Oskar Kohonen, Sami Virpioja, and Mikko Kurimo. 2013. Supervised morphological segmentation in a low-resource learning setting using conditional random fields. In *CoNLL*, pages 29–37.

Cicero Nogueira dos Santos and Bianca Zadrozny. 2014. Learning Character-level Representations for Part-of-Speech Tagging. *Proceedings of the 31st International Conference on Machine Learning*, ICML-14(2011):1818–1826.

Ilya Sutskever, James Martens, and Geoffrey E Hinton. 2011. Generating text with recurrent neural networks. In *Proceedings of the 28th International Conference on Machine Learning (ICML)*, pages 1017–1024.

Clara Vania and Adam Lopez. 2017. From Characters to Words to in Between : Do We Capture Morphology ? *To appear in Proceedings of the 55th Annual Meeting of the Association for Computational Linguistics*.

Linlin Wang, Zhu Cao, Yu Xia, and Gerard de Melo. 2016. Morphological segmentation with window lstm neural networks. In *AAAI*, pages 2842–2848.

Ron J Weiss, Jan Chorowski, Navdeep Jaitly, Yonghui Wu, and Zhifeng Chen. 2017. Sequence-to-sequence models can directly translate foreign speech. *arXiv preprint arXiv:1703.08581*.

LISA: Explaining Recurrent Neural Network Judgments via Layer-wIse Semantic Accumulation and Example to Pattern Transformation

Pankaj Gupta[1,2], Hinrich Schütze[2]

[1]Corporate Technology, Machine-Intelligence (MIC-DE), Siemens AG Munich, Germany
[2]CIS, University of Munich (LMU) Munich, Germany
`pankaj.gupta@siemens.com`
`pankaj.gupta@campus.lmu.de | inquiries@cislmu.org`

Abstract

Recurrent neural networks (RNNs) are temporal networks and cumulative in nature that have shown promising results in various natural language processing tasks. Despite their success, it still remains a challenge to understand their hidden behavior. In this work, we analyze and interpret the cumulative nature of RNN via a proposed technique named as *Layer-wIse-Semantic-Accumulation* (LISA) for explaining decisions and detecting the most likely (i.e., saliency) patterns that the network relies on while decision making. We demonstrate (1) *LISA*: "How an RNN accumulates or builds semantics during its sequential processing for a given text example and expected response" (2) *Example2pattern*: "How the saliency patterns look like for each category in the data according to the network in decision making". We analyse the sensitiveness of RNNs about different inputs to check the increase or decrease in prediction scores and further extract the saliency patterns learned by the network. We employ two relation classification datasets: SemEval 10 Task 8 and TAC KBP Slot Filling to explain RNN predictions via the *LISA* and *example2pattern*.

1 Introduction

The interpretability of systems based on deep neural network is required to be able to explain the reasoning behind the network prediction(s), that offers to (1) verify that the network works as expected and identify the cause of incorrect decision(s) (2) understand the network in order to improve data or model with or without human intervention. There is a long line of research in techniques of interpretability of Deep Neural networks (DNNs) via different aspects, such as explaining network decisions, data generation, etc. Erhan et al. (2009); Hinton (2012); Simonyan et al. (2013) and Nguyen et al. (2016) focused on model

aspects to interpret neural networks via activation maximization approach by finding inputs that maximize activations of given neurons. Goodfellow et al. (2014) interprets by generating adversarial examples. However, Baehrens et al. (2010) and Bach et al. (2015); Montavon et al. (2017) explain neural network predictions by sensitivity analysis to different input features and decomposition of decision functions, respectively.

Recurrent neural networks (RNNs) (Elman, 1990) are temporal networks and cumulative in nature to effectively model sequential data such as text or speech. RNNs and their variants such as LSTM (Hochreiter and Schmidhuber, 1997) have shown success in several natural language processing (NLP) tasks, such as entity extraction (Lample et al., 2016; Ma and Hovy, 2016), relation extraction (Vu et al., 2016a; Miwa and Bansal, 2016; Gupta et al., 2016, 2018c), language modeling (Mikolov et al., 2010; Peters et al., 2018), slot filling (Mesnil et al., 2015; Vu et al., 2016b), machine translation (Bahdanau et al., 2014), sentiment analysis (Wang et al., 2016; Tang et al., 2015), semantic textual similarity (Mueller and Thyagarajan, 2016; Gupta et al., 2018a) and dynamic topic modeling (Gupta et al., 2018d).

Past works (Zeiler and Fergus, 2014; Dosovitskiy and Brox, 2016) have mostly analyzed deep neural network, especially CNN in the field of computer vision to study and visualize the features learned by neurons. Recent studies have investigated visualization of RNN and its variants. Tang et al. (2017) visualized the memory vectors to understand the behavior of LSTM and gated recurrent unit (GRU) in speech recognition task. For given words in a sentence, Li et al. (2016) employed heat maps to study sensitivity and meaning composition in recurrent networks. Ming et al. (2017) proposed a tool, RNNVis to visualize hidden states based on RNN's expected response to

Proceedings of the 2018 EMNLP Workshop BlackboxNLP: Analyzing and Interpreting Neural Networks for NLP, pages 154–164
Brussels, Belgium, November 1, 2018. ©2018 Association for Computational Linguistics

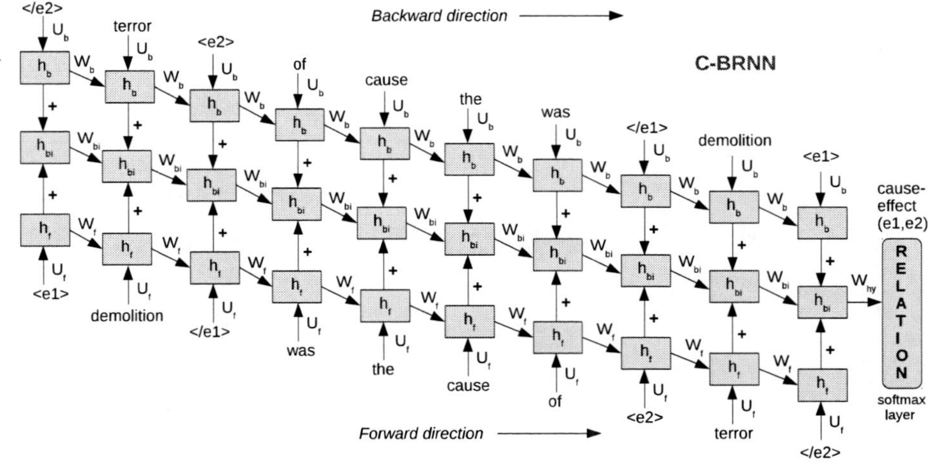

Figure 1: Connectionist Bi-directional Recurrent Neural Network (C-BRNN) (Vu et al., 2016a)

inputs. Peters et al. (2018) studied the internal states of deep bidirectional language model to learn contextualized word representations and observed that the higher-level hidden states capture word semantics, while lower-level states capture syntactical aspects. Despite the possibility of visualizing hidden state activations and performance-based analysis, there still remains a challenge for humans to interpret hidden behavior of the"black box" networks that raised questions in the NLP community as to verify that the network behaves as expected. In this aspect, we address the cumulative nature of RNN with the text input and computed response to answer "how does it aggregate and build the semantic meaning of a sentence word by word at each time point in the sequence for each category in the data".

Contribution: In this work, we analyze and interpret the cumulative nature of RNN via a proposed technique named as *Layer-wIse-Semantic-Accumulation* (LISA) for explaining decisions and detecting the most likely (i.e., saliency) patterns that the network relies on while decision making. We demonstrate (1) *LISA*: "How an RNN accumulates or builds semantics during its sequential processing for a given text example and expected response" (2) *Example2pattern*: "How the saliency patterns look like for each category in the data according to the network in decision making". We analyse the sensitiveness of RNNs about different inputs to check the increase or decrease in prediction scores. For an example sentence that is classified correctly, we identify and extract a saliency

pattern (N-grams of words in order learned by the network) that contributes the most in prediction score. Therefore, the term *example2pattern* transformation for each category in the data. We employ two relation classification datasets: SemEval 10 Task 8 and TAC KBP Slot Filling (SF) Shared Task (ST) to explain RNN predictions via the proposed *LISA* and *example2pattern* techniques.

2   Connectionist Bi-directional RNN

We adopt the bi-directional recurrent neural network architecture with ranking loss, proposed by Vu et al. (2016a). The network consists of three parts: a forward pass which processes the original sentence word by word (Equation 1); a backward pass which processes the reversed sentence word by word (Equation 2); and a combination of both (Equation 3). The forward and backward passes are combined by adding their hidden layers. There is also a connection to the previous combined hidden layer with weight W_{bi} with a motivation to include all intermediate hidden layers into the final decision of the network (see Equation 3). They named the neural architecture as 'Connectionist Bi-directional RNN' (C-BRNN). Figure 1 shows the C-BRNN architecture, where all the three parts are trained jointly.

$$h_{f_t} = f(U_f \cdot w_t + W_f \cdot h_{f_{t-1}}) \tag{1}$$

$$h_{b_t} = f(U_b \cdot w_{n-t+1} + W_b \cdot h_{b_{t+1}}) \tag{2}$$

$$h_{bi_t} = f(h_{f_t} + h_{b_t} + W_{bi} \cdot h_{bi_{t-1}}) \tag{3}$$

where w_t is the word vector of dimension d for a word at time step t in a sentence of length n.

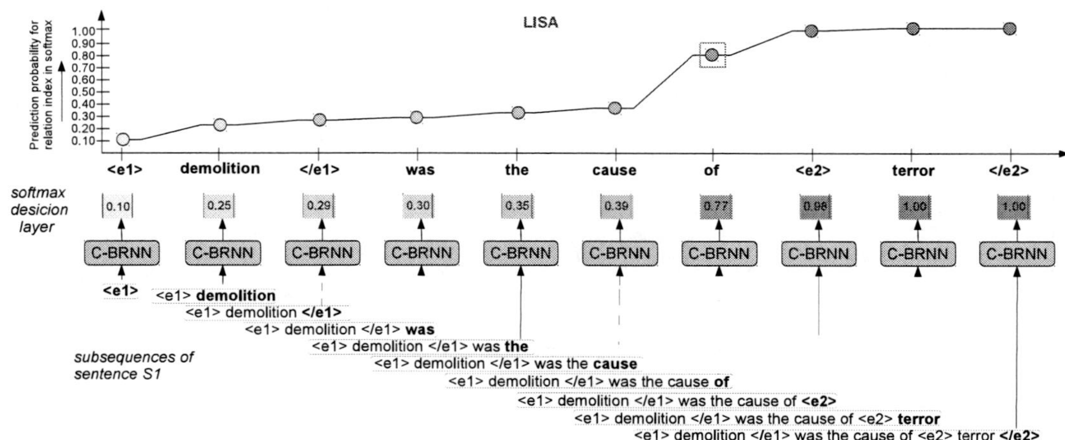

Figure 2: An illustration of Layer-wIse Semantic Accumulation (LISA) in C-BRNN, where we compute prediction score for a (known) relation type at each of the input subsequence. The highlighted indices in the softmax layer signify one of the relation types, i.e., *cause*-effect(e1, e2) in SemEval10 Task 8 dataset. The bold signifies the last word in the subsequence. Note: Each word is represented by N-gram (N=3, 5 or 7), therefore each input subsequence is a sequence of N-grams. E.g., the word 'of' → 'cause of <e2>' for N=3. To avoid complexity in this illustration, each word is shown as a uni-gram.

D is the hidden unit dimension. $U_f \in \mathbb{R}^{d \times D}$ and $U_b \in \mathbb{R}^{d \times D}$ are the weight matrices between hidden units and input w_t in forward and backward networks, respectively; $W_f \in \mathbb{R}^{D \times D}$ and $W_b \in \mathbb{R}^{D \times D}$ are the weights matrices connecting hidden units in forward and backward networks, respectively. $W_{bi} \in \mathbb{R}^{D \times D}$ is the weight matrix connecting the hidden vectors of the combined forward and backward network. Following Gupta et al. (2015) during model training, we use 3-gram and 5-gram representation of each word w_t at timestep t in the word sequence, where a 3-gram for w_t is obtained by concatenating the corresponding word embeddings, i.e., $w_{t-1} w_t w_{t+1}$.

Ranking Objective: Similar to Santos et al. (2015) and Vu et al. (2016a), we applied the ranking loss function to train C-BRNN. The ranking scheme offers to maximize the distance between the true label y^+ and the best competitive label c^- given a data point x. It is defined as-

$$\mathcal{L} = \log(1 + \exp(\gamma(m^+ - s_\theta(x)_{y^+}))) \\ + \log(1 + \exp(\gamma(m^- + s_\theta(x)_{c^-}))) \tag{4}$$

where $s_\theta(x)_{y^+}$ and $s_\theta(x)_{c^-}$ being the scores for the classes y^+ and c^-, respectively. The parameter γ controls the penalization of the prediction errors and m^+ and m are margins for the correct and incorrect classes. Following Vu et al. (2016a), we set $\gamma = 2$, $m^+ = 2.5$ and $m^- = 0.5$.

Model Training and Features: We represent each word by the concatenation of its word embedding and position feature vectors. We use word2vec (Mikolov et al., 2013) embeddings, that are updated during model training. As position features in relation classification experiments, we use position indicators (PI) (Zhang and Wang, 2015) in C-BRNN to annotate target entity/nominals in the word sequence, without necessity to change the input vectors, while it increases the length of the input word sequences, as four independent words, as position indicators (<e1>, </ e1>, <e2>, </e2>) around the relation arguments are introduced.

In our analysis and interpretation of recurrent neural networks, we use the trained C-BRNN (Figure 1) (Vu et al., 2016a) model.

3 LISA and Example2Pattern in RNN

There are several aspects in interpreting the neural network, for instance via (1) *Data*: "Which dimensions of the data are the most relevant for the task" (2) *Prediction* or *Decision*: "Explain why a certain pattern" is classified in a certain way (3) *Model*: "How patterns belonging to each category in the data look like according to the network".

In this work, we focus to explain RNN via *decision* and *model* aspects by finding the patterns that explains "why" a model arrives at a particular decision for each category in the data and verifies that model behaves as expected. To do so, we propose a technique named as LISA that interprets RNN about "how it accumulates and builds meaningful semantics of a sentence word by word" and "how the saliency patterns look like according to the network" for each category in the data while decision making. We extract the saliency patterns via *example2pattern* transformation.

LISA Formulation: To explain the cumulative nature of recurrent neural networks, we show how does it build semantic meaning of a sentence word by word belonging to a particular category in the data and compute prediction scores for the expected category on different inputs, as shown in Figure 2. The scheme also depicts the contribution of each word in the sequence towards the final classification score (prediction probability).

At first, we compute different subsequences of word(s) for a given sequence of words (i.e., sentence). Consider a sequence $\mathbf{S}$ of words $[w_1, w_2, ..., w_k, ..., w_n]$ for a given sentence S of length n. We compute n number of subsequences, where each subsequence $\mathbf{S}_{\leq k}$ is a subvector of words $[w_1, ...w_k]$, i.e., $\mathbf{S}_{\leq k}$ consists of words preceding and including the word w_k in the sequence $\mathbf{S}$. In context of this work, extending a subsequence by a word means appending the subsequence by the next word in the sequence. Observe that the number of subsequences, n is equal to the total number of time steps in the C-BRNN.

Next is to compute RNN prediction score for the category R associated with sentence S. We compute the score via the autoregressive conditional $P(R|\mathbf{S}_{\leq k}, \mathbb{M})$ for each subsequence $\mathbf{S}_{\leq k}$, as-

$$P(R|\mathbf{S}_{\leq k}, \mathbb{M}) = softmax(W_{hy} \cdot h_{bi_k} + b_y) \quad (5)$$

using the trained C-BRNN (Figure 1) model $\mathbb{M}$. For each $k \in [1, n]$, we compute the network prediction, $P(R|\mathbf{S}_{\leq k}, \mathbb{M})$ to demonstrate the cumulative property of recurrent neural network that builds meaningful semantics of the sequence $\mathbf{S}$ by extending each subsequence $\mathbf{S}_{\leq k}$ word by word. The internal state h_{bi_k} (attached to softmax layer as in Figure 1) is involved in decision making for each input subsequence $\mathbf{S}_{\leq k}$ with bias vector $b_y \in \mathbb{R}^C$ and hidden-to-softmax weights matrix $W_{hy} \in \mathbb{R}^{D \times C}$ for C categories.

The *LISA* is illustrated in Figure 2, where each word in the sequence contributes to final classification score. It allows us to understand the network decisions via peaks in the prediction score

---

Algorithm 1 Example2pattern Transformation

> **Input:** sentence S, length n, category R, threshold τ, C-BRNN $\mathbb{M}$, N-gram size N
> **Output:** N-gram saliency pattern $patt$
> 1: **for** k in 1 to n **do**
> 2:   compute N-gram$_k$ (eqn 8) of words in S
> 3: **for** k in 1 to n **do**
> 4:   compute $\mathbf{S}_{\leq k}$ (eqn 7) of N-grams
> 5:   compute $P(R|\mathbf{S}_{\leq k}, \mathbb{M})$ using eqn 5
> 6:   **if** $P(R|\mathbf{S}_{\leq k}, \mathbb{M}) \geq \tau$ **then**
> 7:   **return** $patt \leftarrow \mathbf{S}_{\leq k}[-1]$

---

over different subsequences. The peaks signify the saliency patterns (i.e., sequence of words) that the network has learned in order to make decision. For instance, the input word '*of*' following the subsequence '*<e1> demolition </e1> was the cause*' introduces a sudden increase in prediction score for the relation type *cause-effect*(e1, e2). It suggests that the C-BRNN collects the semantics layer-wise via temporally organized subsequences. Observe that the subsequence '*...cause of*' is salient enough in decision making (i.e., prediction score=0.77), where the next subsequence '*...cause of <e2>*' adds in the score to get 0.98.

Example2pattern for Saliency Pattern: To further interpret RNN, we seek to identify and extract the most likely input pattern (or phrases) for a given class that is discriminating enough in decision making. Therefore, each example input is transformed into a saliency pattern that informs us about the network learning. To do so, we first compute N-gram for each word w_t in the sentence S. For instance, a 3-gram representation of w_t is given by w_{t-1}, w_t, w_{t+1}. Therefore, an N-gram (for N=3) sequence $\mathbf{S}$ of words is represented as $[[w_{t-1}, w_t, w_{t+1}]_{t=1}^n]$, where w_0 and w_{n+1} are PADDING (zero) vectors of embedding dimension.

Following Vu et al. (2016a), we use N-grams (e.g., tri-grams) representation for each word in each subsequence $\mathbf{S}_{\leq k}$ that is input to C-BRNN to compute $P(R|\mathbf{S}_{\leq k})$, where the N-gram (N=3) subsequence $\mathbf{S}_{\leq k}$ is given by,

$$\mathbf{S}_{\leq k} = [[PADDING, w_1, w_2]_1, [w_1, w_2, w_3]_2, ...,$$
$$[w_{t-1}, w_t, w_{t+1}]_t, ..., [w_{k-1}, w_k, w_{k+1}]_k]$$
$$(6)$$

$$\mathbf{S}_{\leq k} = [tri_1, tri_2, ..., tri_t, ...tri_k] \quad (7)$$

for $k \in [1, n]$. Observe that the 3-gram tri_k con-

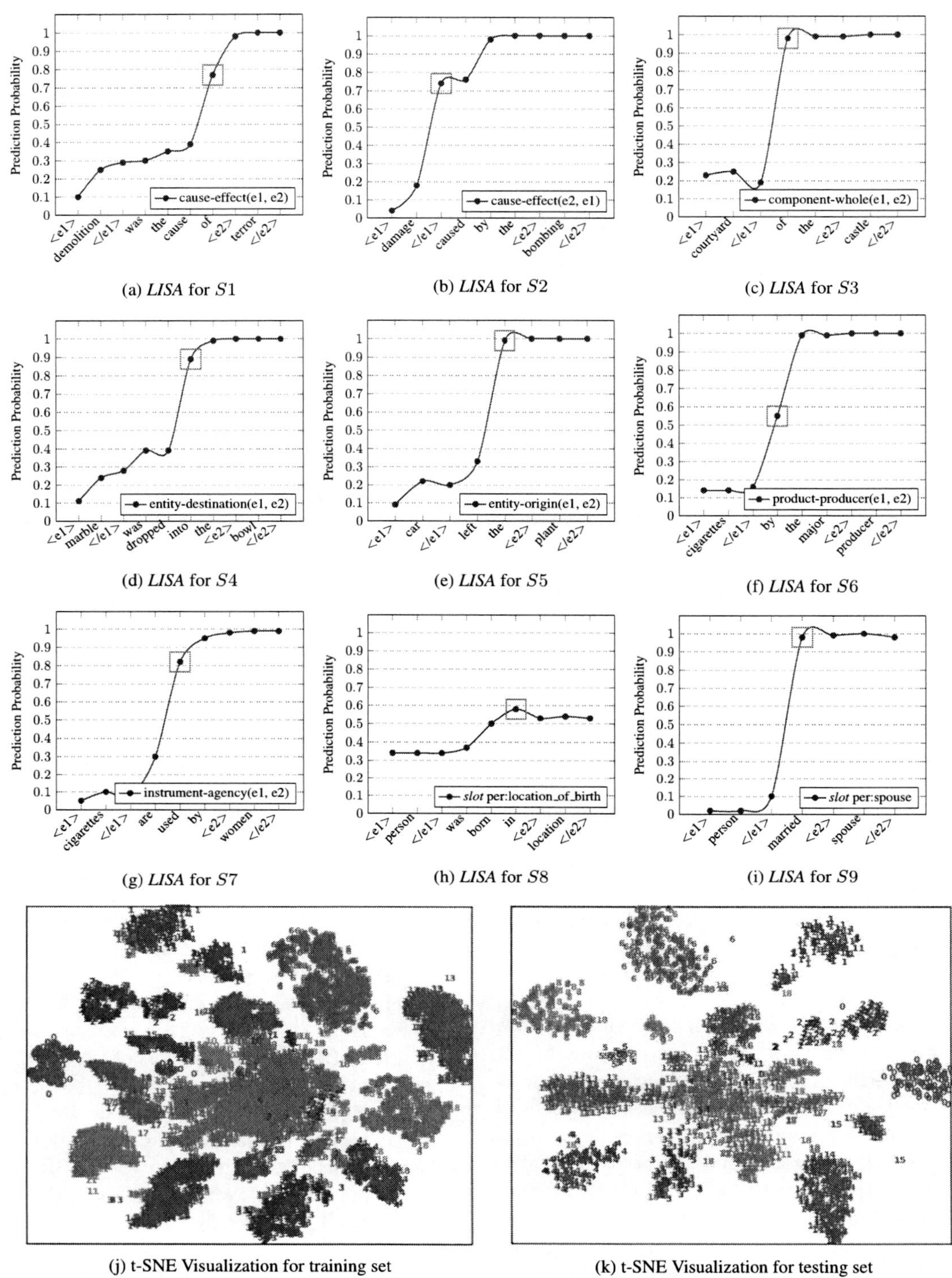

(a) *LISA* for $S1$ (b) *LISA* for $S2$ (c) *LISA* for $S3$

(d) *LISA* for $S4$ (e) *LISA* for $S5$ (f) *LISA* for $S6$

(g) *LISA* for $S7$ (h) *LISA* for $S8$ (i) *LISA* for $S9$

(j) t-SNE Visualization for training set   (k) t-SNE Visualization for testing set

Figure 3: (a-i) Layer-wIse Semantic Accumulation (LISA) by C-BRNN for different relation types in SemEval10 Task 8 and TAC KBP Slot Filling datasets. The square in red color signifies that the relation is correctly detected with the input subsequence (enough in decision making). (j-k) t-SNE visualization of the last combined hidden unit (h_{bi}) of C-BRNN computed using the SemEval10 train and test sets.

ID	Relation/Slot Types	Example Sentences	Example2Pattern
$S1$	cause-effect(e1, e2)	<e1> demolition </e1> was the cause of <e2> terror </e2>	cause of <e2>
$S2$	cause-effect(e2, e1)	<e1> damage </e1> caused by the <e2> bombing </e2>	damage </e1> caused
$S3$	component-whole(e1, e2)	<e1> countyard </e1> of the <e2> castle </e2>	</e1> of the
$S4$	entity-destination(e1,e2)	<e1> marble </e1> was dropped into the <e2> bowl </e2>	dropped into the
$S5$	entity-origin(e1, e2)	<e1> car </e1> left the <e2> plant </e2>	left the <e2>
$S6$	product-produce(e1, e2)	<e1> cigarettes </e1> by the major <e2> producer </e2>	</e1> by the
$S7$	instrument-agency(e1, e2)	<e1> cigarettes </e1> are used by <e2> women </e2>	</e1> are used
$S8$	per:loc_of_birth(e1, e2)	<e1> person </e1> was born in <e2> location </e2>	born in <e2>
$S9$	per:spouse(e1, e2)	<e1> person </e1> married <e2> spouse </e2>	</e1> married <e2>

Table 1: Example Sentences for *LISA* and *example2pattern* illustrations. The sentences $S1$-$S7$ belong to SemEval10 Task 8 dataset and $S8$-$S9$ to TAC KBP Slot Filling (SF) shared task dataset.

sists of the word w_{k+1}, if $k \neq n$. To generalize for $i \in [1, \lfloor N/2 \rfloor]$, an N-gram$_k$ of size N for word w_k in C-BRNN is given by-

$$\text{N-gram}_k = [w_{k-i}, ..., w_k, ..., w_{k+i}]_k \quad (8)$$

Algorithm 1 shows the transformation of an example sentence into pattern that is salient in decision making. For a given example sentence S with its length n and category R, we extract the most salient N-gram (N=3, 5 or 7) pattern $patt$ (the last N-gram in the N-gram subsequence $\mathbf{S}_{\leq k}$) that contributes the most in detecting the relation type R. The threshold parameter τ signifies the probability of prediction for the category R by the model $\mathbb{M}$. For an input N-gram sequence $\mathbf{S}_{\leq k}$ of sentence S, we extract the last N-gram, e.g., tri_k that detects the relation R with prediction score above τ. By manual inspection of patterns extracted at different values (0.4, 0.5, 0.6, 0.7) of τ, we found that $\tau = 0.5$ generates the most salient and interpretable patterns. The saliency pattern detection follows LISA as demonstrated in Figure 2, except that we use N-gram (N =3, 5 or 7) input to detect and extract the key relationship patterns.

4 Analysis: Relation Classification

Given a sentence and two annotated nominals, the task of binary relation classification is to predict the semantic relations between the pairs of nominals. In most cases, the context in between the two nominals define the relationship. However, Vu et al. (2016a) has shown that the extended context helps. In this work, we focus on the building semantics for a given sentence using relationship contexts between the two nominals.

We analyse RNNs for *LISA* and *example2pattern* using two relation classification datsets: (1) SemEval10 Shared Task 8 (Hendrickx

Input word sequence to C-BRNN	*pp*
<e1>	0.10
<e1> **demolition**	0.25
<e1> demolition <**/e1**>	0.29
<e1> demolition </e1> **was**	0.30
<e1> demolition </e1> was **the**	0.35
<e1> demolition </e1> was the **cause**	0.39
<e1> demolition </e1> was the cause **of**	<u>0.77</u>
<e1> demolition </e1> was the cause of <**e2**>	0.98
<e1> demolition </e1> was the cause of <e2> **terror**	1.00
<e1> demolition </e1> was the cause of <e2> terror <**/e2**>	1.00

Table 2: Semantic accumulation and sensitivity of C-BRNN over subsequences for sentence $S1$. Bold indicates the last word in the subsequence. *pp*: prediction probability in the softmax layer for the relation type. The underline signifies that the *pp* is sufficient enough (τ=0.50) in detecting the relation. Saliency patterns, i.e., N-grams can be extracted from the input subsequence that leads to a sudden peak in *pp*, where $pp \geq \tau$.

et al., 2009) (2) TAC KBP Slot Filling (SF) shared task[1] (Adel and Schütze, 2015). We demonstrate the sensitiveness of RNN for different subsequences (Figure 2), input in the same order as in the original sentence. We explain its predictions (or judgments) and extract the salient relationship patterns learned for each category in the two datasets.

4.1 SemEval10 Shared Task 8 dataset

The relation classification dataset of the Semantic Evaluation 2010 (SemEval10) shared task 8 (Hendrickx et al., 2009) consists of 19 relations (9 directed relations and one artificial class `Other`), 8,000 training and 2,717 testing sentences. We split the training data into train (6.5k) and development (1.5k) sentences to optimize the C-BRNN

---

[1] data from the slot filler classification component of the slot filling pipeline, treated as relation classification

Relation	3-gram Patterns	5-gram Patterns	7-gram Patterns
cause-effect(e1,e2)	</e1> cause <e2>	the leading causes of <e2>	is one of the leading causes of
	</e1> caused a	the main causes of <e2>	is one of the main causes of
	that cause respiratory	</e1> leads to <e2> inspiration	</e1> that results in <e2> hardening </e2>
	which cause acne	</e1> that results in <e2>	</e1> resulted in the <e2> loss </e2>
	leading causes of	</e1> resulted in the <e2>	<e1> sadness </e1> leads to <e2> inspiration
cause-effect(e2,e1)	caused due to	</e1> has been caused by	</e1> is caused by a <e2> comet
	comes from the	</e1> are caused by the	</e1> however has been caused by the
	arose from an	</e1> arose from an <e2>	</e1> that has been caused by the
	caused by the	</e1> caused due to <e2>	that has been caused by the <e2>
	radiated from a	infection </e2> results in an	<e1> product </e1> arose from an <e2>
content-container(e1,e2)	in a <e2>	</e1> was contained in a	</e1> was contained in a <e2> box
	was inside a	</e1> was discovered inside a	</e1> was in a <e2> suitcase </e2>
	contained in a	</e1> were in a <e2>	</e1> were in a <e2> box </e2>
	hidden in a	is hidden in a <e2>	</e1> was inside a <e2> box </e2>
	stored in a	</e1> was contained in a	</e1> was hidden in an <e2> envelope
product-produce(e1,e2)	</e1> released by	</e1> issued by the <e2>	<e1> products </e1> created by an <e2>
	</e1> issued by	</e1> was prepared by <e2>	</e1> by an <e2> artist </e2> who
	</e1> created by	was written by a <e2>	</e1> written by most of the <e2>
	by the <e2>	</e1> built by the <e2>	temple </e1> has been built by <e2>
	of the <e1>	</e1> are made by <e2>	</e1> were founded by the <e2> potter
whole(e1, e2) component-	</e1> of the	</e1> of the <e2> device	the <e1> timer </e1> of the <e2>
	of the <e2>	</e1> was a part of	</e1> was a part of the romulan
	part of the	</e1> is part of the	</e1> was the best part of the
	</e1> of <e2>	is a basic element of	</e1> is a basic element of the
	</e1> on a	</e1> is part of a	are core components of the <e2> solutions
entity-destination(e1,e2)	put into a	have been moving into the	</e1> have been moving back into <e2>
	released into the	was dropped into the <e2>	</e1> have been moving into the <e2>
	</e1> into the	</e1> moved into the <e2>	</e1> have been dropped into the <e2>
	moved into the	were released into the <e2>	</e1> have been released back into the
	added to the	</e1> have been exported to	power </e1> is exported to the <e2>
instrument-agency(e1,e2)	</e1> are used	</e1> assists the <e2> eye	cigarettes </e1> are used by <e2> women
	used by <e2>	</e1> are used by <e2>	<e1> telescope </e1> assists the <e2> eye
	</e1> is used	</e1> were used by some	<e1> practices </e1> for <e2> engineers </e2>
	set by the	</e1> with which the <e2>	the best <e1> tools </e1> for <e2>
	</e1> set by	readily associated with the <e2>	<e1> wire </e1> with which the <e2>

Table 3: SemEval10 Task 8 dataset: N-Gram (3, 5 and 7) saliency patterns extracted for different relation types by C-BRNN with PI

network. For instance, an example sentence with relation label is given by-

```
The <e1> demolition </e1> was
the cause of <e2> terror </e2>
and communal divide is just a way
of not letting truth prevail.  →
cause-effect(e1,e2)
```

The terms `demolition` and `terror` are the relation arguments or nominals, where the phrase `was the cause of` is the relationship context between the two arguments. Table 1 shows the examples sentences (shortened to argument1+relationship context+argument2) drawn from the development and test sets that we employed to analyse the C-BRNN for semantic accumulation in our experiments. We use the similar experimental setup as Vu et al. (2016a).

LISA Analysis: As discussed in Section 3, we interpret C-BRNN by explaining its predictions via the semantic accumulation over the subsequences $S_{\leq k}$ (Figure 2) for each sentence S. We select the example sentences $S1$-$S7$ (Table 1) for which the network predicts the correct relation type with high scores. For an example sentence $S1$, Table 2 illustrates how different subsequences are input to C-BRNN in order to compute prediction scores pp in the softmax layer for the relation `cause-effect(e1, e2)`. We use tri-gram (section 3) word representation for each word for the examples $S1$-$S7$.

Figures 3a, 3b, 3c, 3d 3e, 3f and 3g demonstrate the cumulative nature and sensitiveness of RNN via prediction probability (pp) about different inputs for sentences $S1$-$S7$, respectively. For

Slots	N-gram Patterns
per-spouse(e1,e2)	</e1> wife of
	</e1> , wife
	</e1> wife
	</e1> married <e2>
	</e1> marriages to
per-location_of_birth(e1,e2)	was born in
	born in <e2>
	a native of
	</e1> from <e2>
	</e1> 's hometown

Table 4: TAC KBP SF dataset: Tri-gram saliency patterns extracted for slots *per:spouse*(e1, e2) and *per:location_of_birth*(e1,e2)

instance in Figure 3a and Table 2, the C-BRNN builds meaning of the sentence $S1$ word by word, where a sudden increase in *pp* is observed when the input subsequence `<e1> demolition </e1> was the cause` is extended with the next term `of` in the word sequence **S**. Note that the relationship context between the arguments `demolition` and `terror` is sufficient enough in detecting the relationship type. Interestingly, we also observe that the prepositions (such as `of`, `by`, `into`, etc.) in combination with verbs are key features in building the meaningful semantics.

Saliency Patterns via example2pattern Transformation: Following the discussion in Section 3 and Algorithm 1, we transform each correctly identified example into pattern by extracting the most likely N-gram in the input subsequence(s). In each of the Figures 3a, 3b, 3c, 3d 3e, 3f and 3g, the square box in red color signifies that the relation type is correctly identified (when $\tau = 0.5$) at this particular subsequence input (without the remaining context in the sentence). We extract the last N-gram of such a subsequence.

Table 1 shows the *example2pattern* transformations for sentences $S1$-$S7$ in SemEval10 dataset, derived from Figures 3a-3g, respectively with N=3 (in the N-grams). Similarly, we extract the salient patterns (3-gram, 5-gram and 7-gram) (Table 3) for different relationships. We also observe that the relation types `content-container(e1, e2)` and `instrument-agency(e1, e2)` are mostly defined by smaller relationship contexts (e.g, 3-gram), however `entity-destination(e1,e2)` by larger contexts (7-gram).

4.2 TAC KBP Slot Filling dataset

We investigate another dataset from TAC KBP Slot Filling (SF) shared task (Surdeanu, 2013), where we use the relation classification dataset by Adel et al. (2016) in the context of slot filling. We have selected the two slots: *per:loc_of_birth* and *per:spouse* out of 24 types.

LISA Analysis: Following Section 4.1, we analyse the C-BRNN for LISA using sentences $S8$ and $S9$ (Table 1). Figures 3h and 3i demonstrate the cumulative nature of recurrent neural network, where we observe that the salient patterns `born in <e2>` and `</e1> married e2` lead to correct decision making for $S8$ and $S9$, respectively. Interestingly for $S8$, we see a decrease in prediction score from 0.59 to 0.52 on including terms in the subsequence, following the term `in`.

Saliency Patterns via example2pattern Transformation: Following Section 3 and Algorithm 1, we demonstrate the *example2pattern* transformation of sentences $S8$ and $S9$ in Table 1 with tirgrams. In addition, Table 4 shows the tri-gram salient patterns extracted for the two slots.

5 Visualizing Latent Semantics

In this section, we attempt to visualize the hidden state of each test (and train) example that has accumulated (or built) the meaningful semantics during sequential processing in C-BRNN. To do this, we compute the last hidden vector h_{bi} of the combined network (e.g., h_{bi} attached to the softmax layer in Figure 1) for each test (and train) example and visualize (Figure 3k and 3j) using t-SNE (Maaten and Hinton, 2008). Each color represents a relation-type. Observe the distinctive clusters of accumulated semantics in hidden states for each category in the data (SemEval10 Task 8).

6 Conclusion and Future Work

We have demonstrated the cumulative nature of recurrent neural networks via sensitivity analysis over different inputs, i.e., *LISA* to understand how they build meaningful semantics and explain predictions for each category in the data. We have also detected a salient pattern in each of the example sentences, i.e., *example2pattern transformation* that the network learns in decision making. We extract the salient patterns for different categories in two relation classification datasets.

In future work, it would be interesting to analyse the sensitiveness of RNNs with corruption in the salient patterns. One could also investigate visualizing the dimensions of hidden states (activation maximization) and word embedding vectors with the network decisions over time. We forsee to apply *LISA* and *example2pattern* on different tasks such as document categorization, sentiment analysis, language modeling, etc. Another interesting direction would be to analyze the bag-of-word neural topic models such as DocNADE (Larochelle and Lauly, 2012) and iDocNADE (Gupta et al., 2018b) to interpret their semantic accumulation during autoregressive computations in building document representation(s). We extract the saliency patterns for each category in the data that can be effectively used in instantiating pattern-based information extraction systems, such as bootstrapping entity (Gupta and Manning, 2014) and relation extractors (Gupta et al., 2018e).

Acknowledgments

We thank Heike Adel for providing us with the TAC KBP dataset used in our experiments. We express appreciation for our colleagues Bernt Andrassy, Florian Buettner, Ulli Waltinger, Mark Buckley, Stefan Langer, Subbu Rajaram, Yatin Chaudhary, and anonymous reviewers for their in-depth review comments. This research was supported by Bundeswirtschaftsministerium (bmwi.de), grant 01MD15010A (Smart Data Web) at Siemens AG- CT Machine Intelligence, Munich Germany.

References

Heike Adel, Benjamin Roth, and Hinrich Schütze. 2016. Comparing convolutional neural networks to traditional models for slot filling. In *Proceedings of the 2016 Conference of the North American Chapter of the Association for Computational Linguistics: Human Language Technologies*, pages 828–838. Association for Computational Linguistics.

Heike Adel and Hinrich Schütze. 2015. Cis at tac cold start 2015: Neural networks and coreference resolution for slot filling. *Proc. TAC2015*.

Sebastian Bach, Alexander Binder, Grégoire Montavon, Frederick Klauschen, Klaus-Robert Müller, and Wojciech Samek. 2015. On pixel-wise explanations for non-linear classifier decisions by layer-wise relevance propagation. *PloS one*, 10(7):e0130140.

David Baehrens, Timon Schroeter, Stefan Harmeling, Motoaki Kawanabe, Katja Hansen, and Klaus-Robert MÃžller. 2010. How to explain individual classification decisions. *Journal of Machine Learning Research*, 11(Jun):1803–1831.

Dzmitry Bahdanau, Kyunghyun Cho, and Yoshua Bengio. 2014. Neural machine translation by jointly learning to align and translate. *arXiv preprint arXiv:1409.0473*.

Alexey Dosovitskiy and Thomas Brox. 2016. Inverting visual representations with convolutional networks. In *Proceedings of the IEEE Conference on Computer Vision and Pattern Recognition*, pages 4829–4837.

Jeffrey L Elman. 1990. Finding structure in time. *Cognitive science*, 14(2):179–211.

Dumitru Erhan, Yoshua Bengio, Aaron Courville, and Pascal Vincent. 2009. Visualizing higher-layer features of a deep network. *University of Montreal*, 1341(3):1.

Ian J Goodfellow, Jonathon Shlens, and Christian Szegedy. 2014. Explaining and harnessing adversarial examples. *arXiv preprint arXiv:1412.6572*.

Pankaj Gupta, Bernt Andrassy, and Hinrich Schütze. 2018a. Replicated siamese lstm in ticketing system for similarity learning and retrieval in asymmetric texts. In *Proceedings of the Workshop on Semantic Deep Learning (SemDeep-3) in the 27th International Conference on Computational Linguistics (COLING2018)*. The COLING 2018 organizing committee.

Pankaj Gupta, Florian Buettner, and Hinrich Schütze. 2018b. Document informed neural autoregressive topic models. Researchgate preprint doi: 10.13140/RG.2.2.12322.73925.

Pankaj Gupta, Subburam Rajaram, Thomas Runkler, Hinrich Schütze, and Bernt Andrassy. 2018c. Neural relation extraction within and across sentence boundaries. Researchgate preprint doi: 10.13140/RG.2.2.16517.04327.

Pankaj Gupta, Subburam Rajaram, Hinrich Schütze, and Bernt Andrassy. 2018d. Deep temporal-recurrent-replicated-softmax for topical trends over time. In *Proceedings of the 2018 Conference of the North American Chapter of the Association for Computational Linguistics: Human Language Technologies, Volume 1 (Long Papers)*, volume 1, pages 1079–1089, New Orleans, USA. Association of Computational Linguistics.

Pankaj Gupta, Benjamin Roth, and Hinrich Schütze. 2018e. Joint bootstrapping machines for high confidence relation extraction. In *Proceedings of the 16th Annual Conference of the North American Chapter of the Association for Computational Linguistics: Human Language Technologies (Long Papers)*, pages 26–36, New Orleans, USA. Association of Computational Linguistics.

Pankaj Gupta, Thomas Runkler, Heike Adel, Bernt Andrassy, Hans-Georg Zimmermann, and Hinrich Schütze. 2015. Deep learning methods for the extraction of relations in natural language text. Technical report, Technical University of Munich, Germany.

Pankaj Gupta, Hinrich Schütze, and Bernt Andrassy. 2016. Table filling multi-task recurrent neural network for joint entity and relation extraction. In *Proceedings of COLING 2016, the 26th International Conference on Computational Linguistics: Technical Papers*, pages 2537–2547. The COLING 2016 Organizing Committee.

Sonal Gupta and Christopher Manning. 2014. Spied: Stanford pattern based information extraction and diagnostics. In *Proceedings of the Workshop on Interactive Language Learning, Visualization, and Interfaces*, pages 38–44.

Iris Hendrickx, Su Nam Kim, Zornitsa Kozareva, Preslav Nakov, Diarmuid Ó Séaghdha, Sebastian Padó, Marco Pennacchiotti, Lorenza Romano, and Stan Szpakowicz. 2009. Semeval-2010 task 8: Multi-way classification of semantic relations between pairs of nominals. In *Proceedings of the Workshop on Semantic Evaluations: Recent Achievements and Future Directions*, pages 94–99. Association for Computational Linguistics.

Geoffrey E Hinton. 2012. A practical guide to training restricted boltzmann machines. In *Neural networks: Tricks of the trade*, pages 599–619. Springer.

Sepp Hochreiter and Jürgen Schmidhuber. 1997. Long short-term memory. *Neural computation*, 9(8):1735–1780.

Guillaume Lample, Miguel Ballesteros, Sandeep Subramanian, Kazuya Kawakami, and Chris Dyer. 2016. Neural architectures for named entity recognition. In *Proceedings of the 2016 Conference of the North American Chapter of the Association for Computational Linguistics: Human Language Technologies*, pages 260–270. Association for Computational Linguistics.

Hugo Larochelle and Stanislas Lauly. 2012. A neural autoregressive topic model. In F. Pereira, C. J. C. Burges, L. Bottou, and K. Q. Weinberger, editors, *Advances in Neural Information Processing Systems 25*, pages 2708–2716. Curran Associates, Inc.

Jiwei Li, Xinlei Chen, Eduard Hovy, and Dan Jurafsky. 2016. Visualizing and understanding neural models in nlp. In *Proceedings of the 2016 Conference of the North American Chapter of the Association for Computational Linguistics: Human Language Technologies*, pages 681–691. Association for Computational Linguistics.

Xuezhe Ma and Eduard Hovy. 2016. End-to-end sequence labeling via bi-directional lstm-cnns-crf. In *Proceedings of the 54th Annual Meeting of the Association for Computational Linguistics (Volume 1: Long Papers)*, pages 1064–1074. Association for Computational Linguistics.

Laurens van der Maaten and Geoffrey Hinton. 2008. Visualizing data using t-sne. *Journal of machine learning research*, 9(Nov):2579–2605.

Grégoire Mesnil, Yann Dauphin, Kaisheng Yao, Yoshua Bengio, Li Deng, Dilek Hakkani-Tur, Xiaodong He, Larry Heck, Gokhan Tur, Dong Yu, et al. 2015. Using recurrent neural networks for slot filling in spoken language understanding. *IEEE/ACM Transactions on Audio, Speech, and Language Processing*, 23(3):530–539.

Tomas Mikolov, Kai Chen, Greg Corrado, and Jeffrey Dean. 2013. Efficient estimation of word representations in vector space. In *Proceedings of the Workshop at ICLR*.

Tomáš Mikolov, Martin Karafiát, Lukáš Burget, Jan Černocký, and Sanjeev Khudanpur. 2010. Recurrent neural network based language model. In *Eleventh Annual Conference of the International Speech Communication Association*.

Yao Ming, Shaozu Cao, Ruixiang Zhang, Zhen Li, Yuanzhe Chen, Yangqiu Song, and Huamin Qu. 2017. Understanding hidden memories of recurrent neural networks. *arXiv preprint arXiv:1710.10777*.

Makoto Miwa and Mohit Bansal. 2016. End-to-end relation extraction using lstms on sequences and tree structures. In *Proceedings of the 54th Annual Meeting of the Association for Computational Linguistics (Volume 1: Long Papers)*, pages 1105–1116. Association for Computational Linguistics.

Grégoire Montavon, Wojciech Samek, and Klaus-Robert Müller. 2017. Methods for interpreting and understanding deep neural networks. *Digital Signal Processing*.

Jonas Mueller and Aditya Thyagarajan. 2016. Siamese recurrent architectures for learning sentence similarity. In *AAAI*, volume 16, pages 2786–2792.

Anh Nguyen, Alexey Dosovitskiy, Jason Yosinski, Thomas Brox, and Jeff Clune. 2016. Synthesizing the preferred inputs for neurons in neural networks via deep generator networks. In *Advances in Neural Information Processing Systems*, pages 3387–3395.

Matthew Peters, Mark Neumann, Mohit Iyyer, Matt Gardner, Christopher Clark, Kenton Lee, and Luke Zettlemoyer. 2018. Deep contextualized word representations. In *Proceedings of the 2018 Conference of the North American Chapter of the Association for Computational Linguistics: ·Human Language Technologies, Volume 1 (Long Papers)*, pages 2227–2237. Association for Computational Linguistics.

Cicero Nogueira dos Santos, Bing Xiang, and Bowen Zhou. 2015. Classifying relations by ranking with convolutional neural networks. In *Proceedings of ACL*. Association for Computational Linguistics.

Karen Simonyan, Andrea Vedaldi, and Andrew Zisserman. 2013. Deep inside convolutional networks: Visualising image classification models and saliency maps. *arXiv preprint arXiv:1312.6034*.

Mihai Surdeanu. 2013. Overview of the tac2013 knowledge base population evaluation: English slot filling and temporal slot filling. In *TAC*.

Duyu Tang, Bing Qin, and Ting Liu. 2015. Document modeling with gated recurrent neural network for sentiment classification. In *Proceedings of the 2015 Conference on Empirical Methods in Natural Language Processing*, pages 1422–1432. Association for Computational Linguistics.

Zhiyuan Tang, Ying Shi, Dong Wang, Yang Feng, and Shiyue Zhang. 2017. Memory visualization for gated recurrent neural networks in speech recognition. In *Acoustics, Speech and Signal Processing (ICASSP), 2017 IEEE International Conference on*, pages 2736–2740. IEEE.

Ngoc Thang Vu, Heike Adel, Pankaj Gupta, and Hinrich Schütze. 2016a. Combining recurrent and convolutional neural networks for relation classification. In *Proceedings of the North American Chapter of the Association for Computational Linguistics: Human Language Technologies*, pages 534–539, San Diego, California USA. Association for Computational Linguistics.

Ngoc Thang Vu, Pankaj Gupta, Heike Adel, and Hinrich Schütze. 2016b. Bi-directional recurrent neural network with ranking loss for spoken language understanding. In *Proceedings of the Acoustics, Speech and Signal Processing (ICASSP)*, pages 6060–6064, Shanghai, China. IEEE.

Yequan Wang, Minlie Huang, xiaoyan zhu, and Li Zhao. 2016. Attention-based lstm for aspect-level sentiment classification. In *Proceedings of the 2016 Conference on Empirical Methods in Natural Language Processing*, pages 606–615. Association for Computational Linguistics.

Matthew D Zeiler and Rob Fergus. 2014. Visualizing and understanding convolutional networks. In *European conference on computer vision*, pages 818–833. Springer.

Dongxu Zhang and Dong Wang. 2015. Relation classification via recurrent neural network.

Analysing the potential of seq-to-seq models
for incremental interpretation in task-oriented dialogue

Dieuwke Hupkes, Sanne Bouwmeester, and **Raquel Fernández**
Institute for Logic Language and Computation
University of Amsterdam
{d.hupkes,raquel.fernandez}@uva.nl
sanne.bouwmeester1@student.uva.nl

Abstract

We investigate how encoder-decoder models trained on a synthetic dataset of task-oriented dialogues process disfluencies, such as hesitations and self-corrections. We find that, contrary to earlier results, disfluencies have very little impact on the task success of seq-to-seq models with attention. Using visualisations and diagnostic classifiers, we analyse the representations that are incrementally built by the model, and discover that models develop little to no awareness of the structure of disfluencies. However, adding disfluencies to the data appears to help the model create clearer representations overall, as evidenced by the attention patterns the different models exhibit.

1 Introduction

The use of Recurrent Neural Networks (RNNs) to tackle sequential language tasks has become standard in natural language processing, after impressive accomplishments in speech recognition, machine translation, and entailment (e.g., Sutskever et al., 2014; Bahdanau et al., 2015b; Kalchbrenner et al., 2014). Recently, RNNs have also been exploited as tools to model dialogue systems. Inspired by neural machine translation, researchers such as Ritter et al. (2011) and Vinyals and Le (2015) pioneered an approach to open-domain chit-chat conversation based on sequence-to-sequence models (Sutskever et al., 2014). In this paper, we focus on task-oriented dialogue, where the conversation serves to fulfil an independent goal in a given domain. Current neural dialogue models for task-oriented dialogue tend to equip systems with external memory components (Bordes et al., 2017), since key information needs to be stored for potentially long time spans. One of our goals here is to analyse to what extent sequence-to-sequence models without external memory can deal with this challenge.

In addition, we consider language realisations that include disfluencies common in dialogue interaction, such as repetitions and self-corrections (e.g., *I'd like to make a reservation for six, I mean, for eight people*). Disfluencies have been investigated extensively in psycholinguistics, with a range of studies showing that they affect sentence processing in intricate ways (Levelt, 1983; Fox Tree, 1995; Bailey and Ferreira, 2003; Ferreira and Bailey, 2004; Lau and Ferreira, 2005; Brennan and Schober, 2001). Most computational work on disfluencies, however, has focused on detection rather than on disfluency processing and interpretation (e.g., Stolcke and Shriberg, 1996; Heeman and Allen, 1999; Zwarts et al., 2010; Qian and Liu, 2013; ?; ?). In contrast, our aim is to get a better understanding of how RNNs process disfluent utterances and to analyse the impact of such disfluencies on a downstream task—in this case, issuing an API request reflecting the preferences of the user in a task-oriented dialogue.

For our experiments, we use the synthetic dataset bAbI (Bordes et al., 2017) and a modified version of it called bAbI+ which includes disfluencies (Shalyminov et al., 2017). The dataset contains simple dialogues between a user and a system in the restaurant reservation domain, which terminate with the system issuing an API call that encodes the user's request. In bAbI+, disfluencies are probabilistically inserted into user turns, following distributions in human data. Thus, while the data is artificial and certainly simplistic, its goal-oriented nature offers a rare opportunity: by assessing whether the system issues the right API call, we can study, in a controlled way, whether and how the model builds up a relevant semantic/pragmatic interpretation when processing a disfluent utterance—a key aspect that would not be available with unannotated natural data.

Proceedings of the 2018 EMNLP Workshop BlackboxNLP: Analyzing and Interpreting Neural Networks for NLP, pages 165–174
Brussels, Belgium, November 1, 2018. ©2018 Association for Computational Linguistics

2 Data

In this section, we discuss the two datasets we use for our experiments: bAbI (Bordes et al., 2017) and bAbI+ (Shalyminov et al., 2017).

2.1 bAbI

The bAbI dataset consists of a series of synthetic dialogues in English, representing human-computer interactions in the context of restaurant reservations. The data is broken down into six subtasks that individuate different abilities that dialogue systems should have to conduct a successful conversation with a human. We focus on Task 1, which tests the capacity of a system to ask the right questions and integrate the answers of the user to issue an API call that matches the user's preferences regarding four semantic slots: cuisine, location, price range, and party size. A sample dialogue can be found in example (4), Section 4.1.

Data The training data for Task 1 is deliberatively kept simple and small, consisting of 1000 dialogues with on average 5 user and 7 system utterances. An additional 1000 dialogues based on different user queries are available for validation and testing, respectively. The overall vocabulary contains 86 distinct words. There are 7 distinct system utterances and 300 possible API calls.

Baselines Together with the dataset, Bordes et al. (2017) present several baseline models for the task. All the methods proposed are retrieval based, i.e., the models are trained to select the best system response from a set of candidate responses (in contrast to the models we investigate in the present work, which are generative—see Section 3). The baseline models include classical information retrieval (IR) methods such as TF-IDF and nearest neighbour approaches, as well as an end-to-end recurrent neural network. Bordes et al. demonstrate that the end-to-end recurrent architecture—a memory network (Sukhbaatar et al., 2015)—outperforms the classical IR methods as well as supervised embeddings, obtaining a 100% accuracy on retrieving the correct API calls.

2.2 bAbI+

Shalyminov et al. (2017) observe that the original bAbI data lack naturalness and variation common in actual dialogue interaction. To introduce such variation while keeping lexical variation constant, they insert speech disfluencies, using a fixed set of templates that are probabilistically applied to the user turns of the original bAbI Task 1 dataset. In particular, three types of disfluencies are introduced: hesitations (1), restarts (2), and self-corrections (3), in around 21%, 40% and 5% of the user's turns, respectively.[1]

(1) We will be *uhm* eight

(2) Good morning *uhm yeah good morning*

(3) I would like *a French uhm sorry* a Vietnamese restaurant

Eshghi et al. (2017) use the bAbI+ dataset to show that a grammar-based semantic parser specifically designed to process incremental dialogue phenomena is able to handle the bAbI+ data without having been directly exposed to it, achieving 100% accuracy on API-call prediction. They then investigate whether the memory network approach by Bordes et al. (2017) is able to generalise to the disfluent data, finding that the model obtains very poor accuracy (28%) on API-call prediction when trained on the original bAbI dataset and tested on bAbI+. Shalyminov et al. (2017) further show that, even when the model is explicitly trained on bAbI+, its performance decreases significantly, achieving only 53% accuracy.

This result, together with the high level of control on types and frequency of disfluencies offered by the bAbI+ scripts, makes the bAbI+ data an excellent testbed for studying the processing of disfluencies by recurrent neural networks.

3 Generative bAbI+ Modelling

We start with replicating the results of Shalyminov et al. (2017) and Eshghi et al. (2017) using a *generative* rather than retrieval based model. For this replication, we use a vanilla one-layer encoder-decoder model (Sutskever et al., 2014) without any external memory. We train models with and without an attention mechanism (Bahdanau et al., 2015b) and compare their results. We perform a modest grid search over hidden layer and embedding sizes and find that an embedding size of 128 and a hidden layer size of 500 appear to be minimally required to achieve a good performance on the task. We therefore fix the embedding and hidden layer size to 128 and 500, respectively, for all further experiments.

---

[1] The inserted material is in italics in the examples.

train / test	seq2seq		attentive seq2seq		MemN2N
	utterances	API calls	utterances	API calls	API calls
bAbI / bAbI	100 (100)	0.02 (66.4)	100 (100)	100 (100)	100
bAbI+ / bAbI+	100 (100)	0.2 (80.6)	100 (100)	98.7 (99.7)	53
bAbI / bAbI+	81.4 (83.3)	0.00 (58.2)	91.5 (92.8)	50.4 (90.1)	28
bAbI+ / bAbI	100 (100)	0.2 (81.4)	100 (100)	99.2 (100)	99

Table 1: Sequence accuracy (word accuracy in brackets) on the test set for utterances (non-API call responses) and API calls only. The last column shows accuracy on the test set for the retrieval-based memory-network system, as reported by Shalyminov et al. (2017) .

3.1 Training

All models are trained to predict the system utterances of all of the 1000 training dialogues of the bAbI and bAbI+ dataset, respectively, including the final API call. After each user turn, models are asked to generate the next system utterance in the dialogue, given the dialogue history up to that point, which consists of all human and system utterances that previously occurred in that dialogue. The model's parameters are updated using stochastic gradient descent on a cross-entropy loss (using mini-batch size 32), with Adam (Kingma and Ba, 2014) as optimiser (learning rate 0.001). All models are trained until convergence, which was reached after $\sim$20 epochs.

3.2 Evaluation

Following Shalyminov et al. (2017), we use a 2×2 paradigm in which we train models either on bAbI or bAbI+ data and evaluate their performance on the test set of the same dataset, as well as across datasets. We report both the percentage of correct words in the generated responses (*word accuracy*) and the percentage of responses that were entirely correct (*sequence accuracy*). Additionally, we separately report the word and sequence accuracy of the API calls generated at the end of each dialogue. Note that these metrics are more challenging than the retrieval-based ones used by Bordes et al. (2017) and Eshghi et al. (2017), as the correct response has to be generated word by word, rather than merely being selected from a set of already available candidate utterances.

3.3 Results

Our results can be found in Table 1. The results obtained with the bAbI/bAbI and bAbI+/bAbI+ conditions indicate that an encoder-decoder model with attention can achieve near-perfect accuracy on Task 1 (predicting the right API call), whereas

a model without attention cannot (sequence accuracy for API calls is only 0.02% on bAbI/bAbI and 0.2% on bAbI+/bAbI+). This suggests that, in line with what was posed by Bordes et al. (2017), the bAbI Task 1 requires some form of memory that goes beyond what is available in a vanilla sequence-to-sequence model. To solve the task, however, using an attention mechanism suffices— a more complicated memory such as present in memory networks is not necessary.

Furthermore, our results confirm that models trained on data without disfluencies struggle to generalise when these are introduced at testing time (bAbI/bAbI+): While the overall accuracy of the dialogue is still high (91.5% of utterances are correct), API call accuracy falls back to 50.4%. Models trained on data containing disfluencies, however, show near-perfect accuracy on disfluent test data (98.7% on bAbI+/bAbI+)—a result that stands in stark contrast with the findings of Eshghi et al. (2017) and Shalyminov et al. (2017).

4 Generalisation to Disfluent Data

In this section, we analyse the potential for generalisation of the encoder-decoder model with attention by focusing on the bAbI/bAbI+ condition, where the model trained on bAbI data is tested on bAbI+. As shown in Table 1, while the model performs perfectly on the bAbI corpus, it achieves only $\sim$50% accuracy on API call prediction when it is asked to generalised to bAbI+ data. Here we aim to shed light on these results by studying the errors made by the model and visualising the patterns of the attention component of the network.

4.1 Qualitative error analysis

We start by observing that the model faced with the bAbI/bAbI+ condition encounters new lexical items at test time, such as filled pauses (uh) or editing terms (no sorry). These items are all

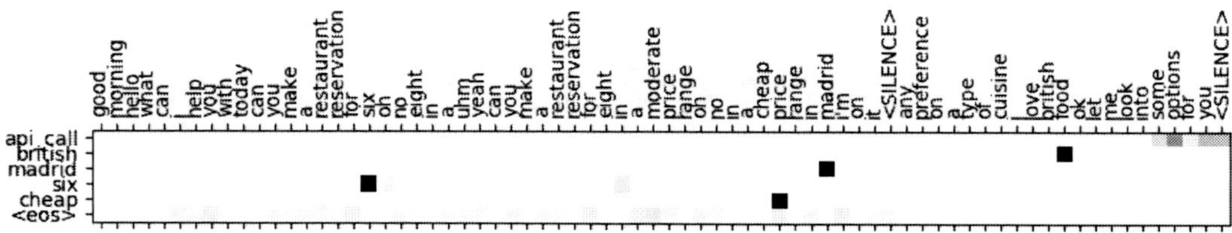

Figure 1: Visualisation of the decoder attention when generating the API call (vertical axis) for the disfluent dialogue in example (4) (horizontal axis). Darker colours indicate higher attention values.

mapped to a single token <unk> for 'unknown'. In addition, the presence of disfluencies increases the length of user utterances: The average utterance length in bAbI is 4.8 tokens, while user utterances in bAbI+ have an average length of 7.6.

Since the inventory of system utterances is very limited (there are 7 types of system outputs), the model has no difficulty learning their surface form. The errors we find, therefore, do not concern the grammaticality of the utterances, but rather when in the course of a dialogue a particular system utterance is offered. We find that utterance errors always involve a jump ahead in the expected sequence of system utterances. For example, around 83% of the utterance errors occur at the beginning of the dialogue. If the first user utterance is disfluent (e.g., `Good morning <unk> <unk> good morning`) and hence longer than expected, the model tends to skip the system's greeting and initial prompt (`Hello, what can I help you with today`) and instead outputs the second system prompt (`I'm on it`), which only makes sense once the user has already provided some task-related information. Utterance errors of this kind, where the model generates an utterance that would be appropriate later on in the dialogue, occur after all disfluency types present in bAbI+: hesitations, restarts, and self-repairs.

The current evaluation setup does not allow us to test whether utterance errors by the system lead to errors in the final API call, since the input sequence given to the encoder is the gold dialogue history and not the dialogue history with system utterances generated by the model. This, however, allows us to conclude that the errors made by the model on around 50% of all API calls are a direct consequence of the disfluencies present in the user utterances. Not surprisingly, API call errors are triggered by self-corrections, which in bAbI+ always involve the mention of two different values for a single semantic slot (see example (4) be-

low). Indeed, the model trained on bAbI achieves near-perfect accuracy when tested on a corpus that does not contain self-correction but only hesitations and restarts. This indicates that the lower accuracy is specifically caused by the presence of multiple potential values for the same API slot in self-corrections.

Manual error inspection shows that the model does not follow a systematic strategy whereby the first mention of a semantic slot is selected, which would lead to all self-corrections being processed incorrectly. As illustrated in (4), the model seems to randomly select between the first and the second mention of a slot in a self-correction structure, which leads to some self-corrections being processed correctly:

```
(4) U:good morning
    S:hello what can I help you with
      today
    U:can you make a reservation for six
      oh no eight in a uhm yeah can you
      make a reservation for eight in a
      moderate price range no in a cheap
      price range in madrid
    S:i'm on it
    U:<silence>
    S:any preference on a type of cuisine
    U:I love british food
    S:ok let me look into some options
      for you
    U:<silence>
    S:<API_call british madrid six cheap>
```

In Figure 1, we visualise the decoder attention of the bAbI model when it generates the (partly incorrect) API call for the dialogue in (4). The plot shows that while generating the different components of the API call, the model strongly relies on its attention mechanism to select the right slot. Furthermore, it confirms the observation that the model is not consistent in its strategy to select a slot after a disfluency: While it incorrectly attends to `six` (rather than `eight`), it correctly selects `cheap` (a repair of `moderate`). In the next section, we will have a closer look at the attention pat-

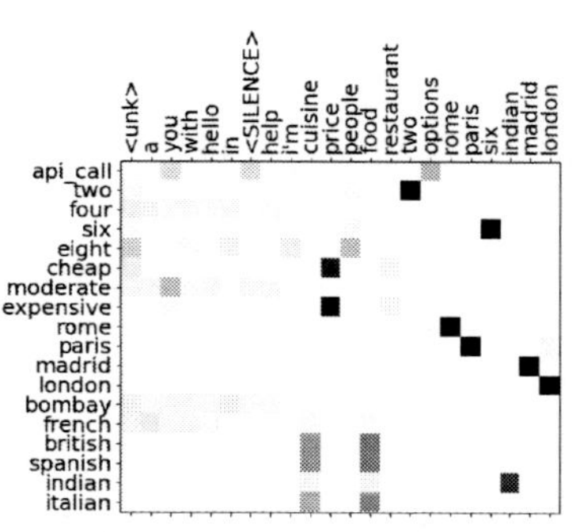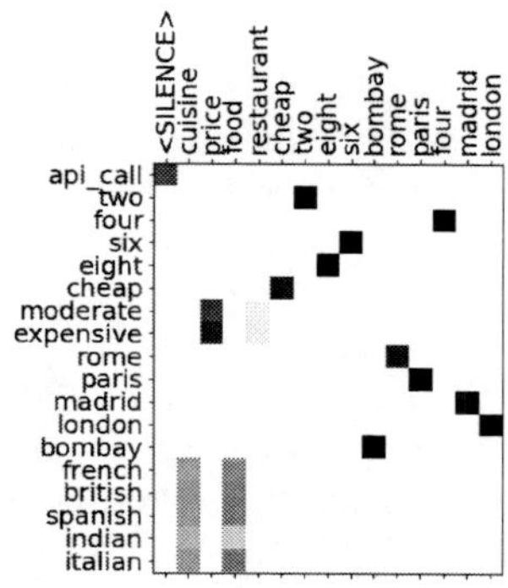

Figure 2: Alignment of in- and output words via the attention for different models tested on bAbI+ data. Left: model trained on bAbI. Right: model trained on bAbI+.

terns of both the bAbI and bAbI+ trained model.

4.2 Comparing attention patterns

To evaluate the network's attention patterns in a more quantitative way, we store all attention weights that the model computes while generating the API calls in the test corpus, and we compute their average for each API-call word. That is, for all words in an API-call, we compute to which words in the dialogue history the decoder was on average attending while it generated that word.

We plot the results in Figure 2, removing for each API-call word (on the vertical axis in the plot) the input words (horizontal axis) whose average attention score was lower 0.2. We observe that the model trained on bAbI (left) not infrequently attends to <unk> while generating API calls, indicating that it did not attend to the correct content word. A striking difference appears comparing the results for the bAbI model with the bAbI+ trained model (Figure 2, right), whose attention scores are much less diffuse. While the bAbI model frequently attends to irrelevant words such as "hello", "a" or "in" (first columns in the plot), these words are not attended at all by the bAbI+ trained model. This difference suggests that the bAbI+ model developed a more clear distinction between different types of words in the input and *benefits* from the presence of disfluencies in the training data rather than being hindered by it.

In the next section, we investigate the representations developed by the bAbI+ model (bAbI+/bAbI+ condition), focussing in particular on how it incrementally processes disfluencies.

5 Disfluency Processing

In contrast to previous work (Eshghi et al., 2017; Shalyminov et al., 2017), our seq2seq model with attention trained on bAbI+ data learns to process disfluent user utterances remarkably well, achieving over 98% sequence accuracy on API calls (see bAbI+/bAbI+ condition in Table 1). In this section, we investigate how the model deals with disfluencies, in particular self-corrections, by drawing inspiration from human disfluency processing.

5.1 The structure of disfluencies

It has been often noted that disfluencies follow regular patterns (Levelt, 1983; Shriberg, 1994). Example (5) shows the structure of a prototypical self-correction, where the *reparandum* (RM) contains the problematic material to be repaired; the utterance is then interrupted, which can optionally be signalled with a filled paused and/or an *editing term* (ET); the final part is the *repair* (R) proper, after which the utterance may continue:

(5) a reservation for *six* {I mean} *eight* in a...
　　　　　　　　　　　 RM　　　ET　　 R

The presence or relationship between these elements serves to classify disfluencies into different types. For example, restarts such as those inserted in the bAbI+ corpus, are characterised by the fact that the reparandum and the repair components are identical (see example (2) in Section 2.2); in contrast to self-corrections, where the repair differs from and is intended to overwrite the material in the reparandum. In hesitations such as (1), there is only a filled pause and no reparandum nor repair.

5.2 Editing terms

The algorithm used to generate the bAbI+ data systematically adds editing expressions (such as `oh no` or `sorry`) to all restarts and self-corrections inserted in the data. However, editing expressions (e.g., *I mean, rather, that is, sorry, oops*) are in fact rare in naturally occurring human conversation. For example, Hough (2015) finds that only 18.52% of self-corrections in the Switchboard corpus contain an explicit editing term. Thus, while psycholinguistic research has shown that the presence of an explicit editing term followed by a correction makes the disfluency easier to handle (Brennan and Schober, 2001), humans are able to process disfluencies without the clues offered by such expressions.

Here we test whether the model relies on the systematic presence of editing expressions in the bAbI+ data. To this end, we created two new versions of the dataset using the code by Shalyminov et al. (2017):[2] One with no editing term in any of the self-corrections or restarts, dubbed "noET"; and one where there is an editing term in 20% of self-corrections and restarts, dubbed "realET" as it reflects a more realistic presence of such expressions. We refer to the original bAbI+ data, which has editing terms in all self-corrections and restarts, as "fullET".

We test to what extent a model trained on fullET, which could rely on the systematic presence of an editing term to detect the presence of a self-correction or restart, is able to process disfluencies in a more natural scenario where editing expressions are only sparsely available (realET). The result indicates that the editing term has very little effect on the model's performance: as shown in Table 2, accuracy goes down slightly, but is still extremely high (98%). This finding persists when the editing terms are left out of the test data entirely (97% accuracy when testing on noET). When models are trained on data containing fewer editing terms (realET and noET) and tested on data with a comparable or smaller percentage of editing terms, we observe a slightly larger drop in accuracy (see Table 2). We conclude that, although editing terms may help the model to develop better representations during training, their presence is not required to correctly process disfluencies at test time.

---

[2]`https://github.com/ishalyminov/babi_tools`

Trained on	Tested on		
	noET	realET	fullET
fullET	97	98	100
realET	94	95	
noET	94		

Table 2: Sequence accuracies of all sequences with and without editing term, averaged over 5 runs.

5.3 Identification of structural components

Disfluencies have regular patterns. However, identifying their components online is not trivial. The comprehender faces what Levelt (1983) calls the *continuation problem*: the need to identify (the beginning and end of the reparandum and the repair onset. Evidence shows that there are no clues (prosodic or otherwise) present during the reparandum. Thus the identification of the disfluency takes place at or after the moment of interruption (typically during the repair). Here there may be prosodic changes, but such clues are usually absent (Levelt and Cutler, 1983). Ferreira et al. (2004) point out that "the language comprehension system is able to identify a disfluency, likely through the use of a combination of cues (in some manner that is as yet not understood)."

We test to what extent our trained encoder-decoder model distinguishes reparanda and editing terms and can identify the boundaries of a repair using *diagnostic classifiers* (Hupkes et al., 2018). Diagnostic classifiers were proposed as a method to qualitatively evaluate whether specific information is encoded in high-dimensional representations—typically the hidden states that a trained neural network goes through while processing a sentence. The technique relies on training simple neural meta-models to predict the information of interest from these representations and then uses the accuracy of the resulting classifiers as a proxy for the extent to which this information is encoded in the representations.

In our case, we aim to identify whether the hidden layer activations reflect if the model is currently processing a reparandum, an editing term, or the repair. To test his, we label each word in the bAbI+ validation corpus according to which of the 3 categories it belongs to and train 3 binary classifiers to classify from the hidden layer activation of the encoder whether the word it just processed belongs to either one of these 3 classes. For an example of such a labelling we refer to Figure 3.

Figure 3: A labelled example sentence to evaluate whether models have distinct representations for reparanda, repairs, and editing terms. For each label, we train a separate binary classifier to predict whether or not a word belongs to the corresponding class.

We hypothesise that while reparanda will not be detectable in the hidden layer activations, as they can only be identified as such a posteriori (Levelt, 1983; Ferreira et al., 2004), editing terms should be easy to detect, since they belong to a class of distinct words. The most interesting classifier we consider is the one identifying repairs, which requires a more structural understanding of the disfluency and the sentence as a whole.

	self-corrections	restarts
Reparandum	15.0 / 89.4	27.4 / 92.6
Editing term	37.3 / 99.4	55.7 / 99.2
Repair	21.3 / 93.5	35.2 / 94.9

Table 3: Precision / recall of diagnostic classifiers to identify reparanda, editing terms and repairs.

The general trends in our results (see Table 3 above) are as expected: Editing terms are more easily recoverable than both reparanda and repairs, and the reparandum has the lowest scores with a precision and recall of 0.15 and 0.89, respectively. However, results for editing terms and repairs are lower than expected. The presence of editing terms is not reliably identifiable given the hidden layer activations of a model (37.3% and 55.7% precision for self-corrections and restarts, respectively), which is surprising given the fact that there is no overlap between editing terms and the rest of the model's vocabulary. Taken together with the results of our previous experiments in Section 5.2 regarding the effect of editing terms on the final sequence accuracy, this indicates that the presence of an editing term causes only minimal changes in the hidden layer activations, and thus leaves only a small trace in the hidden state of the network. The performance of the repair classifier is also low: 21.3% precision on self-correction and 35.2% on restarts. These results suggest that the model has no explicit representations of the structure of disfluencies and instead relies on other cues to infer the right API call.

5.4   Incremental interpretation

Next we analyse how the model processes disfluencies by looking into the interpretation—in terms of task-related predictions—that the model builds incrementally, word by word and utterance by utterance.

Word by word   First, we probe the representations of the *encoder* part of the model while it processes incoming sentences, for which we use again diagnostic classifiers. In particular, we test if information that is given at a particular point in the dialogue (for instance, the user expresses she would like to eat Indian food) is remembered by the encoder throughout the rest of the conversation. We label the words in a dialogue according to what slot information was already provided previously in the dialogue, and test if this information can be predicted by a diagnostic classifier at later points in the dialogue. Note that while in the bAbI data the prediction for a slot changes only once when the user expresses her preference, due to the possibilities of corrections, slot information may change multiple times in the bAbI+ corpus. We train separate diagnostic classifiers for the different slots in the API call: cuisine (10 options), location (10 options), party size (4 options), and price range (3 options).

Our experiments show that the semantic information needed to issue an API call is not accurately predictable from the hidden representations that the encoder builds of the dialogue—see Table 4, where accuracy scores are all relatively low.

Cuisine	31.3
Location	25.9
Price range	57.3
Party size	43.0

Table 4: Accuracy per slot type in the word-by-word experiment.

In Figure 4, we plot the accuracy of the diagnostic classifiers over time, relative to the position at which information appears in the dialogue (that is, the accuracy at position 4 represents the accuracy

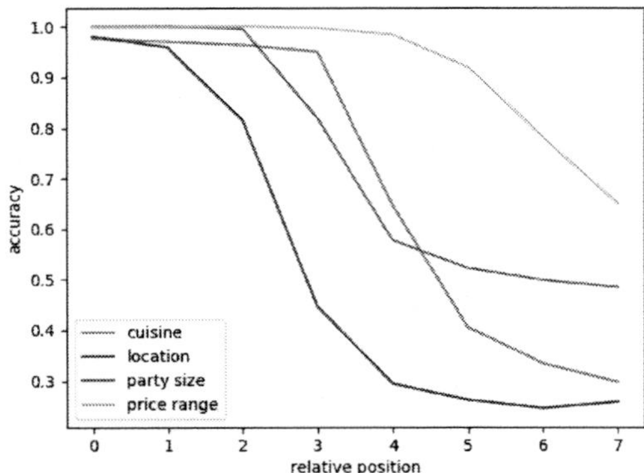

Figure 4: Accuracy at position relative to mention in the dialogue of each type of slot.

4 words after the slot information occurred). The plot illustrates that the encoder keeps traces of semantic slot information for a few time steps after this information appears in the dialogue, but then rapidly 'forgets' it when the dialogue continues.[3] These results confirm our earlier findings that most of the burden for correctly issuing API calls falls on the model's attention mechanism, which needs to select the correct hidden states at the moment an API call should be generated.

Utterance by utterance In a second experiment, we study the incremental development of the API call made by the model's generative component (the *decoder*) by prompting it to generate an API call after every user utterance. To trigger the API calls, we append the utterances normally preceding an API call (let me look some options for you <silence>) to the dialogue history that is fed to the decoder. We apply this trick to elicit an API call after every user utterance in the dialogue. We evaluate the generated API calls by considering only the slots that can already be filled given the current dialogue history. That is, in a dialogue in which the user has requested to eat Italian food in London but has not talked about party size, we exclude the party size slot from the evaluation, and evaluate only whether the generated API call correctly predicts "Italian" and "London".

For models trained on bAbI data, the described method reliably prompted an API call, while it

---

[3]To exclude the possibility that the low accuracy is a consequence of *relocation* of information instead of it being forgotten, we also trained diagnostic classifiers to only start predicting a few words after slot information appears, but this did not result in an increase in accuracy.

bAbI / bAbI	100
bAbI+ / bAbI	100
bAbI / bAbI+	66.6
bAbI+ / bAbI+	99.8

Table 5: Accuracy on triggered API calls utterance by utterance.

was less successful for models trained on bAbI+, where API calls were evoked only in 86% of the time (when testing on bAbI+ data) and 54% of the time (when testing on bAbI data). For our analysis, we consider only cases in which the API call was prompted and ignore cases in which other sentences were generated

As shown in Table 5, we find that the decoders of both the bAbI and bAbI+ models are able to generate appropriate API calls immediately after slots are mentioned in the user utterance (~100% accuracy in the bAbI/bAbI, bAbI+/bAbI, and bAbI+/bAbI+ conditions). However, when confronted with disfluencies, the model trained on the disfluency-free bAbI data is not able to do so reliably (66.6% accuracy with bAbI/bAbI+), following the trend we also observed in Table 1.

6 Conclusions

We have investigated how recurrent neural networks trained in a synthetic dataset of task-oriented English dialogues process disfluencies. Our first conclusion is that, contrary to earlier findings, recurrent networks with attention can learn to correctly process disfluencies, provided they were presented to them at training time. In the current data, they do so without strongly relying on the presence of editing terms or identifying the repair component of disfluent structures. When comparing models trained on data with and without disfluencies, we observe that the attention patterns of the former models are more clear-cut, suggesting that the disfluencies contribute to a better understanding of the input, rather than hindering it.

Furthermore, we find that in an encoder-decoder model with attention, at least for the current task-oriented setting, a large burden of the processing falls on the *generative* part of the model: the decoder aided by the attention mechanism. The encoder, on the other hand, does not incrementally develop complex representations of the dialogue history, limiting its usefulness as a cognitive model of language interpretation. We preliminary conclude that different learning biases are necessary to obtain a more balanced division of labour between encoder and decoder.

Here we have exploited synthetic data, taking advantage of the control this affords regarding types and frequency of disfluency patterns, as well as the direct connection between language processing and task success present in the dataset. In the future, we aim at investigating neural models of disfluency processing applied to more naturalistic data, possibly leveraging eye-tracking information to ground language comprehension (**??**).

References

Dzmitry Bahdanau, Kyunghyun Cho, and Yoshua Bengio. 2015a. Neural machine translation by jointly learning to align and translate. In *Proceedings of the 3rd International Conference on Learning Representations (ICLR)*.

Dzmitry Bahdanau, Kyunghyun Cho, and Yoshua Bengio. 2015b. Neural machine translation by jointly learning to align and translate. In *Proceedings of the 3rd International Conference on Learning Representations (ICLR2015)*.

Karl GD Bailey and Fernanda Ferreira. 2003. Disfluencies affect the parsing of garden-path sentences. *Journal of Memory and Language*, 49(2):183–200.

Antoine Bordes, Y-Lan Boureau, and Jason Weston. 2017. Learning end-to-end goal-oriented dialog. In *Proceedings of the 5th International Conference on Learning Representations (ICLR)*.

Susan E Brennan and Michael F Schober. 2001. How listeners compensate for disfluencies in spontaneous speech. *Journal of Memory and Language*, 44(2):274–296.

Arash Eshghi, Igor Shalyminov, and Oliver Lemon. 2017. Bootstrapping incremental dialogue systems from minimal data: the generalisation power of dialogue grammars. In *Proceedings of the 2017 Conference on Empirical Methods in Natural Language Processing (EMNLP)*, pages 2220–2230. Association for Computational Linguistics.

Fernanda Ferreira and Karl G. D. Bailey. 2004. Disfluencies and human language comprehension. *Trends in Cognitive Sciences*, 8(5).

Fernanda Ferreira, Ellen F. Lau, and Karl G. D. Bailey. 2004. Disfluencies, language comprehension, and tree adjoining grammars. *Cognitive Science*, 28:721–749.

Jean E. Fox Tree. 1995. The effects of false starts and repetitions on the processing of subsequent words in spontaneous speech. *Journal of memory and language*, 34(6):709–738.

Peter A. Heeman and James F. Allen. 1999. Speech repairs, intonational phrases, and discourse markers: modeling speakers' utterances in spoken dialogue. *Computational Linguistics*, 25(4):527–571.

Julian Hough. 2015. *Modelling Incremental Self-Repair Processing in Dialogue*. Ph.D. thesis, Queen Mary University of London.

Dieuwke Hupkes, Sara Veldhoen, and Willem Zuidema. 2018. Visualisation and 'diagnostic classifiers' reveal how recurrent and recursive neural networks process hierarchical structure. *Journal of Artificial Intelligence Research*, 61:907–926.

Nal Kalchbrenner, Edward Grefenstette, and Phil Blunsom. 2014. A convolutional neural network for modelling sentences. In *Proceedings of the 52nd Annual Meeting of the Association for Computational Linguistics*, pages 655–665.

Diederik Kingma and Jimmy Ba. 2014. Adam: A method for stochastic optimization. In *Proceedings of ICLR 2014*, pages 1–13.

Ellen F. Lau and Fernanda Ferreira. 2005. Lingering effects of disfluent material on comprehension of garden path sentences. *Language and Cognitive Processes*, 20:633—666.

Willem J. M. Levelt. 1983. Monitoring and self-repair in speech. *Cognition*, 14(1):41–104.

Willem JM Levelt and Anne Cutler. 1983. Prosodic marking in speech repair. *Journal of semantics*, 2(2):205–218.

Xian Qian and Yang Liu. 2013. Disfluency detection using multi-step stacked learning. In *Proceedings of the 2013 Conference of the North American Chapter of the Association for Computational Linguistics: Human Language Technologies*, pages 820–825.

Alan Ritter, Colin Cherry, and William B. Dolan. 2011. Data-driven response generation in social media. In *Proceedings of the 2011 Conference on Empirical Methods in Natural Language Processing*, pages 583–593. Association for Computational Linguistics.

Igor Shalyminov, Arash Eshghi, and Oliver Lemon. 2017. Challenging neural dialogue models with natural data: Memory networks fail on incremental phenomena. In *Proceedings of the 21st Workshop on the Semantics and Pragmatics of Dialogue (SEM-DIAL)*, pages 125–133.

Elizabeth E. Shriberg. 1994. *Preliminaries to a Theory of Speech Disfluencies*. Ph.D. thesis, University of California at Berkeley, Berkeley, CA.

Andreas Stolcke and Elizabeth Shriberg. 1996. Statistical language modeling for speech disfluencies. In *Conference Proceedings of the IEEE International Conference on Acoustics, Speech, and Signal Processing (ICASSP-96)*, volume 1, pages 405–408.

Sainbayar Sukhbaatar, arthur szlam, Jason Weston, and Rob Fergus. 2015. End-to-end memory networks. In C. Cortes, N. D. Lawrence, D. D. Lee, M. Sugiyama, and R. Garnett, editors, *Advances in Neural Information Processing Systems 28*, pages 2440–2448. Curran Associates, Inc.

Ilya Sutskever, Oriol Vinyals, and Quoc V Le. 2014. Sequence to sequence learning with neural networks. In *Advances in neural information processing systems (NIPS)*, pages 3104–3112.

Oriol Vinyals and Quoc V. Le. 2015. A neural conversational model. In *Proceedings of the 31 st International Conference on Machine Learning (ICML) – Deep Learning Workshop*.

Simon Zwarts, Mark Johnson, and Robert Dale. 2010. Detecting speech repairs incrementally using a noisy channel approach. In *Proceedings of the 23rd international conference on computational linguistics*, pages 1371–1378. Association for Computational Linguistics.

An Operation Sequence Model for Explainable Neural Machine Translation

Felix Stahlberg and **Danielle Saunders** and **Bill Byrne**
Department of Engineering
University of Cambridge, UK
{fs439,ds636,wjb31}@cam.ac.uk

Abstract

We propose to achieve explainable neural machine translation (NMT) by changing the output representation to explain itself. We present a novel approach to NMT which generates the target sentence by monotonically walking through the source sentence. Word reordering is modeled by operations which allow setting markers in the target sentence and move a target-side write head between those markers. In contrast to many modern neural models, our system emits explicit word alignment information which is often crucial to practical machine translation as it improves explainability. Our technique can outperform a plain text system in terms of BLEU score under the recent Transformer architecture on Japanese-English and Portuguese-English, and is within 0.5 BLEU difference on Spanish-English.

1 Introduction

Neural machine translation (NMT) models (Sutskever et al., 2014; Bahdanau et al., 2015; Gehring et al., 2017; Vaswani et al., 2017) are remarkably effective in modelling the distribution over target sentences conditioned on the source sentence, and yield superior translation performance compared to traditional statistical machine translation (SMT) on many language pairs. However, it is often difficult to extract a comprehensible explanation for the predictions of these models as information in the network is represented by real-valued vectors or matrices (Ding et al., 2017). In contrast, the translation process in SMT is 'transparent' as it can identify the source word which caused a target word through word alignment. Most NMT models do not use the concept of word alignment. It is tempting to interpret encoder-decoder attention matrices (Bahdanau et al., 2015) in neural models as (soft) alignments, but previous work has found that the attention weights in NMT are often erratic (Cheng et al., 2016) and differ significantly from traditional word alignments (Koehn and Knowles, 2017; Ghader and Monz, 2017). We will discuss the difference between attention and alignment in detail in Sec. 4. The goal of this paper is explainable NMT by developing a transparent translation process for neural models. Our approach does not change the neural architecture, but represents the translation together with its alignment as a linear sequence of operations. The neural model predicts this operation sequence, and thus simultaneously generates a translation and an explanation for it in terms of alignments from the target words to the source words that generate them. The operation sequence is "self-explanatory"; it does not explain an underlying NMT system but is rather a single representation produced by the NMT system that can be used to generate translations along with an accompanying explanatory alignment to the source sentence. We report competitive results of our method on Spanish-English, Portuguese-English, and Japanese-English, with the benefit of producing hard alignments for better interpretability. We discuss the theoretical connection between our approach and hierarchical SMT (Chiang, 2005) by showing that an operation sequence can be seen as a derivation in a formal grammar.

2 A Neural Operation Sequence Model

Our operation sequence neural machine translation (OSNMT) model is inspired by the operation sequence model for SMT (Durrani et al., 2011), but changes the set of operations to be more appropriate for neural sequence models. OSNMT is not restricted to a particular architecture, i.e. any seq2seq model such as RNN-based, convolutional, or self-attention-based models (Bahdanau et al.,

175

Proceedings of the 2018 EMNLP Workshop BlackboxNLP: Analyzing and Interpreting Neural Networks for NLP, pages 175–186
Brussels, Belgium, November 1, 2018. ©2018 Association for Computational Linguistics

2015; Vaswani et al., 2017; Gehring et al., 2017) could be used. In this paper, we use the recent Transformer model architecture (Vaswani et al., 2017) in all experiments.

In OSNMT, the neural seq2seq model learns to produce a sequence of operations. An OS-NMT operation sequence describes a translation (the 'compiled' target sentence) and explains each target token with a hard link into the source sentence. OSNMT keeps track of the positions of a source-side read head and a target-side write head. The read head monotonically walks through the source sentence, whereas the position of the write head can be moved from marker to marker in the target sentence. OSNMT defines the following operations to control head positions and produce output words.

- POP_SRC: Move the read head right by one token.

- SET_MARKER: Insert a marker symbol into the target sentence at the position of the write head.

- JMP_FWD: Move the write head to the nearest marker right of the current head position in the target sentence.

- JMP_BWD: Move the write head to the nearest marker left of the current head position in the target sentence.

- INSERT(t): Insert a target token t into the target sentence at the position of the write head.

Tab. 1 illustrates the generation of a Japanese-English translation in detail. The neural seq2seq model is trained to produce the sequence of operations in the first column of Tab. 1. The initial state of the target sentence is a single marker symbol X_1. Generative operations like SET_MARKER or INSERT(t) insert a single symbol left of the current marker (highlighted). The model begins with a SET_MARKER operation, which indicates that the translation of the first word in the source sentence is not at the beginning of the target sentence. Indeed, after "translating" the identities '2000' and 'hr', in time step 6 the model jumps back to the marker X_2 and continues writing left of '2000'. The translation process terminates when the read head is at the end of the source sentence. The final translation in plain text can be obtained by removing all markers from the (compiled) target sentence.

2.1 OSNMT Represents Alignments

The word alignment can be derived from the operation sequence by looking up the position of the read head for each generated target token. The alignment for the example in Tab. 1 is shown in Fig. 1. Note that similarly to the IBM models (Brown et al., 1993) and the OSM for SMT (Durrani et al., 2011), our OSNMT can only represent 1:n alignments. Thus, each target token is aligned to exactly one source token, but a source token can generate any number of (possibly non-consecutive) target tokens.

2.2 OSNMT Represents Hierarchical Structure

We can also derive a tree structure from the operation sequence in Tab. 1 (Fig. 2) in which each marker is represented by a nonterminal node with outgoing arcs to symbols inserted at that marker. The target sentence can be read off the tree by depth-first search traversal (post-order).

More formally, synchronous context-free grammars (SCFGs) generate pairs of strings by pairing two context-free grammars. Phrase-based hierarchical SMT (Chiang, 2005) uses SCFGs to model the relation between the source sentence and the target sentence. Multitext grammars (MTGs) are a generalization of SCFGs to more than two output streams (Melamed, 2003; Melamed et al., 2004). We find that an OSNMT sequence can be interpreted as sequence of rules of a tertiary MTG $\mathcal{G}$ which generates 1.) the source sentence, 2.) the target sentence, and 3.) the position of the target side write head. The start symbol of $\mathcal{G}$ is

$$[(S), (X_1), (P_1)]^{\mathsf{T}} \tag{1}$$

which initializes the source sentence stream with a single nonterminal S, the target sentence with the initial marker X_1 and the position of the write head with 1 (P_1). Following Melamed et al. (2004) we denote rules in $\mathcal{G}$ as

$$[(\alpha_1), (\alpha_2), (\alpha_3)]^{\mathsf{T}} \to [(\beta_1), (\beta_2), (\beta_3)]^{\mathsf{T}} \tag{2}$$

where $\alpha_1, \alpha_2, \alpha_3$ are single nonterminals or empty, $\beta_1, \beta_2, \beta_3$ are strings of terminals and nonterminals, and $\alpha_i \to \beta_i$ for all $i \in \{1, 2, 3\}$ with nonempty α_i are the rewriting rules for each of

	Operation	Source sentence	Target sentence (compiled)
		2000 hr の 安定 動作 を 確認 した	X_1
1	SET_MARKER	2000 hr の 安定 動作 を 確認 した	X_2 X_1
2	2000	2000 hr の 安定 動作 を 確認 した	X_2 2000 X_1
3	POP_SRC	2000 hr の 安定 動作 を 確認 した	X_2 2000 X_1
4	hr	2000 hr の 安定 動作 を 確認 した	X_2 2000 hr X_1
5	POP_SRC	2000 hr の 安定 動作 を 確認 した	X_2 2000 hr X_1
6	JMP_BWD	2000 hr の 安定 動作 を 確認 した	X_2 2000 hr X_1
7	SET_MARKER	2000 hr の 安定 動作 を 確認 した	X_3 X_2 2000 hr X_1
8	of	2000 hr の 安定 動作 を 確認 した	X_3 of X_2 2000 hr X_1
9	POP_SRC	2000 hr の 安定 動作 を 確認 した	X_3 of X_2 2000 hr X_1
10	JMP_BWD	2000 hr の 安定 動作 を 確認 した	X_3 of X_2 2000 hr X_1
11	stable	2000 hr の 安定 動作 を 確認 した	stable X_3 of X_2 2000 hr X_1
12	POP_SRC	2000 hr の 安定 動作 を 確認 した	stable X_3 of X_2 2000 hr X_1
13	operation	2000 hr の 安定 動作 を 確認 した	stable operation X_3 of X_2 2000 hr X_1
14	POP_SRC	2000 hr の 安定 動作 を 確認 した	stable operation X_3 of X_2 2000 hr X_1
15	JMP_FWD	2000 hr の 安定 動作 を 確認 した	stable operation X_3 of X_2 2000 hr X_1
16	JMP_FWD	2000 hr の 安定 動作 を 確認 した	stable operation X_3 of X_2 2000 hr X_1
17	was	2000 hr の 安定 動作 を 確認 した	stable operation X_3 of X_2 2000 hr was X_1
18	POP_SRC	2000 hr の 安定 動作 を 確認 した	stable operation X_3 of X_2 2000 hr was X_1
19	POP_SRC	2000 hr の 安定 動作 を 確認 した	stable operation X_3 of X_2 2000 hr was X_1
20	confirmed	2000 hr の 安定 動作 を 確認 した	stable operation X_3 of X_2 2000 hr was confirmed X_1
21	POP_SRC	2000 hr の 安定 動作 を 確認 した	stable operation X_3 of X_2 2000 hr was confirmed X_1

Table 1: Generation of the target sentence "stable operation of 2000 hr was confirmed" from the source sentence "2000 hr の 安定 動作 を 確認 した". The neural model produces the linear sequence of operations in the first column. The positions of the source-side read head and the target-side write head are highlighted. The marker in the target sentence produced by the i-th SET_MARKER operation is denoted with 'X_{i+1}'; X_1 is the initial marker. We denote INSERT(t) operations as t to simplify notation.

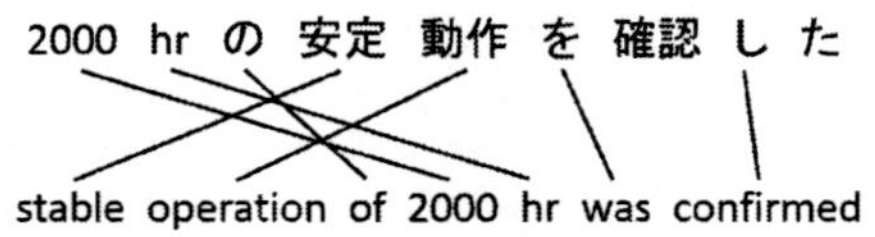

Figure 1: The translation and the alignment derived from the operation sequence in Tab. 1.

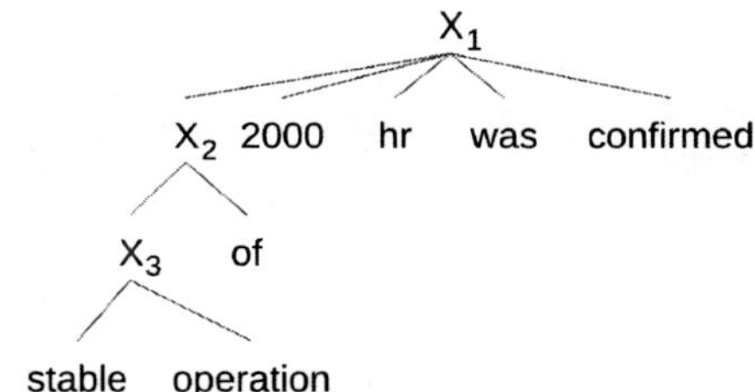

Figure 2: Target-side tree representation of the operation sequence in Tab. 1.

the three individual components which need to be applied simultaneously. POP_SRC extends the source sentence prefix in the first stream by one token.

$$\text{POP\_SRC} : \forall s \in \mathcal{V}_{src} : \begin{bmatrix} (S) \\ () \\ () \end{bmatrix} \to \begin{bmatrix} (sS) \\ () \\ () \end{bmatrix} \quad (3)$$

where $\mathcal{V}_{src}$ is the source language vocabulary. A jump from marker X_i to X_j is realized by replacing P_i with P_j in the third grammar component:

$$\text{JMP} : \forall i, j \in \mathcal{N} : [(), (), P_i]^{\mathsf{T}} \to [(), (), (iP_j)]^{\mathsf{T}} \quad (4)$$

where $\mathcal{N} = \{k \in \mathbb{N} | k \leq n\}$ is the set of the first n natural numbers for a sufficiently large n. The generative operations (SET_MARKER and

Derivation	OSNMT
$[(S), (X_1), P_1]^{\mathsf{T}}$	
$\overset{\text{Eq. 3}}{\to} [(2000\ S), (X_1), P_1]^{\mathsf{T}}$	SET_MARKER
$\overset{\text{Eq. 5}}{\to} [(2000\ S), (X_2 X_1), (P_1)]^{\mathsf{T}}$	2000
$\overset{\text{Eq. 6}}{\to} [(2000\ S), (X_2\ 2000\ X_1), (P_1)]^{\mathsf{T}}$	POP_SRC
$\overset{\text{Eq. 3}}{\to} \begin{bmatrix} (2000\ \text{hr}\ S) \\ (X_2\ 2000\ X_1) \\ (P_1) \end{bmatrix}$	hr
$\overset{\text{Eq. 6}}{\to} \begin{bmatrix} (2000\ \text{hr}\ S) \\ (X_2\ 2000\ \text{hr}\ X_1) \\ (P_1) \end{bmatrix}$	POP_SRC
$\overset{\text{Eq. 3}}{\to} \begin{bmatrix} (2000\ \text{hr}\ の\ S) \\ (X_2\ 2000\ \text{hr}\ X_1) \\ (P_1) \end{bmatrix}$	JMP_BWD
$\overset{\text{Eq. 4}}{\to} \begin{bmatrix} (2000\ \text{hr}\ の\ S) \\ (X_2\ 2000\ \text{hr}\ X_1) \\ (1\ P_2) \end{bmatrix}$	SET_MARKER
$\overset{\text{Eq. 5}}{\to} \begin{bmatrix} (2000\ \text{hr}\ の\ S) \\ (X_3 X_2\ 2000\ \text{hr}\ X_1) \\ (1\ P_2) \end{bmatrix}$	of
$\overset{\text{Eq. 6}}{\to} \begin{bmatrix} (2000\ \text{hr}\ の\ S) \\ (X_3\ \text{of}\ X_2\ 2000\ \text{hr}\ X_1) \\ (1\ P_2) \end{bmatrix}$	...
...	

Table 2: Derivation in $\mathcal{G}$ for the example of Tab. 1.

INSERT(t)) insert symbols into the second component.

$$\text{SET\_MARKER} : \forall i \in \mathcal{N} : \begin{bmatrix} () \\ (X_i) \\ (P_i) \end{bmatrix} \to \begin{bmatrix} () \\ (X_{i+1} X_i) \\ (P_i) \end{bmatrix} \quad (5)$$

$$\text{INSERT} : \forall i \in \mathcal{N}, t \in \mathcal{V}_{trg} : \begin{bmatrix} () \\ (X_i) \\ (P_i) \end{bmatrix} \to \begin{bmatrix} () \\ (t X_i) \\ (P_i) \end{bmatrix} \quad (6)$$

where $\mathcal{V}_{trg}$ is the target language vocabulary. The identity mapping $P_i \to P_i$ in the third component enforces that the write head is at marker X_i. We note that $\mathcal{G}$ is not only context-free but also regular in the first and third components (but not in the second component due to Eq. 5). Rules of the form in Eq. 6 are directly related to alignment links (cf. Fig. 1) as they represent the fact that target token t is aligned to the last terminal symbol in the first stream. We formalize removing markers/nonterminals at the end by introducing a special nonterminal T which is eventually mapped to the end-of-sentence symbol EOS:

$$[(S), (), ()]^{\mathsf{T}} \to [(T), (), ()]^{\mathsf{T}} \quad (7)$$

$$[(T), (), ()]^{\mathsf{T}} \to [(\text{EOS}), (), ()]^{\mathsf{T}} \quad (8)$$

$$\forall i \in \mathcal{N} : [(T), (X_i), ()]^{\mathsf{T}} \to [(T), (\epsilon), ()]^{\mathsf{T}} \quad (9)$$

$$\forall i \in \mathcal{N} : [(T), (), (P_i)]^{\mathsf{T}} \to [(T), (), (\epsilon)]^{\mathsf{T}} \quad (10)$$

Tab. 2 illustrates that there is a 1:1 correspondence between a derivation in $\mathcal{G}$ and an OSNMT operation sequence. The target-side derivation (the second component in $\mathcal{G}$) is structurally similar to a binarized version of the tree in Fig. 2. However, we assign scores to the structure via the corresponding OSNMT sequence which does not need to obey the usual conditional independence assumptions in hierarchical SMT. Therefore, even though $\mathcal{G}$ is context-free in the second component, our scoring model for $\mathcal{G}$ is more powerful as it conditions on the OSNMT history which potentially contains context information. Note that OSNMT is deficient (Brown et al., 1993) as it assigns non-zero probability mass to any operation sequence, not only those with derivation in G.

We further note that subword-based OSNMT can potentially represent any alignment to any target sentence as long as the alignment does not violate the 1:n restriction. This is in contrast to phrase-based SMT where reference translations often do not have a derivation in the SMT system due to coverage problems (Auli et al., 2009).

2.3 Comparison to the OSM for SMT

Our OSNMT set of operations (POP_SRC, SET_MARKER, JMP_FWD, JMP_BWD, and INSERT(t)) is inspired by the original OSM for SMT (Durrani et al., 2011) as it also represents the translation process as linear sequence of operations. However, there are significant differences which make OSNMT more suitable for neural models. First, OSNMT is monotone on the source side, and allows jumps on the target side. SMT-OSM operations jump in the source sentence. We argue that source side monotonicity potentially mitigates coverage issues of neural models (over- and under-translation (Tu et al., 2016)) as the attention can learn to scan the source sentence from left to right. Another major difference is that we use *markers* rather than *gaps*, and do not close a gap/marker after jumping to it. This is an implication of OSNMT jumps being defined on the target side since the size of a span is unknown at inference time.

178

Algorithm 1 Align2OSNMT(a, $\mathbf{x}$, $\mathbf{y}$)

1: $holes \leftarrow \{(0, \infty)\}$
2: $ops \leftarrow \langle\rangle$ {Initialize with empty list}
3: $head \leftarrow 0$
4: **for** $i \leftarrow 1$ **to** $|\mathbf{x}|$ **do**
5:    **for all** $j \in \{j | a_j = i\}$ **do**
6:       $hole\_idx \leftarrow holes.\text{find}(j)$
7:       $d \leftarrow hole\_idx - head$
8:       **if** $d < 0$ **then**
9:          $ops.\text{extend}(\texttt{JMP\_BWD}.\text{repeat}(-d))$
10:       **end if**
11:       **if** $d > 0$ **then**
12:          $ops.\text{extend}(\texttt{JMP\_FWD}.\text{repeat}(d))$
13:       **end if**
14:       $head \leftarrow hole\_idx$
15:       $(s, t) \leftarrow holes[head]$
16:       **if** $s \neq j$ **then**
17:          $holes.\text{append}((s, j - 1))$
18:          $head \leftarrow head + 1$
19:          $ops.\text{append}(\texttt{SET\_MARKER})$
20:       **end if**
21:       $ops.\text{append}(\texttt{y}_j)$
22:       $holes[head] \leftarrow (j + 1, t)$
23:    **end for**
24:    $ops.\text{append}(\texttt{SRC\_POP})$
25: **end for**
26: **return** ops

---

3 Training

We train our Transformer model as usual by minimising the negative log-likelihood of the target sequence. However, in contrast to plain text NMT, the target sequence is not a plain sequence of subword or word tokens but a sequence of operations. Consequently, we need to map the target sentences in the training corpus to OSNMT representations. We first run a statistical word aligner like Giza++ (Och and Ney, 2003) to obtain an aligned training corpus. We delete all alignment links which violate the 1:n restriction of OSNMT (cf. Sec. 2). The alignments together with the target sentences are then used to generate the reference operation sequences for training. The algorithm for this conversion is shown in Alg. 1.[1] Note that an operation sequence represents one specific alignment, which means that the only way for an OSNMT sequence to be generated correctly is if

Corpus	Language pair	# Sentences
Scielo	Spanish-English	587K
Scielo	Portuguese-English	513K
WAT	Japanese-English	1M

Table 3: Training set sizes.

both the word alignment and the target sentence are also correct. Thereby, the neural model learns to align and translate at the same time. However, there is spurious ambiguity as one alignment can be represented by different OSNMT sequences. For instance, simply adding a SET_MARKER operation at the end of an OSNMT sequence does not change the alignment represented by it.

4 Results

We evaluate on three language pairs: Japanese-English (ja-en), Spanish-English (es-en), and Portuguese-English (pt-en). We use the ASPEC corpus (Nakazawa et al., 2016) for ja-en and the health science portion of the Scielo corpus (Neves and Névéol, 2016) for es-en and pt-en. Training set sizes are summarized in Tab. 3. We use byte pair encoding (Sennrich et al., 2016) with 32K merge operations for all systems (joint encoding models for es-en and pt-en and separate source/target models for ja-en). We trained Transformer models (Vaswani et al., 2017)[2] until convergence (250K steps for plain text, 350K steps for OSNMT) on a single GPU using Tensor2Tensor (Vaswani et al., 2018) after removing sentences with more than 250 tokens. Batches contain around 4K source and 4K target tokens. Transformer training is very sensitive to the batch size and the number of GPUs (Popel and Bojar, 2018). Therefore, we delay SGD updates (Saunders et al., 2018) to every 8 steps to simulate 8 GPU training as recommended by Vaswani et al. (2017). Based on the performance on the ja-en dev set we decode the plain text systems with a beam size of 4 and OSNMT with a beam size of 8 using our SGNMT decoder (Stahlberg et al., 2017). We use length normalization for ja-en but not for es-en or pt-en. We report cased `multi-bleu.pl` BLEU scores on the tokenized text to be comparable with the WAT evaluation campaign on ja-en.[3]

---

[1]A Python implementation is available at `https://github.com/fstahlberg/ucam-scripts/blob/master/t2t/align2osm.py`.

[2]We follow the `transformer_base` configuration and use 6 layers, 512 hidden units, and 8 attention heads in both the encoder and decoder.

[3]`http://lotus.kuee.kyoto-u.ac.jp/WAT/evaluation/list.php?t=2&o=4`

Method	BLEU	
	es-en	pt-en
Align on subword level	36.7	38.1
Convert word level alignments	37.1	38.4

Table 4: Generating training alignments on the subword level.

Type	Frequency
Valid	**92.49%**
Not enough SRC_POP	7.28%
Too many SRC_POP	0.22%
Write head out of range	0.06%

Table 5: Frequency of invalid OSNMT sequences produced by an unconstrained decoder on the ja-en test set.

Generating training alignments As outlined in Sec. 3 we use Giza++ (Och and Ney, 2003) to generate alignments for training OSNMT. We experimented with two different methods to obtain alignments on the subword level. First, Giza++ can directly align the source-side subword sequences to target-side subword sequences. Alternatively, we can run Giza++ on the word level, and convert the word alignments to subword alignments in a post-processing step by linking subwords if the words they belong to are aligned with each other. Tab. 4 compares both methods and shows that converting word alignments is marginally better. Thus, we use this method in all other experiments.

Constrained beam search Unconstrained neural decoding can yield invalid OSNMT sequences. For example, the JMP_FWD and JMP_BWD operations are undefined if the write head is currently at the position of the last or first marker, respectively. The number of SRC_POP operations must be equal to the number of source tokens in order for the read head to scan the entire source sentence. Therefore, we constrain these operations during decoding. We have implemented the constraints in our publicly available SGNMT decoding platform (Stahlberg et al., 2017). However, these constraints are only needed for a small fraction of the sentences. Tab. 5 shows that even unconstrained decoding yields valid OSNMT sequences in 92.49% of the cases.

Comparison with plain text NMT Tab. 6 compares our OSNMT systems with standard plain text models on all three language pairs. OSNMT performs better on the pt-en and ja-en test sets, but

Representation	BLEU			
	es-en	pt-en	ja-en	
			dev	test
Plain	37.6	37.5	28.3	28.1
OSNMT	37.1	38.4	28.1	28.8

Table 6: Comparison between plain text and OSNMT on Spanish-English (es-en), Portuguese-English (pt-en), and Japanese-English (ja-en).

slightly worse on es-en. We think that more engineering work such as optimizing the set of operations or improving the training alignments could lead to more consistent gains from using OSNMT. However, we leave this to future work since the main motivation for this paper is explainable NMT and not primarily improving translation quality.

Alignment quality Tab. 7 contains example translations and subword-alignments generated from our Portuguese-English OSNMT model. Alignment links from source words consisting of multiple subwords are mapped to the final subword, visible for the words 'temperamento' in the first example and 'pennisetum' in the second one. The length of the operation sequences increases with alignment complexity as operation sequences for monotone alignments consist only of INSERT(t) and SRC_POP operations (example 1). However, even complex mappings are captured very well by OSNMT as demonstrated by the third example. Note that OSNMT can represent long-range reorderings very efficiently: the movement from 'para' in the first position to 'to' in the tenth position is simply achieved by starting the operation sequence with 'SET_MARKER to' and a JMP_BWD operation later. The first example in particular demonstrates the usefulness of such alignments as the wrong lexical choice ('abroad' rather than 'body shape') can be traced back to the source word 'exterior'.

For a qualitative assessment of the alignments produced by OSNMT we ran Giza++ to align the generated translations to the source sentences, enforced the $1{:}n$ restriction of OSNMT, and used the resulting alignments as reference for computing the alignment error rate (Och and Ney, 2003, AER). Fig. 3 shows that as training proceeds, OSNMT learns to both produce high quality translations (increasing BLEU score) and accurate alignments (decreasing AER).

As mentioned in the introduction, a light-weight way to extract $1{:}n$ alignments from a vanilla atten-

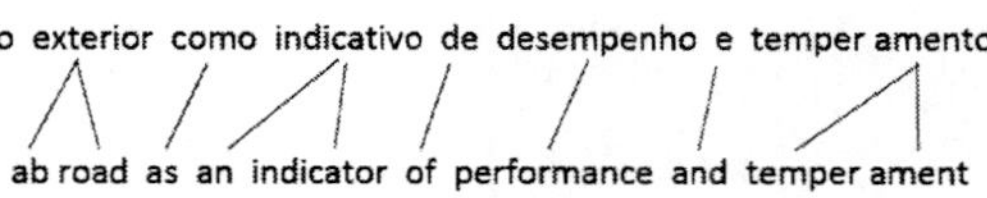

Operation sequence: SRC_POP ab road_ SRC_POP as_ SRC_POP an_ indicator_ SRC_POP of_ SRC_POP performance_ SRC_POP and_ SRC_POP SRC_POP temper ament_ SRC_POP
Reference: the body shape as an indicative of performance and temperament

Operation sequence: behavior_ SRC_POP of_ SRC_POP SET_MARKER clones_ SRC_POP SRC_POP SRC_POP SRC_POP SRC_POP JMP_BWD pen n is et um_ SRC_POP JMP_FWD subjected_ SRC_POP to_ SRC_POP SET_MARKER periods_ SRC_POP SRC_POP JMP_BWD SET_MARKER restriction_ SRC_POP JMP_BWD SET_MARKER water_ SRC_POP JMP_BWD controlled_ SRC_POP
Reference: response of pennisetum clons to periods of controlled hidric restriction

Operation sequence: SET_MARKER to_ SRC_POP analyze_ SRC_POP these_ SRC_POP data_ SRC_POP JMP_BWD SET_MARKER should_ be_ SRC_POP used_ SRC_POP JMP_BWD SET_MARKER methodologies_ SRC_POP¿ JMP_BWD appropriate_ SRC_POP JMP_FWD JMP_FWD JMP_FWD ._ SRC_POP
Reference: to analyze these data suitable methods should be used .

Table 7: Examples of Portuguese-English translations together with their (subword-)alignments induced by the operation sequence. Alignment links from source words consisting of multiple subwords were mapped to the final subword in the training data, visible for 'temperamento' and 'pennisetum'.

Representation	Alignment extraction	AER (in %)	
		dev	test
Plain	LSTM forced decoding	63.9	63.7
Plain	LSTM forced decoding with supervised attention (Liu et al., 2016, *Cross Entropy* loss)	54.9	54.7
OSNMT	OSNMT	24.2	21.5

Table 8: Comparison between OSNMT and using the attention matrix from forced decoding with a recurrent model.

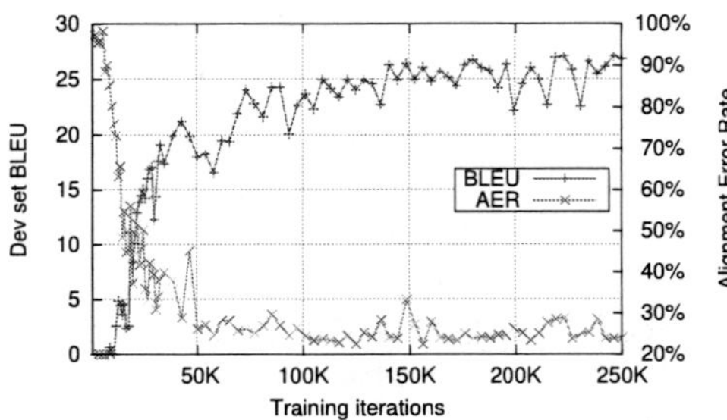

Figure 3: AER and BLEU training curves for OSNMT on the Japanese-English dev set.

tional LSTM-based seq2seq model is to take the maximum over attention weights for each target token. This is possible because, unlike the Transformer, LSTM-based models usually only have a single soft attention matrix. However, in our experiments, LSTM-based NMT was more than 4.5 BLEU points worse than the Transformer on Japanese-English. Therefore, to compare AERs under comparable BLEU scores, we used the LSTM-based models in forced decoding mode on the output of our plain text Transformer model from Tab. 6. We trained two different LSTM models: one standard model by optimizing the like-

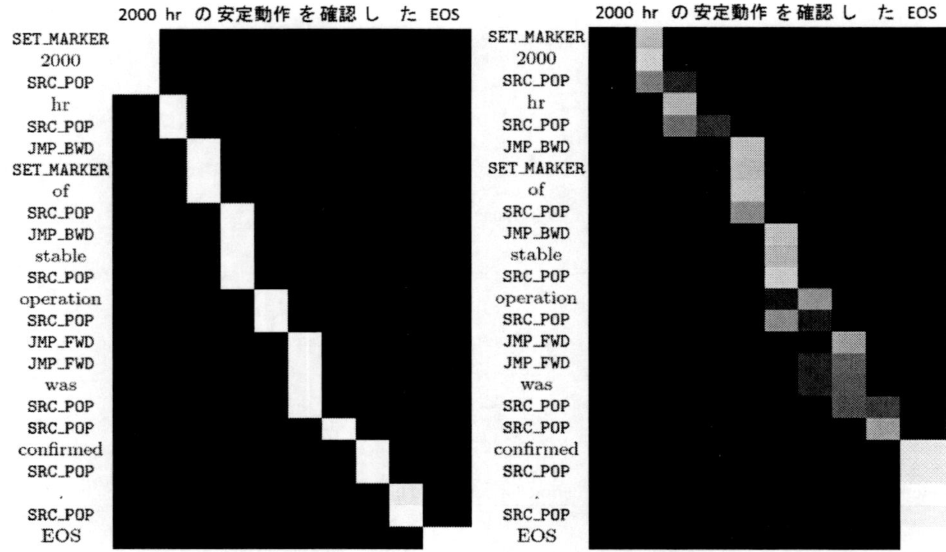

(a) Layer 4, head 1; attending to the source side read head.

(b) Layer 2, head 3; attending to the right trigram context of the read head.

Figure 4: Encoder-decoder attention weights.

lihood of the training set, and a second one with supervised attention following Liu et al. (2016). Tab. 8 shows that the supervised attention loss of Liu et al. (2016) improves the AER of the LSTM model. However, OSNMT is able to produce much better alignments since it generates the alignment along with the translation in a single decoding run.

OSNMT sequences contain target words in source sentence order An OSNMT sequence can be seen as a sequence of target words in source sentence order, interspersed with instructions on how to put them together to form a fluent target sentence. For example, if we strip out all SRC_POP, SET_MARKER, JMP_FWD, and JMP_BWD operations in the OSNMT sequence in the second example of Tab. 7 we get:

> behavior of clones pennisetum subjected to periods restriction water controlled

The word-by-word translation back to Portugese is:

> comportamento de clones pennisetum submetidos a períodos restrição hídrica controlada

This restores the original source sentence (cf. Tab. 7) up to unaligned source words. Therefore, we can view the operations for controlling the write head (SET_MARKER, JMP_FWD, and JMP_BWD) as reordering instructions for the target words which appear in source sentence word order within the OSNMT sequence.

Role of multi-head attention In this paper, we use a standard seq2seq model (the Transformer architecture (Vaswani et al., 2017)) to generate OSNMT sequences from the source sentence. This means that our neural model is representation-agnostic: we do not explicitly incorporate the notion of read and write heads into the neural architecture. In particular, neither in training nor in decoding do we explicitly bias the Transformer's attention layers towards consistency with the alignment represented by the OSNMT sequence. Our Transformer model has 48 encoder-decoder attention matrices due to multi-head attention (8 heads in each of the 6 layers). We have found that many of these attention matrices have strong and interpretable links to the translation process represented by the OSNMT sequence. For example, Fig. 4a shows that the first head in layer 4 follows the source-side read head position very closely: at each SRC_POP operation the attention shifts by

182

one to the next source token. Other attention heads have learned to take other responsibilities. For instance, head 3 in layer 2 (Fig. 4b) attends to the trigram right of the source head.

5   Related Work

Explainable and interpretable machine learning is attracting more and more attention in the research community (Ribeiro et al., 2016; Doshi-Velez and Kim, 2017), particularly in the context of natural language processing (Karpathy et al., 2015; Li et al., 2016; Alvarez-Melis and Jaakkola, 2017; Ding et al., 2017; Feng et al., 2018). These approaches aim to explain (the predictions of) an existing model. In contrast, we change the target representation such that the generated sequences themselves convey important information about the translation process such as the word alignments.

Despite considerable consensus about the importance of word alignments in practice (Koehn and Knowles, 2017), e.g. to enforce constraints on the output (Hasler et al., 2018) or to preserve text formatting, introducing explicit alignment information to NMT is still an open research problem. Word alignments have been used as supervision signal for the NMT attention model (Mi et al., 2016; Chen et al., 2016; Liu et al., 2016; Alkhouli and Ney, 2017). Cohn et al. (2016) showed how to reintroduce concepts known from traditional statistical alignment models (Brown et al., 1993) like fertility and agreement over translation direction to NMT. Some approaches to simultaneous translation explicitly control for reading source tokens and writing target tokens and thereby generate monotonic alignments on the segment level (Yu et al., 2016, 2017; Gu et al., 2017). Alkhouli et al. (2016) used separate alignment and lexical models and thus were able to hypothesize explicit alignment links during decoding. While our motivation is very similar to Alkhouli et al. (2016), our approach is very different as we represent the alignment as operation sequence, and we do not use separate models for reordering and lexical translation.

The operation sequence model for SMT (Durrani et al., 2011, 2015) has been used in a number of MT evaluation systems (Durrani et al., 2014; Peter et al., 2016; Durrani et al., 2016) and for post-editing (Pal et al., 2016), often in combination with a phrase-based model. The main difference to our OSNMT is that we have adapted the set of operations for neural models and are able to use it as stand-alone system, and not on top of a phrase-based system.

Our operation sequence model has some similarities with transition-based models used in other areas of NLP (Stenetorp, 2013; Dyer et al., 2015; Aharoni and Goldberg, 2017). In particular, our POP_SRC operation is very similar to the *step* action of the hard alignment model of Aharoni and Goldberg (2017). However, Aharoni and Goldberg (2017) investigated monotonic alignments for morphological inflections whereas we use a larger operation/action set to model complex word reorderings in machine translation.

6   Conclusion

We have presented a way to use standard seq2seq models to generate a translation together with an alignment as linear sequence of operations. This greatly improves the interpretability of the model output as it establishes explicit alignment links between source and target tokens. However, the neural architecture we used in this paper is representation-agnostic, i.e. we did not explicitly incorporate the alignments induced by an operation sequence into the neural model. For future work we are planning to adapt the Transformer model, for example by using positional embeddings of the source read head and the target write head in the Transformer attention layers.

Acknowledgments

This work was supported in part by the U.K. Engineering and Physical Sciences Research Council (EPSRC grant EP/L027623/1). We thank Joanna Stadnik who produced the recurrent translation and alignment models during her 4th year project.

References

Roee Aharoni and Yoav Goldberg. 2017. Morphological inflection generation with hard monotonic attention. In *Proceedings of the 55th Annual Meeting of the Association for Computational Linguistics (Volume 1: Long Papers)*, pages 2004–2015, Vancouver, Canada. Association for Computational Linguistics.

Tamer Alkhouli, Gabriel Bretschner, Jan-Thorsten Peter, Mohammed Hethnawi, Andreas Guta, and Hermann Ney. 2016. Alignment-based neural machine translation. In *Proceedings of the First Conference on Machine Translation*, pages 54–65, Berlin, Germany. Association for Computational Linguistics.

Tamer Alkhouli and Hermann Ney. 2017. Biasing attention-based recurrent neural networks using external alignment information. In *Proceedings of the Second Conference on Machine Translation*, pages 108–117, Copenhagen, Denmark. Association for Computational Linguistics.

David Alvarez-Melis and Tommi Jaakkola. 2017. A causal framework for explaining the predictions of black-box sequence-to-sequence models. In *Proceedings of the 2017 Conference on Empirical Methods in Natural Language Processing*, pages 412–421. Association for Computational Linguistics.

Michael Auli, Adam Lopez, Hieu Hoang, and Philipp Koehn. 2009. A systematic analysis of translation model search spaces. In *Proceedings of the Fourth Workshop on Statistical Machine Translation*, pages 224–232. Association for Computational Linguistics.

Dzmitry Bahdanau, Kyunghyun Cho, and Yoshua Bengio. 2015. Neural machine translation by jointly learning to align and translate. In *ICLR*, Toulon, France.

Peter E. Brown, Stephen A. Della Pietra, Vincent J. Della Pietra, and Robert L. Mercer. 1993. The mathematics of statistical machine translation: Parameter estimation. *Computational Linguistics*, 19(2).

Wenhu Chen, Evgeny Matusov, Shahram Khadivi, and Jan-Thorsten Peter. 2016. Guided alignment training for topic-aware neural machine translation. *arXiv preprint arXiv:1607.01628*.

Yong Cheng, Shiqi Shen, Zhongjun He, Wei He, Hua Wu, Maosong Sun, and Yang Liu. 2016. Agreement-based joint training for bidirectional attention-based neural machine translation. In *Proceedings of the Twenty-Fifth International Joint Conference on Artificial Intelligence*, IJCAI'16, pages 2761–2767. AAAI Press.

David Chiang. 2005. A hierarchical phrase-based model for statistical machine translation. In *Proceedings of the 43rd Annual Meeting of the Association for Computational Linguistics (ACL'05)*, pages 263–270, Ann Arbor, Michigan. Association for Computational Linguistics.

Trevor Cohn, Cong Duy Vu Hoang, Ekaterina Vymolova, Kaisheng Yao, Chris Dyer, and Gholamreza Haffari. 2016. Incorporating structural alignment biases into an attentional neural translation model. In *Proceedings of the 2016 Conference of the North American Chapter of the Association for Computational Linguistics: Human Language Technologies*, pages 876–885, San Diego, California. Association for Computational Linguistics.

Yanzhuo Ding, Yang Liu, Huanbo Luan, and Maosong Sun. 2017. Visualizing and understanding neural machine translation. In *Proceedings of the 55th Annual Meeting of the Association for Computational*

Linguistics (Volume 1: Long Papers), pages 1150–1159. Association for Computational Linguistics.

Finale Doshi-Velez and Been Kim. 2017. Towards a rigorous science of interpretable machine learning.

Nadir Durrani, Fahim Dalvi, Hassan Sajjad, and Stephan Vogel. 2016. QCRI machine translation systems for IWSLT 16. In *International Workshop on Spoken Language Translation. Seattle, WA, USA*.

Nadir Durrani, Barry Haddow, Philipp Koehn, and Kenneth Heafield. 2014. Edinburgh's phrase-based machine translation systems for WMT-14. In *Proceedings of the Ninth Workshop on Statistical Machine Translation*, pages 97–104, Baltimore, Maryland, USA. Association for Computational Linguistics.

Nadir Durrani, Helmut Schmid, and Alexander Fraser. 2011. A joint sequence translation model with integrated reordering. In *Proceedings of the 49th Annual Meeting of the Association for Computational Linguistics: Human Language Technologies*, pages 1045–1054, Portland, Oregon, USA. Association for Computational Linguistics.

Nadir Durrani, Helmut Schmid, Alexander Fraser, Philipp Koehn, and Hinrich Schütze. 2015. The operation sequence model—combining n-gram-based and phrase-based statistical machine translation. *Computational Linguistics*, 41(2):157–186.

Chris Dyer, Miguel Ballesteros, Wang Ling, Austin Matthews, and Noah A. Smith. 2015. Transition-based dependency parsing with stack long short-term memory. In *Proceedings of the 53rd Annual Meeting of the Association for Computational Linguistics and the 7th International Joint Conference on Natural Language Processing (Volume 1: Long Papers)*, pages 334–343, Beijing, China. Association for Computational Linguistics.

Shi Feng, Eric Wallace, Alvin Grissom II, Mohit Iyyer, Pedro Rodriguez, and Jordan Boyd-Graber. 2018. Pathologies of neural models make interpretations difficult. In *Proceedings of the 2018 Conference on Empirical Methods in Natural Language Processing*. Association for Computational Linguistics.

Jonas Gehring, Michael Auli, David Grangier, Denis Yarats, and Yann N Dauphin. 2017. Convolutional sequence to sequence learning. *ArXiv e-prints*.

Hamidreza Ghader and Christof Monz. 2017. What does attention in neural machine translation pay attention to? In *Proceedings of the Eighth International Joint Conference on Natural Language Processing (Volume 1: Long Papers)*, pages 30–39. Asian Federation of Natural Language Processing.

Jiatao Gu, Graham Neubig, Kyunghyun Cho, and Victor O.K. Li. 2017. Learning to translate in real-time with neural machine translation. In *Proceedings of the 15th Conference of the European Chapter of the Association for Computational Linguistics: Volume*

1, Long Papers, pages 1053–1062. Association for Computational Linguistics.

Eva Hasler, Adrià de Gispert, Gonzalo Iglesias, and Bill Byrne. 2018. Neural machine translation decoding with terminology constraints. In *Proceedings of the 2018 Conference of the North American Chapter of the Association for Computational Linguistics: Human Language Technologies*. Association for Computational Linguistics.

Andrej Karpathy, Justin Johnson, and Li Fei-Fei. 2015. Visualizing and understanding recurrent networks. *arXiv preprint arXiv:1506.02078*.

Philipp Koehn and Rebecca Knowles. 2017. Six challenges for neural machine translation. In *Proceedings of the First Workshop on Neural Machine Translation*, pages 28–39. Association for Computational Linguistics.

Jiwei Li, Xinlei Chen, Eduard Hovy, and Dan Jurafsky. 2016. Visualizing and understanding neural models in NLP. In *Proceedings of the 2016 Conference of the North American Chapter of the Association for Computational Linguistics: Human Language Technologies*, pages 681–691. Association for Computational Linguistics.

Lemao Liu, Masao Utiyama, Andrew Finch, and Eiichiro Sumita. 2016. Neural machine translation with supervised attention. In *Proceedings of COLING 2016, the 26th International Conference on Computational Linguistics: Technical Papers*, pages 3093–3102, Osaka, Japan. The COLING 2016 Organizing Committee.

I. Dan Melamed. 2003. Multitext grammars and synchronous parsers. In *Proceedings of the 2003 Human Language Technology Conference of the North American Chapter of the Association for Computational Linguistics*.

I. Dan Melamed, Giorgio Satta, and Benjamin Wellington. 2004. Generalized multitext grammars. In *Proceedings of the 42nd Annual Meeting of the Association for Computational Linguistics (ACL-04)*.

Haitao Mi, Zhiguo Wang, and Abe Ittycheriah. 2016. Supervised attentions for neural machine translation. In *Proceedings of the 2016 Conference on Empirical Methods in Natural Language Processing*, pages 2283–2288, Austin, Texas. Association for Computational Linguistics.

Toshiaki Nakazawa, Manabu Yaguchi, Kiyotaka Uchimoto, Masao Utiyama, Eiichiro Sumita, Sadao Kurohashi, and Hitoshi Isahara. 2016. ASPEC: Asian scientific paper excerpt corpus. In *LREC*, pages 2204–2208, Portoroz, Slovenia.

Mariana L Neves and Aurélie Névéol. 2016. The Scielo corpus: a parallel corpus of scientific publications for biomedicine. In *LREC*, pages 2942–2948, Portoroz, Slovenia.

Franz Josef Och and Hermann Ney. 2003. A systematic comparison of various statistical alignment models. *Computational Linguistics*, 29(1):19–51.

Santanu Pal, Marcos Zampieri, and Josef van Genabith. 2016. USAAR: An operation sequential model for automatic statistical post-editing. In *Proceedings of the First Conference on Machine Translation*, pages 759–763, Berlin, Germany. Association for Computational Linguistics.

Jan-Thorsten Peter, Andreas Guta, Nick Rossenbach, Miguel Graça, and Hermann Ney. 2016. The RWTH Aachen machine translation system for IWSLT 2016. In *International Workshop on Spoken Language Translation. Seattle, WA, USA*.

Martin Popel and Ondřej Bojar. 2018. Training tips for the transformer model. *arXiv preprint arXiv:1804.00247*.

Marco Ribeiro, Sameer Singh, and Carlos Guestrin. 2016. "Why should I trust you?": Explaining the predictions of any classifier. In *Proceedings of the 2016 Conference of the North American Chapter of the Association for Computational Linguistics: Demonstrations*, pages 97–101. Association for Computational Linguistics.

Danielle Saunders, Felix Stahlberg, Adrià de Gispert, and Bill Byrne. 2018. Multi-representation ensembles and delayed SGD updates improve syntax-based NMT. In *Proceedings of the 56th Annual Meeting of the Association for Computational Linguistics*. Association for Computational Linguistics.

Rico Sennrich, Barry Haddow, and Alexandra Birch. 2016. Neural machine translation of rare words with subword units. In *Proceedings of the 54th Annual Meeting of the Association for Computational Linguistics (Volume 1: Long Papers)*, pages 1715–1725. Association for Computational Linguistics.

Felix Stahlberg, Eva Hasler, Danielle Saunders, and Bill Byrne. 2017. SGNMT – A flexible NMT decoding platform for quick prototyping of new models and search strategies. In *Proceedings of the 2017 Conference on Empirical Methods in Natural Language Processing: System Demonstrations*, pages 25–30. Association for Computational Linguistics. Full documentation available at `http://ucam-smt.github.io/sgnmt/html/`.

Pontus Stenetorp. 2013. Transition-based dependency parsing using recursive neural networks. In *NIPS Workshop on Deep Learning*. Citeseer.

Ilya Sutskever, Oriol Vinyals, and Quoc V Le. 2014. Sequence to sequence learning with neural networks. In Z. Ghahramani, M. Welling, C. Cortes, N. D. Lawrence, and K. Q. Weinberger, editors, *Advances in Neural Information Processing Systems 27*, pages 3104–3112. Curran Associates, Inc.

Zhaopeng Tu, Zhengdong Lu, Yang Liu, Xiaohua Liu, and Hang Li. 2016. Modeling coverage for neural machine translation. In *Proceedings of the 54th Annual Meeting of the Association for Computational Linguistics (Volume 1: Long Papers)*, pages 76–85. Association for Computational Linguistics.

Ashish Vaswani, Samy Bengio, Eugene Brevdo, Francois Chollet, Aidan N Gomez, Stephan Gouws, Llion Jones, Łukasz Kaiser, Nal Kalchbrenner, Niki Parmar, et al. 2018. Tensor2tensor for neural machine translation. *arXiv preprint arXiv:1803.07416*.

Ashish Vaswani, Noam Shazeer, Niki Parmar, Jakob Uszkoreit, Llion Jones, Aidan N Gomez, Ł ukasz Kaiser, and Illia Polosukhin. 2017. Attention is all you need. In *Advances in Neural Information Processing Systems 30*, pages 6000–6010. Curran Associates, Inc.

L Yu, P Blunsom, C Dyer, E Grefenstette, and T Kocisky. 2017. The neural noisy channel. In *Proceedings of the 5th International Conference on Learning Representations (ICLR)*, Toulon, France. Computational and Biological Learning Society.

Lei Yu, Jan Buys, and Phil Blunsom. 2016. Online segment to segment neural transduction. In *Proceedings of the 2016 Conference on Empirical Methods in Natural Language Processing*, pages 1307–1316, Austin, Texas. Association for Computational Linguistics.

Introspection for convolutional automatic speech recognition

Andreas Krug and **Sebastian Stober**
University of Potsdam, Research Focus Cognitive Sciences
Karl-Liebknecht-Str. 24/25, 14476 Potsdam, Germany
`{ankrug, sstober}@uni-potsdam.de`

Abstract

Artificial Neural Networks (ANNs) have experienced great success in the past few years. The increasing complexity of these models leads to less understanding about their decision processes. Therefore, introspection techniques have been proposed, mostly for images as input data. Patterns or relevant regions in images can be intuitively interpreted by a human observer. This is not the case for more complex data like speech recordings. In this work, we investigate the application of common introspection techniques from computer vision to an Automatic Speech Recognition (ASR) task. To this end, we use a model similar to image classification, which predicts letters from spectrograms. We show difficulties in applying image introspection to ASR. To tackle these problems, we propose normalized averaging of aligned inputs (NAvAI): a data-driven method to reveal learned patterns for prediction of specific classes. Our method integrates information from many data examples through local introspection techniques for Convolutional Neural Networks (CNNs). We demonstrate that our method provides better interpretability of letter-specific patterns than existing methods.

1 Introduction

Artificial Neural Networks (ANNs) perform incredibly well in many fields of application, even outperforming humans. In particular, deep learning (DL) has been used with great success in a variety of tasks. The most successful applications of DL are in computer vision, like image classification (Krizhevsky et al., 2012) or segmentation (Chen et al., 2014). Moreover, DL performs well in audio processing, like automatic speech recognition (Bahdanau et al., 2016) or machine translation (Wu et al., 2016). One reason for the success of these models is the increase in their complexity by implementing deeper or wider network layers (Szegedy et al., 2015). While this allows the model to learn more complex patterns for solving its

task, it is becoming more difficult to interpret how it accomplishes it (Yosinski et al., 2015). Several introspection techniques were proposed to shed light on the decision processes in ANNs (Zeiler and Fergus 2014, Springenberg et al. 2014, Selvaraju et al. 2016). However, most of them come with restrictions on the network architecture or the type of task that is solved. In particular, most methods focus on interpretability of ANNs in computer vision. The reason for this is that evaluating the results from introspection techniques on images is intuitive for a person. This is not the case for more complex data like audio waveforms or multi-channel data like Electroencephalography (EEG) recordings. Applying introspection techniques from computer vision to this kind of data is possible, but evaluating the results is hard, as a human expert cannot easily interpret the input data in the first place.

In this work, we investigate the application of several introspection techniques to the domain of Automatic Speech Recognition (ASR). To make the task of ASR similar to image classification, we use a fully-convolutional ANN for letter-wise prediction from audio spectrograms. We identify problems in applying introspection techniques from computer vision to the ASR domain. To overcome these difficulties, we propose normalized averaging of aligned inputs (NAvAI): a data-driven introspection method for interpreting speech recognition.

2 Related Work

In computer vision, Convolutional Neural Networks (CNNs) are the most common choice of network architecture (Szegedy et al., 2015). As we want to adapt techniques from this domain, we focus on introspection methods developed for CNNs.

Introspection techniques for classification tasks in deep learning can roughly be divided into two categories. Firstly, there are local introspection methods, which trace the classification result back to

Proceedings of the 2018 EMNLP Workshop BlackboxNLP: Analyzing and Interpreting Neural Networks for NLP, pages 187–199
Brussels, Belgium, November 1, 2018. ©2018 Association for Computational Linguistics

the original input, for example the deconvolutional network approach by Zeiler and Fergus 2014 or layer-wise relevance propagation (Bach et al., 2015). The second category are global introspection techniques that infer input patterns or characteristics which activate particular neurons, like activation maximization (Erhan et al. 2009, Yosinski et al. 2015).

2.1 Local introspection

Local introspection traces back signals to a particular input source. This means inferring, which parts of an input sample were important for the prediction. The backpropagated signal comes either from pre-softmax activations or the softmax-logits of an ANN classifier's output layer. The common way is to trace back the result of the output layer as a one-hot vector, so only class-specific information are retained (Springenberg et al., 2014). This means that the position of highest activation is set to 1, while all other positions are set to 0.

A simple and fast way to infer the contribution of input values to the classification score is to perform sensitivity analysis. This method computes the (squared) partial derivatives of output scores with respect to the values of a particular input sample (Gevrey et al., 2003). Another method is to use deconvolutional networks, which invert the data flow of a convolutional classifier network to reconstruct the input (Zeiler and Fergus, 2014). The backward pass also includes units that revert max-pooling operations. This is done by storing the maximum positions before pooling in so-called switches (Zeiler and Fergus, 2014).

Another local introspection method is guided backpropagation (Springenberg et al., 2014). This technique is based on gradient backpropagation but integrates information about the forward pass. For a network which uses Rectified Linear Unit (ReLU) activation, the authors propose to only backpropagate positive gradients, where the corresponding forward activation is positive as well (Springenberg et al., 2014). The authors also report that introspection using the deconvolutional network approach by Zeiler and Fergus 2014 performs poorly for higher layers, where neurons can be maximally activated by a wider variety of input signals. Their method does not show this drop in performance for higher layers. Guided backpropagation reveals detailed features in the input which are important for the prediction, but is not strongly class-discriminative.

Selvaraju et al. 2016 introduced the class-discriminative Gradient-weighted Class Activa-tion Mapping (Grad-CAM), which identifies low-resolution regions of importance in the input. Grad-CAM first computes importance weights for each feature map in one layer. This is done by global average pooling gradients of the prediction score with respect to the feature maps. These importance weights are used to compute a weighted sum of forward activations, which represent the influence on the predicted class. The authors use a ReLU on the weighted sums, to only show positive influences on the prediction. By using their method to mask the result of guided backpropagation, which they call guided Grad-CAM, they get both class-specificity and high resolution in relevant input values (Selvaraju et al., 2016).

All of those local introspection methods only reveal information about a single input sample. This could help understanding particular decisions, for example wrong classifications. For revealing decision processes of an ANN as a whole, global introspection is essential.

2.2 Global introspection

The most common global introspection technique is activation maximization (AM) (Erhan et al., 2009). AM is independent of the input and can be used to find patterns which activate particular features. This method optimizes the input, such that the activation of a particular feature is maximized. Such a feature could be a single neuron at any position of the network. For classifiers, the most interesting feature is the output neuron of the predicted class. The optimization target can be the corresponding activation either before or after applying the softmax. It is also possible to visualize optimal inputs for a whole layer, as in Google DeepDream (Mordvintsev et al., 2015). However, the input optimization approach has some drawbacks. Optimal inputs tend to be unnatural and noisy, thus cannot be interpreted (Nguyen et al., 2015). Therefore, it is crucial to regularize, for example by total variation (Mahendran and Vedaldi, 2015) or a Generative Adversarial Network (GAN) objective (Nguyen et al., 2016) to penalize unnatural data. Even with regularized optimization, the optimal input needs to be interpretable. This means a human has to be able to assess, whether patterns in the optimized input are related to a certain class.

2.3 Introspection for audio

The aforementioned local and global introspection techniques are almost exclusively applied to tasks which use images as input. This is due to the intuitive interpretability of relevance mappings onto images for a human observer. Whether an introspection technique performs well is mostly measured by how plausible the result is for a person. This is not an objective quantification, but it indicates how similar the ANN decisions are to the human perception. However, this is not possible for all types of data. For example, when using waveforms as input to an audio-classification task like ASR, it is not intuitive to assess the meaningfulness of important regions or optimal inputs. To our knowledge there are no comparable introspection techniques for ANN in speech recognition tasks. However, this is not the first attempt to understand ANNs for speech recognition. Several studies explored representations of speech in ANNs for acoustic modelling, for example multi-layer perceptrons (Nagamine et al. 2015, Nagamine et al. 2016, Nagamine and Mesgarani 2017) or Deep Belief Networks (Mohamed et al., 2012).

3 Methods

3.1 Automatic Speech Recognition

The use of CNNs for speech is not uncommon. However, they are often used as part of complex hybrid models, for example involving Hidden Markov Models (Abdel-Hamid et al., 2014) or Recurrent Neural Networks (Trigeorgis et al., 2016). Such complex models are much harder to introspect than fully-convolutional ones. CNNs are also used for speech-related tasks different from ASR, like learning spectrum feature representations (Cummins et al., 2017).

For ASR, we implement a fully-convolutional architecture to apply introspection techniques from computer vision. To this end, we are using an architecture based on Wav2Letter (Collobert et al., 2016). This model is a fully-convolutional neural network, which predicts letters from spectrograms. We train the network on z-normalized spectrograms, scaled to 128 mel-frequency bins. Each letter prediction can use 206 time steps due to the receptive field of the convolutions. We use whole-sequence audio recordings from the LibriSpeech corpus (Panayotov et al., 2015). Training and architecture are described in detail in (Kunze et al., 2017). Different to Kunze et al. we slightly changed the number of neurons per layer to powers of two (250 to 256 neurons and 2000 to 2048 neurons). Moreover, we used a vocabulary with repetition characters like Collobert et al. 2016 used with their Auto Segmentation Criterion (ASG) loss.

3.2 Activation Maximization

We visualize important features by computing the optimal input for activating a particular neuron. We used L1- and L2-regularization to avoid unnatural noisy results, both with a scale of 0.001. The optimization was initialized with a 206×128 input (the receptive field size) using a Xavier uniform initializer (Glorot and Bengio, 2010). Training was performed to maximize the activation of a particular neuron, using an Adam optimizer (Kingma and Ba, 2014) with learning rate 0.05 for 250 steps. We applied AM for neurons of different layers to show differences in the complexity of optimal patterns.

3.3 Preparing the data for introspection

Our ASR model predicts all letters for a given speech recording at once, but we are interested in determining the important regions for single predicted letters. Therefore, we perform our analyses on spectrogram frames, which are predicted as only one letter. Based on the receptive field size, we perform introspection on spectrogram frames of width 206. Moreover, we only investigate spectrogram frames predicted as letters 'a' to 'z', because blank and repetition characters would not be interpretable for a human observer. For training and evaluation, our neural network uses same-padding with zeros. To avoid biasing our introspection results due to padding, we only analyze spectrogram frames without padding. Because we are training with whole sentences, most of the letters are predicted from spectrogram frames without padding.

3.4 Local introspection

For a spectrogram frame of interest, we first perform a forward pass through the network, while storing all layers' activations and the output scores. To find important positions in the input data, we perform different methods for propagating back the prediction score. In particular, we are using sensitivity analysis (Gevrey et al., 2003) and layer-wise relevance propagation (LRP) (Montavon et al., 2017). As initial value for the backward pass, we use a vector which is set to 1 for the predicted class and 0 for all other positions. We call this vector $R^{(out)}$.

We did not investigate guided backpropagation, because we rely on getting class-discriminative introspection results. We also did not use Grad-CAM, because of the 1D-convolutions in our network. As our input data is treated as 128 one-dimensional channels, applying Grad-CAM to our network would only identify important regions over the time dimension. This means, we would not be able to identify which frequencies are important.

Sensitivity analysis was performed by computing the partial derivative of $R^{(out)}$ with respect to the input spectrogram frame, as shown in Equation 1. The resulting gradient-based relevances $R^{(0)}$ can be interpreted as positions in the input x, which increase or decrease the prediction score upon change.

$$R_i^{(0)} = \frac{\partial R^{(out)}}{\partial x_i} \tag{1}$$

Different to sensitivity, LRP aims to map high relevances to input positions that have caused $R^{(out)}$. We performed non-Taylor-type LRP, which we adapted from Equation 56 in Bach et al. 2015:

$$R_{i \leftarrow j}^{(l,l+1)} = \frac{z_{ij}}{z_j} \cdot R_j^{(l+1)} \tag{2}$$

where i refers to the neuron in the lower layer l and j to the neuron in the higher layer $l+1$. This original rule means, that relevances are propagated back based on the ratio of local (z_{ij}) and global (z_j) pre-activations. The pre-activations are outputs of the convolution for a neuron j either masking all lower layer neurons but neuron i (local) or not masking any neurons (global). Hence, the ratio $\frac{z_{ij}}{z_j}$ is the relative influence of a neuron i on the pre-activation of neuron j. This allows to distribute the relevance from neuron j to the lower layer neurons while conserving the sum of relevance values (compare Equation 5).

Computing these ratios is computationally expensive for more complex neural networks, as it is necessary to compute the contribution of every value i of the lower layer to every value j of the higher layer through the convolutions. For example, in the input layer of our network, it is necessary to compute local pre-activations from 128×206 input values to 256×80 output values. This corresponds to 500 million local pre-activations in the first layer.

Applying Equation 2 is not straightforward in our speech recognizer network. This is due to two major differences to the image classification networks that Bach et al. 2015 used. Firstly, our network involves negative input values from z-normalized mel-spectrograms. Secondly, after each convolution, batch normalization is applied before the ReLU activation. This allows convolution outputs to change their sign before entering the ReLU activation. In order to account for negative values and the effects of batch normalization, we adapt Equation 2 as follows. We compute the ratio between local and global pre-activations using the absolute value of the global pre-activation. This preserves the sign of local pre-activations for comparison to the convolution output after applying batch normalization. The magnitude

of the neuron influence is not changed. For avoiding division by zero, we add a small value $\epsilon = 1e\text{-}21$ to the absolute value of global pre-activation. This ratio is multiplied with the sign of the output value after applying batch normalization (bn), shown in Equation 3. With this approach, a positive ratio indicates that a local pre-activation supports the output after batch normalization, because they have the same sign. We backpropagate the relevance as shown in Equation 4.

$$r_{ij} = \frac{z_{ij}}{|z_j| + \epsilon} \cdot \text{sgn}(\text{bn}(z_j)) \tag{3}$$

$$R_{i \leftarrow j}^{(l,l+1)} = r_{ij} \cdot R_j^{(l+1)} \tag{4}$$

The original rule in Equation 2 is satisfying the conservation law

$$\sum_i R_{i \leftarrow j}^{(l,l+1)} = R_j^{(l+1)} \tag{5}$$

where no relevance may be lost by distributing the value to lower layer neurons. In our adaptation, this conservation law is not satisfied, because we change the sign of some ratios to correct for batch normalization. As this procedure does not change absolute values, we do not lose any information about the relevances. Furthermore, using the original rule, relevances can become unbounded for negative ratios $\frac{z_{ij}}{z_j}$. To avoid absolute relevances to become very large, we scale the values by the maximum absolute relevance value in each step of LRP. Scaling the relevances is also violating the conservation law in Equation 5. However, the relevances still contain the same information, as the ratio between all relevances is conserved.

3.5 Normalized averaging of aligned inputs

We perform global introspection by analyzing the training data set, in which we want to find common letter-specific patterns. To this end, we propose a novel approach for global introspection, called normalized averaging of aligned inputs (NAvAI). We describe NAvAI for ASR, but applying it to other domains is straight-forward. Our method averages all spectrogram frames predicted as the same letter. This mean spectrogram input should retain information related to the letter and average out values which are related to the context. Averaging only produces meaningful results, if the predicted letter is properly aligned to the spectrogram frame. This means that the position of the predicted letter needs to be the same in all frames. Otherwise, even letter-specific information would get averaged out. Therefore, before computing average frames, NAvAI aligns the spectrogram frames as described below. Computing the average over (aligned) letter-specific spectrogram frames retains information about what is common to all frames. However, this is not necessarily exclusive to spectrogram frames of this particular letter. There might be information, which is contained for all predicted letters. Therefore, our method normalizes the letter-averaged spectrogram frames by subtracting the mean over spectrogram frames predicted as any letter 'a' to 'z'.

3.6 Alignment of spectrogram frames

For proper alignment between predicted letter and spectrogram, we facilitate the introspection techniques from Section 3.4. We follow the hypothesis, that the time step, where a predicted letter actually occurs, is the one that is most important for the prediction score. We infer this position from local introspection results using sensitivity analysis and LRP. Positive relevances from LRP identify values, which have caused the prediction score. Therefore, we use the maximum position from LRP. In contrast, sensitivity can be meaningful both at the maximum and minimum value position. Positive values imply importance of positions, because increasing them would make the prediction more certain. Negative gradients are of interest as well, because they show where a change in input value causes the prediction certainty to drop. Most of the predictions are already very close to being a one-hot vector as softmax-output. Then, there might be no or only a small gradient for increasing the prediction certainty. In this case, the minimum value position from sensitivity might be more appropriate than the maximum value position. The alignment procedure crops the spectrogram frames on one side, such that the determined positions are in the center.

4 Results & Discussion

4.1 Optimal inputs by activation maximization

We performed AM for neurons of different layers. For visualization, we chose neurons which are maximally activated for the prediction of letter 'a' in a randomly chosen spectrogram frame. In the output layer, this neuron corresponds to the predicted letter (here it is the 'a'-neuron). As the outputs of the three topmost layers are one-dimensional, we use the neuron of highest activation. In all other layers, we chose neurons with highest average activation over the time dimension. We only show optimization of strongly activated neurons, because they are evidently sensitive

to some pattern and potentially letter-specific. In Figure 1, we representatively show four different layers of the network. The top row shows optimal inputs for a neuron in the first and second layer. In those layers, AM reveals patterns, which can be interpreted as features in the spectrogram. For example, the input layer neuron detects a shift of intensity towards higher frequencies. The second-layer neuron combines low-level features, so it is sensitive to different changes in frequency intensities, particularly of lower frequencies. In contrast, optimizing neuron

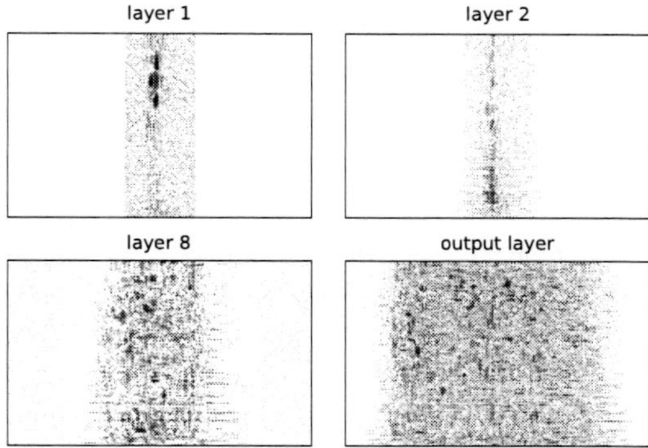

Figure 1: Optimal inputs for neurons in different layers of the network. Each shown neuron has highest activation for predicting letter 'a' in the respective layer. Optimal inputs to bottom layers (top row) are still interpretable as features in the spectrogram. The higher layers (bottom row), in particular the output neuron for 'a' (bottom right), do not look like spectrograms and cannot be interpreted as particular features which the neuron is sensitive to. The axes are equal to the spectrogram frames in Figure 2.

output in higher layers (bottom row) does not reveal any interpretable patterns. Those neurons are sensitive to a large variety of different patterns, so that a single optimal input is not natural anymore. This is a common problem for AM. Still, it is easier to detect unnatural but related patterns in real-world images than in audio spectrograms.

To obtain more natural results, one possibility would be using stronger regularization techniques like a GAN penalty. On the other hand, using stronger regularization interferes with determining the actual learned patterns. Regularizing is therefore favoring results similar to data over actual insight in the model. For our speech recognizer, we can conclude that the model did not learn a single abstract representation for the letters. This is not surprising, as the same letter is not pronounced equally in every context.

In addition, in the output layer, we observed zero-

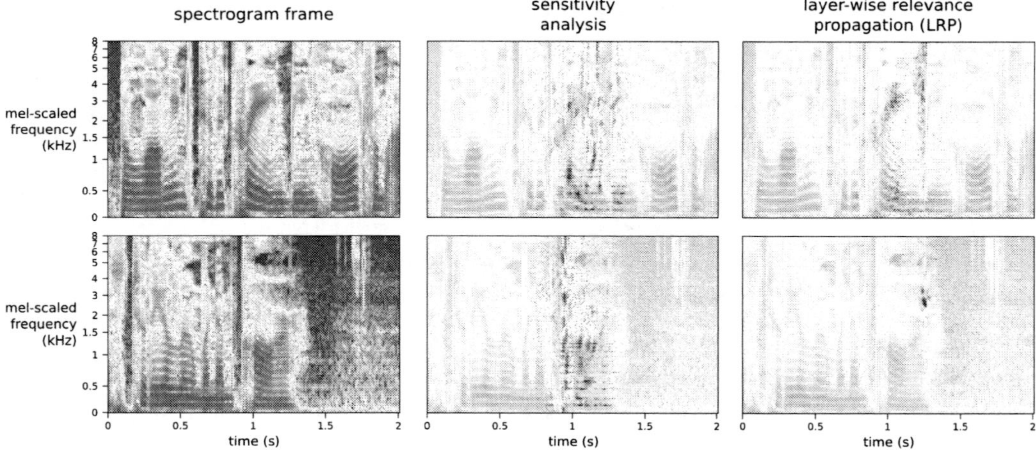

Figure 2: Local introspection using sensitivity analysis and LRP. *Left*: Two spectrogram frames, both predicted as letter 'a'. By propagating the prediction score back through the network, important regions are identified. *Center*: Sensitivity analysis results. *Right*: Relevances using LRP. The results of both methods are visualized as an overlay on top of the original spectrogram. Blue values indicate negative sensitivity/relevance, red indicates positive values.

areas in the beginning and end of the optimal input. This implies that the network capacity is not fully utilized for the prediction and could still be compressed.

4.2 Sensitivity analysis and LRP

We performed sensitivity analysis and LRP for all spectrogram frames. Here, we show characteristics of these methods based on two spectrogram frames predicted as letter 'a'. Figure 2 shows those two spectrogram frames (left) and the local introspection results. The sensitivity values (center) and LRP-based relevances (right) are visualized superimposed on the input spectrogram. Both methods differ strongly in what they identify as important for the prediction.

Sensitivity analysis identifies relevant positions in a larger area and includes more data points than LRP. As we assumed, if the prediction already was certain, sensitivity analysis is resulting in mostly negative values, as in the top example. In the bottom example, there are more positive gradients, indicating a less certain prediction. Moreover, sensitivity analysis identifies important regions close to center of the spectrogram frame.

The relevances backpropagated with LRP are much more position-specific than sensitivity values. The top example shows fewer relevant positions. In the bottom example, relevance is assigned to only two small regions. This indicates that LRP identifies important positions, but emphasizes the most relevant ones. We assume, this is due to having negative

input values. As mentioned above, relevances can become unbounded for negative input values, which we prevented by scaling them. However, this does not reduce possible large differences between weak and strong relevances. We also observe that LRP identifies regions as relevant, which are further away from the center of the spectrogram frame.

Neither sensitivity analysis nor LRP reveal patterns, which can be interpreted as typical letters for the network. Furthermore, different spectrogram frames predicted as the same letter do rarely show common patterns. We would expect that in most cases important regions for predicting letter 'a' are formants in the spectrogram, which are characteristic for vowels. The second example in Figure 2 is one of many examples, where this expectation is not met. Sensitivity analysis shows that the beginning of the utterance is important, because highly sensitive positions are distributed over all frequencies in one time point. This can be explained for the model, since it could have learned the context around the formant pattern. The LRP result is identifying two small regions in the spectrogram both of negative values in the spectrogram. Although this might be valid for what is important for the model, this cannot be interpreted as features of an 'a'.

4.3 Global introspection

We perform global introspection with our novel method NAvAI. We compute letter-specific spectrograms as average over aligned spectrogram frames

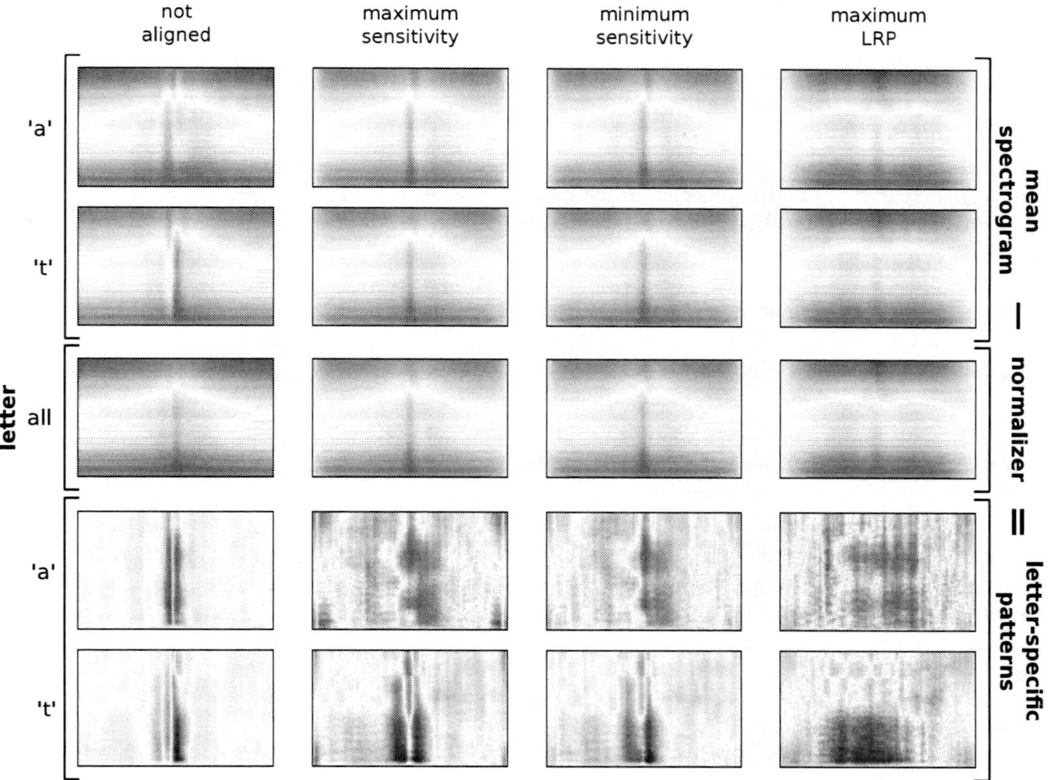

Figure 3: Averaging and normalizing letter-specific spectrogram frames. *Top two rows*: Mean inputs over spectrograms predicted as letter 'a' and 't', respectively. *Middle row*: Average spectrogram frame over all letters, which is used for normalization. *Bottom two rows*: By subtracting the mean over all letters from the letter-averaged spectrograms, we obtain patterns specific to the prediction of certain letters. Each analysis was performed with different alignment methods, of which each is visualized in a column. The *second to fourth column* correspond to aligning the spectrograms frames to the predicted letter based on local introspection. As comparison, the *first column* presents the averaging results for the unaligned spectrogram frames. The axes are equal to the spectrograms in Figure 2. Values in each frame are normalized, such that the absolute maximum is 1.

and normalize them. The alignment procedure crops the frames, so they are centered to the most important position. Because of this, the beginning and end of the averaged frame implicitly has lower values.

Mean spectrogram frames over letters   Figure 3 exemplifies the mean spectrogram frames for letters 'a' and 't' (top two rows). It is not possible to see interpretable differences between particular letters. Therefore, we cannot tell anything about the quality of the alignment methods as well. Interestingly, for all letters there are higher mean values in the center of unaligned mean spectrogram frames where only the position is slightly shifted comparing the letters. This

indicates that the network learned to align the center of the snippet with sounds that have a high value for all frequencies. For example, this could mean that the network can detect release bursts of plosives easily and uses them as a center point the prediction of letters in their context. Alignment by minimum or maximum sensitivity is causing this effect to be less pronounced. With using maximum LRP for alignment this effect vanishes. This is due to LRP identifying important regions further away from the center than sensitivity. The middle row of Figure 3 shows the mean over all letters. If there was nothing in common between the letters, all information would have been averaged out. On the contrary, we can observe that the overall mean is very similar to the letter-specific means. This shows that there is information common to all letters, which overshadows the spectrogram features that are relevant for prediction. More precisely, this information is not only common to the letters, but to spectrograms in general. For example, in speech, there is higher intensity of low frequencies than of high frequencies. This is reflected in the mean spectrograms, where the mean value decreases with higher frequency.

Mean spectrogram frame normalization To reveal where the differences between the letter-specific patterns are, we normalized each letter-averaged spectrogram frame with the mean over all letters. Figure 3 visualizes this procedure, where the mean over all letters (middle row) is subtracted from the exemplary mean frames over letters 'a' and 't' (top two rows). The resulting average spectrogram frames after normalization are shown in the bottom two rows of Figure 3. With normalization, we obtain the final result of our NAvAI method and we are able to observe letter-specific patterns.

Patterns in normalized mean spectrogram frames We emphasize that the normalized frames (bottom two rows of Figure 3) are not spectrograms anymore. Positive (red) and negative (blue) values indicate, where the average over one letter is higher or lower than the mean over all letters, respectively. This can lead to positive values where the (average) spectrogram was negative, and vice versa. Moreover, our method is not identifying which particular features are used by the network for prediction. For example, if NAvAI reveals two formants for a particular letter, it is not certain that both are used for the prediction.

First of all, we averaged spectrogram frames without alignment (first column in Figure 3). There are no letter-specific patterns visible in the resulting frames. For all letters, the normalized frame only shows a transition from positive to negative values (or the other way round) in the center. This simply reflects the above mentioned high intensities in the center, which are slightly shifted for different letters.

With all investigated alignment methods, we can observe a clear difference between the patterns for different letters. For predicting letter 'a', the network is detecting a stronger signal at the center and right of it for sensitivity-based and LRP alignments. Also for all alignments, two formants are clearly visible at around 700 Hz and 2700 Hz. This pattern makes sense, as vowels are combinations of different

formants. While all alignment methods show this pattern, it is more wide-spread across time using LRP.

Similarly, we can observe a letter-specific pattern for the letter 't'. For sensitivity-based alignments, there is a quick change from lower to higher signal and back in the center. This transition occurs in all frequencies, while it is more pronounced in the higher ones. This corresponds to the typical pattern of plosives. Their release burst is characterized by a high intensity of all frequencies in a very short time span. With LRP-based alignment, we did not observe this pattern. From the observations for letter 'a', we know that the signal is more wide-spread for LRP. This is not affecting the observed formant pattern of letter 'a', but it affects the plosive pattern. Here, the signal of interest spans the frequency dimension. Spreading the strong signal wider in the time dimension causes averaging out the interesting pattern. The weaker signal of low frequencies is detected with both sensitivity and LRP, because this is more consistent in the time dimension. The wide spread of signals when aligning by maximum LRP indicates that the letters were not properly aligned to the spectrogram.

The alignment by minimum or maximum sensitivity both revealed letter-specific patterns which also are specific in the time dimension. There is only slight difference between minimum and maximum sensitivity alignment, but the resulting normalized mean spectrogram frames seem to be more specific when aligning at the minimum sensitivity. We cannot guarantee that the alignment centers the spectrograms at the real occurrence of the letter. This can be seen in the typical patterns for 'a', which are right of the center. However, as long as the alignment is consistent, we still get meaningful results. We suspected that the network learns to facilitate release bursts of plosives in the center of prediction frames. If this was true, alignment should not change the center position much for letters that are mostly pronounced as plosives. This idea is supported by the shown results, as there is a much smaller difference between aligned and unaligned mean spectrogram frames for 't' compared to 'a'. Patterns of all letters are provided in Supplemental Material A.

5   Conclusion

Applying local and global introspection methods for image classification CNNs to an ASR task is not straight-forward. There are difficulties due to the real-value space of input data, architectural limitations and interpretability of audio data. We showed that local introspection with sensitivity analysis and LRP does not give much insight into the network. Global introspection with weakly regularized AM was only producing interpretable patterns for lower layers.

We introduced NAvAI as a novel introspection method, which determines class-specific features by averaging over examples for each class. This approach adapts simple averaging to specific properties of the ASR task, by aligning letters to spectrograms through local introspection techniques and normalization. We showed that our method is capable of revealing interpretable patterns, which are common to predicting particular letters. Although demonstrated for ASR, NAvAI is generally applicable to other domains.

This work did not cover, whether there are different patterns corresponding to particular contexts or pronunciation of letters. In future work, the classes will be separated into different pronunciations, for example by facilitating information about phonemes. Although the patterns are interpretable, some knowledge about features in spectrograms is needed. Evaluating the introspection as a sound example would be far more intuitive. Therefore, future work will cover synthesizing sound samples from the intro-spection results or working with waveforms directly. This work pinpointed several issues, where common introspection techniques fail for CNN-based ASR. Following our results, we will further develop or adapt introspection techniques and optimize the architecture towards better applicability of introspection.

Acknowledgments

This research has been funded by the Federal Ministry of Education and Research of Germany (BMBF) and supported by the donation of a GeForce GTX Titan X graphics card from the NVIDIA Corporation.

References

Ossama Abdel-Hamid, Abdel-rahman Mohamed, Hui Jiang, Li Deng, Gerald Penn, and Dong Yu. 2014. Convolutional neural networks for speech recognition. *IEEE/ACM Transactions on audio, speech, and language processing*, 22(10):1533–1545.

Sebastian Bach, Alexander Binder, Grégoire Montavon, Frederick Klauschen, Klaus-Robert Müller, and Wojciech Samek. 2015. On pixel-wise explanations for non-linear classifier decisions by layer-wise relevance propagation. *PloS one*, 10(7):e0130140.

Dzmitry Bahdanau, Jan Chorowski, Dmitriy Serdyuk, Philemon Brakel, and Yoshua Bengio. 2016. End-to-end attention-based large vocabulary speech recognition. In *Acoustics, Speech and Signal Processing (ICASSP), 2016 IEEE International Conference on*, pages 4945–4949. IEEE.

Liang-Chieh Chen, George Papandreou, Iasonas Kokkinos, Kevin Murphy, and Alan L Yuille. 2014. Semantic image segmentation with deep convolutional nets and fully connected crfs. *arXiv preprint arXiv:1412.7062*.

Ronan Collobert, Christian Puhrsch, and Gabriel Synnaeve. 2016. Wav2letter: an end-to-end convnet-based speech recognition system. *CoRR*, abs/1609.03193.

Nicholas Cummins, Shahin Amiriparian, Gerhard Hagerer, Anton Batliner, Stefan Steidl, and Björn W Schuller. 2017. An image-based deep spectrum feature representation for the recognition of emotional speech. In *Proceedings of the 2017 ACM on Multimedia Conference*, pages 478–484. ACM.

Dumitru Erhan, Yoshua Bengio, Aaron Courville, and Pascal Vincent. 2009. Visualizing higher-layer features of a deep network. *University of Montreal*, 1341(3):1.

Muriel Gevrey, Ioannis Dimopoulos, and Sovan Lek. 2003. Review and comparison of methods to study the contribution of variables in artificial neural network models. *Ecological modelling*, 160(3):249–264.

Xavier Glorot and Yoshua Bengio. 2010. Understanding the difficulty of training deep feedforward neural networks. In *Proceedings of the thirteenth international conference on artificial intelligence and statistics*, pages 249–256.

Diederik P Kingma and Jimmy Ba. 2014. Adam: A method for stochastic optimization. *arXiv preprint arXiv:1412.6980*.

Alex Krizhevsky, Ilya Sutskever, and Geoffrey E Hinton. 2012. Imagenet classification with deep convolutional neural networks. In F. Pereira, C. J. C. Burges, L. Bottou, and K. Q. Weinberger, editors, *Advances in Neural Information Processing Systems 25*, pages 1097–1105. Curran Associates, Inc.

Julius Kunze, Louis Kirsch, Ilia Kurenkov, Andreas Krug, Jens Johannsmeier, and Sebastian Stober. 2017. Transfer learning for speech recognition on a budget. In *Proceedings of the 2nd Workshop on Representation Learning for NLP*, pages 168–177. Association for Computational Linguistics.

Aravindh Mahendran and Andrea Vedaldi. 2015. Understanding deep image representations by inverting them. In *Proceedings of the IEEE conference on computer vision and pattern recognition*, pages 5188–5196.

Abdel-rahman Mohamed, Geoffrey Hinton, and Gerald Penn. 2012. Understanding how deep belief networks perform acoustic modelling. In *Acoustics, Speech and Signal Processing (ICASSP), 2012 IEEE International Conference on*, pages 4273–4276. IEEE.

Grégoire Montavon, Sebastian Lapuschkin, Alexander Binder, Wojciech Samek, and Klaus-Robert Müller. 2017. Explaining nonlinear classification decisions with deep taylor decomposition. *Pattern Recognition*, 65:211–222.

Alexander Mordvintsev, Christopher Olah, and Mike Tyka. 2015. Inceptionism: Going deeper into neural networks. *Google Research Blog. Retrieved June*, 20(14):5.

Tasha Nagamine and Nima Mesgarani. 2017. Understanding the representation and computation of multilayer perceptrons: A case study in speech recognition. In *International Conference on Machine Learning*, pages 2564–2573.

Tasha Nagamine, Michael L Seltzer, and Nima Mesgarani. 2015. Exploring how deep neural networks form phonemic categories. In *Sixteenth Annual Conference of the International Speech Communication Association*.

Tasha Nagamine, Michael L Seltzer, and Nima Mesgarani. 2016. On the role of nonlinear transformations in deep neural network acoustic models. In *Interspeech*, pages 803–807.

Anh Nguyen, Alexey Dosovitskiy, Jason Yosinski, Thomas Brox, and Jeff Clune. 2016. Synthesizing the preferred inputs for neurons in neural networks via deep generator networks. In *Advances in Neural Information Processing Systems*, pages 3387–3395.

Anh Nguyen, Jason Yosinski, and Jeff Clune. 2015. Deep neural networks are easily fooled: High confidence predictions for unrecognizable images. In *Proceedings of the IEEE Conference on Computer Vision and Pattern Recognition*, pages 427–436.

Vassil Panayotov, Guoguo Chen, Daniel Povey, and Sanjeev Khudanpur. 2015. Librispeech: an asr corpus based on public domain audio books. In *Acoustics, Speech and Signal Processing (ICASSP), 2015 IEEE International Conference on*, pages 5206–5210. IEEE.

Ramprasaath R. Selvaraju, Abhishek Das, Ramakrishna Vedantam, Michael Cogswell, Devi Parikh, and Dhruv Batra. 2016. Grad-cam: Visual explanations from deep networks via gradient-based localization. *CoRR*, abs/1610.02391.

Jost Tobias Springenberg, Alexey Dosovitskiy, Thomas Brox, and Martin Riedmiller. 2014. Striving for simplicity: The all convolutional net. *arXiv preprint arXiv:1412.6806*.

Christian Szegedy, Wei Liu, Yangqing Jia, Pierre Sermanet, Scott Reed, Dragomir Anguelov, Dumitru Erhan, Vincent Vanhoucke, and Andrew Rabinovich. 2015. Going deeper with convolutions. In *Proceedings of the IEEE conference on computer vision and pattern recognition*, pages 1–9.

George Trigeorgis, Fabien Ringeval, Raymond Brueckner, Erik Marchi, Mihalis A Nicolaou, Björn Schuller, and Stefanos Zafeiriou. 2016. Adieu features? end-to-end speech emotion recognition using a deep convolutional recurrent network. In *Acoustics, Speech and Signal Processing (ICASSP), 2016 IEEE International Conference on*, pages 5200–5204. IEEE.

Yonghui Wu, Mike Schuster, Zhifeng Chen, Quoc V Le, Mohammad Norouzi, Wolfgang Macherey, Maxim Krikun, Yuan Cao, Qin Gao, Klaus Macherey, et al. 2016. Google's neural machine translation system: Bridging the gap between human and machine translation. *arXiv preprint arXiv:1609.08144*.

Jason Yosinski, Jeff Clune, Anh Nguyen, Thomas Fuchs, and Hod Lipson. 2015. Understanding neural networks through deep visualization. *arXiv preprint arXiv:1506.06579*.

Matthew D Zeiler and Rob Fergus. 2014. Visualizing and understanding convolutional networks. In *European conference on computer vision*, pages 818–833. Springer.

A   Supplemental Material

A.1   NAvAI results for letters 'a' to 'i'

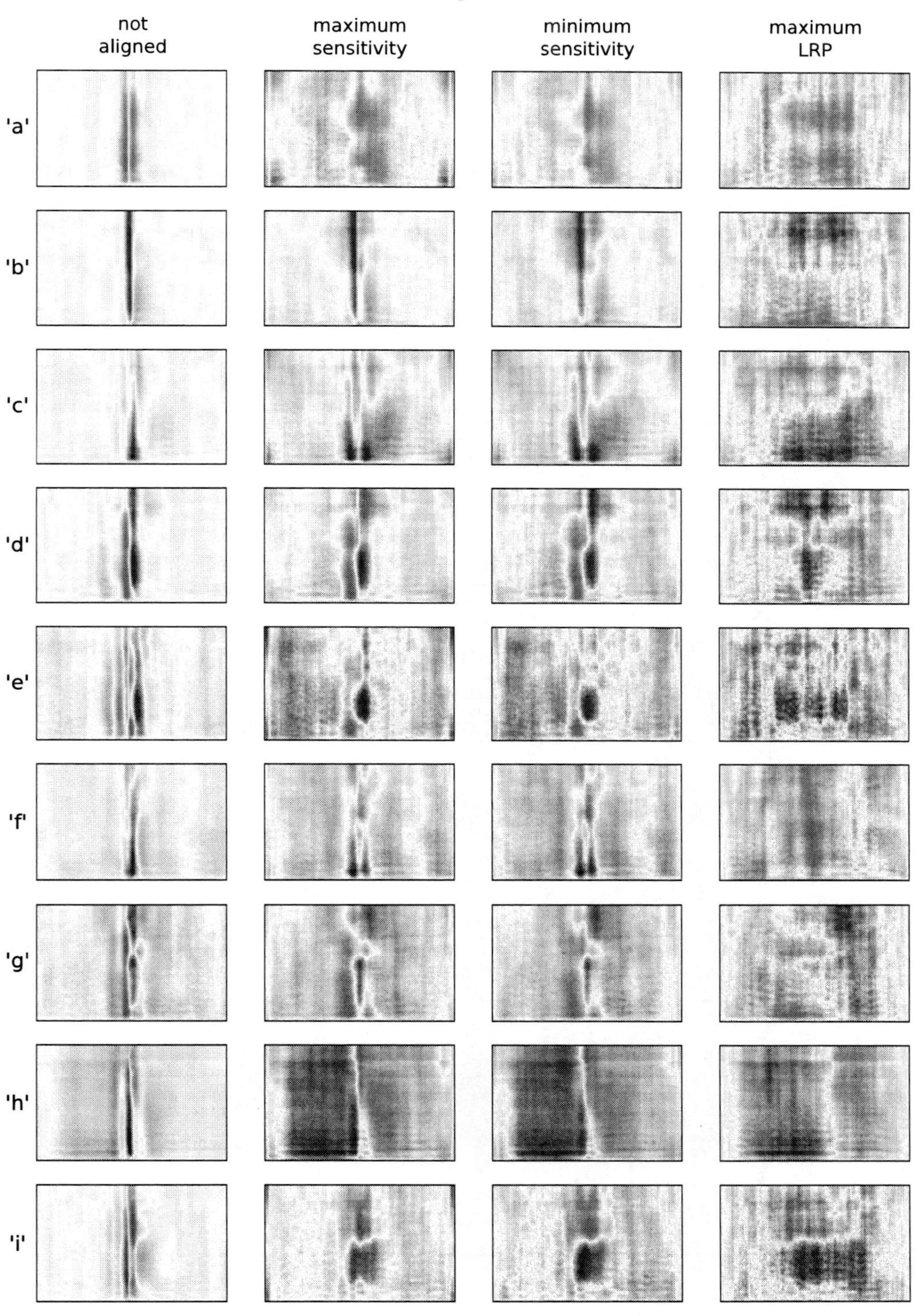

alignment

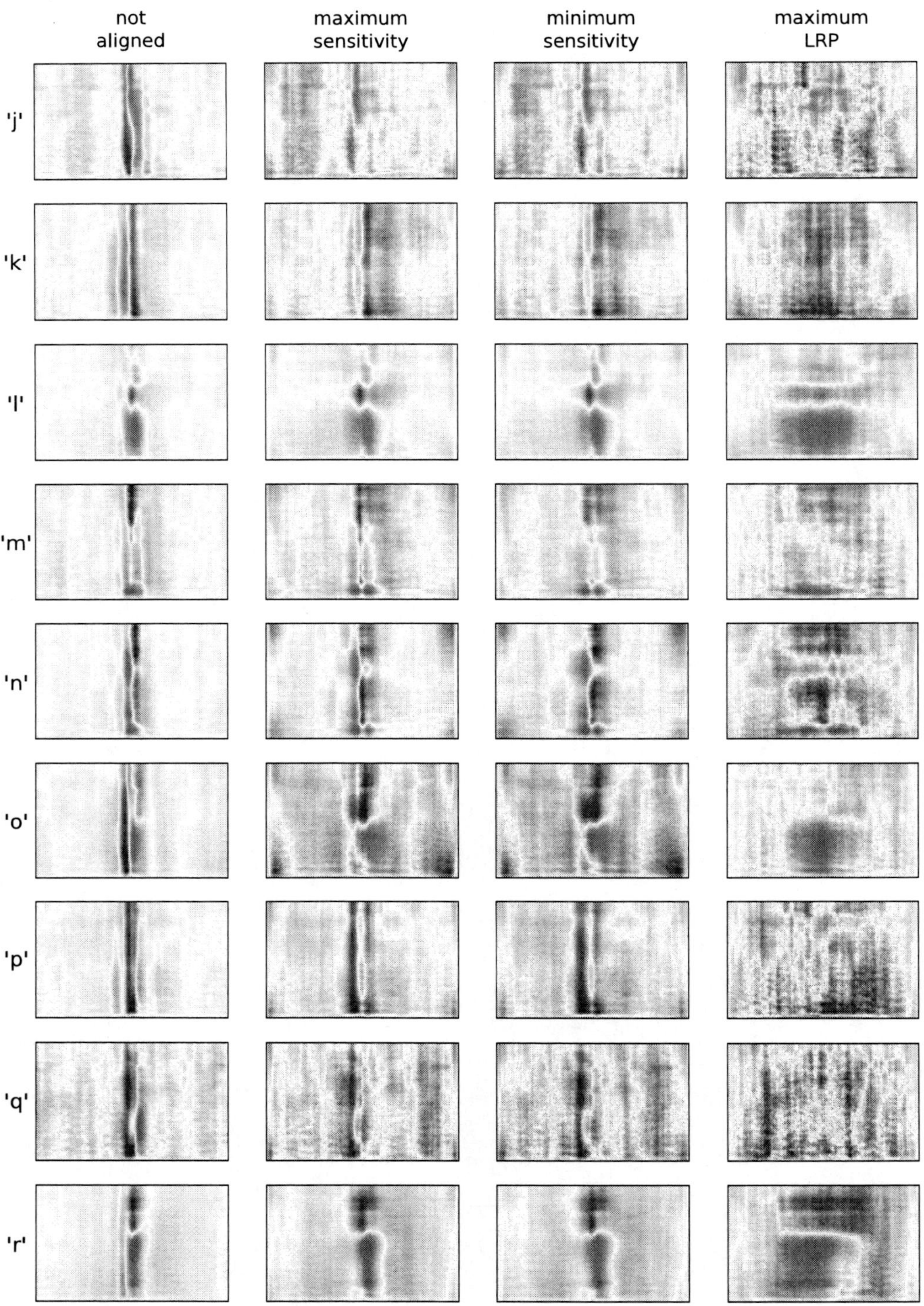

A.3 NAvAI results for letters 's' to 'z'

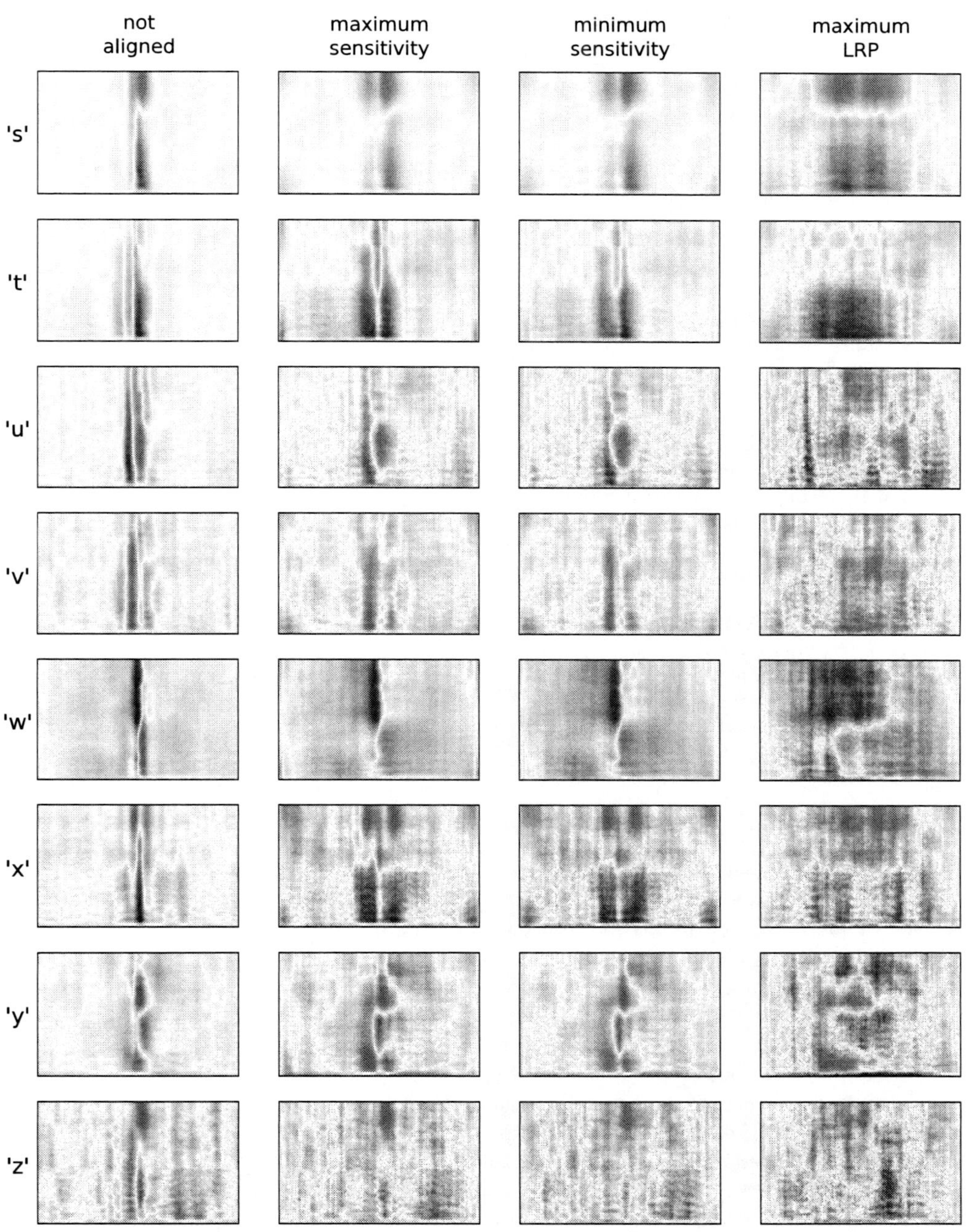

Learning and Evaluating Sparse Interpretable Sentence Embeddings

Valentin Trifonov
ETH Zürich, Switzerland
valentin.trifonov@outlook.com

Octavian-Eugen Ganea
ETH Zürich, Switzerland
octavian.ganea@inf.ethz.ch

Anna Potapenko
National Research University
Higher School of Economics, Russia*
anna.a.potapenko@gmail.com

Thomas Hofmann
ETH Zürich, Switzerland
thomas.hofmann@inf.ethz.ch

Abstract

Previous research on word embeddings has shown that sparse representations, which can be either learned on top of existing dense embeddings or obtained through model constraints during training time, have the benefit of increased interpretability properties: to some degree, each dimension can be understood by a human and associated with a recognizable feature in the data. In this paper, we transfer this idea to sentence embeddings and explore several approaches to obtain a sparse representation. We further introduce a novel, quantitative and automated evaluation metric for sentence embedding interpretability, based on topic coherence methods. We observe an increase in interpretability compared to dense models, on a dataset of movie dialogs and on the scene descriptions from the MS COCO dataset.

1 Introduction

In the word embeddings literature, it has previously been of interest to find interpretable representations: individual dimensions should capture a distinct semantic meaning, such that humans are able to understand why a word is encoded in a particular vector. With a cognitive plausibility argument from Murphy et al. (2012), the interpretability can be linked to sparse representations: they argue that the representation should model a wide range of features in the data and that every sample should be characterized by the presence of a small number of key features. Arora et al. (2016) use this idea to recover and disentangle the different meanings of polysemous words.

The above-named approaches, as well as those by Subramanian et al. (2017); Faruqui et al. (2015), recover an interpretable sparse representation in a separate, post-processing step on top of

the uninterpretable, dense embeddings of the original model (often word2vec or GloVe). This is commonly done using sparse coding or a downstream model. Additionally to understanding a model's intermediate representation, there has been work on constructing models that inherently use a sparse embedded representation by learning it during the training process (Sun et al., 2016; Chen et al., 2017). This is motivated by the idea that the model should include the prior that each word is a sparse combination of disentangled features from the very beginning. In contrast, when computing dense embeddings first, it is less likely that this representation will be easily disentanglable in the post-processing step.

Goh (2016) argues that sparse representations can be used to explain image and sentence embeddings as well. To be precise, the author focuses on encoder-decoder neural networks and uses sparse coding to recover interpretable features in the latent spaces of a variational autoencoder (Kingma and Welling, 2013) and an image captioning system based on (Vinyals et al., 2015).

In this paper, we aim to use sparse methods to disentangle sentence embeddings' dimensions. We focus on a simple sentence autoencoder model, and apply both a sparse-coding-based post-processing technique, as well as model constraints during training time, to obtain sparse vector representations of sentences. We aim to increase the understanding of the latent space, which helps us gain insight into how the inference and learning process works by identifying the patterns in the data that the model learns to recognize and encode in this representation.

To compare our different approaches, as well as measure the improvement compared to the baseline of a dense autoencoder model, we introduce a novel, quantitative and automated metric of the mentioned interpretability properties. It is based

---

*Work done during an internship at ETH Zürich.

Proceedings of the 2018 EMNLP Workshop BlackboxNLP: Analyzing and Interpreting Neural Networks for NLP, pages 200–210
Brussels, Belgium, November 1, 2018. ©2018 Association for Computational Linguistics

on the notion of topic coherence and further develops it for the case of sentences. We observe that the new measure reflects our manual judgment on the interpretability of the embeddings. Additionally, we track reconstruction quality and performance in downstream tasks, showing that sparse approaches can obtain a remarkable increase in interpretability at a moderate cost in quality.

2 Models

Our models are based on a standard recurrent neural network autoencoder following the *Sequence-to-Sequence* architecture (seq2seq; Sutskever et al., 2014). This architecture is based on the encoder-decoder scheme, where an encoder network maps the input to a dense, embedded representation $\mathbf{z}$, and a decoder net reconstructs the input from $\mathbf{z}$. In Section 3, we give a more detailed description of our experimental setup.

2.1 Enforcing Sparsity by Post-Processing Dense Embeddings

Consider a dataset $x_1, \ldots, x_N$ of N sentences. We train a dense autoencoder net with a hidden state size $D' = 500$ to convergence, and compute $\mathbf{Z} = [\mathbf{z}_1, \ldots, \mathbf{z}_N]^\mathsf{T} \in \mathbb{R}^{N \times D'}$, the vector representations of the data arranged as the rows of a matrix. We follow the approaches by Arora et al. (2016); Goh (2016) and compute a sparse representation of size $D = 2000$ on top of $\mathbf{Z}$, where all but k values have to be zero. We do this by solving the following sparse dictionary learning problem:

$$\mathbf{E}, \mathbf{U} = \arg\min_{\mathbf{E}, \mathbf{U}} ||\mathbf{EU} - \mathbf{Z}||_F^2,$$
$$s.t. \ ||\mathbf{e}_i||_0 \leq k, ||\mathbf{u}_j||_2 = 1, \ \forall i, j, \tag{1}$$

whereby we obtain $\mathbf{E} = [\mathbf{e}_1, \ldots, \mathbf{e}_N]^\mathsf{T} \in \mathbb{R}^{N \times D}$, a set of new, sparse vector representations, and $\mathbf{U} = [\mathbf{u}_1, \ldots, \mathbf{u}_D]^\mathsf{T} \in \mathbb{R}^{D \times D'}$, a dictionary of *atoms* found in $\mathbf{Z}$. We solve this problem with the k-SVD algorithm (Aharon et al., 2006, we use an open source implementation called *pyksvd*[1]).

The intuition behind this sparse coding approach is as follows. The atoms $\mathbf{U}$ are intended to represent a wide range of the 2000 most important features that explain the data in the dense latent space of the model. By solving this problem we decompose the intermediate representation $\mathbf{z}_i$ of a sample x_i into a linear combination $\mathbf{e}_i$ of

[1] https://github.com/hoytak/pyksvd

atoms. By constraining $\mathbf{e}_i$ to a fixed and low sparsity level k we aim to disentangle this representation and therefore increase interpretability. We refer to this representation as the k-SVD model.

2.2 Enforcing Sparsity during Embedding Learning

The k-SVD model proposed in the previous section obtains sparse representations through solving two independent problems: finding a fixed-size vector representation for sentences with a neural model and, in a separate step, mapping it to an interpretable, sparse representation. As we mention in the introduction, we conjecture that interpretability can be further increased with an end-to-end approach. In this section, we introduce modifications to the model architecture that will force the neural nets to encode and understand sparse representations of the data during training time.

We propose an additional layer that is inserted between the encoder and decoder net. We map the vector representation $\mathbf{z}$ to a vector $\mathbf{e}$ of the same size in a *sparsity transformation*. The only requirements for this mapping are that the output $\mathbf{e}$ is sparse and differentiable (or that we can define a custom gradient) to allow backpropagation through it. We then feed $\mathbf{e}$ through the decoder net instead of $\mathbf{z}$ and train the whole net end-to-end. In the rest of this section, we propose two mappings for such a sparsity transformation.

k-Sparse.

For this model, we draw inspiration from the *k-Sparse Autoencoder* by Makhzani and Frey (2013). We again introduce a hyperparameter k and define $\mathbf{e}$ by keeping the k largest activations in $\mathbf{z}$, the *support set*, and setting all other units to zero. We backpropagate only through the support set. This is a simple way of enforcing a hard specification for the sparsity level as an integral part of the model.

Sparsemax.

The k-Sparse approach has the drawback of requiring a fixed sparsity level for all samples. To allow for a variable, per-sample sparsity level, we use the *Sparsemax* layer, introduced by Martins and Astudillo (2016). Sparsemax is an alternative to Softmax—however, unlike Softmax, it is able to return sparse probability distributions. It is defined as:

$$\text{Sparsemax}(\mathbf{z}) = \arg \min_{\mathbf{p} \in \Delta^{D-1}} ||\mathbf{z} - \mathbf{p}||_2^2, \quad (2)$$

where D is the dimensionality of $\mathbf{z}$ and Δ^{D-1} is the $(D-1)$-dimensional simplex $= \{\mathbf{p} \in \mathbb{R}^D \mid \mathbf{1}^\mathsf{T}\mathbf{p} = 1, \mathbf{p} \geq 0\}$.

Similar to Softmax, Sparsemax supports a temperature mechanism, where a hyperparameter τ trades off the "confidence" in the output probability of the largest input unit. To be precise, as τ approaches 0, the probability distribution Sparsemax $\left(\frac{\mathbf{z}}{\tau}\right)$ approaches the distribution peaked on the maximum components of $\mathbf{z}$. Additionally to Softmax, Sparsemax has the property that this output distribution becomes increasingly sparse.

Putting this together, we introduce a hyperparameter τ and define a sparsity transformation by defining $\mathbf{e} = \text{Sparsemax} \left(\frac{\mathbf{z}}{\tau}\right)$.

3 Experiments

3.1 Training Details

In our experiments, we use a vocabulary size of 20,000, with the symbolic words `<person>`, `<unk>`, and `<eos>` for names and out-of-vocabulary (OOV) words in the dataset, and the end-of-sentence marker, respectively. We convert words to 100-dimensional word embeddings by looking them up in a trainable matrix $\mathbf{V}$ (note that, in general, this matrix is not sparse—sparsity is only imposed on the latent space of the sentences[2]).

Our encoder and decoder nets are recurrent neural networks that use a single GRU (Cho et al., 2014) layer. They have the same hidden dimensionality but share no parameters. We obtain the model predictions as the Softmax of a learned, affine transformation to 20,000-dimensional space at every time step of the decoder net. We minimize the mean cross-entropy loss over all timesteps. We use a batch size of 64 and the Adam optimization algorithm.

3.2 Data

We train our models on the Cornell Movie-Dialogs Corpus and MS Common Objects in Context datasets (respectively Danescu-Niculescu-Mizil and Lee, 2011; Lin et al., 2014).

The Movie-Dialogs Corpus is a collection of movie lines, therefore it contains a wide variety of different utterences and allows us to explore general-purpose sentence embeddings. We preprocess this data by splitting the movie lines into separate sentences, thereby obtaining more than 500,000 samples. This dataset has no predefined split; we define a validation and test set by setting aside 50,000 samples each.

The MS COCO dataset contains images showing scenes with objects in numerous configurations. Every image contains 5 human-annotated variations of a caption that describe the scene. In our experiments, we use only these captions and refer to this as the COCO Captions data. They total over 600,000 samples and allow us to explore sentence embeddings of a more narrow language: since they merely describe objects and scenes, they tend to follow the same, simple sentence structure. The dataset comes with a predefined training/validation split.

For tokenizing and splitting movie lines into sentences we use the NLP library SpaCy[3]. All our models are implemented in TensorFlow (Abadi et al., 2015).

4 A Quantitative and Automated Evaluation Metric

The most common quantitative interpretability measure for embeddings (in particular word embeddings) is the intrusion test, first introduced in (Chang et al., 2009). This test involves generating 5-tuples of samples, where according to the embeddings model four are related and one stands out. The better human judges identify the intruder, the more interpretable the model is considered.

This evaluation method has the drawback of requiring human attention, thereby it is expensive and slow to evaluate. For our evaluation, we introduce an automated interpretability test, based on topic coherence, that does not require human attention. We describe our method in this section.

A *topic model* defines a set of topics in a corpus of documents and allows us to find the top n most likely words that belong to each topic. *Topic coherence* is an automated evaluation method of the interpretability of topic models, which has been shown to correlate well with human assessments (Newman et al., 2010; Mimno et al., 2011). Given a symmetric similarity measure of

---

[2]On a side note, sparsity can be imposed on the word embeddings by adding an L1-regularizer to $\mathbf{V}$ (Sun et al., 2016; Chen et al., 2017).

[3]https://spacy.io

original	a room with blue walls and a white sink and door .
reconstruction	a room with blue walls and a white sink and windows .
original	two cars parked on the sidewalk on the street
reconstruction	two buses parked on the curb on the street
original	two women waiting at a bench next to a street .
reconstruction	two women sit at a park next to a street .
original	a car that seems to be parked illegally behind a legally parked car
reconstruction	a car that seems to be parked close to a police officer and talking
original	a bathroom sink and various personal hygiene items .
reconstruction	a bathroom sink and various other hygiene items .
original	this is an open box containing four cucumbers .
reconstruction	this is an open box makes delicious doughnuts .

Table 1: Typical sentence reconstruction errors by the k-Sparse, $k = 15$ model, trained on the COCO Captions data.

two words (e.g. pointwise mutual information), the coherence of a topic is defined as the mean pairwise similarity of all pairs of words. The total topic coherence of the model is the mean coherence over all topics.

We devise an evaluation scheme based on topic coherence. Instead of looking at words in topics, we consider the highest-ranked sentences in the dimensions of our embeddings and replace the word similarity measure with a sentence similarity measure. Let $x_d^{(p)}$ be the sample that has rank p in the order given by the d-th dimension in the embedding. For a similarity measure sim_*, the coherence of a single dimension d is defined as:

$$coh_*(d) = \frac{2}{n \cdot (n-1)} \sum_{p=1}^{n-1} \sum_{q=p+1}^{n} sim_*(x_d^{(p)}, x_d^{(q)}).$$

$$(3)$$

The coherence of the model is defined as the mean coherence over all dimensions:

$$coh_*(1, \ldots, D) = \frac{1}{D} \sum_d coh_*(d). \qquad (4)$$

In addition, to determine how much the coherence deteriorates when looking beyond the top ranks, we consider all non-zero samples of a dimension and we evaluate Equation 3 on n sentences sampled at random and without replacement from $\{x_i \mid e_{i,d} \neq 0\}$ instead of $x_d^{(1)}, \ldots, x_d^{(n)}$.

We compute this on the validation set of our data. We strip all stop words from all sentences. We consider $n = 10$ sentences per dimension, unless a dimension has a non-zero value for less than n samples, in which case we compute Equation 3 on all pairs of sentences. In the following, we define three choices for a sentence similarity measure sim_*.

Jaccard Similarity. We regard the sentences as sets of words and compute the Jaccard similarity:

$$sim_{\text{J}}(x_i, x_j) = \frac{|x_i \cap x_j|}{|x_i \cup x_j|}. \qquad (5)$$

BoW Similarity. We consider the Bag-of-Words (BoW) vectors $\mathbf{b}_i, \mathbf{b}_j$ of the two sentences, i.e. the vectors with the number of occurrences of each vocabulary word in x_i, x_j, respectively. The similarity is defined as the cosine of the angle between these vectors:

$$sim_{\text{BoW}}(x_i, x_j) = \frac{\mathbf{b}_i^{\mathsf{T}} \mathbf{b}_j}{||\mathbf{b}_i||_2 \, ||\mathbf{b}_j||_2}. \qquad (6)$$

WMD Similarity. The Jaccard and BoW similarity measures have a drawback in that they do not take semantic relatedness of different words into account. The *Word Mover's Distance* (WMD; Kusner et al., 2015) remedies this problem: the authors define a document distance measure that relies on the word2vec latent space to make a better assessment of the semantic distance of sentences, based on the distance of the words they consist of. We use the negative WMD to obtain a similarity measure:

$$sim_{\text{WMD}}(x_i, x_j) = -\text{WMD}(x_i, x_j). \qquad (7)$$

5 Results

5.1 Reconstruction Quality

We start off by looking at the amount of information lost by our models due to sparsity constraints.

In general, we observe that as the sparsity level is decreased, the reconstructions start to deteriorate. At low values of k, our sparse models often fail to restore the exact meaning or phrasing, but still generate sentences with correct grammar and related topics. For example,

e_{i,d_1}	x_i
1.00	`a person laying on a couch with a laying on him`
1.00	`a cat laying on top of a suitcase laying on the floor .`
1.00	`a man laying on top of a sandy beach laying next to a surfboard .`
1.00	`a person laying on a couch with a cat laying in their arms, covering part of the face .`
1.00	`a woman is laying on a couch with a boy laying his head on her belly, and a cat between her legs .`
1.00	`some cats laying on a dock with their chins laying over the end`
1.00	`a man laying in bed with a gray cat laying on top of him .`
1.00	`a number of cows laying in a lot near cars`
1.00	`a number of items laying on a surface near one another`
1.00	`two cows laying out together underneath a tree .`

(a) This dimension clearly corresponds to sentences that describe a configuration of an object `laying` on another, whether that be people on the couch or items on a surface. Coherence score: $coh_{\text{WMD}}(d_1) = -2.32$.

e_{i,d_2}	x_i
0.94	`a motorcycle parked outside the doors of a building`
0.94	`a blue motorcycle parked outside of a building .`
0.94	`traffic lights on the road showing the street`
0.93	`food in a bowl sitting on a table`
0.92	`a yellow train in an outside train station .`
0.92	`a motorcycle sits on a sidewalk near a building`
0.92	`a car that is outside in the dirt .`
0.92	`a red truck parked outside in the snow .`
0.91	`a boy sitting on a bench at the park`
0.91	`a black motorcycle is parked on a sidewalk`

(b) This dimension seems to capture, with some false positives, different kinds of motor vehicles (`motorcycle`, `train`, `car`, `truck`) that are `parked` (`sit`, `sitting`, `is outside`) somewhere. Coherence score: $coh_{\text{WMD}}(d_2) = -2.83$.

e_{i,d_3}	x_i
0.79	`herd of goats in grassy area with herder .`
0.64	`herd of five zebras grazing in a field`
0.63	`people are sitting in lounge chairs on the beach .`
0.63	`a close up of many large kites near the ground`
0.63	`cows lounge in a field with a mountain backdrop .`
0.62	`close up of the flower extending from a banana tree stalk`
0.61	`a group of object on top of a muddy river .`
0.61	`many plants and umbrellas on the side of the street .`
0.58	`a close up view of sheets that are on a bed`
0.58	`room with cramped quarters holding dining table set and extra chairs .`

(c) It is not clear which features this dimension captures. Coherence score: $coh_{\text{WMD}}(d_3) = -3.12$.

Table 2: Examples of selected dimensions d_1, d_2, d_3 of our k-Sparse, $k = 15$ model, trained on the COCO Captions data. We show the 10 highest-ranked samples x_i and the coherence $coh_{\text{WMD}}(d)$ of each dimension d. We give more examples of high-coherence dimensions in the appendix, in Table 5.

they turn "`waiting at a bench`" into "`sit at a park`", "`sidewalk`" into "`curb`", "`two cars`" into "`two buses`", and similar. The k-SVD model generally does this less than the other models but in some cases it fails as well. See examples of typical reconstruction errors by our k-Sparse, $k = 15$ model in Table 1.

5.2 Highest-Ranked Samples

We examine the top samples in the dimensions of our embedding models and observe that sparse models often group sentences s.t. they have a common syntactic element or talk about a common concept. For example, in our k-Sparse, $k = 15$

model trained on the COCO Captions dataset, we identify dimensions that represent sentences about objects in `water`, people `holding` things, `horse` (and occasionally `bicycle`) riders, sentences starting with common prefixes such as `there is a [...]`, etc. We give examples in Table 2 and in the appendix in Table 5. For some dimensions, this pattern is not only recognizable in the top ranks but for all samples x_i with $e_{i,d} \neq 0$.

We are able to find such patterns in all sparse models, but the lower the sparsity level, the more apparent these patterns become. k-SVD based models exhibit these properties to a lesser extent.

Embeddings model	Jaccard	BoW	WMD
COCO Captions	0.05	0.10	−3.12
Movie-Dialogs	0.08	0.16	−2.06

(a) Mean similarity of random sentences

Embeddings model	Top 10 samples			Random 10 samples		
	Jaccard	BoW	WMD	Jaccard	BoW	WMD
dense, 500 dim. AE	0.08	0.14	−3.00	0.06	0.10	−3.12
k-SVD, $k = 100$	0.07	0.12	−3.08	0.06	0.10	−3.11
k-SVD, $k = 50$	0.08	0.13	−3.03	0.06	0.11	−3.10
k-SVD, $k = 20$	0.11	0.18	−2.88	0.06	0.11	−3.08
k-SVD, $k = 15$	**0.11**	**0.19**	−2.86	0.07	0.12	−3.06
k-Sparse, $k = 100$	0.08	0.14	−3.02	0.06	0.11	−3.09
k-Sparse, $k = 50$	0.09	0.15	−2.96	0.07	0.12	−3.06
k-Sparse, $k = 20$	0.11	0.17	**−2.85**	0.08	0.14	**−3.00**
k-Sparse, $k = 15$	0.11	0.18	−2.86	**0.08**	**0.14**	−3.01
Sparsemax, $\tau = 50$	0.04	0.07	−3.25	0.03	0.06	−3.27
Sparsemax, $\tau = 20$	0.04	0.06	−3.29	0.03	0.05	−3.35
Sparsemax, $\tau = 10$	0.04	0.07	−3.25	0.03	0.06	−3.31

(b) COCO Captions dataset

Embeddings model	Top 10 samples			Random 10 samples		
	Jaccard	BoW	WMD	Jaccard	BoW	WMD
dense, 500 dim. AE	0.20	0.31	−1.85	0.09	0.16	−2.02
k-SVD, $k = 100$	0.17	0.24	−1.99	0.09	0.16	−2.01
k-SVD, $k = 50$	0.17	0.24	−2.01	0.10	0.16	−2.01
k-SVD, $k = 20$	0.20	0.28	−1.91	0.11	0.18	−2.01
k-SVD, $k = 15$	0.20	0.29	−1.88	0.12	0.19	−1.98
k-Sparse, $k = 100$	0.16	0.25	−2.01	0.10	0.18	−2.08
k-Sparse, $k = 50$	0.16	0.25	−1.95	0.11	0.19	−2.05
k-Sparse, $k = 20$	0.19	0.30	−1.82	0.13	0.22	−1.99
k-Sparse, $k = 15$	**0.22**	**0.33**	**−1.76**	0.14	**0.23**	−1.98
Sparsemax, $\tau = 50$	0.12	0.19	−2.13	0.12	0.19	−2.02
Sparsemax, $\tau = 20$	0.13	0.21	−2.02	**0.16**	0.23	**−1.89**
Sparsemax, $\tau = 10$	0.15	0.22	−2.01	0.15	0.22	−1.96

(c) Movie-Dialogs dataset

Table 3: Interpretability of our models, as measured by our topic-coherence-based metric in Equation 4. We evaluate this equation using three different notions of sentence similarity sim_*. In Equation 3, we consider 10 random non-zero samples in addition to the 10 highest-ranked samples.

5.3 Quantitative Evaluation

In Table 2 we additionally report the coherence $coh_{\text{WMD}}(d)$ of the presented dimensions d (see Equations 3, 7). We observe that this score correlates with our empirical assessment of the interpretability of the dimension. For example, we observe on the COCO dataset that, while unrelated groups of sentences usually have a coherence score of < -3, sentences with common or semantically related subjects and objects have higher coherence scores (usually between -2.8 and -2.2). Groups of sentences with very close semantic meaning or large common prefixes have coherence scores around -2 or higher.

We report the topic coherence of our models (Equation 4) in Table 3. As rough reference values for the metrics, we include the mean similarity of pairs of random sentences from the dataset (estimated on 500 randomly sampled pairs), and the topic coherence of a 500-dimensional dense autoencoder model.

In accordance with our empirical observations, we see an increase in interpretability in the sparse models. For example, on the COCO Captions data, a random pair of sentences has a WMD-based similarity of -3.12, and the WMD-based coherence score of a dense autoencoder model is -3. With the additional sparse coding step on top of that, we can increase the coherence to -2.86.

5.4 Downstream Tasks

Additionally to the interpretability properties of sparse sentence embeddings, it is of interest whether sparsity decreases their usefulness in downstream tasks. To evaluate this, we use the

Embeddings model	CR	MR	SUBJ	MPQA	SST2	SST5	TREC	SICK-E	SICK-R	STS14	MRPC
dense, 500 dim. AE	65.99	**59.37**	76.24	**73.01**	60.63	28.96	**77.60**	**75.50**	**0.61**	**0.42**	67.25
k-SVD, $k = 100$	60.48	54.63	69.61	70.73	59.58	25.07	68.20	56.36	0.34	0.18	59.65
k-SVD, $k = 50$	62.54	55.01	70.47	70.70	57.66	25.84	69.80	58.09	0.34	0.17	60.58
k-SVD, $k = 20$	62.41	55.53	70.60	71.16	58.76	25.20	70.40	60.26	0.33	0.17	59.94
k-SVD, $k = 15$	62.91	55.48	70.63	71.25	57.33	23.89	70.20	59.71	0.33	0.16	61.04
k-Sparse, $k = 100$	65.22	56.09	**76.47**	72.04	58.98	27.69	72.80	70.33	0.56	0.37	66.72
k-Sparse, $k = 50$	64.64	57.13	74.74	71.51	59.86	27.42	73.80	71.36	0.55	0.32	66.38
k-Sparse, $k = 20$	64.53	55.98	73.00	71.65	58.43	26.24	75.60	68.20	0.50	0.25	67.48
k-Sparse, $k = 15$	**67.63**	58.24	75.52	71.87	**62.16**	**30.14**	76.80	72.50	0.55	0.23	65.45
Sparsemax, $\tau = 50$	64.58	54.60	66.33	69.13	55.46	27.69	65.80	64.28	0.53	0.19	**67.88**
Sparsemax, $\tau = 20$	63.58	54.58	66.45	70.21	52.94	26.92	64.20	63.95	0.49	0.19	66.90
Sparsemax, $\tau = 10$	63.44	54.60	63.07	69.29	54.53	26.92	61.40	63.02	0.48	0.17	66.49

Table 4: Evaluation of the embeddings from Movie-Dialogs models on various downstream tasks. The values measure classification accuracy or spearman correlation with human-labeled ground truth (see Section 5.4); larger values are better.

SentEval framework (Conneau and Kiela, 2018), which learns downstream models on top of the provided sentence embeddings to solve a variety of transfer tasks.

We report the accuracy on the standard classification problems the framework provides, namely binary sentiment of movie reviews (MR), movie lines (SST2) and product reviews (CR), five-class sentiment of movie lines (SST5), subjectivity/objectivity (SUBJ), binary opinion polarity (MPQA), and six-class question type (TREC) classification. To look at semantic entailment/similarity of pairs of sentences, we report Spearman correlation with human-labelled ground truth on the five-class semantic relatedness (STS14, SICK-R), and three-class semantic entailment (SICK-E) tasks, and accuracy on the binary paraphrase detection (MRPC) task.

We configure the framework to use Logistic Regression for downstream models. More details on the tasks and evaluation methods can be found in the SentEval paper. We evaluate these tasks on the Movie-Dialogs models only, because COCO is unsuited for general-purpose sentence embeddings.

We show the results of this evaluation in Table 4. We again observe that sparse representations perform, in many cases, worse than their dense equivalent, therefore, trading quality for interpretability[4]. However, this does not occur on all tasks: for example, SST2 and SST5 clearly benefit from a sparse representation.

5.5 Discussion

The results of our quantitative evaluation method confirm the tendencies we observed in our empirical evaluation. It appears that embedding dimensions generated by sparse models are coherent to a higher extent—in particular, the lower the sparsity level, the more apparent topics can be found in the embedding dimensions.

The price of good interpretability is a higher reconstruction error. As we impose more sparsity in the representation, the model is forced to "cut corners" and single slots in the embedding are designated broader collections of traits in the data. This results in more coherent topics, however, the narrow information bandwidth reduces the decoder net's ability to reconstruct the exact sentence. The fact that sparse representations carry less information may also explain the lower utility in some of the downstream tasks. Other tasks (e.g. sentiment classification) can be solved with greater accuracy, which suggests that a sparse and interpretable representation discovers more useful features for a simple downstream model like Logistic Regression.

As we force a model to deal with a sparse representation already during the training phase, finding sensible atoms gets incorporated into the encoding and decoding mechanism. We found that, in comparison to extracting this information from a dense model's intermediate representation, this results in an observable and measurable boost in interpretability. We can explain this by the fact that this architecture makes it *part of the model's task* to find a sparse and accurate representation

<hr>

[4]On a side note, we address the noticeable fact that the transfer tasks are solved with low accuracy in general. For numbers comparable to the state of the art literature, more powerful sentence embedding models (such as self-attentive networks, InferSent, SkipThought etc., see Conneau et al., 2017; Kiros et al., 2015) with a higher latent dimensionality, more layers, and a larger and more diverse dataset are required. Further, SentEval provides slower but more powerful MLP downstream models instead of Logistic Regression.

of the data, whereas in a post-processing approach the model focuses on reconstruction only.

On the other side of the coin, this modification interferes with the training process. To be more precise, the model follows a more complex objective, and the sparse layer is limited in the amount of information that can be forward and backpropagated through it at a time—hence we observe convergence at a higher loss value and bigger reconstruction errors.

We note that our Sparsemax-based approach does not perform particularly well in our evaluation, although in some cases it outperforms other approaches when we consider samples beyond the 10 highest-ranked. This can be explained by the fact that the sparsity level is not fixed, and that due to the Sparsemax layer, the embeddings $\mathbf{e}_i$ are valid probability distributions. A high value $e_{i,d}$ does, therefore, not necessarily indicate a strong presence of feature d in sample i, but also a lack of other features. On the other hand, Sparsemax is better at determining feature presence/absence in general, due to not being constrained to find an exact number of features.

6   Related Work

As aforesaid, there has been work in the NLP literature on the interpretability of word embeddings. Murphy et al. (2012) suggest that sparse embeddings can be linked to a disentangled, and thus interpretable, representations. This idea is also applied in (Arora et al., 2016; Faruqui et al., 2015; Subramanian et al., 2017), commonly by solving a sparse dictionary learning problem on top of dense embeddings. In the papers (Sun et al., 2016; Chen et al., 2017; Luo et al., 2015), the authors learn sparse word embeddings during the training phase. Goh (2016) applies above-named approaches to image embeddings, and the intermediate representation of an image captioning model.

Makhzani and Frey (2013) define the k-Sparse autoencoder. They use a k-Sparse layer in a shallow autoencoder trained on the MNIST and NORB datasets, focusing on unsupervised feature learning, improvement in classification accuracy, and a fast alternative to sparse coding. Martins and Astudillo (2016) develop Sparsemax as an alternative to the Softmax layer that is able to output exactly zero probabilities, their work is focused on classification problems and attention mechanisms.

Interpretability metrics are usually of interest for word embeddings, where the predominant evaluation method is the word intrusion test (Chang et al., 2009). Our interpretability metric is based on topic coherence (Newman et al., 2010), a comparison of different variants of this method can be found in (Röder et al., 2015).

7   Conclusion

Being able to understand the intermediate representation of a neural net increases our model understanding. In this paper we have taken a step towards this goal by introducing several sparse methods for a sentence autoencoder, inspired by previous work on word embeddings. The evaluation of our proposed models supports our hypothesis that sparse methods benefit the interpretability of the embedding. It is intuitive that a vector restricted to many zero values inevitably carries less information, and indeed we have found that this increase in interpretability comes at a cost in reconstruction quality and, in some cases, utility in downstream tasks. It is, however, possible to strike a balance and achieve good interpretability without a large penalty.

We have devised a novel, automated method of quantifying said interpretability, based on topic coherence. In our experiments, we observe that this evaluation corresponds to our manual assessment of interpretability. It is fully automated, and therefore cheap and fast to run. It can easily be extended by using different sentence similarity metrics or other topic coherence variants.

An interpretable sentence representation has further applications beyond model understanding: for example, it allows us to develop a sentence similarity measure, that can justify *why* two sentences are similar. It can also help us understand downstream models on top of sentence embeddings. For example, consider the case of a linear classification model: we can inspect the largest positive and negative weights and understand which features in a source sentence influence the model's decision.

For future work, it suggests itself to apply sparsity constraints to more sophisticated sentence embedding models such as *SkipThought* or *InferSent* (respectively Kiros et al., 2015; Conneau et al., 2017). Our methods can also be used to construct sparse encoder-decoder models for further tasks, such as image captioning, machine translation, or recommender systems.

References

Martín Abadi, Ashish Agarwal, Paul Barham, Eugene Brevdo, Zhifeng Chen, Craig Citro, Greg S. Corrado, Andy Davis, Jeffrey Dean, Matthieu Devin, Sanjay Ghemawat, Ian Goodfellow, Andrew Harp, Geoffrey Irving, Michael Isard, Yangqing Jia, Rafal Jozefowicz, Lukasz Kaiser, Manjunath Kudlur, Josh Levenberg, Dandelion Mané, Rajat Monga, Sherry Moore, Derek Murray, Chris Olah, Mike Schuster, Jonathon Shlens, Benoit Steiner, Ilya Sutskever, Kunal Talwar, Paul Tucker, Vincent Vanhoucke, Vijay Vasudevan, Fernanda Viégas, Oriol Vinyals, Pete Warden, Martin Wattenberg, Martin Wicke, Yuan Yu, and Xiaoqiang Zheng. 2015. TensorFlow: Large-scale machine learning on heterogeneous systems. Software available from tensorflow.org.

Michal Aharon, Michael Elad, and Alfred Bruckstein. 2006. rmk-svd: An algorithm for designing overcomplete dictionaries for sparse representation. *IEEE Transactions on signal processing*, 54(11):4311–4322.

Sanjeev Arora, Yuanzhi Li, Yingyu Liang, Tengyu Ma, and Andrej Risteski. 2016. Linear algebraic structure of word senses, with applications to polysemy. *arXiv preprint arXiv:1601.03764*.

Jonathan Chang, Sean Gerrish, Chong Wang, Jordan L Boyd-Graber, and David M Blei. 2009. Reading tea leaves: How humans interpret topic models. In *Advances in neural information processing systems*, pages 288–296.

Yunchuan Chen, Ge Li, and Zhi Jin. 2017. Learning sparse overcomplete word vectors without intermediate dense representations. In *International Conference on Knowledge Science, Engineering and Management*, pages 3–15. Springer.

Kyunghyun Cho, Bart Van Merriënboer, Caglar Gulcehre, Dzmitry Bahdanau, Fethi Bougares, Holger Schwenk, and Yoshua Bengio. 2014. Learning phrase representations using rnn encoder-decoder for statistical machine translation. *arXiv preprint arXiv:1406.1078*.

Alexis Conneau and Douwe Kiela. 2018. Senteval: An evaluation toolkit for universal sentence representations. *arXiv preprint arXiv:1803.05449*.

Alexis Conneau, Douwe Kiela, Holger Schwenk, Loic Barrault, and Antoine Bordes. 2017. Supervised learning of universal sentence representations from natural language inference data. *arXiv preprint arXiv:1705.02364*.

Cristian Danescu-Niculescu-Mizil and Lillian Lee. 2011. Chameleons in imagined conversations: A new approach to understanding coordination of linguistic style in dialogs. In *Proceedings of the Workshop on Cognitive Modeling and Computational Linguistics, ACL 2011*.

Manaal Faruqui, Yulia Tsvetkov, Dani Yogatama, Chris Dyer, and Noah Smith. 2015. Sparse overcomplete word vector representations. *arXiv preprint arXiv:1506.02004*.

Gabriel Goh. 2016. Decoding the thought vector. http://gabgoh.github.io/ThoughtVectors/.

Diederik P Kingma and Max Welling. 2013. Autoencoding variational bayes. *arXiv preprint arXiv:1312.6114*.

Ryan Kiros, Yukun Zhu, Ruslan R Salakhutdinov, Richard Zemel, Raquel Urtasun, Antonio Torralba, and Sanja Fidler. 2015. Skip-thought vectors. In *Advances in neural information processing systems*, pages 3294–3302.

Matt Kusner, Yu Sun, Nicholas Kolkin, and Kilian Weinberger. 2015. From word embeddings to document distances. In *International Conference on Machine Learning*, pages 957–966.

Tsung-Yi Lin, Michael Maire, Serge Belongie, James Hays, Pietro Perona, Deva Ramanan, Piotr Dollár, and C Lawrence Zitnick. 2014. Microsoft coco: Common objects in context. In *European conference on computer vision*, pages 740–755. Springer.

Hongyin Luo, Zhiyuan Liu, Huanbo Luan, and Maosong Sun. 2015. Online learning of interpretable word embeddings. In *Proceedings of the 2015 Conference on Empirical Methods in Natural Language Processing*, pages 1687–1692.

Alireza Makhzani and Brendan Frey. 2013. K-sparse autoencoders. *arXiv preprint arXiv:1312.5663*.

Andre Martins and Ramon Astudillo. 2016. From softmax to sparsemax: A sparse model of attention and multi-label classification. In *International Conference on Machine Learning*, pages 1614–1623.

David Mimno, Hanna M Wallach, Edmund Talley, Miriam Leenders, and Andrew McCallum. 2011. Optimizing semantic coherence in topic models. In *Proceedings of the conference on empirical methods in natural language processing*, pages 262–272. Association for Computational Linguistics.

Brian Murphy, Partha Talukdar, and Tom Mitchell. 2012. Learning effective and interpretable semantic models using non-negative sparse embedding. *Proceedings of COLING 2012*, pages 1933–1950.

David Newman, Jey Han Lau, Karl Grieser, and Timothy Baldwin. 2010. Automatic evaluation of topic coherence. In *Human Language Technologies: The 2010 Annual Conference of the North American Chapter of the Association for Computational Linguistics*, pages 100–108. Association for Computational Linguistics.

Michael Röder, Andreas Both, and Alexander Hinneburg. 2015. Exploring the space of topic coherence measures. In *Proceedings of the eighth ACM international conference on Web search and data mining*, pages 399–408. ACM.

Anant Subramanian, Danish Pruthi, Harsh Jhamtani, Taylor Berg-Kirkpatrick, and Eduard Hovy. 2017. Spine: Sparse interpretable neural embeddings. *arXiv preprint arXiv:1711.08792*.

Fei Sun, Jiafeng Guo, Yanyan Lan, Jun Xu, and Xueqi Cheng. 2016. Sparse word embeddings using l1 regularized online learning. In *Proceedings of the Twenty-Fifth International Joint Conference on Artificial Intelligence*, pages 2915–2921. AAAI Press.

Ilya Sutskever, Oriol Vinyals, and Quoc V Le. 2014. Sequence to sequence learning with neural networks. In *Advances in neural information processing systems*, pages 3104–3112.

Oriol Vinyals, Alexander Toshev, Samy Bengio, and Dumitru Erhan. 2015. Show and tell: A neural image caption generator. In *Computer Vision and Pattern Recognition (CVPR), 2015 IEEE Conference on*, pages 3156–3164. IEEE.

e_{i,d_4}	x_i
0.98	a black cat drinking water out of a water faucet .
0.98	the boats are outside on the water sailing .
0.98	several cows drinking water from a water receptacle .
0.98	a boat speeds down open water spraying water behind it .
0.98	two elephants drink water out of a body of water
0.98	a large body of water covered with boats .
0.98	a person stands on water skis in the water .
0.98	a woman is on the water on water skis .
0.98	small boats on water with setting sun behind distant hills .
0.98	a power boat on a body of water with a large water spray behind .

(a) $coh_{\mathrm{WMD}}(d_4) = -2.21$

e_{i,d_5}	x_i
0.99	white vase holding holding an assortment of flowers
0.99	a man holding holding a tennis racquet on a tennis court .
0.99	a man holding holding a giant remote control .
0.99	two bears holding each other outside the surroundings .
0.99	snowboarder holding a pink board being hugged by man in costume .
0.99	baby holding a teething toy in his hand
0.99	a countertop holding a <unk> bowl across from a shelf holding stemware .
0.99	a bird holding a fish in it's mouth .
0.99	a oven holding two trays of food baking .
0.99	two glasses holding red wine sit on a piece of paper on a wooden surface .

(b) $coh_{\mathrm{WMD}}(d_5) = -2.77$

e_{i,d_6}	x_i
0.97	person riding their skateboard on the street with the cars .
0.94	person riding a skateboard while pushing a stroller
0.94	person riding a horse while the sun sets
0.93	person riding a horse while another horse stands in a field .
0.92	person riding a bicycle while walking two dogs .
0.92	person riding a four wheeler on a beach towards a bridge .
0.91	person riding an elephant as it crosses through a river .
0.91	person riding a horse along shore of a body of water .
0.91	a person riding their bike down a path to a gate with a stop sign .
0.91	person riding down snowy hill on a pair of skis

(c) $coh_{\mathrm{WMD}}(d_6) = -2.21$

e_{i,d_7}	x_i
0.99	there is a brown box on the toilet
0.99	there is a blender with a green mixture in it
0.99	there is a brown bear walking through the woods alone
0.99	there is a clock that is above the building doors
0.99	there is a clock inside of a curvy blue sculpture .
0.99	there is a truck that has something mounted on the top
0.99	there is a boy playing with a tie
0.99	there is a person playing a nintendo wii
0.99	there is a boy playing baseball at the base ball field
0.99	there is a clock on the wall between the two arches .

(d) $coh_{\mathrm{WMD}}(d_7) = -3.47$. Note that this dimension has low coherence because the common feature it brings out (there is a) consists of stop words, which are not considered in our metrics.

e_{i,d_8}	x_i
1.00	a person is surfing on a shallow wave .
1.00	a person is surfing on a medium sized wave .
1.00	a person is surfing in a on a wave
1.00	a person is surfing on a wave in the ocean .
1.00	a person is surfing a huge wave while staying upright .
1.00	a person is surfing on the waves of an empty ocean .
1.00	a person is surfing on a board at the beach
1.00	a person is surfing in a wave pool .
1.00	a person is surfing on a wave at the beach
1.00	a person is surfing a wave on a surfboard .

(e) $coh_{\mathrm{WMD}}(d_8) = -1.47$

Table 5: Highest-ranked samples in a selection of dimensions of our k-Sparse, $k = 15$ model, trained on the COCO Captions data, along with the coherence of the dimension.

What do RNN Language Models Learn about Filler–Gap Dependencies?

Ethan Wilcox[1], **Roger Levy**[2], **Takashi Morita**[3,4], and **Richard Futrell**[5]

[1]Department of Linguistics, Harvard University, `wilcoxeg@g.harvard.edu`
[2]Department of Brain and Cognitive Sciences, MIT, `rplevy@mit.edu`
[3]Primate Research Institute, Kyoto University, `tmorita@alum.mit.edu`
[4]Department of Linguistics and Philosophy, MIT
[5]Department of Language Science, UC Irvine, `rfutrell@uci.edu`

Abstract

RNN language models have achieved state-of-the-art perplexity results and have proven useful in a suite of NLP tasks, but it is as yet unclear what syntactic generalizations they learn. Here we investigate whether state-of-the-art RNN language models represent long-distance **filler–gap dependencies** and constraints on them. Examining RNN behavior on experimentally controlled sentences designed to expose filler–gap dependencies, we show that RNNs can represent the relationship in multiple syntactic positions and over large spans of text. Furthermore, we show that RNNs learn a subset of the known restrictions on filler–gap dependencies, known as **island constraints**: RNNs show evidence for wh-islands, adjunct islands, and complex NP islands. These studies demonstrates that state-of-the-art RNN models are able to learn and generalize about empty syntactic positions.

1 Introduction

Many recent advancements in Natural Language Processing have come from the introduction of Recurrent Neural Networks (RNN) (Elman, 1990; Goldberg, 2017). One class of RNNs, the Long Short-Term Memory RNN (LSTM) (Hochreiter and Schmidhuber, 1997) has been able to achieve impressive results on a suite of NLP tasks, including machine translation, language modeling, and syntactic parsing (Sutskever et al., 2014; Vinyals et al., 2015; Jozefowicz et al., 2016). But the nature of the representations learned by these models is not properly understood. As these models are being deployed with increasing frequency, this poses both engineering, accountability, and theoretical problems.

One promising line of research aims to crack open these 'black boxes' by investigating how LSTM language models perform on specially controlled sentences designed to draw out behavior that indicates representation of a syntactic dependency. Using this method, Linzen et al. (2016) and Gulordava et al. (2018) demonstrated that these models are able to successfully learn the number agreement dependency between a subject and its verb, even when there are intervening elements, and McCoy et al. (2018) found that RNNs learn the hierarchical rules of English auxiliary inversion. In this paper, we broaden and deepen this line of inquiry by examining what LSTMs learn about an unexplored syntactic relationship: the filler–gap dependency. The filler–gap dependency is novel, insofar as learning it requires the network to generalize about the absence of material.

For our purposes, **filler–gap dependency** refers to a relationship between a **filler**, which is a wh-complementizer such as 'what' or 'who', and a **gap**, which is an empty syntactic position licensed by the filler. In example (1a), the filler is 'what' and the gap appears after 'devoured', indicated with underscores. If the filler were not present, the gap would be ungrammatical, as in (1b).

(1) a. I know what the lion devoured __ at sunrise.
    b.*I know that the lion devoured __ at sunrise.

There is also a semantic relationship between the filler and the gap, in the sense that "what" is semantically the direct object of "devoured". In this work, we study the behavior of language models, and so we treat the filler–gap dependency purely as a licensing relationship.

Elman (1991) found that simple distributed models have some success predicting post-verbal gaps in sentences containing object-extracted relative clauses. However, correct representation of filler–gap dependencies and the constraints on them has proven challenging even in hand-engineered symbolic models. Furthermore, they are subject to numerous complex **island constraints** (Ross, 1967). Because of their complex-

Proceedings of the 2018 EMNLP Workshop BlackboxNLP: Analyzing and Interpreting Neural Networks for NLP, pages 211–221
Brussels, Belgium, November 1, 2018. ©2018 Association for Computational Linguistics

ity and ubiquity, these dependencies have figured prominently in arguments that natural language would be unlearnable by children without a great deal of innate knowledge (Phillips, 2013) (cf. Pearl and Sprouse, 2013; Ellefson and Christiansen, 2000)

The remainder of the paper is structured as follows. Section 2 presents our methods in more detail. Section 3 gives evidence that LSTM language models represent the basic filler–gap dependency in multiple syntactic positions despite intervening material. Section 4 investigates whether LSTM language models are sensitive to various constraints: wh-islands, adjunct islands, complex NP islands, and subject islands. We find that the language models are sensitive to some but not all of these constraints. Section 5 concludes.

2 Methods

2.1 Language models

We study the behavior of two pre-existing LSTMs trained on a language modeling objective over English text. Our first model is presented in Jozefowicz et al. (2016) under the name *BIG LSTM+CNN Inputs*; we call it the **Google model**. It was trained on the One Billion Word Benchmark (Chelba et al., 2013) and has two hidden layers with 8196 units each. It uses the output of a character-level Convolutional Neural Network (CNN) as input to the LSTM. This model has the best published perplexity for English text. Our second model is the one presented in the supplementary materials of Gulordava et al. (2018), which we call the **Gulordava model**. Trained on 90 million tokens of English Wikipedia, it has two hidden layers of 650 units each. Our goal in using these models is to provide two samples of the state-of-the-art. As a baseline, we also study an n-gram model trained on the One Billion Word Benchmark (a 5-gram model with modified Kneser-Ney interpolation, fit by KenLM with default parameters) (Heafield et al., 2013).

2.2 Dependent variable: Surprisal

We investigate RNN behavior primarily by studying the **surprisal values** that an RNN assigns to words and sentences. Surprisal is log inverse probability:

$$S(x_i) = -\log_2 p(x_i|h_{i-1}),$$

where x_i is the current word or character, h_{i-1} is the RNN's hidden state before consuming x_i, and the probability is calculated from the RNN's softmax activation. The logarithm is taken in base 2, so that surprisal is measured in bits.

The degree of surprisal for a word or sentence tells us the extent to which that word or sentence is unexpected under the language model's probability distribution. It is known to correlate directly with human sentence processing difficulty (Hale, 2001; Levy, 2008; Smith and Levy, 2013). In this paper, we look for cases where the surprisal associated with an an unusual construction—such as a gap—is ameliorated by the presence of a licensor, such as a wh-word. If the models learn that syntactic gaps require licensing, then sentences with licensors should exhibit lower surprisal than minimally different pairs that lack a proper licensor.

2.3 Experimental design

We test whether the LSTM language models have learned filler–gap dependencies by looking for a 2x2 interaction between the presence of a gap and the presence of a wh-licensor. This interaction indicates the extent to which a wh-licensor reduces the surprisal associated with a gap, so we call it the **wh-licensing interaction**. In studying constraints on filler–gap dependencies, we look for interactions between the wh-licensing interaction and other factors: for example, whether the wh-licensing interaction decreases when a gap is in a syntactic island position as opposed to a syntactically licit position (Section 4).

We use experimental items where the gap is located in an obligatory argument position, e.g. in subject position or as the direct object of a transitive verb, as judged by the authors. The phrase with the gap is embedded inside a complement clause. We chose this paradigm over bare wh-questions because it eliminates do-support and tense manipulation of the main verb, resulting in higher similarity across conditions. Each item appears in four conditions, reflecting a 2×2 experimental design manipulating presence of a wh-licensor and presence of a gap. For example:[1]

(2) a. I know that the lion devoured a gazelle at sunrise. [no wh-licensor, no gap]

   b. *I know what the lion devoured a gazelle at sunrise. [wh-licensor, no gap]

   c. *I know that the lion devoured __ at sunrise. [no wh-licensor, gap]

---

[1] We indicate the gap position with underscores for expository purposes, but these underscores were not included in experimental items.

d. I know what the lion devoured ⎯ at sunrise. [wh-licensor, gap]

We measure surprisal in two places: at the word immediately following a (filled) gap and summed over the whole region from the gap to the end of the embedded clause. We look at immediate-word surprisal because a gap's licitness should have local effects on network expectation. We look at whole-region surprisal because the presence of a filler also changes expectations about overall well-formedness of the sentence—a global phenomenon. Until the final punctuation is reached in (2b) there are potential gap-containing continuations that render the sentence syntactically licit (e.g. 'with ⎯.'). Therefore, we might expect no large spike in surprisal at any one point, but small increases in surprisal when the network encounters filled argument-structure roles and at the end of the sentence. Measuring summed surprisal captures these distributed, global effects.

If the network is learning the licensing relationship between fillers and gaps then two things should be true: First, if a wh-licensor sets up a global expectation for the presence of a gap, then in sentences containing a wh-licensor but no gap we expect higher surprisal in syntactic positions where a gap is likely to occur resulting in higher summed surprisal. That is, $S((2b)) - S((2a))$ should be a large positive number. Second, the presence of a gap in the absence of a wh-licensor should also result in higher surprisal than when the wh-licensor is present, that is $S((2d)) - S((2c))$ should be a large negative number. Given the four sentences in (2), the full wh-licensing interaction is: (S(2b) - S(2a)) - (S(2d) - S(2c)) This represents how well the network learns both parts of the licensing relationship. A positive wh-licensing interaction means the model represents a filler-gap dependency between the wh-word and the gap site; a licensing interaction indistinguishable from zero indicates no such dependency. For the purposes of brevity, we will give examples that mirror item (2d), above, but items of type (2a)–(2c) were also constructed in order to calculate the full licensing interaction.

Following standard practice in psycholinguistics, we derive the statistical significance of the interaction from a mixed-effects linear regression model predicting surprisal given sum-coded conditions (Baayen et al., 2008). We include random intercepts by item; random slopes are not neces-

sary because we do not have repeated observations within items and conditions (Barr et al., 2013). In our figures, error bars represent 95% confidence intervals of the contrasts between conditions, computed by subtracting out the by-item means before calculating the intervals as advocated in Masson and Loftus (2003). [2]

Although our method can indicate whether there is a link between fillers and gaps, the relationship between language model probability and grammaticality is complex (Lau et al., 2017) and interpreting our patterns in terms of grammaticality judgments would require auxiliary assumptions that we don't pursue here. To be clear: our goal is to investigate whether RNNs model the probabilistic dependencies between fillers and gaps *at all*, not whether the outputs of such models can be used to classify sentences as 'grammatical' or not.

3 Representation of filler–gap dependencies

The filler–gap dependency has three basic characteristics. First, the relationship is **flexible**: wh-phrases can license gaps in diverse syntactic positions. Second, the relationship is **robust to intervening material**: syntactic position, not linear distance, determines grammaticality. Third, the relationship is **one-to-one**: except in certain special cases, one wh-phrase licenses one gap. In this section, we demonstrate that the RNNs have learned these three properties of filler–gap dependencies by comparing their performance to a simple *n*-gram baseline model.

3.1 Flexibility of Wh-Licensing

If the RNN has learned the flexibility of the filler–gap dependency, then we predict to find a wh-licensing interaction when the gap appears in subject, object, and indirect object positions:

(3) a. I know who ⎯ showed the presentation to the visitors yesterday. [*subj*]
   b. I know what the businessman showed ⎯ to the visitors yesterday. [*obj*]
   c. I know who the businessman showed the presentation to ⎯ yesterday. [*pp*]

To test the flexibility of the model's filler–gap dependency representation, we created 21 test items containing either an obligatorily ditransitive verb,

---

[2] Our studies were preregistered on `aspredicted.org`: To see the preregistrations go to `aspredicted.org/X.pdf` where $X \in \{\texttt{md5ax}, \texttt{hd2df}, \texttt{mp9dv}, \texttt{uu8b5}, \texttt{rj2sk}\}$.

or a transitive verb with an obligatorily argument-taking preposition, as in (3). The obligatoriness of verb and preposition transitivity was judged by the authors. To control for the infrequent *wh-licensor–verb* bigram when the gap is in subject position, in all cases the embedded clause was separated from the wh-phrase by either an adverbial (e.g. "despite protocol") or by words introducing a secondary embedded clause (e.g. "my brother said"). For each item, we created three variants: *subj*, *obj*, and *pp*, corresponding to the items in Example (3).

The top row of Figure 1 demonstrates how the wh-licensing interaction was calculated for this experiment. The two panels at left show the main effect of wh-licensing, with surprisal in post-gap material shown in (a) and summed whole-clause surprisal in (b). The red bars indicate the effect of a wh-licensor on surprisal in the non-gapped condition, or $S(2b)–S(2a)$, to use the example from 2.3. The blue bars show the effect of a wh-licensor on surprisal in the gapped conditions, or $S(2d)–S(2c)$, to use the same example. The difference between the red bars and the blue bars in each condition is the licensing interaction, which is shown directly in (c) and (d). Not pictured are results from the *n*-gram baseline model, which yielded exactly 0 licensing interaction in all positions.

The bottom row of Figure 1 shows a region-by-region visualization of wh-licensing interaction. Region-by-region behavior is consistent across conditions: The licensing interaction spikes in the immediate post-gap material and returns to near zero levels for the rest of the sentence. The height of the licensing 'spike' in each condition is equivalent to the size of the wh-licensing interaction in (c), and the difference between the bars in (a). Meanwhile, the area under the 'wh-licensing curve' is equivalent to the summed wh-licensing interaction shown in (d) and the difference between the bars in (b). All of these wh-licensing interactions are significant ($p < 0.001$ in all cases).

This experiment was designed to test whether licensing interaction exists in multiple syntactic positions, which we turn to now. In the post-gap material, there is no significant difference in licensing interaction between conditions. But when we sum wh-licensing interaction across the entire embedded clause model behavior does diverge. For the Gulordava model, there is no significant difference between the three variants. For the Google model there is a significant reduction in licensing effect

between the *subj* and *obj* variants ($p < 0.01$) and the *subj* and *pp* variants ($p < 0.001$). The stronger licensing effects for subject gaps indicates that the networks have a stronger expectation for gaps in this position. This matches human online processing results, in so far as gap expectation may be one reason why subject-extracted clauses are easier to process than other clauses (King and Just, 1991). Overall, these experiments provide strong evidence that both models are learning the filler–gap dependency. Furthermore, both RNN models are learning the flexibility of the dependency, as they exhibit similar wh-licensing effects for all three argument roles tested.

3.2 Robustness of Wh-Licensing to Intervening Material

All syntactic dependencies are robust to intervening material. In (4), the dependency is determined by the syntactic relationship between the complementizer 'what' and the position of the gap; modifying the subject doesn't change the relationship, and thus has no effect on filler–gap licensing:

(4) a. I know what your friend gave __ to Sam during the picnic yesterday.

    b. I know what your new friend from the south of France who only just arrived last week gave __ to Sam during the picnic yesterday.

Having shown previously that RNNs have expectations for filler–gap dependencies, in this section we ask how well they are able to maintain those expectations over intervening material. We designed 21 sentences, like those in (4), with an obligatorily transitive verb and either an indirect object or a PP modifier. For each sentence we produced four variants, a short-modified version with 3-5 extra intervening words between the wh-licensor and the gap site, a medium version with 6-8 additional words and a long version, with 8-12 additional words. In all cases the extra material modified the subject of the embedded clause. For each length gradation we produced two further variants: one in which the direct object was extracted (*obj*, as in (4)) and one variant in which the indirect object or prepositional object was extracted (*goal*, where 'Sam' is in (4)). For each variant, we measured the wh-licensing interaction in the post-gap material and across the embedded clause. Treating the number of intervening words as a continuous variable, we calculated the correlation between the length of the intervener and the

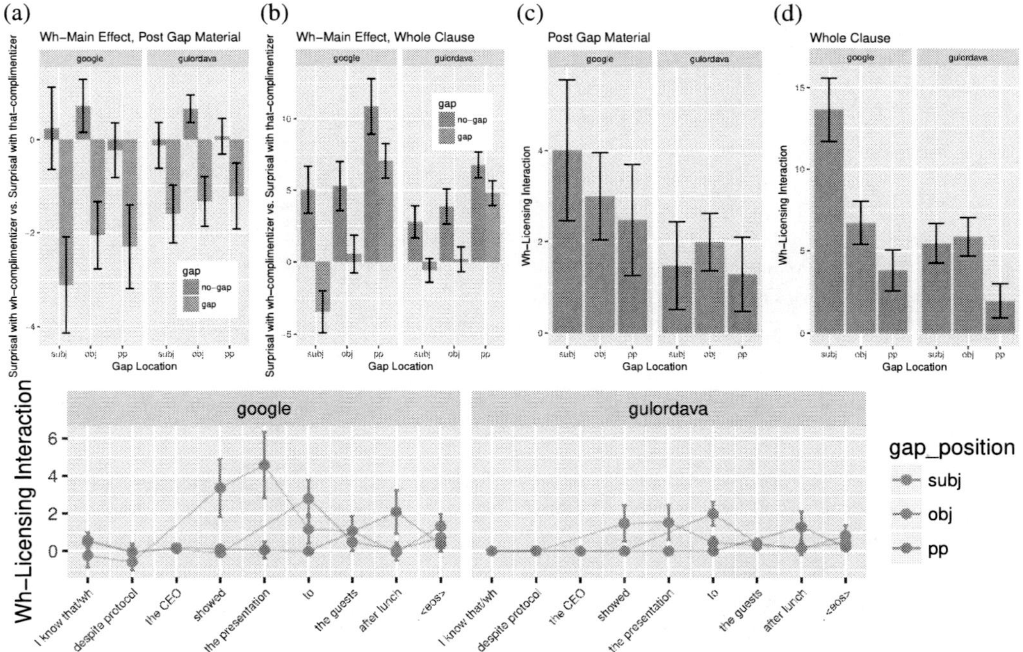

Figure 1: Wh-licensing by syntactic position. Charts (a) and (b) show the effect of wh-licensors on surprisal; (c) and (d) show the wh-licensing interaction by syntactic position. The difference between the non-gapped and gapped conditions (red and blue bars) in (a) and (b) correspond to the total licensing interaction, or the height of the bars in (c) and (d). The bottom chart displays wh-licensing interaction summed across all words within each region.

strength of the wh-licensing interaction. Optimally we would find zero correlation; a negative correlation indicates that the strength of the interaction decays with increasing intervening words.

Results of this study can be seen in Figure 2. First, as a baseline, across the eight experiments shown below, the average number of positive licensing interaction measurements was 86.4%. The vast majority of the time, the presence of both a filler and a gap reduced surprisal superadditively, producing a positive licensing interaction. Moving on to the effect of intervener length itself: For the Google model, intervener length was not a significant predictor of wh-licensing interaction in any of the conditions. For the Gulordava model, intervener length was not a significant predictor of wh-licensing interaction size when measurements were taken across the entire embedded clause. But length did correlate with wh-licensing interaction size when measured in the post-gap material for the object position ($\beta = 0.0289, p = 0.0219$) and goal position ($\beta = 0.0047, p = 0.0432$). These extremely small effect sizes, combined with the otherwise mixed results from both models, indicate

that interveners do not consistently attenuate the size of the licensing interaction.

While inconsistent with the formal linguistic literature on filler–gap dependencies, the negative values of all but one of the correlations are consistent with known effects in human sentence processing, where increasing distance between fillers and gaps usually causes processing slowdown (Grodner and Gibson, 2005; Bartek et al., 2011). In the n-gram baseline, all licensing effects are exactly zero, indicating the n-gram model has no representation of the filler–gap dependency.

3.3 Multiple Gaps

Except for a few special cases, such as with across-the-board (ATB) movement and parasitic gaps, a one-to-one relationship must be maintained between the wh-phrase and the gap it licenses. The presence of two gaps in (5c) violates this one-to-one relationship, accounting for its relative badness compared to (5a) and (5b).

(5) a. I know what the lion devoured __ at sunrise.
   b. I know what __ devoured a mouse at sunrise.
   c. *I know what __ devoured __ at sunrise.

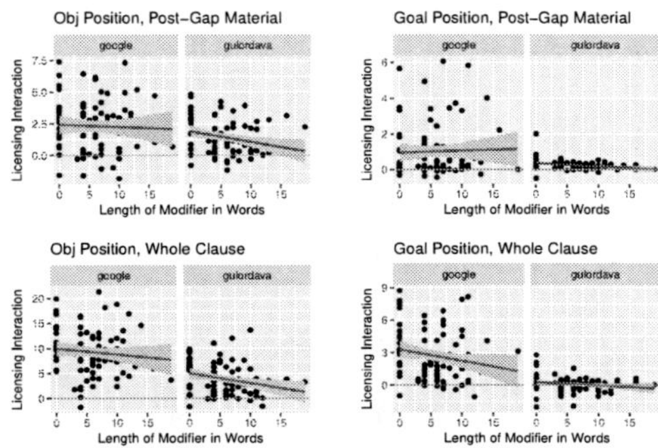

Figure 2: Wh-licensing interaction as a function of intervener length. Zero is marked with a red line.

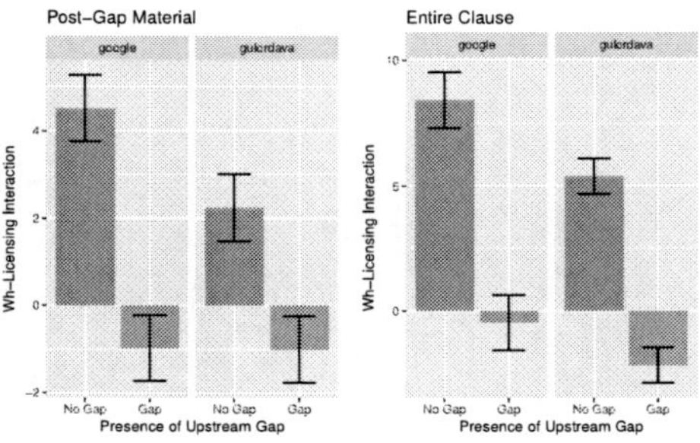

Figure 3: Wh-Licensing Interaction as a function of Double Gapping: Singly-gapped sentences are shown in red, doubly-gapped sentences in blue. Prepositional Phrases following the gap constitute post-gap material.

To test whether RNNs have learned this one-to-one feature of wh-licensing, we created 21 items all with gaps in object position like those in (5), with two variants: one without a subject gap like (5a) (*no-subj-gap*) and one with a subject gap, as in (5c) (*subj-gap*). We took special care to use only obligatorily transitive verbs. Half of the test items contained 'what' and half 'who' as wh-licensors. We measured the wh-licensing interaction for the two RNN models and the *n*-gram model, in both the post-gap PP and across the embedded phrase.

Figure 3 shows the results of this experiment. First, the relatively high bars in the grammatical *no-subject-gap* condition is another example of the RNN learning the filler–gap dependency; the *n*-gram baseline (not shown) exhibits no wh-licensing interaction under this condition. For the two LSTMs, the presence of an upstream gap increases surprisal in the target region, resulting in a significantly lower licensing effect across the board ($p < 0.001$ in all conditions). Meanwhile, the presence of a gap in the baseline condition results in no significant change in wh-licensing interaction. Overall these experiments demonstrate that the LSTMs have learned the last of the three main filler–gap dependency characteristics, and—for the typical object position—expect wh-phrases to be paired with only one gap.

4 Syntactic islands

Even though the filler–gap dependency is flexible and potentially unbounded, it is not entirely unconstrained. Ross (1967) identified five syntactic positions in which gaps are illicit, dubbing them **syntactic islands**. It remains an open question whether these "island constraints" are true gram-

matical constraints, or whether they are effects of processing difficulty or discourse-structural factors (Ambridge and Goldberg, 2008; Hofmeister and Sag, 2010; Sprouse and Hornstein, 2014).

In the following experiments, we examine whether RNN language models have learned constraints on filler–gap dependencies by comparing the wh-licensing interaction in non-islands to that within islands. The strongest evidence for an island constraint would be if the wh-licensing interaction goes to zero for a gap in island position, implying that, in the distribution over strings implied by the network, the appearance of a wh-licensor is totally unrelated to the appearance of a gap in the island position. More generally, we can look for a weakened wh-licensing interaction for island vs. non-island positions, which would mean that the network believes a relationship between the wh-licensor and the island gap is less likely. A positive but nonzero wh-licensing interaction would be in line with human acceptability judgments, which do not always categorically rule out gaps in island positions (Ambridge and Goldberg, 2008), and with human online processing experiments, which have shown that gap expectation is attenuated during processing of areas where gaps cannot occur licitly, but does not always disappear entirely (Stowe, 1986; Traxler and Pickering, 1996; Phillips, 2006). Therefore, in this section we take a significant reduction in the island relative to the non-island case to constitute evidence that the model has 'learned' the constraint.

4.1 Wh-Island Constraint

A gap cannot appear inside doubly nested clauses headed by wh-complementizers. This phenomenon is called the **Wh-Island Constraint** (WHC). (6) gives three sentences that demonstrate this phenomenon. As these three sentence variants will serve as the basis for our experiment we give each variant a condition name, on the top, and a brief description below. We will use this three-row expository technique—name, example, description—for each of the island conditions tested in this section and use condition names to label graphs and figures.

(6) a.
null-comp
I know what Alex said your friend devoured _ at the party.
Extraction from the object position of an embedded clause with a null complementizer. No island violations.

b.
that-comp
I know what Alex said that your friend devoured _ at the party.
Extraction from an embedded clause headed with the complementizer "that." No island violations.

c.
wh-comp
***I know what Alex said whether your friend devoured _ at the party.**
Extraction from an embedded clause headed with the complementizer "whether." WHC violation.

To test whether our LSTM language models have learned this constraint, we constructed 24 items following the conditions in (6). We measured the wh-licensing interactions at the sentence final PP, as well as across the entire embedded clause for both conditions.

Figure 4 shows the wh-licensing interaction for both LSTMs, with non-island conditions in red and green and island conditions in blue. In all conditions, extraction out of a wh-island resulted in a significantly lower licensing interaction than extraction out of a null-headed embedded clause ($p < 0.01$). For the Google model, extraction out of an island resulted in significantly lower wh-licensing interaction than extraction out of a that-headed embedded clause ($p < 0.001$), and while the Gulordava model showed similar behavior, none of the reductions were significant ($p = 0.071$ for the post gap material and $p = 0.052$ for the whole clause measurement). In all cases there was no significant difference between extraction out of the two non-island conditions, except for in the Gulordava model whole-clause condition, where licensing interaction for the *that-comp* condition was significantly lower than the *null-comp* condition ($p < 0.001$). These results indicate that the Google model has learned the wh-island constraint insofar as it has relatively similar expectations for extraction from null-headed

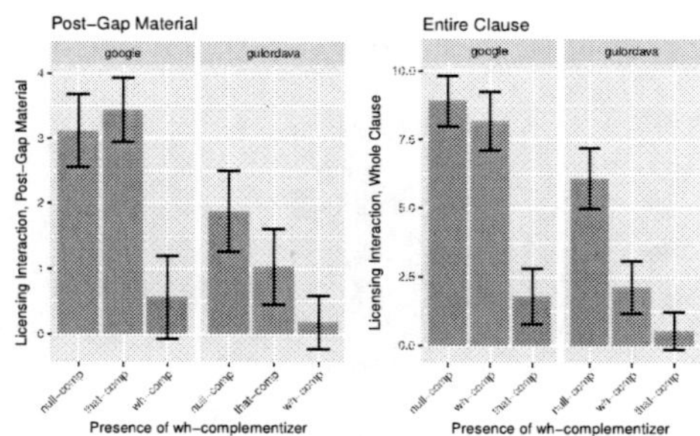

Figure 4: Effect of embedded clause complementizer on wh-licensing interaction. Post-gap material effect is in the left panel, whole-clause effect on the right panel.

and that-headed clauses, which differ from from its expectations about wh-headed clauses. The Gulordava model has learned wh-islands, but gradiently, treating that-headed embedded clauses as a semi-island condition.

4.2 Adjunct Island Constraint

Gaps cannot be licensed in an adjunct clause, as demonstrated by the relative unacceptability of (7b) and (7c), compared to (7a). We will refer to this constraint as the **Adjunct Constraint** (AC).

(7) a.
object
I know what the librarian in the dark blue glasses placed _ on the wrong shelf.
Material is extracted from the object position of the embedded verb. No island violations.

b.
adjunct-back
***I know what the patron got mad after the librarian placed _ on the wrong shelf.**
Material is moved from the object position of an embedded sentential adjunct. AC violation.

c.
adjunct-front
***I know what, after the librarian placed _ on the wrong shelf, the patron got mad.**
Material is moved from an embedded sentential adjunct that has been fronted to before the main verb of the embedded clause. AC violation.

To test whether RNNs were sensitive to the AC we devised 20 items following the variants in (7). Filler material was added to the *object* condition to control for sentence length across variants. We used three different prepositions to construct temporal adjuncts: 'while', 'after' and 'before'. We measured the wh-licensing interaction in the post-gap PP and across the entire embedded clause.

Figure 5 shows the wh-licensing interaction for both models. For the Google model there is a significant ($p < 0.001$) reduction in wh-licensing interaction between the *object* condition and the two adjunct conditions when measurement is taken in the post-gap material. The difference in licensing

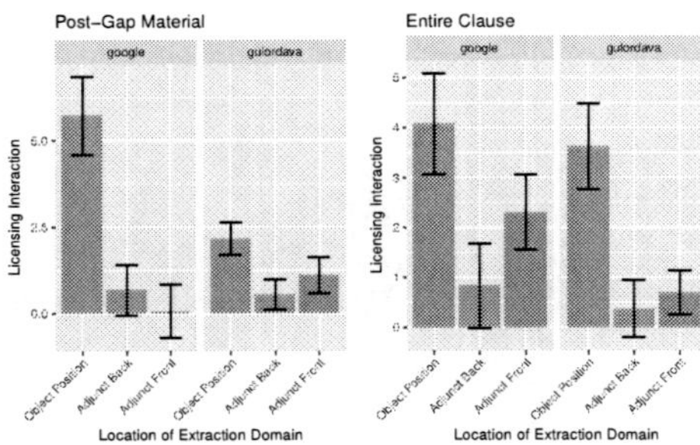

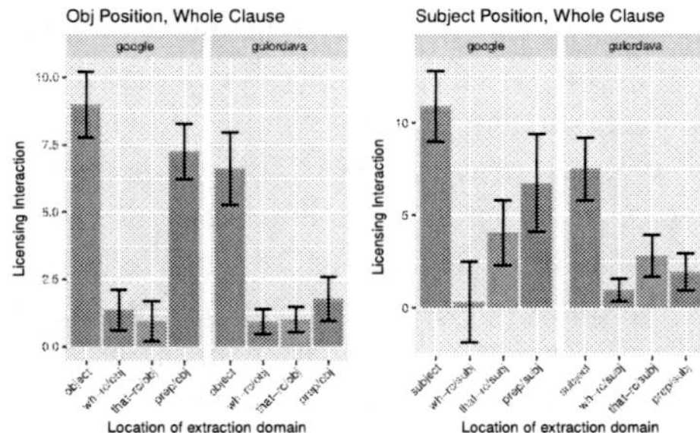

Figure 5: Effect of extraction site on wh-licensing interaction for adjunct islands. Post-gap material effect is in the left panel, whole-clause effect on the right panel.

Figure 6: Effect of extraction site location in complex np islands on wh-licensing interaction, measurement taken across the whole embedded clause. Object position is at left, subject position at right.

is also significant when measurements are taken across the embedded clause ($p < 0.05$ for the *object–adj-front* difference and $p < 0.01$ for the *object–adj-back* difference). The Gulordava model shows similar results. In the post gap material, there is a significant difference when wh-licensing interaction is measured in the post-gap material ($p < 0.05$ for the *object–adj-front* difference; $p < 0.01$ for the *object–adj-back* difference). Results are also significant when the whole embedded clause is measured ($p < 0.01$ for both differences). To sum up: In all cases, the placement of a gap within an adjunct results in a significantly lower licensing interaction. This difference in licensing interaction suggests that the models have learned the AC inasmuch as they have attenuated expectations for wh-licensing within sentential adjuncts.

4.3 Complex NP and Subject Islands

The **Complex NP Constraint** (CNPC) holds that a gap cannot be hosted in a sentential clause dominated by a noun phrase with a lexical head noun. This constraint accounts for the unacceptability of (8b), (8c), (8f) and (8g) below. The CNPC does not apply to other NP modifiers, such as PPs, unless the modified NP occurs in subject position (Huang, 1982). This ban, called the **Subject Constraint** (SC), accounts for the unacceptability of (8h) compared to (8d).

object

(8) a. **I know what the family bought __ last year.**
Extraction of embedded clause object.

that-rc/obj

b. ***I know who the family bought the painting that depicted __ last year.**
Extraction from 'that'-headed relative clause modifying embedded object. CNPC violation.

wh-rc/obj

c. ***I know who the family bought the painting which depicted __ last year.**
Extraction from 'wh'-headed relative clause modifying embedded object. CNPC violation

prep/obj

d. **I know who the family bought the painting by __ last year.**
Extraction from PP attached to embedded object.

subject

e. **I know what __ fetched a high price at auction.**
Extraction of embedded clause subject.

that-rc/subj

f. ***I know who the painting that depicted __ fetched a high price at auction.**
Extraction from 'that'-headed relative clause modifying embedded subject. CNPC violation

wh-rc/subj

g. ***I know who the painting which depicted __ fetched a high price at auction.**
Extraction from 'wh'-headed relative clause modifying embedded subject. CNPC violation.

prep/subj

h. ***I know who the painting by __ fetched a high price at auction.**
Extraction from PP attached to embedded subject. SC violation.

To test whether RNNs were sensitive to the CNPC and SC, we constructed 21 items for the variants shown in (8), which resulted in 8 conditions. For *prep/obj* and *prep/subj* special care was taken to use prepositions that unambiguously attach to the object and subject NP, respectively. As post gap material varied between variants, only whole-clause wh-licensing interaction measurement is given for this experiment.

Results for object variants can be seen in the left panel of Figure 6, and results for the subject variants on the right. In all cases the comparatively large licensing interaction in non-island conditions (*object* and *subject*) shrinks when the extracted material occurs inside a complex NP

218

(the middle bars in each chart). For the Google model the difference is significant for both CNP islands when extraction occurs in object position ($p < 0.001$). For subject position, the difference is significant when the RC is headed by a wh-word (*wh-rc/subj*) ($p < 0.05$), but there is no significant difference when the RC is headed by 'that', as in *wh-that/subj*. For the Gulordava model, both differences are significant in subject ($p < 0.05$) and object position ($p < 0.01$). Of the eight comparisons in 6 between CNPC islands and their non-island counterparts, seven show significant reduction in wh-licensing interaction. These differences indicate that both LSTMs do not generally expect extraction to occur from within complex NPs.

However, the LSTMs demonstrate divergent licensing behavior when extraction occurs from out of a prepositional phrase. If the models were learning the SC, we would expect no significant difference between *object* and *prep/obj*, but a island-like reduction in licensing interaction between the *subject* and *prep/subj* conditions. However, for the Google model there is no significant difference in licensing interaction in any condition, and for the Gulordava model the difference is significant ($p < 0.05$) in all cases. These results demonstrate that neither model has learned the subject constraint, categorizing PPs as either licit extraction domains in all positions (the Google model) or treating them like islands (the Gulordava model).

5   Conclusion

We have provided evidence that state-of-the-art LSTM language models have learned to represent filler–gap dependencies and some of the constraints on them. These results capture the bi-directional nature of the dependency, due to the fact that our measure—wh-licensing interaction—measures both the salutary effect of a gap given the presence of an upstream filler, as well as the salutary effect of a filler given a gap. We found strong licensing effects in both subject, object and indirect object locations, as well as an expectation that the filler–gap relationship was one-to-one and relatively unaffected by grammatically-irrelevant interveners. The models also learned constraints on the dependency, insofar as licensing effect shrank when gaps were located in wh-islands, adjunct islands and most complex NP islands, although the subject constraint was not clearly learned and some trace licensing interaction remained.

While the Google model was trained on ten times more data, contained ten times as many hidden units and uses character CNN embeddings, its performance was not qualitatively more human-like than the Gulordava model. Both models failed to correctly generalize island constraints in two conditions: The Google model failed to learn that-headed Complex-NP Islands, the Gulordava model to learn Wh-Islands, and both failed to learn Subject Islands. These results indicate that— beyond a certain point—increased model size and training regimen give diminishing returns.

In other recent work, Chowdhury and Zamparelli (2018) tested the ability of neural networks to separate grammatical from ungrammatical extractions using similar metrics to ours, finding that their neural networks do not represent the unboundedness of filler–gap dependencies nor certain strong island constraints. We believe the difference between our results and theirs is due to experimental design: They choose to measure the probability of the question mark punctuation as a proxy for the RNNs gap expectation, and use sentence schemata instead of hand-engineered experimental items. While Chowdhury and Zamparelli (2018) conclude that the networks are not learning island-like constraints, but rather displaying sensitivity to syntactic complexity plus order, we demonstrate island-like effects where both the island and the non-island item are equally complex (in e.g. wh-islands). Note also that our work is focused on finding evidence that networks represent the probabilistic contingencies implied by island constraints, without attempting to directly model grammaticality judgments.

Our work shows these dependencies and their constraints can be learned to some extent by a generic sequence model with no obvious inductive bias for hierarchical structures. This is evidence against the idea that such an inductive bias is necessary for language learning, although the amount of data these models are trained on is much larger than the typical input to a child learner.

Acknowledgements

All experimental materials and scripts are available at `https://osf.io/zpfxm/`. EGW would like to acknowledge support from the Mind Brain Behavior Graduate Student Grant, as well as Emmanuel Dupoux and the Cognitive Machine Learning Group at the ENS. RPL gratefully acknowledges support to his laboratory from Elemental Cognition and from the MIT-IBM Watson AI Lab. This work was supported by a GPU Grant from the NVIDIA corporation.

References

Ambridge, Ben and Adele E Goldberg. 2008. The island status of clausal complements: Evidence in favor of an information structure explanation. *Cognitive Linguistics* 19(3):357–389.

Baayen, R.H., D.J. Davidson, and D.M. Bates. 2008. Mixed-effects modeling with crossed random effects for subjects and items. *Journal of memory and language* 59(4):390–412.

Barr, Dale J, Roger Levy, Christoph Scheepers, and Harry J Tily. 2013. Random effects structure for confirmatory hypothesis testing: Keep it maximal. *Journal of Memory and Language* 68(3):255–278.

Bartek, B., Richard L. Lewis, Shravan Vasishth, and M. R. Smith. 2011. In search of on-line locality effects in sentence comprehension. *Journal of Experimental Psychology: Learning, Memory, and Cognition* 37(5):1178–1198.

Chelba, Ciprian, Tomas Mikolov, Mike Schuster, Qi Ge, Thorsten Brants, Phillipp Koehn, and Tony Robinson. 2013. One billion word benchmark for measuring progress in statistical language modeling. *arXiv preprint arXiv:1312.3005* .

Chowdhury, Shammur Absar and Roberto Zamparelli. 2018. Rnn simulations of grammaticality judgments on long-distance dependencies. In *Proceedings of the 27th International Conference on Computational Linguistics*. pages 133–144.

Ellefson, Michelle R and Morten H Christiansen. 2000. Subjacency constraints without universal grammar: Evidence from artificial language learning and connectionist modeling. In *Proceedings of the Annual Meeting of the Cognitive Science Society*. volume 22.

Elman, Jeffrey L. 1991. Distributed representations, simple recurrent networks, and grammatical structure. *Machine learning* 7(2-3):195–225.

Elman, J.L. 1990. Finding structure in time. *Cognitive Science* 14(2):179–211.

Goldberg, Yoav. 2017. Neural network methods for natural language processing. *Synthesis Lectures on Human Language Technologies* 10(1):1–309.

Grodner, Daniel and Edward Gibson. 2005. Consequences of the serial nature of linguistic input for sentential complexity. *Cognitive Science* 29(2):261–290.

Gulordava, K., P. Bojanowski, E. Grave, T. Linzen, and M. Baroni. 2018. Colorless green recurrent networks dream hierarchically. In *Proceedings of NAACL*.

Hale, John T. 2001. A probabilistic Earley parser as a psycholinguistic model. In *Proceedings of the Second Meeting of the North American Chapter of the Association for Computational Linguistics and Language Technologies*. pages 1–8.

Heafield, Kenneth, Ivan Pouzyrevsky, Jonathan H. Clark, and Philipp Koehn. 2013. Scalable modified Kneser-Ney language model estimation. In *Proceedings of the 51st Annual Meeting of the Association for Computational Linguistics*. Sofia, Bulgaria.

Hochreiter, Sepp and Jürgen Schmidhuber. 1997. Long short-term memory. *Neural Computation* 9(8):1735–1780.

Hofmeister, Philip and Ivan A Sag. 2010. Cognitive constraints and island effects. *Language* 86(2):366.

Huang, Cheng-Teh James. 1982. *Logical relations in Chinese and the theory of grammar*. Ph.D. thesis, Massachusetts Institute of Technology, Cambridge, MA.

Jozefowicz, Rafal, Oriol Vinyals, Mike Schuster, Noam Shazeer, and Yonghui Wu. 2016. Exploring the limits of language modeling. *arXiv* 1602.02410.

King, Jonathan and Marcel Adam Just. 1991. Individual differences in syntactic processing: The role of working memory. *Journal of memory and language* 30(5):580.

Lau, Jey Han, Alexander Clark, and Shalom Lappin. 2017. Grammaticality, acceptability, and probability: a probabilistic view of linguistic knowledge. *Cognitive Science* 41(5):1202–1241.

Levy, Roger. 2008. Expectation-based syntactic comprehension. *Cognition* 106(3):1126–1177.

Linzen, Tal, Emmanuel Dupoux, and Yoav Goldberg. 2016. Assessing the ability of LSTMs to learn syntax-sensitive dependencies. *Transactions of the Association for Computational Linguistics* 4:521–535.

Masson, Michael E. J. and Geoffrey R. Loftus. 2003. Using confidence intervals for graphically based data interpretation. *Canadian Journal of Experimental Psychology/Revue canadienne de psychologie expérimentale* 57(3):203.

McCoy, R. Thomas, Robert Frank, and Tal Linzen. 2018. Revisiting the poverty of the stimulus: hierarchical generalization without a hierarchical bias in recurrent neural networks. *arXiv preprint arXiv:1802.09091* .

Pearl, Lisa and Jon Sprouse. 2013. Syntactic islands and learning biases: Combining experimental syntax and computational modeling to investigate the language acquisition problem. *Language Acquisition* 20(1):23–68.

Phillips, Colin. 2006. The real-time status of island phenomena. *Language* pages 795–823.

Phillips, Colin. 2013. On the nature of island constraints II: Language learning and innateness. *Experimental syntax and island effects* pages 132–157.

Ross, John Robert. 1967. *Constraints on variables in syntax*. Ph.D. thesis, Massachusetts Institute of Technology, Cambridge, MA.

Smith, Nathaniel J. and Roger Levy. 2013. The effect of word predictability on reading time is logarithmic. *Cognition* 128(3):302–319.

Sprouse, Jon and Norbert Hornstein. 2014. *Experimental syntax and island effects*. Cambridge University Press.

Stowe, Laurie A. 1986. Parsing wh-constructions: Evidence for on-line gap location. *Language and cognitive processes* 1(3):227–245.

Sutskever, Ilya, Oriol Vinyals, and Quoc V Le. 2014. Sequence to sequence learning with neural networks. In *Advances in Neural Information Processing Systems*. pages 3104–3112.

Traxler, Matthew J and Martin J Pickering. 1996. Plausibility and the processing of unbounded dependencies: An
eye-tracking study. *Journal of Memory and Language*
35(3):454–475.

Vinyals, Oriol, Łukasz Kaiser, Terry Koo, Slav Petrov, Ilya
Sutskever, and Geoffrey Hinton. 2015. Grammar as a foreign language. In *Advances in Neural Information Processing Systems*. pages 2773–2781.

Do Language Models Understand *Anything*?
On the Ability of LSTMs to Understand Negative Polarity Items

Jaap Jumelet
University of Amsterdam
`jaap.jumelet@student.uva.nl`

Dieuwke Hupkes
ILLC, University of Amsterdam
`d.hupkes@uva.nl`

Abstract

In this paper, we attempt to link the inner workings of a neural language model to linguistic theory, focusing on a complex phenomenon well discussed in formal linguistics: (negative) polarity items. We briefly discuss the leading hypotheses about the licensing contexts that allow negative polarity items and evaluate to what extent a neural language model has the ability to correctly process a subset of such constructions. We show that the model finds a relation between the licensing context and the negative polarity item and appears to be aware of the *scope* of this context, which we extract from a parse tree of the sentence. With this research, we hope to pave the way for other studies linking formal linguistics to deep learning.

1 Introduction

In the past decade, we have seen a surge in the development of neural language models (LMs). As they are more capable of detecting long distance dependencies than traditional n-gram models, they serve as a stronger model for natural language. However, it is unclear what kind of properties of language these models encode. This does not only hinder further progress in the development of new models, but also prevents us from using models as explanatory models and relating them to formal linguistic knowledge of natural language, an aspect we are particularly interested in in the current paper.

Recently, there has been an increasing interest in investigating what kind of linguistic information is represented by neural models, (see, e.g., Conneau et al., 2018; Linzen et al., 2016; Tran et al., 2018), with a strong focus on their *syntactic* abilities. In particular, (Gulordava et al., 2018) used the ability of neural LMs to detect noun-verb congruence pairs as a proxy for their awareness of syntactic structure, yielding promising results. In this paper, we follow up on this research by studying a phenomenon that has received much attention by linguists and for which the model requires – besides knowledge of syntactic structure – also a *semantic* understanding of the sentence: negative polarity items (NPIs).

In short, NPIs are a class of words that bear the special feature that they need to be *licensed* by a specific licensing context (LC) (a more elaborate linguistic account of NPIs can be found in the next section). A common example of an NPI and LC in English are *any* and *not*, respectively: The sentence *He didn't buy any books* is correct, whereas *He did buy any books* is not. To properly process an NPI construction, a language model must be able to detect a relationship between a licensing context and an NPI.

Following Linzen et al. (2016); Gulordava et al. (2018), we devise several tasks to assess whether neural LMs (focusing in particular on LSTMs) can handle NPI constructions, and obtain initial positive results. Additionally, we use diagnostic classifiers (Hupkes et al., 2018) to increase our insight in how NPIs are processed by neural LMs, where we look in particular at their understanding of the *scope* of an LCs, an aspect which is also relevant for many other natural language related phenomena.

We obtain positive results focusing on a subset of NPIs that is easily extractable from a parsed corpus but also argue that a more extensive investigation is needed to get a complete view on how NPIs – whose distribution is highly diverse – are processed by neural LMs. With this research and the methods presented in this paper, we hope to pave the way for other studies linking neural language models to linguistic theory.

In the next section, we will first briefly discuss NPIs from a linguistic perspective. Then, in Sec-

Proceedings of the 2018 EMNLP Workshop BlackboxNLP: Analyzing and Interpreting Neural Networks for NLP, pages 222–231
Brussels, Belgium, November 1, 2018. ©2018 Association for Computational Linguistics

tion 3, we provide the setup of our experiments and describe how we extracted NPI sentences from a parsed corpus. In Section 4 we describe the setup and results of an experiment in which we compare the grammaticality of NPI sentences with and without a licensing context, using the probabilities assigned by the LM. Our second experiment is outlined in Section 5, in which we describe a method for scope detection on the basis of the intermediate sentence embeddings. We conclude our findings in Section 6.

2 Negative Polarity Items

NPIs are a complex yet very common linguistic phenomenon, reported to be found in at least 40 different languages (Haspelmath, 1997). The complexity of NPIs lies mostly in the highly idiosyncratic nature of the different types of items and licensing contexts. Commonly, NPIs occur in contexts that are related to negation and modalities, but they can also appear in imperatives, questions and other types of contexts and sentences. This broad range of context types makes it challenging to find a common feature of these contexts, and no overarching theory that describes when NPIs can or cannot occur yet exists (Barker, 2018). In this section, we provide a brief overview of several hypotheses about the different contexts in which NPIs can occur, as well as examples that illustrate that none of these theories are complete in their own regard. An extensive description of these theories can be found in (Giannakidou, 2008), (Hoeksema, 2012), and (Barker, 2018), from which most of the example sentences were taken. These sentences are also collected in Table 1.

Entailment A downward entailing context is a context that licenses entailment to a subset of the initial clause. For example, *Every* is downward entailing, as *Every [student] left* entails that *Every [tall student] left*. In (Ladusaw, 1980), it is hypothesized that NPIs are licensed by downward entailing contexts. Rewriting the previous example to *Every [student with any sense] left* yields a valid expression, contrary to the same sentence with the upward entailing context *some*: *Some [student with any sense] left*. An example of a non-downward entailing context that is a valid NPI licensor is *most*.

Non-veridicality A context is non-veridical when the truth value of a proposition (*veridicality*) that occurs inside its scope cannot be inferred. An example is the word *doubt*: the sentence *Ann doubts that Bill ate some fish* does not entail *Bill ate some fish*. (Giannakidou, 1994) hypothesizes that NPIs are licensed only in non-veridical contexts, which correctly predicts that *doubt* is a valid licensing context: *Ann doubts that Bill ate any fish*. A counterexample to this hypothesis is the context that is raised by the veridical operator *only*: *Only Bob ate fish* entails *Bob ate fish*, but also licenses *Only Bob ate any fish* (Barker, 2018).

2.1 Related constructions

Two grammatical constructions that are closely related to NPIs are Free Choice Items (FCIs) and Positive Polarity Items (PPIs).

Free Choice Items FCIs inhibit a property called *freedom of choice* (Vendler, 1967), and are licensed in contexts of generic or habitual sentences and modal verbs. An example of such a construction is the generic sentence *Any cat hunts mice*, in which *any* is an FCI. Note that *any* in this case is not licensed by negation, modality, or any of the other licensing contexts for NPIs. English is one of several languages in which a word can be both an FCI and NPI, such as the most common example *any*. Although this research does not focus on FCIs, it is important to note that the somewhat similar distributions of NPIs and FCIs can severely complicate the diagnosis whether we are dealing with an NPI or an FCI.

Positive Polarity Items PPIs are a class of words that are thought to bear the property of scoping above negation (Giannakidou, 2008). Similar to NPIs their contexts are highly idiosyncratic, and the exact nature of their distribution is hard to define. PPIs need to be situated in a veridical (often affirmative) context, and can therefore be considered a counterpart to the class of NPIs. A common example of a PPI is *some*, and the variations thereon. It is shown in (Giannakidou, 2008) that there exist multiple interpretations of *some*, influenced by its intonation. The emphatic variant is considered to be a PPI that scopes above negation, while the non-emphatic *some* is interpreted as a regular indefinite article (such as *a*).

	Context type
1. *Every* [*student with* **any** *sense*] *left*	Downward entailing
2. *Ann doubts that* [*Bill* **ever** *ate any fish*]	Non-veridical
3. *I don't* [*have* **any** *potatoes*]	Downward entailing
4. [*Did you see* **anybody**] *?*	Questions

Table 1: Various example sentences containing NPI constructions. The licensing context scope is denoted by square brackets, the NPI itself in boldface, and the licensing operator is underlined. In our experiments we focus mostly on sentences that are similar to sentence 3.

3 Experimental Setup

Our experimental setup consists of 2 phases: first we extract the relevant sentences and NPI constructions from a corpus, and then, after passing the sentences through an LM, we apply several diagnostic tasks to them.

3.1 NPI extraction

For extraction we used the parsed Google Books corpus (Michel et al., 2011).

We focus on the most common NPI pairs, in which the NPI *any* (or any variation thereon) is licensed by a negative operator (*not*, *n't*, *never*, or *nobody*), as they can reliably be extracted from a parsed corpus. As variations of *any* we consider *anybody*, *anyone*, *anymore*, *anything*, *anytime*, and *anywhere* (7 in total including *any*).

We first identify candidate NPI-LC relations looking only at the surface form of the sentence, by selecting sentences that contain the appropriate lexical items. We use this as a pre-filtering step for our second method, in which we extract specific subtrees given the parse tree of the sentence. We consider 6 different subtrees, that are shown in Table 2.

An example of such a subtree that licenses an NPI is the following:

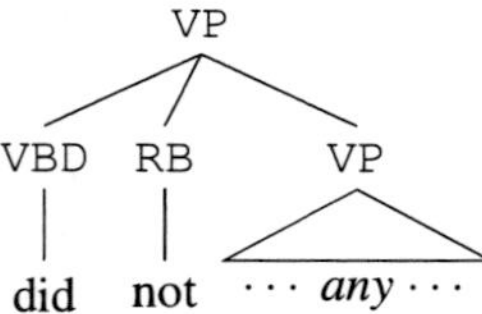

which could, for instance, be a subtree of the parse tree of *Bill did not buy any books*. In this subtree, the scope of the licensor *not* encompasses the VP of the sentence. We use this scope to pinpoint the exact range in which an NPI can reside.

Once all NPI constructions have been extracted, we are able to gain more insight in the distance

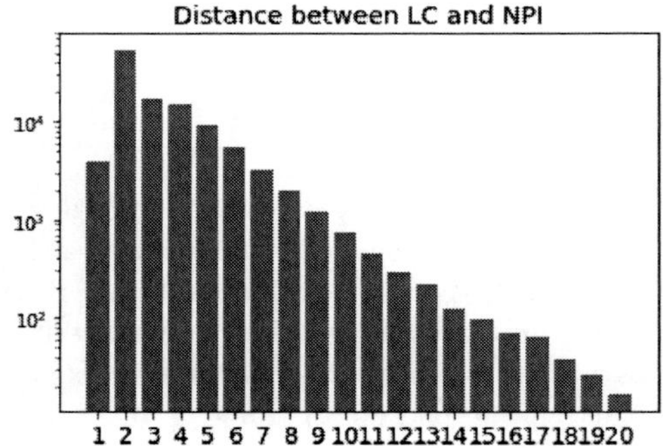

Figure 1: Distribution of distances between NPI and licensing context. Note the log scale on the y-axis.

between the licensing operator and an NPI, which we plot in Figure 1. Note the use of a log scale on the y-axis: in the majority of the constructions (47.2%) the LC and NPI are situated only 2 positions from each other.

3.2 Model

For all our experiments, we use a pretrained 2-layer LSTM language model with 650 hidden units made available by Gulordava et al. (2018).[1] For all tests we used an average hidden final state as initialization, which is computed by passing all sentences in our corpus to the LM, and averaging the hidden states that are returned at the end of each sentence.

We use two different methods to assess the LSTMs ability to handle NPI constructions, which we will discuss in the next two sections: one that is based on the probabilities that are returned by the LM, and one based on its internal activations.

4 Sentence Grammaticality

In our first series of experiments, we focus on the probabilities that are assigned by the model to dif-

---

[1]`github.com/facebookresearch/`
`colorlessgreenRNNs/tree/master/data`

Construction	#	(% / corpus)
All corpus sentences	11.213.916	
Containing any variation of *any*	301.836	(2.69%)
Licensed by negative operator	123.683	(1.10%)
Detected by subtree extractor	112.299	(1.00%)
1. `(VP (VP RB [VP]))` *He did n't [have **any** trouble going along] .*	70.017	
2. `(VP (MD RB [VP]))` *I could not [let **anything** happen to either of them] .*	27.698	
3. `(VP (VP RB [NP/PP/ADJP]))` *"There was n't [**any** doubt in his mind who was preeminent] ."*	8708	
4. `(VP (NP RB [VP]))` *Those words never [lead to **anything** good] .*	3564	
5. `(S (RB [S/SBAR]))` *The trick is not [to process **any** of the information I encounter] .*	1347	
6. `(RB [NP/PP ADVP])` *There was not [a trace of water **anywhere**] .*	930	

Table 2: Various sentence constructions and their counts that were extracted from the corpus. Similar verb POS tags are grouped under VP, except for modal verbs (MD). LC scope is denoted by square brackets.

ferent sequences. More specifically, we compare the exponent of the normalized negative log probability (also referred to as *perplexity*) of different sentences. The lower the perplexity score of a sentence is, the better a model was able to predict its tokens.

4.1 Rewriting sentences

While studying perplexity scores of individual sentences is not very informative, comparing perplexity scores of similar sentences can provide information about which sentence is preferred by the model. We exploit this by comparing the negative polarity sentences in our corpus with an ungrammatical counterpart, that is created by removing or rewriting the licensing context.[2]

To account for the potential effect of rewriting the sentence, we also consider the sentences that originate from replacing the NPI in the original and rewritten sentence with its positive counterpart. In other words, we replace the variations of *any* by those of *some*: *anything* becomes *something*, *anywhere* becomes *somewhere*, etc. We refer to these 4 conditions with the terms **NPI**$_{neg}$, **NPI**$_{pos}$, **PPI**$_{neg}$ and **PPI**$_{pos}$:

NPI$_{neg}$:	*Bill did not buy any books*
NPI$_{pos}$:	* *Bill did buy any books*
PPI$_{neg}$:	# *Bill did not buy some books*
PPI$_{pos}$:	*Bill did buy some books*

PPI$_{neg}$ would be correct when interpreting *some* as indefinite article (*non-emphatic some*). In our setup, **NPI**$_{neg}$ always refers to the original sentence, as we always use a sentence containing an NPI in a negative context as starting point. Of the 7 *any* variations, *anymore* is the only one without a PPI counterpart, and these sentences are therefore not considered for this comparison.

4.2 Comparing sentences

For all sentences, we compute the perplexity of the original sentence, as well as the perplexity of the 3 rewritten versions of it. To discard any influence that the removal of the licensing operator might have on its continuation after the occurrence of the NPI, we compute the perplexity of the sentence up to and including the position of the NPI. I.e., in the example of *Bill did not buy any books* the word *books* would not be taken into account when computing the perplexity.

In addition to perplexity, we also consider the conditional probabilities of the PPIs and NPIs, given the preceding sentence.[3] For example, for

---

[2]*Not* and *never* are removed, *nobody* is rewritten to *everybody*.

[3]We also considered the SLOR score (Pauls and Klein,

$\mathbf{NPI}_{neg}$ we would then compute *P(any | Bill did not buy)*.

4.3 Expectations

We posit the following hypotheses about the outcome of the experiments.

- $PP(\mathbf{NPI}_{neg}) < PP(\mathbf{NPI}_{pos})$: We expect an NPI construction to have a lower perplexity than the rewritten sentence in which the licensing operator has been removed.

- $PP(\mathbf{PPI}_{pos}) < PP(\mathbf{PPI}_{neg})$: Similarly, we expect a PPI to be preferred in the positive counterpart of the sentence, in which no licensing operator occurs.

- $PP(\mathbf{NPI}_{neg}) < PP(\mathbf{PPI}_{neg})$: We expect an NPI to be preferred to a PPI inside a negative context.

- $PP(\mathbf{PPI}_{pos}) < PP(\mathbf{NPI}_{pos})$: We expect the opposite once the licensor for this context has been removed.

4.4 Results

In Figure 2, we plot the distribution of the perplexity scores for each sentence type. The perplexities of the original and rewritten sentence without the NPI are indicated by $\mathbf{SEN}_{neg}$ and $\mathbf{SEN}_{pos}$, respectively. This figure shows that the original sentences have the lowest perplexity, whereas the NPIs in a positive context are deemed most improbable by the model.

More insightful we consider Figure 3, in which we plot the distribution of the relative differences of the perplexity scores and conditional probabilities for each of the above mentioned comparisons, and we report the percentage of sentences that complied with our hypotheses. The relative difference between two values a and b, given by $(a - b)/((a + b)/2)$, neatly maps each value pair in a window between -2 ($a \ll b$) and 2 ($a \gg b$), thereby providing a better insight in the difference between two arrays of scores. We highlight some of the previously mentioned comparisons below.

2012), that was shown in (Lau et al., 2017) to have a strong correlation with human grammaticality judgments. The SLOR score can be seen as a perplexity score that is normalized by the average unigram probability of the sentence. It turned out, however, that this score had such a strong correlation with the perplexity scores (Spearman's ρ of -0.66, Kendall's τ of -0.54), that we omitted a further analysis of the outcome.

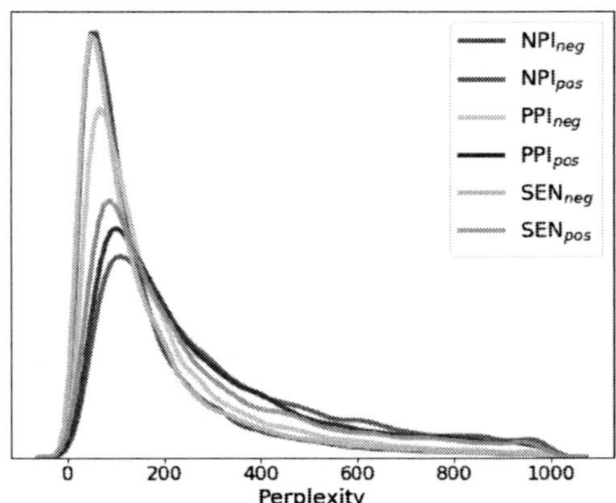

Figure 2: Distribution of perplexity scores for all the sentences.

$PP(\mathbf{NPI}_{neg}) < PP(\mathbf{NPI}_{pos})$ From Figure 3 it is clear that the model has a very strong preference for NPIs to reside inside the negative scope, an observation that is supported by both the perplexity and probability scores. While observable in both plots, this preference is most clearly visible when considering conditional probabilities: the high peak shows that the difference between the probabilities is the most defined of all comparisons that we made.

$PP(\mathbf{NPI}_{neg}) < PP(\mathbf{PPI}_{neg})$ The model has a strong preference for NPIs over PPIs inside negative scope, although this effect is slightly less prevalent in the perplexity scores. This might be partly due to the fact that there exist interpretations for *some* inside negative scope that are correct (the non-emphatic *some*, as described in Section 2). When looking solely at the conditional probabilities the preference becomes clearer, showing similar behavior to the difference between $\mathbf{NPI}_{neg}$ and $\mathbf{NPI}_{pos}$.

$PP(\mathbf{NPI}_{neg}) < PP(\mathbf{PPI}_{pos})$ The original sentences with NPIs are strongly preferred over the rewritten sentences with PPIs, which indicates that the rewriting in general leads to less probable sentences. This finding is confirmed by comparing the perplexities of the original and rewritten sentence *without* the NPI or PPI (dotted line in the left plot in Figure 3): the original sentence containing the licensing context has a lower perplexity than the rewritten sentence in 92.7% of the cases. The profile of the differences between the 2 sentences is somewhat similar to the other comparisons in which the negative context is preferred. Given that

226

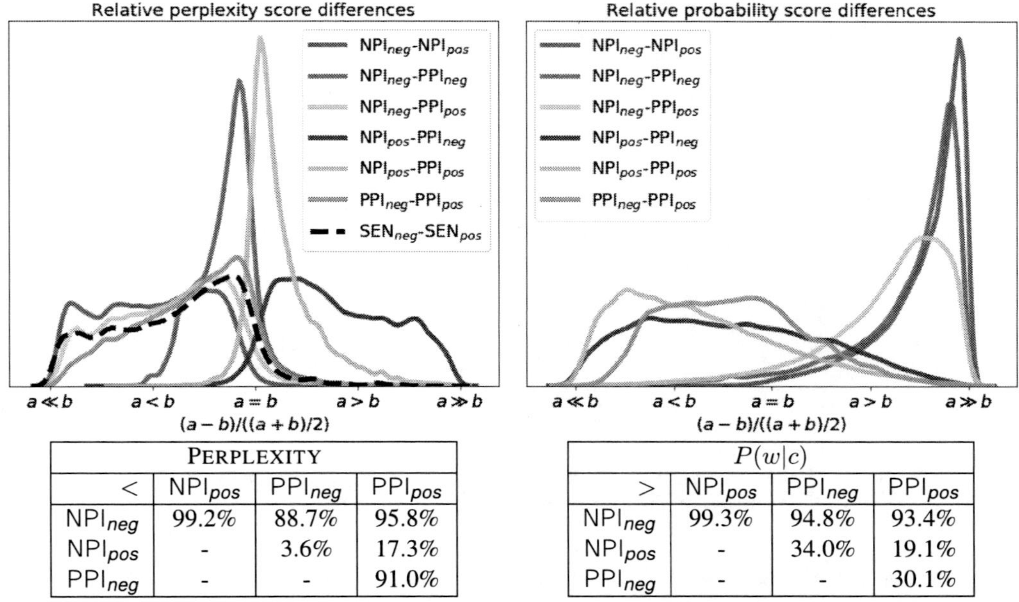

PERPLEXITY			
$<$	NPI_{pos}	PPI_{neg}	PPI_{pos}
NPI_{neg}	99.2%	88.7%	95.8%
NPI_{pos}	-	3.6%	17.3%
PPI_{neg}	-	-	91.0%

$P(w\|c)$			
$>$	NPI_{pos}	PPI_{neg}	PPI_{pos}
NPI_{neg}	99.3%	94.8%	93.4%
NPI_{pos}	-	34.0%	19.1%
PPI_{neg}	-	-	30.1%

Figure 3: Results of perplexity and conditional probability tests. For perplexity a lower score is better, for probability a higher score is better. The plots denote the distribution of the relative differences between the scores of the 6 sentence pairs that are considered.

the considered sentences were taken from natural data, it is not entirely unsurprising that removing or rewriting a scope operator has a negative impact on the probability of the rest of the sentence. This observation, however, does urge care when running experiments like this.

$PP(\mathbf{PPI}_{pos}) < PP(\mathbf{NPI}_{pos})$ When comparing NPIs and PPIs in the rewritten sentences, it turns out that the model does show a clear preference that is not entirely due to a less probable rewriting step. Both the perplexity (17.3%) and probability (19.1%) show that the NPI did in fact strongly depend on the presence of the licensing operator, and not on other words that it was surrounded with. The model is thus able to pick up a signal that makes it prefer a PPI to an NPI in a positive context, even if that positive context was obtained by rewriting it from a negative context.

$PP(\mathbf{PPI}_{neg}) < PP(\mathbf{NPI}_{pos})$ PPIs in a negative context are strongly preferred to NPIs in a faulty positive context: a lower perplexity was assigned to $\mathbf{NPI}_{pos}$ in only 3.6% of the cases. This shows that the model is less strict on the allowed context for PPIs, which might be related to the non-emphatic variant of *some*, as mentioned before.

$PP(\mathbf{PPI}_{neg}) < PP(\mathbf{PPI}_{pos})$ A surprising result is the higher perplexity that is assigned to PPIs inside the original negative context compared to PPIs in the rewritten sentence, which is opposite to what we hypothesized. It is especially remarkable considering the fact that the conditional probability indicates an opposite result (at only 30.1% preference for the original sentence). Once more the outcome of the perplexity comparison might partly be due to the rewriting resulting in a less probable sentence. When solely looking at the conditional probability score, however, we can conclude that the model has a preference for PPIs to reside in positive contexts.

Long distances As shown in Figure 1, most distances between the LC and the NPI are rather short. It might therefore be useful to look at the performance of the model on sentences that contain longer distance dependencies. In Figure 4 the outcomes of the conditional probability task are split out on the distance between the LC and the NPI.

From this plot it follows that the shorter dependencies were mostly responsible for the outcome of our hypotheses. The significant differences between the original sentence and the rewritten sen-

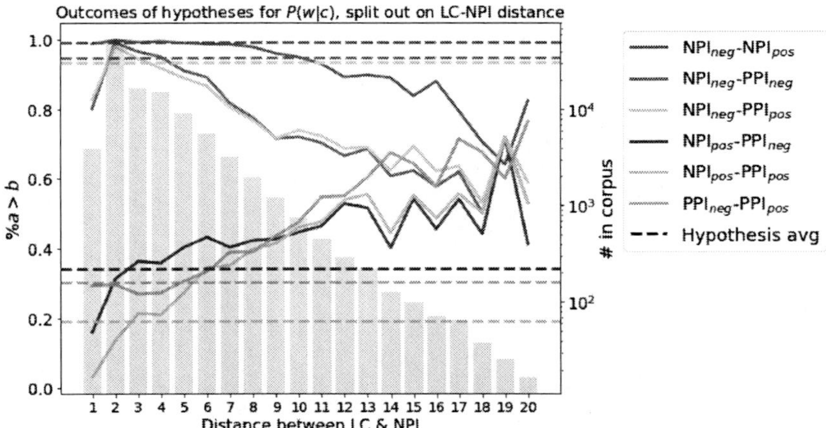

Figure 4: Outcomes for the conditional probability task, split out on the distance between licensing context and NPI. The averages that are reported in Figure 3 are denoted by the dotted lines.

tences **NPI**$_{pos}$ and **PPI**$_{neg}$ becomes less defined when the distance is increased.

This might be partly due to the lower occurrence of these constructions: 47.2% of the sentences in our corpus are situated only 2 positions from each other. Moreover, it would be interesting to see how this behavior matches with that of human judgments.

Conclusion We conclude that the LM is able to detect a signal that indicates a strong relationship between an NPI and its licensing context. By comparing the scores between equivalent sentence constructions we were able to account for possible biases of the model, and showed that the output of the model complied with our own hypotheses in almost all cases.

5 Scope detection

In the previous section, we assessed the ability of a neural LM to handle NPI constructions, based on the probabilities returned by the LM. In the current section, we focus on the hidden states that the LM uses to arrive at a probability distribution over the vocabulary. In particular, we focus on the *scope* of the licensing operator, which determines where an NPI can occur.

Setup

Using the parse tree extraction method described in Section 3, we annotate all sentences in our corpus with the scope of the licensing operator. Following Hupkes et al. (2018), we then train

diagnostic classifiers to predict for each word in the sentence whether it is inside the licensing scope. This is done on the basis of the hidden representation of the LM that is obtained after it just processed this word. We differentiate between 5 different labels: pre-licensing scope words (1), the licensing operator (2), words inside the scope (3), the NPI itself (4), and post-licensing scope words (5). The sentence *The man that died didn't have any relatives, but he died peacefully.*, for example, is annotated as follows:

The$_1$ man$_1$ that$_1$ died$_1$ did$_1$ n't$_2$ have$_3$ any$_4$ relatives$_3$,$_5$ but$_5$ he$_5$ died$_5$ peacefully$_5$.$_5$

The main positions of interest are the transition from within the licensing scope to the post-scope range, and the actual classification of the NPI and LC. Of lesser interest are the pre- and post-licensing scope, as these are both diverse embeddings that do not depend directly on the licensing context itself.

We train our model on the intermediate hidden states of the final layer of the LSTM, using a logistic regression classifier. The decoder of the LM computes the probability distribution over the vocabulary by a linear projection layer from the final hidden state. By using a linear model for classification (such as logistic regression) we can investigate the expressiveness of the hidden state: if the linear model is able to fulfill a classification task, it could be done by the linear decoding layer too.

As a baseline test, we also train a logistic regression model on representations that were acquired by an additive model using GloVe word embeddings (Pennington et al., 2014). Using these embeddings as a baseline we are able to determine the importance of the language model: if it turns out that the LM does not outperform a simple additive model, this indicates that the LM did not add much syntactic information to the word embeddings themselves (or that no syntactic information is required to solve this task). We used 300-dimensional word embeddings that were trained on the English Wikipedia corpus (as is our own LM).

For both tasks (LM and GloVe) we use a subset of 32k NPI sentences which resulted in a total of 250k data points. We use a split of 90% of the data for training, and the other 10% for testing classification accuracy.

Results

The classifier trained on the hidden states of the LM achieved an accuracy of **89.7%** on the test set. The model that was trained on the same dataset using the GloVe baseline scored **72.5%**, showing that the information that is encoded by the LM does in fact contribute significantly to this task. To provide a more qualitative insight into the power of this classifier, we provide 3 remarkable sentences that were classified accurately by the model. Note the correct transition from licensing scope to post-scope, and the correct classification of the NPI and LC in all sentences here.

1. I_1 'd$_1$ <u>never$_2$</u> seen$_3$ **anything$_4$** like$_3$ it$_3$ and$_5$ it$_5$ ...$_5$ was$_5$ ...$_5$ beautiful$_5$.$_5$

2. "$_1$ I_1 do$_1$ <u>n't$_2$</u> think$_3$ I_3 'm$_3$ going$_3$ to$_3$ come$_3$ to$_3$ you$_3$ for$_3$ reassurance$_3$ **anymore$_4$** ,$_5$ "$_5$ Sibyl$_5$ grumbled$_5$.$_5$

3. But$_1$ when$_1$ it$_1$ comes$_1$ to$_1$ you$_1$,$_1$ I_1 'm$_1$ <u>not$_2$</u> taking$_3$ **any$_4$** more$_3$ risks$_3$ than$_3$ we$_3$ have$_3$ to$_3$.$_5$

We ran a small evaluation on a set of 3000 sentences (47020 tokens), of which 56.8% were classified completely correctly. Using the GloVe classifier only 22.1% of the sentences are classified flawlessly. We describe the classification results in the confusion matrices that are displayed in Figure 5.

Looking at the results on the LSTM embeddings, it appears that the post-licensing scope tokens (5) were misclassified most frequently: only

75.2% of those data points were classified correctly. The most common misclassification for this class is class 3: an item inside the licensing scope. This shows that for some sentences it is hard to distinguish the actual border of the licensing scope, although 90.3% of the first post-scope embeddings (i.e. the first embedding after the scope has ended) were classified correctly. The lower performance of the model on this class is mostly due to longer sentences in which a large part of the post-licensing scope was classified incorrectly. This causes the model to pick up a noisy signal that trips up the predictions for these tokens. It is promising, however, that the NPIs (4) and licensing operator items (2) themselves are classified with a very high accuracy, as well as the tokens inside the licensing scope (3). When comparing this to the performance on the GloVe embeddings, it turns out that that classifier has a strong bias towards the licensing scope class (3). This highlights the power of the LSTM embeddings, revealing that is not a trivial task at all to correctly classify the boundaries of the context scope. We therefore conclude that the information that is relevant to NPI constructions can be accurately extracted from the sentence representations, and furthermore that our neural LM has a significant positive influence on encoding that structural information.

6 Conclusion

We ran several diagnostic tasks to investigate the ability of a neural language model to handle NPIs. From the results on the perplexity task we conclude that the model is capable to detect the relationship between an NPI and the licensing contexts that we considered. We showed that the language model is able to pick up a distinct signal that indicates a strong relationship between a negative polarity item and its licensing context. By comparing the perplexities of the NPI constructions to those of the equivalent PPIs, it follows that removing the licensing operator has a remarkably different effect on the NPIs than on the PPIs. This effect, however, does seem to vanish when the distance between the NPI and licensing context is increased. From our scope detection task it followed that the licensing signal that the LM detects can in fact be extracted from the hidden representations, providing further evidence of the ability of the model in handling NPIs. There are many other

LSTM Embeddings					
	Correct label				
Pred.	1	2	3	4	5
1	**14891**	83	408	2	760
2	203	**2870**	42	0	59
3	850	42	**14555**	15	1286
4	13	1	32	**3005**	44
5	520	11	821	0	**6507**
Total	16477	3007	15858	3022	8656

GloVe embeddings					
	Correct label				
Pred.	1	2	3	4	5
1	**11166**	87	1077	0	249
2	178	**1847**	82	0	0
3	4708	1072	**14166**	353	4003
4	17	0	84	**2669**	36
5	408	1	449	0	**4368**
Total	16477	3007	15858	3022	8656

Figure 5: Confusion matrices for the scope detection task trained on the embeddings of an LSTM and the averages of GloVe embeddings.

natural language phenomena related to language scope, and we hope that our methods presented here can provide an inspiration for future research, trying to link linguistics theory to neural models.

The setup of our second experiment, for example, would translate easily to the detection of the nuclear scope of quantifiers. In particular, we believe it would be interesting to look at a wider typological range of NPI constructions, and investigate how our diagnostic tasks translate to other types of such constructions. Furthermore, the findings of our experiments could be compared to those of human judgments syntactic gap filling task. These judgments could also provide more insight into the grammaticality of the rewritten sentences.

The hypotheses that are described in Section 2 and several others that are mentioned in the literature on NPIs are strongly based on a specific kind of entailment relation that should hold for the contexts in which NPIs reside. An interesting follow-up experiment that would provide a stronger link with the literature in formal linguistics on the subject matter, would be based on devising several entailment tasks that are based on the various hypotheses that exists for NPI licensing contexts. It would be interesting to see whether the model is able to detect whether a context is downward entailing, for example, or if it has more difficulty identifying non-veridical contexts. This would then also create a stronger insight in the semantic information that is stored in the encodings of the model. Such experiments would, however, require the creation of a rich artificial dataset, which would give much more control in determining the inner workings of the LSTM, and is perhaps a necessary step to gain a thorough insight in the LM encodings from a linguistic perspective.

Acknowledgements

We thank the reviewers, Samira Abnar, and Willem Zuidema for their useful and constructive feedback. DH is funded by the Netherlands Organization for Scientific Research (NWO), through a Gravitation Grant 024.001.006 to the Language in Interaction Consortium.

References

Chris Barker. 2018. Negative polarity as scope marking. *Linguistics and Philosophy*, pages 1–28.

Alexis Conneau, German Kruszewski, Guillaume Lample, Loïc Barrault, and Marco Baroni. 2018. What you can cram into a single vector: Probing sentence embeddings for linguistic properties. *arXiv preprint arXiv:1805.01070*.

Anastasia Giannakidou. 1994. The semantic licensing of npis and the modern greek subjunctive. *Language and cognition*, 4:55–68.

Anastasia Giannakidou. 2008. Negative and positive polarity items: Variation, licensing, and compositionality. In Claudia Maienborn, Klaus von Heusinger, and Paul Porner, editors, *Semantics: An international handbook of natural language meaning. Berlin: Mouton de Gruyter*, pages 1660–1712.

Kristina Gulordava, Piotr Bojanowski, Edouard Grave, Tal Linzen, and Marco Baroni. 2018. Colorless green recurrent networks dream hierarchically. pages 1195–1205.

M. Haspelmath. 1997. *Indefinite Pronouns*. Oxford Studies in Typology and. Clarendon Press.

Jack Hoeksema. 2012. On the natural history of negative polarity items. *Linguistic Analysis*, 38(1):3.

Dieuwke Hupkes, Sara Veldhoen, and Willem Zuidema. 2018. Visualisation and 'diagnostic classifiers' reveal how recurrent and recursive neural networks process hierarchical structure. *Journal of Artificial Intelligence Research*, 61:907–926.

W.A. Ladusaw. 1980. *Polarity sensitivity as inherent scope relations*. Outstanding dissertations in linguistics. Garland Pub.

Jey Han Lau, Alexander Clark, and Shalom Lappin. 2017. Grammaticality, acceptability, and probability: a probabilistic view of linguistic knowledge. *Cognitive Science*, 41(5):1202–1241.

Tal Linzen, Emmanuel Dupoux, and Yoav Goldberg. 2016. Assessing the ability of lstms to learn syntax-sensitive dependencies. *Transactions of the Association for Computational Linguistics*, 4:521–535.

Jean-Baptiste Michel, Yuan Kui Shen, Aviva Presser Aiden, Adrian Veres, Matthew K. Gray, , Joseph P. Pickett, Dale Hoiberg, Dan Clancy, Peter Norvig, Jon Orwant, Steven Pinker, Martin A. Nowak, and Erez Lieberman Aiden. 2011. Quantitative analysis of culture using millions of digitized books. *Science*, 331(6014):176–182.

Adam Pauls and Dan Klein. 2012. Large-scale syntactic language modeling with treelets. In *Proceedings of the 50th Annual Meeting of the Association for Computational Linguistics: Long Papers-Volume 1*, pages 959–968. Association for Computational Linguistics.

Jeffrey Pennington, Richard Socher, and Christopher Manning. 2014. Glove: Global vectors for word representation. In *Proceedings of the 2014 conference on empirical methods in natural language processing (EMNLP)*, pages 1532–1543.

Ke Tran, Arianna Bisazza, and Christof Monz. 2018. The importance of being recurrent for modeling hierarchical structure. *arXiv preprint arXiv:1803.03585*.

Z. Vendler. 1967. *Linguistics in philosophy*. G - Reference, Information and Interdisciplinary Subjects Series. Cornell University Press.

Closing Brackets with Recurrent Neural Networks

Natalia Skachkova,[*] **Thomas A. Trost**,[*] **Adam Kusmirek** and **Dietrich Klakow**
Spoken Language Systems
Saarland University
Saarland Informatics Campus
66123 Saarbrücken, Germany
`{s9naskac@stud,{thomas.trost,akusmirek,dietrich.klakow}@lsv}.uni-saarland.de`

Abstract

Many natural and formal languages contain words or symbols that require a matching counterpart for making an expression well-formed. The combination of opening and closing brackets is a typical example of such a construction. Due to their commonness, the ability to follow such rules is important for language modeling. Currently, recurrent neural networks (RNNs) are extensively used for this task. We investigate whether they are capable of learning the rules of opening and closing brackets by applying them to synthetic Dyck languages that consist of different types of brackets. We provide an analysis of the statistical properties of these languages as a baseline and show strengths and limits of Elman-RNNs, GRUs and LSTMs in experiments on random samples of these languages. In terms of perplexity and prediction accuracy, the RNNs get close to the theoretical baseline in most cases.

1 Introduction

Brackets are a challenge for language models. They regularly appear in texts, they typically produce long-range dependencies, and a failure to properly close them is readily recognized by a human evaluator as a severe error (Shen et al., 2017). Beyond the syntactical level, many natural languages exhibit brackets-like structures. For example, the German language is infamous for its convoluted sentences with verb-particle constructions, in which words from the beginning have to be properly closed at the end (Dewell, 2011; Müller et al., 2015).

In this paper we present a dedicated study of the capability of Elman-RNNs, GRUs and LSTMs to model expressions with brackets and properly close them. Towards this end, we conduct experiments on Dyck languages, which consist of balanced bracket expressions.

1.1 Related Work

Synthetic datasets and formal languages have long been used for checking the ability of RNNs to capture a particular feature. For example, Elman (1990), Das et al. (1992), or Gers and Schmidhuber (2001) already did such investigations. Recent work in this direction was done by Weiss et al. (2017, 2018).

More specifically, the interplay of RNNs with certain grammatical constructs, brackets and Dyck languages has been the subject of several studies. Karpathy et al. (2016) show that RNNs are capable of capturing bracket structures on real-world datasets. Linzen et al. (2016) study the application of LSTMs to certain grammatical phenomena. RNNs and their variants have been used for recognizing Dyck words (Kalinke and Lehmann, 1998; Deleu and Dureau, 2016). Li et al. (2017) evaluate their nonlinear weighted finite automata model on a Dyck language. Most recently, Bernardy (2018) conducted a very similar study to ours on Dyck languages with a slightly different focus.

1.2 Contributions

In this work, we sample Dyck words in such a way that we can give theoretical lower bounds for the perplexity of a respective language model. This way, we can compare the performance of RNNs with a theoretical baseline and not just with the performance of other architectures.

2 Dyck Languages

We use artificially generated data in order to have a completely controlled environment for the experiments. In particular, the training and test datasets consist of balanced sequences of n different types

---

[*] Both authors contributed equally.

Proceedings of the 2018 EMNLP Workshop BlackboxNLP: Analyzing and Interpreting Neural Networks for NLP, pages 232–239
Brussels, Belgium, November 1, 2018. ©2018 Association for Computational Linguistics

of brackets, $(_1,)_1, (_2,)_2, \ldots$, where n depends on the specific experiment. The set of such sequences forms the so-called *Dyck language* D_n (Duchon, 2000). Elements of D_n are called *Dyck words*. Each D_n is a context-free but not regular formal language (Chomsky, 1956) and can be described by the grammar:

$$S \to \epsilon \tag{1a}$$

$$S \to SS \tag{1b}$$

$$S \to (_iS)_i \quad \forall i \in \{1, \ldots, n\} \tag{1c}$$

Some examples of such Dyck words are:

$$(_1 \, (_1 \,)_1 \,)_1$$
$$(_2 \,)_2 \, (_1 \,)_1 \, (_3 \, (_1 \,)_1 \,)_3$$
$$(_1 \, (_1 \,)_1 \, (_1 \,)_1 \, (_1 \,)_1 \, (_1 \,)_1 \,)_1$$

It is well-known that there are $C_m := \frac{1}{m+1}\binom{2m}{m}$ words of length $2m$ in D_1, where C_m is the m-th *Catalan number* (Chung and Feller, 1949). As the type of each pair of brackets can independently be chosen, it follows that there are $n^m C_m$ words of length $2m$ in D_n. There are obviously no Dyck words with odd length.

2.1 Generation of Dyck Words

Each "sentence" in the datasets is a randomly generated non-empty Dyck word. The first symbol of a word is always an open bracket. From there, the generation proceeds in a sequential manner: With probability p an open bracket is emitted. Otherwise and thus with probability $p - 1$, a matching closed bracket is emitted or the generation terminates if all open brackets already have a matching partner. If not stated otherwise, we assume $0 < p < 1$ in all calculations because the edge cases usually have to be treated differently but do not add significant value to our discussion. The type of bracket is chosen randomly from a uniform distribution but might follow some other distribution for future studies.

2.2 Statistical Properties of Dyck Words

We quickly review some statistical properties of such sequences for explaining choices in the setups and in order to get a baseline for the experiments. It can readily be seen that the sequences of length $2m$ all have the same probability:

$$\frac{1}{n^m}p^{m-1}(1-p)^{m+1} \tag{2}$$

The asymmetry in the exponents is due to leaving out empty sequences. The factor n^{-m} accounts

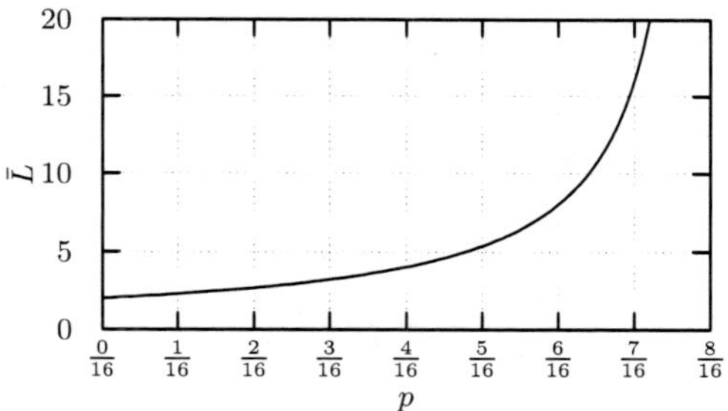

Figure 1: Average length of generated sequences, based on Eq. (4).

for the equally probable choices of brackets types. We can check consistency by considering the normalization condition:

$$\sum_{k=1}^{\infty} C_k p^{k-1}(1-p)^{k+1} = \begin{cases} 1 & \text{for } p \leq \frac{1}{2} \\ \frac{(1-p)^2}{p^2} & \text{for } p > \frac{1}{2} \end{cases} \tag{3}$$

While the result for $p \leq \frac{1}{2}$ is expected, the case $p > \frac{1}{2}$ might appear curious at first. The reason for this behaviour is that the sum only takes finite sequences into account, while there is a nonzero probability for getting infinite sequences for $p > \frac{1}{2}$. This is easily seen for the case $p = 1$, where brackets are never closed so that the overall probability of obtaining a finite sequence is indeed zero.

2.2.1 Average Length

This naturally leads to the question what the average length $\bar{L}$ of the sequences is, depending on p. For $p < \frac{1}{2}$, we find

$$\bar{L} = 2\sum_{k=1}^{\infty} kC_k p^{k-1}(1-p)^{k+1} = \frac{2}{1-2p}. \tag{4}$$

The graph of this function can be seen in Fig. 1. In line with our previous findings, problems with infinite sequences arise for $p \geq \frac{1}{2}$, as the expression (4) diverges for $p = \frac{1}{2}$. For these reasons, we only consider the case $p < \frac{1}{2}$ in the experiments.

2.2.2 Baseline for Perplexity

A prediction system for the next symbol emitted by the generator will not be able to perform arbitrarily well due to the random nature of the process. In order to get a baseline for the performance, we consider the perplexity per symbol PP of the probability distribution of the generated Dyck languages. For a sequence of symbols w

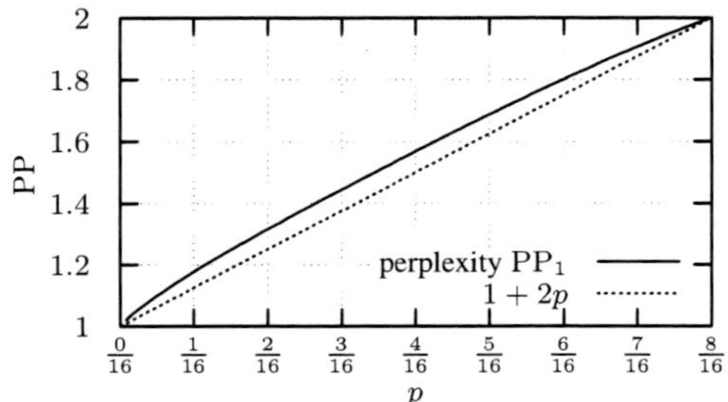

Figure 2: Perplexity PP$_1$ of distribution of D_1, cf. (7). As a reference, the graph of $1+2p$ is given.

with length $|w|$ it is defined as

$$\mathrm{PP} := 2^{-\frac{1}{|w|}\sum_{i=1}^{|w|}\log_2 P(w_i|w_1,\ldots,w_{i-1})}, \quad (5)$$

where $P(w_i|w_1,\ldots,w_{i-1})$ is the probability of the i-th symbol under the model, given the previous $i-1$ symbols. Eq. (5) corresponds to the way in which perplexity is calculated by the software that we use for our experiments (cf. Sec. 3).

We estimate the baseline for the perplexity PP$_n$ for the language D_n by considering (5) under the true probability model in the limit of an infinite amount of samples from the corresponding probability distribution. Under these conditions and for our case, (5) can be transformed into:

$$\log_2 \mathrm{PP}_n = -\lim_{L\to\infty}\lim_{N\to\infty}\frac{\sum_{\ell=1}^{L}\frac{N_\ell}{N}\log_2 P_\ell}{\sum_{\ell=1}^{L}\frac{N_\ell}{N}(2\ell+1)} \quad (6)$$

The numerator contains the sum of the log-probabilities, where P_ℓ is the probability of a Dyck word with 2ℓ brackets. The denominator represents the total number of symbols. Adding one to the length in the term $(2\ell+1)$ accounts for the end-of-sentence symbols that are counted by the software. The limit $L \to \infty$ for the maximum length of a word is taken at the end because the normalization by the number of symbols has to be carried out for a finite value. Finally, N represents the number of samples and N_ℓ stands for the number of words with 2ℓ brackets in the dataset, so that $\frac{N_\ell}{N}$ converges to the probability of generating a word of this length.

All these quantities are known, so that we can obtain the following result:

$$\mathrm{PP}_n = n^{\frac{1}{3-2p}}\frac{1}{\sqrt{p(1-p)}}\left(\frac{p^3}{1-p}\right)^{\frac{1-2p}{6-4p}} \quad (7)$$

While the expression (7) with its singularity at zero does not readily reveal the characteristics of the perplexity, its graph (Fig. 2) shows that it is close to a simple affine function. In the edge cases it behaves just like expected: $p = 0$ means that there is no randomness at all and there is just one possible next symbol. For $p = \frac{1}{2}$ however, opening and closing brackets are equally likely, so that there are always two symbols to choose from without any way to tell which to prefer. The dependence on n must be sublinear because for closing brackets the type is uniquely predictable.

3 Neural Network Architecture

We use three different RNN architectures for our experiments: Elman-RNN (abbreviated as SRNN for *simple* RNN), GRU (*gated recurrent unit*), and LSTM (*long short-term memory*).

For the experiments with SRNNs we use the RNNLM toolkit (version 0.3e) developed by Mikolov et al. (2011b). The SRNN has one hidden layer of arbitrary size N_{hidden} with a sigmoid activation function. At each time step the input vector is built by concatenating the vector of the current word and the output produced by the hidden layer during the previous time step. The next word is predicted by applying the softmax function to the last layer. The RNNLM toolkit offers the possibility to group words into classes (Mikolov et al., 2011a), but this feature is more interesting for boosting efficiency in cases of large vocabularies with a natural frequency distribution. After initializing the weights with random Gaussian noise, the training of the SRNNs is performed using the standard stochastic gradient descent algorithm with an initial learning rate $\alpha = 0.1$ and the recurrent weight is trained by the truncated backpropagation through time algorithm (Rumelhart et al., 1985). We refer to the respective hyperparameter that specifies the number of time steps taken into account as T_{BPTT}.

For the other more elaborate architectures, we make use of TF-NNLM-TK[1] by Oualil et al. (2016) which provides implementations of LSTM and GRU networks. LSTMs and GRUs work similar to SRNNs but exhibit specific units that allow for storing previous activations and for tracking long-term dependencies in a more flexible and efficient way. In the case of LSTMs, the memory state is being handled via input, forget and output

---

[1]https://github.com/uds-lsv/TF-NNLM-TK

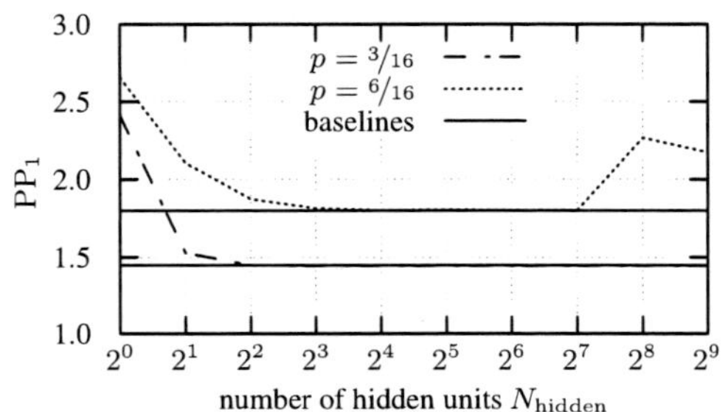

Figure 3: Test perplexity PP_1 vs. number of hidden units N_{hidden} for SRNN. Both curves reach their respective baseline, given in (7).

n	1	2	3	4	5
baseline	1.444	1.881	2.195	2.449	2.667
GRU	1.450	1.900	2.204	2.488	2.691
LSTM	1.451	1.899	2.203	2.486	2.688
RNN	1.445	1.873	2.205	2.445	2.669

(a) For $p = {}^3/_{16}$.

n	1	2	3	4	5
baseline	1.800	2.450	2.934	3.334	3.682
GRU	1.808	2.483	2.995	3.396	3.775
LSTM	1.810	2.481	2.995	3.401	3.771
RNN	1.804	2.494	3.030	3.499	3.885

(b) For $p = {}^6/_{16}$.

Table 1: Baseline respectively mean test perplexity PP_n for T_{BPTT} settings between 1 and 16 in steps of 1 for different architectures (cf. Fig. 4 for a graphical representation of the SRNN values). The standard deviation is roughly around 0.001 and slightly larger for the SRNN.

gate. Those gates allow to decide on the amount of a cell state that should be preserved or forgotten and the amount that should be passed to the cells in the next layer of the network. Similarly, the GRU regulates its memory state using an update and a reset gate that allows to either delete the previous cell state and decide on the amount of the current activation that should be added to the current cell state. For the experiments with LSTMs and GRUs the hyperparameter settings are chosen to be similar to the ones used with the RNNLM toolkit. Weights are again initialized using random Gaussian noise and standard stochastic gradient descent is utilized. The initial learning rate is set to $\alpha = 0.1$ and in later training epochs decayed using a factor of $\gamma = 0.9$. The models are trained for 100 epochs using a batch size of 128 and $T_{BPTT} = 16$ (if not stated otherwise) with learning rate decay starting at epoch 80.

4 Experiments

4.1 Setup and Perplexities

We conduct a number of experiments for investigating the overall performance and the influence of the hyperparameters on the perplexity. For all experiments we use datasets that were artificially generated in the previously described way (cf. Sec 2.1). All training sets contain 131,072 Dyck words, while the test sets contain 10,000 Dyck words that were sampled from the same distribution. In all experiments, the value of p is varied between $1/16$ and $7/16$ in steps of $1/16$. The ratio behind this choice is that $7/16$ yields an average sequence length of 16, which is roughly a typical sentence length for natural languages (Sichel, 1974; Sigurd et al., 2004). The smaller values of p are considered for comparison.

In a first set of experiments, we consider D_1 and vary the number of hidden units between 1 and 512, doubling the hidden layer size in each iteration. Having more than 512 units does not bring much perplexity improvement but slows down the training process considerably. Typical results for the Elman-RNN can be found in Fig. 3. For all values of p, the test time perplexity reaches the baseline. The convergence is slower for larger values of p, which is the expected behavior. For larger values of N_{hidden} there are some increases of PP_1 that are most probably connected to the specific software implementation. Despite that, the models are surprisingly good at recovering the baseline. All in all we conclude that $N_{hidden} = 64$ is a good compromise between optimization for perplexity and speed.

In a second set of experiments, we change T_{BPTT} from 0 to 16, increasing its size by one in each iteration. We limit T_{BPTT} with 16 as this is the maximum expected length of a sentence in our setting. This time, we do not only vary p, but also the number of types of brackets n. Typical results can be seen in Fig. 4. It is striking that T_{BPTT} has hardly any influence on the performance as long as it is larger than zero. This can be exploited for making the comparison easier: The average value of the test perplexities for the different architectures is given in Tab. 1. The values give a good impression of where the curves saturate. Higher values of p and n appear to make the task more

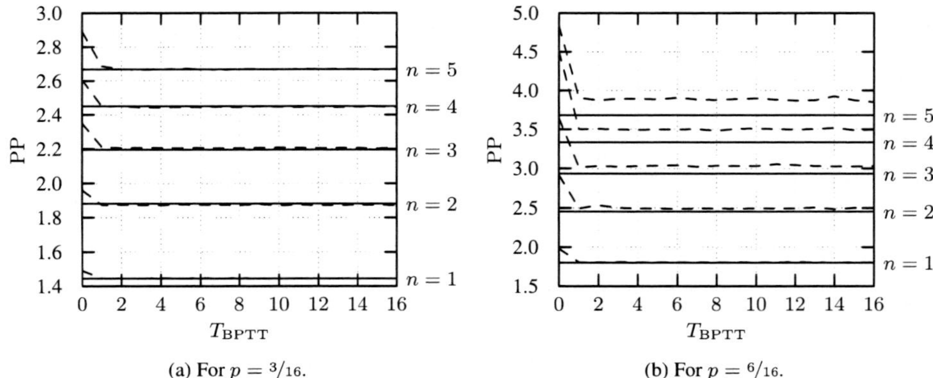

(a) For $p = 3/16$.   (b) For $p = 6/16$.

Figure 4: Test perplexity PP_n vs. hyperparameter T_{BPTT} for Dyck languages with different numbers of types of brackets, obtained with the Elman-RNN. The respective baselines (cf. Eq. (7)) are plotted as solid lines.

p	n	$\bar{L}$	$\bar{\ell}$	SRNN	GRU	LSTM
$3/16$	1	3.191	2.586	1.00	1.000	1.000
$3/16$	2	3.222	2.611	0.978	0.9998	1.000
$3/16$	4	3.183	2.609	0.960	0.9994	1.000
$6/16$	1	8.049	4.976	1.00	0.9997	0.9999
$6/16$	2	7.941	4.936	0.742	0.9982	0.9996
$6/16$	4	8.095	5.079	0.966	0.9959	0.9998

Table 2: Accuracy for the task of finding the last bracket of a Dyck word, together with measured values for the average length $\bar{L}$ of the words and the average length of the task $\bar{\ell}$ (see the text for a definition).

challenging. While all curves rsp. values are close to the baseline in Fig. 4a and Tab. 1a, the gap increases with n in Fig. 4b and Tab. 1b. Given that the average length of Dyck words for $p = 3/16$ is only 3.2, compared to a length of 8 for $p = 6/16$, the differences in the performance is not surprising. While the Elman-RNN performs similar or even slightly better than the other architectures for the easier tasks, the more elaborate methods increasingly outperform it with increasing task difficulty.

4.2 Accuracy

Based on the results of the previous section, the RNNs appear to perform quite well in terms of the perplexity. In order to get a better feeling for the capability of the networks, we consider a second task: Given a Dyck word without the last closing bracket, the RNN has to predict the most likely candidate for this missing symbol. The success is

measured in terms of accuracy, which is the number of successfully finished tasks divided by the total number of tasks. The respective values, based on a dataset of 10000 Dyck words, are given in Tab. 2. Except for one case, the RNNs reach an accuracy close to one. Only one experiment is done per configuration and even harder tasks appear to be solvable, so the lower value is probably just an outlier. GRU and in particular LSTM perform almost perfectly in this task.

Some additional statistics are given in the table. The average word length $\bar{L}$ indeed follows (4). Besides that, a new quantity is introduced here: The average length of the task $\bar{\ell}$ measures how far the algorithm has to look back in order to find the open brackets it has to close on average. The difference between length L and task length ℓ is best illustrated with an example. For the Dyck word

$$(_2 \, (_1 \,)_1 \,)_2 \, \underbrace{(_1 \, (_1 \,)_1 \, (_3 \,)_3 \, \boxed{)_1}}_{\text{task length } \ell \, = \, 6},$$

the length is ten but the task length is six because the first four brackets are irrelevant for determining the last one, which is boxed for emphasis. The task length is the relevant measure for the hardness of the task, because small values of $\bar{\ell}$ would mean that there are hardly any long-range dependencies. For $p = 6/16$, $\bar{\ell}$ lies around five, so we would expect to need at least a five-gram model or something equivalent for achieving good results in this task.

The full frequency distribution of length and task length can be seen in Fig. 6. By far the largest

236

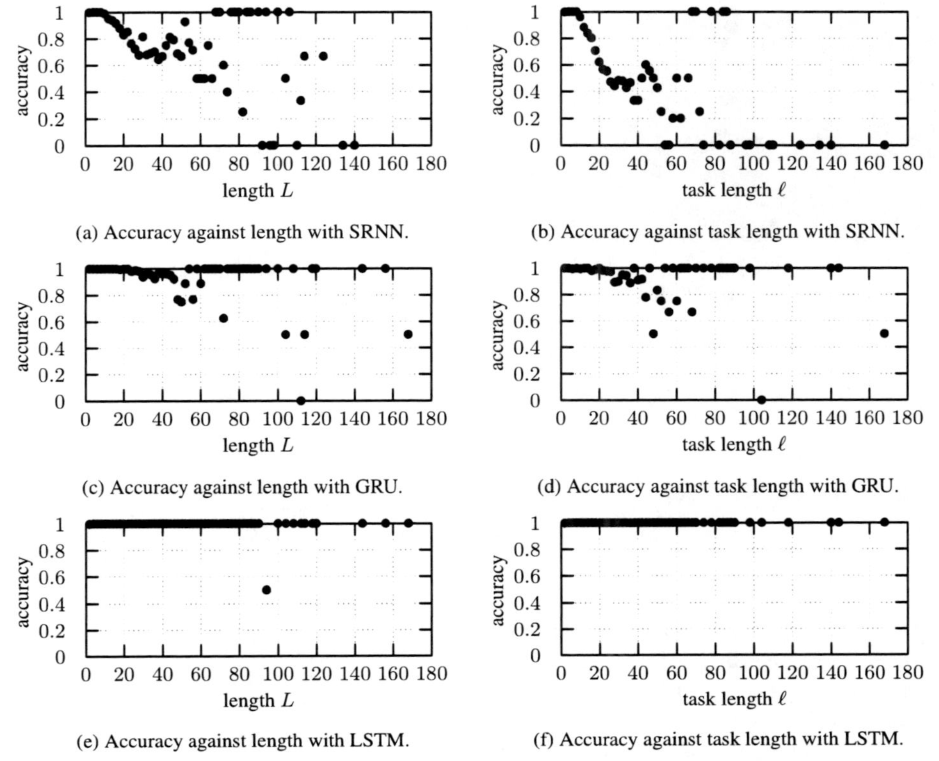

(a) Accuracy against length with SRNN.

(b) Accuracy against task length with SRNN.

(c) Accuracy against length with GRU.

(d) Accuracy against task length with GRU.

(e) Accuracy against length with LSTM.

(f) Accuracy against task length with LSTM.

Figure 5: Accuracy depending on length respectively task length (see the text for a definition) for different architectures. Data from the experiments with $p = 6/16$ and $n = 4$.

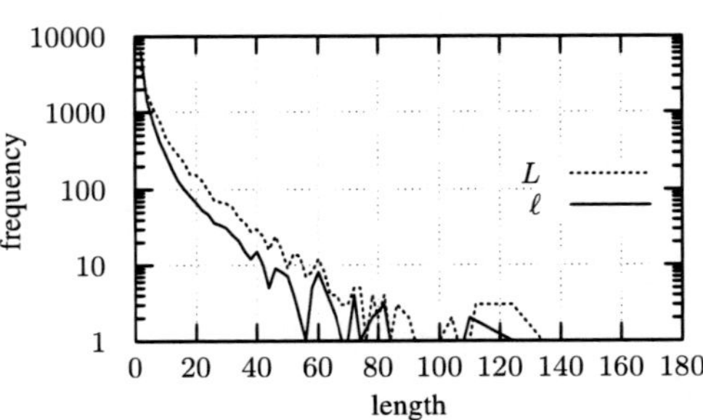

Figure 6: Histogram for length and task length for the experiment with $p = 6/16$ and $n = 4$.

part of the distribution is distributed over small values, so the really long words do not play a big role in the statistics. This naturally raises the question how the RNNs perform for those. Fig. 5 reveals that the performance indeed depends on the length of the sequence respectively the task length and that there are huge differences between the architectures. Only the bigger picture can be compared because the test sets differ between the ar-

chitectures. While the Elman-RNN reaches perfect accuracy for lengths of up to eight symbols, the GRU gets along very well with lengths of up to 20 symbols. After that, the performance breaks in for these networks. Due to the low number of samples, the curve is very noisy for intermediate values, so it is hard to draw conclusions for this region. There is not a single correct guess by the Elman-RNN for task lengths beyond 90. The LSTM once again performs best in this task and exhibits an almost perfect accuracy over the whole spectrum of lengths.

Finally, the kind of error that is made is of interest. A good representation of that is the confusion matrix given in Fig. 7. For our task, the true bracket is always a closing one. Interestingly, the SRNN appears to "understand" that and hardly ever chooses an opening one. Apart from that Fig. 7 reveals that the SRNN does not consider the different types of brackets as equally likely, otherwise the probability mass would be distributed more evenly.

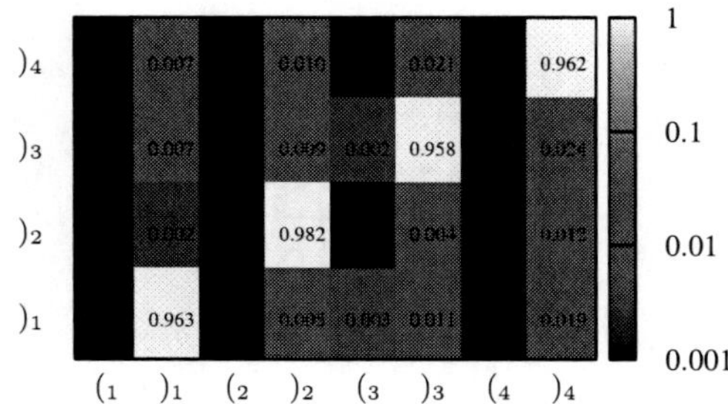

Figure 7: Confusion matrix: Probability of confusing the correct brackets on the y-axis with those on the x-axis, measured with the Elman-RNN for $p = 6/16$ and $n = 4$. Only non-zero values are given in the plot.

5 Conclusion and Outlook

We evaluated the capability of different RNNs to model an artificial language that consists of convoluted bracket expressions. In terms of perplexity, the models easily get close to the theoretical baseline in most cases. For the task of predicting the last bracket of a sequence, the Elman-RNN mostly reaches accuracies between 0.96 and 1 and hardly ever chooses an opening bracket, while GRU and LSTM score almost perfectly. Based on such good results, our plans for future work are to make the task harder by extending the artificial language. This would help to better carve out the weaknesses of particular architectures. In this context, an important point would be some kind of control over the long-range dependencies.

Acknowledgments

This work was supported in part by the German Research Foundation (DFG) as part of SFB1102. We thank Andrea Fischer for fruitful discussions.

References

Jean-Philippe Bernardy. 2018. Can Recurrent Neural Networks Learn Nested Recursion? *Linguistic Issues in Language Technology*, 16(1).

N. Chomsky. 1956. Three models for the description of language. *IEEE Transactions on Information Theory*, 2(3):113–124.

Kai Lai Chung and William Feller. 1949. On Fluctuations in Coin-tossing. *Proceedings of the National Academy of Sciences*, 35(10):605–608.

Sreerupa Das, C. Lee Giles, and Guo-Zheng Sun. 1992. Learning Context-free Grammars: Capabilities and Limitations of a Recurrent Neural Network with an External Stack Memory. In *Proceedings of The Fourteenth Annual Conference of Cognitive Science Society*, page 14, Bloomington, IN, USA.

Tristan Deleu and Joseph Dureau. 2016. Learning Operations on a Stack with Neural Turing Machines. *Computing Research Repository*, arXiv:1612.00827.

Robert B. Dewell. 2011. *The Meaning of Particle / Prefix Constructions in German*, volume 34 of *Human Cognitive Processing*. John Benjamins Publishing Company.

Philippe Duchon. 2000. On the enumeration and generation of generalized Dyck words. *Discrete Mathematics*, 225(1-3):121–135.

Jeffrey L. Elman. 1990. Finding Structure in Time. *Cognitive science*, 14(2):179–211.

Felix A. Gers and Jürgen Schmidhuber. 2001. LSTM recurrent networks learn simple context-free and context-sensitive languages. *IEEE Transactions on Neural Networks*, 12(6):1333–1340.

Yvonne Kalinke and Helko Lehmann. 1998. Computation in recurrent neural networks: From counters to iterated function systems. *Lecture Notes in Computer Science*, 1502:179–190.

Andrej Karpathy, Justin Johnson, and Li Fei-Fei. 2016. Visualizing and Understanding Recurrent Networks. In *International Conference on Learning Representations, Workshop Track*.

Tianyu Li, Guillaume Rabusseau, and Doina Precup. 2017. Neural Network Based Nonlinear Weighted Finite Automata. *Computing Research Repository*, arXiv:1709.04380.

Tal Linzen, Emmanuel Dupoux, and Yoav Goldberg. 2016. Assessing the Ability of LSTMs to Learn Syntax-Sensitive Dependencies. *Transactions of the Association for Computational Linguistics*, 4:521–535.

Tomáš Mikolov, Stefan Kombrink, Lukáš Burget, Jan Černocký, and Sanjeev Khudanpur. 2011a. Extensions of Recurrent Neural Network Language Model. In *Acoustics, Speech and Signal Processing (ICASSP), 2011 IEEE International Conference on*, pages 5528–5531. IEEE.

Tomáš Mikolov, Stefan Kombrink, Anoop Deoras, Lukáš Burget, and Jan Honza Černocký. 2011b. RNNLM – Recurrent Neural Network Language Modeling Toolkit. In *ASRU 2011 Demo Session*, Waikoloa, HI, USA.

Peter O. Müller, Ingeborg Ohnheiser, Susan Olsen, and Franz Rainer. 2015. *Word-Formation: An International Handbook of the Languages of Europe*, volume 40.1 of *Handbooks of Linguistics and Communication Science*. De Gruyter Mouton.

Youssef Oualil, Mittul Singh, Clayton Greenberg, and Dietrich Klakow. 2016. Long-short range context neural networks for language modeling. In *Proceedings of the 2016 Conference on Empirical Methods in Natural Language Processing*, pages 1473–1481, Austin, Texas.

David E. Rumelhart, Geoffrey E. Hinton, and Ronald J. Williams. 1985. Learning Internal Representations by Error Propagation. Technical report, University of California San Diego, La Jolla Institute for Cognitive Science.

Xiaoyu Shen, Youssef Oualil, Clayton Greenberg, Mittul Singh, and Dietrich Klakow. 2017. Estimation of gap between current language models and human performance. In *Proceedings of the 18th Annual Conference of the International Speech Communication Association*, pages 553–557, Stockholm, Sweden.

H. S. Sichel. 1974. On a Distribution Representing Sentence-Length in Written Prose. *Journal of the Royal Statistical Society. Series A (General)*, 137(1):25.

Bengt Sigurd, Mats Eeg-Olofsson, and Joost van Weijer. 2004. Word length, sentence length and frequency – Zipf revisited. *Studia Linguistica*, 58(1):37–52.

Gail Weiss, Yoav Goldberg, and Eran Yahav. 2017. Extracting automata from recurrent neural networks using queries and counterexamples. *Computing Research Repository*, arXiv:1711.09576.

Gail Weiss, Yoav Goldberg, and Eran Yahav. 2018. On the practical computational power of finite precision rnns for language recognition. *Computing Research Repository*, arXiv:1805.04908.

Under the Hood: Using Diagnostic Classifiers to Investigate and Improve how Language Models Track Agreement Information

Mario Giulianelli
University of Amsterdam

Jack Harding
University of Amsterdam

Florian Mohnert
University of Amsterdam

{mario.giulianelli, jack.harding, florian.mohnert}@student.uva.nl

Dieuwke Hupkes
ILLC, University of Amsterdam
d.hupkes@uva.nl

Willem Zuidema
ILLC, University of Amsterdam
w.h.zuidema@uva.nl

Abstract

How do neural language models keep track of number agreement between subject and verb? We show that 'diagnostic classifiers', trained to predict number from the internal states of a language model, provide a detailed understanding of how, when, and where this information is represented. Moreover, they give us insight into when and where number information is corrupted in cases where the language model ends up making agreement errors. To demonstrate the causal role played by the representations we find, we then use agreement information to influence the course of the LSTM during the processing of difficult sentences. Results from such an intervention reveal a large increase in the language model's accuracy. Together, these results show that diagnostic classifiers give us an unrivalled detailed look into the representation of linguistic information in neural models, and demonstrate that this knowledge can be used to improve their performance.

1 Introduction

Machine learning models for estimating the probabilities of potential next words (and hence, for predicting the next word) in a running text have seen enormous improvements in performance over the last few years (Merity et al., 2018). These newer models—all based on deep learning techniques such as LSTMs (Hochreiter and Schmidhuber, 1997)—allow some language technologies, such as speech recognisers, to reach 'human parity'. From their high accuracy and from further analysis, it is clear that LSTM-based language models have learned a great deal about both short and long distance relations in sentences and discourse. In particular, Gulordava et al. (2018) report that for several languages, their LSTM-based language model performs remarkably well on a set of long-distance number agreement tasks.

The Gulordava study, however, does not clarify which components of the LSTM are responsible for storing or processing syntactic features, and how such features are represented. Understanding how trained recurrent networks such as LSTMs might represent syntax and other structural information is currently a key area of research. Popular approaches include visualising the state space of these networks, performing ablations to the network, or using the internal states of the networks for some auxiliary task (e.g., Adi et al., 2016; Kádár et al., 2017; Conneau et al., 2018; Khandelwal et al., 2018).

In this paper, we analyse the phenomenon of subject-verb agreement in English using the *diagnostic classification* approach of Hupkes et al. (2018). We start with replicating the results of Gulordava et al. (2018) on English, and we then show that diagnostic classifiers can be used to give a fine-grained analysis of how neural language models capture structural dependencies. In particular, we examine how information about subject-verb agreement is represented by an LSTM (Section 4), (ii) how that information varies across timesteps (Section 5), and (iii) where and how the problems arise that let the model commit agreement errors (Section 5 and 6). Finally, to demonstrate how precisely and accurately this method can identify the network's internal representations, we (iv) show that we can alter the representation to strongly improve the models ability to predict verb number (Section 7). In the next section, after discussing subject-verb agreement, we outline the data used throughout our experiments.

Proceedings of the 2018 EMNLP Workshop BlackboxNLP: Analyzing and Interpreting Neural Networks for NLP, pages 240–248
Brussels, Belgium, November 1, 2018. ©2018 Association for Computational Linguistics

2 Data

The work in this paper focuses on understanding how recurrent neural language models can understand subject-verb agreement, which is used as a proxy for understanding syntactic structure. In this section, we discuss subject verb agreement and the type of sentences we look at throughout the rest of this paper. We then briefly describe the data that we use for our investigation.

2.1 Subject-verb agreement

Subject-verb agreement is a variable-distance syntactic dependency, and a classic example of a structural dependency in natural language (Chomsky, 1957; Tesnière, 1959). In English, a present tense verb and the head of its syntactic subject must agree on their number (singular or plural). Thus, "The **dog chases** the cat" is grammatical, whilst "The **dog chase** the cat" is not. In principle, subject and verb can be separated by an arbitrary number of tokens, often including other nouns with a potentially different number (for an example, see Figure 1). We call the number of tokens between the subject head and the mean verb the *context size*.

Without any syntactic analysis, it is unclear how to identify all subject-verb pairs in a sentence within an arbitrarily large window of tokens, especially since intervening nouns can themselves be candidates for agreement. To respect subject-verb agreement, a language model needs to detect the grammatical number of both the subject head and the verb, store this information across timesteps, and identify which nouns correspond to which verbs. When intervening nouns carry the opposite grammatical number from the subject head—as do both intervening nouns in the example sentence in Figure 1—we refer to them as *agreement attractors*, or simply *attractors*.

2.2 Datasets

For the experiments described in this paper we use two different datasets. The first is the one introduced by Gulordava et al. (2018), which contains 410 sentences with at least three tokens occurring between subject head and verb. For each of 41 original sentences, nine 'nonce' variants were generated by substituting each context word in the sentence by a random word with the same part-of-speech tag and morphological features. This data construction method is motivated by the fact that grammaticality judgements should not be influenced by the meaningfulness of a sentence, and ensures that frequency-based confounds are avoided. Every sentence in the dataset is annotated with the correct and incorrect verb forms, the morphological features of the former, the position of the subject head and of the verb, the number of agreement attractors, and the type of construction spanning the long-distance dependency.

Additionally, we extract different subsets of the Universal Dependency (UD) corpus (ca. 1.5 million sentences) for our experiments. The large amount of annotated sentences in this dataset allows us to retrieve sets of sentences that satisfy specific conditions relevant to subject-verb agreement. In particular, we can extract sentences with specific context sizes, and fixed numbers of words before the subject and after the verb. We are also able to specify whether the sentences in the set should have an attractor and—if so—at which index (or, in our terminology, *timestep*) the attractor should appear. Similarly, we can ensure that there is no other noun between subject and verb that has the same number as the subject (we call these *helpful nouns*). As we will see, this allows us to examine the dynamic effect of attractors in the way the LSTM processes subject-verb agreement.

In this paper, the specific subset of the universal dependency dataset we use varies from experiment to experiment, as different experiments require different constraints. We will specify our selection of data for each experiment in the relevant sections. To clarify which subset of the UD corpus is used in an experiment, we use the following notation: *UD-Kk-Ll-Mm-Aa*, where k refers to the minimal number of words appearing before the subject, l to the number of words between the subject and verb (the context size), m to the minimal number of words after the verb, and a to the position of the attractor relative to the subject. We use an asterisk to indicate that no restrictions are placed on one of the above mentioned variables; e.g., $A*$ indicates that there may or may not be an attractor. Finally, we denote datasets of sentences that have no attractor with a minus following the attractor index (i.e., $A-$).

3 Replication

We start with replicating the experiment performed in (Gulordava et al., 2018), using the pretrained LM and the English test set made available

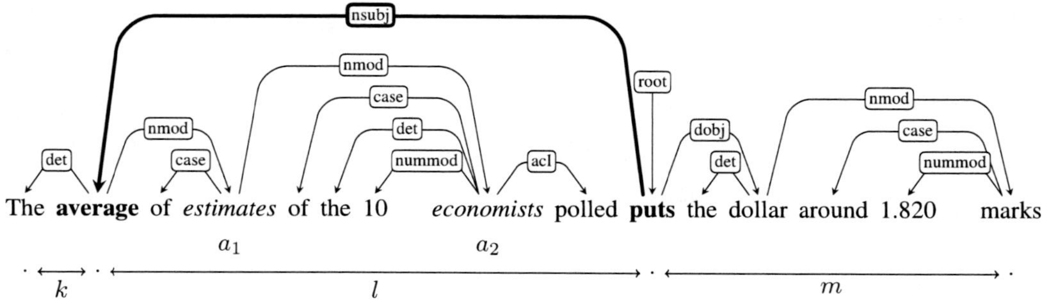

Figure 1: An example dependency parse of a sentence with a singular subject head and main verb (marked in boldface). As the subject *average* and the verb *put* are separated by 7 tokens, the *context size* (l) of this sentence is 7. Within this context, there are two intervening plural nouns, *estimates* (a_1) and *economists* (a_2), which we call *agreement attractors*.

by the authors of the paper.[1] Following Linzen et al. (2016) and Gulordava et al. (2018), we use the LSTM language model to process a corpus of sentences containing long-distance subject-verb relations, and test whether the model assigns a higher probability to the verb that originally occurred in the sentence than to its incongruent counterpart.

	Gulordava et al.	Our Accuracy
Original	81.0	78.1
Nonce	74.1	70.7

Table 1: LM accuracy on both English sets from Gulordava et al. (2018). Reported are the percentages of sentences for which the correct verb form is assigned a higher likelihood under the LM than the incorrect form.

In Table 1 we report both Gulordava's original accuracies, and the results from our replication. Overall we obtain similar results, but our accuracy scores are slightly lower[2] than those reported by Gulordava et al. (2018).

4 Diagnostic Classification to Predict Number

After confirming Gulordava et al. (2018)'s results, we now investigate *how* the LSTM repre-

---

[1] github.com/facebookresearch/ colorlessgreenRNNs/tree/master/data

[2] The results we obtain with our implementation exactly match those we get when running the script publicly shared by Gulordava et al. (2018); we currently have no explanation for the discrepancy in overall scores but consider the differences small enough to proceed with the real purpose of our study: understanding how the models work.

sents the required number information, how this information is built up over time and where in the network the representation resides. To this end, we use diagnostic classifiers (DCs, Hupkes et al., 2018). The key idea of diagnostic classification is to test whether an LSTM's intermediate representations contain information about a particular phenomenon—such as subject-verb agreement—by training another model to recognise the information relevant to the phenomenon in the internal activations of the LSTM. More precisely, given a dataset of intermediate LSTM representations and a set of labels that describe the hypothesis to be tested, a meta model can be trained to predict the correct label from the representations. If the model succeeds in this task (i.e. if it achieves a performance significantly above chance on test data disjoint from the training data), this constitutes evidence that the LSTM is in fact computing or keeping track of the hypothesised information.

Training We create a training set containing 1000 sentences that all have 5 words between subject and verb (i.e. the context size is 5), have at least one word before the subject and after the verb, and for which no attractor based constraints are placed on the training set (*UD-K1-L5-M1-A−*). We run the pretrained LM of Gulordava et al. (2018)—a two layer LSTM model with 650 hidden units—on this corpus, and for both layers we extract activation data for both the hidden and gate activations (the hidden activation h_t and memory cell c_t, and the forget gate f_t, input gate i_t and output gate o_t). For example, for a single sentence of length n we obtain $5 \times 2 \times n$ activation vectors, because we have 2 layers, n timesteps, and 5 types of

	$\mathbf{h_t}$	$\mathbf{c_t}$	$\mathbf{f_t}$	$\mathbf{i_t}$	$\mathbf{o_t}$
Layer 0	**0.74** / 0.57	**0.76** / 0.58	**0.69** / 0.55	**0.68** / 0.56	**0.69** / 0.56
Layer 1	**0.90** / 0.62	**0.91** / 0.65	**0.86** / 0.61	**0.86** / 0.60	**0.87** / 0.60

Table 2: Mean accuracy of DCs (correct/wrong) across timesteps, averaged over datasets drawn from different context sizes and attractor positions (with $K = 0$, $M = 0$, $5 \le L \le 7$ and with a variable number of attractors at different positions).

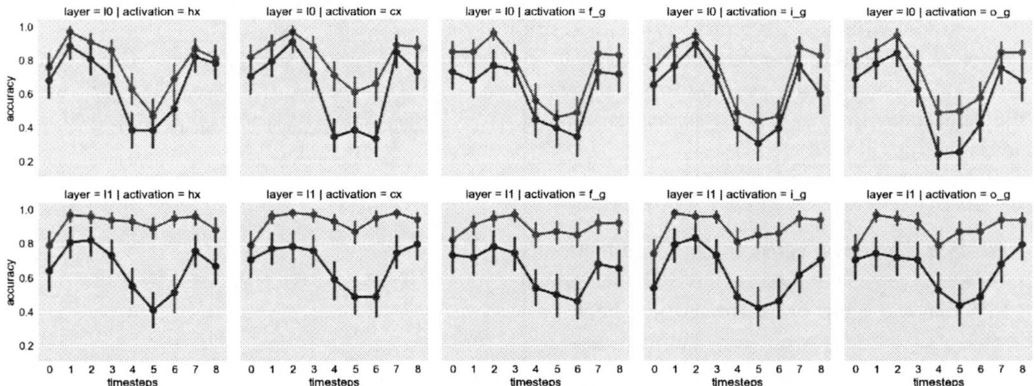

Figure 2: Accuracies over time (on UD-K1-L5-M1-A3) of 10 diagnostic classifiers trained and tested on data from different components of the LSTM. As in this testset one word occurs before the subject, the subject is at timestep 1. Green lines represent sentences for which the LSTM predicts the correct verb, blue lines sentences for which the LSTM assigns a higher probability to the incongruent counterpart.

activations at each time step t: $\mathbf{h_t}, \mathbf{c_t}, \mathbf{f_t}, \mathbf{i_t}, \mathbf{o_t}$). We then label all activations with the number of the main verb of the sentence from which it was generated (either 'singular' or 'plural') and train a separate DCs for each of the 10 components of the LSTM.

Results We test the trained DCs on two test sets, that differ with respect to whether the LM correctly or incorrectly classified the sentences they contain (i.e. a sentence s is in the 'correct' set iff the LM assigns higher probability to the correct form of the sentence than to the incorrect form). Otherwise, the two sets have similar features, containing both sentences from *UD-K1-L5-M1-A3*. While we strive to generate the 'wrong' and 'correct' test sets with 100 sentences each, this is not always possible due to data sparsity. However, we ensure that both test sets have approximately the same size and do contain at least 50 sentences.

In Table 2, we print the average DC accuracies. We observe that for both the 'wrong' and the 'correct' test sets, the accuracies are highest at the second layer (layer 1) across almost all LSTM components, suggesting that the last LSTM layer reaches the level of abstraction which can best capture long-distance dependencies.

In Figure 2, we plot the average DC accuracy at different timesteps when processing sentences (from a set with a context size of 5 and a single attractor located three words after the subject). Unsurprisingly, the DCs obtain their best accuracy scores at (or just after) the subject and verb timestep. This pattern is consistent across context sizes, attractor positions, and number of words before the subject and after the verb, and regardless of whether the LSTM prediction was correct or incorrect. This result illustrates that the LM learns to recognise the number information of subject heads and present tense verbs.

The figure furthermore shows that performance differs between layers and between components. The DC performance of the layer 1 components, moreover, critically differs for 'correct' and 'wrong' sentences, For example, classifiers that make predictions based on $\mathbf{c_t}$ and $\mathbf{h_t}$ activations of 'correct' sentences are the most stable in terms of accuracy, in particular at layer 1. Although all LSTM components outperform the random baseline of 50%, these results imply that the cell state and the hidden activation are the LSTM components that are most specialised at processing number information. We test this claim in Section 5.

Another cause of differences across diagnostic classification error rates is the presence of agreement attractors. Accuracies for the test sets with an attractor are overall lower than those obtained on sentences without an attractor. While the error rate rises in Figure 2 and diverges between 'correct' and 'wrong' at the position of the attractor, the same does not happen for sentences without attractors (not plotted).

5 Representations Across Timesteps

Results so-far show us that number information is most easily retrieved from the internal states of the LM when the noun or verb have just been presented, but not very well from the internal states at intermediate timesteps. The good performance of the LM in predicting the number of the verb, however, indicates that the LM does retain the subject's number information during those intermediate timesteps—but apparently it does so using a *different* representation. In this section, we focus on these changing representations.

In the previous experiment we trained diagnostic classifiers on activation data for all words in the sentence. In contrast, we now train *separate* diagnostic classifiers for each timestep: each DC_t is trained with activation data at timestep t only. We test, however, each DC_t on data from all other timesteps as well. With a total of T timesteps, this gives us $T \times T$ DC-accuracies that together constitute a *Temporal Generalization Matrix* (King and Dehaene, 2014; Fyshe et al., 2016).

In effect, we are forcing each DC to specialise on timestep-specific representations of subject-verb agreement information. If this information is represented uniformly across timesteps, a classifier trained at the subject timestep should also have a high accuracy when applied to the activations corresponding with the timestep in which the attractor occurs. If, on the other hand, information is dynamically encoded, no such generality of classifiers is to be expected.

Data To test the development of the encoding over time, we create a corpus with sentences that are identical with respect to the position of the subject, attractor and main verb. We train on sentences with 5 intervening words between the sub-

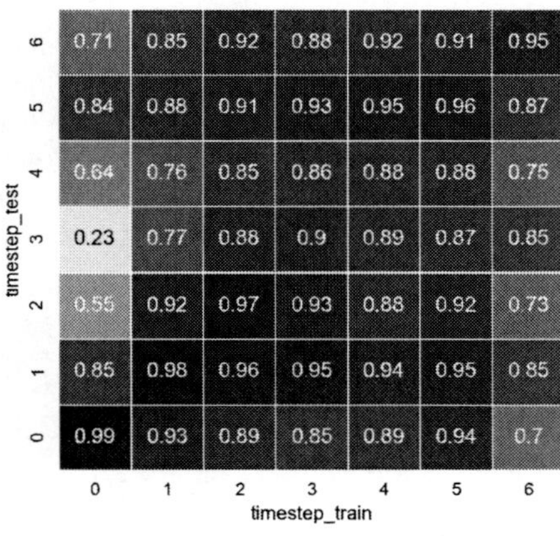

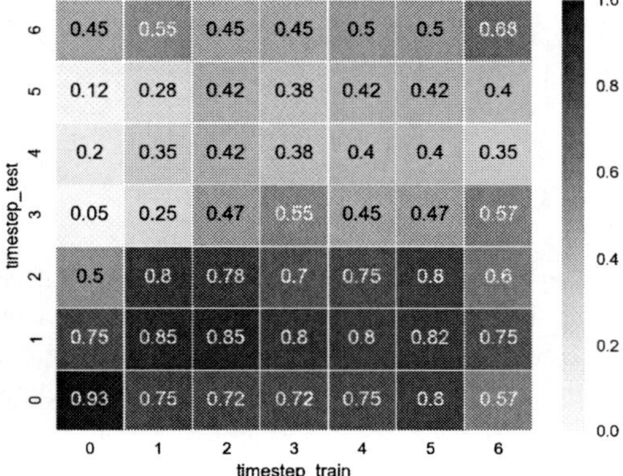

Figure 3: The temporal generalization matrices for DCs trained on memory cell activation at different timesteps, for correctly (top) and incorrectly classified (bottom) sentences. Timestep 0 corresponds to the subject of the sentence, the attractor and main verb of the sentence occur at timesteps 3 and 6, respectively. The corpus used for testing here is *UD-K*-L5-M*-A3*.

ject, containing one attractor 3 timesteps after the subject, and a variable number of words before the subject and after the verb (*UD-K*-L5-M*-A3*). After computing the activations for all sentences, we collect the activations corresponding to all 6 timesteps from subject to verb, in 6 different bins. For each bin, we train a separate DC.

For testing we create again a 'correct' and an 'incorrect' test set, drawing both sets from *UD-K*-L5-M*-A3*. Following the same procedure as for the training data, we split both test sets up into 6 timesteps. In the remainder of this section, position 0 thus always refers to the position of the subject, while the attractor and main verb of the sentence occur at timestep 3 and 6, respectively.

In Figure 3, we plot the Temporal Generalization Matrix for the memory cell ($\mathbf{c}_t^1$) activation data, containing the accuracies of T DC's evaluated on T timestep datasets each. The top figure plots results for 'correct' sentences, the bottom figure for 'incorrect' sentences.

A first observation is that accuracies on the diagonals—which correspond to classifiers that were trained and tested on the same timestep—are typically high for sentences that are processed correctly, while being lower for incorrectly processed sentences. Interestingly, this difference already emerges at the first two timesteps, where no attractor has yet appeared—suggesting that an important part of the problem with misclassified sentences is the encoding of the relevant information already when the subject occurs.

Comparing the plots for correctly and incorrectly processed sentences, we notice that the attractor (timestep 3) has a very large effect on the accuracies for incorrectly classified sentences. For those sentences, the LM's internal states contain no information anymore after the attractor is processed: timesteps 4 and 5 receive below chance accuracies, whereas for correctly processed sentences the attractor prompts only a slight dip in accuracy.

Focussing on the correctly processed sentences, an interesting observation that can be made is the discrepancy between column 0 and 6 (the columns corresponding to the subject and verb of a sentence) and the rest of the columns. While the first and last column generalise poorly to different timesteps, the classifiers trained and tested on timesteps 1-5 show a different pattern: despite potential effects from the attractor at timestep 3, the accuracy scores do not change substantially across timesteps. This implies that the LSTM represents subject-verb agreement information in at least two different ways: a short-term 'surface' level at and around the subject timestep, and a longer-term 'deep' level for successive sequence processing. This deep level information seems to be represented most generically at timestep 4, the classifier for which has the highest accuracy across timesteps.

In the next section, we delve deeper into the representations at this timestep and investigate which components of the LSTM are most crucial in representing this information.

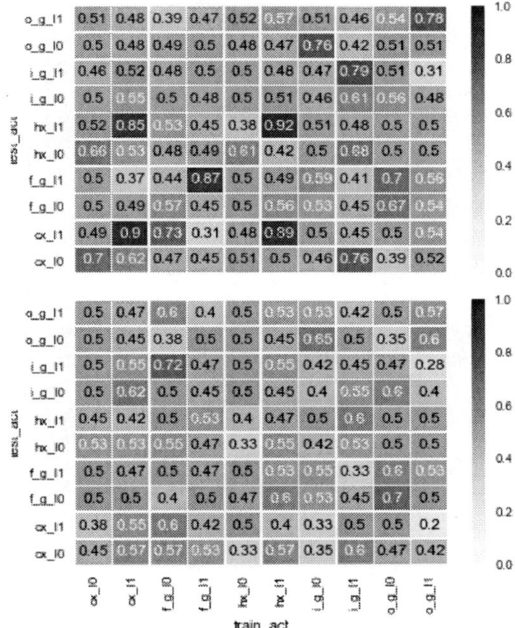

Figure 4: The spatial generalization matrices at timestep 4. Shown are accuracies of DCs trained on activation data of each component separately (horizontal), and tested on each component separately (vertical). Results for correctly (top) and incorrectly (bottom) classified sentences.

6 Comparing Representations Across Components

In this section, we briefly investigate the stability of information across components of the LSTM. Rather than comparing DCs that are trained on different *timesteps*, we now compare DCs that are trained on different *components*. We focus on timestep 4 which, following our previous experiments, optimally represents 'deep' information about subject-verb agreement. For our experiments, we use the same training set as for the previous experiment, with sentences with a context size of 5 and a single attractor located three words after the subject (*UD-K*-L5-M*-A3*).

Figure 4 presents the 'spatial generalization matrix', with DCs trained at timestep 4 with data from each components separately. The matrix shows that deep information is best represented in the hidden activation and memory cell of layer 1, and that the representations in these two components are similar.

245

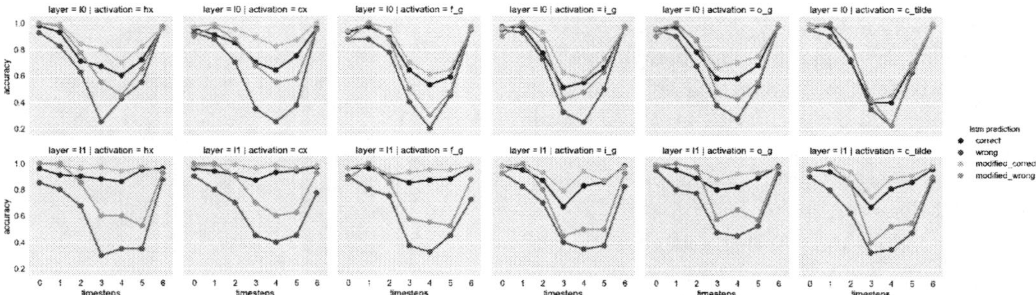

Figure 5: Mean accuracies for each component of the LSTM after an intervention of c_t and h_t at the subject timestep 0. An attractor and the agreeing verb occur at timestep 3 and 6, respectively.

	An	official	estimate	issued	in	2003	suggests	suggest
Original		-11.05	-8.426	-8.472	-1.243	-3.951	-5.753	-5.6979
Intervention		-11.05	-8.426	-8.472	-1.268	-3.97	-5.691	-6.4361

Table 3: Example sentence as processed by the neural language model of Gulordava et al. (2018), without and with our intervention. Shown are perplexities per word, for two versions of the sentence (featuring the verb 'suggests' or 'suggest').

7 Improving the Language Model Using Diagnostic Classifiers

In the experiments presented above, we used diagnostic classifiers to investigate the way the LSTM performs the verb number prediction task. In this section, we take one step further: rather than using DCs to analyse what neural networks are encoding, we try to use them to actively influence their behaviour through what they learned.

We use the same data as we used for the experiments described in the previous section: a corpus of sentences with the subject at timestep 0, one attractor 3 timesteps after (at timestep 3) and the main verb at timestep 6 (*UD-K0-L5-M0-A3*). We train 4 DCs to predict the number of the sentence from the hidden layer activations and memory cell activations for both layers, respectively.

We then use the trained DCs to actively influence the course of processing by the LSTM. We start processing sentences from the Gulordava et al. (2018) corpus, but after processing the subject of a sentence—the point where we discovered information is stored in a corrupted way for 'wrong' sentences—we halt the LSTM's processing, extract the hidden activation and the activation of the memory cell, and apply the trained diagnostic classifier to predict whether the main verb in the sentence is singular or plural. We then slightly adapt the activations based on the error that is de-

fined by the difference between the predicted label and the correct label for this particular sentence. We compute the gradients of this error with respect to the activations of the network, and we modify the activations using the delta-rule (we empirically decided on $\eta = 0.5$). In other words, we change the activations such that the prediction of the diagnostic classifier is slightly closer to the gold label. After adapting the activations, we continue to process the rest of the sentence given the adapted activations.

DC accuracy In Figure 5 we plot the accuracies of DCs trained on different components of the LSTM when we apply them on activations resulting from sentences processed with the above described intervention. Trivially, the intervention increases the accuracy of DCs for the hidden activation and memory cell of the network at timestep 1. More interestingly, this effect persists while the processing of the sentence proceeds—in some cases it grows even stronger—and thus in fact *changes* how the LSTM processes the sentence. This effect is not only visible in the components on which the intervention is done, but also displays in the gate-values, that are not directly updated but only changed indirectly through the interventions in the memory cell and hidden activations.

Language modelling To put our interventions to the test, we now assess the predictions made

246

	without intervention	with intervention
Original	78.1	85.4
Nonce	70.7	75.6

Table 4: Accuracy of the LSTM on the Gulordava et al. (2018) agreement test, with and without an intervention at the subject timestep.

by the LSTM as a consequence of the interventions. First, we confirm that the intervention does not cause strong anomalies in the LSTM, by comparing the perplexity of a small corpus of sentences processed *with* interventions at the subject timestep with sentences processed without any interventions. Table 3 shows an example sentence. We do not find any strong differences, confirming that the intervention is minor with respect to the overall behaviour of the LSTM. On the agreement test described by Gulordava et al. (2018) and conducted earlier in Section 3, however, the intervention *does* have a strong effect, as can be seen in Table 4. The accuracy of predicting the correct verb number increases from 78.1 to 85.4 and from 70.7 to 75.6 for original and nonce sentences, respectively.

These results provide evidence that DCs are able to pick up features that are actually used by the LSTM, rather than relying on idiosyncrasies in the high dimensional spaces that happen to be aligned with the predicted labels. Furthermore, they illustrate how diagnostic classifiers can be used to actively change the course of processing in a recurrent neural network, and with this opens a path that moves from merely *analysing* to actively *influencing* black box neural models.

8   Conclusions

In this paper, we focus on understanding how an LSTM language model processes subject-verb congruence, using a task first presented by Linzen et al. (2016), in which it is tested whether a language model prefers congruent over incongruent verbs. After replicating their results, we train diagnostic classifiers (Hupkes et al., 2018) to discover where and how number information is encoded by the LSTM; we find that number information is encoded *dynamically* over time, rather than remaining constant. Using a cognitive-neuroscience inspired method, we then train different diagnostic classifiers for different timesteps, resulting in a

Temporal Generalisation Matrix, which provides more information about changing representations over time. We find that while number information is stored in very different ways at the beginning and end of a sentence, in between a relatively stable 'deep' representation is maintained. Additionally, we find that for sentences in which the LSTM prefers an incongruent verb over congruent one, the information appears to be stored wrongly already at the beginning of the sentence, far before the verb is to appear.

Combining this information, we invert the process of diagnostic classification, using the classifiers to *influence* rather than merely observe. To this end, we process sentences with our language model and, at the point where we find information to be often corrupted, we intervene by (slightly) changing the hidden activations of the network using a trained DC. After this intervention, we continue processing the sentence as normal. This small intervention has little effect on the overall course of the LSTM, but a very large effect on the verb prediction at the end: the percentage of sentences for which the model prefers the congruent over the incongruent verb rises from 78.1% to 85.4%.

With these results, we not only show that diagnostic classifiers offer a detailed understanding of where and when information is encoded in a neural model, but also that this information can be used post hoc to change the course of the processing of such a model.

Acknowledgements

DH and WZ are funded by the Netherlands Organization for Scientific Research (NWO), through a Gravitation Grant 024.001.006 to the Language in Interaction Consortium.

References

Yossi Adi, Einat Kermany, Yonatan Belinkov, Ofer Lavi, and Yoav Goldberg. 2016. Fine-grained analysis of sentence embeddings using auxiliary prediction tasks. In *International Conference on Learning Representations (ICLR)*.

Noam Chomsky. 1957. *Syntactic Structures*. Mouton and Co., The Hague.

Alexis Conneau, German Kruszewski, Guillaume Lample, Loïc Barrault, and Marco Baroni. 2018. What you can cram into a single vector: Probing sentence embeddings for linguistic properties. In *Association for Computational Linguistics (ACL)*.

Alona Fyshe, Gustavo Sudre, Leila Wehbe, Nicole Rafidi, and Tom M Mitchell. 2016. The semantics of adjective noun phrases in the human brain. *bioRxiv*, page 089615.

Kristina Gulordava, Piotr Bojanowski, Edouard Grave, Tal Linzen, and Marco Baroni. 2018. Colorless green recurrent networks dream hierarchically. In *Proceedings of the 2018 Conference of the North American Chapter of the Association for Computational Linguistics: Human Language Technologies, Volume 1 (Long Papers)*, volume 1, pages 1195–1205.

Sepp Hochreiter and Jürgen Schmidhuber. 1997. Long short-term memory. *Neural computation*, 9(8):1735–1780.

Dieuwke Hupkes, Sara Veldhoen, and Willem Zuidema. 2018. Visualisation and 'diagnostic classifiers' reveal how recurrent and recursive neural networks process hierarchical structure. *Journal of Artificial Intelligence Research*, 61:907–926.

Akos Kádár, Grzegorz Chrupała, and Afra Alishahi. 2017. Representation of linguistic form and function in recurrent neural networks. *Computational Linguistics*, 43(4):761–780.

Urvashi Khandelwal, He He, Peng Qi, and Dan Jurafsky. 2018. Sharp nearby, fuzzy far away: How neural language models use context. In *Association for Computational Linguistics (ACL)*.

JR King and Stanislas Dehaene. 2014. Characterizing the dynamics of mental representations: the temporal generalization method. *Trends in cognitive sciences*, 18(4):203–210.

Tal Linzen, Emmanuel Dupoux, and Yoav Goldberg. 2016. Assessing the ability of lstms to learn syntax-sensitive dependencies. *Transactions of the Association for Computational Linguistics*, 4:521–535.

Stephen Merity, Nitish Shirish Keskar, and Richard Socher. 2018. An analysis of neural language modeling at multiple scales. *arXiv preprint arXiv:1803.08240*.

Lucien Tesnière. 1959. *Eléments de syntaxe structurale*. Klincksieck, Paris.

Iterative Recursive Attention Model for
Interpretable Sequence Classification

Martin Tutek and **Jan Šnajder**
Text Analysis and Knowledge Engineering Lab
Faculty of Electrical Engineering and Computing, University of Zagreb
Unska 3, 10000 Zagreb, Croatia
`{martin.tutek, jan.snajder}@fer.hr`

Abstract

Natural language processing has greatly benefited from the introduction of the attention mechanism. However, standard attention models are of limited interpretability for tasks that involve a series of inference steps. We describe an iterative recursive attention model, which constructs incremental representations of input data through reusing results of previously computed queries. We train our model on sentiment classification datasets and demonstrate its capacity to identify and combine different aspects of the input in an easily interpretable manner, while obtaining performance close to the state of the art.

1 Introduction

The introduction of the attention mechanism (Bahdanau et al., 2014) offered a way to demystify the inference process of neural models. By assigning scalar weights to different elements of the input, we are able to visualize and potentially understand why the model made the decision it made, or discover a deficiency in the model by tracing down a relevant aspect of the input being overlooked by the model. Specifically in natural language processing (NLP), which abounds with variable-length word sequence classification tasks, attention alleviates the issue of learning long-term dependencies in recurrent neural networks (Bengio et al., 1994) by offering the model a glimpse into previously processed tokens.

Attention offers a good retrospective explanation of the classification decision by indicating what parts of the input contributed the most to the decision. However, in many cases the final decision is best interpreted as a result of a series of inference steps, each of which can potentially affect its polarity. A case in point is sentiment analysis, in which contrastive clauses and negations act as polarity switches of the overall sentence sentiment. In such cases, attention will only point to the part of the

input sentence whose polarity matches that of the final decision. However, unfolding the inference process of a model into a series of interpretable steps would make the model more interpretable and allow one to identify its shortcomings.

As a step toward that goal, we propose an extension of the iterative attention mechanism (Sordoni et al., 2016), which we call the *iterative recursive attention model* (IRAM), where the result of an attentive query is nonlinearly transformed and then added to the set of vector representations of the input sequence. The nonlinear transformation, along with reusing the representations obtained in previous steps, allows the model to construct a recursive representation and process the input sequence bit by bit. The upshot is that we can inspect how the model weighs the different parts of the sentence and recursively combines them to give the final decision. We test the model on two sentiment analysis tasks and demonstrate its capacity to isolate different task-related aspects of the input, while reaching performance comparable with the state of the art.

2 Related Work

Attention (Bahdanau et al., 2014) and its variants (Luong et al., 2015) have initially been proposed for machine translation, but are now widely adopted in NLP. Attention has proven especially useful in tasks that involve long text sequences, such as summarization (Rush et al., 2015; See et al., 2017), question answering (Hermann et al., 2015; Xiong et al., 2016; Cui et al., 2017), and natural language inference (Rocktäschel et al., 2015; Yin et al., 2016; Parikh et al., 2016), as well as purely attentional machine translation (Vaswani et al., 2017; Gu et al., 2017).

Thus far, there has been a number of interesting and effective approaches for interpreting the in-

Proceedings of the 2018 EMNLP Workshop BlackboxNLP: Analyzing and Interpreting Neural Networks for NLP, pages 249–257
Brussels, Belgium, November 1, 2018. ©2018 Association for Computational Linguistics

ner workings of recurrent neural networks through methods such as representing them as finite automata (Weiss et al., 2017), extracting inference rules (Zanzotto and Ferrone, 2017), and analyzing saliency of inputs through first-order derivative information (Li et al., 2016; Arras et al., 2017).

Akin to the saliency analysis approaches, we opt not to condense the trained network into a finite set of rules. We differ from (Li et al., 2016; Arras et al., 2017) in that we attempt to decode the steps of the decision process of a recurrent network instead of demonstrating through saliency how the decision changes with respect to the inputs. In the context of sentiment analysis, the main benefit we see in representing the decision process of a recurrent network as a sequence of steps is that it offers a simple way to isolate sentiment-bearing phrases by observing how they get grouped in a single iteration. Secondly, we aim for improved interpretability of functional dependencies such as negation, where we demonstrate that our method first attends on the negated phrase, constructing an intermediate representation, which is then recursively transformed in the next iteration.

Sordoni et al. (2016) introduced the iterative attention mechanism for question answering, where attention alternates between the question and the document, and the query is updated in each step by a GRU cell (Cho et al., 2014). The model combines the weights obtained throughout the iterations to select the final answer, similar to the attention sum reader of Kadlec et al. (2016) and pointer networks of Vinyals et al. (2015).

We believe there is much to gain from the iterative attention mechanism by eliminating the direct link between the intermediate representations and the output, allowing the model to construct its own sequential representation of the input. Our model only connects the last attention step to the output, removing the need for intermediate steps to contain all the information relevant for the final decision. Apart from (Sordoni et al., 2016), related work closest to ours consists of concepts of multi-head attention (Lin et al., 2017; Vaswani et al., 2017), in which all queries are generated at once, pairwise attention (Cui et al., 2017; Xiong et al., 2016), where attention is applied to multiple inputs but is not applied iteratively and hierarchical iterative attention (Yang et al., 2016), where the authors first use a intra-sentence attention mechanism and then combine the intermediate representations with inter-sentence attention. In contrast to their work, we do not predetermine the level on which the attention is applied – in each iteration the mechanism can focus on any element of the input sequence.

3 Model

Throughout the experiments, we will use two variants of our model: (1) the vanilla model and (2) the full model. The vanilla model contains the bare minimum of components needed for the attention mechanism to function as intended. The purpose of the vanilla model is to eliminate any additional confounders for the performance and showcase the interpretability of the model. For the full model, we extend the vanilla model with additional deep learning components commonly employed in state-of-the-art models, to showcase the performance of the model when given capacity akin to competing models.

In both versions of the model, data is processed in three phases: (1) *encoding phase*, which contextualizes the word representations; (2) *attention phase*, which uses iterative recursive attention to isolate and combine the different parts of the input; and (3) *classification phase*, where the learned representation is fed as an input to a classifier.

The vanilla and full model differ only in the encoding phase, while our proposed attention mechanism is employed only in the second phase. We begin with a detailed account of the proposed attention mechanism and its regularization, and continue with a description of the remaining components, highlighting the differences between the vanilla and full models.

3.1 Iterative Recursive Attention

Fig. 1 shows the architecture of the iterative attention mechanism. The mechanism uses a recurrent network, dubbed the *controller*, to refine the attention query throughout T iterations.

Inputs to the mechanism are an initial query $\hat{x}$ and a set of hidden states $H = [h_i, \ldots, h_N]$ constituting the input sequence, both obtained from the encoding step.

As the controller, we use a gated recurrent unit (GRU) (Cho et al., 2014) cell. The input to the controller is the transformed result of the previous query, while the hidden state is the previous query.

For the attention mechanism we use bilinear attention (Luong et al., 2015):

$$\vec{a} = softmax(\vec{q}WH) \qquad (1)$$

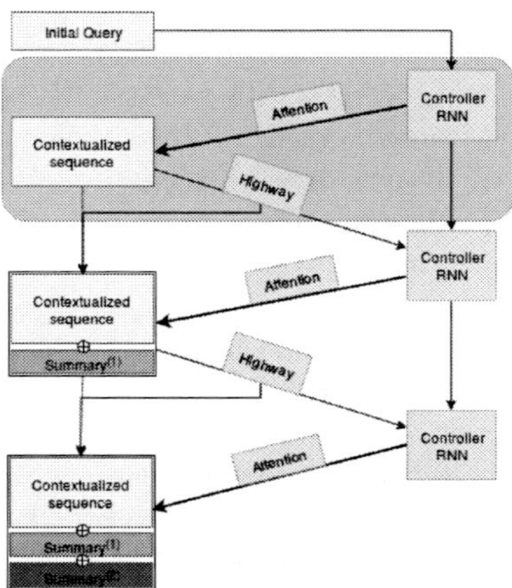

Figure 1: The iterative recursive attention model (IRAM). Green-colored components share their parameters with components of the same type. Highlighted in gray is one iteration of IRAM.

where $\vec{q}$ is the current query vector, W a parameter of size $\mathbb{R}^{d_q \times d_h}$, while d_q and d_h are the dimensionalities of the query and the hidden state, respectively.

The attention weights are then used to compute the input summary in timestep t as a linear combination of the hidden states:

$$\hat{s}^{(t)} = \sum_i^N a_i^{(t)} h_i \qquad (2)$$

As we intend to use $\hat{s}^{(t)}$ in the next iteration of the attention mechanism, we need to allow the network the capacity to discern between the new additions and original inputs. To this end, we use a highway network (Srivastava et al., 2015), which gives the model the option to pass subsets of the summary as-is or transform them with a nonlinearity. If the summary is not transformed with a nonlinearity, it ends up being merely a linear combination of the hidden states, and we gain no information from adding it to the sequence.

The final input summary is thus obtained as $s^{(t)} = Highway(\hat{s}^{(t)})$ and added to the set of hidden states $H = \{h_i, \dots, h_n, s^{(1)}, \dots, s^{(t)}\}$.

3.2 Attention Regularization

Ideally, we want the model to focus on different task-related aspects of the input in each iteration. However, the model is in no way incentivized to learn to propagate information through the sum-

maries and can in principle focus on the same segment in each step.

To prevent this from happening – and push the model to focus on different aspects of the input in every step – we regularize it by minimizing the pairwise dot products between all iterations of attention:

$$L_{attn} = \frac{\gamma}{2T} \sum_{i \neq j} [AA^T]_{ij} \qquad (3)$$

where γ is a hyperparameter determining the regularization strength and $A \in \mathbb{R}^{T \times N+T-1}$ is a matrix containing the attention weights generated in T steps over N inputs by the iterative attention mechanism. The matrix has $N + T - 1$ columns to account for attention over $T - 1$ added summaries, as the summary generated in the last iteration cannot be attended over. In each row t, the matrix has $T - t - 1$ trailing zeroes, corresponding to summaries that are not yet available in iteration t.

Concretely, the attention weight vector in row t of the matrix A consists of:

$$A_t = [\overbrace{a_1, \dots, a_N}^{\text{Input sequence}}, \overbrace{a_{N+1}, \dots, a_{N+t-1}}^{\text{Summaries in } t^- < t}, 0, \dots] \qquad (4)$$

resulting in each element i, j of the regularization matrix AA^T storing the dot product between attention weights in iterations i, j. The regularization expression is a sum over all off-diagonal elements. The diagonal elements are dot products of attention weights in the same iteration so we ignore them. We scale by $\frac{1}{2}$ to account for the symmetrical elements in $A^T A$ and by $\frac{1}{T}$ to account for the number of dot product comparisons.

We note that, while this regularization penalty does encourage the model to focus on different elements of the input sequence, there is still a trivial way for the model to minimize the penalty without learning a meaningful behavior. Since the attention weight over the summary in iteration t is zero in all iterations $t^- < t$, the model can simply attend over any elements of the input sequence in the first iteration, and afterwards propagate the information forward by fully attending only over the summary generated in the previous iteration. We will illustrate this behavior with concrete examples in Section 4.

3.3 Vanilla Encoder

For training, the inputs of the encoding phase are a sequence of words $x = [w_1, \dots, w_N]$ and a class

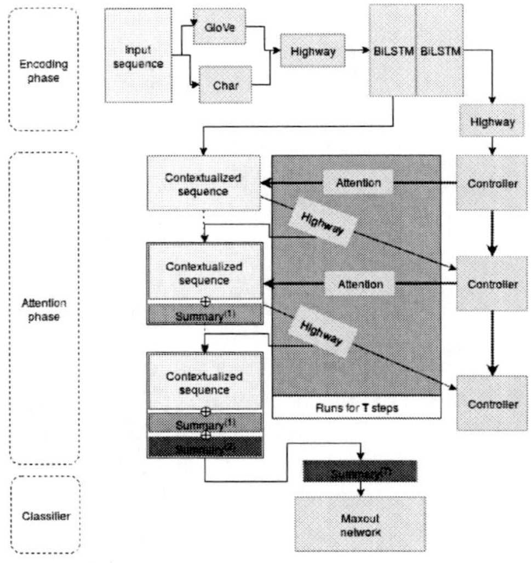

Figure 2: The full version of the iterative recursive attention model (IRAM). Green-colored components share their parameters with components of the same type; blue-colored components each have their own parameters.

label y. The encoder of the vanilla model maps the word indices to dense vector representations using pretrained GloVe vectors (Pennington et al., 2014). The sequence of word vectors is then fed as input to a bidirectional long-short term memory (BiLSTM) network (Hochreiter and Schmidhuber, 1997). The outputs of the BiLSTM are used as the input sequence to the iterative attention step, while the cell state in the last timestep is used as the initial query.

3.4 Full Encoder

There are three key differences between the full encoder and the vanilla encoder. The full encoder uses (1) character n-gram embeddings, (2) an additional highway network, whose task is to fine-tune the word embeddings, and (3) an additional layer of BiLSTM, followed by a highway layer to construct the initial query. For extensions (1) and (2), we took inspiration from McCann et al. (2017), who also use both components. However, unlike McCann et al. (2017), who used a ReLU feedforward network to fine-tune the embeddings for the task, we use a highway network, which we found performs better.

The pretrained character n-gram vectors obtained from (Hashimoto et al., 2016) are first aver-

aged over all character n-grams for a given word and then concatenated to the GloVe embedding. Further on, before feeding the sequence of word embeddings to a recurrent model, we use a two-layer highway network (Srivastava et al., 2015) to fine-tune the embeddings for the task, which is especially beneficial when the input vectors are kept fixed.

To contextualize the input sequence and produce an initial attention query, we use a bidirectional long-short term memory (BiLSTM) network. We split the network conceptually into two parts: the lower l_{ctx} layers are used to transform the input sequence of word embeddings into a sequence of contextualized word representations, while the upper l_{query} layers are used to read and comprehend the now-transformed sequence and capture its relevant aspects into a single vector. The rationale for the split is that recurrent networks are often required to tackle two tasks at once: contextualize the input and comprehend the whole sequence. Intuitively, the split should incite a division of labor between the two parts of the network: contextualization network only has to memorize the local information specific to each word (e.g., verb tense, noun gender) in order to transform its representation, while comprehension network needs to model aspects of meaning pertaining to the entire sequence (e.g., the overall sentiment of the sentence, locations of sentiment bearing phrases).

We use a single ($l_{ctx} + l_{query}$)-layered BiLSTM, where we use the output of the l_{ctx}-th layer, while we use the cell state from the last layer as the sequence representation $\hat{x}$.

Lastly, since the weights of the BiLSTM network are suited toward processing the input sequence rather than preparing the query vector, we add an additional highway layer designed to fine-tune the sentence representation into the initial query.

3.5 Classifier

As input to the classifier, we use the summary vector obtained from the last step of iterative attention $s^{(T)}$. This way we force the network to propagate information through the attention steps, and also because the intermediate summaries do not contribute directly toward the classification and hence need not have the same polarity. The last summary vector is fed into a maxout network (Goodfellow et al., 2013) to obtain the class-conditional probabilities.

Fig. 2 shows the full version of the iterative attention mechanism with all of the aforementioned components.

4 Experiments

4.1 Datasets

We test IRAM on two sentiment classification datasets. The first is the Stanford Sentiment Treebank (SST) (Socher et al., 2013), a dataset derived from movie reviews on Rotten Tomatoes and containing 11,855 sentences labeled into five classes at the sentence level and at the level of each node in the constituency parse tree. The binary version with the neutral class removed contains 56,400 instances, while the fine-grained version with scores ranging from 1 (very negative) to 5 (very positive) contains 94,200 text-sentiment pairs. The second dataset is the Internet Movie Database (IMDb) (Maas et al., 2011), containing 22,500 multi-sentence reviews extracted from positive and negative reviews. We truncate each sentence from this dataset to a maximum length of 200 tokens.

Firstly, we demonstrate and analyze how each component in the vanilla model contributes to the performance and interpretability. We then analyze the full model and evaluate it on the aforementioned datasets.

4.2 Experimental Setup

Unless stated otherwise, all weights are initialized from a Gaussian distribution with zero mean and standard deviation of 0.01. We use the Adam optimizer (Kingma and Ba, 2014) with the AmsGrad modification (Reddi et al., 2018) and $\alpha = 0.0003$. We clip the global norm of the gradients to 1.0 and set weight decay to 0.00003.

We use 300-dimensional GloVe word embeddings trained on the Common Crawl corpus and 100-dimensional character embeddings. We follow the recommendation of Mu et al. (2017) and standardize the embeddings. Dropout of 0.1 is applied to the word embedding matrix.

For both datasets, we set $l_{ctx} = 2$ and $l_{query} = 1$. The highway network for fine-tuning the input embeddings has two layers, while the ones fine-tuning the query and the summary have a single layer. All highway networks' gate biases are initialized to 1, as recommended by Srivastava et al. (2015), as well as the biases of the LSTM forget gates.

The maxout network uses two 200-dimensional layers with a pool size of 4.

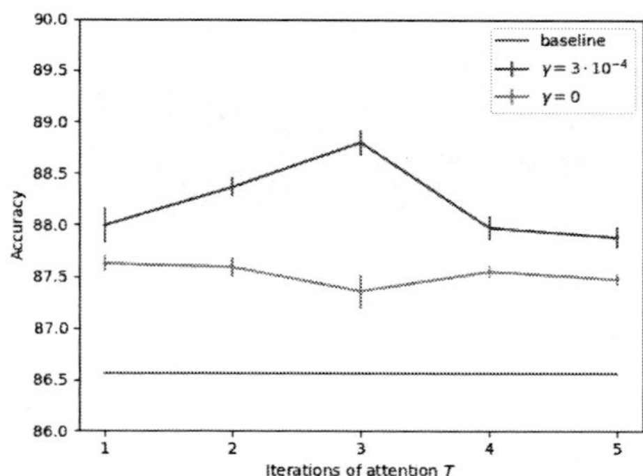

Figure 3: The effect of regularization γ across different values of T

Throughout our experiments, we have experimented with selecting the batch size from $\{32, 64\}$, dropout for the recurrent layers and the maxout classifier from $\{0.1, 0.2, 0.3, 0.4\}$, and the LSTM hidden state size from $\{400, 500, 1000\}$. The word and character n-gram vectors are kept fixed for SST but are learned for the IMDb dataset. These parameters are optimized using cross-validation, and the best configuration is ran on the test set. As IMDb has no official validation set, we randomly select 10% of the dataset and use it for all of the experiments. The values of other hyperparameters were selected through inexhaustive search.

4.3 Analysis of the Vanilla Model

The vanilla model defined in Section 3.3 has two main confounding variables: strength (and presence) of attention regularization (γ) and the number of iterations of the iterative recursive attention mechanism (T). We also would like to examine the difference in performance of the vanilla IRAM compared to some baseline sequence classifier. To this end, we implement a baseline model without the attention mechanism – a maxout classifier over the last hidden state of the encoder BiLSTM. To keep the running time of the experiments feasible, in this section we use only the binary SST dataset.

Effect of regularization. For each experiment in this round, we run every model three times with different random seeds and report the average results along with the standard deviations across the experiments. In Fig. 3 we present the comparison between the performance of the vanilla model with and without regularization. A more telling sign of

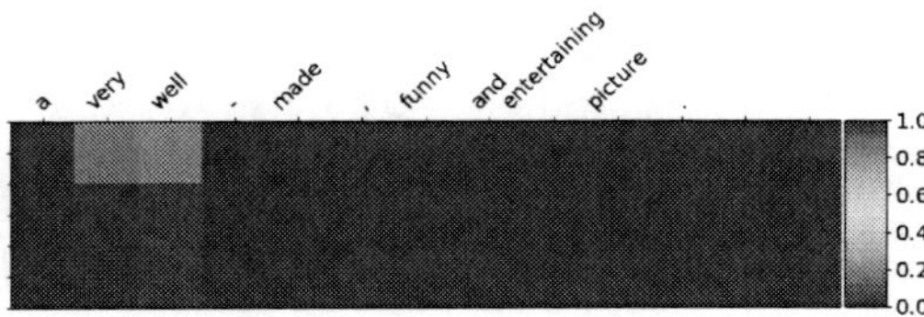

Figure 4: Attention sample for $\gamma = 0$ and $T = 3$

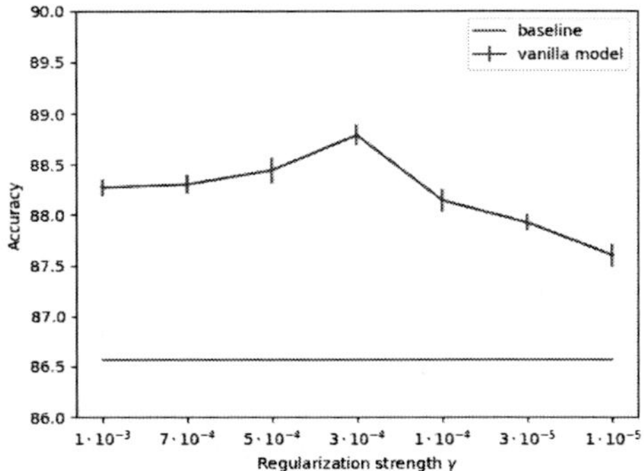

Figure 5: Classification accuracy for different values of γ

SST	
NSE (Munkhdalai and Yu, 2017)	89.7
IRAM	90.1
BCN + CoVe (McCann et al., 2017)	90.3
bmLSTM (Radford et al., 2017)	**91.8**
SST-5	
IRAM	53.7
BCN + CoVe (McCann et al., 2017)	53.7
BCN + ELMo (Peters et al., 2018)	**54.7**
IMDb	
IRAM	91.2
TRNN (Dieng et al., 2016)	93.8
oh-LSTM (Johnson and Zhang, 2016)	**94.1**
Virtual (Miyato et al., 2016)	**94.1**

Table 1: Classification accuracy on the test sets

Removed component	Accuracy
Full model	**90.1**
Vanilla model	88.7
– char n-grams	89.3
– query fine-tune	89.8
– embedding fine-tune	89.3

Table 2: Effect of removing components on performance

the different behavior between the models can be seen through inspecting attention weights.

In Fig. 4 we can see that the attention mechanism, when not regularized, fails to use its capacity and simply attends over the same element in each timestep. The last two columns, which contain the summaries from the first two steps of the iterative attention mechanism, have an attention weight of 0, which means that the model does not pass any information through the summaries nor refine the query. This behavior initially prompted us to add the regularization penalty term.

Through inexhaustive search we isolated a critical range of values for γ, for which we perform a detailed analysis of performance. For this experiment, we fix $T = 3$ as it has exhibited better performance for the vanilla model.

Effect of the number of iterations. Apart from comparing the effect of the existence of regularization, in Fig. 3 we can also observe the effect of the number of timesteps T. Increasing T beyond 3 has a diminishing effect on classification performance, something which we find to be consistent for the IMDB dataset as well.

We attribute this decrease in performance to the fact that SST is relatively simple, containing at most two contrastive aspects in each sentence, making any additional steps unnecessary. While the model could in theory exploit the pass-through mechanism, we believe that this operation adds some noise to the final representations and in turn affects performance slightly.

4.4 Analysis of the Full Model

We now evaluate the full model. Table 1 shows the accuracy scores of our best models (for $T = 3$, $\gamma = 0.0003$) and other state-of-the-art models on the test portions of the SST and IMDb datasets. Our model performs competitively with the best results on SST and SST-5 datasets. It is important to note that our model does not use transfer learning apart from the pretrained word vectors, which is not the case for the competing models.

Ablation study of encoder components. As mentioned in Section 3.4, through adding various components to the model we introduced a number of confounders. In order to determine the effect of each of the added components on the overall score, we evaluate the performance of the full model on the binary SST dataset with the remaining hyperparameters fixed and one of the components removed in isolation.

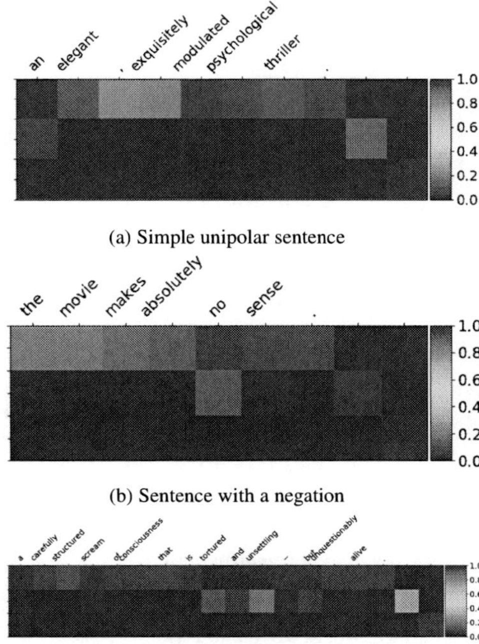

(a) Simple unipolar sentence

(b) Sentence with a negation

(c) Contrastive multipolar sentence

Figure 6: Visualization of attention across sentence words (horizontal) and T=3 time steps (vertical). The last T-1 columns contain the attention weights over the result of the previous attentive query.

4.5 Visualizing Attention

To gain an intuition about the working of IRAM, we visually analyzed its attention mechanism on a number of sentences from our dataset. We limit ourselves to examples from the test set of the SST dataset as the length of examples is manageable for visualization. We isolate three specific cases where the attention mechanism demonstrates interesting results: (1) simple unipolar sentences, (2) sentences with negations, and (3) multipolar sentences.

The least interesting case is the unipolar, as the attention mechanism often does not need multiple iterations. Fig. 6a shows the attention mechanism simply propagating information, since sentiment classification is straightforward and does not require multiple attention steps. This can be seen from most of the attention weight in the second and third steps being on the columns corresponding to the summaries.

The more interesting cases are sentences involving negations and modifiers. Fig. 6b shows the handling of negation: attention is initially on all words except on the negator. In the second step, the mechanism combines the output of the first step with the negation. We interpret this as flipping the sentiment – the model cannot rely solely on recognizing a negative word, and has to account for what that word negates through a functional dependence. These examples highlight one of the drawbacks of recurrent networks which we aim to alleviate. In case a standard attention mechanism is applied to a sentence containing a negator, the hidden representation of the negator has to scale or negate the intensity of an expression. Our model has the capacity to process such sequences iteratively, first constructing the representation of an expression, which is then adjusted by the nonlinear transformation and simpler to combine with the negator in the next step.

Lastly, Fig. 6c shows a contrastive multipolar sentence, where the model in the first step focuses on positive words, and then combines the negative words (*tortured, unsettling*) with the results of the first step. In such cases, the model succeeds to isolate the contrasting aspects of the sentence and attends to them in different iterations of the model, alleviating the burden of simultaneously representing the positive and negative aspects. After both contrastive representations have been formed, the model has the capacity to *weigh* them one against other and compute the final representation.

5 Conclusion

The proposed iterative recursive attention model (IRAM) has the capacity to construct representations of the input sequence in a recursive fashion, making inference more interpretable. We demonstrated that the model can learn to focus on various task-relevant parts of the input, and can propagate the information in a meaningful way to handle the more difficult cases. On the sentiment analysis task, the model performs comparable to the state of the art. Our next goals will be to try to use the iterative attention mechanism to extract tree-like sentence structures akin to constituency parse trees, evaluate the model on more complex datasets as well as extend the model to support an adaptive number of iterative steps.

Acknowledgment

This research has been supported by the European Regional Development Fund under the grant KK.01.1.1.01.0009 (DATACROSS).

References

Leila Arras, Grégoire Montavon, Klaus-Robert Müller, and Wojciech Samek. 2017. Explaining recurrent neural network predictions in sentiment analysis. In *Proceedings of the 8th Workshop on Computational Approaches to Subjectivity, Sentiment and Social Media Analysis*, pages 159–168.

Dzmitry Bahdanau, Kyunghyun Cho, and Yoshua Bengio. 2014. Neural machine translation by jointly learning to align and translate. *arXiv preprint arXiv:1409.0473*.

Yoshua Bengio, Patrice Simard, and Paolo Frasconi. 1994. Learning long-term dependencies with gradient descent is difficult. *IEEE transactions on neural networks*, 5(2):157–166.

Kyunghyun Cho, Bart van Merriënboer, Dzmitry Bahdanau, and Yoshua Bengio. 2014. On the properties of neural machine translation: Encoder–decoder approaches. *Syntax, Semantics and Structure in Statistical Translation*, page 103.

Yiming Cui, Zhipeng Chen, Si Wei, Shijin Wang, Ting Liu, and Guoping Hu. 2017. Attention-over-attention neural networks for reading comprehension. In *Proceedings of the 55th Annual Meeting of the Association for Computational Linguistics (Volume 1: Long Papers)*, volume 1, pages 593–602.

Adji B Dieng, Chong Wang, Jianfeng Gao, and John Paisley. 2016. TopicRNN: A recurrent neural network with long-range semantic dependency. In *ICLR 2016*.

Ian J Goodfellow, David Warde-Farley, Mehdi Mirza, Aaron Courville, and Yoshua Bengio. 2013. Maxout networks. *arXiv preprint arXiv:1302.4389*.

Jiatao Gu, James Bradbury, Caiming Xiong, Victor OK Li, and Richard Socher. 2017. Non-autoregressive neural machine translation. *arXiv preprint arXiv:1711.02281*.

Kazuma Hashimoto, Caiming Xiong, Yoshimasa Tsuruoka, and Richard Socher. 2016. A joint many-task model: Growing a neural network for multiple nlp tasks. *arXiv preprint arXiv:1611.01587*.

Karl Moritz Hermann, Tomas Kocisky, Edward Grefenstette, Lasse Espeholt, Will Kay, Mustafa Suleyman, and Phil Blunsom. 2015. Teaching machines to read and comprehend. In *Advances in Neural Information Processing Systems*, pages 1693–1701.

Sepp Hochreiter and Jürgen Schmidhuber. 1997. Long short-term memory. *Neural computation*, 9(8):1735–1780.

Rie Johnson and Tong Zhang. 2016. Supervised and semi-supervised text categorization using lstm for region embeddings. In *International Conference on Machine Learning*, pages 526–534.

Rudolf Kadlec, Martin Schmid, Ondrej Bajgar, and Jan Kleindienst. 2016. Text understanding with the attention sum reader network. *arXiv preprint arXiv:1603.01547*.

Diederik P Kingma and Jimmy Ba. 2014. Adam: A method for stochastic optimization. *arXiv preprint arXiv:1412.6980*.

Jiwei Li, Xinlei Chen, Eduard Hovy, and Dan Jurafsky. 2016. Visualizing and understanding neural models in nlp. In *Proceedings of NAACL-HLT*, pages 681–691.

Zhouhan Lin, Minwei Feng, Cicero Nogueira dos Santos, Mo Yu, Bing Xiang, Bowen Zhou, and Yoshua Bengio. 2017. A structured self-attentive sentence embedding. *arXiv preprint arXiv:1703.03130*.

Thang Luong, Hieu Pham, and Christopher D Manning. 2015. Effective approaches to attention-based neural machine translation. In *Proceedings of the 2015 Conference on Empirical Methods in Natural Language Processing*, pages 1412–1421.

Andrew L Maas, Raymond E Daly, Peter T Pham, Dan Huang, Andrew Y Ng, and Christopher Potts. 2011. Learning word vectors for sentiment analysis. In *Proceedings of the 49th annual meeting of the association for computational linguistics: Human language technologies-volume 1*, pages 142–150. Association for Computational Linguistics.

Bryan McCann, James Bradbury, Caiming Xiong, and Richard Socher. 2017. Learned in translation: Contextualized word vectors. In *Advances in Neural Information Processing Systems*, pages 6297–6308.

Takeru Miyato, Andrew M Dai, and Ian Goodfellow. 2016. Adversarial training methods for semi-supervised text classification. *arXiv preprint arXiv:1605.07725*.

Jiaqi Mu, Suma Bhat, and Pramod Viswanath. 2017. All-but-the-top: simple and effective postprocessing for word representations. *arXiv preprint arXiv:1702.01417*.

Tsendsuren Munkhdalai and Hong Yu. 2017. Neural semantic encoders. In *Proceedings of the conference. Association for Computational Linguistics. Meeting*, volume 1, page 397. NIH Public Access.

Ankur P Parikh, Oscar Täckström, Dipanjan Das, and Jakob Uszkoreit. 2016. A decomposable attention model for natural language inference. *arXiv preprint arXiv:1606.01933*.

Jeffrey Pennington, Richard Socher, and Christopher Manning. 2014. GloVe: Global vectors for word representation. In *Proceedings of the 2014 conference on empirical methods in natural language processing (EMNLP)*, pages 1532–1543.

Matthew E Peters, Mark Neumann, Mohit Iyyer, Matt Gardner, Christopher Clark, Kenton Lee, and Luke Zettlemoyer. 2018. Deep contextualized word representations. *arXiv preprint arXiv:1802.05365.*

Alec Radford, Rafal Jozefowicz, and Ilya Sutskever. 2017. Learning to generate reviews and discovering sentiment. *arXiv preprint arXiv:1704.01444.*

Sashank J Reddi, Satyen Kale, and Sanjiv Kumar. 2018. On the convergence of Adam and beyond. In *International Conference on Learning Representations.*

Tim Rocktäschel, Edward Grefenstette, Karl Moritz Hermann, Tomáš Kočiský, and Phil Blunsom. 2015. Reasoning about entailment with neural attention. *arXiv preprint arXiv:1509.06664.*

Alexander M Rush, Sumit Chopra, and Jason Weston. 2015. A neural attention model for abstractive sentence summarization. In *Proceedings of the 2015 Conference on Empirical Methods in Natural Language Processing*, pages 379–389.

Abigail See, Peter J Liu, and Christopher D Manning. 2017. Get to the point: Summarization with pointer-generator networks. In *Proceedings of the 55th Annual Meeting of the Association for Computational Linguistics (Volume 1: Long Papers)*, volume 1, pages 1073–1083.

Richard Socher, Alex Perelygin, Jean Wu, Jason Chuang, Christopher D Manning, Andrew Ng, and Christopher Potts. 2013. Recursive deep models for semantic compositionality over a sentiment treebank. In *Proceedings of the 2013 conference on empirical methods in natural language processing*, pages 1631–1642.

Alessandro Sordoni, Philip Bachman, Adam Trischler, and Yoshua Bengio. 2016. Iterative alternating neural attention for machine reading. *arXiv preprint arXiv:1606.02245.*

Rupesh Kumar Srivastava, Klaus Greff, and Jürgen Schmidhuber. 2015. Highway networks. *arXiv preprint arXiv:1505.00387.*

Ashish Vaswani, Noam Shazeer, Niki Parmar, Jakob Uszkoreit, Llion Jones, Aidan N Gomez, Łukasz Kaiser, and Illia Polosukhin. 2017. Attention is all you need. In *Advances in Neural Information Processing Systems*, pages 6000–6010.

Oriol Vinyals, Meire Fortunato, and Navdeep Jaitly. 2015. Pointer networks. In *Advances in Neural Information Processing Systems*, pages 2692–2700.

Gail Weiss, Yoav Goldberg, and Eran Yahav. 2017. Extracting automata from recurrent neural networks using queries and counterexamples. *arXiv preprint arXiv:1711.09576.*

Caiming Xiong, Victor Zhong, and Richard Socher. 2016. Dynamic coattention networks for question answering. *arXiv preprint arXiv:1611.01604.*

Zichao Yang, Diyi Yang, Chris Dyer, Xiaodong He, Alex Smola, and Eduard Hovy. 2016. Hierarchical attention networks for document classification. In *Proceedings of the 2016 Conference of the North American Chapter of the Association for Computational Linguistics: Human Language Technologies*, pages 1480–1489.

Wenpeng Yin, Hinrich Schütze, Bing Xiang, and Bowen Zhou. 2016. ABCNN: Attention-based convolutional neural network for modeling sentence pairs. *Transactions of the Association of Computational Linguistics*, 4(1):259–272.

Fabio Massimo Zanzotto and Lorenzo Ferrone. 2017. Can we explain natural language inference decisions taken with neural networks? inference rules in distributed representations. In *Neural Networks (IJCNN), 2017 International Joint Conference on*, pages 3680–3687. IEEE.

Interpreting Word-Level Hidden State Behaviour of Character-Level LSTM Language Models

Avery Hiebert[†*], Cole Peterson[†], Alona Fyshe[‡], Nishant A. Mehta[†]
[†]Department of Computer Science, University of Victoria, Canada
[‡]Computing Science / Psychology Departments, University of Alberta, Canada
`averyhiebert@gmail.com, cpeterso@uvic.ca`
`alona@ualberta.ca, nmehta@uvic.ca`

Abstract

While Long Short-Term Memory networks (LSTMs) and other forms of recurrent neural network have been successfully applied to language modeling on a character level, the hidden state dynamics of these models can be difficult to interpret. We investigate the hidden states of such a model by using the HDBSCAN clustering algorithm to identify points in the text at which the hidden state is similar. Focusing on whitespace characters prior to the beginning of a word reveals interpretable clusters that offer insight into how the LSTM may combine contextual and character-level information to identify parts of speech. We also introduce a method for deriving word vectors from the hidden state representation in order to investigate the word-level knowledge of the model. These word vectors encode meaningful semantic information even for words that appear only once in the training text.

1 Introduction

Recurrent Neural Networks (RNNs), including Long Short-Term Memory (LSTM) networks (Hochreiter and Schmidhuber, 1997; Gers et al., 2000), have been widely applied to natural language processing tasks including character-level language modeling (Mikolov et al., 2012; Graves, 2013). However, like other types of neural networks, the hidden states and behaviour of a given LSTM can be difficult to understand and interpret, due to both the distributed nature of the hidden state representations and the relatively opaque relationship between the hidden state and the final output of the network. It is also not clear how a character-level LSTM language model takes advantage of orthographic patterns to infer higher-level information.

---

[*]Corresponding author

In this paper, we investigate the hidden state dynamics of a character-level LSTM language model both directly and — through the use of output gate activations — indirectly. As an overview, our main contributions are:

1. We use clustering to investigate similar hidden states (and output gate activations) at different points in a text, paying special attention to whitespace characters. We provide insight into the model's awareness of both orthographic patterns and word-level grammatical information.

2. Inspired by our findings from clustering, we introduce a method for extracting meaningful word embeddings from a character-level model, allowing us to investigate the word-level knowledge of the model.

First, we use the HDBSCAN clustering algorithm (Campello et al., 2013) to reveal locations within a text at which the hidden state of the LSTM is similar, or at which a similar combination of cell state dimensions is relevant (as determined by output gates). Interestingly, focusing on moments when the network must predict the first letter of a word reveals clusters that are interpretable on the level of words and which display both character-level patterns and grammatical structure (i.e. separating parts of speech). We give examples of clusters of similar hidden states that appear to be heavily influenced by local orthographic patterns but also distinguish between different grammatical functions of the pattern — for example, a cluster containing whitespace characters following possessive uses, but not contractive uses, of the affix "'s". This sheds light on the use of orthographic patterns to infer higher-level information.

We also introduce a method for extracting word

Proceedings of the 2018 EMNLP Workshop BlackboxNLP: Analyzing and Interpreting Neural Networks for NLP, pages 258–266
Brussels, Belgium, November 1, 2018. ©2018 Association for Computational Linguistics

embeddings from a character-level model and perform qualitative and quantitative analyses of these embeddings. Surprisingly, this method can assign meaningful representations even to words that appear only once in the text, including associating the rare word "scrutinizingly" with "questioningly" and "attentively", and correctly identifying "deck" as a verb based on a single use despite its lack of meaningful subword components. These results suggests that the model is capable of deducing meaningful information about a word based on the context of a single use. While these embeddings do not achieve state-of-the-art performance on word similarity benchmarks, they do outperform the older methods of Turian et al. (2010) despite the small corpus size and the fact that our language model was not designed with the intent of producing word embeddings.

The rest of the paper is structured as follows: The following section describes related work. Section 3 describes the architecture and training of the LSTM language model used in our experiments. In Section 4, we describe our clustering methods and show examples of the clusters found, as well as a part of speech analysis. In Section 5, we describe and analyze our method for extracting word embeddings from the character-level model. Finally, we conclude and suggest directions for future work.

2 Related Work

2.1 Analyzing Hidden State Dynamics

Many researchers have investigated techniques for understanding the meaning and dynamics of the hidden states of recurrent neural networks. In his seminal paper (Elman, 1990) introducing the simple recurrent network (SRN) (or "Elman network"), Elman uses hierarchical clustering to investigate the hidden states of a word-level RNN modeling a toy language of 29 words. Our approach in Section 4 is in some ways similar, although we use real English data and a character-level LSTM model. This also bears some similarities to a visualization technique used by Krakovna and Doshi-Velez (2016) to investigate a hybrid HMM-LSTM model, although their work uses only 10 k-means clusters and does not deeply investigate clustering. Elman also uses principal component analysis to visualize hidden state over time (1991), and many researchers have used dimensionality reduction methods such as t-SNE

(Van der Maaten and Hinton, 2008) to visualize similarity between word embeddings, as well as other forms of distributed representation. More recently, Li et al. (2016) directly visualize representations over time using heatmaps, and Strobelt et al. (2018) develop interactive tools for visualizing LSTM hidden states and testing hypotheses about distributed representations.

Other researchers have investigated methods for clarifying the function of specific hidden dimensions. Karpathy et al. (2015) use static visualizations to demonstrate the existence of cells in an LSTM language model with interpretable behaviour representing long-term dependencies (such as cells tracking line length or quotations in a text). Another approach is that of Kádár et al. (2017), who introduce a "Top K Contexts" method for interpreting the function of certain hidden dimensions, identifying the K points in a sequence which experience the highest activations for the dimension in question.

2.2 Character-Level Word Embeddings

Multiple researchers have developed methods for creating word embeddings that incorporate subword level (Luong et al., 2013) or character-level (Santos and Zadrozny, 2014; Ling et al., 2015) information in order to better handle rare or out-of-vocabulary words. These approaches differ from our work in Section 5 in that they use architectures specifically designed to create word embeddings, while we create embeddings from the hidden state of a character-level model not designed for this purpose. In addition, we are interested not in the embeddings themselves, but rather in what they tell us about the word-level knowledge of the language model.

Kim et al. (2016) investigate word embeddings created by a character-aware language model; however, the model uses word-level inputs that are further subdivided into character-level information and makes predictions on the word level, while we use an entirely character-level model.

3 Model

In this paper we focus on the task of language modeling on the character level. Given an input sequence of characters, the model is tasked with predicting the log probability of the following character.

We trained two models on different data sets using the same architecture. Most of the paper focuses on the *War and Peace* model, but Section 5 uses embeddings derived from the *Lancaster-Oslo/Bergen Corpus* model when measuring performance against word embedding benchmarks.

3.1 Training Data

Our first model uses a relatively small data set, consisting of the text of *War and Peace* by Tolstoy[1]. This data set was chosen due to its convenience as a sufficiently long but stylistically consistent example of English text. The text contains 3,201,616 characters. We use the first 95% of the data for training and the last 5% for validation.

Our second model uses a slightly larger data set, consisting of the Lancaster-Oslo/Bergen (LOB) corpus (Johansson et al., 1978)[2], which we removed all markup from. This data set draws from a wide variety of fiction and non-fiction texts written in British English in 1961, and contains 5,818,332 characters total. It was chosen for use in Section 5 because it covers a wide range of topics (allowing us to extract word embeddings for a wider vocabulary) while still remaining at a manageable size. We use the last 95% of the data for training and the first 5% for validation.

3.2 Model Architecture and Implementation

We use a simple LSTM architecture consisting of a 256-dimensional character embedding layer, followed by three 512-dimensional LSTM layers, and a final layer producing a log softmax distribution over the set of possible characters. The model was implemented in PyTorch (Paszke et al., 2017) using the default LSTM implementation[3].

This architecture was chosen mostly arbitrarily, and distantly inspired by Karpathy et al. (2015).

3.3 Training

The *War and Peace* model was trained for 170 epochs using stochastic gradient descent and the negative log likelihood loss function, with mini-batches of size 100 and truncated backpropagation through time (BPTT) of 100 time steps. During training, dropout was applied after each LSTM layer with a dropout rate of 0.5. The learning rate

was initially set to 1 and halved every time the loss on the validation data set plateaued. The final model achieved 1.660 bits-per-character (BPC) on the validation data.

The Lancaster-Oslo/Bergen model was trained for 100 epochs using the PyTorch implementation of AdaGrad, with mini-batches of size 100, truncated BPTT of 100 time steps, a dropout rate of 0.5, and an initial learning rate of 0.01.[4] The final model achieved 1.787 BPC on the validation data.

4 Cluster Analysis of Character-Level and Word-Level Patterns

In this section we analyze points in the training text by clustering according to hidden state values and output gate activations, revealing a combination of grammatical and word-level patterns reflected in the hidden state of our language model.

4.1 Data For Clustering

We created two sets of data for use in clustering: a "full" data set and a "whitespace" data set.

To create the "full" data set, we ran our *War and Peace* language model on the first 50,000 characters[5] of the training data and recorded the hidden state (i.e. the values often denoted h_t in the LSTM literature, rather than the cell state c_t) and the sigmoid activations of the output gate of the third LSTM layer at each time step. We focus on the third layer based on the expectation that it will encode more high-level information than earlier layers, an expectation which was supported by brief experimentation on the first layer.

To create the "whitespace" data set, we ran the *War and Peace* model on the first 250,000 characters of the training data and recorded data only for timesteps when the input character was a space or a new line character.

4.2 Basic Clustering Experiment

We chose to use the HDBSCAN clustering algorithm (Campello et al., 2013), since it is designed to work with non-globular clusters of varying density, does not require that an expected number of clusters be specified in advance, and is willing to avoid assigning points to a cluster if they do not

---

[1](Tolstoy, 2009), translated to English by Louise and Aylmer Maude.

[2]retrieved from `http://purl.ox.ac.uk/ota/0167`

[3]We intend to release our code, including the trained models.

[4]Training parameters were not tuned to the data and differ mainly because the models were not trained at the same time, with unrelated experiments intervening.

[5]This smaller data set was used due to the relatively slow speed of the HDBSCAN implementation on high-dimensional data.

Cluster	Sample Cluster Members
4	even wi[s]h to; conversing wi[t]h; case wi[t]h; whi[c]h was; him wi[t]h; his wi[f]e; very wi[t]ty; acts whi[c]h;
7	so[m]ething like; she sa[w] that; Hardenburg sa[y]s; the sa[m]e time; none se[e]med to; words su[g]gested.
14	e[x]plains; e[v]erything; e[x]posed; e[x]pectations; e[l]derly; e[x]pression;
39	thi[s] reception; tha[t] profound; like thi[s]?"; the[y] promised; the[y] have; The[r]e is;
54	who[ ]is; He[ ]spoke; he[ ]indicated; who[ ]had; He[ ]frowned; She[ ]was; who[ ]was; she[ ]said; why[ ]he
56	on[ ]the; for[ ]God's; of[ ]the; of[ ]them; by[ ]imbecility; for[ ]Pierre; of[ ]young people; from[ ]abroad;
62	had[ ]gone; had[ ]the; had[ ]been; have[ ]reference; have[ ]promised; had[ ]also; has[ ]been; has[ ]to;
63	her[ ]house; that[ ]is; his[ ]boats; this[ ]pretty; that[ ]this; prevented her[ ]from; her[ ]age; his[ ]way; her[ ]duties;

Table 1: Example members of clusters found using hidden state values based on the "full" data set. Cluster members (indicated by brackets) are accompanied by text excerpts (separated by semicolons) to give context.

seem to be a good fit for any cluster. We used the Python implementation of McInnes et al. (2017).

Using the "full" data set, we attempted to cluster the time steps according to either hidden state or output gate activations. We used the Euclidean metric and the HDBSCAN parameters min_cluster_size=100 and min_samples=10. This was chosen somewhat arbitrarily and not on the basis of a parameter search; we did briefly try other settings during preliminary research and found that the results were similar[6]. Clustering by hidden state values and clustering by output gate activations both produced a number of interpretable clusters[7].

Table 1 shows a representative sample of the clusters found when using the hidden state for clustering[8]. We found that most clusters seemed to have interpretable meanings on the character level, often including characters near the start of words that begin with a particular character or characters, as in clusters 4, 7, and 14. In some cases, these clusters seem to locate orthographic patterns that

are useful in predicting the following character; for example, the characters in cluster 4 are often followed by an "h", and cluster 39 contains mostly letters at the end of a word (i.e. usually followed by whitespace). However, we did not find clusters that were characterised only by the following characters and not by patterns in the preceding characters.

More interestingly, clusters consisting of points immediately preceding the start of a word tended to reflect word-level information relating to the preceding word. For example, cluster 54 consists of spaces immediately following the pronouns "he" and "she", as well as the interrogative pronoun "who"[9], while cluster 56 consists of spaces following certain prepositions. This was observed in both the clusters based on hidden state and the clusters based on output gate activation. This could be due to the fact that the output gate activations, which also impact the hidden state, can be intepreted as choosing which dimensions of the cell state are relevant for the network's "decision" at a given time, and we would expect that word-level information is relevant when choosing a distribution over the first letter of the next word.

4.3 Whitespace Clustering and Part-of-Speech Analysis

Since the clusters including whitespace tended to reflect word-level grammatical information (as seen in clusters 54, 56, and 62 from Table 1), we performed another round of clustering restricting our focus to only spaces and new lines. Clustering was performed on the "whitespace" data according to either hidden states or output gate activations, again producing many interpretable clusters[10].

For the purposes of word-level analysis, each data point (corresponding to a whitespace character in the text) was equated with the word immediately preceding it. The Stanford Part-of-Speech Tagger (Toutanova et al., 2003) was used to tag the text with part of speech (POS) information, and for each cluster the *precision* (percentage of words in the cluster having a given tag) and *recall* (percentage of words with a given tag falling

---

[6]Of course, allowing smaller clusters results in more clusters, while requiring larger clusters results in fewer, broader clusters, but there were no major qualitative differences in the types of clusters produced.

[7]Clustering by hidden state produced 67 clusters, while clustering by output gate activations produced 87 clusters.

[8]The output gate clusters were similar and are omitted to save space.

[9] This cluster also occasionally includes spaces following the word "why", which may be due to orthographic similarity to "who", or due to the fact that "why" is often followed by a verb, as in "Why is...".

[10]Clustering by hidden states produced 70 clusters, while clustering by output gate activations produced 77 clusters.

Cluster	Sample Members of Cluster	POS - Precision	POS - Recall
HS-35	asked; replied; remarked; continued; replied; cried; cried; repeated; continued; exclaimed; remarked; remarked; continued; declared;	VBD: 100%	VBD: 4.5%
HS-40	will; will; don't; don't; don't; cannot; just; can't; will; will; might; could; shall; will; would; just; would; just; just; don't; don't; could;	MD: 59.2% RB: 18.3% NN: 21.3% [11]	MD: 89.9% RB: 5.1% NN: 2.9%
HS-57	looking; looked; looking; looked; looked; looking; walked; glanced; looking; looking; glancing; looked; looked; looked; looking	VBD: 60.0% VBG: 40.0%	VBD: 2.4% VBG: 4.8%
HS-59	trembled; jumped; tucked; smoothed; smiled; raised; standing; smiled; pushed; smiled; passed; crowding; turning; raised; climbed; watched; turned; changed;	VBD: 59.1% VBG: 31.5% VBN: 8.7%	VBD: 6.0% VBG: 9.7% VBN: 3.3%
HS-62	unnatural; beautiful; beautiful; beautiful; terrified; suppressed; proud-looking; polished; well-garnished; nice-looking; swaggering; wonderful; embittered; alarmed; mournful	JJ: 84.4% VBN: 6.7% VBG: 4.4%	JJ: 4.1% VBN: 0.9% VBG: 0.5%
OG-69	laughter; mother; father; daughter; father; father; matter; daughter; father; manner; officer; father; daughter; mother; laughter; daughter; daughter; father; officer;	NN: 94.1% NNS: 2.9% JJ: 2.9%	NN: 1.9% NNS: 0.3% JJ: 0.1%
OG-74	emancipation; nation; conversation; conversation; opinion conversation; resignation; conversation; conversation; expression;	NN: 95.7% NNP: 4.4%	NN: 3.8% NNP: 0.3%

Table 2: Cluster members and POS statistics. Example cluster members (corresponding to whitespace characters) are drawn uniformly at random from the cluster and are represented by the preceding word. Note that some words appear multiple times since each appearance of the word in the text corresponds to a different data point. POS tags are those used by the Stanford POS tagger. Statistics are reported for the three parts of speech with highest precision.

into the cluster)[12] were calculated with respect to each tag. Since the clusters are based only on data corresponding to whitespace, words not followed by whitespace (approximately 16% of all words) were not counted when calculating recall.

A selection of clusters, example members, and POS statistics can be seen in Table 2. Clusters are designated "OG" or "HS" for "output gate" and "hidden state" respectively, so "HS-35" means the 35th cluster produced when clustering by hidden state values. These clusters were selected to illustrate the interesting patterns present, rather than to represent "typical" clusters.

The resulting clusters based on hidden states were similar to those based on output gate activations. Both approaches resulted in some clusters based on a mix of orthographic and semantic similarity — for example, both produced a cluster consisting primarily of three-letter verbs beginning with "s" (particularly "sat", "saw", and "say"), as well as clusters consisting of possessive uses of the suffix "'s", but not uses of "'s" as a contraction of "is" (as in "it's", "that's", etc.), despite the existence of several such uses in the text.

In fact, some early experimentation resulted in a distinct cluster for the contractive use of "'s", although this does not occur with the parameters we chose for our canonical data. Additionally, in both cases the majority of clusters contained instances of only a single word or a small set of words — for example, a cluster consisting entirely of the word "the", a cluster consisting almost entirely of the words "he" and "she", and a cluster containing only the words "me" and "my". In total, 71% of clusters either contained only one or two words, or were determined by preceding punctuation.

However, there were qualitative differences between the two approaches. Some of the hidden state clusters appear to be based on semantic similarities that go beyond mere grammatical similarity; in particular, cluster HS-35 (as seen in Table 2) contains words related to dialogue (and additional context reveals that members of this cluster always follow the end of a quotation), while cluster HS-57 contains multiple words related to looking (including "gazed", although it does not appear in the table). Additionally, cluster HS-40 finds modal verbs with high precision and 89.9% recall, along with the words "just" and "still", which might be included due to orthographic similarity to "must" and "will".

In contrast, clusters based on output gate activations appear to be somewhat more closely related to orthographic similarities. Several of these clusters display orthographic patterns that corre-

---

[11]Manual inspection suggests that the claimed 22% precision for nouns is actually due to the POS tagger mistaking "don't", "can't" etc. for nouns, probably due to poor tokenization, meaning that the true precision for modal verbs in this cluster is 80% if we consider these to be modal verbs.

[12]Note that when measured in this way, recall will usually be quite low, since most clusters only contain some particular subset of words with a given tag.

late strongly with parts of speech; for example, clusters OG-69 and OG-74 contain "-ion" nouns and "-er" nouns (but not "-er" adjectives) respectively, and rather than including all modal verbs in a single cluster, the output gate clusters group the words "would", "could", and "should" separately from "don't", "won't", and "can't" (which are in turn separate from the cluster containing "will" and "still"). This suggests that character-level patterns correlated with grammatical information could strongly influence output gate activations in a way that contributes to the grammatical understanding of the model[13].

5 Extracting Word Embeddings

As seen in Section 4.3, hidden states after whitespace characters encode word-level information. This suggests a method for deriving word embeddings from a character-level model, in order to better investigate the model's word-level knowledge.

To obtain word embeddings, we ran the *War and Peace* model on the entire text of *War and Peace*, storing hidden state values at each point in the text. We then associated each word appearing at least once in the text[14] with the average hidden state vector for whitespace characters following the word in question. This produced a set of 512-dimensional embeddings for a vocabulary of 15,750 distinct words[15].

Table 3 shows the nearest neighbours[16] of the embeddings of several words, as well as a count of how frequently the word appears in the text. While not all nearest neighbours seem to be relevant (particularly for e.g. "write" and "food"), it nonetheless appears that for words well-represented in the text, these embeddings do reflect meaning (e.g. "loved" is similar to "liked", "soldier" to "officer", and so on). In the case of words that are less well represented (e.g. "write", "food"), the nearest neighbours often seem to be retrieved based more on orthographic similarities; however, "food" is

Word (Occurrences)	5 Nearest Neighbours
prince (1,926)	princess, pwince, princes, platón, phillip
we (1069)	I, tu, you, ve, he
soldier (201)	officer, footman, soldiers, traveler, landowner
loved (120)	liked, longed, saved, lived, lose
frenchman (100)	frenchwoman, englishman, huntsman, coachman, frenchmen
write (61)	wring, wake, wipe, strive, live
food (41)	foot, folk, fool, fear, form
tu (4)	we, I, thou, you, je
untruth (3)	distrust, entreaty, rescript, rupture, ruse
cannonading (2)	undertaking, attacking, outflanking, maintaining tormenting
scrutinizingly (1)	questioningly, challengingly, attentively, imploringly, despairingly
moscovite (1)	honneur, moravian, tshausen, chinese, grenadier
custodian (1)	guardian, battalion, nightmare, republican, mathematician
conduce (1)	convince, conclude, conduced induce, introduce
deck (1)	delve, dwell, descry, deny, decide

Table 3: Sample vocabulary words and the number of times each appears in the text, compared with the 5 nearest neighbours according to our extracted word embeddings.

still associated with nouns, and "write" with verbs, and more generally the embedding usually appears to at least reflect basic part of speech information.

More surprising, however, is the treatment of words that appear only once in the text. In some cases, the embeddings of these words do reflect not only grammatical information but also their actual meaning; the word "moscovite", for example, is correctly associated with the words "moravian" and "chinese" which also describe geographic origin, and the word "scrutinizingly" is associated with "questioningly" and "challengingly". In these cases, since the word "moscovites" and various forms of "scrutinize" do appear more frequently in the text, it is possible that orthographic similarity and an understanding of morphemes such as "-s", "-ing" and "-ly" contribute to these embeddings. This would be consistent with the findings of e.g. Santos and Zadrozny (2014) and others who have used the orthographic information associated with words to develop word embeddings that perform well for rare words and even out-of-vocabulary words.

---

[13]Though the ability of RNNs to learn and represent syntax has been studied in RNNs with explicit access to grammatical structure (Kuncoro et al., 2017), to our knowledge, syntax representations have not been explored in character-level RNNs.

[14]Excluding words that are never followed immediately by a whitespace character (about 16% of all words).

[15]17,510 words in total, but 1,760 are a combination of two words joined by an em-dash. We ignore these "words" in our nearest neighbours analysis.

[16]A tool from scikit-learn (Pedregosa et al., 2011) was used to find nearest neighbours by cosine similarity. Using the Euclidean metric instead gives very similar results.

Task	Pairs Found and Correlation					
	Our Embeddings		Metaoptimize		Skip-Gram	
WS-353	290	0.1376	351	0.1013	353	**0.6392**
WS-353-SIM	164	0.2265	201	0.1507	203	**0.6962**
WS-353-REL	215	0.1384	252	0.0929	252	**0.6094**
MC-30	25	0.1808	30	-0.1351	30	**0.6258**
RG-65	48	0.2051	64	-0.0182	65	**0.5386**
Rare-Word	604	0.1500	1159	0.1085	1435	**0.3878**
MEN	2317	0.1800	2915	0.0908	2999	**0.6462**
MTurk-287	232	0.3681	284	0.0922	286	**0.6698**
MTurk-771	689	0.0920	770	0.1016	771	**0.5679**
YP-130	111	0.1311	124	0.0690	130	**0.3992**
SimLex-999	948	0.0827	998	0.0095	998	**0.3131**
Verb-144	144	**0.3437**	144	0.0553	144	0.2728
SimVerb-3500	3052	0.0098	3447	0.0009	3492	**0.2172**

Table 4: Performance of the word vectors derived from our Lancaster-Oslo/Bergen model on word similarity tasks, compared with scores (taken from `http://wordvectors.org` (Faruqui and Dyer, 2014)) for the Metaoptimize (Turian et al., 2010) and Skip-Gram (Mikolov et al., 2013) embeddings. For each set of embeddings and each task we list the number of word pairs found and the measured correlation (Spearman's rank correlation coefficient).

However, this does not explain the case of "deck". When this word appears in the text, it is used in its sense as a verb. The only other appearance of the string "deck" in the text is the word "decks", referring to the noun form of the word, and yet the embedding for "deck" is correctly similar to other verbs. For this reason, and because the word "deck" is short and does not consist of meaningful sub-word entities, it is unlikely that the verb-ness of "deck" was deduced from the word itself. This suggests that the model was able to determine the part of speech of the word from its use *in a single context* (e.g. the fact that it was preceded by "do not"). A similar mechanism may also be responsible for the understanding of the French word "tu", which is correctly identified as a personal pronoun similar to both "you" (its translation, appearing 3,509 times) and "je" (the French 1st-person singular pronoun, appearing 16 times) despite containing little orthographic information. It should also be noted that while it is not the norm for these embeddings of singleton words to reflect meaning (as in the case of "scrutinizingly"), the majority of embeddings do appear to at least identify part of speech (as in the case of "deck"), suggesting a fairly robust mechanism for determining this information from context.

The goal of this experiment was not to produce high-quality embeddings, but rather to understand the word-level knowledge of a character-level language model. Nonetheless, we decided to evaluate word embeddings obtained in this manner against some word similarity benchmarks. In order to obtain a broader vocabulary, we used word embeddings derived from the model we trained on the Lancaster-Oslo/Bergen corpus. While this training data is still quite small (less than 6 million characters), it covers a wider range of authors, styles, and topics, including fiction, non-fiction, scientific papers and news articles, and thus is better suited to producing general-purpose word embeddings. The embeddings we extracted from this corpus cover a vocabulary of 38,981 words.

We assessed these embeddings using the 13 word similarity tasks of `http://wordvectors.org` (Faruqui and Dyer, 2014), achieving the results shown in Table 4. While these results are far from state-of-the-art, they do outperform the representations of Turian et al. (2010) on all tasks except for MTurk-771. Furthermore, our embeddings perform comparably on the "Rare Words" task compared to several other tasks, despite the small corpus size, presumably due to the use of orthographic and contextual information by the language model.

6 Discussion and Conclusion

In this paper, we used clustering to investigate the type of information reflected in the hidden states and output gate activations of an LSTM language model. Focusing on whitespace characters revealed clusters containing words with meaningful semantic similarities, as well as clusters reflecting orthographic patterns that correlate with grammatical information.

We also described a method for extracting word embeddings from a character-level language model. Analysis suggests that the model is able to learn meaningful semantic information even about words that appear only once in the training text, using some combination of orthographic and contextual information.

Directions for future work related to our clustering analysis could include applying similar techniques to other RNN architectures (e.g. the GRU of Cho et al. (2014)), comparing the effectiveness of different clustering algorithms for this type of analysis, and scaling up the clustering experiments using more computational resources, a more efficient algorithm, and a larger corpus.

Another promising direction is to expand on the findings of Section 5 by analyzing the quality of word embeddings produced from character-level models trained on a larger corpus, and investigating the capability of character level models to produce word embeddings for out-of-vocabulary words when given a small amount of context.

Collectively, our findings regarding clustering analysis and extraction of word embeddings offer interesting insight into the behaviour of character-level recurrent language models, and we hope that they will prove a useful contribution in the ongoing effort to increase the interpretability of recurrent neural networks.

Acknowledgments

This research was supported by NSERC (Natural Sciences and Engineering Research Council), including an Undergraduate Student Research Award for Avery Hiebert, and by CIFAR (Canadian Institute for Advanced Research).

References

Ricardo J. G. B. Campello, Davoud Moulavi, and Joerg Sander. 2013. Density-based clustering based on hierarchical density estimates. In *Advances in Knowledge Discovery and Data Mining*, pages 160–172, Berlin, Heidelberg. Springer Berlin Heidelberg.

Kyunghyun Cho, Bart van Merriënboer, Caglar Gulcehre, Dzmitry Bahdanau, Fethi Bougares, Holger Schwenk, and Yoshua Bengio. 2014. Learning phrase representations using rnn encoder-decoder for statistical machine translation. In *Proceedings of the 2014 Conference on Empirical Methods in Natural Language Processing (EMNLP 2014)*, Doha, Qatar.

Jeffrey L Elman. 1990. Finding structure in time. *Cognitive science*, 14(2):179–211.

Jeffrey L Elman. 1991. Distributed representations, simple recurrent networks, and grammatical structure. *Machine learning*, 7(2-3):195–225.

Manaal Faruqui and Chris Dyer. 2014. Community evaluation and exchange of word vectors at word-vectors.org. In *Proceedings of the 52nd Annual Meeting of the Association for Computational Linguistics: System Demonstrations*, Baltimore, USA. Association for Computational Linguistics.

Felix A Gers, Jürgen Schmidhuber, and Fred Cummins. 2000. Learning to forget: Continual prediction with LSTM. *Neural Computation*, 12(10):2451–2471.

Alex Graves. 2013. Generating sequences with recurrent neural networks. *Computing Research Repository*, arXiv:1308.0850. Version 5.

Sepp Hochreiter and Jürgen Schmidhuber. 1997. Long short-term memory. *Neural Computation*, 9(8):1735–1780.

Stig Johansson, Geoffrey N Leech, and Helen Goodluck. 1978. *Manual of information to accompany the Lancaster-Oslo/Bergen Corpus of British English, for use with digital computer*. Department of English, University of Oslo.

Akos Kádár, Grzegorz Chrupała, and Afra Alishahi. 2017. Representation of linguistic form and function in recurrent neural networks. *Computational Linguistics*, 43(4):761–780.

Andrej Karpathy, Justin Johnson, and Li Fei-Fei. 2015. Visualizing and understanding recurrent networks. In *Workshop track - ICLR 2016*.

Yoon Kim, Yacine Jernite, David Sontag, and Alexander M Rush. 2016. Character-aware neural language models. In *AAAI*, pages 2741–2749.

Viktoriya Krakovna and Finale Doshi-Velez. 2016. Increasing the interpretability of recurrent neural networks using hidden Markov models. In *Proceedings of NIPS 2016 Workshop on Interpretable Machine Learning for Complex Systems*, Barcelona, Spain.

Adhiguna Kuncoro, Miguel Ballesteros, Lingpeng Kong, Chris Dyer, Graham Neubig, and Noah A. Smith. 2017. What do recurrent neural network grammars learn about syntax? In *Proceedings of the 15th Conference of the European Chapter of the Association for Computational Linguistics: Volume 1, Long Papers*, pages 1249–1258. Association for Computational Linguistics.

Jiwei Li, Xinlei Chen, Eduard Hovy, and Dan Jurafsky. 2016. Visualizing and understanding neural models in NLP. In *Proceedings of the 2016 Conference of the North American Chapter of the Association for Computational Linguistics: Human Language Technologies*, pages 681–691, San Diego, California. Association for Computational Linguistics.

Wang Ling, Tiago Luís, Luís Marujo, Rámon Fernandez Astudillo, Silvio Amir, Chris Dyer, Alan W Black, and Isabel Trancoso. 2015. Finding function in form: Compositional character models for open vocabulary word representation. EMNLP.

Thang Luong, Richard Socher, and Christopher Manning. 2013. Better word representations with recursive neural networks for morphology. In *Proceedings of the Seventeenth Conference on Computational Natural Language Learning*, pages 104–113.

Laurens van der Maaten and Geoffrey Hinton. 2008. Visualizing data using t-SNE. *Journal of Machine Learning Research*, 9(Nov):2579–2605.

Leland McInnes, John Healy, and Steve Astels. 2017. hdbscan: Hierarchical density based clustering. *The Journal of Open Source Software*, 2(11):205.

Tomas Mikolov, Kai Chen, Greg Corrado, and Jeffrey Dean. 2013. Efficient estimation of word representations in vector space. In *Workshop Proceedings of the International Conference on Learning Representations (ICLR) 2013*.

Tomáš Mikolov, Ilya Sutskever, Anoop Deoras, Hai-Son Le, Stefan Kombrink, and Jan Černocký. 2012. Subword language modeling with neural networks. *preprint http://www.fit.vutbr.cz/~imikolov/rnnlm/char.pdf*, 8.

Adam Paszke, Sam Gross, Soumith Chintala, Gregory Chanan, Edward Yang, Zachary DeVito, Zeming Lin, Alban Desmaison, Luca Antiga, and Adam Lerer. 2017. Automatic differentiation in PyTorch. In *NIPS 2017 Autodiff Workshop*, Long Beach, California, USA.

F. Pedregosa, G. Varoquaux, A. Gramfort, V. Michel, B. Thirion, O. Grisel, M. Blondel, P. Prettenhofer, R. Weiss, V. Dubourg, J. Vanderplas, A. Passos, D. Cournapeau, M. Brucher, M. Perrot, and E. Duchesnay. 2011. Scikit-learn: Machine learning in Python. *Journal of Machine Learning Research*, 12:2825–2830.

Cícero D Santos and Bianca Zadrozny. 2014. Learning character-level representations for part-of-speech tagging. In *Proceedings of the 31st International Conference on Machine Learning (ICML-14)*, pages 1818–1826.

H. Strobelt, S. Gehrmann, H. Pfister, and A. M. Rush. 2018. LSTMVis: A tool for visual analysis of hidden state dynamics in recurrent neural networks. *IEEE Transactions on Visualization and Computer Graphics*, 24(1):667–676.

Leo Tolstoy. 2009. *War and Peace*. Project Gutenberg, Urbana, IL. Translated by Louise and Aylmer Maude.

Kristina Toutanova, Dan Klein, Christopher D Manning, and Yoram Singer. 2003. Feature-rich part-of-speech tagging with a cyclic dependency network. In *Proceedings of the 2003 Conference of the North American Chapter of the Association for Computational Linguistics on Human Language Technology-Volume 1*, pages 173–180. Association for Computational Linguistics.

Joseph Turian, Lev Ratinov, and Yoshua Bengio. 2010. Word representations: a simple and general method for semi-supervised learning. In *Proceedings of the 48th annual meeting of the association for computational linguistics*, pages 384–394. Association for Computational Linguistics.

Importance of Self-Attention for Sentiment Analysis

Gaël Letarte,* Frédérik Paradis,* Philippe Giguère, François Laviolette
Department of Computer Science and Software Engineering
Université Laval, Québec, Canada
`{gael.letarte, frederik.paradis}.1@ulaval.ca`

Abstract

Despite their superior performance, deep learning models often lack interpretability. In this paper, we explore the modeling of insightful relations between words, in order to understand and enhance predictions. To this effect, we propose the Self-Attention Network (SANet), a flexible and interpretable architecture for text classification. Experiments indicate that gains obtained by self-attention is task-dependent. For instance, experiments on sentiment analysis tasks showed an improvement of around 2% when using self-attention compared to a baseline without attention, while topic classification showed no gain. Interpretability brought forward by our architecture highlighted the importance of neighboring word interactions to extract sentiment.

1 Introduction

Deep neural networks have achieved great successes on numerous tasks. However, they are often seen as black boxes, lacking interpretability. Research efforts in order to solve this issue have steadily increased (Simonyan et al., 2013; Zeiler and Fergus, 2014; Bach et al., 2015; Ribeiro et al., 2016; Fong and Vedaldi, 2017). In language modeling, interpretability often takes place via an attention mechanism in the neural network (Bahdanau et al., 2014; Xu et al., 2015; Sukhbaatar et al., 2015; Choi et al., 2017). In this context, attention essentially allows a network to identify which words in a sentence are more relevant. Beyond interpretability, this often results in improved decision making by the network.

Recently, Vaswani et al. (2017) proposed the *Transformer* architecture for machine translation. It relies only on attention mechanisms, instead of making use of either recurrent or convolutional neural networks. This architecture contains layers called self-attention (or intra-attention) which allow each word in the sequence to pay attention to other words in the sequence, independently of their positions. We modified this architecture, resulting in the following contributions:

- A novel architecture for *text classification* called Self-Attention Network (SANet) that models the interactions between all input word pairs. It is sequence length-agnostic, thanks to a global max pooling layer.
- A study on the impact of this self-attention mechanism on large scale datasets. In particular, we empirically demonstrate the positive impact of self-attention in terms of performance and interpretability for sentiment analysis, compared to topic classification. In the study, we make use of two quantitative metrics (Gini coefficient and diagonality) that exhibit particular behaviors for attention mechanisms in sentiment analysis.

2 Related Work

The majority of text classification techniques either use convolutional or recurrent neural networks on the words or the characters of the sentence (Zhang et al., 2015, 2017; Yang et al., 2016; Conneau et al., 2017; Johnson and Zhang, 2016, 2017; Howard and Ruder, 2018). One notable exception is the *fastText* architecture (Joulin et al., 2016) which essentially employs a bag-of-words approach with word embeddings of the sentence.

Attention mechanisms are a way to add interpretability in neural networks. They were introduced by Bahdanau et al. (2014), where they achieved state-of-the-art in machine translation. Since then, attention mechanisms have been used in other language modeling tasks such as image captioning (Xu et al., 2015), question answer-

---

* Authors contributed equally to this work.

Proceedings of the 2018 EMNLP Workshop BlackboxNLP: Analyzing and Interpreting Neural Networks for NLP, pages 267–275
Brussels, Belgium, November 1, 2018. ©2018 Association for Computational Linguistics

ing (Sukhbaatar et al., 2015; Choi et al., 2017), and text classification (Yang et al., 2016). The concept of *self-attention* (Cheng et al., 2016; Parikh et al., 2016), central to our proposed approach, has shown great promises in natural language processing; It produced state-of-the-art results for machine translation (Vaswani et al., 2017).

In text classification, the focus on interpretability has thus far been limited. Lee et al. (2018) used a convolutional neural network (CNN) with Class Activation Mapping (CAM) (Oquab et al., 2015) to do sentiment analysis. CAM basically uses the weights of the classification layer to derive a heatmap on the input. Wang et al. (2018) used a densely connected CNN (Huang et al., 2017) to apply attention to n-grams. However, their approach limits the range and acuteness of the interactions between the words in the text. Lin et al. (2017) and Yang et al. (2016) both combined an attention mechanism with a recurrent neural network. The main difference with our work is, while being interpretable, these approaches do not perform true word-on-word attention across a whole sequence such as our self-attention layer.

3 SANet: Self-Attention Network

Inspired by the *Transformer* architecture (Vaswani et al., 2017) which performed machine translation without recurrent or convolutional layers, we propose the Self-Attention Network (SANet) architecture targeting instead text classification. One key difference between our approach and Vaswani et al. (2017)'s is that we only perform *input-input* attention with self-attention, as we do not have sequences as output but a text classification. Moreover, we employ global max pooling at the top, which enables our architecture to process input sequences of arbitrary length.

Formally, let $X = [x_1^T; x_2^T; \ldots; x_n^T]$ be the concatenation of a sequence of n vectors giving a matrix $X \in \mathbb{R}^{n \times d}$ such that $x_i \in \mathbb{R}^d$. Vaswani et al. (2017) defined attention as a function with as input a triplet containing queries Q, keys K with associated values V.

$$\text{Att}(Q, K, V) = \text{softmax}\left(QK^T\right) V$$

In the case of self-attention, Q, K and V are linear projections of X. Thus, we define the dot-product

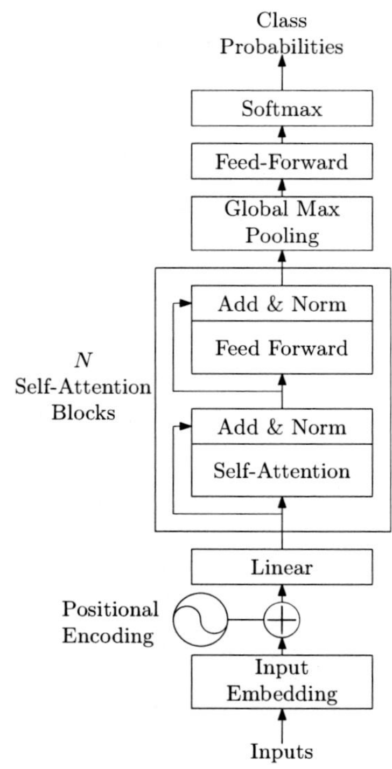

Figure 1: Our Self-Attention Network (SANet), derived from the Transformer architecture (Vaswani et al., 2017). The self-attention block is repeated N times.

self-attention mechanism as follows.

$$\text{Self-Att}(X) = \text{Att}(XW_Q, XW_K, XW_V)$$
$$= \text{softmax}\left(XW_{QK}X^T\right) XW_V$$

Where $W_Q, W_K, W_V, W_{QK} \in \mathbb{R}^{d \times d}$ and $W_{QK} = W_Q W_K^T$. Hence, W_{QK} and W_V are learned parameters.

Our network (depicted in Figure 1) first encodes each word to its embedding. Pre-trained embeddings, like GloVe (Pennington et al., 2014), may be used and fine-tuned during the learning process. Next, to inject information about the order of the words, the positional encoding layer adds location information to each word. We use the positional encoding vectors that were defined by Vaswani et al. (2017) as follows.

$$\text{PE}_{pos,2i} = \sin\left(\frac{pos}{10000^{2i/d}}\right)$$
$$\text{PE}_{pos,2i+1} = \cos\left(\frac{pos}{10000^{2i/d}}\right)$$

Where pos is the position of the word in the sequence and $1 \leq i \leq d$ is the dimension in the positional encoding vector.

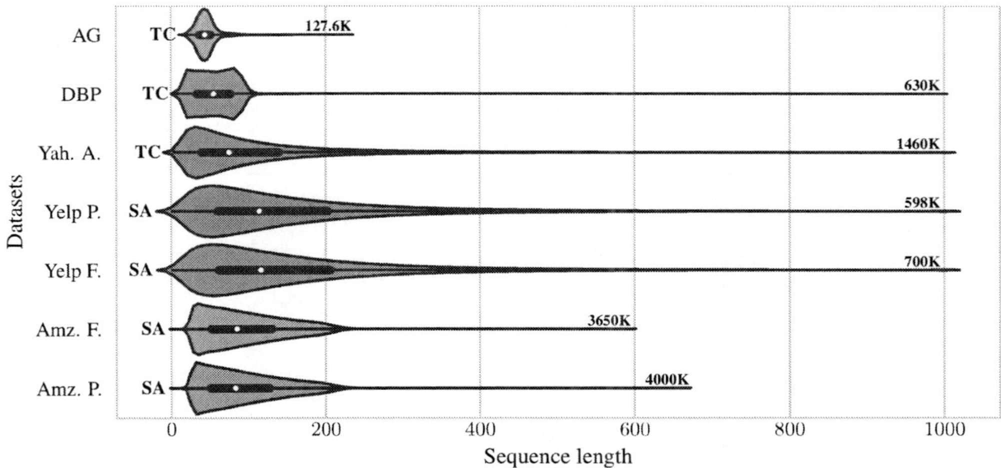

Figure 2: Visualization of sequences length distributions. For each dataset, the total number of examples is presented on the right and task semantics are identified on the left: Topic Classification (TC) or Sentiment Analysis (SA).

A linear layer then performs dimensionality reduction/augmentation of the embedding space to a vector space of dimension d, which is kept constant throughout the network. It is followed by one or several "self-attention blocks" stacked one onto another. These blocks are comprised of a self-attention layer followed by a feed-forward network, both with residual connections. Contrary to Vaswani et al. (2017), we only use a single attention head, with attention performed on the complete sequence with constant d-dimensional inputs.

The feed-forward network consists of a single hidden layer with a ReLU.

$$\text{FFN}(x) = \max(0, xW_1 + b_1)W_2 + b_2$$

Where $W_1, W_2 \in \mathbb{R}^{d \times d}$ are learned parameters. The "Add & Norm" layer is a residual connection defined by $\text{LayerNorm}(x + \text{SubLayer}(x))$, where $\text{SubLayer}(x)$ is the output of the previous layer and LayerNorm is a layer normalization method introduced by Ba et al. (2016). Let x_i be the vector representation of an element in the input sequence. The normalization layer simply normalizes x_i by the mean and the variance of its elements. Throughout this paper, dropout of 0.1 is applied to the output of $\text{SubLayer}(x)$

Finally, since we restrict ourselves to classification, we need a fixed-size representation of the sequence before the classification layer. To achieve this, we apply a global max pooling operation for each dimension across all the n words of the sequence. That is, if $X \in \mathbb{R}^{n \times d}$, then the max pooling on X outputs a vector in $\mathbb{R}^d$. This technique was inspired by global average pooling introduced by Lin et al. (2013) for image classification in CNNs. Global max pooling allows us to handle sequences of any length (up to memory limitations). Thus, our approach is length-agnostic contrary to some approaches based on CNN, where sequences are truncated or padded to obtain a fixed-length representation.

4 Experiments

We evaluated our model on seven large scale text classification datasets introduced by Zhang et al. (2015), grouped into two kinds of tasks. The first one is topic classification: *AG's News* with 4 classes of news articles, *DBPedia* with 14 classes of the Wikipedia ontology and *Yahoo! Answers* containing 10 categories of questions/answers. *Yelp* and *Amazon* reviews involve sentiment analysis with ratings from 1 to 5 stars. Two versions are derived from those datasets: one for predicting the number of stars, and the other involving the polarity of the reviews (negative for 1-2 stars, positive for 4-5 stars).

Each text entry was split into sentences and tokenized using NLTK (Bird et al., 2009). Sequences longer than 1000 tokens were truncated to accommodate GPU memory limitations, only affecting a negligible portion of the texts. See Figure 2 for

Table 1: Test error rates (%) for text classification. In **bold**, the state-of-the-art and in *italic*, our best model. Lin et al. (2017)'s results provided by Wang et al. (2018). Stars (*) indicate attention mechanisms.

Model	Topic Classification			Sentiment Analysis			
	AG	DBP.	Yah. A.	Yelp P.	Yelp F.	Amz. F.	Amz. P.
ngrams/CNN (Zhang et al., 2015)	7.64	1.31	28.26	4.36	37.95	40.43	4.98
fastText (Joulin et al., 2016)	7.5	1.4	27.7	4.3	36.1	39.8	5.4
word-CNN (Johnson and Zhang, 2016)	6.57	0.84	24.85	2.90	32.39	36.24	3.79
HN-ATT* (Yang et al., 2016)	-	-	**24.2**	-	-	36.4	-
VDCNN (Conneau et al., 2017)	8.67	1.29	26.57	4.28	35.28	37.00	4.28
DCNN (Zhang et al., 2017)	-	1.17	25.82	3.96	-	-	-
DPCNN (Johnson and Zhang, 2017)	6.87	0.88	23.90	2.64	30.58	**34.81**	**3.32**
SA-Embedding* (Lin et al., 2017)	8.5	1.7	-	5.1	36.6	40.2	-
ULMFiT (Howard and Ruder, 2018)	**5.01**	**0.80**	-	**2.16**	**29.98**	-	-
DCCNN-ATT* (Wang et al., 2018)	6.4	**0.8**	-	3.5	34.0	37.0	-
Baseline (base model)	7.34	1.30	26.87	6.39	39.98	41.80	6.38
SANet* (base model)	7.86	1.27	26.99	6.26	38.16	40.08	5.55
Baseline (big)	*7.20*	*1.25*	25.90	6.42	38.92	40.58	5.82
SANet* (big)	*7.42*	*1.28*	*25.88*	*4.77*	*36.03*	*38.67*	*4.52*

a visualization of the resulting sequences length distribution and the total number of examples per dataset.

We used 20% of the training texts for validation. The vocabulary was built using every word appearing in the training and validation sets. The words embeddings were initialized using pre-trained word vectors from GloVe (Pennington et al., 2014) when available, or randomly initialized otherwise.

We experimented with two configurations for our proposed SANet. The base model used $N = 1$ self-attention blocks, an embedding size of 100 and a hidden size of $d = 128$. The big model doubled these numbers, i.e. $N = 2$ self-attention blocks, embedding size of 200 and hidden size $d = 256$. For each configuration, we also trained a baseline network without any attention mechanisms, replacing each self-attention layer with a feed forward layer.

Training was performed using SGD with a momentum of 0.9, a learning rate of 0.01 and minibatches of size 128. For the embeddings, a learning rate of 0.001 was applied without momentum. All learning rates were halved for the big model. We trained for 40 epochs and selected the best epoch, based on validation accuracy.

5 Results and Discussion

From a performance perspective, as shown in Table 1, our model based entirely on attention is competitive while offering high level interpretability. There is a notable exception with *Yelp Review Polarity* that will be discussed. Our results also indicate that the increase in depth and representation size in the big model is beneficial, compared to the simpler base model. Most noteworthy, we noticed considerably different behaviors of the attention mechanism depending on the type of task. We offer an analysis below.

5.1 Topic Classification Tasks

On the topic classification task, the self-attention behavior can be described as looking for interactions between important concepts, without considering relative distance. As such, it acts similarly to a bag-of-word approach, while highlighting key elements and their associations. Thus, the attention matrix takes shape of active columns, one per concept. One such matrix is depicted in Figure 3a, where the attention is focused on distanced pairs such as (`microsoft`, `class-action`) or (`settlement`, `billions`) to help SANet predict the *Business* category, while the baseline wrongfully predicts *Sci/Tech*. We observed this column-based structure for attention matrix for every topic classification dataset, see Figure 4 for

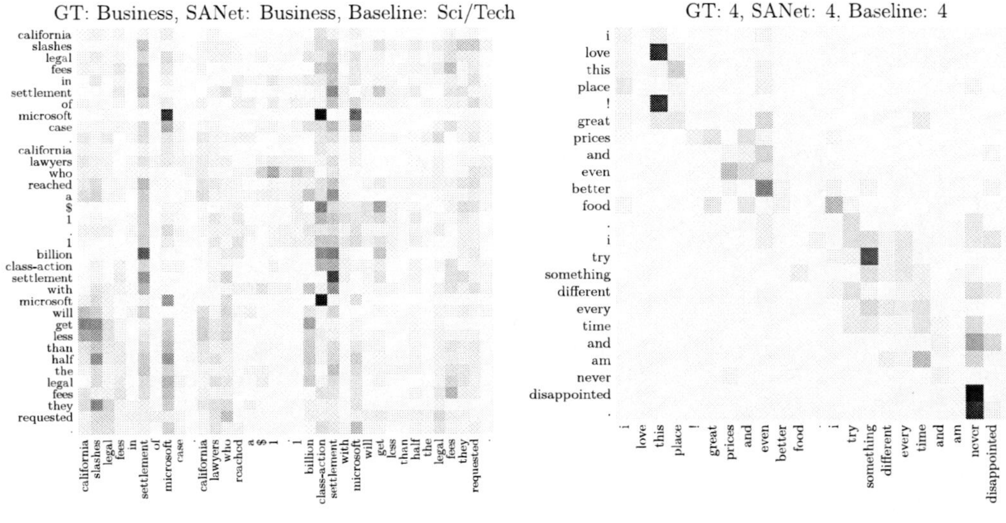

(a) Topic Classification.

(b) Sentiment Analysis. Label 4 means 5-star review

Figure 3: Self-attention different behavior for each text classification task. The attention matrices were extracted from the SANet base model applied on the testing set of each dataset. Words on the y-axis are attending to the words on the x-axis. GT refers to the ground truth.

multiple examples. Although it adds interpretability to the model, our results seem to indicate that self-attention does not improve performances for topic classification, compared to the baseline.

5.2 Sentiment Analysis Tasks

For sentiment analysis tasks, self-attention improves accuracy for every dataset and model configurations that we tested. For *Yelp Review Polarity*, although attention helps, the overall performances remain subpar.

Noticeably for the other datasets, SANet is able to extract subtle interactions between words, with a strong focus on neighboring relation. Hence, the attention matrices are close to being band matrices, with interest concentrated on very small regions near the diagonal. This is observable in Figure 5 where multiple examples from all sentiment analysis datasets are presented. Concentration of the attention around the diagonal indicates that the useful features learned by the attention mechanism consist essentially of skip-bigrams with relatively small gaps. Of note, Wang and Manning (2012) previously observed consistent gains when including word bigram features to extract sentiment. Thus, our model corroborates this intuition about sentiment analysis while yielding interpretable insights on relevant word pairs across

all possible skip-bigrams.

Figure 3b is a typical example of such matrix with a band diagonal structure, for a 5-star Yelp review. A number of positive elements are highlighted by the self-attention mechanism such as *i)* the initial strong sentiment with the interaction between `this` with `love` and `!` *ii)* the favorable comparison with `even` and `better` *iii)* the enticing openness to experiences with `try` and `something` and *iv)* the positive combination of two negative words with `never` and `disappointed`.

Positional encoding helps the self-attention mechanism when interpreting words repetitions, in order to extract sentiment gradation. When repeating three times an adjective before the modified noun, attention on the adjective increases with their proximity to the noun: `horrible` `horrible` `horrible` `service`. Punctuation repetitions exhibit a similar behavior, as in the sentence "love this place!!!", where the words `love` and all three exclamation points apply attention to `this` with varying intensities: `love` `this` place `!` `!` `!`. This particular behavior of the model reinforces our belief that it learns intricate knowledge for the task of sentiment analysis. Entire attention heatmaps for complete sequences can be found in Figure 6.

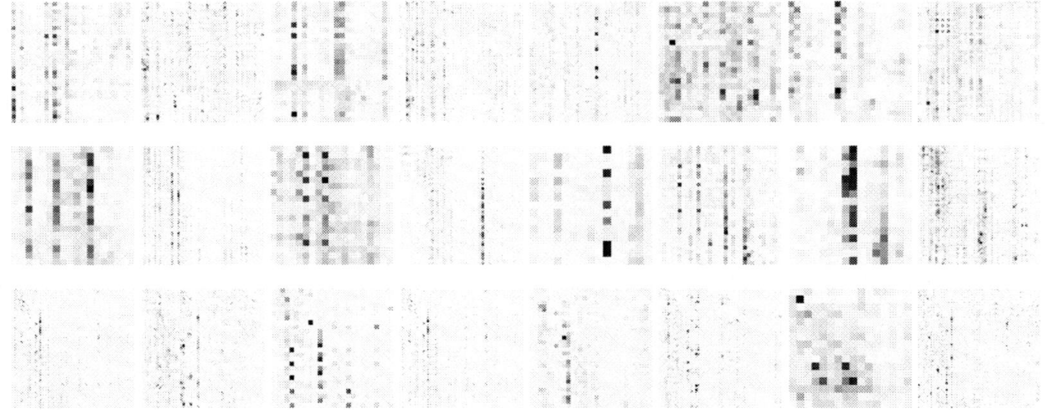

Figure 4: Randomly selected attention matrices for topic classification task. Each row corresponds to a different dataset in this order: *AG's News*, *DBPedia* and *Yahoo! Answers*. The column-based pattern is clearly present in the attention mechanism for topic classification.

Figure 5: Randomly selected attention matrices for sentiment analysis task. Each row corresponds to a different dataset in this order: *Yelp Review Polarity*, *Yelp Review Full*, *Amazon Review Full* and *Amazon Review Polarity*. The diagonal band pattern of the matrices is clearly present in the attention mechanism for sentiment analysis except for the *Yelp Review Polarity* dataset.

5.3 Quantitative Analysis

We now present a quantitative analysis of the attention matrices to support the qualitative intuition stated previously. Two metrics are used in order to assess the properties of the matrices; the first one (Gini coefficient) quantifies the sparsity of the attention, whereas the second one (diagonality) focuses on the diagonal concentration. These two properties are relevant for interpretability issues. The results are presented in Table 2.

The Gini coefficient which measures the inequality in the attention weights distribution is first computed. For topic classification datasets, the mean of the Gini coefficient is 63.57%, whereas, for sentiment analysis datasets, it raises at 87.15% without considering *Yelp Review Polarity*. Thus, for topic classification it reveals that every word

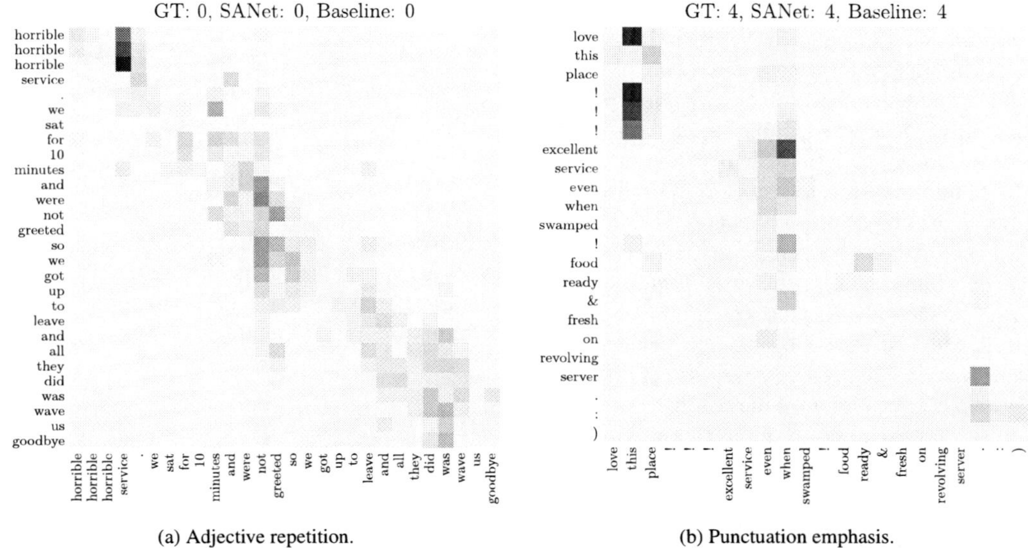

(a) Adjective repetition.

(b) Punctuation emphasis.

Figure 6: Positional encoding impact for sentiment gradation through self-attention mechanism. Both examples are extracted from the testing set of the *Yelp Review Full* dataset. Label 4 means 5-star review and label 0 means 1-star review. Words on the y-axis are attending to the words on the x-axis. GT refers to the ground truth.

Table 2: Quantitative statistics of the self-attention mechanism behavior for the two text classification tasks. Metrics are computed on the testing sets using the SANet base model.

Metric	Topic Classification			Sentiment Analysis			
	AG	DBP.	Yah. A.	Yelp P.	Yelp F.	Amz. F.	Amz. P.
Gini coefficient	55.31	67.94	67.45	65.16	84.18	89.50	87.76
Diagonality (bandwidth = 1)	7.44	8.49	6.34	5.02	23.54	41.77	40.01
Diagonality (bandwidth = 2)	11.86	13.80	9.83	7.89	36.89	62.35	60.34
Diagonality (bandwidth = 3)	16.21	18.88	13.28	10.62	45.49	73.53	71.43
Diagonality (bandwidth = 4)	20.42	23.74	16.59	13.19	50.90	79.49	77.21
Diagonality (bandwidth = 5)	24.48	28.25	19.65	15.62	54.54	83.09	80.56

interacts with multiple other words in the sequence. On the other hand, for sentiment analysis, the attention is focused on a fewer number of word pairs. The second metric will also point out that the sentiment analysis attention is sparse and specifically based on pair of words that are close in the sentence. This structurally corresponds to an attention matrix concentrated near the diagonal and justifies the introduction of the following metric.

This new metric evaluates the resemblance with a band matrix by computing the proportion of attention weights which occur inside the band diagonal of a given bandwidth b, thus the band diagonality or diagonality for short. It expresses the interactions of every element with itself, and the b elements before and after in the sequence. This metric of diagonality was computed for a bandwidth of $b = 1, 2, \ldots, 5$ as presented in Table 2. Results clearly reveal that sentiment analysis attention matrices are structurally close to being band matrices. Notably, with a bandwidth of $b = 3$ for topic classification, 16.12% of the weights occur inside the band diagonal, as for sentiment analysis without considering *Yelp Review Polarity*, 63.48% is located inside the band diagonal.

In our opinion, the combination of these two metrics supports our qualitative observations of the attention matrices. It strengthens the difference in attention behavior between the topic classification and sentiment analysis task. Moreover, this quantitative analysis clearly exposes SANet inability to learn the appropriate attention behavior for sentiment analysis with *Yelp Review Polarity*. Its failure to adequately exploit the self-attention mechanism coincide with its poor performance to extract sentiment. Interestingly, *Yelp Review Polarity* examples are a subset of *Yelp Review Full* with merged classes, for which SANet performs well with the expected attention behavior. The cause of this discrepancy with the Yelp datasets is unknown and left for future work as is some linguistic investigation of the impact of close interacting words in sentiment analysis.

6   Conclusion

In this paper, we introduced the Self-Attention Network (SANet), an attention-based length-agnostic model architecture for text classification. Our experiments showed that self-attention is important for sentiment analysis. Moreover, the improved interpretability of the model through attention visualization enabled us to discover considerably different behaviors of our attention mechanism between the topic classification and sentiment analysis tasks. The interpretable perspective of this work gives insights on the importance of modeling interaction between neighboring words in order to accurately extract sentiment, as noted by (Wang and Manning, 2012) for bigrams. It highlights how interpretability can help us understand models behavior to guide future research. In the future, we hope to apply our Self-Attention Network to other datasets such as bullying detection on social network data and tasks from various fields, such as genomic data in bioinformatics. Finally, we wish to study the properties of the introduced global max pooling layer as a complementary tool for interpretability in a similar way that was done with CAM (Oquab et al., 2015) for global average pooling. The outcome will be some attention on individual words that can take into account the context given by the self-attention mechanism. This contrast with the approach of this paper which focuses on interaction between elements as pairs. Thus we are allowed to expect that these two mechanisms will act in a complementary way to enrich interpretability.

Acknowledgments

We would like to thank Nicolas Garneau, Alexandre Drouin and Jean-Samuel Leboeuf for their advice and insightful comments. This work is supported in part by NSERC. We gratefully acknowledge the support of NVIDIA Corporation with the donation of the Titan Xp GPU used for this research.

This work was done using the PyTorch library (Paszke et al., 2017) with the PyToune framework (Paradis and Garneau).

References

Jimmy Lei Ba, Jamie Ryan Kiros, and Geoffrey E Hinton. 2016. Layer normalization. *arXiv preprint arXiv:1607.06450*.

Sebastian Bach, Alexander Binder, Grégoire Montavon, Frederick Klauschen, Klaus-Robert Müller, and Wojciech Samek. 2015. On pixel-wise explanations for non-linear classifier decisions by layer-wise relevance propagation. *PloS one*, 10(7):e0130140.

Dzmitry Bahdanau, Kyunghyun Cho, and Yoshua Bengio. 2014. Neural machine translation by jointly learning to align and translate. *arXiv preprint arXiv:1409.0473*.

Steven Bird, Ewan Klein, and Edward Loper. 2009. *Natural language processing with Python: analyzing text with the natural language toolkit.* " O'Reilly Media, Inc.".

Jianpeng Cheng, Li Dong, and Mirella Lapata. 2016. Long short-term memory-networks for machine reading. *arXiv preprint arXiv:1601.06733*.

Eunsol Choi, Daniel Hewlett, Jakob Uszkoreit, Illia Polosukhin, Alexandre Lacoste, and Jonathan Berant. 2017. Coarse-to-fine question answering for long documents. In *Proceedings of the 55th Annual Meeting of the Association for Computational Linguistics (Volume 1: Long Papers)*, volume 1, pages 209–220.

Alexis Conneau, Holger Schwenk, Loïc Barrault, and Yann Lecun. 2017. Very deep convolutional networks for text classification. In *Proceedings of the 15th Conference of the European Chapter of the Association for Computational Linguistics: Volume 1, Long Papers*, volume 1, pages 1107–1116.

Ruth C Fong and Andrea Vedaldi. 2017. Interpretable explanations of black boxes by meaningful perturbation. *arXiv preprint arXiv:1704.03296*.

Jeremy Howard and Sebastian Ruder. 2018. Fine-tuned language models for text classification. *arXiv preprint arXiv:1801.06146*.

Gao Huang, Zhuang Liu, Kilian Q Weinberger, and Laurens van der Maaten. 2017. Densely connected convolutional networks. In *Proceedings of the IEEE conference on computer vision and pattern recognition*, volume 1, page 3.

Rie Johnson and Tong Zhang. 2016. Convolutional neural networks for text categorization: Shallow word-level vs. deep character-level. *arXiv preprint arXiv:1609.00718*.

Rie Johnson and Tong Zhang. 2017. Deep pyramid convolutional neural networks for text categorization. In *Proceedings of the 55th Annual Meeting of the Association for Computational Linguistics (Volume 1: Long Papers)*, volume 1, pages 562–570.

Armand Joulin, Edouard Grave, Piotr Bojanowski, and Tomas Mikolov. 2016. Bag of tricks for efficient text classification. *arXiv preprint arXiv:1607.01759*.

Gichang Lee, Jaeyun Jeong, Seungwan Seo, CzangYeob Kim, and Pilsung Kang. 2018. Sentiment classification with word localization based on weakly supervised learning with a convolutional neural network. *Knowledge-Based Systems*.

Min Lin, Qiang Chen, and Shuicheng Yan. 2013. Network in network. *arXiv preprint arXiv:1312.4400*.

Zhouhan Lin, Minwei Feng, Cicero Nogueira dos Santos, Mo Yu, Bing Xiang, Bowen Zhou, and Yoshua Bengio. 2017. A structured self-attentive sentence embedding. *arXiv preprint arXiv:1703.03130*.

Maxime Oquab, Léon Bottou, Ivan Laptev, and Josef Sivic. 2015. Is object localization for free?-weakly-supervised learning with convolutional neural networks. In *Proceedings of the IEEE Conference on Computer Vision and Pattern Recognition*, pages 685–694.

Frédérik Paradis and Nicolas Garneau. PyToune. http://pytoune.org.

Ankur P. Parikh, Oscar Täckström, Dipanjan Das, and Jakob Uszkoreit. 2016. A decomposable attention model for natural language inference. In *Empirical Methods in Natural Language Processing*, pages 2249–2255.

Adam Paszke, Sam Gross, Soumith Chintala, Gregory Chanan, Edward Yang, Zachary DeVito, Zeming Lin, Alban Desmaison, Luca Antiga, and Adam Lerer. 2017. Automatic differentiation in pytorch.

Jeffrey Pennington, Richard Socher, and Christopher Manning. 2014. Glove: Global vectors for word representation. In *Proceedings of the 2014 conference on empirical methods in natural language processing (EMNLP)*, pages 1532–1543.

Marco Tulio Ribeiro, Sameer Singh, and Carlos Guestrin. 2016. Why should i trust you?: Explaining the predictions of any classifier. In *Proceedings of the 22nd ACM SIGKDD International Conference on Knowledge Discovery and Data Mining*, pages 1135–1144. ACM.

Karen Simonyan, Andrea Vedaldi, and Andrew Zisserman. 2013. Deep inside convolutional networks: Visualising image classification models and saliency maps. *arXiv preprint arXiv:1312.6034*.

Sainbayar Sukhbaatar, Jason Weston, Rob Fergus, et al. 2015. End-to-end memory networks. In *Advances in neural information processing systems*, pages 2440–2448.

Ashish Vaswani, Noam Shazeer, Niki Parmar, Jakob Uszkoreit, Llion Jones, Aidan N Gomez, Łukasz Kaiser, and Illia Polosukhin. 2017. Attention is all you need. In *Advances in Neural Information Processing Systems*, pages 6000–6010.

Shiyao Wang, Minlie Huang, and Zhidong Deng. 2018. Densely connected cnn with multi-scale feature attention for text classification. In *Proceedings of the Twenty-Seventh International Joint Conference on Artificial Intelligence, IJCAI-18*.

Sida Wang and Christopher D Manning. 2012. Baselines and bigrams: Simple, good sentiment and topic classification. In *Proceedings of the 50th Annual Meeting of the Association for Computational Linguistics: Short Papers-Volume 2*, pages 90–94. Association for Computational Linguistics.

Kelvin Xu, Jimmy Ba, Ryan Kiros, Kyunghyun Cho, Aaron Courville, Ruslan Salakhudinov, Rich Zemel, and Yoshua Bengio. 2015. Show, attend and tell: Neural image caption generation with visual attention. In *International Conference on Machine Learning*, pages 2048–2057.

Zichao Yang, Diyi Yang, Chris Dyer, Xiaodong He, Alex Smola, and Eduard Hovy. 2016. Hierarchical attention networks for document classification. In *Proceedings of the 2016 Conference of the North American Chapter of the Association for Computational Linguistics: Human Language Technologies*, pages 1480–1489.

Matthew D Zeiler and Rob Fergus. 2014. Visualizing and understanding convolutional networks. In *European conference on computer vision*, pages 818–833. Springer.

Xiang Zhang, Junbo Zhao, and Yann LeCun. 2015. Character-level convolutional networks for text classification. In *Advances in neural information processing systems*, pages 649–657.

Yizhe Zhang, Dinghan Shen, Guoyin Wang, Zhe Gan, Ricardo Henao, and Lawrence Carin. 2017. Deconvolutional paragraph representation learning. In *Advances in Neural Information Processing Systems*, pages 4172–4182.

Firearms and Tigers are Dangerous, Kitchen Knives and Zebras are Not: Testing whether Word Embeddings Can Tell

Pia Sommerauer and Antske Fokkens
Computational Lexicology and Terminology Lab
Vrije Universiteit Amsterdam
De Boelelaan 1105 Amsterdam, The Netherlands
pia.sommerauer@vu.nl, antske.fokkens@vu.nl

Abstract

This paper presents an approach for investigating the nature of semantic information captured by word embeddings. We propose a method that extends an existing human-elicited semantic property dataset with gold negative examples using crowd judgments. Our experimental approach tests the ability of supervised classifiers to identify semantic features in word embedding vectors and compares this to a feature-identification method based on full vector cosine similarity. The idea behind this method is that properties identified by classifiers, but not through full vector comparison are captured by embeddings. Properties that cannot be identified by either method are not. Our results provide an initial indication that semantic properties relevant for the way entities interact (e.g. dangerous) are captured, while perceptual information (e.g. colors) is not represented. We conclude that, though preliminary, these results show that our method is suitable for identifying which properties are captured by embeddings.

1 Introduction

Word embeddings are widely used in NLP and have been shown to boost performance in a large selection of tasks ranging from morphological analysis to sentiment analysis (Lazaridou et al., 2013; Socher et al., 2013; Zhou and Xu, 2015, among many others). Despite a number of different approaches to evaluation, our understanding of what type of information is represented by the vectors remains limited. Most approaches focus on full-vector comparison which treat vectors as points in a space (Yaghoobzadeh and Schütze, 2016), which are evaluated by performance on semantic similarity or relatedness test sets and analogy questions (Mikolov et al., 2013; Turney, 2012). Previous work, however, has shown that high performance does not necessarily mean that

vectors actually contain the information required to solve the task (Rogers et al., 2017; Linzen, 2016). Better understanding of the kind of semantic information captured by word embeddings can increase our understanding of how they help improve downstream tasks. In general, understanding what information is present in (often prominent) input embeddings forms an essential component of gaining deeper understanding of the nature of information and manner in which it travels through the hidden layers of a neural network.

In this paper, we propose a method that investigates what kind of semantic information is encoded in vectors using a human-elicited dataset of semantic properties. We compare the output of supervised classifiers to an approach based on full-vector comparison that cannot access individual dimensions. The assumptions behind this approach are that (1) both full-vector comparison and the supervised classifier will perform well on identifying semantic properties that correlate highly with general similarity; (2) the classifier will outperform full-vector analysis on properties that are reflected by the context, but shared among a diverse set of entities and (3) that neither approach will perform well on properties that are not represented directly or indirectly in the text. The last two outcomes can indicate whether a semantic property is encoded in embeddings (2) or not (3).

The main contribution of this paper lies in the new method and corpus it proposes. To our knowledge, this is the first approach that aims at identifying whether specific semantic properties are captured by individual dimensions or complex patterns in the vector. In addition, we provide specific hypotheses as to which properties are captured well by which method and test them using our approach.[1] Our general hypothesis states that se-

____

[1]The hypotheses and code for our experiments can

Proceedings of the 2018 EMNLP Workshop BlackboxNLP: Analyzing and Interpreting Neural Networks for NLP, pages 276–286
Brussels, Belgium, November 1, 2018. ©2018 Association for Computational Linguistics

mantic properties that are relevant for the way entities interact with the world are well represented (e.g. functions of objects, activities entities are frequently involved in), whereas properties of relatively little consequence for the way entities interact with the world are not (e.g. perceptual properties such as shapes and colors, which either have no function or highly diverse functions). Though preliminary due to the complexity of the task, results indicate that these tendencies hold. Moreover, the overall outcome shows that the method and data are complementary to existing intrinsic evaluation methods.

The rest of this paper is structured as follows. We discuss related work in Section 2. Our method is outlined in Section 3. Section 4 presents our experiments and results. We finish with a critical discussion and overview of future work in Section 5.

2   Related work

Intrinsic evaluation of word embeddings has primarily focused on two main tasks: identifying general semantic relatedness or similarity and the so-called analogy task, where word embeddings have been shown to be able to predict missing components of analogies of the type A is to B as C is to D (Mikolov et al., 2013; Turney, 2012). Furthermore, most intrinsic evaluation methods take full vectors into consideration. The famous examples $Paris - France + Italy \approx Rome$ or $king - man + woman \approx queen$ evoke the suggestion that embeddings can capture semantic properties. The task has, however, been criticized substantially (Linzen, 2016; Gladkova and Drozd, 2016; Gladkova et al., 2016; Drozd et al., 2016, among others).

Gladkova et al. (2016) follow an observation in Levy and Goldberg (2014) on the large differences in performance on different categories in the Google analogy set (Mikolov et al., 2013). They provide a new, more challenging, analogy dataset that improves existing sets on balance (capturing more semantic categories) and size. Linzen (2016) points out more fundamental problems including the observation that the target vector in the analogy task can often be found by simply taking the vector closest to the source. Drozd et al. (2016) show that classifiers picking out the target word from a set of related terms outperform the stan-

be found at: `https://cltl.github.io/semantic_space_navigation`

dardly applied cosine addition or multiplication methods. Though also boosted by the aforementioned proximity bias, these results indicate that standard methods of solving analogies miss information that is captured by embeddings. Rogers et al. (2017) conclude that the analogy evaluation does not reveal if word embedding representations indeed capture specific semantic properties.

On top of that, an embedding may capture specific semantic properties in ways that are not analogous to semantic properties of related categories. Analogy methods assume that semantic properties stand in analogous relation to each other based on the information provided by the context, but there is no reason why (e.g.) things made of wood and things made of plastic result in (combinations of) embedding dimensions that are similar enough to stand in a parallel relation to each other. Our set-up can determine whether the properties are represented without supposing such structures by targeting semantic properties directly rather than in relation to other concepts.

Several approaches have attempted to derive properties collected in property norm datasets from the distribution in naturally occurring texts (Kelly et al., 2014; Baroni et al., 2010; Barbu, 2008). Whereas these approaches yield indications about the potential of distributional models, they do not go beyond full-vector proximity on a low-dimensional SVD model or context words in a transparent, high-dimensional count model. Their focus lies on detecting informative contexts. We follow the idea behind this approach and make a human-elicited property dataset that is created in the same tradition, but larger. Our approach goes beyond the previous work in two ways: first, we add gold negative examples which allows us to go beyond testing for salient properties. Second, we compare full vector proximity to the outcome of a classifier which allows us to verify whether the property is captured for entities that share the property, but are not similar otherwise.

A few other studies go beyond full vector comparisons, moving towards the interpretation of word embedding dimensions. Tsvetkov et al. (2015, 2016) evaluate word embeddings by measuring the correlation between word embedding vectors and count vectors representing co-occurrences of words with WordNet supersenses. While they show that their results have a higher correlation with results obtained from extrinsic evaluations than standardly used intrinsic evaluations, they do not provide insights into what kind of semantic information is represented well. Yaghoobzadeh and Schütze (2016) decompose distributional vectors into individual linguistic aspects by means of a supervised classification approach to test which linguistic phenomena are captured by embeddings. They test their approach on an artificially created corpus and do not provide insights into specific semantic knowledge. Faruqui et al. (2015) transform learned embedding matrices into sparse matrices to make them more interpretable, which is complementary to our approach.

Previous studies provide (indicative) support for the hypothesis that embeddings lack information people get from other modalities than language. Fagarasan et al. (2015) present a method to ground embedding models in perceptual information by mapping distributional spaces to semantic spaces consisting of feature norms. Several approaches to boosting distributional models with visual information show that the additional information improves the performance of word embedding vectors (Roller and Schulte im Walde, 2013; Lazaridou et al., 2014). Whereas this indicates that word embedding models lack visual information, it does not show to what extent different types of properties are encoded. The method proposed in this paper is, to the best of our knowledge, the first approach specifically designed to identify what semantic knowledge is captured in word embeddings. We are not aware of earlier work that provides explicit hypotheses about the kind of information we expect to learn from distributional vectors, making this the first attempt to confirm these hypotheses experimentally.

3 Method

The core of our evaluation consists of testing whether nearest neighbors and classifiers are capable of identifying which embeddings encode a given semantic property. We first describe the dataset and then present the procedure we apply. We complete this section with our hypotheses about the outcome of our evaluation.

3.1 Extended CSLB Data

We use the Centre for Speech, Language and the Brain concept property norms dataset (Devereux et al., 2014, henceforth CSLB). This dataset follows the tradition of the sets created by McRae et al. (2005); Vinson and Vigliocco (2008) and used in Kelly et al. (2014); Baroni et al. (2010); Barbu (2008) and is the largest available semantic property dataset we are aware of. In the collection process, human subjects were given concrete and mostly monosemous concepts and asked to provide a set of semantic features. Polysemous concepts were disambiguated. Properties were elicited by cues such as *has*, *is*, *does* and *made_of*. An empty slot was provided to fill in other relations. The dataset comprises 638 annotated concepts, each of which was presented to 30 participants. Properties listed by at least two participants are included in the published set.

We select features associated with at least 20 concepts. In an exploratory experiment, we count all concepts for which the target feature is listed as positive examples and all other concepts as negative examples. However, the fact that people did not list a property does not necessarily mean that a given concept is a negative example of it. For instance: *falcon* is described by *is_a_bird*, but not by *is_an_animal*.

For proper evaluation, the CSLB dataset should be extended with verified negative examples. We apply two methods to add both positive and (verified) negative properties to CSLB. First, we select properties that necessarily imply the target property (e.g. *is_a_bird* implies *is_an_animal*) or necessarily exclude the target property (e.g. *is_food* almost certainly excludes *has_wheels*). We both manually inspect the extended sets of positive and negative examples per selected property to exclude remaining noise independently, resolving disagreements after discussion.[2]

The resulting dataset has the disadvantage that negative examples largely consist of the same specific categories, e.g. negative examples of *has_wheels* are food, animals and plants. Based on these examples, we cannot tell whether the classifier performs well because embeddings encode the property of having wheels or because it can distinguish vehicles from food, animals and plants. We therefore need to expand the dataset so that it includes diverse negative and positive examples and preferably positive and negative examples that are closely related in semantic space.

Ultimately, we want to verify and increase the

---

[2]All annotations, guiding principles as well as notes about resolving discussions can be found at `https://cltl.github.io/semantic_space_navigation`.

entire dataset and distinguish between things that always or typically have a property (e.g. *bike has_wheels, banana is_yellow*), things that can have a property (e.g. *bikini - is_pink, plate - made_of_metal*) and things that do normally not have a property (e.g. *grape - does_kill, beer - is_pink*). We set up a crowdsourcing task in which we ask participants whether a property applies to a word. Possible answers are *yes, mostly, possibly* and *no*.

This crowdsourcing method has currently been applied to a selection of property-concept pairs that were labeled as false-positives by at least one of our approaches in the initial setup. In addition, we extend the property-concept pairs given to crowd workers by collecting the nearest neighbors of the property centroid and a number of seed words. We aim at (1) identifying negative examples that have a high cosine similarity to positive examples in the dataset and (2) including a broader variety of words. This nearest-neighbors strategy explicitly aims at collecting words that are highly similar to positive examples of a property but are not associated with it. For instance, in order to extend the concept set for the property *has_wheels*, we used the seed words *car, sledge*, and *ship*.[3]

In the experiments reported in this paper, we only consider properties that clearly apply to a concept as positive examples (the *yes* and *mostly* cases) and properties that clearly do not apply as negative examples, leaving disputable cases and the cases that *possibly* apply for future work. We manually checked cases of disagreement in the crowd data and selected or removed data based on these criteria.[4]

3.2 Classification approaches

We use the pretrained Word2vec model based on the Google News corpus.[5] The underlying architecture is a skip-gram with negative sampling model (Mikolov et al., 2013), which learns word vectors by predicting the context given a word.

The overall goal is to investigate whether word vectors capture specific semantic properties or not. We start from the assumption that classifiers can learn properties that are represented in the embedding in a binary classification task. We apply supervised classification to see whether a logistic regression classifier or a neural network are capable of distinguishing embeddings of words that have a specific semantic property from those which do not. Specifically, we use embedding vectors corresponding to words associated or not associated with a semantic target-property (i.e. positive and negative examples) as input for a binary classifier and test whether the classifier can learn to distinguish embeddings of words that have the property from those who do not. However, word embeddings also capture semantic similarity. If a property is shared by similar entities (e.g. most animals with a beak are birds), the classifiers may perform well because of this similarity rather than identifying the actual property. We therefore compare the performance of classifiers to the performance of an approach based on full vector similarity. If only the classifiers score well, this provides an indication that the embedding captures the property. If both methods perform poorly this could mean that the property is not captured.[6]

Supervised classification

As the datasets are limited in size, we evaluate by applying a leave-one-out approach. We employ two different supervised classifiers, which we expect to differ in performance. As a 'vanilla' approach, we use a logistic regression classifier with default settings as implemented in SKlearn. This type of classifier is also used in Drozd et al. (2016) to detect words of similar categories in an improved analogy model.

In addition, we use a basic neural network. Meaningful properties may not always be encoded in individual patterns, but rather arise from a combination of activated dimensions. This is not captured well by a logistic regression model, as it can only react to individual dimensions. In contrast, the neural network can learn from patterns of dimensions. We use a simple multi-layer perceptron (as implemented in SKlearn[7]) with a single hidden layer. We calculate the number of nodes in the hidden layer as follows: (number of input dimensions + number of output dimensions) * 1/3. The

---

[3]The details about our selection and full lists of seed words are provided with our code (see link in Footnote 1).

[4]Some difference in judgment are clearly the result of lack of knowledge (e.g. not knowing a something is an animal). The original outcome of the crowd and final resulting test are provided on the github repository associated with this paper.

[5]https://code.google.com/archive/p/word2vec/

[6]Given the size and balance of our dataset as well as the lack of fine-tuning, we remain careful not to draw firm conclusions at this point.

[7]http://scikit-learn.org/stable/index.html

pretrained Google News vectors have 300 dimensions, resulting in a hidden layer of 100 nodes. We use the recommended settings for small datasets. No parameter tuning was conducted so far due to the limited size of the datasets and the use of a leave-one-out evaluation strategy. We present the runs of several models, as the neural network can react to the order in which the examples are presented as well as the randomly assigned vectors for initialization. While the performance of the model could be optimized further by experimenting with the settings, we find that the set-up presented here already outperforms the logistic regression classifier in many cases.

Full vector similarity

To show that supervised classification can go beyond full vector comparison in terms of cosine similarity, we compare the performance of the classifiers to an n-nearest neighbors approach. We calculate the centroid vector of all positive examples in the training set. The training set consists of all positive examples in the leave-one-out split except for the one we are testing on. We then consider its n-nearest neighbors measured by their cosine distance to the centroid as positive examples. We vary n between 100 and 1,000 in steps of 100. We report the performance of the optimal number of neighbors for each property (which varies per property). In future work, we will add more fine-grained steps and investigate the performance of a classifier using the cosine similarity of words to the centroid as a sole feature.

Variety approximation

The performance of the approaches outlined above depends on to the variety of words associated with a property. We approximate this variety by calculating the average cosine similarity of words associated with a property to one-another. This is done by averaging over the cosine similarities between all possible pairs of words. A high average cosine similarity means that the words associated with a concepts tend to be close to each other in the space, which should mostly apply to words associated with taxonomic categories. In contrast, a low average cosine means a high diversity, which should largely apply to general descriptions.

3.3   Specific hypotheses

We select a number of properties for closer investigation based on the clean and extended dataset described in Section 3.1. We first formulated the hypotheses independently, before discussing and specifying them.[8] Table 1 summarizes the agreed upon expectations. The hypotheses can be categorized in the following way:

Sparse Textual Evidence

We select properties of which we expect that textual evidence is too sparse to be represented by distributional vectors. The properties *is_black*, *is_yellow*, *is_red* and *made_of_wood* have little impact on the way most entities belonging to that class interact with the world. We expect that the only textual evidence indicating them are individual words denoting the properties themselves (e.g. *red*, *black*, *wooden*)[9] and it is unclear how often they are mentioned explicitly. It may, however, be the case that certain subcategories in the datasets are learned regardless of this sparsity, because they happen to coincide with more relevant taxonomic categories such as *red fruits*.

Fine-grained Distinctions in Larger Categories

We expect that a supervised classifier may be able to make more fine-grained distinctions between examples of the same category when these differences are relevant for the way they interact with the world. We select two properties that introduce crucial distinctions in larger categories: *has_wheels* and *is_found_in_seas*. The former applies to a sub-group of vehicles and may be apparent in certain behaviors and contexts only applying to these vehicles (rolling, street, etc). The latter applies to animals, plants and other entities found in water, but it is unclear whether textual evidence is enough to distinguish between seawater and fresh water.

Mixed Groups

We expect that a supervised machine learning approach can find positive examples of a property that are not part of the most common class in the training set. For instance, the majority of positive examples for *is_dangerous* and *does_kill* refer to weapons or dangerous animals. We expect the classifier to (1) find positive examples from less well represented groups and (2) be able to distinguish between positive and negative examples of a well-represented category (e.g. *rhino* v.s. *hippo*

---

[8]Details can be found on the paper's github repository.

[9]In the case of *made_of_wood*, the evidence may be a bit broader, as it might be indicated by different types of wood occurring in the context of furniture.

Property	learnable property
is_an_animal	yes
is_food	yes
is_dangerous	yes
does_kill	yes
is_used_in_cooking	yes
has_wheels	possibly
is_found_in_seas	possibly
is_black	no
is_red	no
is_yellow	no
made_of_wood	no

Table 1: Hypotheses about whether selected semantic properties can be learned by a supervised classifier

for killing). For the property *is_used_in_cooking*, the example words refer to food items as well as utensils. We expect that classifiers can distinguish between cooking-related utensils and other tools.

Polysemy

We expect that machine learning can recognize vector dimensions indicating properties applying to different senses of a word, whereas the nearest-neighbors approach simply assigns the word to its dominant class. For instance, we expect that word vectors that can be used to describe animals as well as food (e.g. *chicken*, *rabbit* or *turkey*) record evidence of both contexts, but end up closer to one of the categories. A supervised machine learning approach should be able to find the relevant dimensions regardless of the cosine similarity to one of the groups and classify the word correctly. We test this by training on a set of monosemous words (animals and food items) and test on a set of polysemous and monosemous examples.

4 Experimental set-up and results

4.1 Concept diversity vs performance

We first investigate the relation between performance and diversity of concepts associated with a property on the full, noisy dataset using a leave-one-out approach. Table 2 shows a selection of the f1-scores achieved on properties in the CSLB dataset in relation to the average cosine similarity of the associated words. A high average cosine similarity means that the concepts overall have similar vector representations and can thus be seen as having a low diversity. The results of the Spearman Rank correlation clearly indicate that scores achieved by nearest neighbors correlate more strongly with the average cosine than the two supervised classification approaches.

feature	cos	f1-neigh	f1-lr	f1-net	type
is_heavy	0.15	0.15	0.17	0.21	op
is_strong	0.15	0.13	0.13	0.34	e
is_thin	0.16	0	0.05	0.1	vp
is_hard	0.16	0.15	0.08	0.26	op
is_expensive	0.16	0	0.28	0.37	e
...	...	...	...	...	
is_black	0.2	0.29	0.23	0.24	vp
is_electric	0.21	0.48	0.5	0.69	vp
is_dangerous	0.21	0.53	0.57	0.59	e
is_colourful	0.21	0.14	0.25	0.32	vp
is_brown	0.21	0.13	0.22	0.33	vp
has_a_handle _handles	0.22	0.44	0.57	0.58	p
has_a_seat _seats	0.22	0.43	0.3	0.48	p
does_smell _is_smelly	0.22	0.08	0.15	0.37	op
made_of_glass	0.22	0.29	0	0.28	vp
has_a_point	0.23	0.38	0.23	0.47	p
does_protect	0.24	0.38	0.26	0.37	f
is_yellow	0.24	0.22	0	0.23	vp
is_soft	0.24	0.12	0	0.16	op
is_red	0.25	0.34	0.13	0.27	vp
is_fast	0.25	0.3	0.31	0.48	vp
is_tall	0.25	0.43	0.57	0.65	vp
is_a_tool	0.26	0.5	0.51	0.47	t
...	...	...	...	...	
is_a_weapon	0.3	0.74	0.56	0.63	t
is_green	0.31	0.45	0.45	0.45	vp
has_a_ blade_blades	0.32	0.68	0.65	0.74	p
is_worn	0.32	0.47	0.86	0.9	f
has_wheels	0.32	0.82	0.83	0.87	p
is_found _in_kitchens	0.33	0.56	0.73	0.76	e
does_fly	0.33	0.57	0.76	0.76	f
has_a_tail	0.33	0.53	0.68	0.69	p
is_an_animal	0.33	0.64	0.76	0.78	t
is_eaten_edible	0.33	0.37	0.88	0.85	f
has_four_legs	0.34	0.67	0.66	0.66	p
is_a_vehicle	0.34	0.76	0.69	0.79	t
does_eat	0.34	0.68	0.71	0.68	f
...	...	...	...	...	
has_a_beak	0.37	0.63	0.83	0.87	p
made_of_cotton	0.37	0.68	0.56	0.64	vp
has_roots	0.37	0.3	0.65	0.72	p
is_a_mammal	0.37	0.69	0.85	0.86	t
does_grow	0.37	0.52	0.81	0.81	e
is_a_plant	0.37	0.43	0.63	0.64	t
has_leaves	0.37	0.41	0.71	0.78	p
...	...	...	...	...	
has_pips_seeds	0.47	0.5	0.08	0.46	p
is_juicy	0.5	0.71	0.48	0.56	op
is_a_vegetable	0.52	0.78	0.75	0.81	t
is_played _does_play	0.53	0.9	0.98	0.98	f
does_make_music	0.55	0.89	0.95	0.92	f
spearman-r		0.72	0.52	0.59	

Table 2: Performance of different approaches in relation to the average cosine similarity of words associated with a property (cos). The last row shows the Spearman Rank correlation between f1-scores and average cosine similarity. Property types are listed under type (p = part, vp = visual-perceptual, op = other-perceptual, e = encyclopaedic, f = functional, t = taxonomic).

Property	pos	neg
full_does_kill	101	69
crowd_does_kill	67	49
full_has_wheels	79	349
full_is_black	42	89
full_is_dangerous	177	104
crowd_is_dangerous	131	84
full_is_found_in_seas	83	72
crowd_is_found_in_seas	47	28
full_is_red	29	80
full_is_used_in_cooking	142	61
full_is_yellow	24	68
full_made_of_wood	87	282
full_is_an_animal_test	37	20
full_is_an_animal_train	166	77
full_is_food_test	37	20
full_is_food_train	97	146

Table 3: Class distribution in dataset consisting of the clean datasets derived from the CSLB set and the additional crowd judgments (marked *full_*). For some properties, we included the dataset consisting of crowd-judgments only, as it is more balanced across semantic categories than the full set (marked *crowd_*). For all properties, a leave-one-out approach was applied to evaluation except for *is_animal* and *is_food*.

4.2 Outcome Specific Hypotheses

We carry out further experiments on a small extended and clean subset, consisting of carefully selected negative examples from the CSLB dataset and crowd annotations validated by the authors. The distribution of positive and negative examples per property is shown in Table 3. For some properties, the sets derived from the CSLB norms alone have an imbalanced distribution of negative examples over semantic categories, as they were selected by means of logical exclusion (e.g. concepts listed under *has_wheels* have been selected as negative examples of *is_food*). Therefore, we add the more balanced but smaller datasets created by crowd-judgments only where enough judgments have been collected. We created additional sets for words part of the food-animal polysemy to test whether supervised classifiers can successfully predict semantic properties of various senses of polysemous words. In the following sections, we will outline the most striking results. Most results confirm, but some contradict our initial hypotheses.

Table 4 shows the f1-scores on the full clean datasets. As hypothesized, the color properties *is_yellow* and *is_red* perform low in all approaches, with slightly better results yielded by supervised learning.

The properties involved in functions and activi-

ties or with high impact on the interaction of entities with the world all perform highly in the classification approaches. For *does_kill*, *is_dangerous* and *is_used_in_cooking*, there is a large difference between the best nearest neighbors approach and the best classification approach (between 60 and 19 points), indicating that the classification approaches are able to infer more information from individual dimensions than is provided by full vector similarity. The property *is_dangerous* has, as can be expected, a particularly high diversity of associated words (comparable to the colors). *Has_wheels* and *is_found_in_seas* can be expected to have high correlations with other taxonomic categories (fish and water animals, vehicles), which is reflected in the lower diversity and comparatively high nearest neighbor performance.

Cases contradicting our expectations are the visual properties *is_black* and *made_of_wood*. Both have comparatively high classification performance with a big difference to the nearest neighbor results. Most likely, this is due to a category bias in the negative examples. For instance, a large portion of the negative examples for *is_made_of_wood* consist of animals and food. In the dataset for *is_black*, a large proportion of the positive examples consists of animals. A classifier can perform highly by simply learning to distinguish these two categories from the rest.

The biases in semantic classes mentioned above partially result from the way we generated the negative examples from the original CSLB dataset. This means that a classifier may learn to distinguish two semantic categories rather than being able to find vector dimensions indicative of the target property. We therefore also present selected results on crowd-only datasets shown in Table 4, which do not have this bias. It can be observed that for all three properties,[10] the performance of the classification approaches drops marginally, whereas it rises for nearest neighbors.

We investigate the outcome on a number of individual examples to gain more insights into whether the subtle differences hypothesized in Section 3 hold. Since we only formulate a general hypothesis for Sparse Textual Evidence, we do not dive deeper into the results for that category here.

---

[10] We only included properties for which we had enough positive and negative examples in our set

Fine-Grained Category Distinctions

The full clean *has_wheels* dataset includes a number of instances for which the classifiers can make more fine-grained distinctions than nearest neighbors. As hypothesized, classifiers, in contrast to nearest-neighbors, can recognize that neither *sled* nor a *skidoo* have wheels, but a *unicycle* a *limousine*, a *train*, *carriage*, an *ambulance*, a *porsche* do. Another fine-grained distinction can be identified in the *is_found_in_seas* crowd-only set: *Sculpin* is correctly identified as a seawater fish by all classifiers but not by nearest-neighbors.

Mixed Groups

Whereas nearest neighbors predominantly identify weapons as *is_dangerous* in the crowd-only set, the classifiers go beyond this category. The neural network approach correctly identifies that *imitation pistol*, *imitation handgun*, and *screwdriver* are negative examples of *is_dangerous*. Furthermore, no animals are labeled as dangerous based on proximity to the centroid, but the classifiers are able to distinguish between some dangerous and non-dangerous animals (e.g. *rhinoceros* is labeled positive, while *giraffe* and *zebra* are labeled as negative). All three classifiers recognize that *meth*, *cocaine* and *oxycodone* are considered dangerous substances, despite the fact that they are far away from the centroid of dangerous things. Of the only two disease-like concepts, *Hepatitis C* and *allergy*, the former is recognized by all classifiers and the latter only by logistic regression. The performance on the smaller, but also weapon-dominated *does_kill* crowd-only set is comparable, but the variety of atypical cases is lower. Among the only two disease-related items, *dengue* is identified by all classifiers and *dengue virus* only by the neural network.

In the crowd-only *is_found_in_seas* set, *seabird* and *gannet* are correctly labeled as positive, even though positive examples almost exclusively consist of fish or underwater-animals, whereas the negative examples encompass a vast variety of animals, including *bird* and some freshwater fish.

Polysemy

For polysemy between food and animals (Table 4), we observe that when trained on pure animal and food words and tested on polysemous animal and food words, the classifiers perform highly with a large difference to nearest neighbors. For food versus pure animal words, the classifier perfor-

property	av-cos	neigh	lr	net1	net2
full_is_yellow	0.23	0.19	0.47	0.64	0.64
full_is_used_in _cooking	0.37	0.29	0.98	0.98	0.98
full_is_black	0.19	0.35	0.75	0.77	0.77
full_is_red	0.23	0.36	0.51	0.54	0.52
full_is_dangerous	0.24	0.58	0.88	0.88	0.87
crowd_is_dangerous	0.26	0.61	0.86	0.86	0.86
full_has_wheels	0.38	0.90	0.96	0.96	0.95
full_is_found_in_seas	0.44	0.87	0.97	0.98	0.98
crowd_is_found _in_seas	0.50	0.87	0.94	0.96	0.96
full_does_kill	0.27	0.67	0.83	0.86	0.82
crowd_does_kill	0.30	0.70	0.82	0.84	0.80
full_made_of_wood	0.17	0.14	0.84	0.85	0.85
full_is_food_test	0.37	0.00	0.36	0.36	0.36
full_is_an _animal_test	0.37	0.52	0.88	0.88	0.88

Table 4: F1 scores achieved by logistic regression (lr) two runs of a neural net classifier (net1 and net2 and the n-best nearest neighbors evaluated with leave-one-out on the full datasets (marked as *full_* and the crow-only sets (marked as *crowd_*).

mance is much lower. We expect the extremely low nearest neighbor performance to be due to the fact that the centroid is calculated over pure food items (without a single animal-related item, not even culinary meat terms such as *pork* or *beef*) which is far away from the animal-region in the space. Despite the classifiers outperforming nearest neighbors, the outcome does not confirm our original hypotheses. We expected that the classifiers could identify that edible animals have both animal properties and food properties, but upon inspection of the results, the classifiers only identified entities with a predominant animal sense correctly as animals and those with a predominant food sense correctly as food.

5 Discussion & Future Work

The experiments presented in this approach have several limitations. First, our semantic datasets are still limited in size. Second, the implication method we applied to generate negative examples led to biases for some properties where most negative examples belong to a small set of (taxonomic) classes. Third, no parameter tuning has been carried out so far. Careful parameter tuning would ensure that the best possible classification approaches are chosen and that the obtained results truly exploit the informative power of the embeddings. Due to the limited size of the dataset and the leave-one-out approach to evaluation, this has not been possible in this preliminary study. Fourth, the experiments presented here only concern a small subsection of semantic properties too limited to draw general conclusions.

Despite these limitations, our results provide preliminary insights that lead us to conclude that the overall idea behind our methods works and opens up promising directions for future work. We first aim to address the limitations of the current dataset. We intend to incorporate other sets designed for similar insights, such as the analogies presented in Drozd et al. (2016) and the SemEval 2018 discriminative property set (Krebs et al., 2018). In addition, we plan to extend and refine the sets with crowd annotations asking for graded judgments (e.g. a property can *mostly* or *possibly* apply) and exploit these judgments in future experiments.

Once we created a bigger and more balanced dataset, we can carry out experiments on different train and test splits in order to overcome the limitations of the leave-one-out evaluation. Furthermore, we will apply careful parameter tuning on a development set in order to ensure our results are representative of the information captured by the embeddings. The increased size of the set will allow us to conduct more experiments that take the distributions of semantic categories in the splits into account as was done for the polysemy set. This way, we ensure that we do not train on examples that belong to the same semantic category as the ones in the test set.

Going beyond the method introduced in this paper, we plan on investigating the type of information encoded in linguistic context by testing which properties can be learned from textual context directly. In addition, applying the method presented by Faruqui et al. (2015) may provide stronger indications about the information represented by word embedding dimensions. Adding these to experiments allows us to trace which information is provided by the context and what ends up being present in word embeddings.

6 Conclusion

The main contribution of this paper is that it introduces a new method aimed at investigating the kind of semantic information captured by word embedding vectors. We have taken the first steps towards constructing a dataset suitable for this investigation on the basis of an existing dataset of human-elicited semantic properties. We introduced a set of hypotheses concerning which semantic properties are captured by embeddings and presented exploratory experiments verifying them.

The current results are limited by the size and balance of our dataset, as discussed in detail in the previous section. Nevertheless, we can report preliminary insights based on our experiments. We show that classifiers, in particular neural networks, can identify which entities have a specific property in cases where this does not follow from general similarity or the overall semantic class the entity belongs to. This can be seen as a first indication that (some) semantic properties are encoded in individual (patterns of) vector dimensions, which can be identified.

The results on the extended datasets partly confirm that visual properties are not well represented by embeddings, while properties relating to function (e.g. cooking, having wheels) and interactions with other entities (e.g. being dangerous or killing) tend to be represented well. Some of these indications could be the result of the bias in our current dataset, but others have been confirmed on the smaller crowd-only sets for properties with enough available data (*is_dangerous* and *does_kill*). Further evidence is provided by the full dataset for *has_wheels* which encompasses a large group of vehicles to which the property does not apply. In addition, we support these indications by qualitative insights through examples of the kinds of distinctions made by the classifiers, but not the nearest neighbor approach. Results achieved for polysemous words and two visual properties currently do not confirm our hypotheses.

Acknowledgements

This research is funded by the PhD in the Humanities Grant provided by the Netherlands Organization of Scientific Research (Nederlandse Organisatie voor Wetenschappelijk Onderzoek, NWO) PGW.17.041 awarded to Pia Sommerauer and NWO VENI grant 275-89-029 awarded to Antske Fokkens. We would like to thank anonymous reviewers for feedback and Piek Vossen for feedback and discussion that helped improve this paper. All remaining errors are our own.

References

Eduard Barbu. 2008. Combining methods to learn feature-norm-like concept descriptions. In *Proceed-*

ings of the ESSLLI Workshop on Distributional Lexical Semantics, pages 9–16.

Marco Baroni, Brian Murphy, Eduard Barbu, and Massimo Poesio. 2010. Strudel: A corpus-based semantic model based on properties and types. *Cognitive science*, 34(2):222–254.

Barry J. Devereux, Lorraine K. Tyler, Jeroen Geertzen, and Billi Randall. 2014. The centre for speech, language and the brain (cslb) concept property norms. *Behavior research methods*, 46(4):1119–1127.

Aleksandr Drozd, Anna Gladkova, and Satoshi Matsuoka. 2016. Word embeddings, analogies, and machine learning: Beyond king-man+ woman= queen. In *COLING*, pages 3519–3530.

Luana Fagarasan, Eva Maria Vecchi, and Stephen Clark. 2015. From distributional semantics to feature norms: grounding semantic models in human perceptual data. In *Proceedings of the 11th International Conference on Computational Semantics*, pages 52–57.

Manaal Faruqui, Yulia Tsvetkov, Dani Yogatama, Chris Dyer, and Noah A. Smith. 2015. Sparse overcomplete word vector representations. In *Proceedings of ACL*.

Anna Gladkova and Aleksandr Drozd. 2016. Intrinsic evaluations of word embeddings: What can we do better? In *Proceedings of the 1st Workshop on Evaluating Vector-Space Representations for NLP*, pages 36–42.

Anna Gladkova, Aleksandr Drozd, and Satoshi Matsuoka. 2016. Analogy-based detection of morphological and semantic relations with word embeddings: what works and what doesn't. In *Proceedings of the NAACL Student Research Workshop*, pages 8–15.

Colin Kelly, Barry Devereux, and Anna Korhonen. 2014. Automatic extraction of property norm-like data from large text corpora. *Cognitive Science*, 38(4):638–682.

Alicia Krebs, Alessandro Lenci, and Denis Paperno. 2018. Semeval-2018 task 10: Capturing discriminative attributes. In *Proceedings of The 12th International Workshop on Semantic Evaluation*, pages 732–740.

Angeliki Lazaridou, Elia Bruni, and Marco Baroni. 2014. Is this a wampimuk? cross-modal mapping between distributional semantics and the visual world. In *Proceedings of the 52nd Annual Meeting of the Association for Computational Linguistics (Volume 1: Long Papers)*, volume 1, pages 1403–1414.

Angeliki Lazaridou, Eva Maria Vecchi, and Marco Baroni. 2013. Fish transporters and miracle homes: How compositional distributional semantics can

help np parsing. In *Proceedings of the 2013 Conference on Empirical Methods in Natural Language Processing*, pages 1908–1913.

Omer Levy and Yoav Goldberg. 2014. Linguistic regularities in sparse and explicit word representations. In *Proceedings of the eighteenth conference on computational natural language learning*, pages 171–180.

Tal Linzen. 2016. Issues in evaluating semantic spaces using word analogies. In *Proceedings of the 1st Workshop on Evaluating Vector-Space Representations for NLP*, pages 13–18.

Ken McRae, George S Cree, Mark S Seidenberg, and Chris McNorgan. 2005. Semantic feature production norms for a large set of living and nonliving things. *Behavior research methods*, 37(4):547–559.

Tomas Mikolov, Wen-tau Yih, and Geoffrey Zweig. 2013. Linguistic regularities in continuous space word representations. In *HLT-NAACL*, volume 13, pages 746–751.

Anna Rogers, Aleksandr Drozd, and Bofang Li. 2017. The (too many) problems of analogical reasoning with word vectors. In *Proceedings of the 6th Joint Conference on Lexical and Computational Semantics (* SEM 2017)*, pages 135–148.

Stephen Roller and Sabine Schulte im Walde. 2013. A multimodal lda model integrating textual, cognitive and visual modalities. In *Proceedings of the 2013 Conference on Empirical Methods in Natural Language Processing*, pages 1146–1157.

Richard Socher, Alex Perelygin, Jean Y. Wu, Jason Chuang, Christopher D. Manning, Andrew Y. Ng, and Christopher Potts. 2013. Recursive deep models for semantic compositionality over a sentiment treebank. In *Proceedings of the 2013 conference on empirical methods in natural language processing*, pages 1631–1642.

Yulia Tsvetkov, Manaal Faruqui, and Chris Dyer. 2016. Correlation-based intrinsic evaluation of word vector representations. In *Proceedings of the 1st Workshop on Evaluating Vector-Space Representations for NLP*, pages 111–115.

Yulia Tsvetkov, Manaal Faruqui, Wang Ling, Guillaume Lample, and Chris Dyer. 2015. Evaluation of word vector representations by subspace alignment. In *Proc. of EMNLP*.

Peter D Turney. 2012. Domain and function: A dual-space model of semantic relations and compositions. *Journal of Artificial Intelligence Research*, 44:533–585.

David P. Vinson and Gabriella Vigliocco. 2008. Semantic feature production norms for a large set of objects and events. *Behavior Research Methods*, 40(1):183–190.

Yadollah Yaghoobzadeh and Hinrich Schütze. 2016. Intrinsic subspace evaluation of word embedding representations. In *Proceedings of the 54th Annual Meeting of the Association for Computational Linguistics (Volume 1: Long Papers)*, volume 1, pages 236–246.

Jie Zhou and Wei Xu. 2015. End-to-end learning of semantic role labeling using recurrent neural networks. In *Proceedings of the 53rd Annual Meeting of the Association for Computational Linguistics and the 7th International Joint Conference on Natural Language Processing (Volume 1: Long Papers)*, volume 1, pages 1127–1137.

An Analysis of Encoder Representations in
Transformer-Based Machine Translation

Alessandro Raganato and **Jörg Tiedemann**
Department of Digital Humanities
University of Helsinki
{alessandro.raganato,jorg.tiedemann}@helsinki.fi

Abstract

The attention mechanism is a successful technique in modern NLP, especially in tasks like machine translation. The recently proposed network architecture of the *Transformer* is based entirely on attention mechanisms and achieves new state of the art results in neural machine translation, outperforming other sequence-to-sequence models. However, so far not much is known about the internal properties of the model and the representations it learns to achieve that performance. To study this question, we investigate the information that is learned by the attention mechanism in Transformer models with different translation quality. We assess the representations of the encoder by extracting dependency relations based on self-attention weights, we perform four probing tasks to study the amount of syntactic and semantic captured information and we also test attention in a transfer learning scenario. Our analysis sheds light on the relative strengths and weaknesses of the various encoder representations. We observe that specific attention heads mark syntactic dependency relations and we can also confirm that lower layers tend to learn more about syntax while higher layers tend to encode more semantics.

1 Introduction

Machine translation (MT) is one of the prominent tasks in Natural Language Processing, tackled in several ways (Bojar et al., 2017). Neural MT (NMT) has become the de-facto standard with a performance that clearly outperforms the alternative approach of Statistical Machine Translation (Luong et al., 2015b; Bojar et al., 2016; Bentivogli et al., 2016). NMT also improves training procedures due to the end-to-end fashion without tedious feature engineering and complex setups. During recent years, a lot of research has been done on NMT, designing new architectures, starting from the plain sequence-to-sequence model (Sutskever et al., 2014; Cho et al., 2014), to an improved version featuring an attention mechanism (Bahdanau et al., 2015; Luong et al., 2015a), to models that only use attention instead of recurrent layers (Vaswani et al., 2017) and models that apply convolution networks (Gehring et al., 2017a,b). Among the different architectures, the Transformer (Vaswani et al., 2017) has emerged as the dominant NMT paradigm.[1] Relying only on attention mechanisms, the model is fast, highly accurate and has been proven to outperform the widely used recurrent networks with attention and ensembling (Wu et al., 2016) by more than 2 BLEU points. Improved translation quality is typically related to better representation of structural information. While other approaches make use of external information to improve the internal representation of NMT models (Arthur et al., 2016; Niehues and Cho, 2017; Alkhouli and Ney, 2017), the Transformer seems to be able to encode a lot of structural information without explicitly incorporating any structural constraints. However, being a rather new architecture, little is known about what the model exactly learns internally. A better understanding of the internal representations of neural models has become a major challenge in NMT (Koehn and Knowles, 2017).

In this work we investigate the kind of linguistic information that is learned by the encoder. We start by training the Transformer system from English to seven languages, with different training set sizes, resulting in models that are not only trained for different target languages but also with expected differences in translation quality. First, we visually inspect the attention weights of the encoders,

---

[1] Most submissions for the WMT18 shared task on news (http://matrix.statmt.org/) employ the Transformer architecture.

Proceedings of the 2018 EMNLP Workshop BlackboxNLP: Analyzing and Interpreting Neural Networks for NLP, pages 287–297
Brussels, Belgium, November 1, 2018. ©2018 Association for Computational Linguistics

in order to find linguistic patterns. As the next step, we exploit the attention weights of the network to build a graph and induce tree structures for each sentence, showing whether syntactic dependencies between words have been learned or not in the spirit of Williams et al. (2018) and Liu and Lapata (2018). Additionally, following previous studies on how to analyze the internal representation of neural systems (Adi et al., 2016; Shi et al., 2016; Belinkov et al., 2017a), we probe the encoder weights of the trained models to address different sequence labeling tasks: Part-of-Speech tagging, Chunking, Named Entity Recognition and Semantic tagging. We evaluate the quality of the decoder on a given task to assess how discriminative the encoder representation is for that task. Lastly, in order to check whether the learned information can be transferred across models, we use the encoder weights of a high-resource language pair to initialize a low-resource language pair, inspired by the work of Zoph et al. (2016). We show that, also for the Transformer, the knowledge of an encoder representation can be shared with other models, helping them to achieve better translation quality.

Overall, our analysis leads to interesting insights about strengths and weaknesses of the attention weights of the Transformer, giving more empirical evidence about the kind of information the model is learning at each layer:

- We find that each layer has at least one attention head that encodes a significant amount of syntactic dependencies.

- Consistent with previous findings on the sequence-to-sequence paradigm, probing the encoder to four different sequence labeling tasks reveals that lower layers tend to encode more syntactic information, whereas upper layers move towards semantic tasks.

- The information about the length of the input sentence starts to vanish after the third layer.

- The study corroborates that attention can be used to transfer knowledge between high- and low-resource languages.

2 Architecture

The architecture of the Transformer system follows the so called encoder-decoder paradigm, trained in an end-to-end fashion. Without using any recurrent layer, the model takes advantage of the positional

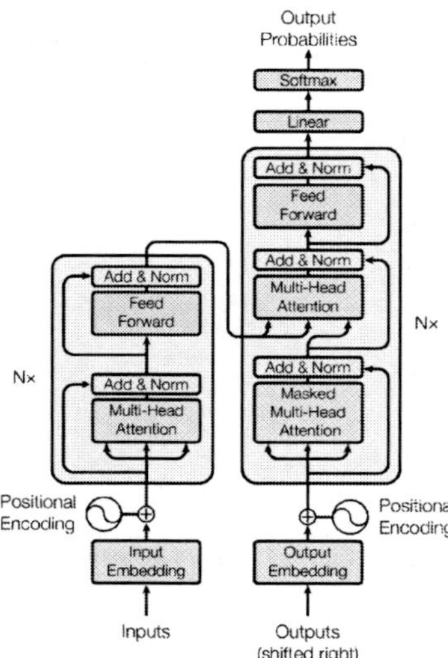

Figure 1: The Transformer architecture (illustration from Vaswani et al. (2017)).

embedding as a mechanism to encode order within a sentence. The encoder, typically stacks 6 identical layers, in which each of them makes use of the so called multi-head attention and of a 2 sublayers feed-forward network, coupled with layer normalization and residual connection (see Figure 1). The multi-head attention mechanism computes attention weights, i.e., a softmax distribution, for each word within a sentence, including the word itself. Specifically:

$$Attention(Q, K, V) = softmax(\frac{QK^T}{\sqrt{d_k}})V \quad (1)$$

where the input consists of queries Q and keys K of dimension d_k, and values V of dimension d_v. The queries, keys and values are linearly projected h times, to allow the model to jointly attend to information from different representation, concatenating the result,

$$MultiHead(Q, K, V) = Concat(head_1, ..., head_h)W^O$$
$$where\ head_i = Attention(QW_i^Q, KW_i^K, VW_i^V)$$

with parameter matrices $W_i^Q \in \mathbb{R}^{d_{model} \times d_k}$, $W_i^K \in \mathbb{R}^{d_{model} \times d_k}$, $W_i^V \in \mathbb{R}^{d_{model} \times d_v}$ and $W^O \in \mathbb{R}^{hd_v \times d_{model}}$.[2]

---

[2] As hyper-parameters we used the *base* version from Vaswani et al. (2017).

288

On top of the multi-head attention there is a feed-forward network that consists of two layers with a ReLU activation in between. Each encoder layer takes as input the output of the previous layer, allowing it to attend to all positions of the previous layer.

The decoder has the same architecture as the encoder, stacking 6 identical layers of multi-head attention with feed-forward networks. However, here there are two multi-head attention sub-layers: i) a decoder self-attention and ii) a encoder-decoder attention. The decoder self-attention attends on the previous predictions made step by step, masked by one position. The second multi-head attention performs an attention between the final encoder representation and the decoder representation.

To summarize, the Transformer model consists of three different attentions: i) the encoder self-attention, in which each position attends to all positions in the previous layer, including the position itself, ii) the encoder-decoder attention, in which each position of the decoder attends to all positions in the last encoder layer, and iii) the decoder self-attention, in which each position attends to all previous positions including the current position.

In this work, we focus on analyzing the structure that is learned by the first type of attention weights of the model, i.e., the encoder self-attention, across different models with different target language and translation quality.

3 Methodology

We aim at analyzing the encoder representation of different models by assessing their quality through several experiments: i) by visualizing the attention weights (Section 5), ii) by inducing tree structure from the encoder weights (Section 6), iii) by probing the encoder as input representation for various prediction tasks (Section 7), and iv) by transferring the knowledge of one encoder to another (Section 8). We start by looking for linguistic patterns through the visualization of the heat-maps of the encoder weights. Next, we use the softmax weights extracted from the multi-head attention to build maximum spanning trees from the input sentences, assessing the quality of the induced tree through dependency parsing. Additionally, we evaluate the ability of the decoder, using a fixed encoder representation as input, on several sequence labeling tasks, measuring how important the input features are for various tasks. As test bed we use four dif-

	#Training sentences
English → Czech	51.391.404
English → German	25.746.259
English → Estonian	1.064.658
English → Finnish	2.986.131
English → Russian	9.140.469
English → Turkish	205.579
English → Chinese	23.861.542

Table 1: Number of training instances used to train each system.

	newstest 2017	newstest 2018
English → Czech	18.11	17.36
English → German	23.37	34.46
English → Estonian	–	13.05
English → Finnish	15.06	10.32
English → Russian	21.30	18.96
English → Turkish	6.93	6.22
English → Chinese	23.10	23.75

Table 2: BLEU score for the newstest2017 and newstest2018 test data.

ferent tasks, ranging from syntax to semantics, i.e, PoS tagging, Chunking, Named Entity Recognition, and Semantic tagging. The assumption is that if a property is well encoded in the input representation then it is easy for the decoder to predict that property. In practice, after training the MT system, we freeze the encoder parameters, and train one decoder layer for each task. The decoder layer is simpler than the original one used for MT; it consists only of one attention head and one feed-forward layer with ReLU activation. Moreover, in order to output the right amount of labels, the decoder also has to learn implicitly the length of the input sentence. Note that our goal is not to beat the state of the art in a given task but rather to analyze the representation of an encoder trained for MT on different tasks referring to different linguistic properties. Finally, to assess whether the knowledge captured within an encoder is general enough to also be used for other models, we test a transfer learning scenario in which we use the encoder representation of a high resource language pair to initialize the encoder of a low resource language pair. Here, we assume that a model is better at encoding abstract linguistic properties if it can share useful information to enhance another weaker model.

4 Model setup

We trained Transformer models[3] from English to seven languages, Czech, German, Estonian, Finnish, Russian, Turkish and Chinese, using the parallel data provided by the WMT18 shared task on news translation.[4] The parallel data come from different sources, mainly from Europarl (Koehn, 2005), News Commentary (Tiedemann, 2012) and ParaCrawl.[5]

The data sets are partially noisy, especially ParaCrawl being on its first release, and to filter out potentially incorrect parallel sentences we used a language identifier[6] to tag each source and target sentence, discarding the sentences that do not match across languages (Stymne et al., 2013; Zariņa et al., 2015). As development set we used the provided newsdev data from the shared task, while using the newstest from WMT 2017 and 2018 as test data. A widely used technique to allow an open vocabulary is byte pair encoding (Sennrich et al., 2016), in which the source and target words are split into subword units. However, in this work we prefer to use the full word forms, allowing us to evaluate and compare the internal representation on standard sequence labeling benchmarks tagged with gold labels on the full word forms. Therefore, we use a large vocabulary of 100K words per language. General statistics on the training data are given in Table 1. As can be seen, we ended up having an heterogeneous amount of data, ranging from 200K for Turkish up to 51M for Czech. We trained each model for maximum 20 epochs, taking the best one according to the development set as model to evaluate. The BLEU score[7] of each model is shown in Table 2. Even though the scores seem low for the Transformer architecture for the MT task, we have to note that each model is trained using full word forms in order to facilitate the analysis of the encoder representation (our results are in line with the comparison between subword units and full word forms done by Sennrich et al. (2016)).

---

[3] We used the OpenNMT framework (Klein et al., 2017).

[4] The provided data are already preprocessed and freely available at http://data.statmt.org/wmt18/translation-task/preprocessed/.

[5] https://paracrawl.eu/

[6] We used the fasttext language identifier tool (Joulin et al., 2016b,a) from https://fasttext.cc/docs/en/language-identification.html

[7] We used the SACREBLEU script (Post, 2018), with signature BLEU+case.mixed+lang.en-{targetLanguage}+numrefs.1+smooth.exp+test.wmt{17,18}+tok.13a+version.1.3.0

We do not aim at beating the best system on the test data, as our main point is to analyze different encoder representations across models with different translation quality and target language.

5 Encoder Evaluation: Visualization

One of the most straightforward ways of understanding the weights of a neural network is by visualizing them. In its base setting, the Transformer employs 6 layers with 8 different attention heads for each of them, making complete visualization difficult. Therefore, we focus only on attention weights with high scores that are visually interpretable.

We discovered four different patterns shared across models: paying attention to the word itself, to the previous and next word and to the end of the sentence (Figure 2). We found that, usually on the first layer, i.e., layer 0, more attention heads focus their weights on the word itself, while on the subsequent layers the network moves the attention more on other words, e.g., on the next and previous word, and to the end of the sentence. This suggests that the transformer tries to find long dependencies between words on higher layers whereas it tends to focus on local dependencies in lower layers.

6 Encoder Evaluation: Inducing Tree Structure

The architecture of the Transformer, linking each word with each other with an attention weight, can be seen as a weighted graph in which the words are the nodes and from which tree structure can be extracted. Even though the models are not trained to produce any trees or to a specific syntax task, we used the attention weights in each layer to extract a tree of the input sentences and inspect whether they reflect a dependency tree.

We evaluated the induced trees on the English PUD treebank from the CoNLL 2017 Shared Task (Zeman et al., 2017). The PUD treebank consists of 1000 sentences randomly taken from on-line newswire and Wikipedia. We measure the performance as Unlabeled Attachment Score (UAS) with the official evaluation script[8] from the shared task, using gold segmentation and tokenization. Plus, given that our weights have no knowledge about the root of the sentence, we decided to use the gold root as starting node for the maximum spanning

---

[8] conll17_ud_eval.py (version 1.1)

		en → cs	en → de	en → et	en → fi	en → ru	en → tr	en → zh
Layer 0	attention head 0	15.06	10.67	8.79	**31.63**	**17.13**	10.99	13.00
	attention head 1	9.94	**32.90**	8.68	12.58	12.02	10.74	15.76
	attention head 2	15.84	10.62	9.60	10.12	12.08	13.69	15.50
	attention head 3	10.62	15.39	**31.38**	8.31	11.08	9.78	22.79
	attention head 4	17.25	18.12	7.76	25.10	11.75	13.20	10.28
	attention head 5	16.71	14.47	24.24	13.63	12.39	27.55	17.19
	attention head 6	**30.26**	26.28	11.76	10.43	11.55	9.90	**33.26**
	attention head 7	15.17	15.31	9.61	9.51	12.13	**31.81**	9.69
Layer 1	attention head 0	10.95	11.73	11.04	11.47	**36.05**	**26.20**	20.33
	attention head 1	10.91	10.65	27.58	10.88	12.66	11.23	10.72
	attention head 2	10.72	10.87	25.80	27.32	25.64	14.46	**35.77**
	attention head 3	12.21	15.06	15.06	20.90	10.45	14.04	9.62
	attention head 4	**35.08**	13.17	11.14	11.01	18.44	15.83	14.17
	attention head 5	29.04	10.69	10.85	12.51	33.23	27.41	10.84
	attention head 6	15.22	**35.94**	13.55	**35.30**	10.27	11.03	11.59
	attention head 7	22.64	35.89	**35.07**	10.10	13.59	11.82	24.09
Layer 2	attention head 0	**35.46**	12.33	7.40	9.01	35.07	20.53	11.02
	attention head 1	10.29	22.62	32.80	10.98	7.63	10.03	11.55
	attention head 2	19.74	9.02	**33.16**	9.00	20.92	9.52	29.40
	attention head 3	16.23	15.82	13.04	13.98	22.27	14.05	10.71
	attention head 4	23.23	11.07	12.58	**29.43**	35.53	10.85	12.98
	attention head 5	16.78	**33.76**	13.80	14.53	**36.08**	**22.56**	**35.80**
	attention head 6	10.17	22.15	10.23	11.30	12.54	19.38	15.16
	attention head 7	32.01	14.97	13.76	18.36	8.84	11.79	22.12
Layer 3	attention head 0	8.28	9.97	11.05	13.89	**35.03**	18.55	13.80
	attention head 1	**35.20**	24.76	7.99	13.72	20.64	**21.53**	13.03
	attention head 2	10.67	10.54	**22.62**	15.14	9.43	17.03	14.78
	attention head 3	31.13	17.36	12.14	**27.24**	9.27	15.67	11.20
	attention head 4	23.89	**35.59**	8.59	12.18	10.36	13.05	14.89
	attention head 5	14.94	10.12	12.37	7.78	12.62	7.18	19.80
	attention head 6	16.02	13.54	13.38	8.70	10.79	8.80	**38.87**
	attention head 7	13.44	11.81	13.02	14.96	29.10	17.83	9.02
Layer 4	attention head 0	14.45	**27.88**	20.86	11.63	12.84	**25.40**	13.34
	attention head 1	10.37	14.37	17.80	**24.00**	10.72	21.11	22.87
	attention head 2	15.06	10.69	11.82	9.52	13.20	11.36	25.25
	attention head 3	13.47	13.47	14.01	10.92	17.11	12.88	12.29
	attention head 4	**29.66**	17.31	19.45	11.82	10.87	11.76	13.55
	attention head 5	28.07	18.14	**32.87**	22.50	13.76	11.06	**35.40**
	attention head 6	13.35	11.27	9.95	15.49	**27.68**	25.13	11.56
	attention head 7	10.84	25.03	14.93	17.32	13.86	14.00	17.52
Layer 5	attention head 0	**36.02**	29.80	17.37	17.49	**35.56**	16.91	16.75
	attention head 1	28.02	27.23	16.68	28.25	13.04	**28.23**	17.71
	attention head 2	20.20	11.14	19.02	33.38	18.49	7.98	13.45
	attention head 3	11.86	8.30	22.45	14.71	19.17	15.76	19.16
	attention head 4	31.71	19.62	**33.68**	31.87	26.42	13.61	27.50
	attention head 5	13.55	15.20	30.73	17.35	11.98	23.13	26.70
	attention head 6	26.02	**35.32**	14.83	24.99	9.77	16.99	**29.73**
	attention head 7	18.63	10.33	15.71	11.01	12.59	25.67	14.79

Table 3: UAS F1-score of the induced trees produced by the attention weights on the English PUD treebank from CoNLL 2017.

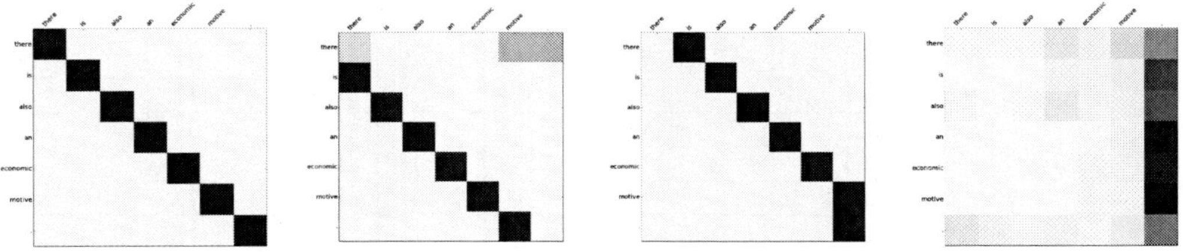

Figure 2: Four examples of the discovered patterns through visualization for the sentence: "there is also an economic motive .".

Sample tree from the attention head 1, layer 3

Sample tree from the attention head 4, layer 3

Figure 3: Sample trees induced by the attention weights from the English-Czech model.

tree algorithm. Specifically, we run the Chu-Liu-Edmonds algorithm (Chu, 1965; Edmonds, 1967) for each attention head of each layer of the models to extract the maximum spanning trees. Table 3 shows the F1-score of the induced structures. For comparison purposes, in this dataset, a state of the art supervised parser (Dozat et al., 2017) reaches 88.22 UAS F1-score and our random baseline, i.e., induced trees with random weights and gold root, achieves 10.1 UAS F1-score on average.[9] Given our findings in Section 5, we also computed a left- and right- branching baseline (with golden root), obtaining 10.39 and 35.08 UAS F1-score respectively.

Although our models are not trained to produce trees, the best dependency trees induced on each layer are far better than the random baseline, suggesting that the models are learning some syntactic relationships. However, the best scores do not achieve results much beyond the right branching baseline, showing that it is difficult to encode more complex and longer dependencies.

Overall, for all language pairs we notice the same performance trend across layers. Comparing

our low resource language pair, English-Turkish, to the other high resource languages, we can see that the models trained with larger dataset are able to induce better syntactic relationships, while among high resource languages all models are in the same ballpark, without any specific correlation with BLEU score, suggesting that it becomes more difficult to induce better dependency relations at a certain point. Figure 3 shows some examples of induced dependency trees. Interestingly enough, we can see that the trees with higher scores follow the patterns found in Section 5, in which each word is linked to the next one, so encoding most compounds and multi-word expressions. From visualizing other trees, even if they do not belong to the best attention head, we can see that they try to capture longer dependencies, as for *dress* and *stuffy* in the example in Figure 3.

7 Encoder Evaluation: Probing Sequence Labeling Tasks

We evaluated the encoder representation through four different sequence labeling tasks: Part-of-Speech (PoS) tagging, Chunking, Named Entity Recognition (NER) and Semantic tagging (SEM). In this test bed we used the trained weights of the encoder, keeping them fixed, training only one de-

___
[9]Even though not comparable in this setting, unsupervised systems developed to build dependency trees achieve on an English dataset UAS F1-score ranging from 27.9 to 51.4 when using the output of a PoS tagger system (Alonso et al., 2017).

		en → cs	en → de	en → et	en → fi	en → ru	en → tr	en → zh
POS	layer 0	91.13 / 7.70	91.06 / 8.20	84.49 / 18.20	86.88 / 25.00	89.47 / 6.00	**68.47** / 52.10	90.81 / 12.20
	layer 1	92.79 / **2.90**	93.12 / 4.60	**87.11** / 18.40	**87.58** / **12.40**	90.67 / 10.60	67.53 / 47.00	**92.60** / **7.90**
	layer 2	**93.20** / 5.40	**93.18** / **4.50**	84.99 / **14.70**	86.41 / 15.20	91.86 / **3.90**	68.13 / **45.40**	91.68 / 13.30
	layer 3	92.24 / 9.50	92.31 / 8.60	84.51 / 16.60	85.16 / 18.70	91.46 / 6.00	66.50 / 53.20	89.52 / 19.00
	layer 4	91.66 / 10.80	90.85 / 13.70	82.65 / 23.70	83.46 / 24.40	**91.98** / 12.00	65.66 / 53.90	86.47 / 22.10
	layer 5	87.14 / 19.10	87.83 / 24.10	82.11 / 23.60	80.41 / 33.30	89.47 / 16.30	62.80 / 54.80	82.95 / 31.30
CHUNK	layer 0	90.28 / 4.37	89.78 / 9.49	86.98 / 13.47	87.75 / **8.90**	88.12 / 6.61	**72.64** / **31.21**	90.37 / 5.42
	layer 1	92.98 / **4.32**	92.91 / 3.58	**88.00** / **11.78**	**88.92** / 10.19	91.16 / **4.03**	71.59 / 40.81	92.76 / **6.71**
	layer 2	**93.56** / 6.56	**93.92** / **3.53**	**88.00** / 12.28	88.65 / 13.22	91.60 / 5.82	70.25 / 37.38	**93.40** / 11.18
	layer 3	93.46 / 12.33	**93.92** / 10.14	87.56 / 14.36	87.41 / 19.93	**92.78** / 5.91	69.20 / 46.17	90.83 / 16.90
	layer 4	92.68 / 14.66	92.83 / 12.77	85.80 / 22.81	86.60 / 20.13	92.73 / 12.72	68.54 / 51.04	89.30 / 19.09
	layer 5	90.87 / 14.46	89.92 / 16.60	85.34 / 19.88	84.04 / 27.14	90.95 / 15.11	65.01 / 53.33	82.82 / 31.71
NER	layer 0	91.18 / 23.75	92.71 / 12.02	87.21 / 33.03	89.38 / 29.53	91.29 / 14.58	86.49 / 39.47	91.72 / **11.05**
	layer 1	93.29 / 9.80	93.36 / 7.27	88.65 / **15.99**	90.14 / **20.77**	92.22 / 10.07	85.66 / 38.14	92.93 / 11.13
	layer 2	**93.83** / 7.11	94.13 / **11.13**	87.46 / 37.30	90.20 / 26.47	**93.20** / 8.12	86.52 / 43.05	**93.72** / 12.35
	layer 3	93.23 / 16.53	**94.32** / 14.85	**88.95** / 33.31	**90.22** / 26.57	93.14 / 9.42	86.82 / **37.68**	93.07 / 18.32
	layer 4	93.72 / 11.81	93.93 / 12.51	88.57 / 40.55	89.14 / 34.28	92.02 / 12.65	**87.21** / 53.99	91.93 / 26.95
	layer 5	92.62 / 21.63	94.11 / 17.35	87.64 / 30.13	89.40 / 31.49	92.33 / 13.98	86.06 / 44.25	92.35 / 30.08
SEM	layer 0	83.99 / 13.56	84.05 / 13.35	81.87 / 14.73	81.99 / 14.69	83.36 / 14.07	79.04 / **16.87**	84.08 / 13.63
	layer 1	84.84 / 12.48	85.27 / 12.16	82.25 / **14.11**	82.70 / 13.97	84.12 / 13.26	78.80 / 17.10	84.93 / 11.88
	layer 2	85.17 / 11.95	85.11 / 12.16	82.28 / 14.25	82.76 / 14.85	84.09 / 13.03	78.26 / 18.09	85.40 / 11.74
	layer 3	85.34 / 12.02	84.77 / 11.45	82.17 / 14.41	82.82 / 14.00	**85.21** / 12.32	**79.22** / 17.28	84.79 / 11.91
	layer 4	85.29 / **11.38**	**85.91** / 9.93	**82.44** / 14.50	**83.19** / **13.77**	84.26 / 12.50	78.36 / 19.26	85.38 / 11.42
	layer 5	**86.27** / 11.68	85.71 / 10.78	82.27 / 14.55	82.96 / 13.84	84.56 / **11.79**	78.67 / 18.78	**85.98** / 10.62

Table 4: Results in terms of precision for each test set (↑, on the left side of each cell), together with the error rate on the sentence length (↓, on the right side of each cell).

	#labels	#training sentences	#testing sentences	average sent. length
PoS	17	12543	1000	21.2
Chunk	22	8042	2012	23.5
NER	9	14987	3684	12.7
SEM	80	62739	4351	6.4

Table 5: Statistics of the evaluation benchmarks used for the probing task.

coder layer using one attention head and one feed-forward layer. We then assess the quality of the encoder representation across stacked layers.

Evaluation Benchmarks. We used a standard benchmark for each task: the Universal Dependencies English Web Treebank v2.0 (Zeman et al., 2017) for PoS tagging, the CoNLL2000 Chunking shared task (Tjong Kim Sang and Buchholz, 2000), the CoNLL2003 NER shared task (Tjong Kim Sang and De Meulder, 2003), and the annotated data from the Parallel Meaning Bank (PMB) for Semantic tagging (Abzianidze et al., 2017). Each benchmark provides its own training, development and test data, except chunking in which we use 10% of the training corpus as validation, and the PMB

in which we used the silver portion for training and the gold portion for test and dev (following the 80-20 split).[10] Table 5 reports general statistics on each benchmark, regarding the granularity of each task, the number of training and testing instances, and the average length of the test sentences.

Evaluation Results. Table 4 reports the performance for each task and stacked layers, together with the error rate for sentence length prediction. For each language pair, we can see that the syntax information, i.e., the PoS task, is encoded mostly in the first 3 layers, corroborating the results in Section 6, while moving towards more semantic tasks, as NER and SEM we can see that in general the decoder needs more encoder layers to achieve better results. Another interesting finding is provided by the length mismatch between the output of the models and the gold labels. Clearly the models encode the information about the sentence length in the first three layers, and then the information starts to vanish with an increase of the error rate. The only exception is given by the SEM task, but as can be seen from the statistics in Table 5, the

---

[10]We used the sem-0.1.0 version.

	newstest 2017	newstest 2018
English → Turkish	6.93	6.22
English TL1 → Turkish	8.72	7.93
English TL2 → Turkish	7.82	6.91

Table 6: BLEU score for the newstest2017 and newstest2018 test data for the transfer learning experiment.

average sentence length is very short and so it is easier to predict. Overall, comparing the performance reached on these probing tasks with the BLEU score of each model, we can see again that the high resource language pairs achieve better results compared to our low resource language pair. Moreover, we notice that in general higher BLEU score correspond to higher probing results, confirming the trend that encoding linguistic proprieties within the encoder representation go on par with better translation quality (Niehues and Cho, 2017; Kiperwasser and Ballesteros, 2018).

8 Encoder Evaluation: Transfer learning

To assess whether the knowledge encoded in the attention units can help other models in a low resource scenario, we additionally carried out an evaluation of the encoder representation in a transfer learning task. Similar to Zoph et al. (2016), we used the encoder weights from one high resource language, i.e., English-German, to train a Transformer system for our low resource language pair, English-Turkish. We provide two experiments: i) initializing and fine tuning the encoder weights (**TL1**), ii) initializing and keeping the encoder weights fixed (**TL2**). Table 6 shows the BLEU scores of the systems evaluated with and without transferring the encoder parameters. Both transfer learning settings are helpful to the decoder to reach a better translation quality, with almost 2 BLEU point more on the best scenario. Starting with a better encoder representation, taken from a high resource language pair, and then fine tuning the parameters on the low resource language achieves the best result, matching and corroborating previous findings on recurrent networks (Zoph et al., 2016).

9 Related Work

The problem of interpreting and understanding neural networks is attracting more and more interest and work, with so many models and new architectures being published continuously each year. One of the first techniques to examine a neural network involves the analysis of activation patterns of the hidden layers (Elman, 1991; Giles et al., 1992). Nowadays, given its popularity, recurrent neural networks are the most evaluated networks, mainly investigated on the structures and linguistic properties they are encoding (Linzen et al., 2016; Enguehard et al., 2017; Kuncoro et al., 2017; Gulordava et al., 2018).

Traditionally, a common way to inspect neural networks is by visualizing the hidden representation trained for a specific task (Ding et al., 2017; Strobelt et al., 2018a,b), and to evaluate them by assessing the properties through downstream tasks (Chung et al., 2014; Greff et al., 2017).

Other recent studies look for hidden linguistic units that provide information on how the network works (Karpathy et al., 2015; Qian et al., 2016; Kádár et al., 2017), while another line of analysis probes the representation learned by a neural network as input to a classifier of another task (Shi et al., 2016; Adi et al., 2016; Belinkov et al., 2017a; Tran et al., 2018).

The most closely related work is by Belinkov et al. (2017b), in which they investigate the representation learned by the encoder of a sequence-to-sequence NMT system across different languages. Unlike them, we studied a neural network without any recurrent layers, which allows us to induce a tree representation from the input sentence, probing the encoder representation towards more downstream tasks, and showing that the attention weights can also be used to transfer knowledge to low-resource languages.

10 Conclusion

In this paper we investigated the kind of information that is captured by the encoder representation of a Transformer model trained for the task of Machine Translation. We analyzed and compared experimentally different models across several languages, including the visualization of weights, building tree structure from each sentence, probing the representation to four different sequence-labeling tasks and by transferring the encoder knowledge to a low resource language. Unlike most previous studies, where the analysis is made only on RNNs, we examined an architecture based on attention only. Our experimental evaluation sheds lights on interesting findings about dependency relations and syntactic and semantic behavior across layers. In future work, we plan to extend the analysis with probing tasks to evaluate other linguistic properties (Conneau et al., 2018) as well as to a recent evaluation dataset (Sennrich, 2017), tackling also the attention weights between the encoder and the decoder.

Acknowledgments

The work in this paper is supported by the Academy of Finland through project 314062 from the ICT 2023 call on Computation, Machine Learning and Artificial Intelligence. We would also like to acknowledge NVIDIA and their GPU grant.

References

Lasha Abzianidze, Johannes Bjerva, Kilian Evang, Hessel Haagsma, Rik van Noord, Pierre Ludmann, Duc-Duy Nguyen, and Johan Bos. 2017. The parallel meaning bank: Towards a multilingual corpus of translations annotated with compositional meaning representations. In *Proceedings of the 15th Conference of the European Chapter of the Association for Computational Linguistics: Volume 2, Short Papers*, pages 242–247, Valencia, Spain. Association for Computational Linguistics.

Yossi Adi, Einat Kermany, Yonatan Belinkov, Ofer Lavi, and Yoav Goldberg. 2016. Fine-grained analysis of sentence embeddings using auxiliary prediction tasks. *arXiv preprint arXiv:1608.04207*.

Tamer Alkhouli and Hermann Ney. 2017. Biasing attention-based recurrent neural networks using external alignment information. In *Proceedings of the Second Conference on Machine Translation*, pages 108–117.

Héctor Martínez Alonso, Željko Agić, Barbara Plank, and Anders Søgaard. 2017. Parsing universal dependencies without training. In *Proceedings of the 15th Conference of the European Chapter of the Association for Computational Linguistics: Volume 1, Long Papers*, volume 1, pages 230–240.

Philip Arthur, Graham Neubig, and Satoshi Nakamura. 2016. Incorporating discrete translation lexicons into neural machine translation. In *Proceedings of the 2016 Conference on Empirical Methods in Natural Language Processing*, pages 1557–1567, Austin, Texas. Association for Computational Linguistics.

Dzmitry Bahdanau, Kyunghyun Cho, and Yoshua Bengio. 2015. Neural Machine Translation by Jointly Learning to Align and Translate. In *ICLR Workshop*.

Yonatan Belinkov, Nadir Durrani, Fahim Dalvi, Hassan Sajjad, and James Glass. 2017a. What do neural machine translation models learn about morphology? In *Proceedings of the 55th Annual Meeting of the Association for Computational Linguistics (Volume 1: Long Papers)*, volume 1, pages 861–872.

Yonatan Belinkov, Lluís Màrquez, Hassan Sajjad, Nadir Durrani, Fahim Dalvi, and James Glass. 2017b. Evaluating layers of representation in neural machine translation on part-of-speech and semantic tagging tasks. In *Proceedings of the Eighth International Joint Conference on Natural Language Processing (Volume 1: Long Papers)*, volume 1, pages 1–10.

Luisa Bentivogli, Arianna Bisazza, Mauro Cettolo, and Marcello Federico. 2016. Neural versus phrase-based machine translation quality: a case study. In *Proceedings of the 2016 Conference on Empirical Methods in Natural Language Processing*, pages 257–267, Austin, Texas. Association for Computational Linguistics.

Ondřej Bojar, Rajen Chatterjee, Christian Federmann, Yvette Graham, Barry Haddow, Shujian Huang, Matthias Huck, Philipp Koehn, Qun Liu, Varvara Logacheva, et al. 2017. Findings of the 2017 conference on machine translation (wmt17). In *Proceedings of the Second Conference on Machine Translation*, pages 169–214.

Ondrej Bojar, Rajen Chatterjee, Christian Federmann, Yvette Graham, Barry Haddow, Matthias Huck, Antonio Jimeno Yepes, Philipp Koehn, Varvara Logacheva, Christof Monz, et al. 2016. Findings of the 2016 conference on machine translation. In *ACL 2016 First Conference on Machine Translation (WMT16)*, pages 131–198. The Association for Computational Linguistics.

Kyunghyun Cho, Bart van Merrienboer, Caglar Gulcehre, Dzmitry Bahdanau, Fethi Bougares, Holger Schwenk, and Yoshua Bengio. 2014. Learning phrase representations using rnn encoder–decoder for statistical machine translation. In *Proceedings of the 2014 Conference on Empirical Methods in Natural Language Processing (EMNLP)*, pages 1724–1734, Doha, Qatar. Association for Computational Linguistics.

Yoeng-Jin Chu. 1965. On the shortest arborescence of a directed graph. *Scientia Sinica*, 14:1396–1400.

Junyoung Chung, Caglar Gulcehre, KyungHyun Cho, and Yoshua Bengio. 2014. Empirical evaluation of gated recurrent neural networks on sequence modeling. *arXiv preprint arXiv:1412.3555*.

Alexis Conneau, Germán Kruszewski, Guillaume Lample, Loïc Barrault, and Marco Baroni. 2018. What you can cram into a single vector: Probing sentence embeddings for linguistic properties. In *Proceedings of the 56th Annual Meeting of the Association for Computational Linguistics (Volume 1: Long Papers)*, pages 2126–2136. Association for Computational Linguistics.

Yanzhuo Ding, Yang Liu, Huanbo Luan, and Maosong Sun. 2017. Visualizing and understanding neural machine translation. In *Proceedings of the 55th Annual Meeting of the Association for Computational*

Linguistics (Volume 1: Long Papers), volume 1, pages 1150–1159.

Timothy Dozat, Peng Qi, and Christopher D Manning. 2017. Stanford's graph-based neural dependency parser at the conll 2017 shared task. *Proceedings of the CoNLL 2017 Shared Task: Multilingual Parsing from Raw Text to Universal Dependencies*, pages 20–30.

Jack Edmonds. 1967. Optimum branchings. *Journal of Research of the National Bureau of Standards, B*, 71:233–240.

Jeffrey L Elman. 1991. Distributed representations, simple recurrent networks, and grammatical structure. *Machine learning*, 7(2-3):195–225.

Émile Enguehard, Yoav Goldberg, and Tal Linzen. 2017. Exploring the syntactic abilities of rnns with multi-task learning. In *Proceedings of the 21st Conference on Computational Natural Language Learning (CoNLL 2017)*, pages 3–14.

Jonas Gehring, Michael Auli, David Grangier, and Yann Dauphin. 2017a. A convolutional encoder model for neural machine translation. In *Proceedings of the 55th Annual Meeting of the Association for Computational Linguistics (Volume 1: Long Papers)*, volume 1, pages 123–135.

Jonas Gehring, Michael Auli, David Grangier, Denis Yarats, and Yann N Dauphin. 2017b. Convolutional sequence to sequence learning. *arXiv preprint arXiv:1705.03122*.

C Lee Giles, Clifford B Miller, Dong Chen, Guo-Zheng Sun, Hsing-Hen Chen, and Yee-Chun Lee. 1992. Extracting and learning an unknown grammar with recurrent neural networks. In *Advances in neural information processing systems*, pages 317–324.

Klaus Greff, Rupesh K Srivastava, Jan Koutník, Bas R Steunebrink, and Jürgen Schmidhuber. 2017. Lstm: A search space odyssey. *IEEE transactions on neural networks and learning systems*, 28(10):2222–2232.

Kristina Gulordava, Piotr Bojanowski, Edouard Grave, Tal Linzen, and Marco Baroni. 2018. Colorless green recurrent networks dream hierarchically. In *Proceedings of the 2018 Conference of the North American Chapter of the Association for Computational Linguistics: Human Language Technologies, Volume 1 (Long Papers)*, volume 1, pages 1195–1205.

Armand Joulin, Edouard Grave, Piotr Bojanowski, Matthijs Douze, Hérve Jégou, and Tomas Mikolov. 2016a. Fasttext.zip: Compressing text classification models. *arXiv preprint arXiv:1612.03651*.

Armand Joulin, Edouard Grave, Piotr Bojanowski, and Tomas Mikolov. 2016b. Bag of tricks for efficient text classification. *arXiv preprint arXiv:1607.01759*.

Akos Kádár, Grzegorz Chrupała, and Afra Alishahi. 2017. Representation of linguistic form and function in recurrent neural networks. *Computational Linguistics*, 43(4):761–780.

Andrej Karpathy, Justin Johnson, and Li Fei-Fei. 2015. Visualizing and understanding recurrent networks. *arXiv preprint arXiv:1506.02078*.

Eliyahu Kiperwasser and Miguel Ballesteros. 2018. Scheduled multi-task learning: From syntax to translation. *Transactions of the Association for Computational Linguistics*, 6:225–240.

Guillaume Klein, Yoon Kim, Yuntian Deng, Jean Senellart, and Alexander M. Rush. 2017. OpenNMT: Open-source toolkit for neural machine translation. In *Proc. ACL*.

Philipp Koehn. 2005. Europarl: A parallel corpus for statistical machine translation. In *MT summit*, volume 5, pages 79–86.

Philipp Koehn and Rebecca Knowles. 2017. Six challenges for neural machine translation. In *Proceedings of the First Workshop on Neural Machine Translation*, pages 28–39.

Adhiguna Kuncoro, Miguel Ballesteros, Lingpeng Kong, Chris Dyer, Graham Neubig, and Noah A. Smith. 2017. What do recurrent neural network grammars learn about syntax? In *Proceedings of the 15th Conference of the European Chapter of the Association for Computational Linguistics: Volume 1, Long Papers*, pages 1249–1258, Valencia, Spain. Association for Computational Linguistics.

Tal Linzen, Emmanuel Dupoux, and Yoav Goldberg. 2016. Assessing the ability of LSTMs to learn syntax-sensitive dependencies. *Transactions of the Association for Computational Linguistics*, 4:521–535.

Yang Liu and Mirella Lapata. 2018. Learning structured text representations. *Transactions of the Association for Computational Linguistics*. To appear.

Thang Luong, Hieu Pham, and Christopher D Manning. 2015a. Effective approaches to attention-based neural machine translation. In *Proceedings of the 2015 Conference on Empirical Methods in Natural Language Processing*, pages 1412–1421.

Thang Luong, Ilya Sutskever, Quoc Le, Oriol Vinyals, and Wojciech Zaremba. 2015b. Addressing the rare word problem in neural machine translation. In *Proceedings of the 53rd Annual Meeting of the Association for Computational Linguistics and the 7th International Joint Conference on Natural Language Processing (Volume 1: Long Papers)*, volume 1, pages 11–19.

Jan Niehues and Eunah Cho. 2017. Exploiting linguistic resources for neural machine translation using multi-task learning. In *Proceedings of the Second Conference on Machine Translation*, pages 80–89.

Matt Post. 2018. A call for clarity in reporting bleu scores. *arXiv preprint arXiv:1804.08771*.

Peng Qian, Xipeng Qiu, and Xuanjing Huang. 2016. Analyzing linguistic knowledge in sequential model of sentence. In *Proceedings of the 2016 Conference on Empirical Methods in Natural Language Processing*, pages 826–835.

Rico Sennrich. 2017. How grammatical is character-level neural machine translation? assessing mt quality with contrastive translation pairs. In *Proceedings of the 15th Conference of the European Chapter of the Association for Computational Linguistics: Volume 2, Short Papers*, volume 2, pages 376–382.

Rico Sennrich, Barry Haddow, and Alexandra Birch. 2016. Neural machine translation of rare words with subword units. In *Proceedings of the 54th Annual Meeting of the Association for Computational Linguistics (Volume 1: Long Papers)*, volume 1, pages 1715–1725.

Xing Shi, Inkit Padhi, and Kevin Knight. 2016. Does string-based neural mt learn source syntax? In *Proceedings of the 2016 Conference on Empirical Methods in Natural Language Processing*, pages 1526–1534.

Hendrik Strobelt, Sebastian Gehrmann, Michael Behrisch, Adam Perer, Hanspeter Pfister, and Alexander M Rush. 2018a. Seq2seq-vis: A visual debugging tool for sequence-to-sequence models. *arXiv preprint arXiv:1804.09299*.

Hendrik Strobelt, Sebastian Gehrmann, Hanspeter Pfister, and Alexander M Rush. 2018b. Lstmvis: A tool for visual analysis of hidden state dynamics in recurrent neural networks. *IEEE transactions on visualization and computer graphics*, 24(1):667–676.

Sara Stymne, Christian Hardmeier, Jörg Tiedemann, and Joakim Nivre. 2013. Tunable distortion limits and corpus cleaning for smt. In *WMT 2013; 8-9 August; Sofia, Bulgaria*, pages 225–231. Association for Computational Linguistics.

Ilya Sutskever, Oriol Vinyals, and Quoc V Le. 2014. Sequence to sequence learning with neural networks. In *Advances in neural information processing systems*, pages 3104–3112.

Jörg Tiedemann. 2012. Parallel data, tools and interfaces in opus. In *Proceedings of the Eight International Conference on Language Resources and Evaluation (LREC'12)*, Istanbul, Turkey. European Language Resources Association (ELRA).

Erik F Tjong Kim Sang and Sabine Buchholz. 2000. Introduction to the conll-2000 shared task: Chunking. In *Proceedings of the 2nd workshop on Learning language in logic and the 4th conference on Computational natural language learning-Volume 7*, pages 127–132. Association for Computational Linguistics.

Erik F Tjong Kim Sang and Fien De Meulder. 2003. Introduction to the conll-2003 shared task: Language-independent named entity recognition. In *Proceedings of the seventh conference on Natural language learning at HLT-NAACL 2003-Volume 4*, pages 142–147. Association for Computational Linguistics.

Ke Tran, Arianna Bisazza, and Christof Monz. 2018. The importance of being recurrent for modeling hierarchical structure. *arXiv preprint arXiv:1803.03585*.

Ashish Vaswani, Noam Shazeer, Niki Parmar, Jakob Uszkoreit, Llion Jones, Aidan N Gomez, Łukasz Kaiser, and Illia Polosukhin. 2017. Attention is all you need. In *Advances in Neural Information Processing Systems*, pages 5998–6008.

Adina Williams, Andrew Drozdov, and Samuel R Bowman. 2018. Do latent tree learning models identify meaningful structure in sentences? *Transactions of the Association of Computational Linguistics*, 6:253–267.

Yonghui Wu, Mike Schuster, Zhifeng Chen, Quoc V Le, Mohammad Norouzi, Wolfgang Macherey, Maxim Krikun, Yuan Cao, Qin Gao, Klaus Macherey, et al. 2016. Google's neural machine translation system: Bridging the gap between human and machine translation. *arXiv preprint arXiv:1609.08144*.

Ieva Zariņa, Pēteris Ņikiforovs, and Raivis Skadiņš. 2015. Word alignment based parallel corpora evaluation and cleaning using machine learning techniques. In *Proceedings of the 18th Annual Conference of the European Association for Machine Translation*.

Daniel Zeman, Martin Popel, Milan Straka, Jan Hajic, Joakim Nivre, Filip Ginter, Juhani Luotolahti, Sampo Pyysalo, Slav Petrov, Martin Potthast, et al. 2017. Conll 2017 shared task: multilingual parsing from raw text to universal dependencies. *Proceedings of the CoNLL 2017 Shared Task: Multilingual Parsing from Raw Text to Universal Dependencies*, pages 1–19.

Barret Zoph, Deniz Yuret, Jonathan May, and Kevin Knight. 2016. Transfer learning for low-resource neural machine translation. In *Proceedings of the 2016 Conference on Empirical Methods in Natural Language Processing*, pages 1568–1575.

Evaluating Syntactic Properties of Seq2seq Output with a Broad Coverage HPSG: A Case Study on Machine Translation

Johnny Tian-Zheng Wei
College of Natural Sciences
University of Massachusetts Amherst
jwei@umass.edu

Khiem Pham
Department of Computer Science
San Jose State University
khiem.pham@sjsu.edu

Brian Dillon
Department of Linguistics
University of Massachusetts Amherst
brian@linguist.umass.edu

Brendan O'Connor
College of Information and Computer Sciences
University of Massachusetts Amherst
brenocon@cs.umass.edu

Abstract

Sequence to sequence (seq2seq) models are often employed in settings where the target output is natural language. However, the syntactic properties of the language generated from these models are not well understood. We explore whether such output belongs to a formal and realistic grammar, by employing the English Resource Grammar (ERG), a broad coverage, linguistically precise HPSG-based grammar of English. From a French to English parallel corpus, we analyze the parseability and grammatical constructions occurring in output from a seq2seq translation model. Over 93% of the model translations are parseable, suggesting that it learns to generate conforming to a grammar. The model has trouble learning the distribution of rarer syntactic rules, and we pinpoint several constructions that differentiate translations between the references and our model.

French	Une situation grotesque.
Reference	It is a grotesque situation.
NMT Output	A generic_adj situation.

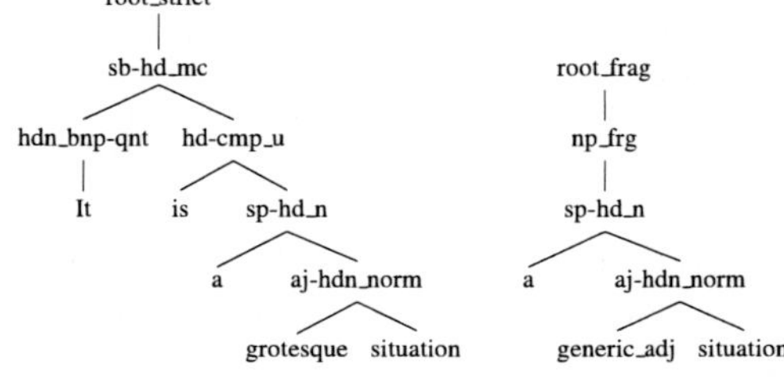

Figure 1: A test set source-reference pair and the NMT translation. Below are parser derivations in the ERG of both the reference and NMT translation. The ERG is described in §2. Non-syntactic rules have been omitted. The NMT model is trained and tested only on sentence pairs where the reference is parseable by the ERG. The NMT translation may not always be parseable. Analysis on model output parseability in §4.1.

1 Introduction

Sequence to sequence models (seq2seq; Sutskever et al., 2014; Bahdanau et al., 2014) have found use cases in tasks such as machine translation (Wu et al., 2016), dialogue agents (Vinyals and Le, 2015), and summarization (Rush et al., 2015), where the target output is natural language. However, the decoder side in these models is usually parameterized by gated variants of recurrent neural networks (Hochreiter and Schmidhuber, 1997), and are general models of sequential data not explicitly designed to generate conforming to the grammar of natural language.

The syntactic properties of seq2seq output is our central interest. We focus on machine translation as a case study, and situate our work among those of artificial language learning, where we train our translation model exclusively on sentence pairs where the target-side output is in our grammar, and test our models by evaluating the output with respect to a grammar. We attempt to understand seq2seq output with the English Resource Grammar (Flickinger, 2000), a broad coverage, linguistically precise HPSG-based grammar of English, and explore the advantages and potential of using such an approach.

This approach has three appealing properties in evaluating seq2seq output. First, the language of the ERG is a departure from studies on unrealistic artificial languages with regular or context-free grammars, which give exact analyses on grammars that bear little relation to human language

Proceedings of the 2018 EMNLP Workshop BlackboxNLP: Analyzing and Interpreting Neural Networks for NLP, pages 298–305
Brussels, Belgium, November 1, 2018. ©2018 Association for Computational Linguistics

(Weiss et al., 2018; Gers and Schmidhuber, 2001). In fact, about 85% of the sentences found in Wikipedia are parseable by the ERG (Flickinger et al., 2010). Second, our methodology directly evaluates sequences the model outputs in practice with greedy or beam search, in contrast to methods rescoring pre-generated contrastive pairs to test implicit model knowledge (Linzen et al., 2016; Sennrich, 2016). Third, the linguistically precise nature of the ERG gives us detailed analyses of the linguistic constructions exhibited by reference translations and parseable seq2seq translations for comparison.

Figure 1 shows an example from our analysis. Each testing example records the reference derivation, the model translation, and the derivation of that translation, if applicable. The derivations richly annotate the rule types and the linguistic constructions present in the translations.

Our analysis in §4.1 presents results on parseability by the ERG and summarizes its relation to surface level statistics using Pearson correlation. In §4.2 we manually annotate a small sample of NMT output without ERG derivations for grammaticality. We find that 60% of exhaustively unparseable NMT translations are ungrammatical by humans. We also identify that 18.3% of the ungrammatical sentences could be corrected by fixing agreement attachment errors. We conduct a discriminatory analysis in §4.4 on reference and NMT rule usage to guide a qualitative analysis on our NMT output. In analyzing specific samples, we find a general trend that our NMT model prefers to translate literally.

2 Head-phrase Structure Grammars

A head-phrase structure grammar (HPSG; Pollard and Sag, 1994) is a highly lexicalized constraint based linguistic formalism. Unlike statistical parsers, these grammars are hand-built from lexical entries and syntactic rules. The English Resource Grammar (Flickinger, 2000) is an HPSG-based grammar of English, with broad coverage of linguistic phenomena, around 35K unique lexical entries, and handling of unknown words with both generic part-of-speech conditioned lexical types (Adolphs et al., 2008) and a comprehensive set of class based generic lexical entries captured by regular expressions. The syntactic rules give fine-grained labels to the linguistic constructions

present.[1] While the ERG produces both syntactic and semantic annotations, we focus only on syntactic derivations in this study.

Suitable to our task, the ERG was engineered to capture as many grammatical strings as possible, while correctly rejecting ungrammatical strings. Parseability under the ERG should have linguistic reality in grammaticality. Ideally, there will be no parses for any ungrammatical string, and at least one parse for all grammatical strings, which can be unpacked in order of scores assigned by the included maximum entropy model. We make a distinction between parseability and grammaticality. For our purposes of evaluating with a specified grammar, we consider the parseability of sentences under the ERG in §4.1, regardless of human grammaticality judgments. In §4.2, we manually annotate unparseable sentences for English grammaticality.

All experiments are conducted with the 1214 version of the ERG, and the LKB/PET was used for all parsing (Copestake and Flickinger, 2000). We use the default parsing configuration (command line option "--erg+tnt"), which uses a parsing timeout of 60 seconds. A sentence is labeled unparseable either if the search space contains no derivations or if not a single derivation is found within the search space before the timeout. Figure 1 shows a simplified derivation tree.

3 Experimental Setup

This section details our setup of a French to English (FR → EN) neural machine translation system which we now refer to as NMT. Our goal was to test a baseline system for comparable results to machine translation and seq2seq models.

Dataset. From 2M French to English sentence pairs in the Europarl v7 parallel corpora (Koehn, 2005), we subset 1.6M where the English/reference sentence was parseable by the ERG. For these 1.6M sentence pairs, we record the best tree of the English sentence as determined by the maximum entropy model included in the ERG. All sentence pairs we now consider have at least one English translation within our grammar, and we make no constraint on French. About 1.4M pairs were used for training, 5K for validation, and the remaining 200K reserved for analysis.

Out of vocabulary tokens. On the source-side

---

[1] A list of rules types and their descriptions can be found at `http://moin.delph-in.net/ErgRules`.

	Strict		**Informal**		**Unpar-**
Source	**Full**	**Frag**	**Full**	**Frag**	**seable**
Ref	64.7	2.4	31.5	1.4	0.0
NMT	60.5	3.0	28.1	1.6	6.8
Δ	-4.2	+0.6	-3.4	+0.2	+6.8

Table 1: The distribution of root node conditions for the reference and NMT translations on the 200K analysis sentence pairs. Root node conditions are taken from the recorded best derivation. The best derivation is chosen by the maximum entropy model included in the ERG.

Feature	Equation	r
LP NMT	$\log P_m(S_o)$	0.313
LP Unigr. (src-fr)	$\log P_u(S_i)$	0.289
LP Unigr. (ref-en)	$\log P_u(S_r)$	0.273
LP Unigr. (out-en)	$\log P_u(S_o)$	0.304
Length Output	$|S_o|$	-0.320
Mean LP	$\frac{\log P_m(S_o)}{|S_o|}$	0.093
Norm LP	$-\frac{\log P_m(S_o)}{\log P_u(S_o)}$	0.057

Table 2: Pearson's r of surface statistics against the binary parseability variable. Parseable is denoted with +1. S_i, S_r, S_o are the input, reference, and NMT output sentences, respectively. We abbreviate log probability as "LP." $P_m(S)$ is the probability of S occurring under the NMT model, and $P_u(S)$ is the probability of S occurring under a unigram model.

French sentences, simple rare word handling was applied, where all tokens with a frequency rank over 40K were replaced with an "UNK" token. However, when handling rare words in the target-side English sentences, "UNK" will significantly degrade ERG parsing performance on model output. We replace our output tokens based on the lexical entries recognized by the ERG in our best parses (as in Figure 1's NMT output). This form of rare word handling is similar to the 10K PTB dataset (Mikolov et al., 2011), but with more detailed part-of-speech and regular expression conditioned "UNK" tokens. After preprocessing, we had a source vocabulary size of 40000, and a target vocabulary size of 36292.

Model. Our translation model is a word-level neural machine translation system with an attention mechanism (**?**). We used an encoder and decoder with 512 dimensions and 2 layers each, and word embeddings of size 1024. Dropout rates of 0.3 on the source, target, and hidden layers were applied. A dropout of 0.4 was applied to the word embedding, which was tied for both input and output. The model was trained for about 20 hours with early stopping on validation perplexity with patience 10 on a single Nvidia GPU Titan X (Maxwell). We used the NEMATUS (Sennrich et al., 2017) implementation, a highly ranked system in WMT16.

Translations. After training convergence on the 1M sentence pairs, the saved model is used for translation on the 200K sentences pairs left for analysis. A beam size of 5 is used to search for the best translation under our NMT model. We parse these translations with the ERG and record the best tree under the maximum entropy model. We have parallel data of the French sentence, the human/reference English translation, the NMT English translation, the parse of the reference trans-

lation, and the parse of NMT translation (if it was grammatical). Note that the NMT translation may have no parse.

4 Results

4.1 Parseability

The NMT translations for the 200K test split were parsed. Parsing a sentence with the ERG yields one of four cases:

- Parseable. A derivation is found and recorded by the parser before the timeout. The best derivation is chosen by the included maximum entropy in the ERG. About 93.2% of the sentences were parseable.

- Unparseable due to resource limitations. The parser reached its limit of either memory or time before finding a derivation. This constitutes about 3.2% of all cases, and 47% of unparsable cases.

- Unparseable due to parser error. The parser encountered an error in retrieving lexical entries or instantiating the parsing chart. This constitutes about 0.5% of all cases, and 8% of unparsable cases.

- Unparseable due to exhaustion of search space. The parser exhausted the entire search space of derivations for a sentence, and concludes that it does not have a derivation in

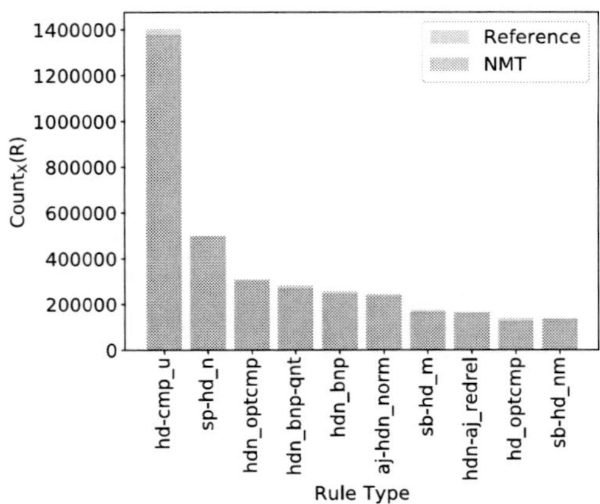

Figure 2: Count of rule usage for the 10 most frequent rules in the derivations of the reference and grammatical NMT translations.

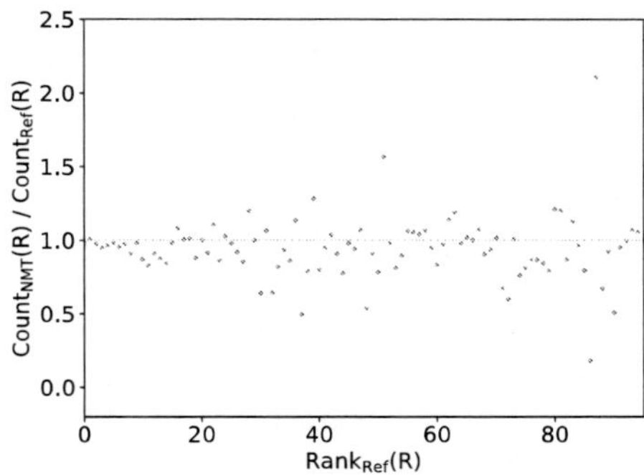

Figure 3: The ratio of each rule's count in grammatical NMT translations over count in reference translations, ordered by the rule's frequency rank in reference derivations. Only rules with over 1000 usages in the set of reference derivations are shown.

the ERG. This constitutes about 3.1% of all cases, and 45% of unparsable cases.

The distribution of the root node conditions for the reference and NMT translation derivations are listed in table 1, along with the parseability of the NMT translations. Root node conditions are used by the ERG to denote whether the parser had to relax punctuation and capitalization rules, with "strict" and "informal", and whether the derivation is of a full sentence or a fragment, with "full" and "frag". Fragments can be isolated noun, verb, or prepositional phrases. Both full sentence root node conditions saw a decrease in usage, with the strict full root condition having the largest drop out of all conditions. Both fragments have a small increase in usage.

We summarize the parseability of NMT translations with a few surface level statistics. In addition to log probabilities from our translation model, we provide several transformations of these scores, which were inspired by work in unsupervised acceptability judgments (Lau et al., 2015). In table 2, we calculate Pearson's r for each statistic and the binary parseability variable. The r coefficient is effectively a normalized difference in means.

From the correlation coefficients, we see that the probabilities from the NMT and unigram models are all indicative of parseability. The higher the probabilities, the more likely the translation is to be grammatical. Length is the only exception with a negative coefficient, where the longer a sentence is, the less likely a translation is gram-

matical. Length has the strongest correlation of all our features, but this correlation may be due to limitations in the ERG's ability to parse longer sentences, instead of the NMT model's to generate longer grammatical sentences. We see that the LP NMT has a higher correlation with grammaticality than the unigram models, but not by a large amount. Coefficients for length and LP NMT have the two greatest magnitudes.

4.2 Grammaticality

Out of the 14K unparseable NMT translations, there are 6.2K translations where the parser concluded unparseability after exhausting the search space for derivations. We will refer to these examples as "exhaustively unparseable." To understand the relation between English grammaticality and exhaustive unparseability under the ERG, two linguistics undergraduates (including the first author) labeled a random sample of 100 NMT translations from this subset. We sampled only those translations with less than 10 words to limit annotator confusion. Annotators were instructed to assign a binary grammatical judgment to each sentence, ignoring the coherence and meaning of the translation, to the best of their abilities. Punctuation was ignored in all annotations, although the ERG is sensitive to punctuation. When the sentence was ungrammatical, subject-verb agreement and noun phrase agreement errors were annotated.

Within our random sample, 60 sentences were labeled as ungrammatical. Of these ungrammatical sentences, 5 could be made grammatical if a

Reference		NMT	
Rule Type	**Annotations**	**Rule Type**	**Annotations**
xp_brck-pr	Paired bracketed phrase	j_sbrd-pre	Pred.subord phr fr.adj, prehead
cl-cl_runon	Run-on sentence w/two clauses	n-j_j-cpd	Compound from noun+adj
np-hdn_cpd	Compound proper-name+noun	j_n-ed	Adj-phr from adj + noun+ed
vp_sbrd-prd-prp	Pred.subord phr from prp-VP	aj-np_int-frg	Fragment intersctv modif + NP
hd-aj_int-sl	Hd+foll.int.adjct, gap in adj	vp_sbrd-prd-aj	Pred.subord phr from adjctv phr
hd-aj_vmod	Hd+foll.int.adjct, prec. NP cmp	np_frg	Fragment NP
vp_np-ger	NP from verbal gerund	flr-hd_nwh	Filler-head, non-wh filler
mrk-nh_atom	Paired marker + phrase	hdn-aj_rc-pr	NomHd+foll.rel.cl, paired pnct
vp_sbrd-pre	Pred.subord phr fr.VP, prehead	sb-hd_mc	Head+subject, main clause
num_prt-det-nc	Partitive NP fr.number, no cmp	num-n_mnp	Measure NP from number+noun

Table 3: The most discriminatory features of both the reference and NMT translations. Features are ranked by a logistic regression without an intercept and an L1 penalty $C = 0.01$, trained with LIBLINEAR within scikit-learn. Description of rule types are taken from the annotations in the ErgRules website.

subject-verb agreement error was corrected, and 5 other translations could be made grammatical by correcting an article or determiner attachment to a noun. One translation exhibited both forms of agreement attachment errors. Agreement attachment errors are better studied phenomenon (Linzen et al., 2016; Sennrich, 2016). However, correcting these errors only fixes 18.3% of ungrammaticality that we observed in our sample.

Out of the 100 sampled NMT translations that have no ERG derivations, we found 35 to be grammatical. 5 test examples were excluded. These include two cases where the source sentences were empty, and three cases where the sentence was parliament session information. Both annotators found annotating to be challenging, and possibly better annotated on an ordinal scale. Out of the exhaustively unparseable random sample, 37% was found to be grammatical. The ERG may have grammar gaps for near grammatical sentences.

4.3 Rule Counts

This section and those following will analyze the rules present in the derivations of the reference and the grammatical NMT translations. We consider only the appearance of the rule, disregarding the context it appears in, and define $\text{Count}_X(R)$ as the number of times rule R appears in the set $X \in \{\text{Ref}, \text{NMT}\}$ of derivations. In figure 2, we plot the counts of the 10 most frequent rule types in the reference and NMT translations. The rules were taken from the best derivations as determined by the included maximum entropy classifier in the ERG. Note that we have about 200K

reference derivations and 189K NMT derivations we aggregate statistics from, as about 7% of the NMT translations are unparseable. We see that both distributions seem to be Zipfian, and that the rule counts in the NMT translations match the reference closely.

In figure 3, for each rule R, we plot the ratio $\text{Count}_{\text{NMT}}(R)/\text{Count}_{\text{Ref}}(R)$ of derivations against the rank of the rule type. The rank is computed from the set of reference derivations. The variance of the ratio seems to increase as the rank of the rule increases. While the occurrences of rarer constructions is low in the NMT translations, it seems not to match the usage in the reference translation dataset. This suggests that NMT has trouble learning the usage of rarer syntactic constructions.

4.4 Discriminative Rules

This section aims to understand which usage of rules distinguish the reference from the NMT translations. The analysis in this section is largely inspired by work in syntactic stylometrics (Feng et al., 2012; Ashok et al., 2013), where we vectorize each derivation as a bag of rules, and fit a logistic regression without an intercept to predict whether a derivation was from the set of reference or NMT translations. In total, there are 392K examples and we prepare an 80/20 training validation split. The model is fit with an L1 sparsity penalty of $C = 0.01$ with the LIBLINEAR solver in scikit learn (Pedregosa et al., 2011). On the validation set, the logistic regression achieves an accuracy of about 59.0% on the validation set up from the 51.9% majority class baseline. Of the 204 rules used as features, only 71 were non-zero. There are 47 rules that are discriminatory towards reference translations (positive weights), and 24 rules that are discriminatory towards NMT translations (negative weights). Table 3 shows the 10 most discriminative rules for each set.

4.5 Qualitative Analysis

We provide qualitative analysis for a few of the most discriminative rules for both the reference and NMT translations. When exploring discriminatory rules in the reference, we sampled for sentence pairs where the reference translation that contained the rule of interest, and the NMT translation did not. We only sampled within sentences with a length of less than 12. Our qualitative analysis is written after we looked through many samples, and we attempted to list a few of our general observations for each rule.

The "cl-cl_runon" rule type indicates a runon sentence with two conjoined clauses. This rule has a positive coefficient, and discriminates towards reference translations. An example is given below:

French	je le répète , vous avez raison .
Reference	i repeat ; you are quite right .
NMT Output	i repeat , you are right .

In this case, the NMT used a comma to conjoin two clauses instead of using a semi-colon, which is more similar in punctuation to the source sentence. In every case we saw, the NMT model seems to follow the French style of conjunction more closely, mirroring the punctuation of the source sentence. Reference translations seem to be more spurious in the usage of semicolons or periods. In more concerning cases, short conjoined clauses were dropped by the NMT translations; e.g. "thank you .".

We now analyze "np_frg" which denotes a noun phrase fragment. This rule that has a negative coefficient, and discriminates towards NMT translations. We give an example below:

French	quel paradoxe !
Reference	what a paradox this is !
NMT Output	what a paradox !

When looking through samples, we saw many examples where the expletive is dropped. This is similar to the case for the previous rule as it is a literal translation of the French source. In NMT translations we observed increases in the formal and strict fragment root conditions, and we believe these translations are a factor.

5 Related Work

Previous work in recurrent neural network based recognizers on artificial languages has studied the performance on context-free and limited context-sensitive languages (Gers and Schmidhuber, 2001). More recent research in this setting provide methods to extract the exact deterministic finite automaton represented by the RNN based recognizers of regular languages (Weiss et al., 2018). These studies give exact analyses of RNN recognizers for simple artificial languages.

In the evaluation of language models in natural language settings, recent work analyzes the rescoring of grammatical and ungrammatical sentence pairs based on specific linguistic phenomenon such as agreement attraction (Linzen et al., 2016). These contrastive pairs have also found use in evaluating seq2seq models through rescoring with the decoder side of neural machine translation systems (Sennrich, 2016). Both studies on contrastive pairs evaluate implicit grammatical knowledge of a language model.

HPSG-based grammars have found use in evaluating human produced language. To determine the degree of syntactic noisiness in social media text, parseability under the ERG was examined for newspaper and Twitter texts (Baldwin et al., 2013). In predicting grammaticality of L2 language learners with linear models, the parseability of sentences with the ERG was found to be a useful feature (Heilman et al., 2014). These studies suggest parseability in the ERG has some degree of linguistic reality.

Our work combines analysis of neural seq2seq models with an HPSG-based grammar, which begins to let us understand the syntactic properties in the model output. Recent work most similar to ours is in evaluating multimodel deep learning models with the ERG (Kuhnle and Copestake, 2017). While their work uses the ERG for language generation to test language understanding, we evaluate language generation with the parsing capabilities of the ERG, and study the syntactic properties.

6 Conclusion

Neural sequence to sequence models do not have any explicit biases towards inducing underlying grammars, yet was able to generate sentences conforming to an English-like grammar at a high rate. We investigated parseability and differences in syntactic rule usage for this neural seq2seq model, and these two analyses were made possible by the English Resource Grammar. Future work will involve using human ratings and machine translation quality estimation datasets to understand which syntactic biases are preferable for machine translation systems. The ERG also produces Minimal Recursion Semantics (MRS; Copestake et al., 2005), a semantic representation which our work does not yet explore. By matching the semantic forms produced, we can make evaluations of language generation systems on a semantic level as well. In using these deep resources for evaluation, there is a shortcoming in the biased coverage of the grammar. Future work will also study how to evaluate our models despite these limitations. We hope this paper spurs others' interest in HPSG-based or language-like grammar evaluations of neural networks.

Acknowledgments

This work was facilitated by the Center for Study of Language and Information REU site at Stanford University, where the first and second author were roommates. Andrew McCallum and IESL provided computing resources. Dan Flickinger, Chris Potts, and the anonymous reviewers provided helpful comments. Nicholas Thomlin co-annotated the grammaticality judgments. Technical support on DELPH-IN was provided by Michael Goodman and Stephen Oepen. The first author received mentorship from Omer Levy, Roy Schwarz, Chenhao Tan, Nelson Liu, and Noah Smith in the summer of 2017, and from Ari Kobren, Nicholas Monath, and Haw-Shiuan Chang in the years prior. The second author received mentorship from Guangliang Chen.

References

Peter Adolphs, Stephan Oepen, Ulrich Callmeier, Berthold Crysmann, Dan Flickinger, and Bernd Kiefer. 2008. Some fine points of hybrid natural language parsing. In *Proceedings of the International Conference on Language Resources and Evaluation, LREC 2008, 26 May - 1 June 2008, Marrakech, Morocco*.

Vikas Ganjigunte Ashok, Song Feng, and Yejin Choi. 2013. Success with style: Using writing style to predict the success of novels. In *Proceedings of the 2013 Conference on Empirical Methods in Natural Language Processing, EMNLP 2013, 18-21 October 2013, Grand Hyatt Seattle, Seattle, Washington, USA, A meeting of SIGDAT, a Special Interest Group of the ACL*, pages 1753–1764.

Dzmitry Bahdanau, Kyunghyun Cho, and Yoshua Bengio. 2014. Neural machine translation by jointly learning to align and translate. *CoRR*, abs/1409.0473.

Timothy Baldwin, Paul Cook, Marco Lui, Andrew MacKinlay, and Li Wang. 2013. How noisy social media text, how diffrnt social media sources? In *Sixth International Joint Conference on Natural Language Processing, IJCNLP 2013, Nagoya, Japan, October 14-18, 2013*, pages 356–364.

Ann Copestake, Dan Flickinger, Carl Pollard, and Ivan A. Sag. 2005. Minimal recursion semantics: An introduction. *Research on Language and Computation*, 3(2):281–332.

Ann A. Copestake and Dan Flickinger. 2000. An open source grammar development environment and broad-coverage English grammar using HPSG. In *Proceedings of the Second International Conference on Language Resources and Evaluation, LREC 2000, 31 May - June 2, 2000, Athens, Greece*.

Song Feng, Ritwik Banerjee, and Yejin Choi. 2012. Characterizing stylistic elements in syntactic structure. In *Proceedings of the 2012 Joint Conference on Empirical Methods in Natural Language Processing and Computational Natural Language Learning, EMNLP-CoNLL 2012, July 12-14, 2012, Jeju Island, Korea*, pages 1522–1533.

Dan Flickinger. 2000. On building a more efficient grammar by exploiting types. *Natural Language Engineering*, 6(1):15–28.

Dan Flickinger, Stephan Oepen, and Gisle Ytrestøl. 2010. Wikiwoods: Syntacto-semantic annotation for English wikipedia. In *Proceedings of the International Conference on Language Resources and Evaluation, LREC 2010, 17-23 May 2010, Valletta, Malta*.

Felix A. Gers and Jürgen Schmidhuber. 2001. LSTM recurrent networks learn simple context-free and context-sensitive languages. *IEEE Trans. Neural Networks*, 12(6):1333–1340.

Michael Heilman, Aoife Cahill, Nitin Madnani, Melissa Lopez, Matthew Mulholland, and Joel R. Tetreault. 2014. Predicting grammaticality on an ordinal scale. In *Proceedings of the 52nd Annual Meeting of the Association for Computational Linguistics, ACL 2014, June 22-27, 2014, Baltimore, MD, USA, Volume 2: Short Papers*, pages 174–180.

Sepp Hochreiter and Jürgen Schmidhuber. 1997. Long short-term memory. *Neural Computation*, 9(8):1735–1780.

Philipp Koehn. 2005. Europarl: A parallel corpus for statistical machine translation. In *MT summit*, volume 5, pages 79–86.

Alexander Kuhnle and Ann A. Copestake. 2017. Deep learning evaluation using deep linguistic processing. *CoRR*, abs/1706.01322.

Jey Han Lau, Alexander Clark, and Shalom Lappin. 2015. Unsupervised prediction of acceptability judgements. In *Proceedings of the 53rd Annual Meeting of the Association for Computational Linguistics and the 7th International Joint Conference on Natural Language Processing of the Asian Federation of Natural Language Processing, ACL 2015, July 26-31, 2015, Beijing, China, Volume 1: Long Papers*, pages 1618–1628.

Tal Linzen, Emmanuel Dupoux, and Yoav Goldberg. 2016. Assessing the ability of lstms to learn syntax-sensitive dependencies. *TACL*, 4:521–535.

Tomas Mikolov, Anoop Deoras, Stefan Kombrink, Lukás Burget, and Jan Cernocký. 2011. Empirical evaluation and combination of advanced language modeling techniques. In *INTERSPEECH 2011, 12th Annual Conference of the International Speech Communication Association, Florence, Italy, August 27-31, 2011*, pages 605–608.

F. Pedregosa, G. Varoquaux, A. Gramfort, V. Michel, B. Thirion, O. Grisel, M. Blondel, P. Prettenhofer, R. Weiss, V. Dubourg, J. Vanderplas, A. Passos, D. Cournapeau, M. Brucher, M. Perrot, and E. Duchesnay. 2011. Scikit-learn: Machine learning in Python. *Journal of Machine Learning Research*, 12:2825–2830.

Carl Pollard and Ivan A. Sag. 1994. *Head-Driven Phrase Structure Grammar*. The University of Chicago Press, Chicago.

Alexander M. Rush, Sumit Chopra, and Jason Weston. 2015. A neural attention model for abstractive sentence summarization. In *Proceedings of the 2015 Conference on Empirical Methods in Natural Language Processing, EMNLP 2015, Lisbon, Portugal, September 17-21, 2015*, pages 379–389.

Rico Sennrich. 2016. How grammatical is character-level neural machine translation? assessing MT quality with contrastive translation pairs. *CoRR*, abs/1612.04629.

Rico Sennrich, Orhan Firat, Kyunghyun Cho, Alexandra Birch, Barry Haddow, Julian Hitschler, Marcin Junczys-Dowmunt, Samuel Läubli, Antonio Valerio Miceli Barone, Jozef Mokry, and Maria Nadejde. 2017. Nematus: a toolkit for neural machine translation. In *Proceedings of the Software Demonstrations of the 15th Conference of the European Chapter of the Association for Computational Linguistics*, pages 65–68, Valencia, Spain. Association for Computational Linguistics.

Ilya Sutskever, Oriol Vinyals, and Quoc V. Le. 2014. Sequence to sequence learning with neural networks. In *Advances in Neural Information Processing Systems 27: Annual Conference on Neural Information Processing Systems 2014, December 8-13 2014, Montreal, Quebec, Canada*, pages 3104–3112.

Oriol Vinyals and Quoc V. Le. 2015. A neural conversational model. *CoRR*, abs/1506.05869.

Gail Weiss, Yoav Goldberg, and Eran Yahav. 2018. Extracting automata from recurrent neural networks using queries and counterexamples. In *Proceedings of the 35th International Conference on Machine Learning, ICML 2018, Stockholmsmässan, Stockholm, Sweden, July 10-15, 2018*, pages 5244–5253.

Yonghui Wu, Mike Schuster, Zhifeng Chen, Quoc V. Le, Mohammad Norouzi, Wolfgang Macherey, Maxim Krikun, Yuan Cao, Qin Gao, Klaus Macherey, Jeff Klingner, Apurva Shah, Melvin Johnson, Xiaobing Liu, Lukasz Kaiser, Stephan Gouws, Yoshikiyo Kato, Taku Kudo, Hideto Kazawa, Keith Stevens, George Kurian, Nishant Patil, Wei Wang, Cliff Young, Jason Smith, Jason Riesa, Alex Rudnick, Oriol Vinyals, Greg Corrado, Macduff Hughes, and Jeffrey Dean. 2016. Google's neural machine translation system: Bridging the gap between human and machine translation. *CoRR*, abs/1609.08144.

Context-Free Transductions with Neural Stacks

Yiding Hao,* **William Merrill,*** **Dana Angluin, Robert Frank,**
Noah Amsel, Andrew Benz, and **Simon Mendelsohn**
Department of Linguistics, Yale University
Department of Computer Science, Yale University
`firstname.lastname@yale.edu`

Abstract

This paper analyzes the behavior of stack-augmented recurrent neural network (RNN) models. Due to the architectural similarity between stack RNNs and pushdown transducers, we train stack RNN models on a number of tasks, including string reversal, context-free language modelling, and cumulative XOR evaluation. Examining the behavior of our networks, we show that stack-augmented RNNs can discover intuitive stack-based strategies for solving our tasks. However, stack RNNs are more difficult to train than classical architectures such as LSTMs. Rather than employ stack-based strategies, more complex networks often find approximate solutions by using the stack as unstructured memory.

1 Introduction

Recent work on recurrent neural network (RNN) architectures has introduced a number of models that enhance traditional networks with differentiable implementations of common data structures. Appealing to their Turing-completeness (Siegelmann and Sontag, 1995), Graves et al. (2014) view RNNs as computational devices that learn transduction algorithms, and develop a trainable model of random-access memory that can simulate Turing machine computations. In the domain of natural language processing, the prevalence of context-free models of natural language syntax has motivated stack-based architectures such as those of Grefenstette et al. (2015) and Joulin and Mikolov (2015). By analogy to Graves et al.'s Neural Turing Machines, these stack-based models are designed to simulate pushdown transducer computations.

From a practical standpoint, stack-based models may be seen as a way to optimize networks for discovering dependencies of a hierarchical

---

*Equal contribution.

nature. Additionally, stack-based models could potentially facilitate interpretability by imposing structure upon the recurrent state of an RNN. Classical architectures such as Simple RNNs (Elman, 1990), Long Short-Term Memory networks (LSTM, Hochreiter and Schmidhuber, 1997), and Gated Recurrent Unit networks (GRU, Cho et al., 2014) represent state as black-box vectors. In certain cases, these models can learn to implement classical data structures using state vectors (Kirov and Frank, 2011). However, because state vectors are fixed in size, the inferred data structures must be represented in a fractal encoding requiring arbitrary position. On the other hand, differentiable stacks typically increase in size throughout the course of the computation, so their performance may better scale to larger inputs. Since the ability of a differentiable stack to function correctly intrinsically requires that the information it contains be represented in the proper format, examining the contents of a network's stack throughout the course of its computation could reveal hierarchical patterns that the network has discovered in its training data.

This paper systematically explores the behavior of stack-augmented RNNs on simple computational tasks. While Yogatama et al. (2018) provide an analysis of stack RNNs based on their Multipop Adaptive Computation Stack model, our analysis is based on the existing Neural Stack model of Grefenstette et al. (2015), as well as a novel enhancement thereof. We consider tasks with optimal strategies requiring either finite-state memory or a stack, or possibly a combination of the two. We show that Neural Stack networks have the ability to learn to use the stack in an intuitive manner. However, we find that Neural Stacks are more difficult to train than classical architectures. In particular, our models prefer not to employ stack-based strategies when other forms of memory are

Proceedings of the 2018 EMNLP Workshop BlackboxNLP: Analyzing and Interpreting Neural Networks for NLP, pages 306–315
Brussels, Belgium, November 1, 2018. ©2018 Association for Computational Linguistics

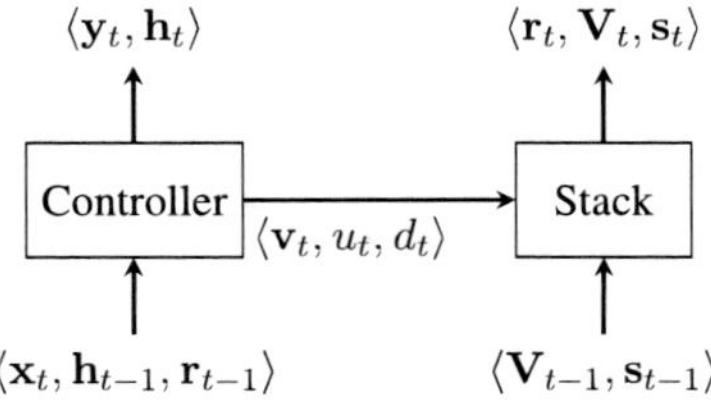

Figure 1: The Neural Stack architecture.

available, such as in networks with both LSTM memory and a stack.

A description of our models, including a review of Grefenstette et al.'s Neural Stacks, appears in Section 2. Section 3 discusses the relationship between stack-augmented RNN models and pushdown transducers, motivating our intuition that Neural Stacks are a suitable architecture for learning context-free structure. The tasks we consider are defined in Section 4, and our experimental paradigm is described in Section 5. Section 6 presents quantitative evaluation of our models' performance as well as qualitative description of their behavior. Section 7 concludes.

2 Models

The neural network models considered in this paper are based on the Neural Stacks of Grefenstette et al. (2015), a family of stack-augmented RNN architectures.[1] A Neural Stack model consists of two modular components: a *controller* executing the computation of the network and a *stack* implementing the data model of the network. At each time step t, the controller receives an input vector $\mathbf{x}_t$ and a *read vector* $\mathbf{r}_{t-1}$ representing the material at the top of the stack at the end of the previous time step. We assume that the controller may adhere to any feedforward or recurrent structure; if the controller is recurrent, then it may also receive a recurrent state vector $\mathbf{h}_{t-1}$. Based on $\mathbf{x}_t$, $\mathbf{r}_{t-1}$, and possibly $\mathbf{h}_{t-1}$, the controller computes an output $\mathbf{y}_t$, a new recurrent state vector $\mathbf{h}_t$ if applicable, and a tuple $\langle \mathbf{v}_t, u_t, d_t \rangle$ containing instructions for manipulating the stack. The stack takes these instructions and produces $\mathbf{r}_t$, the vector corresponding to the material at the top of the stack after popping and pushing operations have been performed on the basis of $\langle \mathbf{v}_t, u_t, d_t \rangle$. The

---

[1]Code for our PyTorch (Paszke et al., 2017) implementation is available at https://github.com/viking-sudo-rm/StackNN.

contents of the stack are represented by a recurrent state matrix $\mathbf{V}_t$ and a strength vector $\mathbf{s}_t$. This schema is shown in Figure 1.

Having established the basic architecture, the remainder of this section introduces our models in full detail. Subsection 2.1 describes how the stack computes $\mathbf{r}_t$ and updates $\mathbf{V}_t$ and $\mathbf{s}_t$ based on $\langle \mathbf{v}_t, u_t, d_t \rangle$. Subsection 2.2 presents the various kinds of controllers we consider in this paper. Subsection 2.3 presents an enhancement of Grefenstette et al.'s schema that allows the network to perform computations of varying duration.

2.1 Differentiable Stacks

A stack at time t consists of sequence of vectors $\langle \mathbf{V}_t[1], \mathbf{V}_t[2], \ldots, \mathbf{V}_t[t] \rangle$, organized into a matrix $\mathbf{V}_t$ whose ith row is $\mathbf{V}_t[i]$. By convention, $\mathbf{V}_t[t]$ is the "top" element of the stack, while $\mathbf{V}_t[1]$ is the "bottom" element. Each element $\mathbf{V}_t[i]$ of the stack is associated with a *strength* $\mathbf{s}_t[i] \in [0, 1]$. The strength of a vector $\mathbf{V}_t[i]$ represents the "degree" to which the vector is on the stack: a strength of 1 means that the vector is "fully" on the stack, while a strength of 0 means that the vector has been popped from the stack. The strengths are organized into a vector $\mathbf{s}_t = \langle \mathbf{s}_t[1], \mathbf{s}_t[2], \ldots, \mathbf{s}_t[t] \rangle$.

At each time step, the stack *pops* a number of items from the top, *pushes* a new item to the top, and *reads* a number of items from the top, in that order. The behavior of the popping and pushing operations is determined by the instructions $\langle \mathbf{v}_t, u_t, d_t \rangle$. The value obtained from the reading operation is passed back to the controller as the recurrent vector $\mathbf{r}_t$. Let us now describe each of the three operations.

Popping reduces the strength $\mathbf{s}_{t-1}[t-1]$ of the top element from the previous time step by u_t. If $\mathbf{s}_{t-1}[t-1] \geq u_t$, then the strength of the $(t-1)$st element after popping is simply $\mathbf{s}_t[t-1] = \mathbf{s}_{t-1}[t-1] - u_t$. If $\mathbf{s}_{t-1}[t-1] \leq u_t$, then we consider the popping operation to have "consumed" $\mathbf{s}_{t-1}[t-1]$, and the strength $\mathbf{s}_{t-1}[t-2]$ of the next element is reduced by the "left-over" strength $u_t - \mathbf{s}_{t-1}[t-1]$. This process is repeated until all strengths in $\mathbf{s}_{t-1}$ have been reduced. For each $i < t$, we compute the left-over popping strength $\mathbf{u}_t[i]$ for the ith item as follows.

$$\mathbf{u}_t[i] =$$
$$\begin{cases} u_t, & i = t-1 \\ \mathrm{ReLU}(\mathbf{u}_t[i+1] - \mathbf{s}_{t-1}[i+1]), & i < t-1 \end{cases}$$

The strengths are then updated accordingly.

$$\mathbf{s}_t[i] = \mathrm{ReLU}\left(\mathbf{s}_{t-1}[i] - \mathbf{u}_t[i]\right)$$

The pushing operation simply places the vector $\mathbf{v}_t$ at the top of the stack with strength d_t. Thus, $\mathbf{V}_t$ and $\mathbf{s}_t[t]$ are updated as follows.

$$\mathbf{s}_t[t] = d_t \qquad \mathbf{V}_t[i] = \begin{cases} \mathbf{v}_t, & i = t \\ \mathbf{V}_{t-1}[i], & i < t \end{cases}$$

Note that $\mathbf{s}_t[1]$, $\mathbf{s}_t[2]$, ..., $\mathbf{s}_t[t-1]$ have already been updated during the popping step.

The reading operation "reads" the elements on the top of the stack whose total strength is 1. If $\mathbf{s}_t[t] = 1$, then only the top element is read. Otherwise, the next element is read using the "left-over" strength $1 - \mathbf{s}_t[t]$. As in the case of popping, we may define a series of left-over strengths $\rho_t[1]$, $\rho_t[2]$, ..., $\rho_t[t]$ corresponding to each item in the stack.

$$\rho_t[i] = \begin{cases} 1, & i = t \\ \mathrm{ReLU}\left(\rho_t[i+1] - \mathbf{s}_t[i+1]\right), & i < t \end{cases}$$

The result $\mathbf{r}_t$ of the reading operation is obtained by computing a sum of the items in the stack weighted by their strengths, including only items with sufficient left-over strength.

$$\mathbf{r}_t = \sum_{i=1}^{t} \min\left(\mathbf{s}_t[i], \rho_t[i]\right) \cdot \mathbf{V}_t[i]$$

2.2 Controllers

We consider two types of controllers: *linear* and *LSTM*. The linear controller is a feedforward network consisting of a single linear layer. The network output is directly extracted from the linear layer, while the stack instructions are passed through the sigmoid function, denoted σ.

$$u_t = \sigma\left(\mathbf{W}_u \cdot \left[\begin{array}{c|c} \mathbf{x}_t & \mathbf{r}_{t-1} \end{array}\right]^{\mathsf{T}} + b_u\right)$$

$$d_t = \sigma\left(\mathbf{W}_d \cdot \left[\begin{array}{c|c} \mathbf{x}_t & \mathbf{r}_{t-1} \end{array}\right]^{\mathsf{T}} + b_d\right)$$

$$\mathbf{v}_t = \sigma\left(\mathbf{W_v} \cdot \left[\begin{array}{c|c} \mathbf{x}_t & \mathbf{r}_{t-1} \end{array}\right]^{\mathsf{T}} + \mathbf{b_v}\right)$$

$$\mathbf{y}_t = \mathbf{W_y} \cdot \left[\begin{array}{c|c} \mathbf{x}_t & \mathbf{r}_{t-1} \end{array}\right]^{\mathsf{T}} + \mathbf{b_y}$$

The LSTM controller maintains two state vectors: the *hidden state* $\mathbf{h}_t$ and the *cell state* $\mathbf{c}_t$. The output and stack instructions are produced by passing $\mathbf{h}_t$ through a linear layer. As in the linear controller, the stack instructions are additionally passed through the sigmoid function.

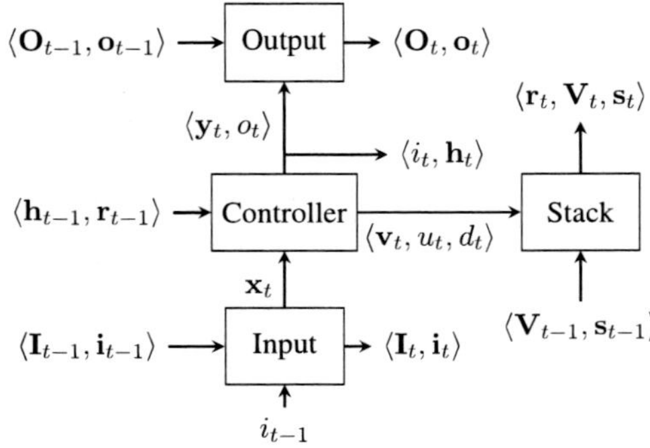

Figure 2: Our enhanced architecture with buffers.

2.3 Buffered Networks

One limitation of many RNN architectures, including Neural Stacks, is that they can only compute *same-length* transductions: at each time step, the network must accept exactly one input vector and produce exactly one output vector. This limitation prevents Neural Stacks from producing output sequences that may be longer or shorter than the input sequence. It also prohibits Neural Stack networks from performing computation steps without reading an input or producing an output (i.e., ε-transitions on input or output), even though such computation steps are a common feature of stack transduction algorithms.

A well-known approach to overcoming this limitation appears in Sequence-to-Sequence models such as Sutskever et al. (2014) and Cho et al. (2014). There, the production of the output sequence is delayed until the input sequence has been fully read by the network. Output vectors produced while reading the input are discarded, and the input sequence is padded with blank symbols to indicate that the network should be producing an output.

The delayed output approach solves the problem of fixed-length outputs, and we adopt it for the String Reversal task described in Section 4. However, delaying the output does not allow our networks to perform streaming computations that may interrupt the process of reading inputs or emitting outputs. An alternative approach is to allow our networks to perform ε-transitions. While Graves (2016) achieves this by dynamically repeating inputs and marking them with flags, we augment the Neural Stack architecture with two differentiable buffers: a read-only input buffer and a write-only output buffer. At each time step t, the input vector $\mathbf{x}_t$ is obtained by popping from the input buffer with strength i_{t-1}. In addition to the output vector and stack instructions, the controller must produce an input buffer pop strength i_t and an output buffer push strength o_t. The output vector is then enqueued to the output buffer with strength o_t. This enhanced architecture is shown in Figure 2.

The implementation of the input and output buffers is based on Grefenstette et al. (2015)'s Neural Queues, a first-in-first-out variant of the Neural Stack. Like the stack, the input buffer at time t consists of a matrix of vectors $\mathbf{I}_t$ and a vector of strengths $\mathbf{i}_t$. Similarly, the output buffer consists of a matrix of vectors $\mathbf{O}_t$ and a vector of strengths $\mathbf{o}_t$. The input buffer is initialized so that $\mathbf{I}_0$ is a matrix representation of the full input sequence, with an initial strength of 1 for each item.

At time t, items are dequeued from the "front" of the buffer with strength i_{t-1}.

$$\iota_t[j] = \begin{cases} i_{t-1}, & j = 1 \\ \mathrm{ReLU}(\iota_t[j-1] - \mathbf{i}_{t-1}[j]), & j > 1 \end{cases}$$

$$\mathbf{i}_t[j] = \mathrm{ReLU}\left(\mathbf{i}_{t-1}[j] - \iota_t[j]\right)$$

Next, the input vector $\mathbf{x}_t$ is produced by reading from the front of the buffer with strength 1.

$$\xi_t[j] = \begin{cases} 1, & j = 1 \\ \mathrm{ReLU}\left(\xi_t[j-1] - \mathbf{i}_t[j]\right), & j > 1 \end{cases}$$

$$\mathbf{x}_t = \sum_{j=1}^{n} \min\left(\mathbf{i}_t[j], \xi_t[j]\right) \cdot \mathbf{I}_t[j]$$

Since the input buffer is read-only, there is no push operation. This means that unlike $\mathbf{V}_t$ and $\mathbf{O}_t$, the number of rows of $\mathbf{I}_t$ is fixed to a constant n. When the controller's computation is complete, the output vector $\mathbf{y}_t$ is enqueued to the "back" of the output buffer with strength o_t.

$$\mathbf{O}_t[j] = \begin{cases} \mathbf{y}_t, & j = t \\ \mathbf{O}_{t-1}[j], & j < t \end{cases}$$

$$\mathbf{o}_t[j] = \begin{cases} o_t, & j = t \\ \mathbf{o}_{t-1}[j], & j < t \end{cases}$$

After the last time step, the final output sequence is obtained by repeatedly dequeuing the front of the output buffer with strength 1 and reading the front of the output with strength 1. These dequeuing and reading operations are identical to those defined for the input buffer.

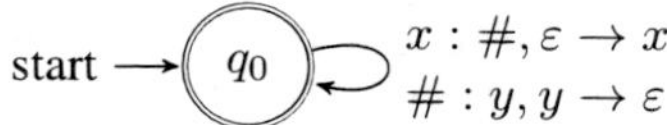

Figure 3: A PDT for the String Reversal task.

3 Pushdown Transducers

Our decision to use a stack for NLP tasks rather than some other differentiable data structure is motivated by the success of context-free grammars (CFGs) in describing the hierarchical phrase structure of natural language syntax. A classic theoretical result due to Chomsky (1962) shows that CFGs generate exactly those sets of strings that are accepted by nondetermininstic pushdown automata (PDAs), a model of computation that augments a finite-state machine with a stack. When enhanced with input and output buffers, we consider Neural Stacks to be an implementation of *deterministic pushdown transducers* (PDTs), a variant of PDAs that includes an output tape.

Formally, a PDT is described by a *transition function* of the form $\delta(q, x, s) = \langle q', y, s' \rangle$, interpreted as follows: if the machine receives an x from the input buffer and pops an s from the top of the stack while in state q, then it sends a y to the output buffer, pushes an s' to the stack, and transitions to state q'. We assume that δ is only defined for finitely many configurations $\langle q, x, s \rangle$. These configurations, combined with their corresponding values of δ, represent all the possible actions of a pushdown transducer.

To illustrate, let us construct a PDT that computes the function $f\left(w\#^{|w|}\right) = \#^{|w|}w^R$, where w^R is the reverse of w and $\#^{|w|}$ is a sequence of $\#$s of the same length as w. We can begin to compute f using a single state q_0 by pushing each symbol of w onto the stack while emitting $\#$s as output. When the machine has finished reading w, the stack contains the symbols of w in reverse order. In the remainder of the computation, the machine pops symbols from the stack one at a time and sends them to the output buffer. A pictoral representation of this PDT is shown in Figure 3. Each circle represents a state of the PDT, and each action $\delta(q, x, s) = \langle q', y, s' \rangle$ is represented by an arrow from q to q' with the label "$x : y, s \to s'$." Observe that the two labels of the arrow from q_0 to itself encode a transition function implementing the algorithm described above.

Given a finite state transition function, there exists an LSTM that implements it. In fact, Weiss et al. (2018) show that a deterministic k-counter automaton can be simulated by an LSTM. Thus, any deterministic PDT can be simulated by the buffered stack architecture with an LSTM controller.

4 Tasks

The goal of this paper is to ascertain whether or not stack-augmented RNN architectures can learn to perform PDT computations. To that end, we consider six tasks designed to highlight various features of PDT algorithms. Four of these tasks—String Reversal, Parenthesis Prediction, and the two XOR Evaluation tasks—have simple PDT implementations. The PDTs for each of these tasks differ in their memory requirements: they require either finite-state memory or stack-structured memory, or a combination of the two. The remaining two tasks—Boolean Formula Evaluation and Subject–Auxiliary Agreement—are designed to determine whether or not Neural Stacks can be applied to complex use cases that are thought to be compatible with stack-based techniques.

4.1 String Reversal

In the String Reversal task, the network must compute the function f from the previous section. As discussed there, the String Reversal task can be performed straightforwardly by pushing all input symbols to the stack and then popping all symbols from the stack. The purpose of this task is to serve as a baseline test for whether or not a controller can learn to use a stack in principle. Since in the general case, correctly producing w^R requires recording w in the stack, we evaluate the network solely based on the portion of its output where w^R should appear, immediately after reading the last symbol of w.

4.2 XOR Evaluation

We consider two tasks that require the network to implement the XOR function. In the *Cumulative XOR Evaluation* task, the network reads an input string of 1s and 0s. At each time step, the network must output the XOR of all the input symbols it has seen so far. The *Delayed XOR Evaluation* task is similar, except that the most recent input symbol is excluded from the XOR computation.

As shown in the left of Figure 4, the XOR Evaluation tasks can be computed by a PDT without using the stack. Thus, we use XOR Evaluation to test the versatility of the stack by assessing whether a feedforward controller can learn to use it as unstructured memory.

The Cumulative XOR Evaluation task presents the linear controller with a theoretical challenge because single-layer linear networks cannot compute the XOR function (Minsky and Papert, 1969). However, in the Delayed XOR Evaluation task, the delay between reading an input symbol and incorporating it into the XOR gives the network two linear layers to compute XOR when unravelled through time. Therefore, we expect that the linear model should be able to perform the Delayed XOR Evaluation task, but not the Cumulative XOR Evaluation task.

The discrepancy between the Cumulative and the Delayed XOR Evaluation tasks for the linear controller highlights the importance of timing in stack algorithms. Since the our enhanced architecture from Subsection 2.3 can perform ε-transitions, we expect it to perform the Cumulative XOR Evaluation task with a linear controller by learning to introduce the necessary delay. Thus, the XOR tasks allow us to test whether our buffered model can learn to optimize the timing of its computation.

4.3 Parenthesis Prediction

The Parenthesis Prediction task is a simplified language modelling task. At each time step t, the network reads the tth symbol of some string and must attempt to output the $(t + 1)$st symbol. The strings are sequences of well-nested parentheses generated by the following CFG.

$$S \to S\,T \mid T\,S \mid T$$
$$T \to (\,T\,) \mid (\,)$$
$$T \to [\,T\,] \mid [\,]$$

We evaluate the network only when the correct prediction is) or]. This restriction allows for a deterministic PDT solution, shown in the right of Figure 4.

Unlike String Reversal and XOR Evaluation, the Parenthesis Prediction task relies on both the stack and the finite-state control. Thus, the Parenthesis Prediction task tests whether or not Neural Stack models can learn to combine different

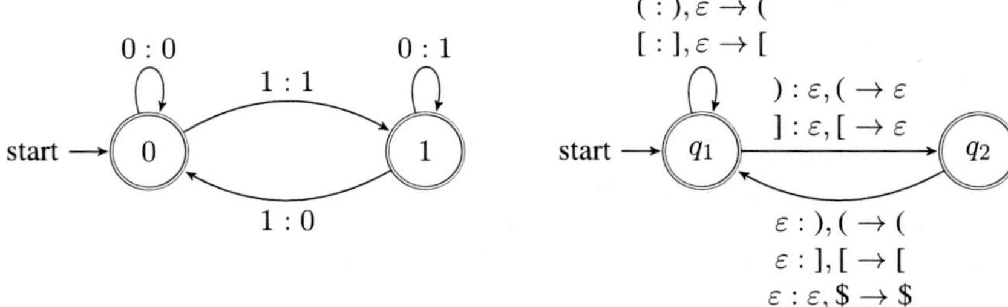

Figure 4: PDTs for Cumulative XOR Evaluation (left) and Parenthesis Prediction (right) tasks. The symbol $ represents the bottom of the stack.

types of memory. Furthermore, since context-free languages can be canonically represented as homomorphic images of well-nested parentheses (Chomsky and Schützenberger, 1959), the Parenthesis Prediction task may be used to gauge the suitability of Neural Stacks for context-free language modelling.

4.4 Boolean Formula Evaluation

In the Boolean Formula Evaluation task, the network reads a boolean formula in reverse Polish notation generated by the following CFG.

$$S \rightarrow S\,S \lor \mid S\,S \land$$
$$S \rightarrow T \mid F$$

At each time step, the network must output the truth value of the longest sub-formula ending at the input symbol.

The Boolean Formula Evaluation task tests the ability of Neural Stacks to infer complex computations over the stack. In this case, the network must store previously computed values on the stack and evaluate boolean operations over these stored values. This technique is reminiscent of shift-reduce parsing, making the Boolean Formula Evaluation task a testing ground for the possibility of applying Neural Stacks to natural language parsing.

4.5 Subject–Auxiliary Agreement

The Subject–Auxiliary Agreement task is inspired by Linzen et al. (2016), who investigate whether or not LSTMs can learn structure-sensitive long-distance dependencies in natural language syntax. There, the authors train LSTM models that perform language modelling on prefixes of sentences drawn from corpora. The last word of each prefix is a verb, and the models are evaluated solely on whether or not they prefer the correct form of the verb over the incorrect ones. In sentences with embedded clauses, the network must be able to identify the subject of the verb among several possible candidates in order to conjugate the verb.

Here, we consider sentences generated by a small, unambiguous CFG that models a fragment of English.

$$S \rightarrow \text{NPsing has} \mid \text{NPplur have}$$
$$\text{NP} \rightarrow \text{NPsing} \mid \text{NPplur}$$
$$\text{NPsing} \rightarrow \text{the lobster (PP} \mid \text{Relsing)}$$
$$\text{NPplur} \rightarrow \text{the lobsters (PP} \mid \text{Relplur)}$$
$$\text{PP} \rightarrow \text{in NP}$$
$$\text{Relsing} \rightarrow \text{that has VP} \mid \text{Relobj}$$
$$\text{Relplur} \rightarrow \text{that have VP} \mid \text{Relobj}$$
$$\text{Relobj} \rightarrow \text{that NPsing has devoured}$$
$$\text{Relobj} \rightarrow \text{that NPplur have devoured}$$
$$\text{VP} \rightarrow \text{slept} \mid \text{devoured NP}$$

As in the Parenthesis Prediction task, the network performs language modelling, but is only evaluated when the correct prediction is an auxiliary verb (i.e., *has* or *have*).

5 Experiments

We conducted four experiments designed to assess various aspects of the behavior of Neural Stacks. In each experiment, models are trained on a generated dataset consisting of 800 input–output string pairings encoded in one-hot representation. Training occurs in mini-batches containing 10 string pairings each. At the end of each epoch, the model is evaluated on a generated development set of 100 examples. Training terminates when five consecutive epochs fail to exceed the highest development accuracy attained. The sizes of the LSTM controllers' recurrent state vectors are fixed to 10, and, with the exception of Experiment 2 described below, the sizes of the vectors placed on the stack are fixed to 2. After training is complete, each trained model is evaluated on a testing set of 1000 generated strings, each of which is at least roughly twice as long as the strings used for training. 10 trials are performed for each set of experimental conditions.

Experiment 1 tests the propensity of trained Neural Stack models to use the stack. We train both the standard Neural Stack model and our enhanced buffered model from Subsection 2.3 to perform the String Reversal task using the linear controller. To compare the stack with unstructured memory, we also train the standard Neural Stack model using the LSTM controller as well as an LSTM model without a stack. Training and development data are obtained from sequences of 0s and 1s randomly generated with an average length of 10. The testing data have an average length of 20.

Experiment 2 considers the XOR Evaluation tasks. We train standard models with a linear controller on the Delayed XOR task and an LSTM controller on the Cumulative XOR task to test the network's ability to use the stack as unstructured state. We also train both a standard and a buffered model on the Cumulative XOR Evaluation task using the linear controller to test the network's ability to use our buffering mechanism to infer optimal timing for computation steps. Training and development data are obtained from randomly generated sequences of 0s and 1s fixed to a length of 12. The testing data are fixed to a length of 24. The vectors placed on the stack are fixed to a size of 6.

In Experiment 3, we attempt to perform the Parenthesis Prediction task using standard models with various types of memory: a linear controller with no stack, which has no memory; a linear controller with a stack, which has stack-structured memory; an LSTM controller with no stack, which has unstructured memory; and an LSTM controller with a stack, which has both stack-structured and unstructured memory.

Sequences of well-nested parentheses are generated by the CFG from the previous section. The training and development data are obtained by randomly sampling from the set of strings of derivation depth at most 6, which contains strings of length up to 20. The testing data are of depth 12

and length up to 110.

Experiment 4 compares the standard models with linear and LSTM controllers against a baseline consisting of an LSTM controller with no stack. Whereas Experiments 1–3 presented the network with tasks designed to showcase various features of the Neural Stack architecture, the goal of this experiment is to gauge the extent to which stack-structured memory may improve the network's performance on more sophisticated tasks. We train the three types of models on the Boolean Formula Evaluation task and the Subject–Auxiliary Agreement task. Data for both tasks are generated by the CFGs given in Section 4. The boolean formulae for training and development are randomly sampled from the set of strings of derivation depth at most 6, having a maximum length of 15, while the testing data are sampled from derivations of depth at most 7, with a maximum length of 31. The sentence prefixes are of depth 16 and maximum length 23 during the training phase, and depth 32 and maximum length 49 during the final evaluation round.

6   Results

Our results are shown in Table 1. The networks we trained were able to achieve a median accuracy of at least 90.0% during the training phase in 10 of the 13 experimental conditions involving a stack-augmented architecture. However, many of these conditions include trials in which the model performed considerably worse during training than the median. This suggests that while stack-augmented networks are able to perform our tasks in principle, they may be more difficult to train than traditional RNN architectures. Note that there is substantially less variation in the performance of the LSTM networks without a stack.

In Experiment 1, the standard network with the linear controller performs perfectly both during the training phase and in the final testing phase. The buffered network performed nearly as well during the training phase, but its performance failed to generalize to longer strings. The LSTM network achieved roughly the same performance both with and without a stack, substantially worse than the linear controller. The left-most graphic in Figure 5 shows that the linear controller pushes a copy of its input to the stack and then pops the copy to produce the output. As suggested by an anonymous reviewer, we also consid-

Task	Buffered	Controller	Stack	Min	Med	Max	Min	Med	Max
Reversal	No	Linear	Yes	49.9	**100.0**	**100.0**	49.3	**100.0**	**100.0**
Reversal	Yes	Linear	Yes	55.3	98.7	99.4	49.5	60.4	74.7
Reversal	No	LSTM	Yes	81.2	89.3	94.4	**67.2**	71.0	73.7
Reversal	No	LSTM	No	**83.0**	86.5	92.5	64.8	68.6	73.3
XOR	No	Linear	Yes	51.1	53.5	54.4	50.7	51.9	51.9
XOR	No	LSTM	Yes	**100.0**	**100.0**	**100.0**	**99.7**	**100.0**	**100.0**
XOR	Yes	Linear	Yes	51.0	99.8	**100.0**	50.4	96.0	99.1
Delayed XOR	No	Linear	Yes	**100.0**	**100.0**	**100.0**	**100.0**	**100.0**	**100.0**
Parenthesis	No	Linear	Yes	72.8	97.0	99.3	59.9	80.3	83.2
Parenthesis	No	Linear	No	70.0	71.8	73.3	59.9	60.5	60.7
Parenthesis	No	LSTM	Yes	**100.0**	**100.0**	**100.0**	**85.8**	**86.8**	**88.9**
Parenthesis	No	LSTM	No	**100.0**	**100.0**	**100.0**	83.5	85.8	88.0
Formula	No	Linear	Yes	87.4	92.0	97.3	87.8	91.2	96.2
Formula	No	LSTM	Yes	**98.0**	**98.7**	**99.4**	**96.8**	**97.7**	**98.4**
Formula	No	LSTM	No	95.4	98.5	99.3	95.3	97.6	**98.4**
Agreement	No	Linear	Yes	53.3	73.5	93.9	51.8	68.8	85.8
Agreement	No	LSTM	Yes	95.6	**98.5**	99.7	82.4	**88.8**	**91.2**
Agreement	No	LSTM	No	**96.2**	98.1	**100.0**	**83.7**	88.2	90.6

Table 1: The minimum, median, and maximum accuracy (%) attained by the 10 models for each experimental condition during the last epoch of the training phase (left) and the final testing phase (right).

ered a variant of this task in which certain alphabet symbols are excluded from the reversed output. The center graphic in Figure 5 shows that for this task, the linear controller learns a strategy in which only symbols included in the reversed output are pushed to the stack. The rightmost graphic shows that LSTM controller behaves differently from the linear controller, exhibiting uniform pushing and popping behavior throughout the computation. This suggests that under our experimental conditions, the LSTM controller prefers to rely on its recurrent state for memory rather than the stack, even though such a strategy does not scale to the final testing round.

The models in Experiment 2 perform as we expected. The unbuffered model with the linear controller performed at chance, in line with the inability of the linear controller to compute XOR. The rest of the models were able to achieve accuracy above 95.0% both in the training phase and in the final testing phase. The buffered network was successfully able to delay its computation in the Cumulative XOR Evaluation task. The leftmost graphic in Figure 6 illustrates the network's behavior in the Delayed XOR Evaluation task, and shows that the linear controller uses the stack as unstructured memory—an unsurprising observation given the nature of the task. Note that the

vectors pushed onto the stack in the presence of input symbol 1 vary between two possible values that represent the current parity.

In Experiment 3, the linear model without a stack performs fairly well during training, achieving a median accuracy of 71.8%. This is because 43.8% of (s and [s in the training data are immediately followed by)s and]s, respectively, so it is possible to attain 71.9% accuracy by predicting) and] when reading (and [and by always predicting] when reading) or]. Linear models with the stack perform better, but as shown by the rightmost graphic in Figure 6, they do not make use of a stack-based strategy (since they never pop), but instead appear to use the top of the stack as unstructured memory. The LSTM models perform slightly better, achieving 100% accuracy during the training phase. However, the LSTM controller still suffers significantly in the final testing phase with or without a stack, suggesting that the LSTM models are not employing a stack-based strategy.

In Experiment 4, the Boolean Formula Evaluation task is performed easily, with a median accuracy exceeding 90.0% for all models both on the development set and the testing set. This is most likely because, on average, three quarters of the nodes in a boolean formula either require no context for evaluation (because they are atomic)

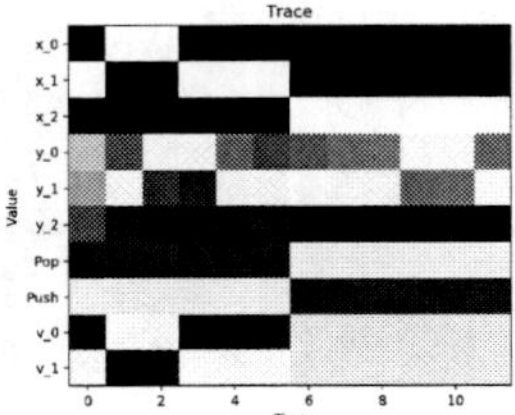
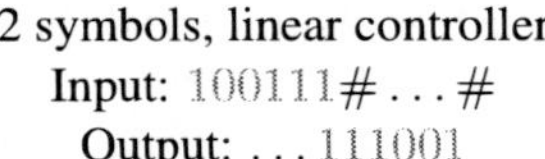

2 symbols, linear controller
Input: 100111#...#
Output: ...111001

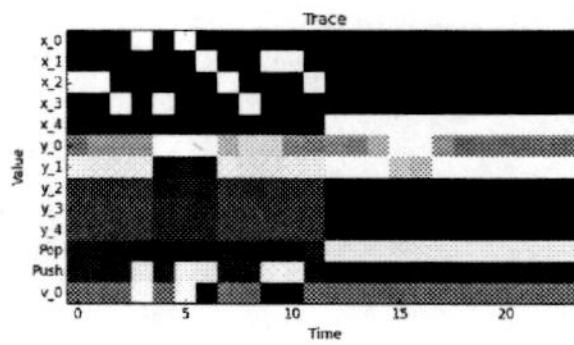

4 symbols, linear controller
Input: 223030123112#...#
Output: ...11100...

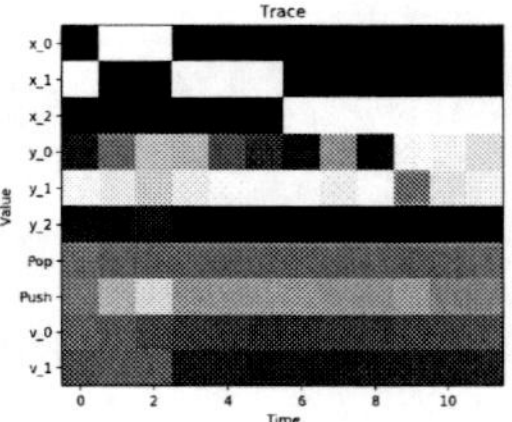

2 symbols, LSTM controller
Input: 100111#...#
Output: ...111001

Figure 5: Diagrams of network computation on the Reversal task with linear and LSTM controllers. In each diagram, the input may consist of 2 or 4 distinct alphabet symbols, but only the symbols 0 and 1 are included in the output. Columns indicate the pop strengths, push strengths, and pushed vectors throughout the course of the computation, along with the input and predicted output in one-hot notation. Lighter colors indicate higher values.

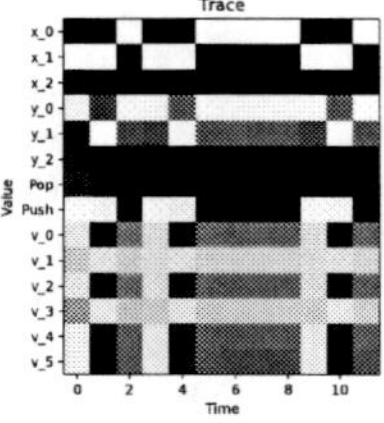

Delayed XOR, linear controller
Input: 110110000110
Output: 010010000010

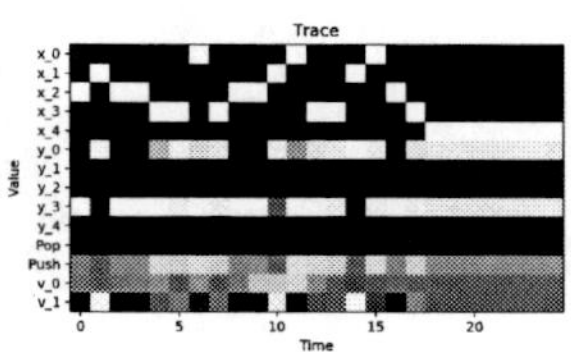

Parenthesis, linear controller
Input: [(([[]])][[()]()[]
Output:])]]]]]]]])]]])]]

Figure 6: Diagrams of network computation for the Delayed XOR and Parenthesis tasks with a linear controller.

or make use of limited context (because they are boolean formulas of depth one). The linear controller performed worse on average than the LSTM models on the agreement task, though the highest-performing linear models achieved a comparable accuracy to their LSTM counterparts. Again, the performance of the LSTM networks is unaffected by the presence of the stack, suggesting that our trained models prefer to use their recurrent state over the stack.

7 Conclusion

We have shown in Experiments 1 and 2 that it is possible in principle to train an RNN to operate a stack and input–output buffers in the intended way. There, the tasks involved have only one optimal solution: String Reversal cannot be performed without recording the string, and the linear controller cannot solve Cumulative XOR Evaluation without introducing a delay. In the other experi-

ments, our models were able to find approximate solutions that rely on unstructured memory, and the stack-augmented LSTMs always favored such solutions over using the stack.

As we saw in Experiments 3 and 4, training examples that require full usage of the stack are rare in practice, making the long-term benefits of stack-based strategies unattractive to greedy optimization. However, the usage of a stack is necessary for a general solution to all of the problems we have explored, with the exception of the XOR Evaluation tasks. While gradual improvements in performance may be obtained by optimizing the usage of unstructured memory, the discrete nature of most stack-based solutions means that finding such solutions often requires a substantial level of serendipity. Our results then raise the question of how to incentivize controllers toward stack-based strategies during training. We leave this question to future work.

References

Kyunghyun Cho, Bart van Merrienboer, Caglar Gulcehre, Dzmitry Bahdanau, Fethi Bougares, Holger Schwenk, and Yoshua Bengio. 2014. Learning Phrase Representations using RNN Encoder–Decoder for Statistical Machine Translation. In *Proceedings of the 2014 Conference on Empirical Methods in Natural Language Processing (EMNLP)*, pages 1724–1734, Doha, Qatar. Association for Computational Linguistics.

N. Chomsky and M. P. Schützenberger. 1959. The Algebraic Theory of Context-Free Languages. In P. Braffort and D. Hirschberg, editors, *Studies in Logic and the Foundations of Mathematics*, volume 26 of *Computer Programming and Formal Systems*, pages 118–161. North-Holland Publishing Company, Amsterdam, Netherlands.

Noam Chomsky. 1962. Context-free grammars and pushdown storage. Technical Report 65, MIT Research Laboratory for Electronics, Cambridge, MA, USA.

Jeffrey L. Elman. 1990. Finding Structure in Time. *Cognitive Science*, 14(2):179–211.

Alex Graves. 2016. Adaptive Computation Time for Recurrent Neural Networks. *Computing Research Repository*, arXiv:1603.08983.

Alex Graves, Greg Wayne, and Ivo Danihelka. 2014. Neural Turing Machines. *Computing Research Repository*, arXiv:1410.5401.

Edward Grefenstette, Karl Moritz Hermann, Mustafa Suleyman, and Phil Blunsom. 2015. Learning to Transduce with Unbounded Memory. *Computing Research Repository*, arXiv:1506.02516v3.

Sepp Hochreiter and Jürgen Schmidhuber. 1997. Long Short-Term Memory. *Neural Computation*, 9(8):1735–1780.

Armand Joulin and Tomas Mikolov. 2015. Inferring Algorithmic Patterns with Stack-Augmented Recurrent Nets. In *Advances in Neural Information Processing Systems 28*, pages 190–198, Montreal, Canada. Curran Associates, Inc.

Christo Kirov and Robert Frank. 2011. Processing of nested and cross-serial dependencies: an automaton perspective on SRN behaviour. *Connection Science*, 24(1):1–24.

Tal Linzen, Emmanuel Dupoux, and Yoav Goldberg. 2016. Assessing the Ability of LSTMs to Learn Syntax-Sensitive Dependencies. *Transactions of the Association for Computational Linguistics*, 4(0):521–535.

Marvin Minsky and Seymour A. Papert. 1969. *Perceptrons: An Introduction to Computational Geometry*. MIT Press, Cambridge, MA, USA.

Adam Paszke, Sam Gross, Soumith Chintala, Gregory Chanan, Edward Yang, Zachary DeVito, Zeming Lin, Alban Desmaison, Luca Antiga, and Adam Lerer. 2017. Automatic differentiation in PyTorch. In *NIPS 2017 Autodiff Workshop*, Long Beach, CA, USA. OpenReview.

H. T. Siegelmann and E. D. Sontag. 1995. On the Computational Power of Neural Nets. *Journal of Computer and System Sciences*, 50(1):132–150.

Ilya Sutskever, Oriol Vinyals, and Quoc V Le. 2014. Sequence to Sequence Learning with Neural Networks. In *Advances in Neural Information Processing Systems 27*, pages 3104–3112, Montreal, Canada. Curran Associates, Inc.

Gail Weiss, Yoav Goldberg, and Eran Yahav. 2018. On the Practical Computational Power of Finite Precision RNNs for Language Recognition. *Computing Research Repository*, arXiv:1805.04908.

Dani Yogatama, Yishu Miao, Gabor Melis, Wang Ling, Adhiguna Kuncoro, Chris Dyer, and Phil Blunsom. 2018. Memory Architectures in Recurrent Neural Network Language Models. In *ICLR 2018 Conference Track*, Vancouver, Canada. OpenReview.

Learning Explanations from Language Data

David Harbecke*   Robert Schwarzenberg*   Christoph Alt
German Research Center for Artificial Intelligence (DFKI)
Alt-Moabit 91c, 10559 Berlin, Germany
{firstname.lastname}@dfki.de

Abstract

PatternAttribution is a recent method, introduced in the vision domain, that explains classifications of deep neural networks. We demonstrate that it also generates meaningful interpretations in the language domain.

1 Introduction

In the last decade, deep neural classifiers achieved state-of-the-art results in many domains, among others in vision and language. Due to the complexity of a deep neural model, however, it is difficult to explain its decisions. Understanding its decision process potentially allows to improve the model and may reveal new knowledge about the input.

Recently, Kindermans et al. (2018) claimed that "popular explanation approaches for neural networks (...) do not provide the correct explanation, even for a simple linear model." They show that in a linear model, the weights serve to cancel noise in the input data and thus the weights show how to extract the signal but not what the signal is. This is why explanation methods need to move beyond the weights, the authors explain, and they propose the methods "PatternNet" and "PatternAttribution" that learn explanations from data. We test their approach in the language domain and point to room for improvement in the new framework.

2 Methods

Kindermans et al. (2018) assume that the data x passed to a linear model $w^T x = y$ is composed of signal (s) and noise (d, from distraction) $x = s + d$. Furthermore, they also assume that there is a linear relation between signal and target $y a_s = s$ where a_s is a so called signal base vector, which is in fact the "pattern" that PatternNet finds for us. As

mentioned in the introduction, the authors show that in the model above, w serves to cancel the noise such that

$$w^T d = 0, \quad w^T s = y. \tag{1}$$

They go on to explain that a good signal estimator $S(x) = \hat{s}$ should comply to the conditions in Eqs. 1 but that these alone form an ill-posed quality criterion since $S(x) = u(w^T u)^{-1} y$ already satisfies them for any u for which $w^T u \neq 0$. To address this issue they introduce another quality criterion over a batch of data $\mathbf{x}$:

$$\rho(S) = 1 - \max_{v} \text{corr}(\overbrace{w^T \mathbf{x}}^{y}, v^T \overbrace{(\mathbf{x} - S(\mathbf{x}))}^{\hat{d}}) \tag{2}$$

and point out that Eq. 2 yields maximum values for signal estimators that remove most of the information about $\mathbf{y}$ in the noise.

We argue that Eq. 2 still is not exhaustive. Consider the artificial estimator

$$S_m(x) = mx + (1 - m)s = s + md$$

which arguably is a a bad signal estimator for large m as its estimation contains scaled noise, md. Nevertheless, it still satisfies Eqs. 1 and yields maximum values for Eq. 2 since

$$x - S_m(x) = (1 - m)(x - s) = (1 - m)d$$

is again just scaled noise and thus does not correlate with the output y. To solve this issue, we propose the following criterion:

$$\rho'(S) := \max_{v_1} \text{corr}(w^T \mathbf{x}, v_1^T S(\mathbf{x}))$$
$$- \max_{v_2} \text{corr}(w^T \mathbf{x}, v_2^T (\mathbf{x} - S(\mathbf{x}))).$$

The minuend measures how much noise is left in the signal, the subtrahend measures how much signal is left in the noise. Good signal estimators split

Proceedings of the 2018 EMNLP Workshop BlackboxNLP: Analyzing and Interpreting Neural Networks for NLP, pages 316–318
Brussels, Belgium, November 1, 2018. ©2018 Association for Computational Linguistics

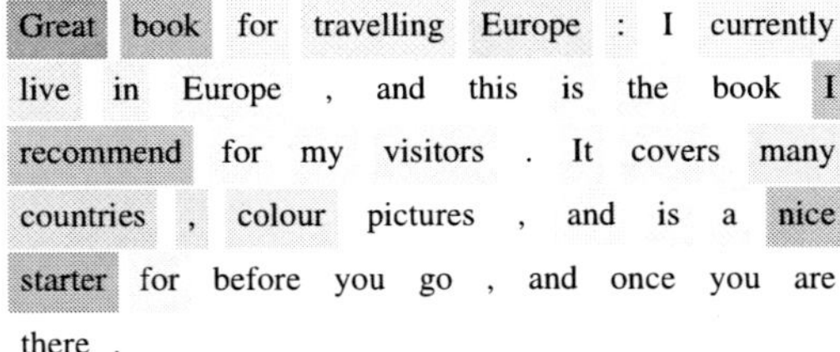

Figure 1: Contributions to positive classification.

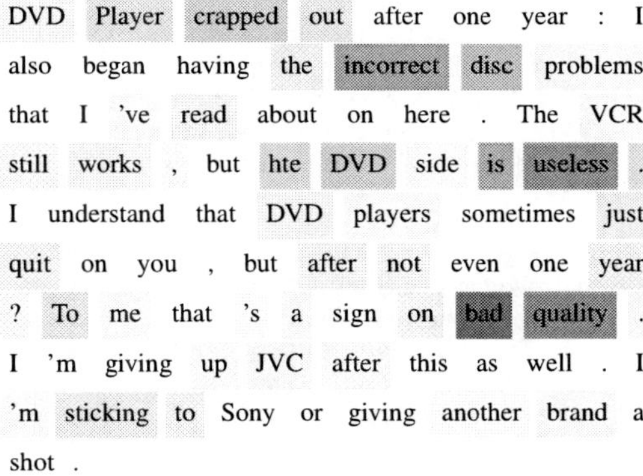

Figure 2: Contributions to negative classification.

signal and noise well and thus yield large $\rho'(S)$. We leave it to future research to evaluate existing signal estimators with our new criterion.

For our experiments, the authors equip us with expressions for the signal base vectors a_s for simple linear layers and ReLU layers. For the simple linear model, for instance, it turns out that $a_s = \text{cov}(\mathbf{x}, \mathbf{y})/\sigma_\mathbf{y}^2$. To retrieve contributions for PatternAttribution, in the backward pass, the authors replace the weights by $w \odot a_s$.

3 Experiments

To test PatternAttribution in the NLP domain, we trained a CNN text classifier (Kim, 2014) on a subset of the Amazon review polarity data set (Zhang et al., 2015). We used 150 bigram filters, dropout regularization and a dense FC projection with 128 neurons. Our classifier achieves an F_1 score of 0.875 on a fixed test split. We then used Kindermans et al. (2018) PatternAttribution to retrieve neuron-wise signal contributions in the input vector space.[1]

To align these contributions with plain text, we summed up the contribution scores over the word vector dimensions for each word and used the accumulated scores to scale RGB values for word highlights in the plain text space. Positive scores are highlighted in red, negative scores in blue. This approach is inspired by Arras et al. (2017a). Example contributions are shown in Figs. 1 and 2.

4 Results

We observe that bigrams are highlighted, in particular no highlighted token stands isolated. Bigrams with clear positive or negative sentiment contribute heavily to the sentiment classification. In contrast, stop words and uninformative bigrams make little to no contribution. We consider these

meaningful explanations of the sentiment classifications.

5 Related Work

Many of the approaches used to explain and interpret models in NLP mirror methods originally developed in the vision domain, such as the recent approaches by Li et al. (2016), Arras et al. (2017a), and Arras et al. (2017b). In this paper we implemented a similar strategy.

Following Kindermans et al. (2018), however, our approach improves upon the latter methods for the reasons outlined above. Furthermore, PatternAttribution is related to Montavon et al. (2017) who make use of Taylor decompositions to explain deep models. PatternAttribution reveals a good root point for the decomposition, the authors explain.

6 Conclusion

We successfully transferred a new explanation method to the NLP domain. We were able to demonstrate that PatternAttribution can be used to identify meaningful signal contributions in text inputs. Our method should be extended to other popular models in NLP. Furthermore, we introduced an improved quality criterion for signal estimators. In the future, estimators can be deduced from and tested against our new criterion.

---

[1]Our experiments are available at `https://github.com/DFKI-NLP/language-attributions`.

* Co-first authorship.

This research was partially supported by the German Federal Ministry of Education and Research through the projects DEEPLEE (01IW17001) and BBDC (01IS14013E).

References

Leila Arras, Franziska Horn, Grégoire Montavon, Klaus-Robert Müller, and Wojciech Samek. 2017a. "What is relevant in a text document?": An interpretable machine learning approach. *PLOS ONE*, 12(8).

Leila Arras, Grégoire Montavon, Klaus-Robert Müller, and Wojciech Samek. 2017b. Explaining recurrent neural network predictions in sentiment analysis. In *Proceedings of the 8th EMNLP Workshop on Computational Approaches to Subjectivity, Sentiment and Social Media Analysis*, pages 159–168.

Yoon Kim. 2014. Convolutional neural networks for sentence classification. In *Proceedings of the 2014 Conference on Empirical Methods in Natural Language Processing (EMNLP)*, pages 1746–1751.

Pieter-Jan Kindermans, Kristof T. Schütt, Maximilian Alber, Klaus-Robert Müller, Dumitru Erhan, Been Kim, and Sven Dähne. 2018. Learning how to explain neural networks: PatternNet and PatternAttribution. In *International Conference on Learning Representations (ICLR)*.

Jiwei Li, Xinlei Chen, Eduard Hovy, and Dan Jurafsky. 2016. Visualizing and understanding neural models in NLP. In *Proceedings of NAACL-HLT*, pages 681–691.

Grégoire Montavon, Sebastian Lapuschkin, Alexander Binder, Wojciech Samek, and Klaus-Robert Müller. 2017. Explaining nonlinear classification decisions with deep taylor decomposition. *Pattern Recognition*, 65:211–222.

Xiang Zhang, Junbo Zhao, and Yann LeCun. 2015. Character-level convolutional networks for text classification. In *Advances in Neural Information Processing Systems (NIPS)*, pages 649–657.

How much should you ask?
On the question structure in QA systems.

Dominika Basaj[*1], Barbara Rychalska[*2], Przemysław Biecek[3], and Anna Wróblewska[4]

d.basaj, b.rychalska, p.biecek, a.wroblewska@mini.pw.edu.pl
[1,2,3,4]Warsaw University of Technology, Warsaw, Poland
[1]Tooploox, Wroclaw, Poland

Abstract

Datasets that boosted state-of-the-art solutions for Question Answering (QA) systems prove that it is possible to ask questions in natural language manner. However, users are still used to query-like systems where they type in keywords to search for answer. In this study we validate which parts of questions are essential for obtaining valid answer. In order to conclude that, we take advantage of LIME - a framework that explains prediction by local approximation. We find that grammar and natural language is disregarded by QA. State-of-the-art model can answer properly even if 'asked' only with a few words with high coefficients calculated with LIME. According to our knowledge, it is the first time that QA model is being explained by LIME.

1 Introduction

Release of SQuAD (Rajpurkar et al., 2016) dataset boosted development of state-of-the-art solutions in Question Answering (QA) systems. Questions asked in natural way give opportunity for human-computer interaction. However, in real life scenario, users are used to 'querying' rather than 'asking'. This assumption inspired us to investigate whether QA systems trained on SQuAD dataset could be used by people who prefer to write faster and more intuitive queries. Our experiments indicate that indeed, QA system returns true answer once we type in just selected keywords without keeping the sentence structure. We conclude that QA systems have a very limited understanding of natural language. They rather learn to distinguish specific words. This indifference to semantics-altering edits is called overstability (Jia and Liang, 2017). Research on this issue was also recently

conducted by Mudrakarta et al. (2018) who compute importance of words by application of Integrated Gradients.

Inspired by LIME (Ribeiro et al., 2016) we perturb questions and score newly created examples with context held constant. We prove that we can remove up to over 90% of words in question and still get the right answer.

The contribution of our study is the following:

1. We use LIME in QA model for determining which parts of question are substantial for obtaining right answer. We obtain valid results although QA systems are not natural candidates for explanation with LIME, since they do not solve a regular classification problem.

2. We show that QA models disregard grammar and syntax and thus can give the right answer once queried with most important keywords, which are the words with high coefficients returned by LIME. Our findings can serve as a starting point for development of QA models that are immune to adversarial examples and as a result - generalize better.

We use QA system developed by Chen et al. (2017). We pick this model for its good performance combined with simplicity and popularity of the algorithm, which in its basic form builds the core of many other QA models.

2 Experiments

In order to query QA system with most important words indicated by coefficients estimated with LIME, we design a two-step algorithm. **First**, we adjust the logic of LIME to our problem, which is perturbing questions while holding the context unchanged. We treat each word in context as a separate class and words in question serve as features. This way, we run LIME in a multiclass setting, with a varied number of ćlasses"for each run.

---

*Both authors contributed equally.

319

Proceedings of the 2018 EMNLP Workshop BlackboxNLP: Analyzing and Interpreting Neural Networks for NLP, pages 319–321
Brussels, Belgium, November 1, 2018. ©2018 Association for Computational Linguistics

Question	Answer
What type of rock is found at the Grand Canyon?	sedimentary
type of rock Grand Canyon	sedimentary
type	sedimentary

Table 1: Questions and answers after removing important words.

Word/PoS/Phrase	% occurences
wh-word + 0 or more words (any)	51 %
1 word (any)	32 %
1 noun	18 %
who	16 %
wh-word + 1 word (any)	13 %
what	12 %
7 and more words	10 %

Table 2: Most common words and phrases found in root questions.

We inspect coefficients estimated for ground truth class (first word in answer). **Second**, once we estimate the influence of each feature, we iteratively remove one word starting with lowest coefficients. After each removal we ask reduced question until we are left with only one word. We call the shortest form of question that still gives the right answer a *root question*. We treat as a right answer a returned span of tokens in which we can locate at least one word from ground truth i.e: *question*: To promote accessibility of the works, what did Luther remove? *ground truth*: impediments and difficulties *QA answer*: impediments and difficulties so that other people may read it without hindrance.

We inspect 800 examples, analyzing questions for which the QA system predicted right answers.

Results. Table 1 presents example of algorithm performance. In this particular case we observe that by leaving only one word *type* we still get the right answer. As shown in figure 1 this word has the highest LIME coefficient. This is quite surprising as one-word question does not convey sufficient information about what we want to ask. Figure 2 shows distribution of percentages of removed words from question that do not disturb the answer. It is left-skewed indicating that a large proportion of question can be removed. We observe that root questions consist mostly of *wh*-words and nouns, as displayed in table 2.

This behavior can be partly traced down to the characteristics of SQuAD dataset. Due to the shortness and focus on just single topic in contexts, the network needs just a single keyword to infer the likely remainder of the question. For example, if we query "type"in a text about rocks in Grand Canyon, it is almost guaranteed that context mentions just single "type"which refers to the rock itself.

Moreover, we observe that there are questions which start off with wrong answer, but when we remove one or more words they start to consistently give valid answers. Based on this, we can hypothesize that although performance of QA systems does not depend on grammar, there are still some underlying dependencies between words.

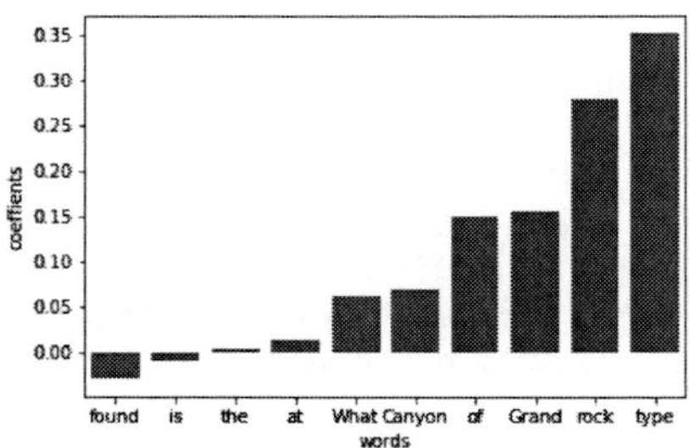

Figure 1: LIME coefficients estimated per word.

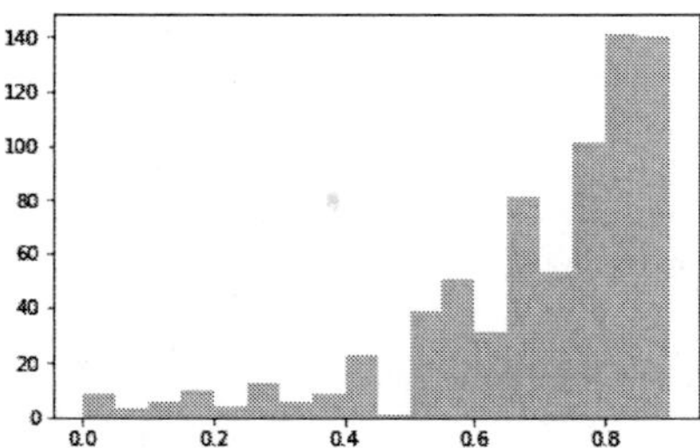

Figure 2: Distribution of percentages of removed question words that still give a valid answer.

3 Summary

In this study we show that QA models do not need grammar to answer questions correctly once they are left with keywords. It indicates that actually model does not really encode what we want to ask, but rather recognizes specific words and associates them with the answer. It means that words that we as humans perceive as important part of questions are disregarded in reality. This might indicate a problem with the underlying dataset, as root questions contain too little information to be considered valid in a real world setting. Our study sets a direction for decreasing their overstability by highlighting drawbacks of QA models.

References

Danqi Chen, Adam Fisch, Jason Weston, and Antoine Bordes. 2017. Reading Wikipedia to answer open-domain questions. In *Association for Computational Linguistics (ACL)*.

Robin Jia and Percy Liang. 2017. Adversarial examples for evaluating reading comprehension systems. In *Proceedings of the 2017 Conference on Empirical Methods in Natural Language Processing*, pages 2021–2031. Association for Computational Linguistics.

Pramod Kaushik Mudrakarta, Ankur Taly, Mukund Sundararajan, and Kedar Dhamdhere. 2018. Did the model understand the question? *CoRR*, abs/1805.05492.

Pranav Rajpurkar, Jian Zhang, Konstantin Lopyrev, and Percy Liang. 2016. Squad: 100, 000+ questions for machine comprehension of text. *CoRR*, abs/1606.05250.

Marco Tulio Ribeiro, Sameer Singh, and Carlos Guestrin. 2016. "why should i trust you?": Explaining the predictions of any classifier. In *Knowledge Discovery and Data Mining (KDD)*.

Does it care what you asked?
Understanding Importance of Verbs in Deep Learning QA System

Barbara Rychalska[*1], Dominika Basaj[*2], Przemysław Biecek[3], and Anna Wróblewska[4]

d.basaj, b.rychalska, p.biecek, a.wroblewska@mini.pw.edu.pl
[1,2,3,4]Warsaw University of Technology, Warsaw, Poland
[2]Tooploox, Wroclaw, Poland

Abstract

In this paper we present the results of an investigation of the importance of verbs in a deep learning QA system trained on SQuAD dataset. We show that main verbs in questions carry little influence on the decisions made by the system - in over 90% of researched cases swapping verbs for their antonyms did not change system decision. We track this phenomenon down to the insides of the net, analyzing the mechanism of self-attention and values contained in hidden layers of RNN. Finally, we recognize the characteristics of the SQuAD dataset as the source of the problem. Our work refers to the recently popular topic of adversarial examples in NLP, combined with investigating deep net structure.

1 Introduction

Recent advances in interpretability for NLP focus on the problem of adversarial examples (Ribeiro et al., 2018) (Jia and Liang, 2017) which lead systems to mistakenly change output. In case of QA systems, either questions or contexts are modified, and it is shown that seemingly small changes in semantics flip system decisions.

In this paper we take a different approach: we create heavy differences in meaning by generating questions with their meaning negated, and observe system outputs. Our initial hypothesis was that verbs together with nouns should be of paramount importance to the system, as they are the main creators of meaning in language. We find that reversing verb meaning disturbs system output in 9.5% of cases, with little influence on decision certainty. We then proceed to explain this phenomenon by observing the behavior of deep net architecture and the characteristics of the SQuAD dataset (Rajpurkar et al., 2016) itself.

As a basis of our research we use the QA system described in Chen et al. (2017). We pick this model for its good performance and state-of-the-art approach.

2 Negating Question Meaning

The first step we take is to measure the impact of verb meaning in question on system output. **First**, we swap verbs in questions for their antonyms using WordNet (Miller, 1995). For auxiliary verbs, we insert their negations (e.g. *is - isn't*). If an antonym is not found in WordNet, we substitute a random verb without assuring that its meaning matches the context. Examples of modified questions are presented in Table 1. **Next**, we test how many system outputs for original questions match the outputs for questions with reversed meaning of verbs. As matching we classify identical answers and also some cases with minimal differences in meaning (where we are sure that the system is attending to the same answer), such as *18th overall* vs. *18th*, or *School of Architecture* vs. *Notre Dame School of Architecture*. The test was conducted on SQuAD development set.

In total, we obtained an accurate match (no system decision change) in 90.5% of all tested cases. Mean decision certainty expressed in softmax stayed similar at 0.60 for modified questions and 0.61 for original questions.

3 Experiments

Attempting to understand the behavior of the system we take inspiration from works focusing on visualizing deep net internals (Li et al., 2015; Karpathy et al., 2015). We apply measures specific to the mechanisms present in our tested system: question self-attention and hidden layers of the RNN. We run experiments on SQuAD development set.

Question self-attention As described in Chen et al. (2017), question self-attention learns to encode importance of each question word. We inspect attention scores b_j for each token during prediction and measure averaged absolute scores for

Proceedings of the 2018 EMNLP Workshop BlackboxNLP: Analyzing and Interpreting Neural Networks for NLP, pages 322–324
Brussels, Belgium, November 1, 2018. ©2018 Association for Computational Linguistics

---

*Both authors contributed equally."

Original question	Question with verb antonym
Q: How many teams **participate** in the Notre Dame Bookstore Basketball tournament?	**Q:** How many teams **drop out** in the Notre Dame Bookstore Basketball tournament?
Q: Which art museum **does** Notre Dame administer?	**Q:** Which art museum **doesn't** Notre Dame administer?

Table 1: Examples of sentences obtained with inserting verb antonyms.

PoS	Attention
Total Verbs	2.32
Total Nouns	5.43
Other PoS	2.39
AUX Verbs	0.63
Non-AUX Verbs	4.16
Non-NE Nouns	5.21
NE Nouns	5.83

Table 2: Average absolute attention scores for parts of speech. We show scores for all verbs, all nouns, all PoS other than nouns and verbs, auxiliary verbs (AUX Verbs), all verbs other than auxiliary (Non-AUX Verbs), all nouns which are not named entities (Non-NE Nouns) and nouns which are named entities (NE Nouns).

words. As shown in Table 2, indeed question attention learned to devalue verbs. Statistical importance of differences between distributions (in particular, of verbs vs. nouns) was confirmed with Kolmogorov-Smirnov test, which showed p-values smaller than 0.001.

Hidden LSTM Layers. Next, we analyze 3-layer LSTM RNN, whose outputs are used to compute question attention. We gather the outputs of all layers and visualize them using heatmaps, as in Figure 1. We observe that variances in numbers appearing in lower layers are distinctively smaller than in the third layer. Furthermore, nouns (in particular named entities) exhibit greater variances than other parts of speech, which aligns with observations for attention scores. Indeed, correlation between entropy scores counted for last hidden layer vectors and attention scores equals -0.91 Pearson's r, and and appropriate variance-attention correlation equals 0.85 Pearson's r and 0.96 Spearman's correlation, as displayed in Figure 2. It suggests that importance of parts of speech is encoded already by the LSTM network.

Diagnosis of Dataset. We observe that in fact the system correctly aligned to the characteristics of the contexts appearing in SQuAD. Most often a specific noun (commonly a named entity, or a combination thereof) appears in a single sentence in single context, so contrasting verbs is not needed to extract the answer. To combat this problem, enhancement of the dataset would be ne-

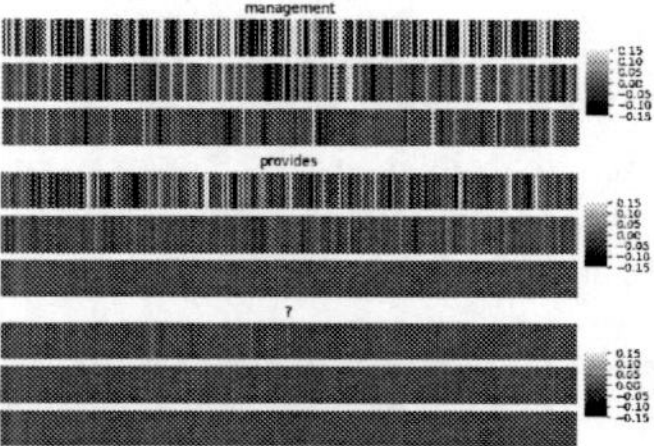

Figure 1: Visualization of values in LSTM hidden layers for a noun (top), verb (middle) and question mark (bottom). Each heatmap shows the 256 values returned by each layer, in 3 layers for each word.

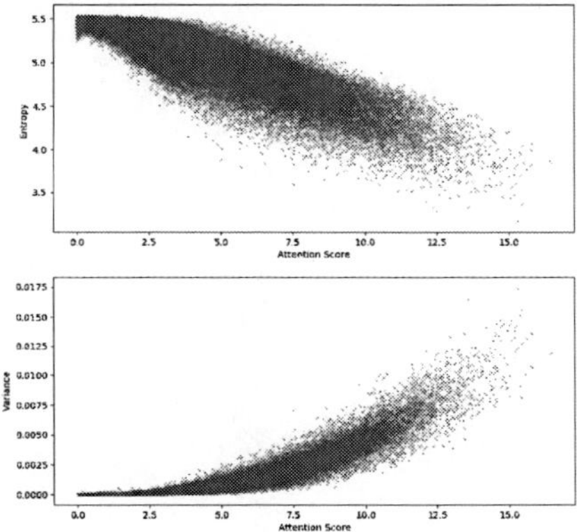

Figure 2: Scatterplot of entropy (top) and variance scores (bottom) in hidden layers (y-axis) and absolute attention scores (x-axis).

eded to include more sentences with repeating nouns (subjects and objects) and varying verbs describing their actions and relations.

Summary. We observe low importance of verbs in QA system training on SQuAD dataset and identify shortcomings in the underlying data. Our findings have confirmation in values yielded by network itself. We show that values in hidden layers and attention scores are correlated with importance of words in the question. This work confirms the usefulness of visualization and explanation of deep learning NLP models.

References

Danqi Chen, Adam Fisch, Jason Weston, and Antoine Bordes. 2017. Reading Wikipedia to answer open-domain questions. In *Association for Computational Linguistics (ACL)*.

Robin Jia and Percy Liang. 2017. Adversarial examples for evaluating reading comprehension systems. *CoRR*, abs/1707.07328.

Andrej Karpathy, Justin Johnson, and Fei-Fei Li. 2015. Visualizing and understanding recurrent networks. *CoRR*, abs/1506.02078.

Jiwei Li, Xinlei Chen, Eduard H. Hovy, and Dan Jurafsky. 2015. Visualizing and understanding neural models in NLP. *CoRR*, abs/1506.01066.

George A Miller. 1995. Wordnet: a lexical database for english. *Communications of the ACM*, 38(11):39–41.

Pranav Rajpurkar, Jian Zhang, Konstantin Lopyrev, and Percy Liang. 2016. Squad: 100, 000+ questions for machine comprehension of text. *CoRR*, abs/1606.05250.

Marco Túlio Ribeiro, Sameer Singh, and Carlos Guestrin. 2018. Semantically equivalent adversarial rules for debugging nlp models.

Interpretable Textual Neuron Representations for NLP

Nina Poerner, Benjamin Roth, Hinrich Schütze
Center for Information and Language Processing
LMU Munich, Germany
poerner@cis.lmu.de

Abstract

Input optimization methods, such as Google Deep Dream, create interpretable representations of neurons for computer vision DNNs. We propose and evaluate ways of transferring this technology to NLP. Our results suggest that gradient ascent with a gumbel softmax layer produces n-gram representations that outperform naive corpus search in terms of target neuron activation. The representations highlight differences in syntax awareness between the language and visual models of the Imaginet architecture.

1 Introduction

Deep Neural Networks (DNNs) have led to advances in Natural Language Processing, but they are hard to interpret. This is partly due to the fact that their smallest components, i.e., neurons, lack interpretable representations.

For computer vision problems, Simonyan et al. (2014) propose to use gradient ascent to find an input image that maximizes the activation of a neuron of interest. Using these image representations, one can for instance show that lower level neurons in vision CNNs specialize in patterns such as stripes (Mordvintsev et al., 2015).

Applying gradient ascent input optimization to NLP is not straightforward, as discrete symbols are not open to continuous manipulation. A common alternative approach is to search existing corpora for optimal documents or n-grams (e.g., Kádár et al. (2017), Aubakirova and Bansal (2016)). As this strategy only covers the space of existing inputs, we assume that it may lead to incorrect assumptions. For instance, the representation of a given neuron may suggest that syntax was learned, when in reality this is due to a lack of ungrammatical inputs in the corpus.

In the following, we propose and test methods for gradient ascent input optimization in NLP. Our

quantitative assessment suggests that one method, which is based on the gumbel softmax trick, produces inputs that are more highly activating than corpus search. By applying this method to the Imaginet architecture, we confirm that a language model pays attention to syntax to some degree, while a visual model looks for key content words and ignores function words.

2 Input optimization for NLP

In the following, we denote as $f(\mathbf{E})$ the activation of some neuron of interest when forward-feeding a sequence of embedding vectors $\mathbf{E} = [\mathbf{e}_1 \dots \mathbf{e}_T]$.

2.1 Embedding optimization

One straightforward approach to NLP input optimization is to treat $\mathbf{E}$ like Simonyan et al. (2014) treat images, i.e., to apply gradient ascent directly to the embedding vectors, while keeping other model parameters constant: $\text{argmax}_{\mathbf{E}}\big[f(\mathbf{E})\big]$. However, there is no guarantee that the optimal vectors will correspond to the embedding vectors of real words, or even be close to them. In our experiments, the average cosine proximity to the closest real-word embedding is 0.24, suggesting that there is a divergence between the training goal (finding embedding vectors) and the real goal (finding a representation made up of real words).

2.2 Word optimization

Note that the embedding operation can be written as $\mathbf{E} = \mathbf{XM}$, where $\mathbf{X} \in \{0,1\}^{T \times V}$ is a matrix of one-hot vectors and $\mathbf{M}$ is the embedding matrix for all V known words. If we relax the requirement that $\mathbf{X}$ be one-hot, we can perform gradient ascent directly on $\mathbf{X}$, while keeping $\mathbf{M}$ constant: $\text{argmax}_{\mathbf{X}}\big[f(\mathbf{XM})\big]$. This approach has the undesirable effect that entries in $\mathbf{X}$ can become very large or negative, and therefore unlike the one-hot vectors seen in training.

325

Proceedings of the 2018 EMNLP Workshop BlackboxNLP: Analyzing and Interpreting Neural Networks for NLP, pages 325–327
Brussels, Belgium, November 1, 2018. ©2018 Association for Computational Linguistics

To enforce positive vectors that sum to one, we can use the softmax function across the vocabulary axis: $\mathrm{argmax}_{\mathbf{X}}\left[f(\mathbf{P}^{\mathrm{smx}}\mathbf{M})\right]$, where $\mathbf{p}_t^{\mathrm{smx}} = \mathrm{softmax}(\mathbf{x}_t)$. However, this input can still be unlike the inputs seen during training, as the optimal distribution may be smooth.

To remedy this situation, we use the gumbel softmax trick (Jang et al. (2017), Maddison et al. (2017)): $\mathrm{argmax}_{\mathbf{X}}\left[f(\mathbf{P}^{\mathrm{gbl}}\mathbf{M})\right]$, where

$$\mathbf{p}_t^{\mathrm{gbl}} = \mathrm{softmax}\left[\tau^{-1}\left(\log(\mathbf{p}_t^{\mathrm{smx}}) + \mathbf{g}_t\right)\right]$$

and $g_{t,v} \sim -\log(-\log(\mathcal{U}(0,1)))$. By slowly annealing τ, we are able to transition from a uniform probability distribution to a "spiky" one where probability mass is concentrated on few words.

3 Experiment

3.1 Model

We re-implement the Imaginet architecture from Kádár et al. (2017). It consists of a joint word embedding layer (embedding size 1024) and two separate unidirectional GRUs (hidden size 1024 each). One GRU serves as a language model, while the other predicts visual features of a scene described in the input sentence. The model is trained on 566435 MSCOCO captions with visual features taken from Chrupała et al. (2017)[1].

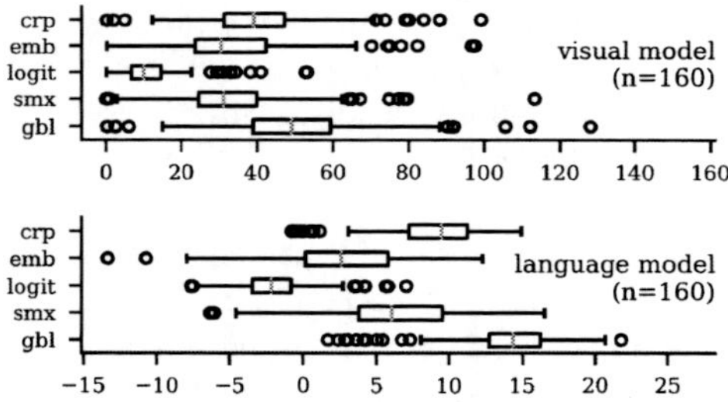

Figure 1: Activation after input optimization for randomly selected projection layer neurons. crp: corpus search; emb: embedding opt.; logit: word opt. w/o softmax; smx: word opt. w/ softmax; gbl: word opt. w/ gumbel softmax.

3.2 Quantitative evaluation

We evaluate the input optimization methods by the activation that they achieve in 160 randomly chosen neurons of the language and visual model projection layers. For embedding optimization, representations are derived by finding the nearest real-word neighbor of the optimized embeddings in the

embedding space. For word optimization, we take the argmax over the vocabulary dimension of $\mathbf{X}$.

We find that while representations from embedding, logit and softmax optimization are not competitive, the gumbel softmax trick outperforms the corpus search strategy in terms of target neuron activation.

3.3 Qualitative observations

Table 1 shows optimal 5-grams for some neurons.

We observe that, contrary to what corpus search suggests, optimal inputs for the visual model rarely contain function words, i.e., the model seems to ignore them. Optimal inputs for the language model sometimes display grammatically correct structures with function words directly before the predicted word (e.g., "stare to their [left]", "under an [umbrella]", see Table 1). This suggests that the language model pays attention to function words and has indeed learned some syntax, as suggested by Kádár et al. (2017).

method	optimal 5-gram	target neuron activation
crp	pizza a sandwich and appetizers	48.44
gbl	fangs calzone raspberries sandwhich pizzas	64.46
	315th neuron in visual projection layer	
crp	fighter jet flying in formation	31.25
gbl	propelleor phrases jetliners treetops flight	37.82
	657th neuron in visual projection layer	
crp	a woman sitting under an	13.28
gbl	campbell lawn raincoat under an	17.54
	314th neuron ("umbrella") in language model projection layer	
crp	the view through a car	10.42
gbl	logging jeep watch through cracked	14.87
	957th neuron ("windshield") in language model projection layer	
crp	a giraffe looks to its	10.64
gbl	fest stares stares to their	13.22
	973th neuron ("left") in language model projection layer	

Table 1: Examples of optimal 5-grams via corpus search and via gradient ascent with gumbel softmax. Spelling errors stem from the Imaginet dictionary.

4 Conclusion

The gumbel softmax trick makes it possible to extend the input optimization method to NLP, and to find interpretable textual neuron representations via gradient ascent. Our experimental results suggest that this technique exceeds naive search on a large in-domain corpus in terms of target neuron activation. The representations also show interesting differences in syntax awareness based on target modality in Imaginet.

---

[1] https://zenodo.org/record/804392/files/data.tgz

References

Malika Aubakirova and Mohit Bansal. 2016. Interpreting neural networks to improve politeness comprehension. In *Empirical Methods in Natural Language Processing*, pages 2035–2041, Austin, USA.

Grzegorz Chrupała, Lieke Gelderloos, and Afra Alishahi. 2017. Representations of language in a model of visually grounded speech signal. In *Annual Meeting of the Association for Computational Linguistics*, pages 613–622, Vancouver, Canada.

Eric Jang, Shixiang Gu, and Ben Poole. 2017. Categorical reparameterization with gumbel-softmax. In *International Conference on Learning Representations*, Toulon, France.

Akos Kádár, Grzegorz Chrupała, and Afra Alishahi. 2017. Representation of linguistic form and function in recurrent neural networks. *Computational Linguistics*, 43(4):761–780.

Chris J Maddison, Andriy Mnih, and Yee Whye Teh. 2017. The concrete distribution: A continuous relaxation of discrete random variables. In *International Conference on Learning Representations*, Toulon, France.

Alexander Mordvintsev, Christopher Olah, and Mike Tyka. 2015. DeepDream – a code example for visualizing neural networks. *Google Research*.

Karen Simonyan, Andrea Vedaldi, and Andrew Zisserman. 2014. Deep inside convolutional networks: Visualising image classification models and saliency maps. In *International Conference on Learning Representations*, Banff, Canada.

Language Models Learn POS First

Naomi Saphra and **Adam Lopez**
`n.saphra@ed.ac.uk`   `alopez@ed.ac.uk`
Institute for Language, Cognition, and Computation
University of Edinburgh

1   Introduction

A glut of recent research shows that language models capture linguistic structure. Linzen et al. (2016) found that LSTM-based language models may encode syntactic information sufficient to favor verbs which match the number of their subject nouns. Liu et al. (2018) suggested that the high performance of LSTMs may depend on the linguistic structure of the input data, as performance on several artificial tasks was higher with natural language data than with artificial sequential data.

Such work answers the question of *whether* a model represents linguistic structure. But how and when are these structures acquired? Rather than treating the training process itself as a black box, we investigate how representations of linguistic structure are learned over time. In particular, we demonstrate that different aspects of linguistic structure are learned at different rates, with part of speech tagging acquired early and global topic information learned continuously.

2   Methods

2.1   Concentration

We measure the degree to which a neural network has "structured" its representation x of a particular word in a sequence through *concentration*.

$$c(x) = \frac{\|x\|_2}{\|x\|_1} \qquad (1)$$

The more similar in value the cells of x are, the smaller its l2/l1 ratio is. Thus if a neural network relies heavily on a small number of cells in an activation pattern, the activation is very concentrated. Likewise, a concentrated gradient is mainly modifying a few specific pathways. For example, it might modify a neuron associated with particular inputs like parentheses (Karpathy et al., 2015), or properties like sentiment (Radford et al., 2017).

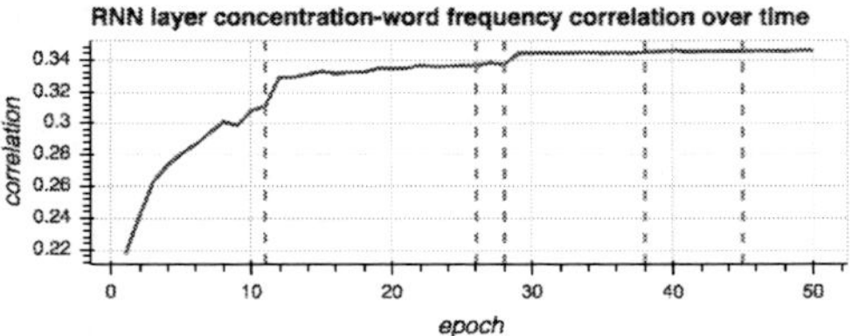

Figure 1: Correlation between mean concentration of a word gradient and word frequency. Vertical dashes mark when the optimizer rescales step size.

2.2   SVCCA

Existing work investigates how language model layers encode tags by training taggers on the activations produced by each layer (Belinkov et al., 2018). We use an alternative technique, SVCCA (Raghu et al., 2017), which interprets an arbitrary selection of neurons in terms of how they relate to another selection of neurons from any network run on the same input data. This method treats a selection of neurons as a subspace, spanned by their activations. Given any 2 sets of neurons, SVCCA projects the 2 distinct views of the same data onto a shared subspace which maximizes correlation between the 2 views.

Intuitively, if both views encode the same semantic information, the correlation in the shared subspace will be high. If the 2 views are encoding disjoint properties, the correlation will be low.

3   Experiments

All experiments are conducted on 1.6GB of English Wikipedia (70/10/20 train/dev/test split) with a 2-layer LSTM language model featuring tied weights in the softmax and embedding layers.

3.1   Gradient Concentration During Training

Over time, the model learns to shape weight structure around familiar words, with more frequent

Proceedings of the 2018 EMNLP Workshop BlackboxNLP: Analyzing and Interpreting Neural Networks for NLP, pages 328–330
Brussels, Belgium, November 1, 2018. ©2018 Association for Computational Linguistics

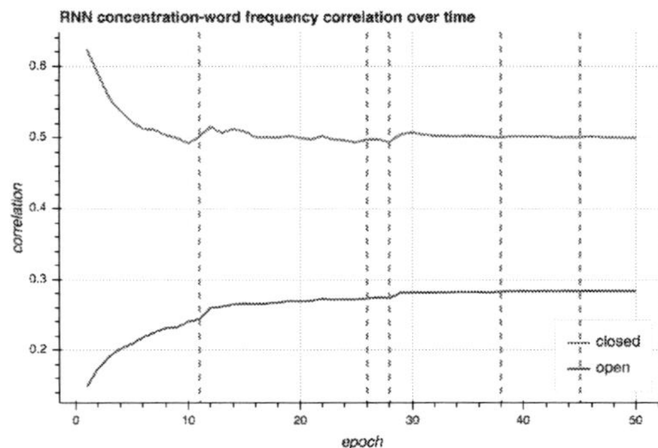

Figure 2: Correlation between mean concentration of a word gradient and word frequency.

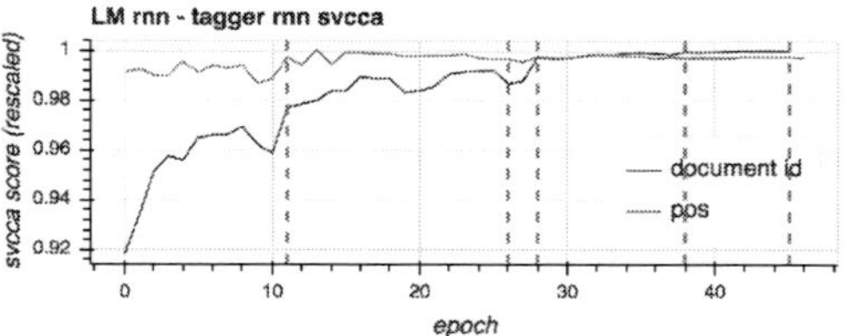

Figure 3: SVCCA correlation scores between LM and taggers. Values are rescaled so maximum score is 1.

words being more concentrated in their gradient. We can inspect this correlation between word frequency and concentration over time in the gradients passed backwards from the decoder layer to the RNN layer in Figure 1. It is clear that frequent words are more concentrated in their representation, and further that generally words become more concentrated in their representation over time. These observations support the idea that gradient concentration can measure the degree to which a word is relied on in shaping specialized structures within the representation.

However, Figure 2 shows that this correlation follows dramatically different trends for open POS classes (e.g., nouns and verbs) and closed classes (e.g., pronouns and prepositions). Initially, frequent words from closed classes are highly concentrated, but soon stabilize, while frequent words from open classes continue to become more concentrated. Why might this pattern emerge?

Closed classes offer clear signals about the current part of speech in a sequence. Open classes, however, contain words which are often ambiguous, such as "report", which may be a noun or verb. Open classes may also offer murkier syntactic signals because there are far more words that may occur in a particular open class POS role. We posit that early in training, closed classes are therefore essential for learning how to prototype syntactic structure, and are essential for shaping network structure. However, open classes are essential for modeling global sentence topic, so their importance in training continues to increase after part of speech tags are effectively modeled.

3.2 Structure Encoding Over Time

Concentration experiments imply that a network first learns syntax, but topic significance continues to rise later. We test this claim directly.

As a proxy for syntactic representation, we use the task of POS tagging, as in (Belinkov et al., 2017). For document-global topic information, we classify the sequence by which Wikipedia article it came from. Both taggers are single layer LSTMs.

We applied SVCCA to the RNN layers of our language model and each tagger in order to find the correlation between the language model representation and the tagger representation. Indeed, Figure 3 illustrates that the POS structure is effectively represented immediately, and continues to be learned in the early stages of training before the first optimizer step size rescale. After that point, POS structure actually slightly declines and stabilizes below its peak value. Meanwhile, topic structure continues to increase over the course of training.

4 Conclusions

The SVCCA results imply that early in training, representing syntax and POS is the natural way to get initial high performance. However, as training progresses, these low-level aspects of linguistic structure sees diminishing returns from committing more parameters to their representation. Instead, later training realizes more gains from refining representations of global topic.

The concentration experiments tell the same story through a different lens. Early in training, structure is dictated by the closed POS classes, which give clear signals about syntax. However, small collections of directions within the network are increasingly responsive to words from open classes, which are more useful for modeling topic.

Our next step in this work is to develop ways of interpreting syntactic structures during training.

References

Yonatan Belinkov, Nadir Durrani, Fahim Dalvi, Hassan Sajjad, and James Glass. 2017. What do Neural Machine Translation Models Learn about Morphology? In *Proceedings of the 55th Annual Meeting of the Association for Computational Linguistics (Volume 1: Long Papers)*, pages 861–872, Vancouver, Canada. Association for Computational Linguistics.

Yonatan Belinkov, Llus Mrquez, Hassan Sajjad, Nadir Durrani, Fahim Dalvi, and James R. Glass. 2018. Evaluating Layers of Representation in Neural Machine Translation on Part-of-Speech and Semantic Tagging Tasks. *CoRR*, abs/1801.07772.

Andrej Karpathy, Justin Johnson, and Li Fei-Fei. 2015. Visualizing and Understanding Recurrent Networks. *arXiv:1506.02078 [cs]*. ArXiv: 1506.02078.

Tal Linzen, Emmanuel Dupoux, and Yoav Goldberg. 2016. Assessing the Ability of LSTMs to Learn Syntax-Sensitive Dependencies. *arXiv:1611.01368 [cs]*. ArXiv: 1611.01368.

Nelson F. Liu, Omer Levy, Roy Schwartz, Chenhao Tan, and Noah A. Smith. 2018. LSTMs Exploit Linguistic Attributes of Data. *arXiv:1805.11653 [cs]*. ArXiv: 1805.11653.

Alec Radford, Rafal Jozefowicz, and Ilya Sutskever. 2017. Learning to Generate Reviews and Discovering Sentiment. *arXiv:1704.01444 [cs]*. ArXiv: 1704.01444.

Maithra Raghu, Justin Gilmer, Jason Yosinski, and Jascha Sohl-Dickstein. 2017. SVCCA: Singular Vector Canonical Correlation Analysis for Deep Learning Dynamics and Interpretability. *arXiv:1706.05806 [cs, stat]*. ArXiv: 1706.05806.

Predicting and interpreting embeddings for out of vocabulary words in downstream tasks

Nicolas Garneau,* Jean-Samuel Leboeuf,* Luc Lamontagne
Département d'informatique et de génie logiciel
Université Laval, Québec, Canada
{nicolas.garneau, jean-samuel.leboeuf}.1@ulaval.ca,
luc.lamongtagne@ift.ulaval.ca

Abstract

We propose a novel way to handle out of vocabulary (OOV) words in downstream natural language processing (NLP) tasks. We implement a network that predicts useful embeddings for OOV words based on their morphology and on the context in which they appear. Our model also incorporates an attention mechanism indicating the focus allocated to the left context words, the right context words or the word's characters, hence making the prediction more interpretable. The model is a "drop-in" module that is jointly trained with the downstream task's neural network, thus producing embeddings specialized for the task at hand. When the task is mostly syntactical, we observe that our model aims most of its attention on surface form characters. On the other hand, for tasks more semantical, the network allocates more attention to the surrounding words. In all our tests, the module helps the network to achieve better performances in comparison to the use of simple random embeddings.

1 Introduction and motivation

Goldberg (2017) emphasizes the fact that out of vocabulary (OOV) words represent a problem often underestimated for NLP tasks such as part of speech tagging (POS) or named entity recognition (NER) (Collobert et al., 2011; Turian et al., 2010). Due to the lack of proper ways to handle OOV words, researchers often resort to simply assign random embeddings to unknown words or to map them to a unique "unknown" embedding, hoping their model will generalize well nonetheless.

An interesting way to handle OOV words is the Mimick model (Pinter et al., 2017). This model aims to predict embeddings such as GloVe (Pennington et al., 2014) for OOV words by training a recurrent network on the characters of the words.

While being simple, this model improves the accuracy of POS tagging as well as morphosyntactic attribute tagging on the Universal Dependencies corpus (De Marneffe et al., 2014).

We propose an extension to this model by taking into account not only the surface form of a word (i.e. its characters) but also the embeddings of its surrounding words. We hypothesize that context words provide useful semantic and syntactic information to model unknown word embeddings, hence complementing cues given by its characters. For this purpose, we introduce a module that can make, for the same word in different contexts, different predictions. It can also learn "specialized" embeddings for a specific downstream task which we evaluate for two sequence labeling tasks. Furthermore, we add to our model an attention/interpretation mechanism to determine which of the left context, right context or the surface form of a word receives more attention during prediction. Our experimental results are depicted in a quantitative and qualitative analysis.

2 Architecture

To test our ideas, we developed an OOV prediction module comprising the following components. First, the left context, right context and word characters are fed to three bi-LSTMs to produce separate encodings. These three hidden states are then passed to a linear layer on which a softmax is applied to determine their relative importance (i.e. their degree of attention). The output of this layer is then used to produce a weighted sum of the hidden states. Finally, a simple layer computes an embedding from this sum.

To evaluate the contribution of this OOV prediction scheme to sequence labeling tasks, we use a bi-LSTM architecture on the resulting word embeddings and apply a softmax on the hidden state of each word to predict tags.

---

*Authors contributed equally to this work.

331

Proceedings of the 2018 EMNLP Workshop BlackboxNLP: Analyzing and Interpreting Neural Networks for NLP, pages 331–333
Brussels, Belgium, November 1, 2018. ©2018 Association for Computational Linguistics

Task	Metric	Random Emb.	Our module
NER	F1	77.56	**80.62**
POS	acc.	91.41	**92.58**

Table 1: Comparison of our OOV embeddings prediction scheme against random embeddings.

Task	Tag	Ex	Word	Left	Right
	O	1039	**0.81**	0.08	0.11
	B-PERS	63	0.21	0.31	**0.49**
	I-PER	119	0.16	**0.52**	0.32
	B-ORG	40	0.26	0.30	**0.44**
NER	I-ORG	3	0.27	0.31	**0.42**
	B-LOC	13	0.23	0.30	**0.47**
	I-LOC	2	0.16	**0.48**	0.36
	B-MISC	47	**0.40**	0.21	0.39
	I-MISC	5	**0.41**	0.26	0.33
	NNP	308	0.29	0.31	**0.40**
	NN	46	**0.45**	0.20	0.35
POS	CD	827	**0.86**	0.05	0.09
	NNS	23	**0.37**	0.24	**0.39**
	JJ	100	**0.49**	0.15	0.36

Table 2: Average weights assigned to word characters, left context and right context by the attention mechanism for NER and for POS tagging.

3   Experimental results and discussion

We evaluate the performance gain that our module can offer by solving two sequence labeling tasks, NER and POS tagging, using the *CoNLL 2003 shared task* dataset. We compare our module to a baseline where OOV words are assigned random embeddings. Table 1 shows the results we obtain. We can observe the clear advantage of proper handling of OOV words can provide. For both tasks, we gain a significant margin on the baseline, with

more than 3% of the F1 score for NER.

We can see from Table 2 that the network focuses more on the context for a semantic task such as NER. An interesting phenomenon is a focus on the right context when the entity is of type *B* and on the left context when the entity is of type *I*. We can also note that for the syntactic task (POS), the network tends to focus on the context for proper nouns (NNP), which corroborates our observations for the NER task. However, morphology plays a more important role to predict embeddings for other lexical categories. Embeddings for quantities (CD) are mostly predicted from their numerical characters.

We further qualitatively analyze the behavior of the network for a given OOV word appearing in different contexts in Table 3. When the target OOV word *langmore* is preceded by *john* or *australian*, the network gives high importance to these context words. However, an interesting phenomenon happens when a sentence begins with this word: the network shifts its attention from the left context to the right one and also assigns more importance to the morphology of the word, thus showing the network has truly learned where it can extract useful information.

4   Future works

In our future works, we plan to apply the attention mechanism specifically on the characters of the OOV word and the words that compose the context instead of using the hidden state of the respective elements only. We are also looking forward to testing our attention model in different languages and on other NLP tasks such as machine translation. We hope to present the full results and the architecture of our model in more details in a paper to be published relatively soon.

Word	Left	Right	Examples
0.24	**0.38**	**0.38**	<BOS> *langmore* **, a persistent campaigner for interventionist economic**
0.15	**0.59**	0.26	<BOS> **australian parliamentarian john** *langmore* has formally resigned from his lower house
0.15	**0.61**	0.24	**had received today from mr john vance** *langmore* , a letter resigning his place as
0.15	**0.69**	0.16	<BOS> **rtrs - australian mp john** *langmore* formally resigns . <EOS>
0.17	**0.40**	**0.43**	<BOS> *langmore* **, 57 , announced in november that**

Table 3: Qualitative example on the OOV word *langmore* which is an entity of type PER. We can cleary see that depending on the context, the weights may shift drastically.

References

Ronan Collobert, Jason Weston, Léon Bottou, Michael Karlen, Koray Kavukcuoglu, and Pavel Kuksa. 2011. Natural language processing (almost) from scratch. *Journal of Machine Learning Research*, 12(Aug):2493–2537.

Marie-Catherine De Marneffe, Timothy Dozat, Natalia Silveira, Katri Haverinen, Filip Ginter, Joakim Nivre, and Christopher D Manning. 2014. Universal stanford dependencies: A cross-linguistic typology. In *LREC*, volume 14, pages 4585–4592.

Yoav Goldberg. 2017. Neural network methods for natural language processing. volume 10, chapter 8, pages 83–97.

Jeffrey Pennington, Richard Socher, and Christopher Manning. 2014. Glove: Global vectors for word representation. In *Proceedings of the 2014 conference on empirical methods in natural language processing (EMNLP)*, pages 1532–1543.

Yuval Pinter, Robert Guthrie, and Jacob Eisenstein. 2017. Mimicking word embeddings using subword rnns. *arXiv preprint arXiv:1707.06961*.

Joseph Turian, Lev Ratinov, and Yoshua Bengio. 2010. Word representations: a simple and general method for semi-supervised learning. In *Proceedings of the 48th annual meeting of the association for computational linguistics*, pages 384–394. Association for Computational Linguistics.

Probing sentence embeddings for structure-dependent tense

Geoff Bacon
Department of Linguistics
UC Berkeley
bacon@berkeley.edu

Terry Regier
Department of Linguistics and
Cognitive Science Program
UC Berkeley
terry.regier@berkeley.edu

1   Introduction

Learning universal sentence representations which accurately model sentential semantic content is a current goal of natural language processing research (Subramanian et al., 2018; Conneau et al., 2017; Wieting et al., 2016; Kiros et al., 2015). A prominent and successful approach is to train recurrent neural networks (RNNs) to encode sentences into fixed length vectors (Conneau et al., 2018; Nie et al., 2017). Many core linguistic phenomena that one would like to model in universal sentence representations depend on syntactic structure (Chomsky, 1965; Everaert et al., 2015). Despite the fact that RNNs do not have explicit syntactic structural representations, there is some evidence that RNNs can approximate such structure-dependent phenomena under certain conditions (Gulordava et al., 2018; McCoy et al., 2018; Linzen et al., 2016; Bowman et al., 2015), in addition to their widespread success in practical tasks.

In this work, we assess RNNs' ability to learn the structure-dependent phenomenon of main clause tense. To test whether sentence representations derived from RNNs capture main clause tense, we attempt to predict the tense from the representation. This approach is called *probing*, and was introduced by Ettinger et al. (2016) and subsequently used by Adi et al. (2017) and others.

Conneau et al. (2018) probed English sentence representations from various RNN architectures for main clause tense and concluded that these architectures, along with a bag-of-vectors (BoV) baseline, capture tense very well (84-91% accuracy). However, this result was based on a test set in which the tense category (i.e. past or present) to be predicted was the most common tense category in the sentence for 95.2% of sentences. The high performance of the BoV model on this test set

is not entirely surprising, given that Köhn (2015, 2016) showed a wide variety of word embedding models capture tense at the word level very well. The high performance of the RNN models is not strong evidence that they are sensitive to the structure-dependence of main clause tense. As suggested by Linzen et al. (2016), these models may be learning a flawed heuristic that only works in grammatically simple examples.

Our goal is to determine whether RNNs learn to perform structure-dependent computation or whether they merely learn practical heuristics. To do this, we extend the experimental setup of Adi et al. (2017), which has a two step nature. First, we train autoencoders for English, Spanish, French and Italian where both the encoder and decoder are either Simple Recurrent Networks (SRNs, Elman, 1990) or Long Short-Term Memory networks (LSTMs, Hochreiter and Schmidhuber, 1997). Second, we use the trained encoder to obtain sentence representations and probe those representations for main clause tense. We investigate whether probing performance is affected by eight potential distractors, one of which is other words in the sentence with tense categories that differ from the tense of the main clause (e.g. *we know who <u>won</u>*). To the extent that the representations are *in*sensitive to structure-dependence, we expect to see probing performance negatively affected by distractors. We compare the RNNs to three BoV baseline models.

In this extended abstract, we report on our work in progress. We have completed data collection and preprocessing, designed our experiments and obtained complete results from our BoV baselines.

2   Data

A guiding principle in our choice of data sources was availability across multiple languages, be-

Proceedings of the 2018 EMNLP Workshop BlackboxNLP: Analyzing and Interpreting Neural Networks for NLP, pages 334–336
Brussels, Belgium, November 1, 2018. ©2018 Association for Computational Linguistics

cause we are interested in cross-linguistic generality. To train sentence embedding models (i.e. RNNs and BoV), we extracted one million sentences between 5 and 70 tokens in length from each language's Wikipedia, in line with Adi et al. (2017). This yields between 25 and 29 million tokens per language.

Our labelled probing data are sentences from Universal Dependencies treebanks (UD, Nivre et al., 2016). Because of the way the UD schema annotates tense in multiword verb phrases, extracting main clause tense is not straightforward. Therefore, for each language we developed between five and seven heuristic rules in terms of UD annotations to extract tense. A random sample of 100 sentences for each language shows that our heuristics produce the correct tense in at least 98% of sentences.

To ensure the sentence embedding models see all word types needed for the probing task during training, the embedding vocabulary is set to the union of the 50k most frequent word types in the Wikipedia data and all word types in the probing data. Resulting vocabulary sizes range from 53k to 68k, with OOV rates in the Wikipedia data between 2 and 4% per language. We remove sentences from the probing task that require word types not seen in the Wikipedia data. This results in between 12k and 31k sentences per language in the probing task. We split these into 70% train and 30% test sets, with the constraint that no word form that is responsible for main clause tense in the training set also appears in the test set, following Conneau et al. (2018).

3   Experimental setup

In line with Adi et al. (2017), we trained word embeddings on the Wikipedia data using skipgram (Mikolov et al., 2013), with hierarchical softmax and a window size of five, for five epochs. We trained 50 sets of embeddings per language, with dimension sizes from 20 to 1000 in steps of 20. Our three BoV baselines consist of combining these word embeddings by summing, averaging and using Smooth Inverse Frequency (Arora et al., 2017). Here, we report results from summing, which in contrast to related experiments (Conneau et al., 2018; Arora et al., 2017), consistently and significantly outperforms the other two baselines. For the probing task, we use L1-regularized logistic regression with ten-fold cross validation.

4   Baseline results

Here, we present results for one of our eight distractors. Figure 1 shows the effect on probing performance of the number of words in the sentence with tense categories that differ from the main clause tense. In all four languages, as the number of such conflicting tensed forms in the sentence increases, error rates on the probing task also tend to increase. This is expected given that BoV is not sensitive to syntactic structure, and serves as a baseline for our upcoming work using RNNs.

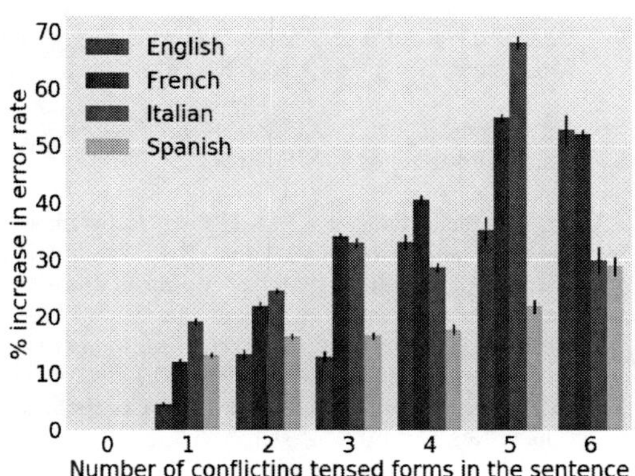

Figure 1: The effect of conflicting tensed words on probing performance for our summed BoV baseline. We measure the absolute percentage increase in error rate over the error rate when no conflicting tensed words are in the sentence. Each bar represents this quantity averaged across all 50 sets of embeddings per language. Error bars are 95% confidence intervals.

Adi et al. (2017) found a negative correlation between performance on one of their probing tasks (content prediction) and sentence length. Surprisingly, we find no correlation between performance of any of our baseline models and sentence length.

5   Remaining work

Our goal is to understand to what extent RNNs show a similar insensitivity to structure-dependence. Our next step is to train SRN- and LSTM-based autoencoders on the Wikipedia data and assess their representations in our probing task. Due to our careful choice of data sources, future work can extend our analysis to any language with i) a sizable Wikipedia, ii) a UD corpus, and iii) tense.

References

Yossi Adi, Einat Kermany, Yonatan Belinkov, Ofer Lavi, and Yoav Goldberg. 2017. Fine-grained analysis of sentence embeddings using auxiliary prediction tasks. *arXiv preprint arXiv:1608.04207*.

Sanjeev Arora, Yingyu Liang, and Tengyu Ma. 2017. A simple but tough-to-beat baseline for sentence embeddings. In *International Conference on Learning Representations*.

Samuel R Bowman, Christopher D Manning, and Christopher Potts. 2015. Tree-structured composition in neural networks without tree-structured architectures. In *Proceedings of the 2015 International Conference on Cognitive Computation: Integrating Neural and Symbolic Approaches-Volume 1583*, pages 37–42. CEUR-WS. org.

Noam Chomsky. 1965. *Aspects of the Theory of Syntax*. Cambridge, MA. MIT Press.

Alexis Conneau, Douwe Kiela, Holger Schwenk, Loïc Barrault, and Antoine Bordes. 2017. Supervised learning of universal sentence representations from natural language inference data. In *Proceedings of the 2017 Conference on Empirical Methods in Natural Language Processing*, pages 670–680, Copenhagen, Denmark. Association for Computational Linguistics.

Alexis Conneau, Germán Kruszewski, Guillaume Lample, Loïc Barrault, and Marco Baroni. 2018. What you can cram into a single vector: Probing sentence embeddings for linguistic properties. In *Proceedings of the 56th Annual Meeting of the Association for Computational Linguistics (Volume 1: Long Papers)*, pages 2126–2136. Association for Computational Linguistics.

Jeffrey L Elman. 1990. Finding structure in time. *Cognitive science*, 14(2):179–211.

Allyson Ettinger, Ahmed Elgohary, and Philip Resnik. 2016. Probing for semantic evidence of composition by means of simple classification tasks. In *Proceedings of the 1st Workshop on Evaluating Vector-Space Representations for NLP*, pages 134–139.

Martin BH Everaert, Marinus AC Huybregts, Noam Chomsky, Robert C Berwick, and Johan J Bolhuis. 2015. Structures, not strings: linguistics as part of the cognitive sciences. *Trends in cognitive sciences*, 19(12):729–743.

Kristina Gulordava, Piotr Bojanowski, Edouard Grave, Tal Linzen, and Marco Baroni. 2018. Colorless green recurrent networks dream hierarchically. In *Proceedings of the 2018 Conference of the North American Chapter of the Association for Computational Linguistics: Human Language Technologies, Volume 1 (Long Papers)*, pages 1195–1205. Association for Computational Linguistics.

Sepp Hochreiter and Jürgen Schmidhuber. 1997. Long short-term memory. *Neural computation*, 9(8):1735–1780.

Ryan Kiros, Yukun Zhu, Ruslan R Salakhutdinov, Richard Zemel, Raquel Urtasun, Antonio Torralba, and Sanja Fidler. 2015. Skip-thought vectors. In *Advances in neural information processing systems*, pages 3294–3302.

Arne Köhn. 2015. What's in an embedding? analyzing word embeddings through multilingual evaluation. In *Proceedings of the 2015 Conference on Empirical Methods in Natural Language Processing*, pages 2067–2073. Association for Computational Linguistics.

Arne Köhn. 2016. Evaluating embeddings using syntax-based classification tasks as a proxy for parser performance. In *Proceedings of the 1st Workshop on Evaluating Vector-Space Representations for NLP*, pages 67–71. Association for Computational Linguistics.

Tal Linzen, Emmanuel Dupoux, and Yoav Goldberg. 2016. Assessing the ability of LSTMs to learn syntax-sensitive dependencies. *Transactions of the Association for Computational Linguistics*, 4:521–535.

R Thomas McCoy, Tal Linzen, and Robert Frank. 2018. Revisiting the poverty of the stimulus: hierarchical generalization without a hierarchical bias in recurrent neural networks. *arXiv preprint arXiv:1802.09091*.

Tomas Mikolov, Ilya Sutskever, Kai Chen, Greg S Corrado, and Jeff Dean. 2013. Distributed representations of words and phrases and their compositionality. In *Advances in neural information processing systems*, pages 3111–3119.

Allen Nie, Erin D. Bennett, and Noah D. Goodman. 2017. Dissent: Sentence representation learning from explicit discourse relations. *CoRR*, abs/1710.04334.

Joakim Nivre, Marie-Catherine De Marneffe, Filip Ginter, Yoav Goldberg, Jan Hajic, Christopher D Manning, Ryan T McDonald, Slav Petrov, Sampo Pyysalo, Natalia Silveira, et al. 2016. Universal dependencies v1: A multilingual treebank collection. In *LREC*.

Sandeep Subramanian, Adam Trischler, Yoshua Bengio, and Christopher J Pal. 2018. Learning general purpose distributed sentence representations via large scale multi-task learning. In *International Conference on Learning Representations*.

John Wieting, Mohit Bansal, Kevin Gimpel, and Karen Livescu. 2016. Towards universal paraphrastic sentence embeddings. In *International Conference on Learning Representations*.

Collecting Diverse Natural Language Inference Problems
for Sentence Representation Evaluation

Adam Poliak[1]   **Aparajita Haldar**[1,2]   **Rachel Rudinger**[1]   **J. Edward Hu**[1]
Ellie Pavlick[3]   **Aaron Steven White**[4]   **Benjamin Van Durme**[1]
[1]Johns Hopkins University, [2] BITS Pilani, Goa Campus, India
[3]Brown University, [4]University of Rochester

Abstract

We present a large scale collection of diverse natural language inference (NLI) datasets that help provide insight into how well a sentence representation encoded by a neural network captures distinct types of reasoning. The collection results from recasting 13 existing datasets from 7 semantic phenomena into a common NLI structure, resulting in over half a million labeled context-hypothesis pairs in total. Our collection of diverse datasets is available at http://www.decomp.net/, and will grow over time as additional resources are recast and added from novel sources.

1 Introduction

A plethora of new natural language inference (NLI)[1] datasets has been created in recent years (Bowman et al., 2015; Williams et al., 2017; Lai et al., 2017; Khot et al., 2018). However, these datasets do not provide clear insight into what type of reasoning or inference a model may be performing. For example, these datasets cannot be used to evaluate whether competitive NLI models can determine if an event occurred, correctly differentiate between figurative and literal language, or accurately identify and categorize named entities. Consequently, these datasets cannot answer how well sentence representation learning models capture distinct semantic phenomena necessary for general natural language understanding (NLU).

To answer these questions, we introduce the **D**iverse **NLI** **C**ollection (DNC), a large-scale NLI dataset that tests a model's ability to perform diverse types of reasoning. DNC is a collection of NLI problems, each requiring a model to perform a unique type of reasoning. Each NLI dataset contains labeled context-hypothesis pairs that we re-

---

[1]The task of determining if a hypothesis would likely be inferred from a context, or premise; also known as Recognizing Textual Entailment (RTE) (Dagan et al., 2006, 2013).

Event Factuality	▶ Find him before he finds the dog food The finding did not happen	✓
	▶ I'll need to ponder The pondering happened	✗
Relation Extraction	▶ Ward joined Tom in their native Perth Ward was born in Perth	✓
	▶ Stefan had visited his son in Bulgaria Stefan was born in Bulgaria	✗
Puns	▶ Kim heard masks have no face value Kim heard a pun	✓
	▶ Tod heard that thrift is better than annuity Tod heard a pun	✗

Table 1: Example sentence pairs for different semantic phenomena. ▶ indicates the line is a context and the following line is its corresponding hypothesis. ✓ and ✗ respectively indicate that the context entails, or does not entail the hypothesis.

cast from semantic annotations for specific structured prediction tasks. Table 1 includes a sample of NLI pairs that test specific types of reasoning.

We extend various prior works on challenge NLI datasets (Zhang et al., 2017), and define recasting as leveraging existing datasets to create NLI examples (Glickman, 2006; White et al., 2017). We recast annotations from a total of 13 datasets across 7 NLP tasks into labeled NLI examples. The tasks include event factuality, named entity recognition, gendered anaphora resolution, sentiment analysis, relationship extraction, pun detection, and lexicosyntactic inference (Table 2). Currently, DNC contains over half a million labeled examples that can be used to probe a model's ability to capture different types of semantic reasoning necessary for general NLU. In short, this work answers a recent plea to the community to test "more kinds of inference" than in previous challenge sets (Chatzikyriakidis et al., 2017).

Proceedings of the 2018 EMNLP Workshop BlackboxNLP: Analyzing and Interpreting Neural Networks for NLP, pages 337–340
Brussels, Belgium, November 1, 2018. ©2018 Association for Computational Linguistics

2 Motivation & Background

Compared to eliciting NLI datasets directly, i.e. asking humans to author contexts and/or hypothesis sentences, recasting can 1) help determine whether an NLU model performs distinct types of reasoning; 2) limit types of biases observed in previous NLI data; and 3) generate examples cheaply, potentially at large scales.

NLU Insights Popular NLI datasets, e.g. Stanford Natural Language Inference (SNLI) (Bowman et al., 2015) and its successor Multi-NLI (Williams et al., 2017), were created by eliciting hypotheses from humans. Crowd-source workers were tasked with writing one sentence each that is entailed, neutral, and contradicted by a caption extracted from the Flickr30k corpus (Young et al., 2014). Although these datasets are widely used to train and evaluate sentence representations, a high accuracy is not indicative of what types of reasoning NLI models perform. Workers were free to create any type of hypothesis for each context and label. Such datasets cannot be used to determine how well an NLI model captures many desired capabilities of language understanding systems, e.g. paraphrastic inference, complex anaphora resolution (White et al., 2017), or compositionality (Pavlick and Callison-Burch, 2016; Dasgupta et al., 2018). By converting prior annotation of a specific phenomenon into NLI examples, recasting allows us to create a diverse NLI benchmark that tests a model's ability to perform distinct types of reasoning.

Limit Biases Studies indicate that many NLI datasets contain significant biases. Examples in the early Pascal RTE datasets could be correctly predicted based on syntax alone (Vanderwende and Dolan, 2006; Vanderwende et al., 2006). Statistical irregularities, and annotation artifacts, within class labels allow a hypothesis-only model to significantly outperform the majority baseline on at least six recent NLI datasets (Poliak et al., 2018). Class label biases may be attributed to the human-elicited protocol. Moreover, examples in such NLI datasets may contain racial and gendered stereotypes (Rudinger et al., 2017).

We limit some biases by not relying on humans to generate hypotheses. Recast NLI datasets may still contain some biases, e.g. non-uniform distributions over NLI labels caused by the distribution of labels in the original dataset that we re-

Phenomena	Dataset
Event Factuality	Decomp (Rudinger et al., 2018b) UW (Lee et al., 2015) MeanTime (Minard et al., 2016)
Named Entity Recognition	Groningen (Bos et al., 2017) CoNLL (Tjong Kim Sang and De Meulder, 2003)
Gendered Anaphora	Winogender (Rudinger et al., 2018a)
Lexicosyntactic Inference	VerbCorner (Hartshorne et al., 2013) MegaVeridicality (White and Rawlins, 2018) VerbNet (Schuler, 2005)
Puns	(Yang et al., 2015) SemEval 2017 Task 7 (Miller et al., 2017)
Relationship Extraction	FACC1 (Gabrilovich et al., 2013)
Sentiment Analysis	(Kotzias et al., 2015)

Table 2: List of each type of semantic phenomena paired with its corresponding dataset(s) we recast.

cast.[2] Experimental results using hypothesis-only models (Poliak et al., 2018; Gururangan et al., 2018; Tsuchiya, 2018) can indicate to what degree the recast datasets retain some biases that may be present in the original semantic datasets.

NLI Examples at Large-scale Generating NLI datasets from scratch is costly. Humans must be paid to generate or label natural language text. This linearly scales costs as the amount of generated NLI-pairs increases. Existing annotations for a wide array of semantic NLP tasks are freely available. By leveraging existing semantic annotations already invested in by the community we can generate and label NLI pairs at little cost and create large NLI datasets to train data hungry models.

Why These Semantic Phenomena? A long term goal is to develop NLU systems that can achieve human levels of understanding and reasoning. Investigating how different architectures and training corpora can help a system perform human-level general NLU is an important step in this direction. DNC contains recast NLI pairs that are easily understandable by humans and can be used to evaluate different sentence encoders and NLU systems. These semantic phenomena cover distinct types of reasoning that an NLU system may often encounter in the wild. While higher performance on these benchmarks might not be conclusive proof of a system achieving human-level reasoning, a system that does poorly should not be viewed as performing human-level NLU. We argue that these semantic phenomena play integral roles in NLU. There exist more semantic phenomena which are integral to NLU (Allen, 1995) and we plan to include them in future versions of DNC.

---

[2]In a corpus with part-of-speech tags, the distribution of labels for the word "the" will likely peak at the Det tag.

References

James Allen. 1995. *Natural language understanding.* Pearson.

Johan Bos, Valerio Basile, Kilian Evang, Noortje J Venhuizen, and Johannes Bjerva. 2017. The groningen meaning bank. In *Handbook of Linguistic Annotation*, pages 463–496. Springer.

Samuel R. Bowman, Gabor Angeli, Christopher Potts, and Christopher D. Manning. 2015. A large annotated corpus for learning natural language inference. In *Proceedings of the 2015 Conference on Empirical Methods in Natural Language Processing (EMNLP)*. Association for Computational Linguistics.

Stergios Chatzikyriakidis, Robin Cooper, Simon Dobnik, and Staffan Larsson. 2017. An overview of natural language inference data collection: The way forward? In *Proceedings of the Computing Natural Language Inference Workshop*.

Alexis Conneau, Douwe Kiela, Holger Schwenk, Loïc Barrault, and Antoine Bordes. 2017. Supervised learning of universal sentence representations from natural language inference data. In *Proceedings of the 2017 Conference on Empirical Methods in Natural Language Processing*, pages 670–680, Copenhagen, Denmark. Association for Computational Linguistics.

Robin Cooper, Dick Crouch, Jan Van Eijck, Chris Fox, Johan Van Genabith, Jan Jaspars, Hans Kamp, David Milward, Manfred Pinkal, Massimo Poesio, et al. 1996. Using the framework. Technical report.

Ido Dagan, Oren Glickman, and Bernardo Magnini. 2006. The pascal recognising textual entailment challenge. In *Machine learning challenges. evaluating predictive uncertainty, visual object classification, and recognising tectual entailment*, pages 177–190. Springer.

Ido Dagan, Dan Roth, Mark Sammons, and Fabio Massimo Zanzotto. 2013. Recognizing textual entailment: Models and applications. *Synthesis Lectures on Human Language Technologies*, 6(4):1–220.

I. Dasgupta, D. Guo, A. Stuhlmüller, S. J. Gershman, and N. D. Goodman. 2018. Evaluating Compositionality in Sentence Embeddings. *ArXiv e-prints*.

Evgeniy Gabrilovich, Michael Ringgaard, and Amarnag Subramanya. 2013. Facc1: Freebase annotation of clueweb corpora, version 1 (release date 2013-06-26, format version 1, correction level 0). *Note: http://lemurproject. org/clueweb09/FACC1/Cited by*, 5.

Oren Glickman. 2006. *Applied textual entailment.* Ph.D. thesis, Bar Ilan University.

Suchin Gururangan, Swabha Swayamdipta, Omer Levy, Roy Schwartz, Samuel Bowman, and Noah A. Smith. 2018. Annotation artifacts in natural language inference data. In *Proc. of NAACL*.

Joshua K Hartshorne, Claire Bonial, and Martha Palmer. 2013. The verbcorner project: Toward an empirically-based semantic decomposition of verbs. In *Proceedings of the 2013 Conference on Empirical Methods in Natural Language Processing*, pages 1438–1442.

Tushar Khot, Ashish Sabharwal, and Peter Clark. 2018. SciTail: A textual entailment dataset from science question answering. In *AAAI*.

Dimitrios Kotzias, Misha Denil, Nando De Freitas, and Padhraic Smyth. 2015. From group to individual labels using deep features. In *Proceedings of the 21th ACM SIGKDD International Conference on Knowledge Discovery and Data Mining*, pages 597–606. ACM.

Alice Lai, Yonatan Bisk, and Julia Hockenmaier. 2017. Natural language inference from multiple premises. In *Proceedings of the Eighth International Joint Conference on Natural Language Processing (Volume 1: Long Papers)*, pages 100–109, Taipei, Taiwan. Asian Federation of Natural Language Processing.

Kenton Lee, Yoav Artzi, Yejin Choi, and Luke Zettlemoyer. 2015. Event detection and factuality assessment with non-expert supervision. In *Proceedings of the 2015 Conference on Empirical Methods in Natural Language Processing*, pages 1643–1648.

Tristan Miller, Christian Hempelmann, and Iryna Gurevych. 2017. Semeval-2017 task 7: Detection and interpretation of english puns. In *Proceedings of the 11th International Workshop on Semantic Evaluation (SemEval-2017)*, pages 58–68, Vancouver, Canada. Association for Computational Linguistics.

Anne-Lyse Minard, Manuela Speranza, Ruben Urizar, Begona Altuna, Marieke van Erp, Anneleen Schoen, and Chantal van Son. 2016. Meantime, the newsreader multilingual event and time corpus. In *Language Resources and Evaluation Conference (LREC)*.

Ramakanth Pasunuru and Mohit Bansal. 2017. Multi-task video captioning with video and entailment generation. In *Proceedings of the 55th Annual Meeting of the Association for Computational Linguistics (Volume 1: Long Papers)*, volume 1, pages 1273–1283.

Ellie Pavlick and Chris Callison-Burch. 2016. Most "babies" are "little" and most "problems" are "huge": Compositional entailment in adjective-nouns. In *Proceedings of the 54th Annual Meeting of the Association for Computational Linguistics (Volume 1: Long Papers)*, pages 2164–2173. Association for Computational Linguistics.

Adam Poliak, Jason Naradowsky, Aparajita Haldar, Rachel Rudinger, and Benjamin Van Durme. 2018. Hypothesis only baselines in natural language inference. In *The Seventh Joint Conference on Lexical and Computational Semantics (*SEM)*.

Rachel Rudinger, Chandler May, and Benjamin Van Durme. 2017. Social bias in elicited natural language inferences. In *Proceedings of the First ACL Workshop on Ethics in Natural Language Processing*, pages 74–79, Valencia, Spain. Association for Computational Linguistics.

Rachel Rudinger, Jason Naradowsky, Brian Leonard, and Benjamin Van Durme. 2018a. Gender bias in coreference resolution. In *Proceedings of the Annual Meeting of the North American Association of Computational Linguistics (NAACL)*.

Rachel Rudinger, Aaron Steven White, and Benjamin Van Durme. 2018b. Neural models of factuality. In *Proceedings of the Annual Meeting of the North American Association of Computational Linguistics (NAACL)*.

Karin Kipper Schuler. 2005. Verbnet: A broad-coverage, comprehensive verb lexicon.

Erik F. Tjong Kim Sang and Fien De Meulder. 2003. Introduction to the conll-2003 shared task: Language-independent named entity recognition. In *Proceedings of the Seventh Conference on Natural Language Learning at HLT-NAACL 2003 - Volume 4*, CONLL '03, pages 142–147, Stroudsburg, PA, USA. Association for Computational Linguistics.

Masatoshi Tsuchiya. 2018. Performance impact caused by hidden bias of training data for recognizing textual entailment. In *11th International Conference on Language Resources and Evaluation (LREC2018)*.

Lucy Vanderwende and William B Dolan. 2006. What syntax can contribute in the entailment task. In *Machine Learning Challenges. Evaluating Predictive Uncertainty, Visual Object Classification, and Recognising Tectual Entailment*, pages 205–216. Springer.

Lucy Vanderwende, Arul Menezes, and Rion Snow. 2006. Microsoft research at rte-2: Syntactic contributions in the entailment task: an implementation. In *Second PASCAL Challenges Workshop*.

Aaron Steven White, Pushpendre Rastogi, Kevin Duh, and Benjamin Van Durme. 2017. Inference is everything: Recasting semantic resources into a unified evaluation framework. In *Proceedings of the Eighth International Joint Conference on Natural Language Processing (Volume 1: Long Papers)*, pages 996–1005, Taipei, Taiwan. Asian Federation of Natural Language Processing.

Aaron Steven White and Kyle Rawlins. 2018. The role of veridicality and factivity in clause selection. In *Proceedings of the 48th Annual Meeting of the North East Linguistic Society*, page to appear, Amherst, MA. GLSA Publications.

Adina Williams, Nikita Nangia, and Samuel R Bowman. 2017. A broad-coverage challenge corpus for sentence understanding through inference. *arXiv preprint arXiv:1704.05426*.

Diyi Yang, Alon Lavie, Chris Dyer, and Eduard Hovy. 2015. Humor recognition and humor anchor extraction. In *Proceedings of the 2015 Conference on Empirical Methods in Natural Language Processing*, pages 2367–2376. Association for Computational Linguistics.

Peter Young, Alice Lai, Micah Hodosh, and Julia Hockenmaier. 2014. From image descriptions to visual denotations: New similarity metrics for semantic inference over event descriptions. *Transactions of the Association for Computational Linguistics*, 2:67–78.

Sheng Zhang, Rachel Rudinger, Kevin Duh, and Benjamin Van Durme. 2017. Ordinal common-sense inference. *Transactions of the Association of Computational Linguistics*, 5(1):379–395.

Interpretable Word Embedding Contextualization

Kyoung-Rok Jang
School of Computing
KAIST
Daejeon, South Korea
`kyoungrok.jang@kaist.ac.kr`

Sung-Hyon Myaeng
School of Computing
KAIST
Daejeon, South Korea
`myaeng@kaist.ac.kr`

Sang-Bum Kim
Naver Corp.
Seongnam-si, South Korea
`sangbum.kim@navercorp.com`

Abstract

In this paper, we propose a method of calibrating a word embedding, so that the semantic it conveys becomes more relevant to the context. Our method is novel because the output shows clearly which senses that were originally presented in a target word embedding become stronger or weaker. This is possible by utilizing the technique of using sparse coding to recover senses that comprises a word embedding.

1 Introduction

In this paper we propose a method of generating contextualized word embeddings. What we mean by 'contextualized' is that standard embeddings such as Skip-gram and GloVe are modified to reflect their contexts. For instance, *apple* appeared in fruit-implying context should become more similar to *fruit* than it was in the prior state.

We need contextualized embeddings because not all information contained in an embedding is helpful for modelling accurately the meaning of a word in context (e.g. company-related senses of *apple* in fruit-implying context). Since word embeddings are trained on unconstrained variation of contexts, using word embeddings as-is is like taking the risk of feeding our subsequent models (e.g. classifiers) with noises that are not relevant to the given context.

We formulate our task as calibrating senses contained in embeddings so that contextually relevant senses (e.g. fruit-ness) becomes stronger and the others (e.g. company-ness) become weaker. To achieve this we utilize the technique of recovering standard word embeddings as linear composition of different senses, proposed by (Murphy et al., 2012; Faruqui et al., 2015; Arora et al., 2016). After applying the technique word embeddings are

transformed into high dimensional (e.g. 2,500) and sparse (only small portion of dimensions are nonzero) embeddings. This makes our method *interpretable* since extracted senses can give us "a succinct description of which other words co-occur with a specific word sense". More detailed explanation is presented in Section 3.

Using the technique we first decompose word embeddings of a target word (to be contextualized) and context words into linear composition of senses, then identify strong senses extracted from context and regard them as contextually relevant. Finally we use the contextually relevant senses for calibrating the senses contained in a target word.

2 Task and Model

2.1 Task

We show that our method is effective by applying it to Word Sense Discrimination (WSD) task. For brevity we present only one instance of sense discrimination: discriminating *apple* as a *fruit* or a *company* depending on given context. The result is described in Section 3

2.2 Embedding Decomposition

To contextualize a target word's embedding, we should first decompose the participating word embeddings (i.e. target and context words) into linear composition of different senses. As a result we obtain high dimensional and sparse embeddings, in which few 'activated' dimensions represent significant senses reside in a word embedding.

For our preliminary experiment we use Nonnegative Sparse Embedding (NNSE) proposed by (Murphy et al., 2012). We use NNSE partly because pre-trained word embeddings are publicly available at it's official website[1].

---

[1] https://www.cs.cmu.edu/ bmurphy/NNSE/

Proceedings of the 2018 EMNLP Workshop BlackboxNLP: Analyzing and Interpreting Neural Networks for NLP, pages 341–343
Brussels, Belgium, November 1, 2018. ©2018 Association for Computational Linguistics

2.3 Contextualization

Figure 1 shows the baseline method of performing word sense discrimination only using embeddings of a target word and context words (Kober et al., 2017). Basically it takes a sum of a target word and context word embeddings, and then decide whether the target word in the context has the same sense by calculating cosine similarity. In our work, we modify the composition (i.e. contextualization) step.

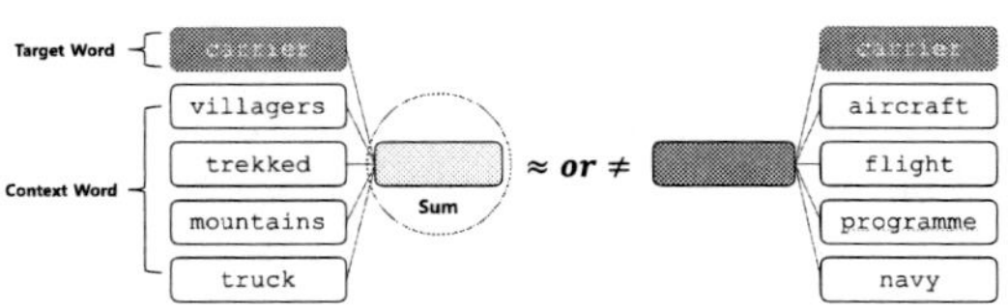

Figure 1: The baseline method. The red circle indicates the step where we make our modification.

We first retrieve NNSE embeddings of a target word and context words. We then generate $emb_{context}$ by summing all the context embeddings to identify contextually relevant dimensions (i.e. senses) (Figure 2).

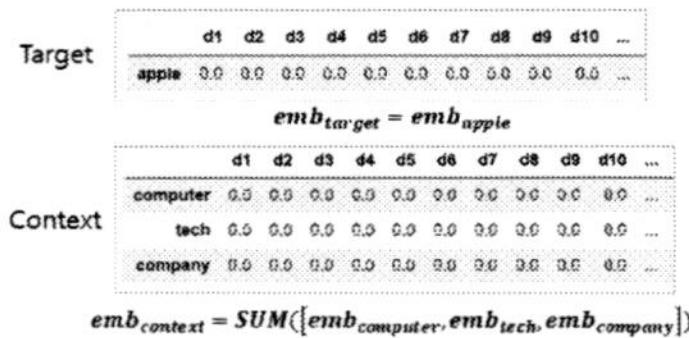

Figure 2: Calculation of target and context embedding. Since NNSE is sparse, the visual part of embeddings in this figure has all zero values.

We hypothesize that the dimensions of $emb_{context}$ that have zero value are irrelevant to the context. This is because in NNSE, a specific dimension is activated only when it represents a significant sense contained in word embeddings. So if a dimension is still deactivated after the sum of all context words, it means that the sense the dimension represents must have low importance.

So we turn off such atoms as well in the target word embedding by applying element-wise multiplication between a target word and a context embedding (Equation 1). This weakens senses that are irrelevant to context.

$$emb_{contextualized} = emb_{target} * emb_{context} \quad (1)$$

Finally, we normalize our contextualized embedding then use it in our task (Equation 2). This strengthens concepts that are relevant to context.

$$\frac{emb_{contextualized}}{\|emb_{contextualized}\|_2} \quad (2)$$

3 Preliminary Experiment and Result

In our experiment we attempt to discriminate *company* and *fruit* senses of *apple* by contextualizing with a relevant context.

Figure 3 shows the calibrated senses of *apple*. In the figure, 'd2104' means it is 2104th dimension of the embedding, and the list of words in the figure is an interpretation of the dimension (i.e. sense), which can be derived by sorting the whole vocabulary by the strength of the specific dimension in reverse order. The score is the strength of the dimension. Note that the identified dimensions are all extracted from *apple* embedding, while the values are calibrated.

The figure shows that our contextualization method is able to strengthen and weaken the senses of *apple* by reflecting the given context.

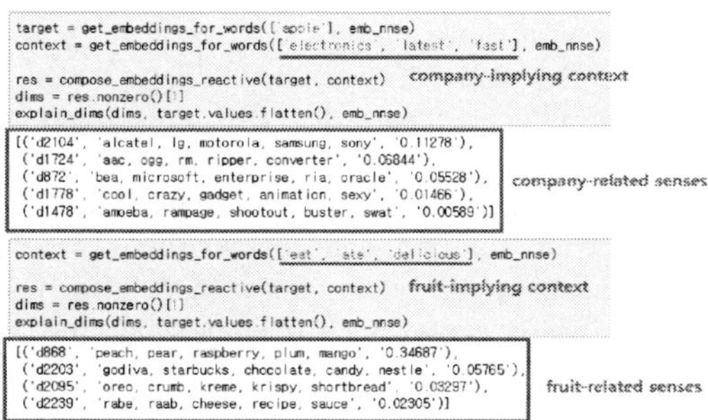

Figure 3: The calibrated senses of *apple*.

4 Discussion and Future Work

We showed that our method could be both interpretable and effective in performing a word sense discrimination task. Our method can be utilized not only to discriminate senses but to decide types of named entities or any other tasks that require inferring the context specific meaning of words. As a future work, we will try to elaborate our method and prove the efficacy of our method by testing on well-known tasks.

References

Sanjeev Arora, Yuanzhi Li, Yingyu Liang, Tengyu Ma, and Andrej Risteski. 2016. Linear Algebraic Structure of Word Senses, with Applications to Polysemy.

Manaal Faruqui, Yulia Tsvetkov, Dani Yogatama, Chris Dyer, and Noah Smith. 2015. Sparse Overcomplete Word Vector Representations.

Thomas Kober, Julie Weeds, John Wilkie, Jeremy Reffin, and David Weir. 2017. One Representation per Word - Does it make Sense for Composition? In *Proceedings of the 1st Workshop on Sense, Concept and Entity Representations and their Applications*, pages 79–90.

Brian Murphy, Partha Pratim Talukdar, and Tom Mitchell. 2012. Learning Effective and Interpretable Semantic Models using Non-Negative Sparse Embedding. *Proceedings of COLING 2012: Technical Papers*, (December 2012):1933–1950.

State Gradients for RNN Memory Analysis

Lyan Verwimp, Hugo Van hamme, Vincent Renkens, Patrick Wambacq
ESAT – PSI, KU Leuven
Kasteelpark Arenberg 10
3001 Heverlee, Belgium
`{firstname}.{lastname}@kuleuven.be`

Abstract

We present a framework for analyzing what the state in RNNs remembers from its input embeddings. We compute the gradients of the states with respect to the input embeddings and decompose the gradient matrix with Singular Value Decomposition to analyze which directions in the embedding space are best transferred to the hidden state space, characterized by the largest singular values. We apply our approach to LSTM language models and investigate to what extent and for how long certain classes of words are remembered on average for a certain corpus. Additionally, the extent to which a specific property or relationship is remembered by the RNN can be tracked by comparing a vector characterizing that property with the direction(s) in embedding space that are best preserved in hidden state space.

1 Introduction

Recurrent neural networks (RNNs) are the current state of the art in many speech and language technology applications, but they are often called 'black-box' models since it is hard for humans to interpret what exactly the network has learned. We present a framework to investigate what the states of RNNs remember from their input and for how long. We apply our approach to the current state of the art in language modeling, long short-term memory (Hochreiter and Schmidhuber, 1997) (LSTM) LMs (Sundermeyer et al., 2012), but it can be applied to other types of RNNs too and to other models with continuous word representations as input.

2 Average memory of the RNN

Our framework is inspired by backpropagation, but instead of computing the gradient of the loss, we compute the gradient of the state with respect to the input embedding, the 'state gradient', to capture the influence of the input on the state. To examine how long input words are remembered by the RNN, we calculate the gradient with a certain delay – with respect to the input word embedding a few time steps earlier. The gradient matrix $\bar{\mathbf{G}}_\tau$ (averaged over all time steps), where τ is a certain delay, is decomposed with Singular Value Decomposition (SVD):

$$\bar{\mathbf{G}}_\tau = \mathbf{U} \, \boldsymbol{\Sigma} \, \mathbf{V}^T = \sigma_1 \, \mathbf{u}_1 \, \mathbf{v}_1^T + \sigma_2 \, \mathbf{u}_2 \, \mathbf{v}_2^T + \dots \quad (1)$$

We can interpret $\mathbf{V}$ as directions in the embedding space, $\boldsymbol{\Sigma}$ as the extent to which the directions in the embedding space can be found in the hidden state space and $\mathbf{U}$ as corresponding directions in the hidden state space. Hence, the directions with the largest singular values (SVs) (lowest index) are directions in embedding space that are best remembered by the RNN.

In order to investigate how well the RNN remembers on a corpus level, we can track the largest SV or the sum of all SVs with respect to the delay τ. For an LM trained on Penn Treebank, we observe an exponential decay of the SVs with respect to the delay: much of the information that is present in the cell state about a specific word is quickly forgotten. However, on average, some information is still remembered even after processing more than 20 words. The ratio of the largest SV with respect to the sum of all SVs becomes larger as the delay increases, indicating that the memory becomes more selective.

We can also compare the SVs based on gradient matrices averaged over specific classes of words or individual words. We observe for example that pronouns have a larger effect on the cell state than other parts-of-speech for a delay of 0, which makes sense because they determine which verb conjugation should follow.

344

Proceedings of the 2018 EMNLP Workshop BlackboxNLP: Analyzing and Interpreting Neural Networks for NLP, pages 344–346
Brussels, Belgium, November 1, 2018. ©2018 Association for Computational Linguistics

3 Tracking a specific property

We can also track whether a specific relationship encoded in the input embedding is remembered by the RNN. It has been shown that relationships between word embeddings can be characterized as vector offsets (Mikolov et al., 2013). We compare a vector characterizing a specific property to the directions in the embedding space that are best remembered (the directions in $\mathbf{V}^T$ corresponding to the largest SVs), to see if and how well the property is remembered in the hidden state.

Firstly, we define a specific property as the difference between the averaged embeddings for the classes separated by that property:

$$\mathbf{d}_{a-b} = \bar{\mathbf{e}}_a - \bar{\mathbf{e}}_b \tag{2}$$

where $\bar{\mathbf{e}}_a$ and $\bar{\mathbf{e}}_b$ are the result of averaging all embeddings of words belonging to classes a and b respectively. In order to check whether this definition makes sense for a specific property, we first test whether the embeddings of the two classes are linearly separable by training a linear classifier.

We propose two methods to investigate the extent to which a property is remembered. Firstly, we can compare $\mathbf{d}$ with $\mathcal{H}_n$, which is the subspace of the embedding space spanned by the directions that are best remembered, the n largest right-singular vectors. To be able to do this, we make the orthogonal projection of $\mathbf{d}$ on $\mathcal{H}_n$:

$$\mathbf{y} = \text{proj}_{\mathcal{H}_n}\, \mathbf{d} = \mathbf{V}_n\, \mathbf{V}_n^T\, \mathbf{d} \tag{3}$$

where $\mathbf{V}_n$ is the matrix containing the n first columns of $\mathbf{V}$. Assuming $\mathbf{d}$ is normalized to unit length, we can calculate the cosine similarity between $\mathbf{y}$ and $\mathbf{d}$ as follows:

$$\cos(\mathbf{d}, \mathbf{y}) = \frac{\mathbf{d}^T\, \mathbf{V}_n\, \mathbf{V}_n^T\, \mathbf{d}}{\|\mathbf{d}\|\, \|\mathbf{V}_n\, \mathbf{V}_n^T\, \mathbf{d}\|} = \left\|\mathbf{V}_n^T\, \mathbf{d}\right\| \tag{4}$$

The cosine similarity between $\mathbf{d}$ and $\mathcal{H}_n$ is a measure of how close $\mathbf{d}$ is to the top n directions that are best remembered in the RNN state.

A second option is comparing $\mathbf{d}$ with the direction in embedding space that is *best* remembered. To do this, we multiply $\mathbf{d}$ with the average gradient matrix:

$$r = \left\|\bar{\mathbf{G}}_\tau \times \mathbf{d}\right\| \tag{5}$$

If $\mathbf{d}$ would be the embedding direction that is best remembered in the state, then it would be equal to

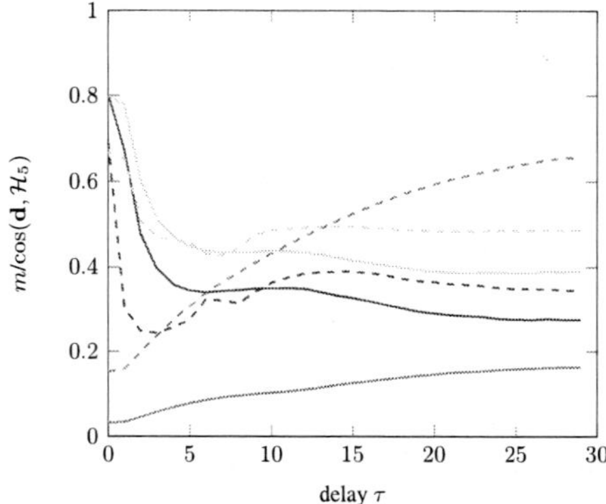

Figure 1: m (full lines) and $\cos(\mathbf{d}, \mathcal{H}_5)$ (dotted lines) for sg-pl (blue) and common-proper (green) nouns with respect to the delay for a PTB LM. Gray lines: $\sigma_1 / \sum \sigma$ (full) and $\sum_{n=1}^5 \sigma_n / \sum \sigma$ (dotted).

$\mathbf{v}_1$ and r would be equal to σ_1. Hence, in order to get a relative measure of how well the difference between two classes is remembered, we compare r with σ_1 and obtain a 'extent to which the property is remembered, relative to the property that is best remembered', or the 'relative memory' m:

$$m = \frac{r}{\sigma_1} \tag{6}$$

In Figure 1, we plot m and $\cos(\mathbf{d}, \mathcal{H}_5)$ for the properties singular-plural (sg-pl) noun and common-proper (cm-pr) noun. Prior experiments with a linear classifier showed that these properties can be characterized as a difference vector. According to both measures the sg-pl distinction is slightly better remembered for a delay of 0, while for the other delays the cm-pr distinction is better remembered. In all plots, there is a sharp decrease after a delay of 1 or 2, indicating that the properties seem mostly important on the short term. We also plot the ratio of σ_1 and the sum of the 5 largest SVs with respect to the sum of all SVs (gray lines). Notice that if τ increases, the ratio increases too, which confirms our observation in section 2 that the memory becomes more selective over time.

4 Conclusion

We analyze the memory of an RNN by computing the gradients of its state with respect to its input. The state gradient matrix is decomposed with SVD, and the resulting singular values and directions with the highest singular values are inspected to investigate for how long and how well the RNN remembers its input.

References

Sepp Hochreiter and Jürgen Schmidhuber. 1997. Long short-term memory. *Neural Computation*, 9(8):1735–1780.

Tomas Mikolov, Wen-tau Yih, and Geoffrey Zweig. 2013. Linguistic regularities in continuous space word representations. In *Conference of the North American Chapter of the Association for Computational Linguistics (NAACL)*, pages 746–751.

Martin Sundermeyer, Ralf Schlüter, and Hermann Ney. 2012. LSTM Neural Networks for Language Modeling. In *INTERSPEECH*, pages 1724–1734.

Extracting Syntactic Trees from Transformer Encoder Self-Attentions

David Mareček and **Rudolf Rosa**
Institute of Formal and Applied Linguistics
Faculty of Mathematics and Physics
Charles University, Prague, Czechia
{marecek,rosa}@ufal.mff.cuni.cz

1 Introduction

Interpreting neural networks is a popular topic, and there are many works focusing on analyzing networks with respect to learning syntax (Shi et al., 2016; Linzen et al., 2016; Blevins et al., 2018).

In particular, Vaswani et al. (2017) showed that the self-attentions in their Transformer architecture may be directly interpreted as syntactic dependencies between tokens. However, there is a potential problem in the fact that the attention mechanism on deeper layers operates on the previous-layer neurons, which already comprise mixed information from multiple source tokens.

Our goal is to infer source sentence tree structures form the encoder's self-attention energies used in the Transfomer neural machine translation (NMT) system. We would like to visualize how the self-attention mechanism connects individual words (or wordpieces) of the sentence, to create various tree structures (e.g. constituency trees, undirected trees, dependency trees), and to discuss their characteristics with respect to the existing syntactic theories and annotations. We would also like to discuss results across various languages and natural language processing (NLP) tasks.

In this abstract, we present our preliminary results, analyzing the encoder in English-to-German NMT within the NeuralMonkey toolkit (Helcl and Libovický, 2017). We introduce aggregation of self-attention through layers to get a distribution over the input tokens for each encoder position and layer (Section 2). We then propose algorithms for constructing two types of syntactic trees (Sections 3 and 4), apply them to 42 sentences sampled from PennTB (Marcus et al., 1993), and compare the resulting structures to established syntax annotation styles, such as that of PennTB, UD (Nivre et al., 2016), or PDT (Böhmová et al., 2003).

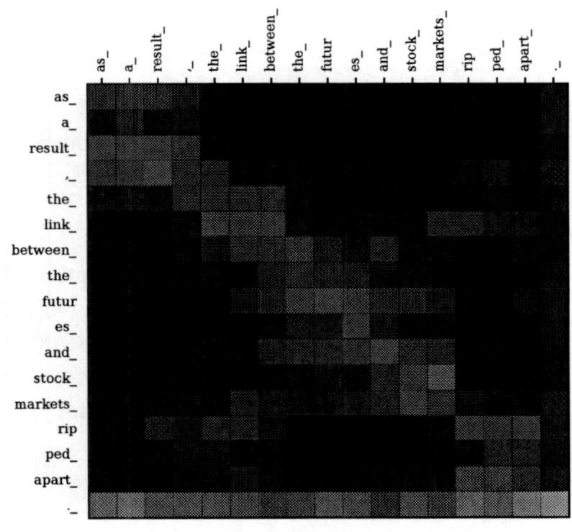

Figure 1: Aggregated encoder's self-attentions after the 6th layer. Each column contains a distribution over the source wordpieces for one encoder position.

2 Aggregated self-attention visualization

We use the default setting: encoder is composed of 6 layers, each consisting of a 16-head self-attention mechanism and a fully connected feed-forward network, both bridged by residual connections. Each position in one layer can attend to all positions in the previous layer; the attention to the same position is boosted by the residual connection. When translating a single sentence by Transformer, we would like to capture how much each input token affects each particular position on each layer in the encoder. This is done by aggregating the attention distributions through the layers. For each layer, we collect the self-attention distribution to the previous layer and add +1 to the same-position attention for the residual connection. The output is then normalized. So far, we take the attention distribution as the average attention over all the 16 heads.

Proceedings of the 2018 EMNLP Workshop BlackboxNLP: Analyzing and Interpreting Neural Networks for NLP, pages 347–349
Brussels, Belgium, November 1, 2018. ©2018 Association for Computational Linguistics

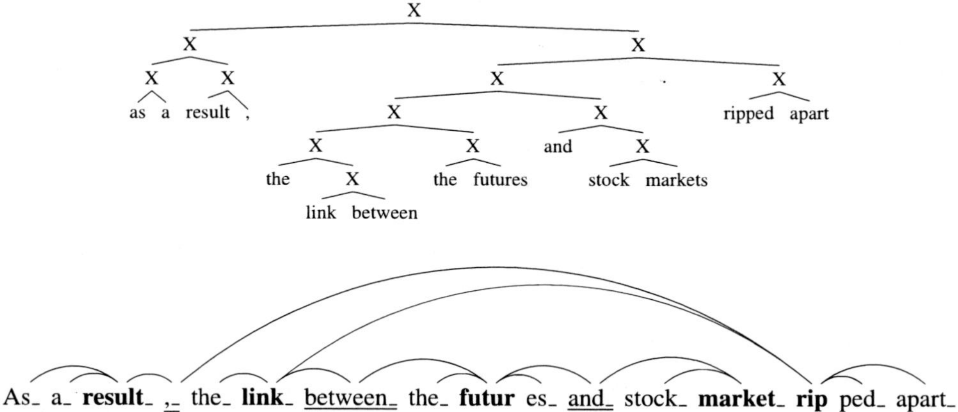

Figure 2: A binary constituency tree and an undirected tree, generated by the proposed algorithms.

3 Constituency trees extraction

In Figure 1, we can see that the self-attention mechanism is quite strong within phrases. That led us to an idea of extracting phrase-structure trees from that. We define the score of a constituent with span from position i to position j as

$$score(i, j) = \frac{\sum_{x \in [i,...,j]} \sum_{y \in [i,...,j]} w[x, y]}{j - i + 1},$$

where $w[x, y]$ is the attention weight of the token y in the position x. We then build a binary constituency tree by recurrently splitting the sentence. When splitting a phrase with span (i, j), we look for a position k maximizing the scores of the two resulting phrases:

$$\arg\max_{k} (score(i, k) \cdot score(k + 1, j)).$$

We also rejoin wordpieces into words, assigning zero scores to constituents separating pieces of a single word. One example is shown in Figure 2.

When compared to PennTB, clauses, noun phrases, or shorter verb phrases are often well recognized. The differences are mainly inside them[1] and in composing them together forming clauses.

4 Undirected trees extraction

First, for each pair of tokens i, j, we calculate a *coattention score*, expressing how common it is for the tokens to be attended to at the same time:

$$score(i, j) = \sum_{m \in [1, N-1]} w[m, i] \cdot w[m, j]$$

We then construct an undirected tree[2] maximizing the coattention scores along its edges, using the algorithm of Kruskal (1956); see the bottom tree in Figure 2. We have found the resulting trees to bear surprising similarities to standard syntactic dependency trees (which, however, are directed).

For example, we observe many flat treelets, resembling headed syntactic phrases; the "phrase heads" (**bold**) are mostly content words, while the function words are mostly attached as leaf nodes (as in UD). We hypothesize that the encoder tries to concentrate the representation of the whole phrase onto the position of a single token – ideally one that already carries a lot of meaning.

Furthermore, the phrase treelets are then typically connected to each other via these heads (as in UD), and/or via a sort of connector tokens at phrase boundaries (underlined), such as commas, conjunctions, or prepositions (as in PDT).

5 Future work

In future, we would like to (1) analyze how the trees evolve through layers, (2) employ unsupervised or supervised selection of "more syntactic" heads, and (3) perform the experiments on more language pairs; especially, we hope that translation into multiple languages could push the encoder to use a more syntactic internal representation.

---

[1] This is also caused by very flat noun phrases representations in PennTB compared to our binary branching.

[2] We also tried to construct directed graphs, (i.e. a standard dependency tree), where the edges could be directly viewed as dependencies, but we did not find any sensible way of defining the coattention scores assymetrically; rather than parent-child dependencies, many relations seem to be more general, without a clear direction.

References

Terra Blevins, Omer Levy, and Luke Zettlemoyer. 2018. Deep RNNs encode soft hierarchical syntax. In *Proceedings of the 56th Annual Meeting of the Association for Computational Linguistics (Volume 2: Short Papers)*, pages 14–19, Melbourne, Australia. Association for Computational Linguistics.

Alena Böhmová, Jan Hajič, Eva Hajičová, and Barbora Hladká. 2003. The Prague dependency treebank. In *Treebanks*, pages 103–127. Springer.

Jindřich Helcl and Jindřich Libovický. 2017. Neural Monkey: An open-source tool for sequence learning. *The Prague Bulletin of Mathematical Linguistics*, (107):5–17.

Joseph B Kruskal. 1956. On the shortest spanning subtree of a graph and the traveling salesman problem. *Proceedings of the American Mathematical society*, 7(1):48–50.

Tal Linzen, Emmanuel Dupoux, and Yoav Goldberg. 2016. Assessing the ability of LSTMs to learn syntax-sensitive dependencies. *Transactions of the Association for Computational Linguistics*, 4:521–535.

Mitchell P. Marcus, Mary Ann Marcinkiewicz, and Beatrice Santorini. 1993. Building a large annotated corpus of English: The Penn treebank. *Comput. Linguist.*, 19(2):313–330.

Joakim Nivre, Marie-Catherine de Marneffe, Filip Ginter, Yoav Goldberg, Jan Hajič, Christopher Manning, Ryan McDonald, Slav Petrov, Sampo Pyysalo, Natalia Silveira, Reut Tsarfaty, and Daniel Zeman. 2016. Universal Dependencies v1: A multilingual treebank collection. In *Proceedings of the 10th International Conference on Language Resources and Evaluation (LREC 2016)*, pages 1659–1666, Portoro, Slovenia. European Language Resources Association.

Xing Shi, Inkit Padhi, and Kevin Knight. 2016. Does string-based neural MT learn source syntax? In *EMNLP*, pages 1526–1534.

Ashish Vaswani, Noam Shazeer, Niki Parmar, Jakob Uszkoreit, Llion Jones, Aidan N Gomez, Lukasz Kaiser, and Illia Polosukhin. 2017. Attention is all you need. In I. Guyon, U. V. Luxburg, S. Bengio, H. Wallach, R. Fergus, S. Vishwanathan, and R. Garnett, editors, *Advances in Neural Information Processing Systems 30*, pages 6000–6010. Curran Associates, Inc.

Portable, layer-wise task performance monitoring for NLP models

Thomas Lippincott
Johns Hopkins University
`tom@cs.jhu.edu`

1 Introduction

There is a long-standing interest in understanding the internal behavior of neural networks (Touretzky and Pomerleau, 1989; Zhou et al., 2017; Raghu et al., 2017; Alishahi et al., 2017). Deep neural architectures for natural language processing (NLP) are often accompanied by explanations for their effectiveness, from general observations (e.g. RNNs can represent unbounded dependencies in a sequence) to specific arguments about linguistic phenomena (early layers encode lexical information, deeper layers syntactic). The recent ascendancy of DNNs is fueling efforts in the NLP community to explore these claims (Belinkov et al., 2017; Dalvi et al., 2017; Karpathy et al., 2015; Kadar et al., 2016; Kohn, 2015; Qian et al., 2016a). Previous work has tended to focus on easily-accessible representations like word or sentence embeddings (Kohn, 2015; Qian et al., 2016b; Adi et al., 2016), with deeper structure requiring more ad hoc methods to extract and examine (Belinkov and Glass, 2017; Poliak et al., 2018). In this work, we introduce **Vivisect**, a toolkit that aims at a general solution for broad and fine-grained monitoring in the major DNN frameworks, with minimal change to research patterns. Vivisect is general enough to serve as a less-polished version of the widely-used TensorBoard tool, but has several priorities that set it apart:

- Minimal invasiveness (e.g. no SummaryOps)

- Low resource use (only keep final metrics)

- Uniform support for major DNN frameworks

- Monitor performance on auxiliary tasks

The first three points are largely ergonomic, though we hope that feature parity between the major DNN research frameworks will yield answers to previously-daunting questions, such as why seemingly-identical implementations of a deep architecture perform differently. The fourth point is the most important: when made aware of task labels from various linguistic modalities, Vivisect will train lightweight linear classifiers and clusterers using each of the model's internal representations as features. A lightweight web server aggregates and plots these scores as a function of other variables (e.g. training epoch) to give insight into what linguistic information is captured by different parts of the model, and how they evolve over time.

Vivisect has evolved out of a focus on neural machine translation models, but is designed with generalization as a fundamental principle. Therefore, it includes mechanisms for deciding what and when calculations are made, and on which parts of a model. There are simple APIs for registering additional metrics and entire DNN frameworks. Vivisect is provided as a code repository and optional prebuilt Docker image.

2 Client usage

To use Vivisect with a PyTorch Module, Tensorflow Session, or MXNet Block, one can minimally add three lines to existing code:

```
from vivisect import probe, flush
probe(model, vivisect_host, vivisect_port)
flush(vivisect_host, vivisect_port)
```

This will monitor all operations in the computation graph, using a Vivisect server at the given host and port. This is accomplished by traversing the computation graph, and at each operation, overriding the forward method (similarly for operation backward methods and parameter update methods). **probe** accepts two optional arguments: a callback **which(model, operation)** that determines whether to attach to each operation, and

Proceedings of the 2018 EMNLP Workshop BlackboxNLP: Analyzing and Interpreting Neural Networks for NLP, pages 350–352
Brussels, Belgium, November 1, 2018. ©2018 Association for Computational Linguistics

when(model, operation) that determines whether the operation should be monitored at the current state.

3   Server architecture

Vivisect has a client and server arrangement so that the computational aspects of monitoring can be off-loaded to other servers, and without writing data to disk. Figure 1 shows the data flow, where all dashed edges are transmitting JSON objects with fields *values* and *metadata*.

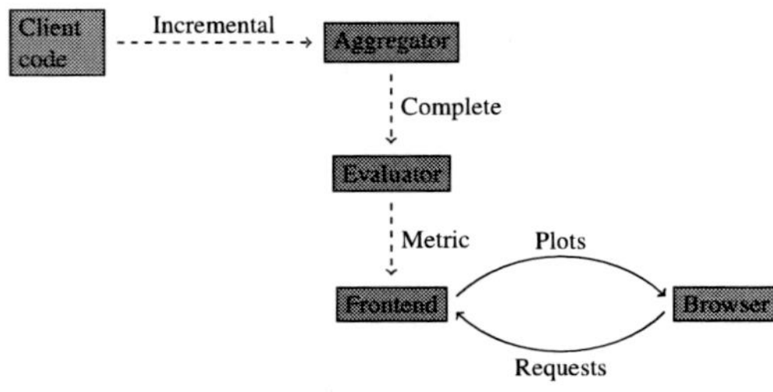

Figure 1: System diagram of Vivisect

(1) The client code, where the model is being trained or applied, sends *incremental* data points to the aggregator whenever a monitored parameter, activation, or gradient is used. These typically don't represent a full input for computing a metric (e.g. we want to monitor full epochs, but are getting activations for each mini-batch). (2) The aggregator keeps track of the metadata fields until it satisfies some condition (e.g. the *epoch* metadata field increases for the given model), constructs a *complete* data point by combining the appropriate arrays and metadata, and sends this to the *evaluator*. (3) The evaluator uses each complete data point to calculate arbitrary scalar-valued *metrics*, which it ships (again, with appropriate metadata) to the *frontend*. (4) The frontend is a simple web server on top of a sqlite database, into which it inserts each metric value, along with corresponding metadata like the model name and epoch. It uses this database to dynamically serve visualizations of the metrics along various axes, with the canonical use-case of how different activations perform as features for a classification task, as a function of epoch.

4   Beyond intrinsic measurements

Tracking and visualizing intrinsic properties of a model's internal state is useful, but well-covered by existing tools like Tensorboard and its variants. Vivisect's goal is to employ user-specified information about the model's input and output (in the latter case, during training or dev/eval) to test intuitions about how linguistic information is organized internally. The user can register such information with the server:

```
from vivisect import register_targets
register_targets(vivisect_host, vivisect_port,
                 name="Training classes",
                 targets=y_train,
                 model_pattern="Gluon MLP")
```

In this case, y_train are just the N-length sequence of classes that the model is being trained to identify, but since it is now registered, whenever the evaluator sees a CDP of appropriate dimension from a matching model, it trains a linear classifier and a k-means clustering using the CDP and calculates macro f-score and mutual information, respectively. These values are passed along in the same fashion as the intrinsic metrics, producing figures that compare how well the hidden layers are encoding this information:

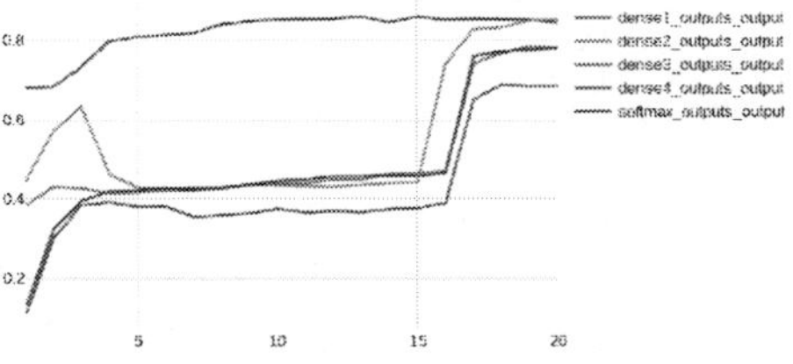

Figure 2: An example figure from the Vivisect frontend showing mutual information between clustering based on the given layer and reference labels

Figure 2 tells a simple story: for this small data set, information about the class is already captured on the surface in the shallow layers, and the model learns to preserve it as training progresses.

5   Ongoing work

Our immediate goal prior to the workshop is to employ Vivisect in training a large machine translation model with targets from several linguistic modalities not explicit in the model, at a minimum, part-of-speech and NER tagging at the word level, and topic ID at the sentence level, and present visualization and analysis.

References

Yossi Adi, Einat Kermany, Yonatan Belinkov, Ofer Lavi, and Yoav Goldberg. 2016. Fine-grained analysis of sentence embeddings using auxiliary prediction tasks. *CoRR*, abs/1608.04207.

Afra Alishahi, Marie Barking, and Grzegorz Chrupaa. 2017. Encoding of phonology in a recurrent neural model of grounded speech. *In Proceedings of the SIGNLL Conference on Computational Natural Language Learning*.

Yonatan Belinkov, Nadir Durrani, Fahim Dalvi, Hassan Sajjad, and James R. Glass. 2017. What do neural machine translation models learn about morphology? *CoRR*, abs/1704.03471.

Yonatan Belinkov and James R. Glass. 2017. Analyzing hidden representations in end-to-end automatic speech recognition systems. *CoRR*, abs/1709.04482.

Fahim Dalvi, Nadir Durrani, Hassan Sajjad, Yonatan Belinkov, and Stephan Vogel. 2017. Understanding and improving morphological learning in the neural machine translation decoder. *In Proceedings of the 8th International Joint Conference on Natural Language Processing*.

Akos Kadar, Grzegorz Chrupaa, and Afra Alishahi. 2016. Representation of linguistic form and function in recurrent neural networks. *arXiv preprint*.

Andrej Karpathy, Justin Johnson, and Fei-Fei Li. 2015. Visualizing and understanding recurrent networks. *arXiv preprint*.

Arne Kohn. 2015. Whats in an embedding? analyzing word embeddings through multilingual evaluation. *In Proceedings of the 2015 Conference on Empirical Methods in Natural Language Processing*.

Adam Poliak, Yonatan Belinkov, James R. Glass, and Benjamin Van Durme. 2018. On the evaluation of semantic phenomena in neural machine translation using natural language inference. *CoRR*, abs/1804.09779.

Peng Qian, Xipeng Qiu, , and Xuanjing Huang. 2016a. Analyzing linguistic knowledge in sequential model of sentence. *In Proceedings of the 2016 Conference on Empirical Methods in Natural Language Processing*.

Peng Qian, Xipeng Qiu, and Xuanjing Huang. 2016b. Investigating language universal and specific properties in word embeddings. *In Proceedings of the 54th Annual Meeting of the Association for Computational Linguistics*.

M. Raghu, J. Gilmer, J. Yosinski, and J. Sohl-Dickstein. 2017. SVCCA: Singular Vector Canonical Correlation Analysis for Deep Learning Dynamics and Interpretability. *ArXiv e-prints*.

TensorBoard. 2017. https://github.com/tensorflow/tensorboard.

David S. Touretzky and Dean A. Pomerleau. 1989. What's hidden in the hidden layers? *BYTE*, 14(8):227–233.

Bolei Zhou, David Bau, Aude Oliva, and Antonio Torralba. 2017. Interpreting deep visual representations via network dissection. *CoRR*, abs/1711.05611.

GLUE: A Multi-Task Benchmark and Analysis Platform for Natural Language Understanding

Alex Wang[1], Amanpreet Singh[1], Julian Michael[2], Felix Hill[3], Omer Levy[2], and Samuel R. Bowman[1]

[1]New York University, New York, NY
[2]Paul G. Allen School of Computer Science & Engineering, University of Washington, Seattle, WA
[3]DeepMind, London, UK

```
{alexwang,amanpreet,bowman}@nyu.edu
{julianjm,omerlevy}@cs.washington.edu
felixhill@google.com
```


Human ability to understand language is *general, flexible*, and *robust*. In contrast, most NLU models above the word level are designed for a specific task and struggle with out-of-domain data. If we aspire to develop models with understanding beyond the detection of superficial correspondences between inputs and outputs, then it is critical to develop a unified model that can execute a range of linguistic tasks across different domains.

To facilitate research in this direction, we present the General Language Understanding Evaluation (GLUE, gluebenchmark.com): a benchmark of nine diverse NLU tasks, an auxiliary dataset for probing models for understanding of specific linguistic phenomena, and an on-line platform for evaluating and comparing models. For some benchmark tasks, training data is plentiful, but for others it is limited or does not match the genre of the test set. GLUE thus favors models that can represent linguistic knowledge in a way that facilitates sample-efficient learning and effective knowledge-transfer across tasks. While none of the datasets in GLUE were created from scratch for the benchmark, four of them feature privately-held test data, which is used to ensure that the benchmark is used fairly.

We evaluate baselines that use ELMo (Peters et al., 2018), a powerful transfer learning technique, as well as state-of-the-art sentence representation models. The best models still achieve fairly low absolute scores. Analysis with our diagnostic dataset yields similarly weak performance over all phenomena tested, with some exceptions.

The GLUE benchmark   GLUE consists of nine English sentence understanding tasks covering a broad range of domains, data quantities, and difficulties. As the goal of GLUE is to spur development of generalizable NLU systems, we design the benchmark such that good performance should re-

Corpus	|Train|	Task	Domain
	Single-Sentence Tasks		
CoLA	8.5k	acceptability	misc.
SST-2	67k	sentiment	movie reviews
	Similarity and Paraphrase Tasks		
MRPC	3.7k	paraphrase	news
STS-B	7k	textual sim.	misc.
QQP	364k	paraphrase	online QA
	Inference Tasks		
MNLI	393k	NLI	misc.
QNLI	108k	QA/NLI	Wikipedia
RTE	2.5k	NLI	misc.
WNLI	634	coref./NLI	fiction books

Table 1: Task descriptions and statistics. **Bold** denotes tasks for which there is privately-held test data. All tasks are binary classification, except STS-B (regression) and MNLI (three classes).

quire models to share substantial knowledge (e.g., trained parameters) across tasks, while maintaining some task-specific components. Though it is possible to train a model per task and evaluate the resulting set of models on this benchmark, we expect that inclusion of several data-scarce tasks will ultimately render this approach uncompetitive.

The nine tasks include two tasks with single-sentence inputs: Corpus of Linguistic Acceptability (CoLA; Warstadt et al. 2018) and Stanford Sentiment Treebank (SST-2; Socher et al. 2013) Three tasks involve detecting semantic similarity: Microsoft Research Paraphrase Corpus (MRPC, (Dolan and Brockett, 2005)), Quora Question Pairs[1] (QQP), and Semantic Textual Similarity Benchmark (STS-B; Cer et al. 2017). The remaining four tasks are formatted as natural language inference (NLI) tasks, such as the Multi-Genre NLI corpus (MNLI; Williams et al. 2018) and Recog-

---

[1] data.quora.com/First-Quora-Dataset-Release-Question-Pairs

353

Proceedings of the 2018 EMNLP Workshop BlackboxNLP: Analyzing and Interpreting Neural Networks for NLP, pages 353–355
Brussels, Belgium, November 1, 2018. ©2018 Association for Computational Linguistics

Model	Avg	Single Sentence		Similarity and Paraphrase			Natural Language Inference			
		CoLA	SST-2	MRPC	QQP	STS-B	MNLI	QNLI	RTE	WNLI
Single-task	64.8	**35.0**	90.2	68.8/80.2	**86.5/66.1**	55.5/52.5	**76.9/76.7**	61.1	50.4	**65.1**
Multi-task	**69.0**	18.9	**91.6**	**77.3/83.5**	85.3/63.3	72.8/71.1	75.6/75.9	81.7	**61.2**	**65.1**
CBoW	58.9	0.0	80.0	73.4/81.5	79.1/51.4	61.2/58.7	56.0/56.4	75.1	54.1	62.3
Skip-Thought	61.5	0.0	81.8	71.7/80.8	82.2/56.4	71.8/69.7	62.9/62.8	74.7	53.1	**65.1**
InferSent	64.7	4.5	85.1	74.1/81.2	81.7/59.1	75.9/75.3	66.1/65.7	79.8	58.0	**65.1**
DisSent	62.1	4.9	83.7	74.1/81.7	82.6/59.5	66.1/64.8	58.7/59.1	75.2	56.4	**65.1**
GenSen	66.6	7.7	83.1	76.6/83.0	82.9/59.8	**79.3/79.2**	71.4/71.3	**82.3**	59.2	**65.1**

Table 2: Baseline performance on the GLUE tasks. For MNLI, we report accuracy on the matched and mismatched test sets. For MRPC and QQP, we report accuracy and F1. For STS-B, we report Pearson and Spearman correlation. For CoLA, we report Matthews correlation (Matthews, 1975). For all other tasks we report accuracy. All values are scaled by 100. A similar table is presented on the online platform.

nizing Textual Entailment (RTE; aggregated from Dagan et al. 2006, Bar Haim et al. 2006, Giampiccolo et al. 2007, Bentivogli et al. 2009), as well as versions of SQuAD (Rajpurkar et al., 2016) and Winograd Schema Challenge (Levesque et al., 2011) recast as NLI (resp. QNLI, WNLI). Table 1 summarizes the tasks. Performance on the benchmark is measured per task as well as in aggregate, averaging performance across tasks.

Diagnostic Dataset To understand the types of knowledge learned by models, GLUE also includes a dataset of hand-crafted examples for probing trained models. This dataset is designed to highlight common phenomena, such as the use of world knowledge, logical operators, and lexical entailments, that models must grasp if they are to robustly solve the tasks. Each of the 550 examples is an NLI sentence pair tagged with the phenomena demonstrated. We ensure that the data is reasonably diverse by producing examples for a wide variety of linguistic phenomena, and basing our examples on naturally-occurring sentences from several domains. We validate our data by using the hypothesis-only baseline from Gururangan et al. (2018) and having six NLP researchers manually validate a random sample of the data.

Baselines To demonstrate the benchmark in use, we apply multi-task learning on the training data of the GLUE tasks, via a model that shares a BiLSTM between task-specific classifiers. We also train models that use the same architecture but are trained on a single benchmark task. Finally, we evaluate the following pretrained models: average bag-of-words using GloVe embeddings (CBoW), Skip-Thought (Kiros et al., 2015), InferSent (Conneau et al., 2017), DisSent (Nie et al., 2017), and GenSen (Subramanian et al., 2018).

Tags	Sentence Pair
Quantifiers *Double Negation*	I have never seen a hummingbird not flying. I have never seen a hummingbird.
Active/Passive	Cape sparrows eat seeds, along with soft plant parts and insects. Cape sparrows are eaten.
Named Entities *World Knowledge*	Musk decided to offer up his personal Tesla roadster. Musk decided to offer up his personal car.

Table 3: Diagnostic set examples. Systems must predict the relationship between the sentences, either *entailment*, *neutral*, or *contradiction* when one sentence is the premise and the other is the hypothesis, and vice versa. Examples are tagged with the phenomena demonstrated. We group each phenomena into one of four broad categories.

We find that our models trained directly on the GLUE tasks generally outperform those that do not, though all models obtain fairy low absolute scores. Probing the baselines with the diagnostic data, we find that performance on the benchmark correlates with performance on the diagnostic data, and that the best baselines similarly achieve low absolute performance on the linguistic phenomena included in the diagnostic data.

Conclusion We present the GLUE benchmark, consisting of: (i) a suite of nine NLU tasks, built on established annotated datasets and covering a diverse range of text genres, dataset sizes, and difficulties; (ii) an online evaluation platform and leaderboard, based primarily on private test data; (iii) an expert-constructed analysis dataset. Experiments indicate that solving GLUE is beyond the capability of current transfer learning methods.

References

Roy Bar Haim, Ido Dagan, Bill Dolan, Lisa Ferro, Danilo Giampiccolo, Bernardo Magnini, and Idan Szpektor. 2006. The second PASCAL recognising textual entailment challenge.

Luisa Bentivogli, Ido Dagan, Hoa Trang Dang, Danilo Giampiccolo, and Bernardo Magnini. 2009. The fifth PASCAL recognizing textual entailment challenge.

Daniel Cer, Mona Diab, Eneko Agirre, Inigo Lopez-Gazpio, and Lucia Specia. 2017. Semeval-2017 task 1: Semantic textual similarity-multilingual and cross-lingual focused evaluation. In *11th International Workshop on Semantic Evaluations*.

Alexis Conneau, Douwe Kiela, Holger Schwenk, Loïc Barrault, and Antoine Bordes. 2017. Supervised learning of universal sentence representations from natural language inference data. In *Proceedings of the 2017 Conference on Empirical Methods in Natural Language Processing, EMNLP 2017, Copenhagen, Denmark, September 9-11, 2017*, pages 681–691.

Ido Dagan, Oren Glickman, and Bernardo Magnini. 2006. The PASCAL recognising textual entailment challenge. In *Machine learning challenges. evaluating predictive uncertainty, visual object classification, and recognising tectual entailment*, pages 177–190. Springer.

William B Dolan and Chris Brockett. 2005. Automatically constructing a corpus of sentential paraphrases. In *Proceedings of IWP*.

Danilo Giampiccolo, Bernardo Magnini, Ido Dagan, and Bill Dolan. 2007. The third PASCAL recognizing textual entailment challenge. In *Proceedings of the ACL-PASCAL workshop on textual entailment and paraphrasing*, pages 1–9. Association for Computational Linguistics.

Suchin Gururangan, Swabha Swayamdipta, Omer Levy, Roy Schwartz, Samuel R. Bowman, and Noah A. Smith. 2018. Annotation artifacts in natural language inference data. In *Proceedings of the North American Chapter of the Association for Computational Linguistics: Human Language Technologies*.

Ryan Kiros, Yukun Zhu, Ruslan R Salakhutdinov, Richard Zemel, Raquel Urtasun, Antonio Torralba, and Sanja Fidler. 2015. Skip-Thought vectors. In *Advances in neural information processing systems*, pages 3294–3302.

Hector J Levesque, Ernest Davis, and Leora Morgenstern. 2011. The Winograd schema challenge. In *Aaai spring symposium: Logical formalizations of commonsense reasoning*, volume 46, page 47.

Brian W Matthews. 1975. Comparison of the predicted and observed secondary structure of t4 phage lysozyme. *Biochimica et Biophysica Acta (BBA)-Protein Structure*, 405(2):442–451.

Allen Nie, Erin D Bennett, and Noah D Goodman. 2017. Dissent: Sentence representation learning from explicit discourse relations. *arXiv preprint 1710.04334*.

Matthew E Peters, Mark Neumann, Mohit Iyyer, Matt Gardner, Christopher Clark, Kenton Lee, and Luke Zettlemoyer. 2018. Deep contextualized word representations. In *Proceedings of NAACL 2018*.

Pranav Rajpurkar, Jian Zhang, Konstantin Lopyrev, and Percy Liang. 2016. SQuAD: 100,000+ questions for machine comprehension of text. In *Proceedings of the 2016 Conference on Empirical Methods in Natural Language Processing*, pages 2383–2392. Association for Computational Linguistics.

Richard Socher, Alex Perelygin, Jean Wu, Jason Chuang, Christopher D Manning, Andrew Ng, and Christopher Potts. 2013. Recursive deep models for semantic compositionality over a sentiment treebank. In *Proceedings of the 2013 conference on empirical methods in natural language processing*, pages 1631–1642.

Sandeep Subramanian, Adam Trischler, Yoshua Bengio, and Christopher J. Pal. 2018. Learning general purpose distributed sentence representations via large scale multi-task learning. In *Proceedings of ICLR*.

Alex Warstadt, Amanpreet Singh, and Samuel R Bowman. 2018. Neural network acceptability judgments. *arXiv preprint 1805.12471*.

Adina Williams, Nikita Nangia, and Samuel R. Bowman. 2018. A broad-coverage challenge corpus for sentence understanding through inference. In *Proceedings of NAACL 2018*.

Explicitly modeling case improves neural dependency parsing

Clara Vania and Adam Lopez
Institute for Language, Cognition and Computation
School of Informatics
University of Edinburgh
`c.vania@ed.ac.uk, alopez@inf.ed.ac.uk`

Abstract

Neural dependency parsing models that compose word representations from characters can presumably exploit morphosyntax when making attachment decisions. How much do they know about morphology? We investigate how well they handle morphological case, which is important for parsing. Our experiments on Czech, German and Russian suggest that adding explicit morphological case—either oracle or predicted—improves neural dependency parsing, indicating that the learned representations in these models do not fully encode the morphological knowledge that they need, and can still benefit from targeted forms of explicit linguistic modeling.

1 Introduction

Parsing morphologically rich languages (MRLs) is difficult due to the complex relationship of syntax to morphology. But the success of neural networks offer an appealing solution to this problem by computing word representation from characters. Character-level models (Ling et al., 2015; Kim et al., 2016) learn relationship between similar word forms and have shown to be effective for parsing MRLs (Ballesteros et al., 2015; Dozat et al., 2017; Shi et al., 2017; Björkelund et al., 2017). Does that mean that we can do away with explicit modeling of morphology altogether? Consider two challenges in parsing MRLs raised by Tsarfaty et al. (2010, 2013):

- *Can we represent words abstractly so as to reflect shared morphological aspects between them?*
- *Which types of morphological information should we include in the parsing model?*

It is tempting to hypothesize that character-level models effectively solve the first problem. For the second, Tsarfaty et al. (2010) and Seeker and Kuhn (2013) reported that morphological case is beneficial across morphologically rich languages with extensive case systems, where *case syncretism* is pervasive and often hurts parsing performance. But these studies focus on vintage parsers; do neural parsers with character-level representations also solve this second problem?

We attempt to answer this question by asking whether an explicit model of morphological case helps dependency parsing, and our results show that it does. Furthermore, a pipeline model in which we feed predicted case to the parser outperforms multi-task learning in which case prediction is an auxiliary task. These results suggest that neural dependency parsers do not adequately infer this crucial linguistic feature directly from the input text.

2 Dependency Parsing Model

We use a neural graph-based dependency parser similar to that of Kiperwasser and Goldberg (2016) and Zhang et al. (2017) for all our experiments. We treat our parser as a black box and experiment only with the input representations of the parser. Let $w = w_1, \ldots, w_{|w|}$ be an input sentence of length $|w|$ and let w_0 denote an artificial ROOT token. For each input token w_i, we compute the context-independent representation, $\mathbf{e}(w_i)$ with a bidirectional LSTM (bi-LSTM) over characters. We concatenate the result with its part-of-speech (POS) representation, $\mathbf{t}_i$: $\mathbf{x}_i = [\mathbf{e}(w_i); \mathbf{t}_i]$. We then feed $\mathbf{x}_i$ to a word-level bi-LSTM encoder to learn a contextual word representation $\mathbf{w}_i$. The model uses these representations to compute the probability $p(h_i, \ell_i \mid w, i)$ of head $h_i \in \{0, ..., |w|\}/i$ and label ℓ_i of word w_i.

3 Experiments

We experiment with three fusional languages with extensive case systems: Czech, German, and Rus-

Proceedings of the 2018 EMNLP Workshop BlackboxNLP: Analyzing and Interpreting Neural Networks for NLP, pages 356–358
Brussels, Belgium, November 1, 2018. ©2018 Association for Computational Linguistics

Language	Input	Dev	Test
Czech	word	89.9	89.3
(68.5K)	char	91.2	90.6
	char (multi-task)	91.6	91.0
	char + predicted case	**92.2**	**91.8**
	char + gold case	92.3	91.9
	char + full analysis	92.5	92.0
German	word	86.7	84.5
(14.1K)	char	87.5	84.5
	char (multi-task)	**87.9**	84.4
	char + predicted case	87.8	**86.4**
	char + gold case	90.2	86.9
	char + full analysis	89.7	86.5
Russian	word	89.5	90.1
(48.8K)	char	91.6	92.4
	char (multi-task)	92.2	92.6
	char + predicted case	**92.5**	**93.3**
	char + gold case	92.8	93.5
	char + full analysis	92.6	93.3

Table 1: Label Attachment Score (LAS) results. For each language, we show the number of training sentences.

sian; and we consider four forms of input ($\mathbf{e}(w_i)$, §2): **word** (embedding), **char**acters, characters with **gold** case, and characters with **predicted** case. For the latter two, we append the case label to the character sequence, e.g. ⟨b, a, t, Acc⟩ represents *bat* with accusative case. Using the same method, we also supply the gold **full analysis**, to tease out the importance of case specifically. Finally, we experiment with **multi-task** learning (MTL; Søgaard and Goldberg, 2016; Coavoux and Crabbé, 2017), using the bi-LSTM states of the lower layer of the bi-LSTM encoder to predict case feature. Table 1 summarizes the results.

Effect of case We found that the oracle condition of adding gold case improves the parsing performance for all languages, and indeed explains all of the gains of a full morphological analysis. In German, *case syncretism* is pervasive—a single surface form can represent multiple cases—and we see improvement of up to 2.4 LAS points on test set. This results suggest that the character-level models still struggle to disambiguate case when they learn only from the input text.

Language	%case	Dev		Test	
		PL	MT	PL	MT
Czech	66.5	95.4	**96.7**	95.2	**96.6**
German	36.2	**92.6**	92.0	90.8	**91.4**
Russian	55.8	95.8	**96.5**	95.9	**96.5**

Table 2: Case accuracy for case-annotated tokens, for pipeline (**PL**) vs. multitask (**MT**) setup. **%case** shows percentage of training tokens annotated with case.

We then look at the performance when we replace gold case with predicted case. We train a morphological tagger to predict case information. The tagger has the same structure as the parser's encoder, with an additional feedforward neural network with one hidden layer followed by a softmax layer. We found that predicted case improves accuracy, although the effect is different across languages. These results are interesting, since in vintage parsers, predicted case usually harmed accuracy (Tsarfaty et al., 2010). However, we note that our taggers use gold POS, which might help.

Pipeline model vs. Multi-task learning In general, MTL models achieve similar or slightly better performance than the character-only models, suggesting that supplying case in this way is beneficial. However, we found that using predicted case in a pipeline model gives more improvements than MTL. We also observe an interesting pattern in which MTL achieves better tagging accuracy than the pipeline model but lower performance in parsing (Table 2). This is surprising since it suggests that the MTL model must learn to effectively encode case in the model's representation, but must not effectively use it for parsing.

4 Conclusion

Vintage dependency parsers rely on hand-crafted feature engineering to encode morphology. The recent success of character-level models for many NLP tasks motivates us to ask whether their learned representations are powerful enough to completely replace this feature engineering. By empirically testing this using a single feature known to be important—morphological case—we have shown that they are not. Experiments with multi-task learning suggest that although MTL gives better performance, it is still underperformed by a traditional pipeline model.

References

Miguel Ballesteros, Chris Dyer, and Noah A. Smith. 2015. Improved transition-based parsing by modeling characters instead of words with lstms. In *Proceedings of the 2015 Conference on Empirical Methods in Natural Language Processing*, pages 349–359, Lisbon, Portugal. Association for Computational Linguistics.

Anders Björkelund, Agnieszka Falenska, Xiang Yu, and Jonas Kuhn. 2017. IMS at the CoNLL 2017 ud shared task: Crfs and perceptrons meet neural networks. In *Proceedings of the CoNLL 2017 Shared Task: Multilingual Parsing from Raw Text to Universal Dependencies*, pages 40–51, Vancouver, Canada. Association for Computational Linguistics.

Maximin Coavoux and Benoit Crabbé. 2017. Multilingual lexicalized constituency parsing with word-level auxiliary tasks. In *Proceedings of the 15th Conference of the European Chapter of the Association for Computational Linguistics: Volume 2, Short Papers*, pages 331–336. Association for Computational Linguistics.

Timothy Dozat, Peng Qi, and Christopher D. Manning. 2017. Stanford's graph-based neural dependency parser at the CoNLL 2017 shared task. In *Proceedings of the CoNLL 2017 Shared Task: Multilingual Parsing from Raw Text to Universal Dependencies*, pages 20–30, Vancouver, Canada. Association for Computational Linguistics.

Yoon Kim, Yacine Jernite, David Sontag, and Alexander Rush. 2016. Character-aware neural language models. In *Proceedings of the 2016 Conference on Artificial Intelligence (AAAI)*.

Eliyahu Kiperwasser and Yoav Goldberg. 2016. Simple and accurate dependency parsing using bidirectional lstm feature representations. *Transactions of the Association for Computational Linguistics*, 4:313–327.

Wang Ling, Chris Dyer, Alan W Black, Isabel Trancoso, Ramon Fermandez, Silvio Amir, Luis Marujo, and Tiago Luis. 2015. Finding function in form: Compositional character models for open vocabulary word representation. In *Proceedings of the 2015 Conference on Empirical Methods in Natural Language Processing*, pages 1520–1530, Lisbon, Portugal. Association for Computational Linguistics.

Wolfgang Seeker and Jonas Kuhn. 2013. Morphological and syntactic case in statistical dependency parsing. *Computational Linguistics*, 39(1):23–55.

Tianze Shi, Felix G. Wu, Xilun Chen, and Yao Cheng. 2017. Combining global models for parsing universal dependencies. In *Proceedings of the CoNLL 2017 Shared Task: Multilingual Parsing from Raw Text to Universal Dependencies*, pages 31–39, Vancouver, Canada. Association for Computational Linguistics.

Anders Søgaard and Yoav Goldberg. 2016. Deep multi-task learning with low level tasks supervised at lower layers. In *Proceedings of the 54th Annual Meeting of the Association for Computational Linguistics (Volume 2: Short Papers)*, pages 231–235. Association for Computational Linguistics.

Reut Tsarfaty, Djamé Seddah, Yoav Goldberg, Sandra Kübler, Marie Candito, Jennifer Foster, Yannick Versley, Ines Rehbein, and Lamia Tounsi. 2010. Statistical parsing of morphologically rich languages (spmrl): What, how and whither. In *Proceedings of the NAACL HLT 2010 First Workshop on Statistical Parsing of Morphologically-Rich Languages*, SPMRL '10, pages 1–12, Stroudsburg, PA, USA. Association for Computational Linguistics.

Reut Tsarfaty, Djamé Seddah, Sandra Kübler, and Joakim Nivre. 2013. Parsing morphologically rich languages: Introduction to the special issue. *Comput. Linguist.*, 39(1):15–22.

Xingxing Zhang, Jianpeng Cheng, and Mirella Lapata. 2017. Dependency parsing as head selection. In *Proceedings of the 15th Conference of the European Chapter of the Association for Computational Linguistics: Volume 1, Long Papers*, pages 665–676, Valencia, Spain. Association for Computational Linguistics.

Language Modeling Teaches You More Syntax than Translation Does: Lessons Learned Through Auxiliary Task Analysis

Kelly W. Zhang[1]
kz918@nyu.edu

Samuel R. Bowman[1,2,3]
bowman@nyu.edu

[1]Dept. of Computer Science
New York University
60 Fifth Avenue
New York, NY 10011

[2]Center for Data Science
New York University
60 Fifth Avenue
New York, NY 10011

[3]Dept. of Linguistics
New York University
10 Washington Place
New York, NY 10003

1 Introduction

Recently, researchers have found that deep LSTMs (Hochreiter and Schmidhuber, 1997) trained on tasks like machine translation learn substantial syntactic and semantic information about their input sentences, including part-of-speech (Belinkov et al., 2017a,b; Blevins et al., 2018). These findings begin to shed light on why pretrained representations, like ELMo and CoVe, are so beneficial for neural language understanding models (Peters et al., 2018; McCann et al., 2017). We still, though, do not yet have a clear understanding of how the choice of pretraining objective affects the type of linguistic information that models learn. With this in mind, we compare four objectives—language modeling, translation, skip-thought, and autoencoding—on their ability to induce syntactic and part-of-speech information, holding constant the quantity and genre of the training data, as well as the LSTM architecture.

2 Methodology

We control for the data domain by exclusively training on datasets from WMT 2016 (Bojar et al., 2016). We train models on all tasks using the parallel En-De corpus, which allows us to make fair comparisons across all tasks. We also augment the parallel data with a large monolingual corpus from WMT to examine how the performance of the unsupervised tasks scales with more data.

We analyze representations learned by language models and by the *encoders* of sequence-to-sequence models.[1] Following Belinkov et al. (2017a), after pretraining, we fix the LSTM model parameters and use the hidden states to train auxiliary classifiers on several probing tasks. We

use two syntactic evaluation tasks: part-of-speech (POS) tagging on Penn Treebank WSJ (Marcus et al., 1993) and Combinatorial Categorical Grammar (CCG) supertagging on CCG Bank (Hockenmaier and Steedman, 2007). CCG supertagging allows us to measure the degree to which models learn syntactic structure above the word. We also measure how much LSTMs simply memorize input sequences with a word identity prediction task.

3 Results

Comparing Pretraining Tasks For all pretraining dataset sizes, bidirectional language model (BiLM) and translation encoder representations outperform skip-thought and autoencoder representations on both POS and CCG tagging. Translation encoders, however, slightly underperform BiLMs, even when both models are trained on the same amount of data. Furthermore, BiLMs trained on the smallest amount of data (1 million sentences) outperform models trained on all other tasks using larger dataset sizes (5 million sentences for translation, and 63 million sentences for skip-thought and autoencoding). Especially since BiLMs do not require aligned data to train, the superior performance of BiLM representations on these tasks suggests that BiLMs (like ELMo) are better than translation encoders (like CoVe) for transfer learning of syntactic information.

Untrained Baseline Surprisingly, we find that the untrained LSTM baseline—frozen after random initialization—performs quite well on syntactic tagging tasks (a few percentage points behind BiLMs) when using all auxiliary data; however, decreasing the amount of *classifier* training data leads to a significantly greater drop in the untrained encoder performance compared to trained encoders. We hypothesize that the classifiers can recover neighboring word identity information—

---

[1]All our encoders are 2-layer, bidirectional LSTMs (500-D in each direction)—except for our large *forward* language models, which are 1000-D and unidirectional.

Proceedings of the 2018 EMNLP Workshop BlackboxNLP: Analyzing and Interpreting Neural Networks for NLP, pages 359–361
Brussels, Belgium, November 1, 2018. ©2018 Association for Computational Linguistics

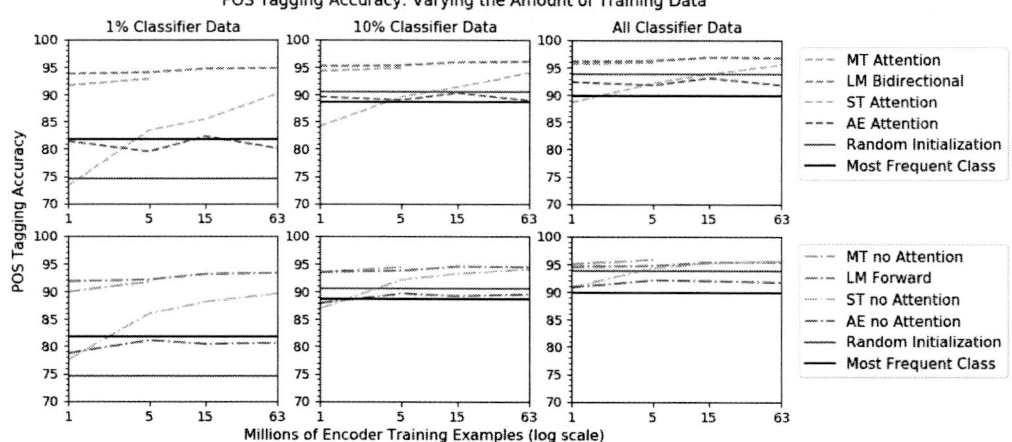

Figure 1: POS accuracies when training on different amounts of encoder and classifier data. We show results for the best performing layer of each model. The most frequent class baseline is word-conditional.

even from untrained LSTMs representations—and thus perform well on tagging tasks by memorizing word configurations and their associated tags from the training data. We test this hypothesis directly with the word identity task.

Word Identity For this task, we train classifiers to take LSTM hidden states and predict the identities of the words from different time steps. For example, for the sentence "I love NLP ." and a time step shift of -2, we would train the classifier to take the hidden state for "NLP" and predict the word "I". While trained encoders outperform untrained ones on both POS and CCG tagging, we find that all trained LSTMs *underperform* untrained ones on word identity prediction. This finding confirms that trained encoders genuinely capture substantial syntactic features, beyond mere word identity, that the auxiliary classifiers can use.

Effect of Depth Belinkov et al. (2017a) find that, for translation models, the first layer consistently outperforms the second on POS tagging. We find that this pattern holds for all our models, except BiLMs, where the first and second layers perform equivalently. This pattern occurs even in untrained models, which suggests that POS information is stored on the lower layer not necessarily because the training tasks encourage this, but due to properties of the deep LSTM architecture. For CCG supertagging though, the second layer performs better than the first in some cases (first layer performs best for untrained LSTMs). Which layer

performs best appears to be independent of absolute performance on the supertagging task.

On word identity prediction, we find that for both trained and untrained models, the first layer outperforms the second layer when predicting the identity of the *immediate* neighbors of a word. However, the second layer tends to outperform the first at predicting the identity of more distant neighboring words. As is the case for convolutional neural networks, our findings suggest that depth in recurrent neural networks has the effect of increasing the "receptive field" and allows the upper layers to have representations that capture a larger context. These results reflect the findings of Blevins et al. (2018) that for trained models, upper levels of LSTMs encode more abstract syntactic information, since more abstract information generally requires larger context information.

4 Conclusion

By controlling for the genre and quantity of the training data, we make fair comparisons between several data-rich training tasks in their ability to induce syntactic information. Our results suggest that for transfer learning, bidirectional language models like ELMo (Peters et al., 2018) capture more useful features than translation encoders— and that this holds even on genres for which data is not abundant. Our work also highlights the interesting behavior of untrained LSTMs, which show an ability to preserve the contents of their inputs better than trained models.

References

Yonatan Belinkov, Nadir Durrani, Fahim Dalvi, Hassan Sajjad, and James R. Glass. 2017a. What do Neural Machine Translation Models Learn about Morphology? *ACL*.

Yonatan Belinkov, Lluís Màrquez, Hassan Sajjad, Nadir Durrani, Fahim Dalvi, and James Glass. 2017b. Evaluating Layers of Representation in Neural Machine Translation on Part-of-Speech and Semantic Tagging Tasks. *IJCNLP*.

Terra Blevins, Omer Levy, and Luke Zettlemoyer. 2018. Deep RNNs Learn Hierarchical Syntax. *ACL*.

Ondrej Bojar, Rajen Chatterjee, Christian Federmann, Yvette Graham, Barry Haddow, Matthias Huck, Antonio Jimeno Yepes, Philipp Koehn, Varvara Logacheva, Christof Monz, Matteo Negri, Aurelie Neveol, Mariana Neves, Martin Popel, Matt Post, Raphael Rubino, Carolina Scarton, Lucia Specia, Marco Turchi, Karin Verspoor, and Marcos Zampieri. 2016. Findings of the 2016 Conference on Machine Translation (WMT16). *ACL*.

Sepp Hochreiter and Jüergen Schmidhuber. 1997. Long Short-Term Memory. *Neural Computation*, 9(8):1735–1780.

Julia Hockenmaier and Mark Steedman. 2007. CCGbank: A Corpus of CCG Derivations and Dependency Structures Extracted from the Penn Treebank. *Computational Linguistics*.

Mitchell P. Marcus, Mary Ann Marcinkiewicz, and Beatrice Santorini. 1993. Building a Large Annotated Corpus of English: The Penn Treebank. *Computational Linguistics*.

Bryan McCann, James Bradbury, Caiming Xiong, and Richard Socher. 2017. Learned in Translation: Contextualized Word Vectors. *NIPS*.

Matthew E. Peters, Mark Neumann, Mohit Iyyer, Matt Gardner, Christopher Clark, Kenton Lee, and Luke Zettlemoyer. 2018. Deep contextualized word representations. *NAACL*.

Representation of Word Meaning in the Intermediate Projection Layer of a Neural Language Model

Steven Derby[1]   Paul Miller[1]   Brian Murphy[1,2]   Barry Devereux[1]

[1] Queen's University Belfast, Belfast, United Kingdom
[2] BrainWaveBank Ltd., Belfast, United Kingdom
{sderby02, p.miller, brian.murphy, b.devereux}@qub.ac.uk

Abstract

Performance in language modelling has been significantly improved by training recurrent neural networks on large corpora. This progress has come at the cost of interpretability and an understanding of how these architectures function, making principled development of better language models more difficult. We look inside a state-of-the-art neural language model to analyse how this model represents high-level lexico-semantic information. In particular, we investigate how the model represents words by extracting activation patterns where they occur in the text, and compare these representations directly to human semantic knowledge.

1 Introduction & Related Work

Language modelling involves learning to predict the next word in a sequence of words, using large text corpora as the training input. Language models must therefore learn to represent information from the preceding context which is relevant for future word prediction, and, intuitively, this should include information about the syntactic structure of the context and the meanings of constituent words. Today's state-of-the-art language models make use of Recurrent Neural Networks (RNNs) with Long Short-Term Memory cells (LSTMs) (Hochreiter and Schmidhuber, 1997) which can handle time series information by remembering salient information over latent variables (Mikolov et al., 2010). Because of their wide applicability, there has been much interest in developing a better understanding of the inner workings of RNN models, and, in particular, researchers have investigated how syntactic knowledge is encoded and processed by such networks (Dyer et al., 2016; Linzen et al., 2016; Jozefowicz et al., 2016; McCoy et al., 2018; Gulordava et al., 2018). Karpathy et al. (2015) performed an in-depth analysis of the types of errors RNN's make, in order to understand how recurrent mechanisms can encode long-term dependency information. Linzen et al. (2016) present a more direct analysis by examining LSTM language models' ability to understand difficult long-range dependencies such as the form of a verb linked to a noun subject. Recently, researchers have started to study the semantic embeddings generated by these networks (Chrupała et al., 2015), especially for those focused on encoding visual grounding (Kiela et al., 2017; Yoo et al., 2017). However, compared to syntax, there has been relatively less work on how LSTM networks represent lexical semantic knowledge.

In this work, we evaluate latent semantic knowledge present in the LSTM activation patterns produced before and after the word of interest. We evaluate whether these activations predict human similarity ratings, human-derived property knowledge, and brain imaging data. In this way, we test the model's ability to encode important semantic information relevant to word prediction, and it's relationship with human cognitive semantic representations.

2 Language Model Data

We make use of a state-of-the-art LSTM neural language model known as lm_1b (Jozefowicz et al., 2016), which consists of two LSTM layers followed by low-dimensional projections. To construct representations from the language model's LSTM projection layer, we first select a subset of 62.5 million sentences from the One Billion Word dataset (Chelba et al., 2013). We then choose a predefined set of target words, based on the overlap of words in the lm_1b vocabulary with words used in three evaluation datasets, described in Section 3. To derive a model of the lexical representation for each of our target words using the language model, we sample 100 sentences for each word in which that word occurs, and process each of those sentences using lm_1b. More specifically, at the location in the sentence where the specific

Proceedings of the 2018 EMNLP Workshop BlackboxNLP: Analyzing and Interpreting Neural Networks for NLP, pages 362–364
Brussels, Belgium, November 1, 2018. ©2018 Association for Computational Linguistics

word of interest has just been processed, we record the 1024-dimensional projection of the activations of the first LSTM layer in the network and then average all these vectors (from 100 sentences) to get the final vector. On the assumption that the effects of context "average out" over the 100 different sampled sentences for each word, we take the average vector to be a representation of the lexical content of the concept, independent of context. Furthermore, we also build a model of lexical representation by recording the LSTM activations at the word just *before* the target word is presented to the network.

3 Experiments & Results

3.1 Comparison to Similarity Judgments

We first investigate how well similarities between our model vectors predict human similarity judgments. We use WordSim353 (Finkelstein et al., 2001) a set of 353 pairs of words along with human ratings. We split WordSim353 into semantic similarity and semantic relatedness datasets, following Agirre et al. (2009). On the hypothesis that the representations we derived from the language model reflect lexical content, we predicted that similarity, as calculated from the model, would more closely correspond to semantic similarity (i.e. shared hypernyms) than semantic relatedness. We also anticipated that correlations with human judgments would be stronger for the 'after' model than the 'before' model, since the word explicitly affects activations in the network only after it is encountered (however, the 'before' model provides an interesting test of whether lexical information can be predicted, drawing an analogy with models of human language comprehension (Kuperberg, 2016)).

For both the before and after models, correlations were stronger for the human semantic similarity ratings than for semantic relatedness, with the strongest correlation achieved for the 'after' model and similarity ratings ($r=0.30$). Furthermore, the after model more closely corresponded to the human similarities than the before model, though the before model still shows some correlation ($r=0.21$), indicating that the model may indeed encode information about upcoming concepts before they occur.

3.2 Property Knowledge Prediction

To directly investigate how the language model encodes lexico-semantic content, we analysed whether the derived lexical representations can predict human-derived properties of the same concepts. We used a dataset of human-elicited property knowledge (the CSLB norms; Devereux et al. (2014)), which lists semantic properties for concepts (e.g. *leaf* has the properties *is-green* & *grows-on-trees*). To test how well the model representations can predict these properties, we largely follow Collell and Moens (2016) and Lucy and Gauthier (2017). For each property, we train an $L2$-regularized logistic regression to predict whether that property is true for a given concept. We train two sets of logistic regression models to predict properties from the vectors in the 'before' and 'after' models. We use 5-fold cross validation with stratified sampling to ensure at least one positive case occurs in the validation fold. To get the final score of the decodability of a property for each model, we average the F1 scores over each test fold. Interestingly, semantic features were more decodable before the noun than afterwards.

3.3 Comparison to Brain Imaging Data

We compared the before and after representations from the language model to fMRI and MEG brain imaging data for 60 concepts available in Brain-Bench (Xu et al., 2016). We use the "2 vs 2" test described in Xu et al. (2016) for all pairs of concepts to measure the correspondence between the models and the brain data. The 'before' and 'after' models perform similarly, though (somewhat surprisingly) the before model performs slightly better on fMRI data than the after model. However, both models perform above chance, indicating that these models are correlated with brain representations of the same nouns.

4 Conclusions

Our results suggest that LSTM language models not only encode probabilistic syntactic knowledge but also represent the semantic content of words in a way which is at least somewhat consistent with measures of human conceptual knowledge. Language models' ability to predict human property knowledge allows us to draw initial comparisons between these models and activation (and pre-activation) of lexical information in human language comprehension.

Acknowledgements

This work was partly funded by a Microsoft Azure for Research Award.

References

Eneko Agirre, Enrique Alfonseca, Keith Hall, Jana Kravalova, Marius Paşca, and Aitor Soroa. 2009. A study on similarity and relatedness using distributional and wordnet-based approaches. In *Proceedings of Human Language Technologies: The 2009 Annual Conference of the North American Chapter of the Association for Computational Linguistics*, pages 19–27. Association for Computational Linguistics.

Ciprian Chelba, Tomas Mikolov, Mike Schuster, Qi Ge, Thorsten Brants, Phillipp Koehn, and Tony Robinson. 2013. One billion word benchmark for measuring progress in statistical language modeling. *arXiv preprint arXiv:1312.3005*.

Grzegorz Chrupała, Akos Kádár, and Afra Alishahi. 2015. Learning language through pictures. *arXiv preprint arXiv:1506.03694*.

Guillem Collell and Marie-Francine Moens. 2016. Is an image worth more than a thousand words? on the fine-grain semantic differences between visual and linguistic representations. In *Proceedings of COLING 2016, the 26th International Conference on Computational Linguistics: Technical Papers*, pages 2807–2817. The COLING 2016 Organizing Committee.

Barry J Devereux, Lorraine K Tyler, Jeroen Geertzen, and Billi Randall. 2014. The centre for speech, language and the brain (cslb) concept property norms. *Behavior research methods*, 46(4):1119–1127.

Chris Dyer, Adhiguna Kuncoro, Miguel Ballesteros, and Noah A Smith. 2016. Recurrent neural network grammars. *arXiv preprint arXiv:1602.07776*.

Lev Finkelstein, Evgeniy Gabrilovich, Yossi Matias, Ehud Rivlin, Zach Solan, Gadi Wolfman, and Eytan Ruppin. 2001. Placing search in context: The concept revisited. In *Proceedings of the 10th international conference on World Wide Web*, pages 406–414. ACM.

Kristina Gulordava, Piotr Bojanowski, Edouard Grave, Tal Linzen, and Marco Baroni. 2018. Colorless green recurrent networks dream hierarchically. In *Proceedings of the 2018 Conference of the North American Chapter of the Association for Computational Linguistics: Human Language Technologies, Volume 1 (Long Papers)*, pages 1195–1205. Association for Computational Linguistics.

Sepp Hochreiter and Jürgen Schmidhuber. 1997. Long short-term memory. *Neural computation*, 9(8):1735–1780.

Rafal Jozefowicz, Oriol Vinyals, Mike Schuster, Noam Shazeer, and Yonghui Wu. 2016. Exploring the limits of language modeling. *arXiv preprint arXiv:1602.02410*.

Andrej Karpathy, Justin Johnson, and Li Fei-Fei. 2015. Visualizing and understanding recurrent networks. *arXiv preprint arXiv:1506.02078*.

Douwe Kiela, Alexis Conneau, Allan Jabri, and Maximilian Nickel. 2017. Learning visually grounded sentence representations. *arXiv preprint arXiv:1707.06320*.

& Jaeger T. F. Kuperberg, G. R. 2016. What do we mean by prediction in language comprehension? *anguage, Cognition and Neuroscience*, 31(1):32–59.

Tal Linzen, Emmanuel Dupoux, and Yoav Goldberg. 2016. Assessing the ability of lstms to learn syntax-sensitive dependencies. *arXiv preprint arXiv:1611.01368*.

Li Lucy and Jon Gauthier. 2017. Are distributional representations ready for the real world? evaluating word vectors for grounded perceptual meaning. *arXiv preprint arXiv:1705.11168*.

R. Thomas McCoy, Robert Frank, and Tal Linzen. 2018. Revisiting the poverty of the stimulus: hierarchical generalization without a hierarchical bias in recurrent neural networks. In *Proceedings of the 40th Annual Conference of the Cognitive Science Society*.

Tomáš Mikolov, Martin Karafiát, Lukáš Burget, Jan Černocký, and Sanjeev Khudanpur. 2010. Recurrent neural network based language model. In *Eleventh Annual Conference of the International Speech Communication Association*.

Haoyan Xu, Brian Murphy, and Alona Fyshe. 2016. Brainbench: A brain-image test suite for distributional semantic models. In *Proceedings of the 2016 Conference on Empirical Methods in Natural Language Processing*, pages 2017–2021.

Kang Min Yoo, Youhyun Shin, and Sang-goo Lee. 2017. Improving visually grounded sentence representations with self-attention. *arXiv preprint arXiv:1712.00609*.

Interpretable Structure Induction Via Sparse Attention

Ben Peters[†]   **Vlad Niculae**[†] and **André F.T. Martins**[†‡]
[†]Instituto de Telecomunicações, Lisbon, Portugal
[‡]Unbabel, Lisbon, Portugal
benzurdopeters@gmail.com, vlad@vene.ro, andre.martins@unbabel.com.

1   Introduction

Neural network methods are experiencing wide adoption in NLP, thanks to their empirical performance on many tasks.   Modern neural architectures go way beyond simple feedforward and recurrent models: they are complex pipelines that perform soft, differentiable computation instead of discrete logic. Inspired by pioneering work by, e.g. Kohonen et al. (1981); Das et al. (1992); Schmidhuber (1992), such modern differentiable architectures include neural memories (Sukhbaatar et al., 2015) and attention mechanisms (Bahdanau et al., 2015). The price of such soft computing is the introduction of dense dependencies, which make it hard to disentangle the patterns that trigger a prediction. Our recent work on **sparse** and **structured** latent computation (Martins and Astudillo, 2016; Niculae and Blondel, 2017; Niculae et al., 2018; Malaviya et al., 2018) presents a promising avenue for enhancing interpretability of such neural pipelines. Through this extended abstract, we aim to discuss and explore the potential and impact of our methods.

The principle of *parsimony* suggests that simpler explanations are more plausible and interpretable.   Our perspective is similar to prior work on regularizing model weights (Hastie et al., 2015), but with a twist: instead of model sparsity that tells us which "static" groups of variables are relevant for a task, we now have a "dynamic" form of sparsity that tells us, for a particular input object, where we should attend to produce a decision.

- **sparsity**: shrinking probabilities to zero to prune entire parts of the input when explaining a prediction (Martins and Astudillo, 2016);

- **regularization**: injecting prior assumptions, such as that neighbouring words should be fused together (Niculae and Blondel, 2017);

- **constraints**: constraining probabilities within lower and upper bounds, to prevent words from receiving too much or too little attention (Malaviya et al., 2018);

- **structure**: learning latent structure predictors (e.g. aligners or parsers), to induce a **compact representation** as a small, interpretable set of global structures (Niculae et al., 2018).

2   Attention Mechanisms

The key background for our work is the concept of attention.   Attention mechanisms and memory networks are able to "point" to relevant items (e.g. words or pixels) that determine the final prediction, approximating a discrete choice (argmax) with a soft, differentiable one (softmax). Let $\mathbf{H} = [\boldsymbol{h}_1, \ldots, \boldsymbol{h}_L] \in \mathbb{R}^{D \times L}$ be a matrix whose columns are vectors encoding the L different choices (for example, words in a sentence). An attention mechanism maps a $\mathbf{H}$ and a control state $\boldsymbol{s}$ to a probability distribution $\boldsymbol{p} \in \triangle^L$ over the L choices.[1] This can be split into (i) generating **scores** for each choice, e.g., $z_i = \boldsymbol{v}^\top \tanh(\mathbf{W}\boldsymbol{h}_i + \mathbf{U}\boldsymbol{s})$ for $i \in \{1, \ldots, L\}$ and (ii) mapping the scores to a probability distribution. Common attention uses (Bahdanau et al., 2015; Luong et al., 2015) $\boldsymbol{p} = \mathsf{softmax}(\boldsymbol{z})$, i.e., $p_i = \exp(z_i)/\sum_j \exp(z_j)$. Since $\mathsf{softmax}$ is strictly positive, this leads to dense probability distributions. However, putting nonzero weight on every choice is not ideal for interpretability (Fig. 1, center); instead, we explore sparse selection, identifying a small set of choices responsible for a prediction. Niculae and Blondel (2017) proposed the general family

$$\Pi_\Omega(\boldsymbol{z}) = \operatorname*{argmax}_{\boldsymbol{p} \in \triangle^L} \boldsymbol{z}^\top \boldsymbol{p} - \Omega(\boldsymbol{p}), \qquad (1)$$

recovering $\mathsf{softmax}$ for $\Omega(\boldsymbol{p}) = -\sum_j p_j \log p_j$.

---

[1]We denote by $\triangle^L = \{\boldsymbol{p} \in \mathbb{R}^L \mid \sum_{i=1}^L p_i = 1, p_i \geq 0, \forall i\}$ the $(L-1)$-dimensional probability simplex.

Proceedings of the 2018 EMNLP Workshop BlackboxNLP: Analyzing and Interpreting Neural Networks for NLP, pages 365–367
Brussels, Belgium, November 1, 2018. ©2018 Association for Computational Linguistics

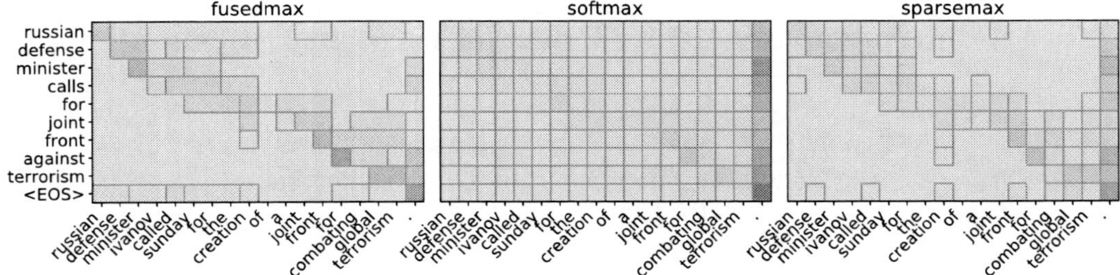

Figure 1: Attention weights for a sequence-to-sequence sentence compression instance. Traditional softmax attention (middle) yields dense weights, which are less interpretable than the sparse weights from sparsemax (right) or fusedmax (left); the latter further enhances interpretability by clustering probabilities of adjacent words. Image courtesy of Niculae and Blondel (2017).

Sparse attention. Martins and Astudillo (2016) proposed sparsemax, which replaces softmax with a Euclidean projection, remaining differentiable while also yielding sparse probabilities. This can be obtained by setting $\Omega = \frac{1}{2}\|\cdot\|_2^2$ in Eqn 1. The resulting probabilities are substantially more interpretable, as the contribution of irrelevant words is now shrunk to **exactly 0** (Fig. 1, right).

Regularized attention. Parsimony goes beyond sparsity: prior assumptions may encourage selecting groups or clusters with equal probability. Niculae and Blondel (2017) propose two linguistically-motivated regularized attention mechanisms: **fusedmax**, which tends to *group adjacent words together*, and **oscarmax**, which may *cluster non-adjacent words*, suitable for languages with flexible word order. Such mechanisms can select interpretable segments (Fig. 1, left).

Constrained attention. Some forms of parsimony must be strictly enforced using constraints, rather than simply encouraged via regularization. One such constraint is to add an upper bound to the cumulative attention an input variable may receive. This can be done using **constrained softmax** (Martins and Kreutzer, 2017) or its sparse analogue, **constrained sparsemax** (Malaviya et al., 2018). Constraining attention weights can be interpreted as specifying the *fertility* (Brown et al., 1993) of the alignments between the source and target, in machine translation.

3 Structured Attention

In this section, we consider *combinatorial* representations. Across application domains, but especially in NLP, many objects of interest can be represented by such structures: syntactic and dependency trees, sequential labellings, alignments.

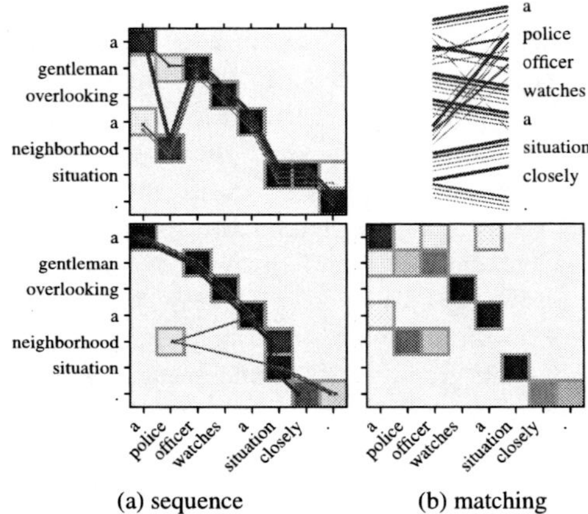

Figure 2: Structured alignment on SNLI (Niculae et al., 2018). The premise is on the y-axis, the hypothesis on the x-axis. Sequential alignment encourages monotonic alignments, matching induces a single symmetrical alignment.

Allowing hidden layers to output structured representations can be valuable for modelling perspective but also for interpretability: discrete structures provide organized representations, in contrast to unstructured vectors of neuron activations.

SparseMAP (Niculae et al., 2018) allows handling discrete structures within end-to-end differentiable neural networks, able to automatically select only a few global structures. On natural language inference, for a word-to-word alignment joint attention mechanism, SparseMAP can induce structured alignments as illustrated in Fig. 2.

4 Conclusion

Building upon the principle of parsimony, we propose sparse, regularized, constrained and structured hidden layers. We seek to discuss the potentials of these strategies with an expert community on black-box interpretability.

Acknowledgments

This work was supported by the European Research Council (ERC StG DeepSPIN 758969) and by the Fundação para a Ciência e Tecnologia through contract UID/EEA/50008/2013.

References

Dzmitry Bahdanau, Kyunghyun Cho, and Yoshua Bengio. 2015. Neural machine translation by jointly learning to align and translate. In *Proc. of ICLR*.

Peter F Brown, Vincent J Della Pietra, Stephen A Della Pietra, and Robert L Mercer. 1993. The mathematics of statistical machine translation: Parameter estimation. *Computational Linguistics*, 19(2):263–311.

Sreerupa Das, C Lee Giles, and Guo-Zheng Sun. 1992. Learning context-free grammars: Capabilities and limitations of a recurrent neural network with an external stack memory. In *Proceedings of The Fourteenth Annual Conference of Cognitive Science Society. Indiana University*, page 14.

Trevor Hastie, Robert Tibshirani, and Martin Wainwright. 2015. *Statistical Learning with Sparsity: The Lasso and Generalizations*. Chapman & Hall/CRC.

Teuvo Kohonen, Erkki Oja, and Pekka Lehtio. 1981. Storage and processing of information in distributed associative memory systems. *Parallel Models of Associative Memory*, pages 129–167.

Thang Luong, Hieu Pham, and Christopher D Manning. 2015. Effective approaches to attention-based neural machine translation. In *Proc. of EMNLP*.

Chaitanya Malaviya, Pedro Ferreira, and André F. T. Martins. 2018. Sparse and constrained attention for neural machine translation. In *Proc. of ACL*.

André F. T. Martins and Ramón Astudillo. 2016. From softmax to sparsemax: A sparse model of attention and multi-label classification. In *Proc. of ICML*.

André FT Martins and Julia Kreutzer. 2017. Learning what's easy: Fully differentiable neural easy-first taggers. In *Proc. of EMNLP*, pages 349–362.

Vlad Niculae and Mathieu Blondel. 2017. A regularized framework for sparse and structured neural attention. In *Proc. of NIPS*.

Vlad Niculae, André F. T. Martins, Mathieu Blondel, and Claire Cardie. 2018. SparseMAP: Differentiable sparse structured inference. In *Proc. of ICML*.

Jürgen Schmidhuber. 1992. Learning to control fast-weight memories: An alternative to dynamic recurrent networks. *Neural Computation*, 4(1):131–139.

Sainbayar Sukhbaatar, Arthur Szlam, Jason Weston, and Rob Fergus. 2015. End-to-end memory networks. In *Proc. of NIPS*.

Debugging Sequence-to-Sequence Models with SEQ2SEQ-VIS

Hendrik Strobelt*
IBM Research,
MIT-IBM AI Lab
hendrik@strobelt.com

Sebastian Gehrmann*
Harvard SEAS
gehrmann@seas.harvard.edu

Michael Behrisch
Harvard SEAS
behrisch@g.harvard.edu

Adam Perer
IBM Research
adam.perer@us.ibm.com

Hanspeter Pfister
Harvard SEAS
pfister@g.harvard.edu

Alexander M. Rush
Harvard SEAS
srush@seas.harvard.edu

1 Introduction

Neural attention-based sequence-to-sequence models (seq2seq) (Sutskever et al., 2014; Bahdanau et al., 2014) have proven to be accurate and robust for many sequence prediction tasks. They have become the standard approach for automatic translation of text, at the cost of increased model complexity and uncertainty. End-to-end trained neural models act as a black box, which makes it difficult to examine model decisions and attribute errors to a specific part of a model. The highly connected and high-dimensional internal representations pose a challenge for analysis and visualization tools. The development of methods to understand seq2seq predictions is crucial for systems in production settings, as mistakes involving language are often very apparent to human readers. For instance, a widely publicized incident resulted from a translation system mistakenly translating "good morning" into "attack them" leading to a wrongful arrest (Hern, 2017).

In this work, we present the visual analysis tool SEQ2SEQ-VIS that allows interaction and "what if"-style exploration of trained seq2seq models through each stage of the translation process. The aim is to identify which patterns have been learned, to detect errors within a model, and to understand the model through counterfactual scenarios. In order to investigate the origin of an error within a seq2seq model, we separate errors within each translation stage into the following categories: (1) representation errors, in which an *encoder* or *decoder* misrepresent a word within a given context (2) alignment errors, in which the *attention* focuses on the wrong word, and (3) decoding errors, in which the *prediction* assigns a wrong probability distribution over words, or the *beam search* fails to include the correct solution.

We define three steps within an analysis that aim to understand the prediction process, understand how an output relates to training data, and examine causal relationships between inputs and outputs.

Examine Model Outputs: SEQ2SEQ-VIS shows a separate visual representation for the output of each stage of the seq2seq pipeline.

Connect Outputs to Samples: SEQ2SEQ-VIS connects the encoder and decoder of a seq2seq model to relevant training examples by showing a neighborhood of examples with the most similar internal states.

Test Alternative Decisions: SEQ2SEQ-VIS enables "what if" explorations and causal relationship testing by manipulation of inputs, attention, and outputs.

The full system is shown in Figure 1. It combines visualizations for the external components with internal representations from specific examples and nearest-neighbor lookups over a corpus of precomputed examples. The entire system integrates with OpenNMT (Klein et al., 2017), one of the largest open source seq2seq libraries.

2 Debugging Use Case

This case study follows the example in Figure 1 and involves a model trainer (Strobelt et al., 2018b) who is building a German-to-English translation model on the IWSLT '14 dataset (Mauro et al., 2012)). The user observes that a specific example was mistranslated. She finds the source sentence: *Die längsten Reisen fangen an, wenn es auf den Straßen dunkel wird.* The correct translation for this sentence is *The longest journeys begin, when it gets dark in the streets.* The model produces the mistranslation: *The longest journey begins, when it gets to the streets.* SEQ2SEQ-VIS shows the tokenized input sentence in blue and the corresponding translation of the model in yellow (on the top). The user observes that the model does not translate the word *dunkel* into *dark.* This mistake exemplifies several goals that motivated the development of

Proceedings of the 2018 EMNLP Workshop BlackboxNLP: Analyzing and Interpreting Neural Networks for NLP, pages 368–370
Brussels, Belgium, November 1, 2018. ©2018 Association for Computational Linguistics

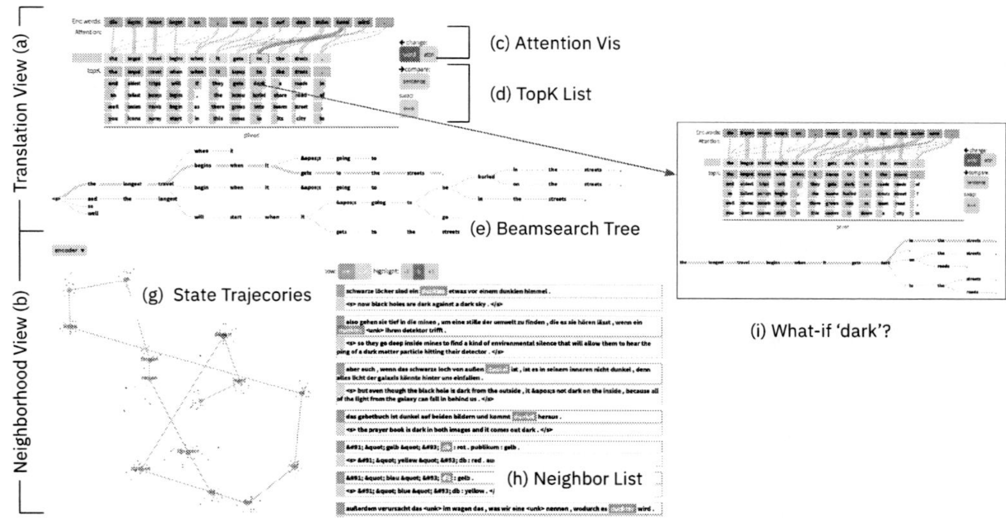

Figure 1: Seq2Seq-Vis tool. See `http://seq2seq-vis.io` for interactive demo and video.

`Seq2Seq-Vis`. The user would like to examine the system's decisions, connect to training examples, and test possible changes:

Nearest neighbors to examine encoder and decoder: `Seq2Seq-Vis` lets the user examine similar encoder/decoder states for any example. We define *neighborhood* as the twenty training examples with the closest states in vector space. SEQ2SEQ-VIS displays the neighborhood for a specific encoder state in a list of training set examples with red highlights for the word with the closest state. Figure 1(h) shows that the nearest neighbors for *dunkel* match similar use of the word from training data. Overall, the encoder seems to perform well in this case. A similar analysis can be done for the decoder.

Graphical test for Attention error: Another possible issue is that the attention may not focus on the corresponding source token *dunkel*. The previous test revealed many examples in the neighborhood that place *dark* after *gets*, which matches the valid translation. In Figure 1(c) the analyst can observe that the highlighted connection following *get* to the correct next word *dunkel* is very strong. Therefore, the user can assume that the attention is well set for predicting *dark* in this position.

What-if testing for Prediction and Search error: The combination of decoder state and attention is used to compute the probability over possible next words. It may be that an error occurs in this decision, leading to a poor probability of the word *dark*. The tool shows the most likely next words and their probabilities in Figure 1(d). Here, the model mistakenly assigns a higher probability to *to* than *dark*. However, both options are very close in probability, indicating that the model is almost equally split between the two choices. These local mistakes should be automatically fixed by the beam search, which is shown in Figure 1(e). In this case, the analyst finds that *dark* is never considered within the search. The analyst has identified a search error, where the approximations made by beam search cut off the better global option in favor of better local choices. To investigate whether the model would produce the correct answer the analyst can test a counterfactual, what would have happened if she had forced the translation to use *dark* at this critical position? By clicking on *dark* she can produce this probe (shown in Figure 1(i)), which yields the correct translation.

3 Conclusion

We have shown SEQ2SEQ-VIS, an interactive tool for finding errors in seq2seq models. It utilizes approaches to debugging in which black-box decisions are connected to easily understandable visual presentations. In future work, we will extend this work to improve models based on feedback from SEQ2SEQ-VIS. A longer description of the system, and additional use-cases can be found in Strobelt et al. (2018a).

References

Dzmitry Bahdanau, Kyunghyun Cho, and Yoshua Bengio. 2014. Neural machine translation by jointly learning to align and translate. *arXiv preprint arXiv:1409.0473*.

Alex Hern. 2017. Facebook translates 'good morning' into 'attack them', leading to arrest. *The Guardian*.

Guillaume Klein, Yoon Kim, Yuntian Deng, Jean Senellart, and Alexander Rush. 2017. Opennmt: Open-source toolkit for neural machine translation. *Proceedings of ACL 2017, System Demonstrations*, pages 67–72.

Cettolo Mauro, Girardi Christian, and Federico Marcello. 2012. Wit3: Web inventory of transcribed and translated talks. In *Conference of European Association for Machine Translation*, pages 261–268.

Hendrik Strobelt, Sebastian Gehrmann, Michael Behrisch, Adam Perer, Hanspeter Pfister, and Alexander M Rush. 2018a. Seq2seq-vis: A visual debugging tool for sequence-to-sequence models. *arXiv preprint arXiv:1804.09299*.

Hendrik Strobelt, Sebastian Gehrmann, Hanspeter Pfister, and Alexander M Rush. 2018b. Lstmvis: A tool for visual analysis of hidden state dynamics in recurrent neural networks. *IEEE transactions on visualization and computer graphics*, 24(1):667–676.

Ilya Sutskever, Oriol Vinyals, and Quoc V Le. 2014. Sequence to sequence learning with neural networks. In *Advances in neural information processing systems*, pages 3104–3112.

Grammar Induction with Neural Language Models: An Unusual Replication

Phu Mon Htut[1]
pmh330@nyu.edu

Kyunghyun Cho[1,2]
kyunghyun.cho@nyu.edu

Samuel R. Bowman[1,2,3]
bowman@nyu.edu

[1]Center for Data Science
New York University
60 Fifth Avenue
New York, NY 10011

[2]Dept. of Computer Science
New York University
60 Fifth Avenue
New York, NY 10011

[3]Dept. of Linguistics
New York University
10 Washington Place
New York, NY 10003

1 Introduction

Grammar induction is the task of learning syntactic structure without the expert-labeled treebanks (Charniak and Carroll, 1992; Klein and Manning, 2002). Recent work on *latent tree learning* offers a new family of approaches to this problem by inducing syntactic structure using the supervision from a downstream NLP task (Yogatama et al., 2017; Maillard et al., 2017; Choi et al., 2018). In a recent paper published at ICLR, Shen et al. (2018) introduce such a model and report near state-of-the-art results on the target task of language modeling, and the first strong latent tree learning result on constituency parsing. During the analysis of this model, we discover issues that make the original results hard to trust, including tuning and even training on what is effectively the test set. Here, we analyze the model under different configurations to understand what it learns and to identify the conditions under which it succeeds. We find that this model represents the first empirical success for neural network latent tree learning, and that neural language modeling warrants further study as a setting for grammar induction.

2 Background and Experiments

We analyze the **Parsing-Reading-Predict-Network** (PRPN; Shen et al., 2018), which uses convolutional networks with a form of structured attention (Kim et al., 2017) rather than recursive neural networks (Goller and Kuchler, 1996; Socher et al., 2011) to learn trees while performing straightforward backpropagation training on a language modeling objective. The structure of the model seems rather suboptimal: Since the parser is trained as part of a language model, it makes parsing greedily, with *no* access to any words to the right of the point where each parsing decision must be made.

The experiments on language modeling and

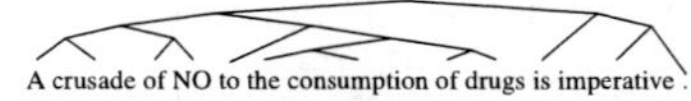

Figure 1: Parses from PRPN-LM trained on AllNLI.

parsing are carried out using different configurations of the model—PRPN-LM tuned for language modeling, and PRPN-UP for (unsupervised) parsing. PRPN-LM is much larger than PRPN-UP, with embedding layer that is 4 times larger and the number of units per layer that is 3 times larger. In the PRPN-UP experiments, we observe that the WSJ data is not split, such that the test data is used without parse information for training. This implies that the parsing results of PRPN-UP may not be generalizable in the way usually expected of machine learning evaluation results.

We train PRPN on sentences from two datasets: The full WSJ and AllNLI, the concatenation of SNLI (Bowman et al., 2015) and MultiNLI (Williams et al., 2018b). We then evaluate the constituency trees produced by these models on the full WSJ, WSJ10[1], and the MultiNLI development set.

3 Results

Table 1 shows results with all the models under study, plus several baselines, on WSJ and WSJ10. Unexpectedly, the PRPN-LM models achieve *higher* parsing performance than PRPN-UP. This shows that any tuning done to separate PRPN-UP from PRPN-LM was not necessary, and that the results described in the paper can be largely reproduced by a unified model in a fair setting. Moreover, the PRPN models trained on the larger, out-of-domain AllNLI perform better than those trained on WSJ. Surprisingly, PRPN-LM tained on out-of-domain AllNLI achieves the best F1 score on full WSJ among all the models

---

[1]A processed subset of WSJ in which the sentences contain no punctuation and no more than 10 words.

Proceedings of the 2018 EMNLP Workshop BlackboxNLP: Analyzing and Interpreting Neural Networks for NLP, pages 371–373
Brussels, Belgium, November 1, 2018. ©2018 Association for Computational Linguistics

Model	Training Data	Stopping Criterion	Vocab Size	Parsing F1				Depth WSJ	Accuracy on WSJ by Tag				
				WSJ10		WSJ			ADJP	NP	PP	INTJ	
				$\mu\,(\sigma)$	max	$\mu\,(\sigma)$	max						
PRPN-UP	AllNLI Train	UP	76k	67.5 (0.6)	68.6	38.1 (0.7)	39.1	5.9	27.8	63.0	31.4	52.9	
PRPN-UP	AllNLI Train	LM	76k	66.3 (0.8)	68.5	39.8 (0.6)	40.7	5.9	26.5	53.0	32.9	52.9	
PRPN-LM	AllNLI Train	LM	76k	52.4 (4.9)	58.1	42.5 (0.7)	**<u>43.6</u>**	6.2	**<u>34.2</u>**	60.1	**<u>60.0</u>**	**<u>64.7</u>**	
PRPN-UP	WSJ Full	UP	15.8k	64.7 (3.2)	70.9	26.6 (1.9)	31.6	5.9	19.3	48.7	19.2	44.1	
PRPN-UP	WSJ Full	LM	15.8k	64.3 (3.3)	70.8	26.5 (1.9)	31.4	5.9	18.8	48.1	19.1	44.1	
PRPN-UP	WSJ Train	UP	15.8k	63.5 (3.5)	70.7	26.6 (2.5)	34.2	5.9	21.3	57.2	19.4	47.1	
PRPN-UP	WSJ Train	LM	15.8k	62.2 (3.9)	70.3	26.4 (2.5)	34.0	5.9	22.3	56.2	19.1	44.1	
PRPN-LM	WSJ Train	LM	10k	70.5 (0.4)	<u>71.3</u>	38.3 (0.3)	38.9	5.9	26.0	**64.4**	25.5	50.0	
PRPN-LM	WSJ Train	UP	10k	66.1 (0.5)	67.2	34.0 (0.9)	36.3	5.9	32.0	58.3	19.6	44.1	
300D ST-Gumbel	AllNLI Train	NLI	–	–	–	*19.0 (1.0)*	*20.1*	–	*15.6*	*18.8*	*9.9*	59.4	
w/o Leaf GRU	AllNLI Train	NLI	–	–	–	*22.8 (1.6)*	*25.0*	–	18.9	24.1	*14.2*	51.8	
300D RL-SPINN	AllNLI Train	NLI	–	–	–	*13.2 (0.0)*	*13.2*	–	*1.7*	*10.8*	*4.6*	50.6	
w/o Leaf GRU	AllNLI Train	NLI	–	–	–	*13.1 (0.1)*	*13.2*	–	*1.6*	*10.9*	*4.6*	50.0	
CCM	WSJ10 Train	–	–	–	71.9	–	–	–	–	–	–	–	
DMV+CCM	WSJ10 Train	–	–	–	77.6	–	–	–	–	–	–	–	
UML-DOP	WSJ10 Train	–	–	–	**82.9**	–	–	–	–	–	–	–	
Random Trees	–	–	–	–	34.7	21.3 (0.0)	21.4	5.3	17.4	22.3	16.0	40.4	
Balanced Trees	–	–	–	–	–	21.3 (0.0)	21.3	4.6	22.1	20.2	*9.3*	55.9	

Table 1: Unlabeled parsing F1 test results broken down by training data and by early stopping criterion. The *Accuracy* columns represent the fraction of ground truth constituents of a given type that correspond to constituents in the model parses. Italics mark results that are worse than the random baseline. Results with RL-SPINN and ST-Gumbel are from Williams et al. (2018a). WSJ10 baselines are from Klein and Manning (2002, CCM), Klein and Manning (2005, DMV+CCM), and Bod (2006, UML-DOP).

Model	Stopping Criterion	F1 wrt.			Depth
		LB	RB	SP	
300D SPINN	NLI	19.3	36.9	70.2	6.2
w/o Leaf GRU	NLI	21.2	39.0	63.5	6.4
300D SPINN-NC	NLI	19.2	36.2	70.5	6.1
w/o Leaf GRU	NLI	20.6	38.9	64.1	6.3
300D ST-Gumbel	NLI	32.6	37.5	23.7	4.1
w/o Leaf GRU	NLI	30.8	35.6	27.5	4.6
300D RL-SPINN	NLI	95.0	13.5	18.8	8.6
w/o Leaf GRU	NLI	99.1	10.7	18.1	8.6
PRPN-LM	LM	25.6	26.9	45.7	4.9
PRPN-UP	UP	19.4	41.0	46.3	4.9
PRPN-UP	LM	19.9	37.4	**48.6**	4.9
Random Trees	–	27.9	28.0	27.0	4.4
Balanced Trees	–	21.7	36.8	21.3	3.9

Table 2: Unlabeled parsing F1 on the MultiNLI development set for models trained on AllNLI. *F1 wrt.* shows F1 with respect to strictly right- and left-branching (LB/RB) trees and with respect to the Stanford Parser (SP) trees supplied with the corpus; The evaluations of SPINN, RL-SPINN, and ST-Gumbel are from Williams et al. (2018a). SPINN is a supervised parsing model, and the others are latent tree models.

we experimented, even though its performance on WSJ10 is the lowest of all. Under all the configurations we tested, PRPN yields much better performance than that seen with the baselines from Yogatama et al. (2017, called RL-SPINN) and Choi et al. (2018, called ST-Gumbel), despite the fact that the model was tuned exclusively for WSJ10 parsing (Table 1 and 2). This suggests that PRPN is strikingly effective at latent tree learning.

Additionally, Table 2 shows that both PRPN-UP models achieve F1 scores of 46.3 and 48.6 respectively on the MultiNLI dev set, setting the state of the art in parsing on this dataset among latent tree models. We conclude that PRPN does acquire some substantial knowledge of syntax, and that this knowledge agrees with Penn Treebank (PTB) grammar significantly better than chance.

Moreover, we replicate the language modeling perplexity of 61.6 reported in the paper using PRPN-LM trained on WSJ, which indicates that PRPN-LM is effective at both parsing and language modeling.

4 Conclusion

In our analysis of the PRPN model, we find several experimental problems that make the results difficult to interpret. However, in the analyses going well beyond the scope of the original paper, we find that PRPN is nonetheless robust. It represents a viable method for grammar induction and the first success for latent tree learning. We expect that it heralds further work on language modeling as a tool for grammar induction research.

References

Rens Bod. 2006. An All-Subtrees Approach to Unsupervised Parsing. *Proceedings of the 21st International Conference on Computational Linguistics and the 44th annual meeting of the Association for Computational Linguistics*, pages 865–872.

Samuel R. Bowman, Gabor Angeli, Christopher Potts, and Christopher D. Manning. 2015. A large annotated corpus for learning natural language inference. In *Proceedings of the Conference on Empirical Methods in Natural Language Processing (EMNLP)*. Association for Computational Linguistics.

Eugene Charniak and Glen Carroll. 1992. Two experiments on learning probabilistic dependency grammars from corpora. In *Proceedings of the AAAI Workshop on Statistically-Based NLP Techniques*, page 113.

Jihun Choi, Kang Min Yoo, and Sang-goo Lee. 2018. Learning to compose task-specific tree structures. In *Proceedings of the Thirty-Second Association for the Advancement of Artificial Intelligence Conference on Artificial Intelligence (AAAI-18)*, volume 2.

Christoph Goller and Andreas Kuchler. 1996. Learning task-dependent distributed representations by backpropagation through structure. In *Proceedings of International Conference on Neural Networks (ICNN'96)*.

Yoon Kim, Carl Denton, Luong Hoang, and Alexander M. Rush. 2017. Structured attention networks.

Dan Klein and Christopher D. Manning. 2002. A generative constituent-context model for improved grammar induction. In *Proceedings of the 40th Annual Meeting on Association for Computational Linguistics - ACL '02*, page 128.

Dan Klein and Christopher D. Manning. 2005. Natural language grammar induction with a generative constituent-context model. *Pattern Recognition*, 38(9):1407–1419.

Jean Maillard, Stephen Clark, and Dani Yogatama. 2017. Jointly learning sentence embeddings and syntax with unsupervised Tree-LSTMs. arXiv preprint 1705.09189.

Yikang Shen, Zhouhan Lin, Chin wei Huang, and Aaron Courville. 2018. Neural language modeling by jointly learning syntax and lexicon. In *International Conference on Learning Representations*.

Richard Socher, Cliff Chiung-Yu Lin, Andrew Ng, and Chris Manning. 2011. Parsing Natural Scenes and Natural Language with Recursive Neural Networks. In *Proceedings of the 28th International Conference on Machine Learning*, pages 129–136.

Adina Williams, Andrew Drozdov, and Samuel R. Bowman. 2018a. Do latent tree learning models identify meaningful structure in sentences? *Transactions of the Association for Computational Linguistics (TACL)*.

Adina Williams, Nikita Nangia, and Samuel R. Bowman. 2018b. A broad-coverage challenge corpus for sentence understanding through inference. In *Proceedings of the North American Chapter of the Association for Computational Linguistics (NAACL)*.

Dani Yogatama, Phil Blunsom, Chris Dyer, Edward Grefenstette, and Wang Ling. 2017. Learning to Compose Words into Setences with Reinforcement Learning. *Proceedings of the International Conference on Learning Representations*, pages 1–17.

Does Syntactic Knowledge in Multilingual Language Models Transfer Across Languages?

Prajit Dhar   **Arianna Bisazza**
Leiden Institute of Advanced Computer Science
Leiden University, The Netherlands
`{p.dhar,a.bisazza}@liacs.leidenuniv.nl`

Abstract

Recent work has shown that neural models can be successfully trained on multiple languages simultaneously. We investigate whether such models learn to share and exploit common syntactic knowledge among the languages on which they are trained. This extended abstract presents our preliminary results.

1 Introduction

Recent work has shown that state-of-the-art neural models of language and translation can be successfully trained on multiple languages simultaneously without changing the model architecture (Östling and Tiedemann, 2017; Johnson et al., 2017). In some cases this leads to improved performance compared to models only trained on a specific language, suggesting that multilingual models learn to share useful knowledge cross-lingually through their learned representations. While a large body of research exists on the multilingual mind, the mechanisms explaining knowledge sharing in computational multilingual models remain largely unknown: What kind of knowledge is shared among languages? Do multilingual models mostly benefit from a better modeling of lexical entries or do they also learn to share more abstract linguistic categories?

We focus on the case of language models (LM) trained on two languages, one of which (L1) is over-resourced with respect to the other (L2), and investigate whether the *syntactic* knowledge learned for L1 is transferred to L2. To this end we use the long-distance agreement benchmark recently introduced by Gulordava et al. (2018).

2 Background

The recent advances in neural networks have opened the way to the design of architecturally simple multilingual models for various NLP tasks, such as language modeling or next word prediction (Tsvetkov et al., 2016; Östling and Tiedemann, 2017; Malaviya et al., 2017; Tiedemann, 2018), translation (Dong et al., 2015; Zoph et al., 2016; Firat et al., 2016; Johnson et al., 2017), morphological reinflection (Kann et al., 2017) and more (Bjerva, 2017). A practical benefit of training models multilingually is to transfer knowledge from high-resource languages to low-resource ones and improve task performance in the latter. Here we aim at understanding *how* linguistic knowledge is transferred among languages, specifically at the syntactic level, which to our knowledge has not been studied so far.

Assessing the syntactic abilities of monolingual neural LMs trained without explicit supervision has been the focus of several recent studies: Linzen et al. (2016) analyzed the performance of LSTM LMs at an English subject-verb agreement task, while Gulordava et al. (2018) extended the analysis to various long-range agreement patterns in different languages. The latter study found that state-of-the-art LMs trained on a standard log-likelihood objective capture non-trivial patterns of syntactic agreement and can approach the performance levels of humans, even when tested on syntactically well-formed but meaningless (*nonce*) sentences.

Cross-language interaction during language production and comprehension by *human* subjects has been widely studied in the fields of bilingualism and second language acquisition (Kellerman and Sharwood Smith; Odlin, 1989; Jarvis and Pavlenko, 2008) under the terms of *language transfer* or *cross-linguistic influence*. Numerous studies have shown that both the lexicons and the grammars of different languages are not stored independently but together in the mind of bilinguals and second-language learners, leading to observ-

Proceedings of the 2018 EMNLP Workshop BlackboxNLP: Analyzing and Interpreting Neural Networks for NLP, pages 374–377
Brussels, Belgium, November 1, 2018. ©2018 Association for Computational Linguistics

able lexical and syntactic transfer effects (Kootstra et al., 2012). For instance, through a cross-lingual syntactic priming experiment, Hartsuiker et al. (2004) showed that bilinguals recently exposed to a given syntactic construction (passive voice) in their L1 tend to reuse the same construction in their L2.

While the neural networks in this study are not designed to be plausible models of the human mind learning and processing multiple languages, we believe there is interesting potential at the intersection of these research fields.

3 Experiment

We consider the scenario where L1 is over-resourced compared to L2 and train our bilingual models by *joint training* on a mixed L1/L2 corpus so that supervision is provided simultaneously in the two languages (Östling and Tiedemann, 2017; Johnson et al., 2017). We leave the evaluation of pre-training (or transfer learning) methods (Zoph et al., 2016; Nguyen and Chiang, 2017) to future work.

The monolingual LM is trained on a small L2 corpus (LM_{L2}). The bilingual LM is trained on a shuffled mix of the same small L2 corpus and a large L1 corpus, where L2 is oversampled to approximately match the amount of L1 sentences (LM_{L1+L2}). See Table 1 for the actual training sizes. For our preliminary experiments we have chosen French as the helper language (L1) and Italian as the target language (L2). Since French and Italian share many morphosyntactic patterns, accuracy on the Italian agreement tasks is expected to benefit from adding French sentences to the training data *if* syntactic transfer occurs.

Data and training details: We train our LMs on French and Italian Wikipedia articles extracted using the WikiExtractor tool.[1] For each language, we maintain a vocabulary of the 50k most frequent tokens, and replace the remaining tokens by <unk>. For the bilingual LM, all words are prepended with a language tag so that vocabularies are completely disjoint. Their union (100K types) is used to train the model. This is the least optimistic scenario for linguistic transfer but also the most controlled one. In future experiments we plan to study how transfer is affected by varying degrees of vocabulary overlap.

Following the setup of Gulordava et al. (2018), we train 2-layer LSTM models with embedding and hidden layers of 650 dimensions for 40 epochs. The trained models are evaluated on the Italian section of the syntactic benchmark provided by Gulordava et al. (2018), which includes various non-trivial number agreement constructions.[2] Note that all models are trained on a regular corpus likelihood objective and do not receive any specific supervision for the syntactic tasks.

4 Results and Conclusions

Table 1 shows the results of our preliminary experiments. The unigram baseline simply picks, for each sentence, the most frequent word form between singular or plural. As an upper-bound we report the agreement accuracy obtained by a monolingual model trained on a large L2 corpus.

Table 1: Accuracy on the Italian agreement set by the unigram baseline, monolingual and bilingual LMs.

Model	Training (#tok)	Agreement$_{IT}$ Orig.	Nonce
Unigram	—	54.9	54.5
$LSTM_{IT}$	$10M_{IT}$	80.7	79.9
$LSTM_{FR+IT}$	$80M_{FR} + 8 \times 10M_{IT}$	82.4	77.5
$LSTM_{IT}$ (large)	$80M_{IT}$	88.2	82.6

The effect of mixing the small Italian corpus with the large French one does not appear to be major. Agreement accuracy increases slightly in the original sentences, where the model is free to rely on collocational cues, but decreases slightly in the nonce sentences, where the model must rely on pure grammatical knowledge. Thus there is currently no evidence that syntactic transfer occurs in our setup. A possible explanation is that the bilingual model has to fit the knowledge from two language systems into the same number of hidden layer parameters and this may cancel out the benefits of being exposed to a more diverse set of sentences. In fact, the bilingual model achieves a considerably worse perplexity than the monolingual one (69.9 vs 55.62) on an Italian-only held-out set. For comparison, Östling and Tiedemann (2017) observed slightly better perplexities when mixing a small number of related languages, however

---

[1]https://github.com/attardi/
wikiextractor

[2]For more details on the benchmark and LM configurations refer to https://github.com/
facebookresearch/colorlessgreenRNNs

their setup was considerably different (character-level LSTM with highly overlapping vocabulary).

This is work in progress. We are currently looking for a bilingual LM configuration that will result in better target language perplexity and, possibly, better agreement accuracy. We also plan to extend the evaluation to other, less related, language pairs and different multilingual training techniques. Finally, we plan to examine whether lexical syntactic categories (POS) are represented in a shared space among the two languages.

Acknowledgments

This research was partly funded by the Netherlands Organization for Scientific Research (NWO) under project number 639.021.646. The experiments were conducted on the DAS computing system (Bal et al., 2016).

References

Henri Bal, Dick Epema, Cees de Laat, Rob van Nieuwpoort, John Romein, Frank Seinstra, Cees Snoek, and Harry Wijshoff. 2016. A medium-scale distributed system for computer science research: Infrastructure for the long term. *Computer*, 49(5):54–63.

Johannes Bjerva. 2017. One model to rule them all: Multitask and multilingual modelling for lexical analysis. *CoRR*, abs/1711.01100.

Daxiang Dong, Hua Wu, Wei He, Dianhai Yu, and Haifeng Wang. 2015. Multi-task learning for multiple language translation. In *Proceedings of the 53rd Annual Meeting of the Association for Computational Linguistics and the 7th International Joint Conference on Natural Language Processing (Volume 1: Long Papers)*, pages 1723–1732, Beijing, China. Association for Computational Linguistics.

Orhan Firat, Kyunghyun Cho, and Yoshua Bengio. 2016. Multi-way, multilingual neural machine translation with a shared attention mechanism. In *Proceedings of the 2016 Conference of the North American Chapter of the Association for Computational Linguistics: Human Language Technologies*, pages 866–875, San Diego, California. Association for Computational Linguistics.

Kristina Gulordava, Piotr Bojanowski, Edouard Grave, Tal Linzen, and Marco Baroni. 2018. Colorless green recurrent networks dream hierarchically. In *Proceedings of the 2018 Conference of the North American Chapter of the Association for Computational Linguistics: Human Language Technologies, Volume 1 (Long Papers)*, pages 1195–1205. Association for Computational Linguistics.

Robert J. Hartsuiker, Martin J. Pickering, and Eline Veltkamp. 2004. Is syntax separate or shared between languages?: Cross-linguistic syntactic priming in spanish-english bilinguals. *Psychological Science*, 15(6):409–414.

Scott Jarvis and Anna Pavlenko. 2008. *Crosslinguistic influence in language and cognition*. Routledge.

Melvin Johnson, Mike Schuster, Quoc Le, Maxim Krikun, Yonghui Wu, Zhifeng Chen, Nikhil Thorat, Fernand a Vigas, Martin Wattenberg, Greg Corrado, Macduff Hughes, and Jeffrey Dean. 2017. Google's multilingual neural machine translation system: Enabling zero-shot translation. *Transactions of the Association for Computational Linguistics*, 5:339–351.

Katharina Kann, Ryan Cotterell, and Hinrich Schütze. 2017. One-shot neural cross-lingual transfer for paradigm completion. In *Proceedings of the 55th Annual Meeting of the Association for Computational Linguistics (Volume 1: Long Papers)*, pages 1993–2003, Vancouver, Canada. Association for Computational Linguistics.

Eric Kellerman and ed. Sharwood Smith, Michael. *Crosslinguistic influence in second language acquisition*. Pergamon.

Gerrit Jan Kootstra, Janet G. Van Hell, and Ton Dijkstra. 2012. Priming of code-switches in sentences: The role of lexical repetition, cognates, and language proficiency. *Bilingualism: Language and Cognition*, 15(4):797819.

Tal Linzen, Emmanuel Dupoux, and Yoav Goldberg. 2016. Assessing the ability of lstms to learn syntax-sensitive dependencies. *Transactions of the Association for Computational Linguistics*, 4:521–535.

Chaitanya Malaviya, Graham Neubig, and Patrick Littell. 2017. Learning language representations for typology prediction. In *Proceedings of the 2017 Conference on Empirical Methods in Natural Language Processing*, pages 2529–2535. Association for Computational Linguistics.

Toan Q. Nguyen and David Chiang. 2017. Transfer learning across low-resource, related languages for neural machine translation. In *Proceedings of the Eighth International Joint Conference on Natural Language Processing (Volume 2: Short Papers)*, pages 296–301, Taipei, Taiwan. Asian Federation of Natural Language Processing.

Terence Odlin. 1989. *Language Transfer: Cross-Linguistic Influence in Language Learning*. Cambridge Applied Linguistics. Cambridge University Press.

Robert Östling and Jörg Tiedemann. 2017. Continuous multilinguality with language vectors. In *Proceedings of the 15th Conference of the European Chapter of the Association for Computational Linguistics: Volume 2, Short Papers*, pages 644–649, Valencia, Spain. Association for Computational Linguistics.

Jörg Tiedemann. 2018. Emerging language spaces learned from massively multilingual corpora. *CoRR*, abs/1802.00273.

Yulia Tsvetkov, Sunayana Sitaram, Manaal Faruqui, Guillaume Lample, Patrick Littell, David Mortensen, Alan W Black, Lori Levin, and Chris Dyer. 2016. Polyglot neural language models: A case study in cross-lingual phonetic representation learning. In *Proceedings of the 2016 Conference of the North American Chapter of the Association for Computational Linguistics: Human Language Technologies*, pages 1357–1366, San Diego, California. Association for Computational Linguistics.

Barret Zoph, Deniz Yuret, Jonathan May, and Kevin Knight. 2016. Transfer learning for low-resource neural machine translation. In *Proceedings of the 2016 Conference on Empirical Methods in Natural Language Processing*, pages 1568–1575, Austin, Texas. Association for Computational Linguistics.

Exploiting Attention to Reveal Shortcomings in Memory Models

Kaylee Burns
UC Berkeley
kayleeburns@berkeley.edu

Aida Nematzadeh
DeepMind
nematzadeh@google.com

Erin Grant
UC Berkeley
eringrant@berkeley.edu

Alison Gopnik
UC Berkeley
gopnik@berkeley.edu

Thomas L. Griffiths
Princeton University
tomg@princeton.edu

Abstract

The decision making processes of deep networks are difficult to understand and while their accuracy often improves with increased architectural complexity, so too does their opacity. Practical use of machine learning models, especially for question and answering applications, demands a system that is interpretable. We analyze the attention of a memory network model to reconcile contradictory performance on a challenging question-answering dataset that is inspired by theory-of-mind experiments. We equate success on questions to task classification, which explains not only test-time failures but also how well the model generalizes to new training conditions.

1 Reasoning about Beliefs

Possessing a capacity similar to human reasoning has been argued to be necessary for the success of artificial intelligence systems (*e.g.*, Levesque et al., 2011). One well-studied domain that requires reasoning is question answering, where simply memorizing and looking up information is often not enough to correctly answer a question.

Recent research has focused on developing neural models that succeed in such scenarios (Sukhbaatar et al., 2015; Henaff et al., 2017). As a benchmark to evaluate these models, Weston et al. (2016) released a dataset – Facebook bAbi – that provides a set of toy tasks, each examining a specific type of reasoning. However, the bAbi tasks are already too simple for the current models, which fail at only one or two (out of 20) tasks (Rae et al., 2016; Santoro et al., 2017).

Considering humans' reasoning abilities can provide inspiration for more complex tasks. People reason not just about their own observations and beliefs but also about others' mental states (such as beliefs and intentions). The capacity to recognize that others can have mental states different than one's own – *theory of mind* – marks an important milestone in the development of children and has been extensively studied by psychologists (for a review, see Flavell, 2004). Recently, Nematzadeh et al. (2018) released a dataset inspired by the theory-of-mind experiments from Baron-Cohen et al. (1985). The dataset is based on three tasks designed to capture increasingly complex theory-of-mind reasoning: *true-*, *false-*, and *second-order false-belief* tasks. Examples of each task type are given in Figure 1. In the true-belief task, Sally observes the world and as a result she has a first-order *true-belief* about the location of the milk – her belief matches reality. In the false-belief task, Sally's first-order belief differs from reality (*i.e.*, she has a *false-belief*) because she was absent when the state of the world changed. In the second-order false-belief task, Sally observes the new location of the milk; thus, she has a *true-belief* about the milk's location. However, Anne's belief about Sally's mental state does not match reality because Anne does not know that Sally has observed the change in the environment. As a result, Anne has a *false belief* about Sally's beliefs.

The dataset from Nematzadeh et al. (2018) contains 4 question types: 2 related to world state and 2 related to beliefs (Table 1). These questions enable us to test whether a model can reason about first-order and second-order beliefs and know the initial and current location of an object; thus, we can distinguish between when a model answers a question by chance and when it actually understands the entire state of the world. Table 2 gives the answers for the 12 combinations of task type and question. Our analysis will focus on the two belief questions proposed.

We use these tasks to generate a training set with 10 000 examples with each of the 12 combinations of task and question types, randomly

Proceedings of the 2018 EMNLP Workshop BlackboxNLP: Analyzing and Interpreting Neural Networks for NLP, pages 378–380
Brussels, Belgium, November 1, 2018. ©2018 Association for Computational Linguistics

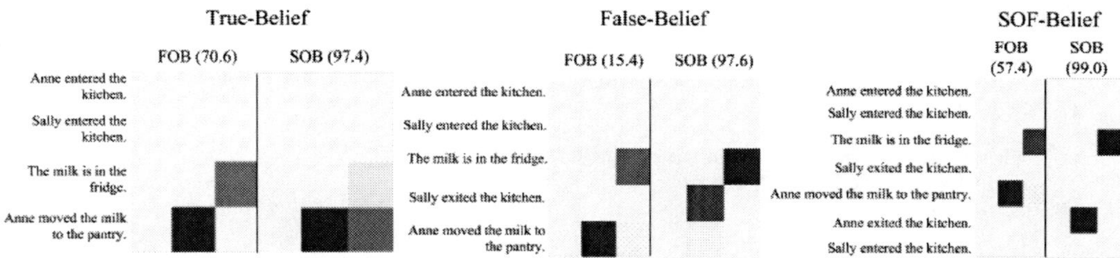

Figure 1: The attention of MemN2N in response to first-order (all left) and second-order (all right) belief questions. To correctly answer the second order belief question, the model needs to identify the true belief task from other tasks (see Table 2). To this end, the model can use the presence of "exit" to classify true-belief from non-true-belief tasks. There is no analogous identifier for the first-order question, where the model fails.

Memory	Where was the milk at the beginning?
Reality	Where is the milk really?
First-order	Where will Sally look for the milk?
Second-order	Where does Sally think that Anne searches for the milk?

Table 1: Examples of the four question types.

	True Belief	False Belief	Second-Order FB
Memory	first	first	first
Reality	second	second	second
First-order	second	first	second
Second-order	second	first	first

Table 2: The correct answer to each question. Here, "first" and "second" are the the initial and actual locations of the object of interest.

grouped into sets of 5 to form stories. Each story in the test set contains 4 tasks, but there is only one question present at the end. Because questions that come closer to the beginning of a story have fewer distractors (*i.e.*, potential answer words) that may confound a model, they are easier to answer.

2 Experiments

We train MemN2N (Sukhbaatar et al., 2015) jointly over all task types without noise, but evaluate success on a test set with noise sentences generated randomly at different positions (*i.e. ToM* (noised)). We first examine how the model performs across a range of parameter and initialization values. Because MemN2N models are very sensitive to the network initialization, for each set of parameters, the best result out of 10 runs is used for each configuration of hyperparameters. To understand why failures occur, we plot the average attention over all instances of each task-question combination. Figure 1 shows the average attention of the best performing 3-hop model on the first-order (left) and second-order (right) belief tasks. Only the attention over memory slots with relevant

story sentences is displayed.

Surprisingly, the model is successful on the "harder" second-order belief question but not on the first-order one. Indeed, the pattern of attention across hops in response to the second-order belief question is more varied across task conditions and attends to sentences that provide information about agents' transition in the world (*i.e.*, "Sally exited the kitchen"). On the other hand, the left hand side of the figure shows that, in response to the first-order belief question, the attention is not sensitive to the task type (*i.e.*, true-, false- or second-order- belief).

Considering each belief question as a task classification, as shown in Table 2, can explain this result. The answer to the first-order question is different for false-belief and second-order false-belief tasks while it is the same for the second-order question. Given the similarity of these 2 tasks (*e.g.*, Sally moves between rooms in both tasks, both contain the word "exited"), the "classification" problem is much easier when the two questions have the same answer. To answer the first-order question correctly – where the answers are different for the false-belief and second-order false-belief tasks – the model needs to learn to distinguish between between these very similar tasks.

To further test this hypothesis, we created an inaccurate version of the *ToM* dataset where the answer to the false belief question was modified to be the second location of the object as opposed to the first. With the difficulty of classifying false-belief from second-order false belief tasks removed, the models were able to successfully answer all of the first order belief questions.

References

Simon Baron-Cohen, Alan M Leslie, and Uta Frith. 1985. Does the autistic child have a theory of mind? *Cognition*, 21(1):37–46.

John H Flavell. 2004. Theory-of-mind development: Retrospect and prospect. *Merrill-Palmer Quarterly*, 50(3):274–290.

Mikael Henaff, Jason Weston, Arthur Szlam, Antoine Bordes, and Yann LeCun. 2017. Tracking the world state with recurrent entity networks. In *International Conference on Learning Representations*.

Hector J Levesque, Ernest Davis, and Leora Morgenstern. 2011. The winograd schema challenge. In *AAAI Spring Symposium: Logical Formalizations of Commonsense Reasoning*, volume 46, page 47.

Aida Nematzadeh, Kaylee Burns, Erin Grant, Alison Gopnik, and Thomas L. Griffiths. 2018. Evaluating theory of mind in question answering. In *Conference on Empirical Methods in Natural Language Processing*, volume abs/1604.06045.

Jack W. Rae, Jonathan J. Hunt, Tim Harley, Ivo Danihelka, Andrew W. Senior, Greg Wayne, Alex Graves, and Timothy P. Lillicrap. 2016. Scaling memory-augmented neural networks with sparse reads and writes. In *Proceedings of 30th Conference on Neural Information Processing Systems*.

Adam Santoro, David Raposo, David G. T. Barrett, Mateusz Malinowski, Razvan Pascanu, Peter Battaglia, and Timothy P. Lillicrap. 2017. A simple neural network module for relational reasoning. In *International Conference on Learning Representations*.

Sainbayar Sukhbaatar, Jason Weston, Rob Fergus, et al. 2015. End-to-end memory networks. In *Proceedings of 29th Conference on Neural Information Processing Systems*, pages 2440–2448.

Jason Weston, Antoine Bordes, Sumit Chopra, and Tomas Mikolov. 2016. Towards AI-complete question answering: A set of prerequisite toy tasks. In *International Conference on Learning Representations*.

End-to-end Image Captioning Exploits Distributional Similarity in Multimodal Space *

Pranava Madhyastha   **Josiah Wang**   **Lucia Specia**

Department of Computer Science
University of Sheffield
{p.madhyastha,j.k.wang,l.specia}@sheffield.ac.uk

Image description generation, or image captioning (IC), is the task of automatically generating a textual description for a given image. The generated text is expected to describe, generally in a single sentence, what is visually depicted in the image, for example the entities/objects present in the image, their attributes, the actions/activities performed, entity/object interactions (including quantification), the location/scene, etc. (e.g. *"a man riding a bike on the street"*). Significant progress has been made with *end-to-end* approaches to tackling this problem, where parallel image–description datasets such as Flickr30k (Young et al., 2014) and MSCOCO (Chen et al., 2015) are used to train a CNN-RNN based neural network IC system (Vinyals et al., 2017; Karpathy and Fei-Fei, 2015; Xu et al., 2015). Such systems have demonstrated impressive performance in the COCO captioning challenge[1] according to automatic metrics, seemingly even surpassing human performance in many instances (e.g. CIDEr score > 1.0 vs. human's 0.85) (Chen et al., 2015). However, in reality, the performance of end-to-end systems is still far from satisfactory according to metrics based on human judgement[2]. This task is thus currently far from being a solved problem.

We challenge the common assumption that end-to-end IC systems are able to achieve strong performance because they have learned to 'understand' and infer semantic information from visual representations, i.e. they can for example induce that *"a boy is playing football"* by learning directly from mid-level image features and the corresponding textual descriptions in an implicit manner, without explicitly modeling the presence of

boy, ball, green field, etc. in the image. It is believed that IC models have managed to infer that the phrase *football* is associated with some 'green-like' area in the image and is thus generated in the output description, or that the word *boy* is generated because of some CNN activations corresponding to a young person. However, there seems to be no concrete evidence that this is the case. Instead, we hypothesize that the apparent strong performance of end-to-end systems is attributed to the fact that they exploit the *distributional similarity* in the multimodal feature space. To our best knowledge, our work is the first to provide empirical analysis of visual representations for the task of image captioning.

By 'distributional similarity' we mean that IC models essentially attempt to match images from the training set that are most similar to a test image, and generate a caption from the most similar training instances, or generate a 'novel' description from a combination of training instances, for example by 'averaging' the descriptions.

Previous work has alluded to this fact (Karpathy, 2016; Vinyals et al., 2017), but it has not been thoroughly investigated. This phenomenon could also be in part attributed to the fact that the datasets are repetitive and simplistic, with a virtually constant and predictable linguistic structure (Lebret et al., 2015; Devlin et al., 2015; Vinyals et al., 2017).

We empirically evaluate end-to-end IC systems where we vary the input image representation but keep the RNN text generation model constant. Our experiment demonstrates that regardless of the image representation (a continuous image embedding or a sparse, low-dimensional vector), end-to-end IC systems seem to utilize a visual-semantic subspace for IC. We also analyze various types of image representations and their transformed versions.

---

*This is an abridged version of a recently published BMVC paper (Madhyastha et al., 2018)

[1] http://cocodataset.org/
#captions-challenge2015

[2] http://cocodataset.org/
#captions-leaderboard

Proceedings of the 2018 EMNLP Workshop BlackboxNLP: Analyzing and Interpreting Neural Networks for NLP, pages 381–383
Brussels, Belgium, November 1, 2018. ©2018 Association for Computational Linguistics

We visualize the initial visual subspace and the learned joint visual semantic subspace and observe that the visual semantic subspace has learned to cluster images with similar visual and linguistic information together, further validating our claims of distributional similarity[3].

	Representation	B-4	M	C	S
	Random	0.07	0.11	0.07	0.03
Softmax	VGG19	0.19	0.20	0.61	0.13
	ResNet152	0.19	0.20	0.62	0.12
Penultimate	VGG19 (fc7)	0.22	0.21	0.69	0.14
	ResNet152 (pool5)	0.23	0.22	0.74	0.15
Embeddings	Top-k	0.19	0.20	0.63	0.13
BOO	Gold-Binary	0.22	0.22	0.75	0.15
	Gold-Counts	0.23	0.22	0.81	0.16
	YOLO-Coco	0.22	0.22	0.75	0.15
	YOLO-9k	0.21	0.20	0.68	0.13
Pseudo-random	Pseudorandom-Binary	0.21	0.21	0.73	0.14
	Pseudorandom-Counts	0.23	0.22	0.80	0.15

Table 1: Results on the MSCOCO test split, where we vary only the image representation and keep other parameters constant. The captions are generated with $beam = 1$. We report **BLEU** (BLEU-4), **Meteor**, **CIDEr** and **SPICE** scores.

We tabulate our observations from our experiments in Table 1 where we used standard end-to-end IC model (Vinyals et al., 2017) which is conditioned on the various image representations. We observe that utilizing standard bottleneck representations (penultimate) are slightly better than using the ImageNet class posteriors (softmax). However, we observe that better captions are obtained by using representations from explicit object detections.

We also introduce *pseudo-random vectors* which are derived from object-level representations as a control to evaluate IC systems. The pseudo-random representation is obtained using the object type information, but without actual object features. More specifically, $I_{pseudo} =$

---

[3]Our visualization and analysis can be found here:
`https://github.com/sheffieldnlp/whatIC`

Method	B-1	B-2	B-3	B-4	M	C	S
PCA	0.66	0.48	0.34	0.24	0.22	0.75	0.15
ICA	0.66	0.48	0.34	0.24	0.22	0.74	0.15
PPCA	0.66	0.48	0.34	0.24	0.22	0.76	0.15
FULL	0.66	0.48	0.33	0.23	0.22	0.74	0.15

Table 2: Performance of compressed Pool5 representations.

$\sum_{o \in \text{Objects}} f \times \phi_o$, where $\phi_o \in \mathcal{R}^d$ is an object-specific random vector and f is a scalar representing counts of the object category. Our results in Table 1 show that the models that utilize pseudo-random representations are able to perform competitively. The models in the current setup are remarkably capable of separating structure from noisy input. We further visualized the initial and projected representations in the setup and observed that while the initial pseudo-random representations were noisy, the projected ones closely resembled the bag-of-objects representations.

We then perform experiments where IC models are conditioned on image representations *factorized and compressed to a lower dimensional space*. We experimented with three exploratory factor analysis based methods – Principal Component Analysis (PCA) (Halko et al., 2011), Probabilistic Principal Component Analysis (PPCA) (Tipping and Bishop, 1999) and Independent Component Analysis (ICA) (Hyvärinen et al., 2004). In all cases, we obtain 80-dimensional factorized representations on *ResNet152 pool5* (2048D) that is commonly used in IC. We summarize this experiment in Table 2. We observe that the representations obtained by all the factor models seem to retain the necessary representational power to produce appropriate captions equivalent to the original representation. This seems contradictory as we expected a loss in the information content when compressing it to arbitrary 80-dimensions. We observe that high dimensional image embeddings that are factorized to a lower dimensional representation and used as input to an IC model result in virtually no loss in performance, further strengthening our claim that IC models only perform similarity matching rather than image understanding. We conclude that the model is able to learn from a seemingly weak, structured information and is able to result in a performance that is close to that of a model that uses the full representation.

The observations above strengthen our distributional similarity hypothesis – that end-to-end IC performs image matching and generates captions for a test image from similar image(s) from the training set – rather than performing actual image understanding. Our findings provide novel insights into what end-to-end IC systems are actually doing, which previous work only suggests or hints at.

References

Xinlei Chen, Hao Fang, Tsung-Yi Lin, Ramakrishna Vedantam, Saurabh Gupta, Piotr Dollár, and C. Lawrence Zitnick. 2015. Microsoft COCO captions: Data collection and evaluation server. *arXiv preprint arXiv:1504.00325*.

Jacob Devlin, Hao Cheng, Hao Fang, Saurabh Gupta, Li Deng, Xiaodong He, Geoffrey Zweig, and Margaret Mitchell. 2015. Language models for image captioning: The quirks and what works. In *Proceedings of the Association for Computational Linguistics (ACL)*, pages 100–105.

Nathan Halko, Per-Gunnar Martinsson, Yoel Shkolnisky, and Mark Tygert. 2011. An algorithm for the principal component analysis of large data sets. *SIAM Journal on Scientific computing*, 33(5):2580–2594.

Aapo Hyvärinen, Juha Karhunen, and Erkki Oja. 2004. *Independent component analysis*, volume 46. John Wiley & Sons.

Andrej Karpathy. 2016. *Connecting Images and Natural Language*. Ph.D. thesis, Department of Computer Science, Stanford University.

Andrej Karpathy and Li Fei-Fei. 2015. Deep visual-semantic alignments for generating image descriptions. In *Proceedings of the IEEE Conference on Computer Vision & Pattern Recognition (CVPR)*, pages 3128–3137.

Remi Lebret, Pedro Pinheiro, and Ronan Collobert. 2015. Phrase-based image captioning. In *Proceedings of the International Conference on Machine Learning (ICML)*, pages 2085–2094.

Pranava Madhyastha, Josiah Wang, and Lucia Specia. 2018. End-to-end image captioning exploits distributional similarity in multimodal space. In *Proceedings of the British Machine Vision Conference (BMVC)*.

Michael E Tipping and Christopher M Bishop. 1999. Probabilistic principal component analysis. *Journal of the Royal Statistical Society*, 61(3):611–622.

Oriol Vinyals, Alexander Toshev, Samy Bengio, and Dumitru Erhan. 2017. Show and tell: Lessons learned from the 2015 MSCOCO image captioning challenge. *IEEE Transactions on Pattern Analysis and Machine Intelligence*, 39(4):652–663.

Kelvin Xu, Jimmy Ba, Ryan Kiros, Kyunghyun Cho, Aaron C Courville, Ruslan Salakhutdinov, Richard S Zemel, and Yoshua Bengio. 2015. Show, attend and tell: Neural image caption generation with visual attention. In *Proceedings of the International Conference on Machine Learning (ICML)*, volume 14, pages 77–81.

Peter Young, Alice Lai, Micah Hodosh, and Julia Hockenmaier. 2014. From image descriptions to visual denotations: New similarity metrics for semantic inference over event descriptions. *Transactions of the Association for Computational Linguistics*, 2:67–78.

Limitations in learning an interpreted language with recurrent models

Denis Paperno

Loria, Centre national de la recherche scientifique (CNRS)

Campus Scientifique, BP 239, 54506 Vandoeuvre-lès-Nancy, France

paperno@ucla.edu

Abstract

In this submission I report work in progress on learning simplified interpreted languages by means of recurrent models. The data is constructed to reflect core properties of natural language as modeled in formal syntax and semantics. Preliminary results suggest that LSTM networks do generalise to compositional interpretation, albeit only in the most favorable learning setting.

Motivation. Despite showing impressive performance on certain tasks, neural networks are still far from showing natural language understanding at a human level, cf. Paperno et al. (2016). In a sense, it is not even clear what kind of neural architecture is capable of learning natural language semantics in all its complexity, with recurrent and convolutional models being currently tried on various tasks.

One can hope to make progress towards the challenging goal of natural language understanding by taking into account what is known about language structure and language processing in humans. With this in mind, it is possible to formulate certain preliminary desiderata for an adequate natural language understanding model.

First, language processing in humans is known to be sequential; people process and interpret linguistic input on the fly, without any lookahead and without waiting for the linguistic structure to be completed. This property, which has serious potential consequences for the cognitive architecture (Christiansen and Chater, 2016), gives a certain degree of cognitive plausibility to unidirectional recurrent models compared to other neural architectures, at last in their current implementations.

Second, natural language can exploit recursive structures: natural language syntax consists of constructions, represented in formal grammars as rewrite rules, which can recursively embed other constructions of the same kind. For example, noun phrases can in principle consist of a single proper noun (e.g. *Ann*) but can also, among other possibilities, be built from other noun phrases recursively via the possessive construction, as in *Ann's child, Ann's child's friend, Ann's child's friend's parent* etc. The possessive construction can be described by the rewrite rule NP $\longrightarrow$ NP*'s* N.

Third, the recursive syntactic structure drives compositional semantic interpretation. The meaning of the noun phrase *Ann's child's friend* is not merely the sum of the meanings of the individual words (in which case it would have been semantically equivalent to *Ann's friend's child*). Rather, to interpret a complex expression correctly, one has to follow the syntactic structure, first identifying the meaning of the smaller constituent (*Ann's friend*), and then computing the meaning of the whole on its basis.

Fourth, semantic compositionality can be formalized as function application, with one constituent in a complex structure corresponding to an argument of a function that another constituent encodes. For instance, in *Ann's child*, we can think of *Ann* as denoting an individual and *child* as denoting a function from individuals to individuals. In formal semantics, function argument application as a semantic compositionality mechanism extends to a wide range of syntactic constructions.

Finally, natural language interpretation, while being sensitive to syntactic structure, is robust to syntactic variation. For example, humans are equally capable of learning to interpret and using left-branching structures such as NP $\longrightarrow$ NP*'s* N (*Ann's child*) and right-branching structures such as NP $\longrightarrow$ *the* N*of* NP (*the child of Ann*).

The task. To summarize, in order to mimic human language capacities, an artificial system has to be able to learn interpreted languages with compositionally interpreted recursive structures, while

Proceedings of the 2018 EMNLP Workshop BlackboxNLP: Analyzing and Interpreting Neural Networks for NLP, pages 384–386
Brussels, Belgium, November 1, 2018. ©2018 Association for Computational Linguistics

being adaptive to surface variation in the syntactic patterns. To test whether neural systems can fit the bill, we define toy interpreted languages based on a fragment of English. The vocabulary includes four names (*Ann, Bill, Dick, George*), interpreted as individual identifiers, four function-denoting nouns (*child, parent, friend, enemy*), and grammatical elements (*of, 's, the*). Our languages contain either left-branching (NP $\longrightarrow$ NP *'s* N, *Ann's child*) or right-branching structures (*the child of Ann*, NP $\longrightarrow$ *the* N *of* NP).

The interpretation is defined model-theoretically. We randomly generate a model where each proper name corresponds to a distinct individual and each function denoted by a common noun is total. In such a model, each well-formed expression of the language is interpreted as an individual identifier. The denotation of any expression can be calculated by recursive application of functions to arguments, guided by the syntactic structure of the expression.

The task given to the neural systems is to identify the individual that corresponds to each expression; e.g. *Ann's child's friend* is the same person as *George*. Since there is just a finite number of individuals in our models, this boils down formally to a string classification task, assigning each expression to one of the set of individuals in the model.

Systems and data. We tested two standard systems: a vanilla recurrent neural network (RNN) and a long short-term memory network (LSTM) on the task. Both systems were implemented in PyTorch and used hidden layers of 256 units.

We used all expressions of the language up to complexity n as experimental data; development and testing data was randomly selected among examples of maximal complexity. Examples of smaller complexity, i.e. 1 and 2, were always included in the training partition since they are necessary to learn the interpretation of lexical items. We also set a curriculum whereby the system was at first given training examples of minimal complexity, with more complex examples added gradually in the process of training.

Results and discussion. We found the RNN system to struggle already at a basic level; it never achieved perfect accuracy even for minimally complex structures (e.g. *Ann's child*), so assessing its recursive compositionality abilities is out of question. Accuracies across LSTM experimental setups are summarized in Table 1.

branching	3	4	5	6	7
right branching	0	.17	.21	.23	.26
left branching	**1**	**1**	**1**	**1**	**1**
left, slow curriculum	.17	.33	.96	**1**	**1**
left, no curriculum	.17	.21	.19	.21	.26

Table 1: System accuracy as a function of the language, curriculum and data complexity. Random baseline is .25.

rec.in train	0.0	0.2	0.4	0.6	0.8
average accuracy	0	.65	.67	.92	**.98**

Table 2: Percentage of complexity 3 data included in training data vs. average test accuracy over 10 runs.

We find that LSTM does learn to do compositional interpretation in our task, but only in the best scenario. First, and unsurprisingly, a curriculum is essential for the LSTM to generalize to unseen compositional examples. Informally, the system has to learn to interpret words first, and recursive semantic composition has to be learned later.

Second, although the recurrent architecture seems naturally adapted for processing complex left-branching structures, the system has to be trained on a lot of examples of composition before it generalizes; cf. Table 2. Unlike (presumably) in humans, recursive compositionality does not come for free and has to be learned from extensive data. This observation goes in line with other findings in related literature (Liska et al., 2018; Hupkes et al., 2018; Lake and Baroni, 2017).

Third, the LSTM only generalized correctly in the case of left-branching structures; for right branching, the accuracy of recursive composition in the end stays just above the chance level (25%). This means that the system only learned to apply composition following the linear sequence of the input and failed when the order of compositionality as determined by the syntactic structure runs opposite to the linear order.

The last two observations suggest that learning recursive structure remains a challenge for LSTM networks, which excel only in sequential, left-to-right processing. If recursion, as has been claimed, is a core distinguishing property of human language and cognition (Hauser et al., 2002; Chomsky, 2014), we may need to ensure that learning systems designed for language incorporate proper biases towards recursive processing.

Acknowledgments

The research has been supported by CNRS PEPS ReSeRVe grant. I also thank Germán Kruszewski for useful input on the topic.

References

Noam Chomsky. 2014. Minimal recursion: exploring the prospects. In *Recursion: Complexity in cognition*, pages 1–15. Springer.

Morten H. Christiansen and Nick Chater. 2016. The now-or-never bottleneck: A fundamental constraint on language. *Behavioral and Brain Sciences*, 39.

Marc D. Hauser, Noam Chomsky, and W. Tecumseh Fitch. 2002. The faculty of language: What is it, who has it, and how did it evolve? *science*, 298(5598):1569–1579.

Dieuwke Hupkes, Anand Singh, Kris Korrel, Germán Kruszewski, and Elia Bruni. 2018. Learning compositionally through attentive guidance. *CoRR*, abs/1805.09657.

Brenden M. Lake and Marco Baroni. 2017. Still not systematic after all these years: On the compositional skills of sequence-to-sequence recurrent networks. *CoRR*, abs/1711.00350.

Adam Liska, Germán Kruszewski, and Marco Baroni. 2018. Memorize or generalize? searching for a compositional RNN in a haystack. *CoRR*, abs/1802.06467.

Denis Paperno, German Kruszewski, Angeliki Lazaridou, Quan Ngoc Pham, Raffaella Bernardi, Sandro Pezzelle, Marco Baroni, Gemma Boleda Torrent, and Raquel Fernandez. 2016. The lambada dataset: word prediction requiring a broad discourse context. In *Proceedings of the 54th Annual Meeting of the Association for Computational Linguistics (Volume 1: Long Papers). Berlin: Association for Computational Linguistics*, pages 1525–1534. ACL (Association for Computational Linguistics).

Author Index